world development report 2004

Making Services Work for Poor People

world development report 2004

Making Services Work for Poor People

A Copublication of the World Bank
and Oxford University Press

Contents

Boxes

Figures

Tables

Acknowledgments

This Report has been prepared by a team led by Shantayanan Devarajan and Ritva Reinikka, and comprising Junaid Ahmad, Stephen Commins, Deon Filmer, Jeffrey Hammer, Lant Pritchett, Shekhar Shah, and Agnès Soucat, with additional contributions by Nazmul Chaudhury. The team was assisted by Claudio E. Montenegro and Manju Rani. Bruce Ross-Larson and Meta de Coquereaumont were the principal editors. The work was carried out under the general direction of Nicholas H. Stern.

The team was advised by a panel of experts led by Emmanuel Jimenez and comprising Martha Ainsworth, Abhijit Banerjee, Timothy Besley, John Briscoe, Anne Case, Luis Crouch, Angus Deaton, David G. de Groot, Anil Deolalikar, Esther Duflo, Vivien Foster, Anne-Marie Goetz, Jonathan D. Halpern, Joel Hellman, Charles Humphreys, R. Mukami Kariuki, Elizabeth King, Michael Kremer, Kenneth Leonard, Maureen Lewis, Benjamin Loevinsohn, Michael Mertaugh, Allister Moon, Howard Pack, Samuel Paul, Sanjay Pradhan, Michael Walton, and Dale Whittington.

Many others inside and outside the World Bank provided helpful comments, wrote background papers and other contributions, and participated in consultation meetings. These contributors and participants are listed in the Bibliographical Note. The Development Data Group contributed to the data appendix and was responsible for the Selected World Development Indicators. Much of the background research was supported by several generous trust fund grants from the UK Department for International Development, and the Dutch, Finnish and Norwegian Governments.

The team undertook a wide range of consultations for this Report, which included workshops in Berlin, Brussels, Cairo, Colombo, Dhaka, Geneva, Havana, Helsinki, Kampala, New Delhi, Paris, Pretoria, Tokyo, Washington D.C., and a series of video conferences with participants from Africa, East and South Asia, Europe, Latin America, and the Middle East. The participants in these workshops and video conferences included researchers, government officials, and staff of nongovernmental and private-sector organizations.

Rebecca Sugui served as executive assistant to the team; Leila Search as program assistant and technical support; and Endy Shri Djonokusomo and Ofelia Valladolid as team assistants. Evangeline Santo Domingo served as resource management assistant.

Book design, editing, and production were coordinated by the Production Services Unit of the World Bank's Office of the Publisher, under the supervision of Susan Graham and Ilma Kramer.

Abbreviations and Data Notes

Abbreviations

ACE	Community Education Association (El Salvador)	MWSS	Metro-Manila Waterworks and Sewerage System
BCG	Bacillus Calmette-Guérin	NGO	Nongovernmental organization
BRAC	Bangladesh Rural Advancement Committee	ODA	Official development aid
DAC	Development Assistance Committee (OECD)	OECD	Organisation for Economic Co-operation and Development
DPT	Diphtheria-pertussis-tetanus		
Educo	Educación con Participación de la Comunidad (Education with the Participation of Communities, El Salvador)	PRI	Institutional Revolutionary Party (Mexico)
		Progresa	El Programa de Educación, Salud y Alimentación de México (Education, Health, and Nutrition Program of Mexico)
EPRDF	Ethiopia People's Revolutionary Democratic Front	PRONASOL	Programa Nacional de Solidaridad (National Solidarity Program of Mexico)
GDP	Gross domestic product	REB	Rural electricity board
GNI	Gross national income	SIDA	Swedish International Development Agency
HIPC	Heavily indebted poor country	TIMSS	Third International Mathematics and Science Study
ICRG	International Country Risk Guide		
IDT	Impres Desa Tertinggal (Indonesia)	USAID	U.S. Agency for International Development
KDP	Kecamatan Development Program (Indonesia)	VERC	Village education resource center
LICUS	Low-income country under stress	WHO	World Health Organization
MKSS	Mazdoor Kisan Shakti Sanghathan (India)	WSP	Water and Sanitation Program

Data Notes

The countries included in regional and income groupings in this Report are listed in the Classification of Economies table at the end of the Selected World Development Indicators. Income classifications are based on GNP per capita; thresholds for income classifications in this edition may be found in the Introduction to Selected World Development Indicators. Group averages reported in the figures and tables are unweighted averages of the countries in the group unless noted to the contrary.

The use of the word *countries* to refer to economies implies no judgment by the World Bank about the legal or other status of a territory. The term *developing countries* includes low- and middle-income economies and thus may include economies in transition from central planning, as a matter of convenience. The term *developed countries* or *industrial countries* may be used as matter of convenience to denote the high-income economies.

Dollar figures are current U.S. dollars, unless otherwise specified. *Billion* means 1,000 million; *trillion* means 1,000 billion.

Foreword

We enter the new millennium with great hopes. For the first time in human history, we have the possibility of eradicating global poverty in our lifetime. One hundred and eighty heads of state signed the Millennium Declaration in October 2000, pledging the world to meeting the Millennium Development Goals by 2015. In Monterrey, Mexico, in the spring of 2002, the world's nations established a partnership for increasing external assistance, expanding world trade, and deepening policy and institutional reforms to reach these goals. Foreign aid, which declined during the 1990s, has begun to increase again.

But the first few years of the 21st century bring heightened challenges. HIV/AIDS and other diseases, illiteracy, and unclean water threaten to dash the hopes of millions, possibly billions, of people that they might escape poverty. Tragically, conflict has undermined development in many countries. Peace and development go hand in hand. And even as we learn how to make development assistance more effective, aid continues to be criticized for not being effective enough.

This year's *World Development Report*, the 26th in the World Bank's flagship series, helps to re-ignite and reinforce our hopes by confronting these challenges. Development is not just about money or even about numerical targets to be achieved by 2015, as important as those are. It is about people. The WDR focuses on basic services, particularly health, education, water, and sanitation, seeking ways of making them work for poor people. Too often, services fail poor people. These failures may be less spectacular than financial crises, but their effects are continuing and deep nonetheless. The report shows that there are powerful examples of services working for poor people. Services work when they include *all* the people, when girls are encouraged to go to school, when pupils and parents participate in the schooling process, when communities take charge of their own sanitation. They work when societies can curtail corruption—which hurts poor people more than it hurts the better off—particularly when it hits basic health services, which poor people need desperately. They work when we take a comprehensive view of development—recognizing that a mother's education will help her baby's health, that building a road or a bridge will enable children to go to school.

Services work especially well when we recognize that resources and their effective use are inseparable. More effective use makes additional resources more productive—and the argument for aid more persuasive. External resources can provide strong support for changes in policy and practice that can bring more effective use. This is how we can scale up to achieve the Millennium Development Goals.

To improve service delivery, the WDR recommends institutional changes that will strengthen relationships of accountability—between policymakers, providers, and citizens. These changes will not come overnight. Solutions must be tailored not to some imaginary "best practice" but to the realities of the country or the town or the village. One size will not fit all. But I am convinced that this new way of thinking about service delivery, and indeed about development effectiveness, will bear fruit, particularly when matched with adequate resources and a desire to assess what works and what does not, and to decide what must be scaled up and, indeed, what must be scaled down.

In short, this year's WDR is central to the World Bank's two-pronged strategy for development—investing in and empowering people, and improving the climate for investment. Next year's WDR will focus on the second of these. Together, these reports form part of the World Bank's contribution to meeting the challenge the global community has set for itself—to eradicate poverty in our lifetime.

James D. Wolfensohn

Overview

I go to collect water four times a day, in a 20-litre clay jar. It's hard work! . . . I've never been to school as I have to help my mother with her washing work so we can earn enough money. . . . Our house doesn't have a bathroom. . . . If I could alter my life, I would really like to go to school and have more clothes.

Elma Kassa, a 13-year-old girl
from Addis Ababa, Ethiopia

Too often, services fail poor people—in access, in quantity, in quality. But the fact that there are strong examples where services do work means governments and citizens can do better. How? By putting poor people at the center of service provision: by enabling them to monitor and discipline service providers, by amplifying their voice in policymaking, and by strengthening the incentives for providers to serve the poor.

Freedom from illness and freedom from illiteracy—two of the most important ways poor people can escape poverty—remain elusive to many. To accelerate progress in human development, economic growth is, of course, necessary. But it is not enough. Scaling up will require both a substantial increase in external resources and more effective use of all resources, internal and external. As resources become more productive, the argument for additional resources becomes more persuasive. And external resources can provide strong support for changes in practice and policy to bring about more effective use. The two are complementary—that is the essence of the development partnership that was cemented in Monterrey in the spring of 2002.

This Report builds an analytical and practical framework for using resources, whether internal or external, more effectively by making services work for poor people. We focus on those services that have the most direct link with human development—education, health, water, sanitation, and electricity.

Governments and citizens use a variety of methods of delivering these services—central government provision, contracting out to the private sector and nongovernmental organizations (NGO)s, decentralization to local governments, community participation, and direct transfers to households. There have been spectacular successes and miserable failures. Both point to the need to strengthen accountability in three key relationships in the service delivery chain: between poor people and providers, between poor people and policymakers, and between policymakers and providers. Foreign-aid donors should reinforce the accountability in these relationships, not undermine it.

Increasing poor clients' choice and participation in service delivery will help them monitor and discipline providers. Raising poor citizens' voice, through the ballot box and widely available information, can increase their influence with policymakers—and reduce the diversion of public services to the non-poor for political patronage. By rewarding the effective delivery of services and penalizing the ineffective, policymakers can get providers to serve poor people better.

Innovating with service delivery arrangements will not be enough. Societies should learn from their innovations by systematically evaluating and disseminating information about what works and what doesn't. Only then can the innovations be scaled up to improve the lives of poor people around the world.

The challenge is formidable, because making services work for poor people involves changing not only service delivery arrangements but also public sector institutions. It also involves changing the way much foreign aid is transferred. As governments, citizens, and donors create incentives for these changes, they should be selective in the problems they choose to address. They should be realistic about implementation difficulties. And they should be patient.

The problem

Poverty has many dimensions. In addition to low income (living on less than $1 a day), illiteracy, ill health, gender inequality, and environmental degradation are all aspects of being poor. This is reflected in the Millennium Development Goals, the international community's unprecedented agreement on the goals for reducing poverty (box 1). The multidimensional nature of poverty is also reflected in the World Bank's two-pronged strategy for development—investing in people and improving the investment climate. That five of the eight goals and one of the two prongs of the strategy for development concern health and education signals how central human development is to human welfare.

But progress in human development has lagged behind that in reducing income poverty (figure 1). The world as a whole is on track to achieve the first goal—reducing by half the proportion of people living on less than $1 a day—thanks mainly to rapid economic growth in India and China, where many of the world's poor live.[1] But the world is off track in reaching the goals for primary education, gender equality, and child mortality.

To reach all of these goals, economic growth is essential. But it will not be enough. The projected growth in per capita GDP will by itself enable five of the world's six developing regions to reach the goal for reducing income poverty (table 1). But that growth will enable only two of the regions to achieve the primary enrollment goal and none of them to reach the child mortality goal. If the economic growth projected for Africa doubles, the region will reach the income poverty goal—but still fall short of the health and education goals. In Uganda, despite average annual per capita GDP growth of 3.9 percent in the past decade, child mortality is stagnating—and only partly due to the AIDS epidemic.[2]

Because growth alone will not be enough to reach the goals, the international community has committed itself—in a series of recent meetings in Monterrey, Doha, and Johannesburg—to greater resource trans-

Figure 1   Progress in human development: off track

People living on less than $1 a day

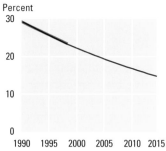

Primary school completion rate

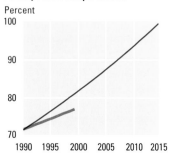

Ratio of girls to boys in primary and secondary school

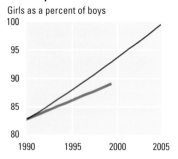

Under-five mortality rate

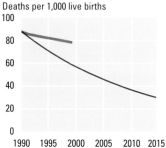

Note: Blue line is the trend line to reach the Millenium Development Goal. The red line shows the actual progress to date.
Source: www.developmentgoals.org.

BOX 1   *The eight Millennium Development Goals*

With starting points in 1990, each goal is to be reached by 2015:

1. **Eradicate extreme poverty and hunger**
    Halve the proportion of people living on less than one dollar a day.
    Halve the proportion of people who suffer from hunger.

2. **Achieve universal primary education**
    Ensure that boys and girls alike complete primary schooling.

3. **Promote gender equality and empower women**
    Eliminate gender disparity at all levels of education.

4. **Reduce child mortality**
    Reduce by two-thirds the under-five mortality rate.

5. **Improve maternal health**
    Reduce by three-quarters the maternal mortality ratio.

6. **Combat HIV/AIDS, malaria, and other diseases**
    Reverse the spread of HIV/AIDS.

7. **Ensure environmental sustainability**
    Integrate sustainable development into country policies and reverse loss of environmental resources.
    Halve the proportion of people without access to potable water.
    Significantly improve the lives of at least 100 million slum dwellers.

8. **Develop a global partnership for development**
    Raise official development assistance.
    Expand market access.

Three points about the Millennium Development Goals: First, to be enduring, success in reaching the goals must be based on systemwide reforms to support progress. Second, focusing on these outcomes does not imply focusing on education and health services alone. Health and education outcomes depend on too many other factors for that to work—everything from parents' knowledge and behavior, to the ease and safety of reaching a health clinic or school, or the technology available for producing outcomes (see crate 1.1). Third, in countries that have already achieved universal primary completion or low infant and maternal mortality rates, the spirit of the Millennium Development Goals—time-bound, outcome-based targets to focus strategies—remains important.

Table 1 Economic growth alone is not enough to reach all the Millennium Development Goals

	Annual average GDP per capita growth 2000–2015* (percent per year)	People living on less than $1 a day		Primary school completion rate		Under-five mortality	
		Target (percent)	2015 growth alone (percent)	Target (percent)	2015 growth alone (percent)	Target (per 1,000 births)	2015 growth alone (per 1,000 births)
East Asia	5.4	14	4	100	100	19	26
Europe and Central Asia	3.6	1	1	100	100	15	26
Latin American and the Caribbean	1.8	8	8	100	95	17	30
Middle East and North Africa	1.4	1	1	100	96	25	41
South Asia	3.8	22	15	100	99	43	69
Africa	1.2	24	35	100	56	59	151

*GDP growth projections from World Bank (2003a).
Note: Elasticity assumed between growth and poverty is –1.5; primary completion rate is 0.62; under-five mortality is –0.48.
Sources: World Bank (2003a), Devarajan (2002).

fers by developed countries and better policies and institutions in developing countries. The level of resource transfers is difficult to calculate precisely. Some estimates are converging around a figure of $40 billion to $60 billion a year in additional foreign aid—so long as the money is accompanied by policy and institutional reforms to enhance the productivity of domestic and external resources.[3]

Focusing on the human development goals, this Report describes the reforms in services needed to achieve them. Ensuring basic health and education outcomes is the responsibility of the state (box 2). But many governments are falling short on their obligation, especially to poor people. In Armenia and Cambodia, child mortality rates for the poorest fifth of the population are two to three times those for the richest fifth. Only about 60 percent of the adolescents in the poorest fifth of the population in the Arab Republic of Egypt and Peru have completed primary school, while all those from the richest fifth have.

To meet this responsibility, governments and citizens need to make the services that contribute to health and education—water, sanitation, energy, transport, health, and education—work for poor people. Too often, these services are failing. Sometimes, they are failing everybody—except the rich, who can opt out of the public system. But at other times, they are clearly failing poor people.

Services are failing poor people in four ways

How do we know that these services are failing poor people? First, while governments devote about a third of their budgets to health and education, they spend very little of it on poor people—that is, on the services poor people need to improve their health and education. Public spending on health and education is typically enjoyed by the non-poor (figure 2). In Nepal 46 percent of education spending accrues to the richest fifth, only 11 percent to the poorest. In India the richest fifth receives three times the curative health care subsidy of the poorest fifth.[4] Even though clean water is critical to health outcomes, in Morocco only 11 percent of the poorest fifth of the population has access to

---

BOX 2 *Services—a public responsibility*

By financing, providing, or regulating the services that contribute to health and education outcomes, governments around the world demonstrate their responsibility for the health and education of their people. Why? First, these services are replete with market failures—with externalities, as when an infected child spreads a disease to playmates or a farmer benefits from a neighbor's ability to read. So the private sector, left to its devices, will not achieve the level of health and education that society desires. Second, basic health and basic education are considered fundamental human

rights. The Universal Declaration of Human Rights asserts an individual's right to "a standard of living adequate for the health and well-being of himself and of his family, including … medical care … [and a right to education that is] … free, at least in the elementary and fundamental stages." No matter how daunting the problems of delivery may be, the public sector cannot walk away from health and education. The challenge is to see how the government—in collaboration with the private sector, communities, and outside partners—can meet this fundamental responsibility.

Figure 2   More public spending for the rich than for the poor
Share of public spending that accrues to the richest and poorest fifths

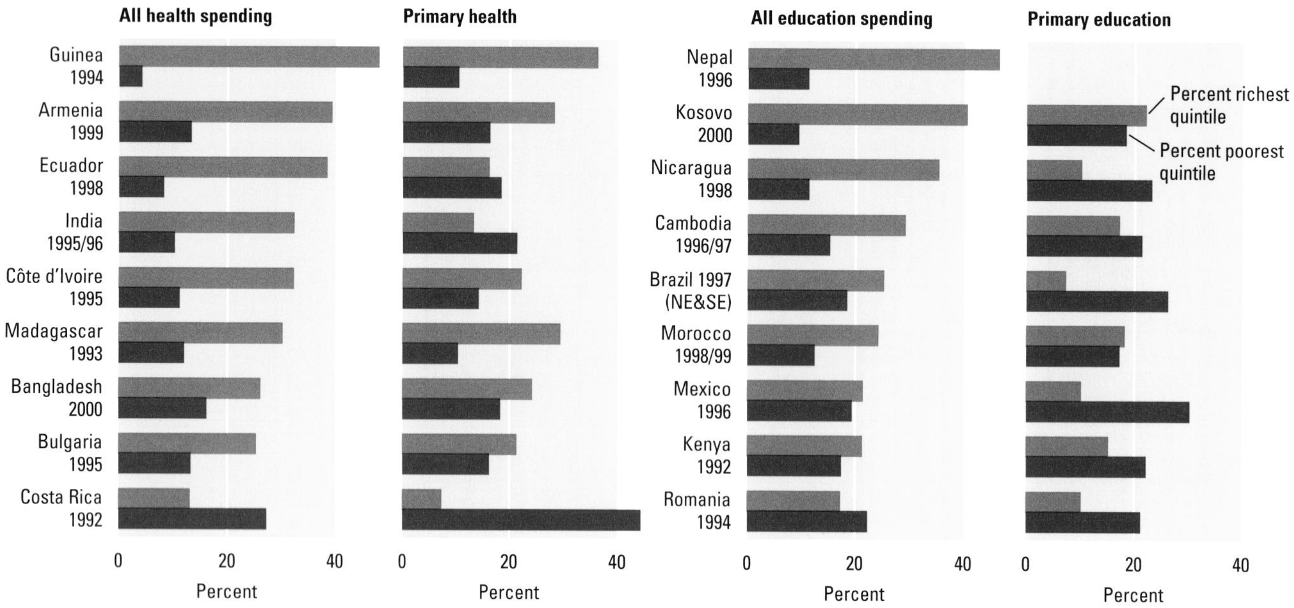

Source: Compiled from various sources by World Bank staff.

safe water, while everybody in the richest fifth does (figure 3).

Second, even when public spending can be reallocated toward poor people—say, by shifting to primary schools and clinics—the money does not always reach the frontline service provider. In the early 1990s in Uganda the share of nonsalary spending on primary education that actually reached primary schools was 13 percent. This was the average: poorer schools received well below the average.[5]

Third, even if this share is increased—as the Ugandans have done—teachers must be present and effective at their jobs, just as doctors and nurses must provide the care that patients need. But they are often mired in a system where the incentives for effective service delivery are weak, wages may not be paid, corruption is rife, and political patronage is a way of life. Highly trained doctors seldom wish to serve in remote rural areas. Since those who do serve there are rarely monitored, the penalties for not being at work are low. A survey of primary health care facilities in Bangladesh found the absentee rate among doctors to be 74 percent.[6] When present, some service providers treat poor people badly. "They treat us like animals," says a patient in West Africa.[7]

By no means do all frontline service providers behave this way. Many, often the majority, are driven by an intrinsic motivation to serve. Be it through professional pride or a genuine commitment to help poor people (or both), many teachers and health workers deliver timely, efficient, and courteous services, often in difficult circumstances—collapsing buildings, overflowing latrines—and with few resources—clinics without drugs, classes without textbooks.[8] The challenge is to reinforce this experience—to replicate the professional ethics, intrinsic motivation, and other incentives of these providers in the rest of the service work force.

The fourth way services fail poor people is the lack of demand. Poor people often don't send their children to school or take them to a clinic. In Bolivia 60 percent of the children who died before age five had not seen a formal provider during the illness culminating in their death. Sometimes the reason is the poor quality of the service—missing materials, absent workers, abusive treatment. At other times it is because they are poor. Even when the services are free, many poor rural families cannot afford the time it takes to travel the nearly 8 kilometers to the nearest primary school in Mali or the 23 kilometers to the nearest medical facility in Chad.[9]

Weak demand can also be due to cultural factors, notably gender. Some parents refuse to send their daughters to school. Husbands have been known to prevent their wives from going to clinics—even for deliveries. And the social distance between poor people and service providers (70 percent of nurses and midwives in rural Niger had been raised in the city) is often a deterrent.

Alternative service delivery arrangements

Ensuring access to basic services such as health, education, water, energy, and sanitation is a public responsibility today, but it has not always been. Nor do governments discharge this responsibility solely through central-government provision. Throughout history and around the world, societies have tried different arrangements—with mixed results.

- Some governments contract services out—to the private sector, to NGOs, even to other public agencies. In the aftermath of a civil war Cambodia introduced two forms of contracting for the delivery of primary health care ("contracting out" whole services and "contracting in" some services). Randomly assigning the arrangements across 12 districts (to avoid systematic bias), it found that health indicators, as well as use by the poor, increased most in the districts contracting out.[10] Whether this can be scaled up beyond 12 districts in Cambodia is worth exploring.
- Governments also sell concessions to the private sector—in water, transport, electricity—with some very good and some very bad results. Privatizing water in Cartagena, Colombia, improved services and access for the poor. A similar sale in Tucuman, Argentina, led to riots in the streets and a reversal of the concession.
- Some societies transfer responsibility (for financing, provision, and regulation) to lower tiers of government. Again, the record has varied—with potentially weaker capacity and greater political patronage at the local level and the reduced scope for redistribution sometimes outweighing the benefits from greater local participation. Local-

Figure 3   Water, water everywhere, nor any drop to drink
Percent of households who use an improved water source (selected countries)

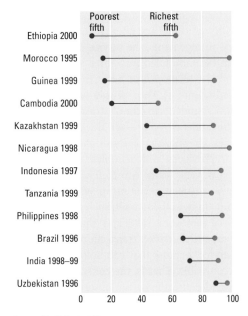

Source: World Bank staff.

government delivery of infrastructure in South Africa improved service provision in a short time.[11] But decentralizing social assistance in Romania weakened the ability and incentives of local councils to deliver cash transfers to the poor.[12] The program is now being recentralized.
- Responsibility is sometimes transferred to communities—or to the clients themselves. El Salvador's Community-Managed Schools Program (Educo) gives parents' associations the right to hire and fire teachers. That, plus the monthly visits to the schools by the parents' associations, has reduced teacher—and student—absenteeism, improving student performance.
- Still other programs transfer resources and responsibility to the household. Mexico's Education, Health, and Nutrition Program (Progresa) gives cash to families if their children are enrolled in school and they regularly visit a clinic. Numerous evaluations of the program show consistently that it increased school enrollment (eight percentage points for girls and five for boys at the secondary level) and improved children's health (illness among young children fell 20 percent).[13]

The framework of relationships—between clients, providers, and policymakers

To help understand the variety of experiences with traditional and alternative service delivery arrangements, the service delivery chain can be unbundled into three sets of actors, and the relationships between them examined (figure 4). Poor people—as patients in clinics, students in schools, travelers on buses, consumers of water—are the clients of services. They have a relationship with the front-line providers, with schoolteachers, doctors, bus drivers, water companies. Poor people have a similar relationship when they buy something in the market, such as a sandwich (or a samosa, a salteña, a shoo-mai). In a competitive-market transaction, they get the "service" because they can hold the provider accountable. That is, the consumer pays the provider directly; he can observe whether or not he has received the sandwich; and if he is dissatisfied, he has power over the provider with repeat business or, in the case of fraud, with legal or social sanctions.

For the services considered here—such as health, education, water, electricity, and sanitation—there is no direct accountability of the provider to the consumer. Why not? For various good reasons, society has decided that the service will be provided not through a market transaction but through the government taking responsibility (see box 2). That is, through the "long route" of accountability—by clients as citizens influencing policymakers, and policymakers influencing providers. When the relationships along this long route break down, service delivery fails (absentee teachers, leaking water pipes) and human development outcomes are poor.

Figure 4   The framework of accountability relationships

Consider the first of the two relationships along the long route—the link between poor people and policymakers or politicians (figure 4). Poor people are citizens. In principle, they contribute to defining society's collective objectives, and they try to control public action to achieve those objectives. In practice, this does not always work. Either they are excluded from the formulation of collective objectives or they cannot influence public action because of weaknesses in the electoral system. Free public services and "no-show" jobs are handed out as political patronage, with poor people rarely the beneficiaries.

Even if poor people can reach the policymaker, services will not improve unless the policymaker can ensure that the service provider will deliver services to them. In Cambodia, policymakers were able to specify the services required to the NGOs with whom they contracted. But for many services, such as student learning or curative care, the policymaker may not be able to specify the nature of the service, much less impose penalties for underperformance of the contract. Teacher and health-worker absenteeism is often the result.

Given the weaknesses in the long route of accountability, service outcomes can be improved by strengthening the short route—by increasing the client's power over providers. School voucher schemes (Colombia's PACES) or scholarships (Bangladesh's Female Secondary School Assistance Program, in which schools receive a grant based on the number of girls they enroll) enable clients to exert influence over providers through choice. El Salvador's Educo program and Guinea's revolving drug scheme (where co-payments inspired villagers to stop theft) are ways for client participation to improve service provision.[14]

Turn now to a closer look at the individual relationships in the service delivery chain—why they break down, how they can be strengthened.

Citizens and politicians/policymakers—stronger voice

Poor citizens have little clout with politicians. In some countries the citizenry has only a weak hold on politicians. Even if there is a well-functioning electoral system, poor people may not be able to influence politicians about public services: they may not be well informed about the quality of public services (and politicians know this); they may vote along ethnic or ideological lines, placing less weight on public services when evaluating politicians; or they may not believe the candidates who promise better public services—because their term in office is too short to deliver on the promise—and they may vote instead for candidates who provide ready cash and jobs.

As a result, public services often become the currency of political patronage and clientelism. Politicians give "phantom" jobs to teachers and doctors. They build free public schools and clinics in areas where their supporters live. Former Boston mayor James Curley strengthened his political base by concentrating public services in the Irish Catholic areas while denying them to the Protestants, who eventually moved to the suburbs.[15]

In 1989 Mexico introduced PRONASOL (Programa Nacional de Solidaridad, or National Solidarity Program), a poverty alleviation program that spent 1.2 percent of GDP annually on water, electricity, nutrition, and education construction in poor communities. Assessments of the six-year program found that it reduced poverty by only about 3 percent. Had the budget been distributed to maximize its impact on poverty, the expected decline would have been 64 percent. It would have been 13 percent even with an untargeted, universal proportional transfer to the whole population. The reason becomes apparent when one examines the political affiliation of communities that received PRONASOL spending. Municipalities dominated by the Institutional Revolutionary Party (PRI), the party in power, received significantly higher per capita transfers than those voting for another party (figure 5).[16]

Just as a well-functioning democracy does not guarantee that poor people will benefit from public services, some one-party states get good health and education outcomes—even among the poor. Cuba has among the best social indicators in Latin America—at a much lower income than its peers, such as Chile and Costa Rica. China reduced infant

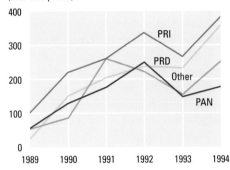

Figure 5 It paid to vote for PRI
PRONASOL expenditures according to party in municipal government

Average expenditures per capita
(real 1995 pesos)

Note: PRI = Institutional Revolutionary Party; PRD = Party of the Democratic Revolution;
PAN = National Action Party.
Source: Estévez, Magaloni, and Diaz-Cayeros (2002).

mortality dramatically, and achieved nearly universal primary enrollment. To be sure, in China, cases during the earliest phase of the outbreak of severe acute respiratory syndrome in 2002 were not openly reported—thus making its further spread almost inevitable. And Cubans, who had high levels of health and education in the 1950s, remain poor on other dimensions.[17]

The lesson seems to be that the citizen-policymaker link is working either when citizens can hold policymakers accountable for public services that benefit the poor or when the policymaker cares about the health and education of poor people. These politics are "pro-poor."

What can be done when the politics are not pro-poor? Societies can still introduce various intermediate elements to make public institutions more accountable. Participatory budgeting in Porto Allegre, Brazil, started as a means for the citizens to participate in budget formulation and then to hold the municipal government accountable for executing the budget.

Perhaps the most powerful means of increasing the voice of poor citizens in policymaking is better information. When the government of Uganda learned that only 13 percent of recurrent spending for primary education was arriving in primary schools, it launched a monthly newspaper campaign on the transfer of funds. That campaign galvanized the populace, inducing the government

to increase the share going to primary schools (now over 80 percent) and compelling school principals to post the entire budget on the schoolroom door.

The media can do much to disseminate information about public services. Higher newspaper circulation in Indian districts is associated with better local-government performance in distributing food and drought relief.[18] The more people who can read, the stronger the influence of the media. In Kerala, India, this led to a virtuous cycle of literacy leading to better public services, which raised literacy even more.[19]

But information is not enough. People must also have the legal, political, and economic means to press demands against the government. Most citizens in Uttar Pradesh, India, know that government services are dismal, and know that everyone else knows that—and yet most do not feel free to complain.[20]

Policymakers and providers— stronger compacts

Strengthening poor people's voice can make policymakers *want* to improve services for the poor. But they still may not be *able* to. Well-intentioned policymakers often cannot offer the incentives and do the monitoring to ensure that providers serve the poor. The absenteeism of teachers, the rude treatment of patients, and the siphoning of pharmaceuticals are symptoms of the problem.

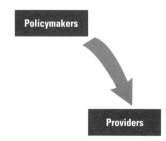

Even in the private sector, where the incentives presumably are better aligned, performance is not much better—for the same reasons that private markets are not the solution to these problems in the first place. Private providers fail to reach the very poor. Weak regulation leads to poor-quality health services in India's private sector. Ineffectively privatizing water incites riots in the streets of Cochabamba.

In the former Soviet Union, state and party control over providers ensured compliance with delivery norms for free services. Services worked, and levels of health status, particularly for the poorer Central Asian republics, were much higher than for other countries at their level of income. But the breakup of the Soviet Union weakened state control over providers, and health and education services collapsed.

Solving the problem requires mentally, and sometimes physically, separating the policymaker from the provider—and thinking of the relationship between the two as a compact. The provider agrees to deliver a service, in return for being rewarded or penalized depending on performance. The compact may be an explicit contract with a private or nonprofit organization—or between tiers of government, as in Johannesburg, South Africa.[21] Or it could be implicit, as in the employment agreements of civil servants.

Separating the policymaker from the provider is not easy, for those who benefit from the lack of separation may resist it. Teachers' unions in Uttar Pradesh, India, blocked an attempt to put teacher hiring, firing, and attendance under the control of the village *panchayat*. On the other hand, health professionals in Brazil participated in a national coalition that prepared the plan for health reforms and municipal health councils.[22] The separation usually happens because of a fiscal crisis (Johannesburg), a major political change (decentralization in Latin America), or a legacy of history (public regulation of water providers in the Netherlands).

Even with a separation of policymaker and provider, the compacts cannot be too explicit. It is difficult to specify precisely what the schoolteacher should do at every point in the day. Too much specificity can lead to inflexibility. Parisian taxi drivers, to make a point about excessive regulations, sometimes meticulously follow the rules in the *Code de la route*—slowing traffic in the French capital to a snail's pace.[23]

Since the contract cannot be fully specified, policymakers look to other means of eliciting pro-poor services from providers. One way is to choose providers who have an intrinsic motivation to serve the poor. A study of faith-based health care providers in Uganda estimates that they work for 28 percent less than government and private for-profit staff, and yet provide a significantly higher quality of care than the public sector.[24] Another way is to increase incentives to serve the poor or work in underserved areas. But one study of Indonesia shows that it would require multiples of current pay levels to get doctors to live in West Papua, for instance (where the vacancy rate is 60 percent).[25] A third way is to solicit bids for services and use the competition in the bidding process to monitor and discipline providers. Many water concessions are managed this way. A recent innovation in Madhya Pradesh, India, allows NGOs to compete for concessions to primary schools, with payments conditional on higher test scores based on independent measurement.

As with the citizen-politician relationship, a critical element in the policymaker-provider relationship is information. The policymaker can specify a contract based only on what he can observe—on what information is available. There has to be a method for monitoring providers and for having that information reach the policymaker. New technologies, including e-government, can make this easier.[26]

So can some ingenious methods using human beings. When Ceará, Brazil, hired a cadre of district health workers, the government sent their names to the applicants who were not selected, inviting them to report any problems with service in the health clinics. More fundamentally, these output-based incentive schemes require rigorous program evaluation, so that the policymaker knows and understands what is working and what isn't. Evaluation-based information, important not only for monitoring providers, also enables the rest of the world to learn about service delivery.

Clients and providers—more choices, more participation

Given the difficulties in strengthening the long route of accountability, improving the short route—the client-provider relationship—deserves more consideration. There is no question that this relationship is broken for hundreds of millions of poor people. *Voices of the Poor* and other surveys point to the helplessness that poor people feel before providers—nurses hitting mothers during childbirth, doctors refusing to treat patients of a lower caste.[27] Unlike most private providers, public water companies funded through budgetary transfers often ignore their customers.

These are but symptoms of the larger problem: many service delivery arrangements neglect the role of clients, especially poor clients, in making services work better.

Clients can play two roles in strengthening service delivery. First, for many services, clients can help tailor the service to their needs, since the actual mix cannot be specified in advance. In some parts of Pakistan, girls are more likely to attend school if there is a female teacher. The construction of separate latrines for girls has had a strong effect on girls' enrollment in primary schools. When the opening hours of health clinics are more convenient for farmers, visits increase. Second, clients can be effective monitors of providers, since they are at the point of service delivery. The major benefit of Educo came from the weekly visits of the community education association to schools. Each additional visit reduced student absenteeism (due to teacher absenteeism) by 3 percent.[28]

How can the role of clients in revealing demand and monitoring providers be strengthened? By increasing poor people's choice and participation in service delivery. When clients are given a choice among service providers, they reveal their demand by "voting with their feet." Female patients who feel more comfortable with female doctors can go to one. The competition created by client choice also disciplines providers. A doctor may refuse to treat lower-caste patients, but if he is paid by the number of patients seen, he will be concerned when the waiting room is empty. Reimbursing schools based on the number of students (or female students) they enroll creates implicit competition among schools for students, increasing students' choice.

School voucher programs—as in Bangladesh, Chile, Colombia, Côte d'Ivoire, and Czech Republic—are explicitly aimed at improving education quality by increasing parents' choices. The evidence on these schemes is mixed, however. They seem to have improved student performance among some groups. But the effects on the poor are ambiguous because universal voucher schemes tend to increase sorting—with richer students concentrating in the private schools.[29] When the voucher is restricted to poor or disadvantaged groups, the effects are

Poor people → Providers

better.[30] The Colombia program showed lower repetition rates and higher performance on standardized tests for students participating in the scheme—with the effect for girls higher than that for boys.[31] Even in network systems such as urban water provision, it is possible to give poor communities choice—by allowing the poor to approach independent providers, introducing flexibility in service standards such as lifeline rates, and so on.

When there is no choice of providers, increasing poor people's participation in service provision—giving them the ability to monitor and discipline the provider, for example—can achieve similar results. Clients can play the role of monitors since they are present at the point of service. But they need to have an incentive to monitor.

In Bangladesh, thanks to reduced import tariffs, households were able to purchase tubewells that tapped ground sources—shallow aquifers—for drinking water. Unfortunately, no one arranged for the monitoring of water quality—a public good—so the arsenic in the water went undetected. If the stakes are high enough, communities tackle the problem. When the Zambian government introduced a road fund financed by a charge on trucks, truck drivers took turns policing a bridge crossing to make sure that overloaded trucks did not cross. Of course such co-payments or user fees reduce demand—and so should not be used when the demand effects outweigh the increase in supply, as in primary education. But for water, electricity, and other services whose benefits are enjoyed mainly by the user, charging for them has the added benefit of increasing the consumer's incentive to monitor the provider. Farmers in Andhra Pradesh, India, are finding that, when they pay for their water, the irrigation department becomes more accountable to them. In the words of one farmer, "We will never allow the government to again give us free water."[32]

Donors and recipients— strengthening accountability, not undermining it

Improving service outcomes for poor people requires strengthening the three relationships in the chain—between client and provider, between citizen and policymaker, and between policymaker and provider. In their zeal to get services to the poor, donors often bypass one or more of these relationships. The typical mode of delivering aid—a project—is often implemented by a separate unit outside the compact, bypassing the relationship between policymakers and providers. The project is typically financed by earmarked funds subject to donor-mandated fiduciary requirements. It and other donor initiatives, including global "funds," bypass the citizen-policymaker relationship where the budget is concerned. To be sure, when the existing relationship is dysfunctional, it may be necessary to go around it. But the cases where the benefits outweigh the costs are probably fewer than imagined.

Recognizing the gap between ends and means, some donors and recipients try to use foreign aid to strengthen, not weaken, the links in the service delivery chain. One approach is to incorporate donor assistance in the recipient's budget, shifting to the recipient's accountability system. In Uganda assistance from Germany, Ireland, the Netherlands, Norway, United Kingdom, and the World Bank is all part of the country's budget, the outcome of a coordinated and participatory process.

Another approach is for donors to pool their assistance in a single "pot" and to harmonize their fiduciary standards around that of the rest of the government. The sectorwide approach to health, education, transport, and other sectors is a step in this direction. Possibly the biggest payoff comes when donors help generate knowledge—as when donor-financed impact evaluation studies reveal what works and what doesn't in service delivery, or when donors pool technical assistance resources at the retail level, as in the multi-donor Water and Sanitation Program. Knowledge is essential to scaling up service delivery. Although it emerges locally, it is a global public good—precisely what aid is designed to finance.

What not to do

The picture painted so far of the difficulties in government-led service delivery may lead some to conclude that government should give up and leave everything to the private sector. That would be wrong. If individuals are left to their own devices, they will not provide levels of education and health that they collectively desire (see box 2). Not only is this true in theory, but in practice no country has achieved significant improvement in child mortality and primary education without government involvement. Furthermore, as mentioned earlier, private sector or NGO participation in health, education, and infrastructure is not without problems—especially in reaching poor people. The extreme position is clearly not desirable.

Some aid donors take a variant of the "leave-everything-to-the-private-sector" position. If government services are performing so badly, they say, why give more aid to those governments? That would be equally wrong. There is now substantial research showing that aid is productive in countries with good policies and institutions, and those policies and institutions have recently been improving.[33] The reforms detailed in this Report (aimed at recipient countries and aid agencies) can make aid even more productive. When policies and institutions are improving, aid should increase, not decrease, to realize the mutually shared objective of poverty reduction, as specified in the Millennium Development Goals.

At the same time, simply increasing public spending—without seeking improvements in the efficiency of that spending—is unlikely to reap substantial benefits. The productivity of public spending varies enormously across countries. Ethiopia and Malawi spend roughly the same amount per person on primary education—with very different outcomes. Peru and Thailand spend vastly different amounts—with similar outcomes.

On average, the relationship between public spending on health and education and the outcomes is weak or nonexistent. A simple scatter plot of spending and outcomes shows a clear line with a significant slope—because richer countries spend more on health and education and have better outcomes. But controlling for the effect of per capita income, the relationship between public spending on health and under-five mortality rates is not statistically significant (figure 6). That is not surprising: most public spending on health and education goes to

Figure 6   Increased public spending is not enough

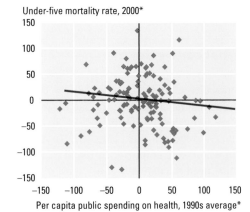

Under-five mortality rate, 2000*

Per capita public spending on health, 1990s average*

*Public spending and child mortality are given as the percent deviation from rate predicted by GDP per capita.
Note: For the regression line shown, the coefficient is –0.148 and the t-statistic is 1.45.
Source: GDP per capita and public spending data, World Development Indicators database; under-5 mortality, UNICEF.

the non-poor, much of it fails to reach the frontline service provider, and service providers face weak incentives to deliver services effectively.

Linked to the "simply-increase-public-spending" approach is one that advocates for more foreign aid without accompanying measures to improve the productivity of foreign aid. This can be just as misleading—and not just for the same reasons that simply increasing public expenditure is misleading. Sometimes the modes of delivering foreign aid, by undermining rather than strengthening service delivery in the recipient country, can reduce the productivity of public spending in the medium run.

Finally, when faced with disappointing health and education outcomes, especially for poor people, it is tempting to recommend a technical solution that addresses the proximate cause of the problem. Why not give vitamin A supplements, de-worm schoolchildren, and train teachers better? Why not develop a "minimum package" of health interventions for everybody? Although each intervention is valuable, recommending them alone will not address the fundamental institutional problems that precluded their adoption in the first place.[34] Lack of knowledge about the right technical solution is probably not the binding constraint. What is needed is a set of institutional arrangements that will give policymakers, providers, and citizens the incentives to adopt the solution and adapt it to local conditions.

What can be done?

The varied experience with traditional and innovative modes of service delivery clearly shows that no single solution fits all services in all countries. The framework of account-ability relationships explains why. In different sectors and countries, different relation-ships need strengthening. In education the biggest payoff may come from strengthen-ing the client-provider link, as with vouch-ers in Colombia or scholarships for girls in Bangladesh. But that may not be so in immunization campaigns.

Furthermore, poor people are often trapped in a system of dysfunctional service-delivery relationships. Making just one link more effective may not be enough—it may even be counterproductive—if there are seri-ous problems elsewhere in the service deliv-ery chain. In water or curative health care, tightening the policymaker-provider link could make providers respond more to the demands of their superiors—and less to their poor clients. Relying on user groups, often generously funded by donors, may inhibit the development of genuinely demo-cratic local governments. Finally, countries, and regions within countries, vary enor-mously in the conditions that make service innovations work. A failed state mired in conflict will be overstretched in resources and institutional capacity, and able to man-age only certain interventions. Countries with high prevalence of HIV/AIDS will require short- and long-term adaptations of the service delivery systems.

Does this mean there are no general lessons about making services work for poor people? No. The experience with ser-vice delivery, viewed through the lens of this Report, suggests a constellation of solutions, each matching various charac-teristics of the service and the country or region. While no one size fits all, perhaps eight sizes do. Even eight may be too few, which is why some of the "sizes" are adjustable, like waistbands.

The eight sizes can be arrived at by answering a series of questions.

yes

Pro-poor?

no

Pro-poor or clientelist politics?

How much is the political system in the country geared toward pro-poor public ser-vices—and how much does it suffer from clientelist politics and corruption? This is the most difficult dimension for an outside actor, such as a donor, to address: the recipient of the advice may also be the source of the prob-lem. And politics do not change overnight.

Even so, at least three sets of policy instru-ments can be deployed where the politics are more clientelist than pro-poor.

- First is choosing the level of government responsible for the service. Countries dif-fer in the patronage politics and capabili-ties of different tiers of government— and this should inform the service delivery arrangement.

- Second, if politicians are likely to capture the rents from free public services and distribute them to their clients, an arrangement that reduces the rents may leave the poor better off. This might include transparent and publicly known rules for allocation, such as per-student grants to schools, or conditional transfers to households, as in Progresa. In some cases it may include fees to reduce the value of the politicians' distribution deci-sions. India's power sector was nationally owned and run because it was a network (and therefore not amenable to head-to-head competition). But the huge rents from providing subsidized electricity have been diverted to people who are not poor—all within a parliamentary democ-racy. Reducing those rents by raising power tariffs or having the private sector provide electricity, even if it violates the principles of equity—they are already violated in the existing system—may be the only way of improving electricity ser-vices to the poor.

- Third, better information—that makes citizens more aware of the money allo-cated to their services, the actual condi-tions of services, and the behavior of policymakers and providers—can be a powerful force in overcoming clientelist politics. The role of a free and vibrant press and improving the level of public discourse cannot be overstated.

Homogeneous or heterogeneous clients?

The answer to this question depends on the service. Students with disabilities have special needs for quality education but not for immunization. Heterogeneity is also defined by regional or community preferences. Whether a girl goes to school may depend on whether there are separate latrines for boys and girls. If that depends on local preferences, the village should have a say in design. Previously homogeneous societies, such as Sweden and Norway, are changing with increased immigration. They are giving more discretion to local communities in tailoring the education system to suit the linguistic abilities of their members.

The more that people differ in their desires, the greater the benefits from decentralizing the decision. In the most extreme case—when individual preferences matter—the appropriate solution will involve individual choices of service (if there is the possibility of competition) and such interventions as cash transfers, vouchers, or capitation payments to schools or medical providers. If there are shared preferences, as in education, or free-rider problems as in sanitation, the community is the correct locus of decision-making. The appropriate policy will then involve local-government decisions in a decentralized setting—or depending on political realities, community decisions (as for social investment funds) and user groups (such as parents in school committees).

Easy or hard to monitor?

Services can be distinguished by the difficulty of monitoring service outputs. The difficulty depends on the service and on the institutional capacity of government to do the monitoring. At one extreme are the services of teachers in a classroom or doctors in a clinic. Both transactions allow much discretion by the provider that cannot be observed easily. A doctor has much more discretion in treating a patient than an electrician switching on a power grid. And it is difficult to know when high-quality teaching or health care is being provided. It may be possible to test students. But test scores tell very little about the teacher's ability or effort, since they depend at least as much on students' socioeconomic status or parental involvement. More easily monitored are immunizations and clean latrines—all measurable by a quantitative, observable indicator.

Of course it depends on who is doing the monitoring. Parents can observe whether the teacher is in attendance, and what their children are learning, more easily than some central education authority. Better management information systems and e-government can make certain services easier to monitor. And monitoring costs can be reduced by judicious choice of providers—such as some NGOs, which may be trustworthy without formal monitoring. In short, the difficulty of monitoring is not fixed: it can vary over time and with policies.

Eight sizes fit all

Now examine different combinations of these characteristics, to see which service delivery arrangement would be a good fit—and which would be a misfit (figure 7). To be sure, none of the characteristics can be easily divided into such clean categories, because countries and services lie on a continuum. Even so, by dividing the salient characteristics, and looking at various combinations, the "eight sizes fit all" approach can be applied to the considerations spelled out earlier.

Central government financing with contracting (1). In a favorable political context, with agreement on what government should do, an easy-to-monitor service such as immunization could be delivered by the public sector, or financed by the public sector and contracted out to the private or nonprofit sector, as with primary health centers in Cambodia.[35] Infrastructure services could be managed by a national utility or provided by the private sector with regulatory oversight.

Note that the particular configuration in which this arrangement will work is special. In the developed countries there is much discussion of a set of reforms, started in New Zealand, that involve greater use of explicit contracts—either from the government to the private sector, or from central ministries to the ministries responsible for specific services. The New Zealand reforms are justified by a well-established public sector ethos,

Figure 7 Eight sizes fit all?

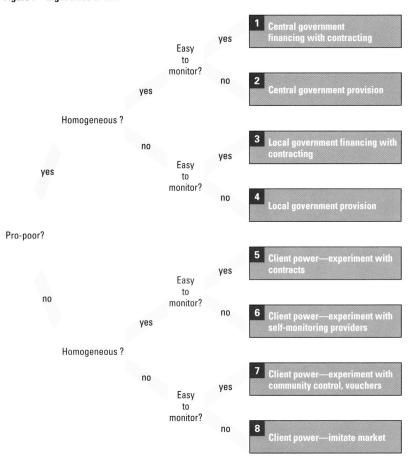

reasonable management information systems, and supporting institutions, including legal systems, to allow contract enforcement. These features increase the "monitorability" of certain services by reducing the gap between contracted and realized outcomes.

These preconditions do not exist in many developing countries, so the template of these reforms cannot be used mechanically.[36] If there is no good legal system and the civil service is subject to bribes (a form of clientelist politics), private sector contracts might be a major source of corruption. In these countries, government should perhaps be even more output-oriented—not as a means of tweaking a well-functioning system but as a way of getting the system to provide much greater improvements in services and generating new information.

Central government provision (2). When the service is difficult to monitor—explicit con-

tracts are difficult to write or enforce—but the politics are pro-poor and clients homogeneous, the traditional, centralized public sector is the appropriate delivery system. The French education system, which administers a uniform service centrally, is one of the best examples.[37] But too many countries fall into the trap of thinking that just because the service is difficult to monitor, it must be delivered by the government. When students are heterogeneous, when the politics of the country are not geared toward poor people, government control of the education system—with no participation by students, parents, or local communities— can leave the poor worse off.

Local government financing with contracting (3). With heterogeneous preferences, local governments should be involved in services. When local politics are pro-poor (but national politics aren't), local governments could be more reliable financiers of services, and vice versa. Easily monitored services such as water or electricity can be contracted out to public or private utilities, as in Johannesburg.

Local government (or deconcentrated central government) provision (4). For difficult-to-monitor services, such as education (for quality), management responsibility might be ceded to parent groups when the politics are conducive, as in the Educo program. Giving clients a choice through vouchers enables them to express their heterogeneous preferences. And the competition created by clients having a choice may improve service quality—as with water vouchers in Chile or sanitation vouchers in Bangladesh.

Client power (5, 6, 7, 8). When publicly financed services are subject to capture—the politics are not pro-poor—the best thing to do is to strengthen the client's power as much as possible. But that can be difficult. Even means-tested voucher schemes or subsidies could be diverted to the non-poor. Transparent, rule-based programs, such as Progresa in Mexico, are needed to make it difficult to hide middle-class capture.

In services such as water and electricity, governments intervene to regulate monopoly providers and protect the poor—and not because there are significant externalities. So separating the policymaker from the provider, and making the provider accountable to the client through prices, can strengthen client power and lead to better results. Poor people can be protected from high prices if charges rise with use (with an initial, free amount). Allowing small, independent water providers to compete with the local monopoly can also discipline provision and keep prices down.

But prices—without accompanying subsidies or transfers to poor people—cannot be used to strengthen client power in education because of the externalities in primary education. A market-based allocation would not be in society's interest. The same applies to health services with externalities, such as immunization. In curative health care, the asymmetry of information between client and provider makes strengthening client power problematic. Better information on preventive care or on how to choose medical providers (possibly disseminated by nonprofit organizations) can ameliorate the problem. In extreme cases, it may be that only community groups or altruistic nonprofits can effectively provide these services to poor people.[38]

These service delivery arrangements represent efforts to balance problems with the long route of accountability (clientelist politics, hard-to-monitor services) with the short route. The reason societies choose the long route is that there are market failures or concerns with equity that make the traditional short route—consumers' power over providers—inadequate. But the "government failures" associated with the long route may be so severe that, in some cases, the market solution may actually leave poor people better off.

Eight sizes fit all with adjustable waistbands

The foregoing simplified scheme captures only part of the story. At least two features are left out.

Failed states. Countries where the state is failing (often countries in conflict) need service delivery arrangements different from those where the state is fairly strong. Primary school completion rates in Senegal and the Democratic Republic of Congo are about 40 percent.

In Senegal—a stable democracy—the reforms in education, including those that strengthen client-provider links, would go through the government (to strengthen the policymaker-provider links as well). In the Democratic Republic of Congo—where conflict has significantly weakened the state—ways should be found to empower communities to improve education services—even if it means bypassing government ministries in the short to medium term. Social funds and community-driven development are examples. They can be effective in improving service outcomes, but concerns about their sustainability and scalability—and whether they crowd out the growth of local government capacity—should not be overlooked.

History. The country's history can also have a bearing on which service delivery arrangements are likely to succeed. Until the 19th century, the education systems of Britain and France were private and the church was the dominant provider. The government had an incentive to develop an oversight mechanism to ensure that the schools taught more than just religion. That proved valuable when education was nationalized in these countries: the systems continued to run with strong regulatory oversight.

Water providers in the Netherlands started as private companies, making the concept of water as an economic good, and charging for it, acceptable. When the system was shifted to municipal ownership, pricing remained. Even if the Dutch never introduce private participation in water, they have achieved the separation between policymaker and provider. In sum, a country's history can generate the incentives for certain institutions to develop—and those institutions can make the difference in whether a particular service arrangement succeeds or fails.

Sectoral service reforms

What do these conclusions tell us about the reform agenda in individual sectors? In *education* there is a tradeoff between the need for greater central authority to capture societywide benefits, such as social cohesion, and the need for greater local influence because student learning is difficult to monitor at the central level. The tradeoff is sharper when the concern is the quality of education rather than the quantity. In Indonesia centralized public delivery of education has enrolled children in schools, but it has been less successful in teaching them valuable skills. To increase the quality of education, therefore, reforms should concentrate on increasing the voice and participation of clients—but not neglect the importance of central government oversight. In practical terms, this would call for more community management of schools and demand-side subsidies to poor people, but with continuing stress on nationally determined curricula and certification.

Governments intervene in *health* to control communicable diseases, protect poor people from impoverishing health expenditures, and disseminate information about home-based health and nutrition practices. Each of these activities is different, yet they are often provided by the same arrangement, such as a central government public health system. They should be differentiated.

- Information about hand washing, exclusive breastfeeding, and nutrition can be delivered (and even financed) by NGOs and other groups, delivery that works best when reinforced by the community.
- Outreach services, such as immunizations, can be contracted out but should be publicly financed.
- Clinical care is the service the client is least able to monitor, but the case in which government failures might swamp market failures. Where the politics are extremely pro-rich, even public financing of these services (with private provision) can be counterproductive for poor people. The non-poor can capture this financing, leaving no curative services for the poor—and no room in the budget for public health services. Strengthening client power, through either demand-side subsidies or co-payments, can improve matters for poor people, even if there is asymmetric information between client and provider.

In the *infrastructure* sectors—such as water, sanitation, transport, and energy—the rationale for government intervention is dif-

ferent from that in education and health, and so should be the policy responses. The main reason for government involvement in water and energy provision is that those services are provided through networks, so direct competition is not possible. Governments also intervene to ensure access by poor people to these services. So the role of government is to regulate and in some cases subsidize production and distribution. There are few advantages to the government's providing the service itself, which explains why the past decade has seen many privatizations, concessions, and the like in water and energy.

Whether delivered by a private or public company, the service needs to be regulated. Who that regulator is will determine service outcomes. At the very least, when the company is public, the regulator should be separate from the provider (when the policymaker and provider are indistinguishable, making this separation is all the more difficult). The situation is worse when water or energy is subsidized, because the sizable rents from this subsidy—the benefits of below-market-rate services—can be captured by politicians, who use them to curry favor with their rich clients rather than the poor.

Sanitation is different because individuals can offload their refuse onto their neighbors. So subsidies to individual households will not solve the collective action problem. Instead, using community-level subsidies, and giving communities the authority to allocate them, puts the locus of authority where the external effects of individual behavior can be contained.

Scaling up

How can all these reforms be scaled up so that developing countries will have a chance of meeting the Millennium Development Goals? First, as noted at the beginning of this Report, additional resources—external and internal—will be needed to capitalize on these reforms. Second, these reforms must be embedded in a public sector responsible for ensuring poor people's access to basic services. This means that the sectoral reforms must be linked to ongoing (or nascent) public sector reforms in such areas as budget management, decentralization, and public administration reform. It also means that a well-functioning public sector is a crucial underpinning of service delivery reform. In the same vein, there should be reform in donor practices—such as harmonizing procedures and making more use of budget support—to strengthen recipient countries' efforts to improve service outputs.

Third, a recurring theme in this Report is what information can do—as a stimulant for public action, as a catalyst for change, and as an input for making other reforms work. Even in the most resistant societies, the creation and dissemination of information can be accelerated. Surveys of the quality of service delivery conducted by the Public Affairs Centre in Bangalore, India, have increased public demand for service reform. The surveys have been replicated in 24 Indian states. The public expenditure tracking survey in Uganda is another example, as is the Probe report on India's education system.

Beyond surveys, the widespread and systematic evaluation of service delivery can have a profound effect on progress toward the Millennium Development Goals. Evaluations based on random assignments, such as Mexico's Progresa, or other rigorous evaluations give confidence to policymakers and the public that what they are seeing is real. Governments are constantly trying new approaches to service delivery. Some of them work. But unless there is some systematic evaluation of these programs, there is no certainty that they worked because of the program or for other reasons. Based on the systematic evaluations of Progresa, the government has scaled up the program to encompass 20 percent of the Mexican people.

The benefits of systematic program evaluation go beyond the program and the country. These evaluations tell policymakers in other countries what works and what doesn't. They are global public goods—which might explain why they are so scarce.[39] If these evaluations are global public goods, the international community should finance them. One possibility would be to protect the 1.5 percent of World Bank loans that is supposed to be used for evaluation (but rarely is), so that this sum—about $300 million a year—could be used to administer rigorous evaluations of projects and disseminate the results worldwide.

In addition to creating and disseminating information, other reforms to improve service delivery will require careful consideration of the particular setting. There is no silver bullet to improve service delivery. It may be known how to educate a child or stop an infant from dying. But institutions are needed that will educate a generation of children or reduce infant mortality by two-thirds. These do not crop up overnight. Nor will a single institutional arrangement generate the desired results. Everything from publicly financed central government provision to user-financed community provision can work (or fail to work) in different circumstances.

Rather than prescribe policies or design the optimal institution, this Report describes the incentives that will give rise to the appropriate institution in a given context. Decentralization may not be the optimal institutional design. But it may give local governments the incentives to build regulatory capacity that, in turn, could make water and energy services work better for poor people. NGO service provision might be effective in the medium run, as it has been in education in Bangladesh. But the incentives it creates for the public sector to stay out of education make it much harder to scale up or improve quality—as Bangladesh is discovering today. Many of these institutions cut across the public sector—budgetary institutions, intergovernmental relations, the civil service—which reinforces the notion that service delivery reform should be embedded in the context of public sector reform

In addition to looking for incentives to generate the appropriate institutions, governments should be more selective in what they choose to do. The experience with service delivery teaches us the importance of implementation. Singapore and Nigeria (both former British colonies) have similarly designed education systems. But in implementation, the outcomes, especially for poor people, could not be more different. Governments and donors often overlook implementation difficulties when designing policies. There may be benefits to having the central government administer schools (such as social cohesion). But the problems with central provision of a hard-to-monitor activity such as primary education are so great, especially among heterogeneous populations, that the government should rethink its position of centrally controlled schools. Selectivity is not just about choosing from the available design options—it is about choosing with an eye toward options that can be implemented.

That there is no silver bullet, that we should be looking for incentives that give rise to appropriate institutions, that we need to be more realistic about implementation in choosing among options—all imply that these reforms will take time. Even if we know what is to be done, it may be difficult to get it done. Despite the urgent needs of the world's poor people, and the many ways services have failed them, quick results will be hard to come by. Many of the changes involve fundamental shifts in power—something that cannot happen overnight. Making services work for poor people requires patience. But that does not mean we should be complacent. Hubert Lyautey, the French marshal, once asked his gardener how long a tree would take to reach maturity. When the gardener answered that it would take 100 years, Marshal Lyautey replied, "In that case, plant it this afternoon."

Services can work for poor people but too often they fail

With seven other children to care for, Maria's mother, Antonia Souza Lima, explained that she could not afford the time—an hour-and-a-half walk—or the 40-cent bus fare to take her listless baby to the nearest medical post. Maria seemed destined to become one of the 250,000 Brazilian children who die every year before turning 5. But in a new effort to cut the devastating infant mortality rate here, a community health worker recently started to walk weekly to the Lima household, bringing oral rehydration formula for Maria and hygiene advice for her mother, who has a television set but no water filter. Once a month, the 7,240 workers in the Ceará health program enter the homes of four million people, the poor majority of a state where most people's incomes are less than $1 a day. Erismar Rodrigues de Lima, a neighbor of the Limas, listened intently to instructions on filtering drinking water. "I am the first member of my family to ever receive prenatal care," said the 22-year-old woman, who is expecting a baby in June.

From the *New York Times*[40]

I go to collect water four times a day, in a 20-litre clay jar. It's hard work! . . . I've never been to school as I have to help my mother with her washing work so we can earn enough money. I also have to help with the cooking, go to the market to buy food, and collect twigs and rubbish for the cooking fire. Our house doesn't have a bathroom. I wash myself in the kitchen once a week, on Sunday. At the same time I change my clothes and wash the dirty ones. When I need the toilet I have to go down to the river in the gully behind my house. I usually go with my friends as we're only supposed to go after dark when people can't see us. In the daytime I use a tin inside the house and empty it out later. If I could alter my life, I would really like to go to school and have more clothes.

Elma Kassa, a 13-year-old girl
from Addis Ababa, Ethiopia[41]

Citizens and governments can make services that contribute to human development work better for poor people—and in many cases they have. But too often services fail poor people. Services are failing because they are falling short of their potential to improve outcomes. They are often inaccessible or prohibitively expensive. But even when accessible, they are often dysfunctional, extremely low in technical quality, and unresponsive to the needs of a diverse clientele. In addition, innovation and evaluation—to find ways to increase productivity—are rare.

Many services contribute to improving human welfare, but this Report focuses on services that contribute directly to improving health and education outcomes—health services, education services, and such infrastructure services as water, sanitation, and energy. "Services" include what goes on in schools, clinics, and hospitals and what teachers, nurses, and doctors do. They also include how textbooks, drugs, safe water, and electricity reach poor people, and what information campaigns and cash transfers can do to enable poor people to improve outcomes directly. Much of all this is relevant for other sectors, such as police services, so the Report features examples from those sectors as well.

Just how bad can services be? Testimonies show that they can be very bad. In Adaboya, Ghana, poor people say that their "children must walk four kilometers to attend school because, while there is a school building in the village, it sits in disrepair and cannot be used in the rainy season."[42] In Potrero Sula, El Salvador, villagers complain that "the health post here is useless because there is no doctor or nurse, and it is only open two days a week until noon."[43] A common response in a client survey by women who had given birth at rural health centers in the Mutasa district of Zimbabwe is that they were hit by staff during delivery.[44]

This chapter illustrates many types of failures—inaccessible or unaffordable services, and various shortfalls in quality—using testimonials from poor people, compilations

Figure 1.1   Child mortality is substantially higher in poor households

Deaths per 1,000 live births

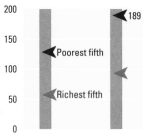

Central African Republic 1994–95

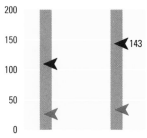

Bolivia 1997

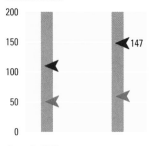

Cambodia 2000

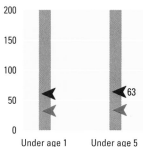

Armenia 2000

Under age 1   Under age 5

Note: Fifths based on asset index quintiles.
Source: Analysis of Demographic and Health Survey data.

of data from several countries, and in-depth studies. The chapter also provides examples of services that are working for poor people. Learning from success and understanding the sources of failure require a framework for analysis. Chapters 3 to 6 of the Report present and develop that framework; Chapters 7 to 11 consider options and issues for reform.

Outcomes are substantially worse for poor people

Just how bad are outcomes? Rates of illness and death are high—and rates of school enrollment, completion, and learning are low—especially for poor people (box 1.1). In Cambodia under-five mortality is 147 per 1,000 births among the poorest fifth of the population; in Armenia it is 63 (figure 1.1).[45] Many children are unlikely to complete even primary schooling. Among adolescents 15 to 19 years old in Egypt, only 60 percent in the poorest fifth have completed the five years of primary school (figure 1.2). In Peru only 67 percent of youths in the poorest fifth have finished the six-year primary cycle, even though almost all started school. In both countries nearly all adolescents in the richest fifth of the population completed primary

school.[46] These countries are not special cases. Worldwide more than 100 million children of primary school age are not in primary school.[47] Almost 11 million children, roughly the population of Greece or Mali, die before their fifth birthday.[48]

Most countries have rich-poor differentials in education or health outcomes. This is not necessarily evidence of services failing poor people—there are many determinants of outcomes (see crate 1.1 at the end of this chapter).[49] Comparing outcomes for richer and poorer people within countries highlights two things. First, it shows the absolutely bad outcomes among the poor—for example, in Bolivia 143 children of every 1,000 from the poorest quintile died before their fifth birthday, and in Niger fewer than 10 percent of adolescents from the poorest quintile completed grade 6. Second, within-country comparisons give a sense of the possible—that is, specific goals already being reached within a country.

Affordable access to services is low—especially for poor people

In many of the poorest countries, access to schools, health clinics, clean water, sanitation

---

BOX 1.1   *Who are "poor people"?*

Defining who is "poor" is always a difficult proposition because there are several concepts of poverty. Perhaps most familiar is the one used to identify the poor in sample surveys in low-income countries: that is based on a composite measure of total household consumption per member (with adjustments for household size and composition).[50] "Poor people" are then defined as those living in households below a particular threshold of this measure of consumption, such as below $1 or $2 a day, or below a nationally defined level.

An alternative approach divides the population into various groups, for example, quintiles, according to a ranked ordering of the measure. The poorest quintile or poorest fifth, for example, is the 20 percent of people who live in households with the lowest values of the consumption measure.

Many surveys, including some used in this Report, do not include consumption data, which are difficult to collect. One approach to assigning people to quintiles is to aggregate indicators of a household's asset ownership and housing characteristics into an index, and then to rank households according to this index. To distinguish these approaches in this Report, quintiles based on the

latter method are typically referred to as "asset" or "wealth" quintiles (since asset ownership and housing characteristics are arguably reflections of a household's wealth).[51]

But poverty based on consumption, "wealth," or an alternative derived from income, is not the only social disadvantage that creates difficulties in the demand for and provision of services. Gender can exclude women from both household and public demands for better services. In many countries ethnicity or other socially constructed categories of disadvantage are important barriers. People with physical and mental disabilities are often not accommodated by education and health services.

Even broader concepts of poverty are relevant to effective services. "Poor people" include people experiencing any of the many dimensions of poverty—and those vulnerable or at risk of poverty—in low-income and lower middle-income countries.[52] So poor people can be seen as the "working class," or "*popular*" in Spanish, or simply just "not rich." Even in middle-income countries the "poor" includes a large part of the population: much of the population cannot insulate itself from the consequences of failures of public services.

facilities, rural transport, and other services is limited. For children in Aberagerema village in Papua New Guinea, the nearest school is in Teapopo village, an hour away by boat, two hours by canoe.[53] This is not unusual: the average travel time to the nearest school in that country is one hour.[54] The availability of services varies dramatically across countries. Typically, however, poor people need to travel substantial distances to reach health and education services—and often much longer distances than richer people in the same country. In rural Nigeria children from the poorest fifth of the population need to travel more than five times farther than children in the richest fifth to reach the nearest primary school, and more than seven times farther to reach the nearest health facility (table 1.1). And traveling theses distances can be hard. In Lusikisiki village, South Africa, it may be necessary to hire neighbors to carry a sick person uphill to even reach the nearest road, which may be inaccessible during the rainy season.[55]

On top of this, staff are getting rarer in some parts of the world. There is mounting evidence that AIDS is reducing the pool of people able to become teachers or health professionals (box 1.2), and international labor markets are making it hard to keep qualified medical staff in poor countries (chapters 6 and 8).

Coverage of other services is also far from universal. More than a billion people worldwide have no access to an improved water source, and 2.5 billion do not have access to improved sanitation. In Africa only half the rural population has access to improved water or improved sanitation. In Asia only 30 percent of the rural population has access to improved sanitation.[56] Again, there are large variations across and within countries. In Cambodia 96 percent of the richest fifth of the population has access to an improved drinking water source, but just 21 percent of the poorest fifth does (figure 1.3). In Morocco in 1992, 97 percent of the richest fifth of the population had access to an improved water source, but just 11 percent of the poorest fifth did. In Peru the corresponding shares are 98 percent and 39 percent.[57]

This need not be. Indonesia expanded access to primary education in the mid-1970s by using its oil windfall to build new schools

and hire more teachers. Primary enrollment doubled between 1973 and 1986, reaching 90 percent—though the story on quality is less positive.[58] Despite a limited budget El Salvador expanded access to schooling in poor rural communities after a civil war in the 1980s by using innovative institutional arrangements (see Educo spotlight).

The exact relationship between use of services and prices or family income varies, but for poor people, lower incomes and higher prices are associated with less use.[59] Poor people spend a lot of their money on services: 75 percent of all health spending in low-income countries is private, 50 percent in middle-income countries.[60] Based on government sources, these broad aggregates are probably underestimates, hiding the heavier burden on poor people. And poor people often need to pay more for the same goods. For example, poor people often pay higher prices to water sellers than the better-off pay to utilities (chapter 9). In Ghana the approximate price paid per liter for water purchased by the bucket was between 5 and 16 times higher than the charge for public supply, even though women and children often had to walk a long distance to purchase the water. In Pune, India, low-income purchasers of water paid up to 30 times the sale price of the metered water that middle- and upper-income households used.[61]

The poor also lack the collateral needed to formally borrow to pay for expensive services for which they lack insurance, and therefore resort to informal moneylenders who charge very high interest rates. If this financing channel is unavailable, they use more expensive traditional or private providers who often provide more flexibility in the terms of payment.[62]

This need not be. In Egypt making health insurance available to school children in the early 1990s almost doubled the probability of a health facility visit among the poorest fifth of the population, substantially reducing the rich-poor gap.[63] In Mexico an innovative program—Progresa—provided parents with cash transfers if they attended health education lectures (where they also received nutrition supplements), and family members got regular medical checkups. The impact of this combination of higher income and facility visits was

Figure 1.2   The poor are less likely to start school, more likely to drop out
Percent of 15- to 19-year-olds who have completed each grade or higher

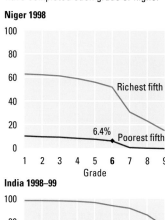
Niger 1998

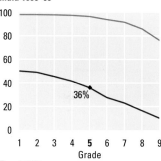
India 1998–99

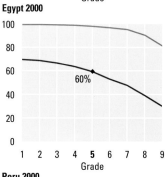
Egypt 2000

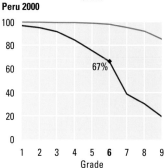
Peru 2000

Notes: The grade number boldfaced denotes the end of the primary cycle. Fifths based on asset index quintiles.
Source: Analysis of Demographic and Health Survey data.

Table 1.1 The nearest school or health center can be quite far
Mean distance to nearest facility in rural areas among the poorest and richest wealth quintiles in 19 developing countries

	GNI per capita	Distance to the nearest primary school (kilometers)			Distance to the nearest medical facility (kilometers)		
		Poorest fifth	Richest fifth	Ratio	Poorest fifth	Richest fifth	Ratio
Bangladesh 1996–97	374	0.2	0.1	1.6	0.9	0.7	1.3
Benin 1996	395	1.5	0.0	—	7.5	2.8	2.7
Bolivia 1993–94	1004	1.2	0.0	—	11.8	2.0	6.0
Burkina Faso 1992–93	336	2.9	0.8	3.9	7.8	2.6	3.0
Central African Republic 1994–95	819	6.7	0.8	8.9	14.7	7.7	1.9
Cameroon 1991	611	2.6	0.7	3.8	7.0	5.4	1.3
Chad 1998	250	9.9	1.3	7.6	22.9	4.8	4.8
Côte d'Ivoire 1994	788	1.4	0.0	—	10.5	3.4	3.1
Dominican Rep. 1991	1261	0.6	0.4	1.3	6.3	1.3	5.0
Haiti 1994–95	336	2.2	0.3	6.4	8.0	1.1	7.2
India 1998–99	462	0.5	0.2	2.3	2.5	0.7	3.6
Madagascar 1992	303	0.6	0.3	1.8	15.5	4.7	3.3
Mali 1995–96	281	7.9	5.2	1.5	13.6	6.7	2.0
Morocco 1992	1388	3.7	0.3	13.1	13.5	4.7	2.9
Niger 1998	217	2.2	1.5	1.5	26.9	9.7	2.8
Nigeria 1999	266	1.8	0.3	5.5	11.6	1.6	7.1
Senegal 1992–93	933	3.8	2.3	1.7	12.8	10.0	1.3
Tanzania 1991–92	224	1.2	0.6	1.9	4.7	3.0	1.6
Uganda 1995	290	1.4	0.9	1.5	4.7	3.2	1.5
Zimbabwe 1994	753	3.0	3.5	0.8	8.6	6.3	1.4

Note: Gross national income (GNI) per capita is that at the time of the survey, expressed in 2001 dollars. Medical facility encompasses health centers, dispensaries, hospitals, and pharmacies. Although some of these data are a bit dated, they are the latest that were collected in a consistent manner across these countries. The situation in some countries may be different today.
Source: Analysis of Demographic and Health Survey data.

significant: illnesses among children under five fell by about 20 percent (see spotlight).

Quality—a range of failures

Lack of access and unaffordability are just two ways services fail. In low- and middle-income countries alike, if services are available at all they are often of low quality. So, many poor people bypass the closest public facility to go to more costly private facilities or choose better quality at more distant public facilities. An in-depth study of the Iringa district in Tanzania, a poor rural area, showed that patients bypassed low-quality facilities in favor of those offering high-quality consultations and prescriptions, staffed by more knowledgeable physicians, and better stocked with basic supplies.[64] A study in Sri Lanka found similar behavior, with patient demand for quality varying with the severity of the illness.[65]

One result: underused publicly funded clinics. In the Sheikhupura district of rural Punjab, Pakistan, only about 5 percent of sick children were taken for treatment to rural primary health care facilities; half went to private dispensaries, and the others to private doctors.[66] When quality improves, the demand for services increases—even among poor clients.[67]

Services are often dysfunctional

Ensuring that positions are filled, that staff report for work, and that they are responsive to all their clients is a major challenge. The more skilled the workers, the less likely they are to accept a job as a teacher or a health worker in a remote area. A recent study in Bangladesh found 40 percent vacancy rates for doctor postings in poor areas.[68] In Papua New Guinea, with a substantial percentage of teaching positions unfilled, many schools closed because they could not get teachers.[69] Incentive payments might encourage professionals to work in remote areas, but they can

BOX 1.2   *HIV/AIDS is killing teachers*

Many countries lack reliable data on AIDS-related deaths and HIV prevalence among teachers, but the available information suggests rising teacher mortality in the presence of HIV/AIDS. For example:

- In the Central African Republic 85 percent of teachers who died between 1996 and 1998 were HIV-positive. On average they died 10 years before they were due to retire.
- In Zambia 1,300 teachers died in the first 10 months of 1998, compared with 680 teachers in 1996.
- In Kenya teacher deaths rose from 450 in 1995 to 1,500 in 1999 (reported by the Teaching Service Commission), while in one of Kenya's eight provinces 20 to 30 teachers die each month from AIDS.
- HIV-positive teachers are estimated at more than 30 percent in parts of Malawi and Uganda, 20 percent in Zambia, and 12 percent in South Africa.

Sources: Coombe (2000), Gachuhi (1999), Kelly (1999), Kelly (2000), UNAIDS (2000), World Bank (2002h).

be expensive. A study in Indonesia estimated that doctors would need to be paid several times their current salaries to induce them to go to the most remote areas.[70]

Even when positions are filled, staff absence rates can be high. In random visits to 200 primary schools in India, investigators found no teaching activity in half of them at the time of visit.[71] Recent random samples of schools and health clinics in several developing countries found absence rates over 40 percent, with higher rates in remote areas and for some kinds of staff—although there is wide variation within countries (tables 1.2 and 1.3). Earlier studies have found similar results. Up to 45 percent of teachers in Ethiopia were absent at least one day in the week before a visit—10 percent of them for three days or more.[72] Health workers in rural health centers in Honduras worked only 77 percent of the possible days in the week before a visit.[73] In rural Côte d'Ivoire only 75 percent of doctors were in attendance on the day before a visit.[74]

Staff alone cannot ensure high-quality services. They also need the right materials—books in schools, drugs in clinics. Studies in Ghana and Nigeria in the early 1990s found

Figure 1.3   Water, water everywhere, nor any drop to drink

Percent of households who use an improved water source, poorest and richest fifths

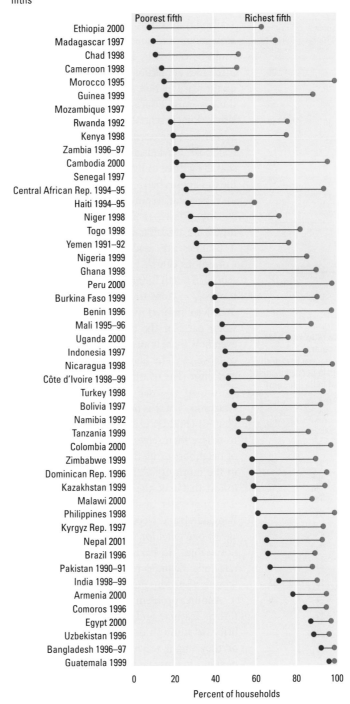

Note: The poorest fifth in one country may correspond to the standard of living in the middle fifth in another country. Within-country inequalities reflect inequality in access to water and in the wealth index used to construct quintiles. An "improved" water source, as defined by UNICEF, provides adequate quality and quantity of water (that is, a household connection or a protected well, not an unprotected well or bottled water).

Source: Analysis of Demographic and Health Survey data.

Table 1.2 Staff are often absent
Absence rates among teachers and health care workers in public facilities (percent)

	Primary schools	Primary health facilities
Bangladesh	—	35
Ecuador	16	—
India*	25	43
Indonesia	18	42
Papua New Guinea	15	19
Peru	13	26
Zambia	17	—
Uganda	26	35

*Average for 14 states.

Table 1.3 Absence rates vary a lot—even in the same country
Absence rates among teachers and health care workers in public facilities in different states of India (percent)

	Primary schools	Primary health facilities
Andhra Pradesh	26	—
Assam	34	58
Uttar Pradesh	26	42
Bihar	39	58
Uttar Anchal	33	45
Rajasthan	24	39
Karnataka	20	43
West Bengal	23	43
Gujarat	15	52
Haryana	24	35
Kerala	23	—
Punjab	37	—
Tamil Nadu	21	—
Orissa	23	35

Notes for tables 1.2 and 1.3: The absence rate is the percentage of staff who are supposed to be present but are not on the day of an unannounced visit. It includes staff whose absence is "excused" and "not excused" and so includes, for example, staff in training, performing nonteaching "government" duties, as well as shirking.
— indicates data not available.
Sources for tables 1.2 and 1.3: Chaudhury and others (2003), Habyarimana and others (2003), and NRI and World Bank (2003). Data should be considered preliminary.

that about 30 percent of public clinics lacked drugs.[75] A quarter of rural clinics in Côte d'Ivoire had no antibiotics.[76] By itself, the availability of drugs in a health facility is an ambiguous measure of quality: stockouts could be caused by high demand. But when medicines are lacking in clinics and available on the black market, as is often the case, something is amiss. Educational materials are similarly lacking in schools. In Nepal a study found as many as six students sharing local-language textbooks. In Madagascar textbooks had to be shared by three to five students, and only half the classrooms had a usable chalk board.[77]

When staff report to work—as many do conscientiously—and when complementary inputs are available, service quality will suffer if facilities are inadequate or in disrepair. Conditions can be horrific. An account of a school in north Bihar in India describes classrooms ". . . close to disintegration. Six children were injured in three separate incidents when parts of the building fell down, and even now there is an acute danger of terminal collapse. . . . The playground is full of muck and slime. The overflowing drains could easily drown a small child. Mosquitoes are swarming. There is no toilet. Neighbors complain of children using any convenient place to relieve themselves, and teachers complain of neighbors using the playground as a toilet in the morning."[78] The same study in India found that half the schools visited had no drinking water available. In rural areas of Bangladesh and Nepal a study found an average of one toilet for 90 students, half of them not usable.[79] In Pakistan there were no separate toilet facilities for girls in 16 percent of schools visited in one study.[80]

Another problem is corruption in various forms. Teachers and principals might solicit bribes to admit students or give better grades, or they might teach poorly to increase the demand for private tuition after hours. Surveys in 11 Eastern and Central European countries found that the health sector was considered one of the most corrupt.[81] Officially only 24 percent of health spending in Europe and Central Asia is estimated to be private, but this fails to include the informal payments—gratuities and bribes—that many patients pay. More than 70 percent of patients make such payments in Azerbaijan, Poland,

and the Russian Federation—more than 90 percent in Armenia.[82]

Corruption hurts patients elsewhere too. For example, studies based on data from the mid-1990s found that informal payments substantially increased the price of health services in Guinea and Uganda.[83] A recent review of case studies in Latin America found widespread corruption in hospitals, ranging from theft and absenteeism to kickbacks for procurement.[84] Villagers in one North African country where people are covered by "free medical care" reported in a discussion group that "there isn't a single tablet in the clinic and the doctor has turned it into his private clinic."[85]

Again, this need not be. In Benin cost-sharing in health clinics—in line with the Bamako Initiative—and revolving drug-funds increased the availability of drugs in clinics that previously provided services free but almost never had any drugs. Use increased in all the clinics that introduced these measures (see spotlight).[86] Innovative arrangements can encourage teachers to report for work. In Nicaragua between 1995 and 1997 teacher attendance increased by twice as much in primary schools that were granted autonomy as in state schools managed through the bureaucratic system.[87] In India a large-scale basic education program in the 1990s doubled the toilets and drinking water facilities in schools in districts where it was implemented. Stakeholders can mobilize to reduce corruption. Public sector unions have organized an anticorruption network (UNICORN) that is supporting national initiatives to protect whistleblowers.

The technical quality of services is often very low

Services also fail poor people when technical quality is low—that is, when inputs are combined in ways that produce outcomes in inefficient, ineffective, or harmful ways. For example, health workers with low skills give the wrong medical advice or procedure, or schools use ineffective teaching methods. Gross inefficiency was identified as the reason for soaring expenditures in a hospital in the Dominican Republic.[88] A multicountry study of health facilities in the mid-1990s found shockingly low cases of proper assessments of diarrhea in children under five, and even fewer cases correctly treated or advised. For example, in Zambia only 30 percent of cases were correctly assessed, and only 19 percent correctly rehydrated.[89] Another study in Egypt found only 14 percent of acute cases of diarrhea were treated appropriately with oral rehydration salts.[90] A recent study in Benin found that one in four sick children received unnecessary or dangerous drugs from health workers.[91] In India the contamination of injection needles used by registered medical practitioners was alarmingly widespread.[92]

Even though technical quality is more difficult to identify in basic education, some indicators raise alarm. For example, spending is ineffectively allocated, with substantially more going to teacher salaries relative to other factors that would be more efficient.[93] Or time is misspent: in five Middle Eastern and North African countries primary school students spend only about 65 percent of the potential time actually on task.[94] In Indonesia first and second grade students officially spend only 2.5 hours a day in school, and absences and classroom time spent on administrative tasks reduced time spent learning even further.[95]

Services are not responsive to clients

Services also fail in the interaction between provider and client. Clients are diverse: they differ by economic status, religion, ethnicity, gender, marital status, age, social status, caste. They may also differ in the constraints on their time, their access to information and social networks, or their civic skills and ability to act collectively. The inequalities between these groups are mirrored in the relationship between clients and providers.[96] In India districts with a higher proportion of lower castes and some religious groups have fewer doctors and nurses per capita, and health outreach workers are less likely to visit lower-caste and poor households.[97] Clients report that they value health facilities that are open at convenient times, with staff who treat them with respect. In El Salvador infrequent and inconvenient operating hours greatly reduced the use of health posts. According to focus group respondents: "Health posts operate only twice a week. Waiting time is three hours on average. Only those who arrive by 8 a.m. get a consultation."[98] In Sub-Saharan Africa school

often starts at 8 a.m. while girls are still fetching water, and school holidays are at odds with local market dates.

The "social distance" between providers and their clients can be large. In Niger, a mainly rural country, a study found 43 percent of the parents of nurses and midwives were civil servants, and 70 percent of them had been raised in the city. All of them went to work by car—a rarity in that country.[99] Sad consequences of the social distance between providers and clients are not hard to find. In Egypt participants in a discussion group complained about the attitude of staff at the local rural hospital, with one respondent summing up the experience: "They have their noses up in the air and neglect us."[100] In South Africa a focus group member comments about a primary health care provider: "Sometimes I feel as if apartheid has never left this place. . . . They really have a way of making you feel like you are a piece of rubbish."[101]

Services must be relevant—filling a perceived need—or there will be little demand for them (box 1.3). If primary schools teach skills relevant only for secondary school—and not for life outside of school—only children from richer families who expect to continue to the secondary level will deem it worthwhile to complete primary school. In Ghana one respondent claimed: "School is useless: children spend time in school and then they're unemployed and haven't learned to work on the land."[102] In India one component of an integrated childhood development program failed when beneficiaries rejected the food

---

BOX 1.3 *School services for girls are not in high demand in Dhamar Province, Yemen*

"At the back of the classroom of 40 boys sat 2 girls....What did the girls want to be when they grew up? 'A teacher,' one said. 'A doctor,' said the other. But less than a quarter of the women in Yemen are literate, and they must follow the path of the traditional village women, who usually marry in their teens and have an average of 10 children. In the countryside of Dhamar Province, one of the country's poorest, there are few professional activities for anyone, much less for women. Besides, most parents won't let their daughters go to school—deeming it unac-

ceptable for them either to learn alongside boys or to walk to class in the street."

In Yemen girls make up about one in three students at the primary level, one in four at the secondary level. More than 75 percent of women over 15 are illiterate, compared with 35 percent of men. Girls' education is not the only problem, however. The net enrollment rate for boys is only 75 percent at the primary level, 70 percent at the secondary level.

Sources: Mayer (1997), World Bank (2002g).

grain supplied. Eventually the program changed what it offered to match varying preferences in different parts of the country.

And again, this need not be. In the Nioki area of Zaire (now the Democratic Republic of Congo), where the use of health services declined substantially between 1987 and 1991, it increased in clinics with nurses who had good interpersonal skills.[103] Among indigenous peoples in Bolivia, Ecuador, Guatemala, Mexico, Paraguay, and Peru, promoting bilingual and intercultural education contributed to improved schooling outcomes.[104] An innovative public health campaign among sex workers in Sonagachi, India, trained "peer educators" to pass information to their co-workers. Disseminating information in this way resulted in more condom use and substantially less HIV infection than in other cities. The approach had knock-on effects as well: sex workers organized a union and effectively lobbied for legalization, reduction in police harassment, and other rights.[105]

Little evaluation, little innovation, stagnant productivity

In most settings there are few evaluations of new interventions, and so no effective innovation and improvement in the productivity of services. Evaluating innovative service arrangements—such as new forms of accountability—is rarer still. If systems don't build in ways of learning about how to do things better, it should be no surprise when they stagnate. Relying on research from other countries, while useful, is not enough. Finding out how a particular intervention works in each country setting is crucial, since history, politics, and institutions determine what works, what doesn't, and why.

Once again, this need not be. Although rarely carried out, some programs have tried to incorporate evaluation components to learn about the program. Mexico's Progresa explicitly included randomization and evaluation in its design. The results of the evaluation—well documented and disseminated in the media—helped solidify support for the program. They showed what was most effective, contributing to the program's extension to a large part of the country's poor people (see spotlight). But even without an experi-

mental design, it is possible to learn about systems and to innovate. For example, the Probe study in India documented a variety of shortcomings of the quality of primary schools. The widely publicized results contributed to mobilizing support for reform.[106]

Making services work to improve outcomes

Many of the examples discussed so far describe failures in the public sector's provision of services, but they are not the only story. The 20th century has seen enormous improvements in living standards. Life expectancy has improved dramatically in nearly every country. The expansion of schooling has been similarly remarkable. In nearly every country illiteracy has been reduced dramatically, enrollment rates have gone up, and the average schooling of the population has more than doubled. Civil service bureaucracies providing good services have been integral elements of those successes. In many settings staff must overcome major obstacles—including threats to their own safety—in order to teach children or provide care to the sick.

What do services that work look like? Safe and pleasant schools with children learning to read and write. Primary clinics with health workers dispensing proper advice and medicine. Water networks distributing safe and dependable water. Direct subsidies to poor children and their families encouraging demand. Services that are accessible, affordable, and of good quality—helping to improve outcomes for poor people.

Governments take on a responsibility to make services work in order to promote health and education outcomes. Chapter 2 addresses the reasons for this responsibility, dwelling on three seemingly straightforward ways to discharge it: relying solely on economic growth, allocating public spending, or applying technical fixes. None of them is enough by itself. Making services work requires improving the institutional arrangements for producing them. Chapters 3 to 6 of this Report develop a framework for analyzing those arrangements. Chapters 7 to 11 apply the framework and draw lessons for governments and donors.

C R A T E 1 . 1 *Determinants of health and education outcomes—within, outside, and across sectors*

Health and education outcomes are determined by more than the availability and quality of health care and schooling. Better nutrition helps children learn. Better refrigeration and transport networks help keep medicines safe. Many factors determine outcomes on both the demand and the supply sides, linked at many levels. The demand for health and education is determined by individuals and households weighing the benefits and costs of their choices and the constraints they face. The supply of services that affect health and education outcomes starts with global technological knowledge and goes all the way to whether teachers report for work and communities maintain water pumps.

Demand: individuals and households
Benefits and costs determine how much an individual invests in education or health. What are the benefits? Higher levels of education and health are associated with higher productivity—and higher earnings. Investing in human capital is a way to get those

returns. But the returns might vary for different people, such as lower expected earnings for women or for ethnic minorities. In these cases one would expect different levels of investment: different desired levels of schooling, for instance. A crucial element of demand is the degree to which individuals rather than society reap the rewards. Goods with large positive externalities—in the extreme, public goods—will be demanded at less than the socially optimal level.

What are the costs? There are direct costs: user fees, transport costs, textbook fees, drug costs. Some of these can be borne by families—though not all families. Coping mechanisms for those that cannot are often hard to use. For example, the lack of insurance markets can make it hard to absorb the financial burden of sudden illness. Or the inability to borrow against future earnings can make it hard to borrow for schooling investments.

Indirect costs can also be large. For example, children often contribute to household

income by working inside or outside the home (looking after siblings, working on the family farm). The value of this contribution is forgone if they spend substantial time in school.

The total cost of illness includes days of work lost recovering, seeking care, or looking after the ill. Richer families can cope better with these costs, which leads to a direct association between income and outcomes. In addition, better health and education are often valued in themselves. As incomes increase families demand more of them, which again results in an association between income and outcomes.

The production of health and education depends on the knowledge and practices of adults in households. This works through both the demand for human capital and the generation of outcomes. A review of four hygiene interventions that targeted hand washing in poor countries found 35 percent less diarrhea-related illness among children who received the interventions. And factors

The determinants of supply and demand operate through many channels

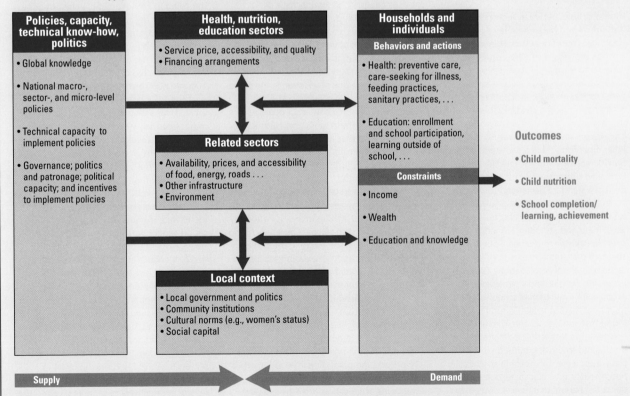

(continued)

CRATE 1.1 *Determinants of health and education outcomes—within, outside, and across sectors (continued)*

in the home complement schooling: books and reading at home contribute to literacy.

Investments in the human capital of children are sensitive to the allocation of power within households: families in which the bargaining power of women is stronger tend to invest more in health and education. A study in Brazil found that demand for calories and protein was up to 10 times more responsive to women's than men's income. This result, strongest in societies that proscribe women's roles, tends to affect girls more than boys.

More generally, the roles and responsibilities of different household members can affect how investments are made. A woman in Egypt says: "We face a calamity when my husband falls ill. Our life comes to a halt until he recovers." Her husband's earnings are crucial for sustaining the family. Since productivity is related to illness, households respond. In Bangladesh a study found that household members who engaged in more strenuous activities received more nutritious food. Daughters' education might be less valuable to parents if sons typically look after them in their old age, so parents might be less willing to send girls to school.

Demand: links between sectors at individual and household levels
Health and nutritional status directly affects a child's probability of school enrollment and capacity to learn and succeed in school. Malnutrition among children was associated with significant delays in school enrollment in Ghana. Improving child health and nutrition at the pre-primary level has long-term impacts on development. A study in the Philippines found that a one-standard-deviation increase in early-age child health increased subsequent test scores by about a third of a standard deviation.

Improving the health and nutritional status of students positively affects school enrollment and attendance. A longitudinal study in Pakistan found that a one-third of a standard deviation increase in child height increased school enrollment by 19 percentage points for girls and 4 percentage points for boys. An evaluation of school-based mass treatment for deworming in rural Kenya found that student absenteeism fell by a quarter—but test scores did not appear to be affected. Improving nutrition is not as simple as supplementary feeding at school: households can reallocate resources with the effect of "sharing" that food. A study in the Philippines found no such sharing in general,

but for a school snack program there was sharing in poorer families.

Parents' education has intergenerational effects on the health, nutritional status, and schooling of their children. Adult female education is one of the most robust correlates of child mortality in cross-national studies, even controlling for national income. Similarly, mother's education is a strong determinant of lower mortality at the household level, though the relationship weakens when other household and community socioeconomic characteristics are controlled for. A large part of this effect might not be general education but specific health knowledge, perhaps acquired using literacy and numeracy skills learned in school, as a study in Morocco found. The effects can also be interspatial: a study in Peru found that the education of a mother's neighbors significantly increases the nutritional status of her children. Parents' education is similarly associated with the schooling of their children, though the magnitude of the effect—and the relative roles of mother's and father's education—vary substantially across countries.

Access to—and use of—safe water, as well as adequate sanitation, have direct effects on health status. Hand washing is a powerful health practice, but it requires sufficient quantities of water. An eight-country study found that going from no improved water to "optimal" water was associated with a 6-percentage-point reduction in the prevalence of diarrhea in children under three years of age (from a base of 25 percent) in households without sanitation. Nutritional status was likewise associated with access to improved water. But not all studies find strong associations between water source and better health.

The water source is only part of the story: in Bangladesh water accessed through tubewells—an "improved" source— is frequently contaminated with arsenic. One study found that arsenic levels higher than the World Health Organization's maximum acceptable level are associated with twice the level of diarrhea in children under age six. Extremely high levels of arsenic are associated with shorter stature among adolescents.

The same eight-country study mentioned above found that going to "optimal" sanitation from none was associated with a 10-percentage-point drop in recent diarrhea in households with no improved water source. As in education, there are spillover effects: sanitation practices at the community

level impact everyone's health. In Peru the sanitation investments of a family's neighbors were associated with better nutritional status for that family's children.

The use of safe energy sources affects both health and education. Indoor air pollution—from using dirty cooking and heating fuels—hurts child health. One review of studies found that the probability of respiratory illness, or even death, was between two and five times higher in houses where exposure to indoor air pollution was high. A study in Guatemala found birth weights 65 grams lower among newborns of women who used wood as a domestic cooking fuel. Coping with the cold, in cold climates, affects health and imposes substantial direct and indirect costs on households. Education is affected as well: schools have to close when there is not enough heat, and it is hard to imagine that working on schoolwork at home is an option when indoor temperatures are below freezing.

Supply: global developments
At any given income, health and education outcomes have been improving. A continuing trend in improvements in health going back several decades is interpreted as advances in technologies and leaps in knowledge about health and hygiene. More recently, at a national income of $600 per capita, predicted child mortality fell from 100 per 1,000 births to 80—a full 20 percent reduction—between 1990 and 2000. If this association were sustained, major headway would be made toward the Millennium Development Goal through these changes alone. Major breakthroughs in immunizations for malaria—or HIV— could have a huge impact on mortality at all income levels.

Recent years have seen major developments in global funding for health and education expenditures. Debt relief through the Heavily Indebted Poor Countries initiative is tied to increases in expenditures on these sectors. New assistance, delivered through multisectoral products such as Poverty Reduction Support Credits, requires explicit strategies for human development investments. Global funds for health and the "Fast-Track Initiative" for education are international pledges to support initiatives in the sectors (chapter 11). Easing financial constraints goes hand in hand with using resources effectively to support services that work for poor people.

C R A T E 1 . 1 *Determinants of health and education outcomes—within, outside, and across sectors (continued)*

Supply: national resources

National income is strongly associated with child mortality and primary school completion. Income and health and education outcomes build on each other. More income leads to better human development outcomes, and better health and education can lead to increased productivity and better incomes. Studies that have tried to disentangle these relationships typically find income to be a robust and strong determinant of outcomes.

National endowments are also a strong determinant. Geography and climate sometimes make it tougher to overcome health problems. For example, areas conducive to mosquito survival have great difficulty in combating malaria—and widely dispersed populations are difficult to serve through traditional school systems.

The performance of public expenditure in producing outcomes varies substantially across countries. There are large differences in achievements at similar levels of expenditure and similar achievements with very large differences in expenditures—conditional on income. Spending more through the public sector is not always associated with improved outcomes. This is not to say that spending cannot be helpful—but the way resources are used is crucial to their effectiveness.

Supply: political, economic, and policy context

Governance affects the efficiency of expenditures: in corrupt settings money that is ostensibly earmarked for improving human development outcomes is diverted. Staffs ostensibly delivering services do not. But the effects of poor governance can be deeper. Famines are caused as much by human factors as by nature. And the repercussions run across national borders. For example, a drought combined with misguided policies and bad governance in Zimbabwe resulted in a regional food shortage.

Managing public expenditures can be a critical link in ensuring that allocated expenditures get put to uses that improve outcomes. "Cash budgeting" in Zambia led to unpredictable social service spending and deep cuts in spending on rural infrastructure.

Conflict leaves long-lived scars on health and education. Children in war-torn countries are hard to find, hard to get into school, and hard to keep in school. During Sierra Leone's recent civil war, tens of thousands of children attended primary school but hundreds of thousands did not. Wars, including civil wars, lead to "lost generations" of undernourished and undereducated children. These deficiencies are difficult—if not impossible—to make up for. When children have been out of school for a long time, it is hard to return. And bad health and poor nutrition at an early age affect children throughout their lives.

Periods of national economic and social crisis can result in bad health and education outcomes. This is clear in Russia's recent history: adult mortality has increased dramatically over the past 10 years. Sustained economic depression can severely compromise children's health and have cascading effects on subsequent development and learning. The evidence of shorter-term economic crises is more mixed. In middle-income environments school enrollments might increase as the opportunity cost of time for young people falls. Even in Indonesia, a relatively poor country, the deep economic and social crisis of the late 1990s had smaller impacts on outcomes than initially feared. This was partly because broad social safety nets were rapidly put in place.

Supply: the local context of government and communities

Decentralization can be a powerful tool for moving decisionmaking closer to those affected by it. Doing so can strengthen the links and accountability between policymakers and citizens—local governments are potentially more accountable to local demands. It can also strengthen them between policymakers and providers—local governments are potentially more able to monitor providers. But local governments should not be romanticized. Like national governments they are vulnerable to capture—and this might be easier for local elites on a local scale.

Community-level institutions, shaped by cultural norms and practices, can facilitate or hinder an environment for improving outcomes. A review of safe-water projects in Central Java, Indonesia, associates success with greater social capital. In Rajasthan, India, manifestations of "mutually beneficial collective action" were associated with watershed conservation and development activities more generally. A broader review of the literature suggests that participatory approaches to implementing projects are more successful in communities with less economic inequality and less social and ethnic heterogeneity.

Supply: services and their financing

Services themselves are important. Inaccessible or poor-quality services raise the effective price of health care and schooling, which results in higher mortality and lower educational achievement. Poor-quality schools deter enrollment and reduce attainment and achievement, especially among children of poor families. Health clinics where the technical skills of staff are so bad as to be dangerous will lead to higher mortality. Lack of water will significantly hurt child health.

Financing arrangements matter. Absorbing the burden of unpredictable large expenditures through health insurance can reduce impoverishment, which in turn will affect outcomes. Financing primary schooling might seem relatively minor: direct costs are typically small. Even so, a lack of access to credit has been found to be associated with lower school enrollment. Borrowing to pay the direct costs of primary school is almost unheard of, but there could be second-round effects if the lack of access to credit means that families need children to engage in home production.

Supply: services working together to produce outcomes

Links among services are critical. Vaccines can become less effective, ineffective, or even dangerous if they get too hot, freeze, or are exposed to light. The ability to transport and store vaccines properly thus determines the success of immunization campaigns. In cold climates schools and health facilities often need to close because of the lack of heating, and dependable energy sources can directly affect health and education outcomes. The accessibility of services can be a deterrent to their use: roads and adequate transport contribute to the total cost of using a service. Since the expected return to education determines the benefits of schooling, labor markets that are not fundamentally distorted (for example, through discriminatory practices toward marginalized groups) can contribute to higher education achievement. Services therefore need to work together to promote improved outcomes.

Source: Sources are detailed in Filmer (2003a).

Conditional cash transfers to reduce poverty in Mexico

Progresa, the Education, Health, and Nutrition Program of Mexico, transferred money directly to families on the condition that family members went for health checkups, mothers went for hygiene and nutrition information sessions, and children attended school. By documenting success through rigorous evaluation, the program has improved, scaled up, and taught others.[107]

When Ernesto Zedillo became Mexico's president in 1995, a fifth of the population could not afford the minimum daily nutritional requirements, 10 million Mexicans lacked access to basic health services, more than 1.5 million children were out of school, and student absenteeism and school desertions were three times higher in poor and remote areas than in the rest of the country. The country had a history of unproductive poverty alleviation programs. Worse, the 1994–95 economic crisis left the government with even fewer resources—and greater demands, as more people were falling into poverty.

The administration decided that a new approach to poverty alleviation was needed. The Education, Health, and Nutrition Program of Mexico, called Progresa, introduced a set of conditional cash transfers to poor families—if their children were enrolled in school and if family members visited health clinics for checkups and nutrition and hygiene information.

The program was intended to remedy several shortcomings of earlier programs. First, it would counter the bias in poor families toward present consumption by bolstering investment in human capital. Second, it would recognize the interdependencies among education, health, and nutrition. Third, to stretch limited resources, it would link cash transfers to household behavior, aiming at changing attitudes. Fourth, to reduce political interference, the program's goals, rules, requirements, and evaluation methods would be widely publicized.

The program has been rigorously evaluated, and evaluators have exploited the randomized way the program was rolled out. The results have been impressive. To emphasize the apolitical nature of the program, the government suspended the growth of the program for six months prior to the election in 2000—to show that Progresa was not a political tool.

When President Vincente Fox was elected, his government embraced the program, built on it using the evaluation results, expanded it to urban areas, and renamed it *Oportunidades*. By the end of 2002 the program had about 21 million beneficiaries—roughly a fifth of the Mexican population.

Designing a comprehensive program

Children over seven were eligible for education transfers. Benefits increased by grade (since opportunity costs increase with age) and were higher for girls in middle school, to encourage their enrollment. To retain the benefits, children needed to maintain an 85 percent attendance record and could not repeat a grade more than once.

Eligible families could also receive a monthly stipend if members got regular medical checkups and mothers attended monthly nutrition and hygiene information sessions. Households with children under three could also receive a micronutrient supplement.

The transfers went to mothers, who were thought more responsible for caring for children. The program imposed a monthly ceiling of $75 per family. In 1999 the average monthly transfer was around $24 per family, nearly 20 percent of mean household consumption before the program. Transfers were also inflation-indexed every six months (today the maximum is $95 and the average is $35).

Highly centralized, the program has just one intermediary between program officials and beneficiaries—a woman community promoter chosen by a general assembly of households in targeted communities. She can also liaise between beneficiaries and education and health providers.

By the end of 1999 the program covered some 2.6 million rural families—about 40 percent of rural families and a ninth of all families in Mexico. The program budget was almost $780 million, or 0.2 percent of gross domestic product and 20 percent of the federal poverty alleviation budget.

Almost 60 percent of program transfers went to households in the poorest 20 percent of the national income distribution and more than 80 percent to the poorest 40 percent. This is impressive. The median targeting effectiveness in 77 safety net programs from around the world was to have 65 percent of benefits go to the poorest 40 percent (according to one recent study).

Even with careful targeting and monitoring, the program's administrative costs were less than 9 percent of total costs—substantially lower than earlier poverty alleviation efforts in Mexico. Despite its initial large scale, the program did not cover all the poor, particularly in urban areas.

Boosting enrollments

Girls' enrollment in middle school rose from 67 percent to around 75 percent, and boys' from 73 percent to 78 percent. Most of the increase came from increases in the transition from primary to middle school (figure 1). The program worked primarily by keeping children in school, not by encouraging those who had dropped out to return. It also helped reduce the incidence of child labor.

Figure 1 Higher school retention, more transitions from primary to middle school
Expected grade completion before and after intervention, and with and without Progresa

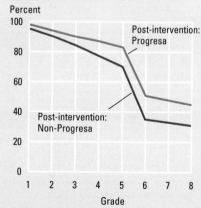

Note: Among children who enroll.
Source: Schultz (2001).

Labor force participation decreased by about 20 percent for boys. Still, a substantial number of children from poor families continue to combine work with school.

The impacts on learning are less clear. Teachers report improvements, attributing them to better attendance, student interest, and nutrition. But a study conducted one year after the program started found no difference in test scores.

Improving nutrition and health

The program helped reduce the incidence of low height for age among children one to three years old. (Before the program stunting was very high, at 44 percent.) Annual mean growth in height was 16 percent for children covered by the program. On average, height increased by 1–4 percent, and weight by 3.5 percent. These gains were achieved despite evidence that some households did not regularly receive nutrition supplements and that supplements were often "shared" with older children. Part of the effect can be attributed to spending more on food and to consuming more nutritious food, as recommended by the nutrition information sessions. There were also positive spillover effects for nonbeneficiaries in the same community.

The program substantially increased preventive health care visits. Visits by pregnant women in their first trimester rose 8 percent, keeping babies and mothers healthier. Illnesses dropped 25 percent among newborns and 20 percent among children under five (figure 2). The prevalence of anemia in children two to four years old declined 19 percent. Adult health improved too.

Reducing poverty

The program is not only raising incomes temporarily, it should help raise future productivity and earnings of the children benefiting. Modeling exercises find that nutritional supplements alone would boost lifetime earnings by about 3 percent and edu-

Figure 2   Improving child health
Percentage of children reported to have had an illness.

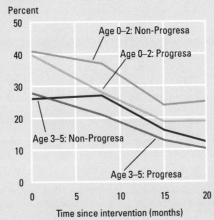

Note: Age at start of intervention.
Source: Gertler (2000).

cation impacts would increase them by 8 percent. A general equilibrium analysis of Progresa found that the welfare impact was 60 percent higher than that of the highly distortionary food subsidies that Mexico used previously.

Evaluating impacts

Progresa was unusual in integrating evaluation from the beginning, enabling it to assess impacts fairly precisely. To ensure political credibility, the evaluation was contracted out to a foreign-based research group, the International Food Policy Research Institute.

Phasing in communities in a random fashion—required for budgetary purposes—allowed the construction of 186 control and 320 treatment groups. Having the control groups enabled evaluators to "wash out" confounding factors, including time trends and shocks (economic and climatic). Eventually all control communities were incorporated in the program. Both quantitative and qualitative evaluations were conducted, the latter using semistructured interviews, focus groups, and workshops.

The evaluation design captures the many determinants of outcomes. But it has limitations. Policymakers would benefit from knowing how the program could be manipulated to improve impacts. For example, what is the impact of conditioning the transfers rather than giving pure unconditioned transfers? In addition, households in the control group might have been affected by the intervention or by knowing that they might receive it in the future, an effect that would muddy the comparisons.

Evaluations can address these issues, but the complexity (and expense) increases substantially. Alternative approaches that rely on modeling—imposing additional assumptions on the analysis—might be necessary. Such analyses are currently underway.

Evidence makes the difference

A conditional cash transfer program can be a powerful way of promoting education, health, and nutritional outcomes on a massive scale. The success of the Progresa program has led to similar programs, especially in other Latin American countries (Colombia, Honduras, Jamaica, and Nicaragua).

Evaluation was not an afterthought. It continually fed back into improving program operations. And its rigor increased confidence in the validity of assessments of the program's effects.

Evaluation was important for domestic and international political and economic support—and thus contributed to program sustainability. Unlike previous programs, this one was not abandoned after a change in government. Clear and credible evidence of large benefits for the country's poor contributed to maintaining the integrity of the program's design (albeit with a name change). It also made it easier to get support from the Inter-American Development Bank for a major expansion of the program.

Governments should make services work

The responsibility that governments take on for basic health and education can be discharged in many ways—among them, fostering economic growth, increasing public spending, and applying technical interventions. Each can contribute to better outcomes. But if they are not supporting services that work—services that result from effective institutional arrangements—they will not make a large sustainable difference. Making services work requires changing the institutional relationships among key actors. Subsequent chapters of this Report develop and apply a framework to understand how and why those relationships play out for different services.

Economic growth, though a major determinant of human development outcomes, would need to be substantially faster than it has been in most countries to make dramatic improvements through that channel alone. Public spending makes improvements possible, but the improvements will fall short if spending fails to reach poor people—either because it goes for things the poor do not use or because it is diverted along the way—or if services are not made more productive. Applying technical interventions—combining inputs to produce outputs and outcomes more effectively—is also important. But simply adjusting inputs without reforming the institutions that produce inefficiencies will not lead to sustainable improvements.

A public responsibility

Governments—and the societies they represent—often see improving outcomes in health and education as a public responsibility. They are supported in this by the international endorsement of the Millennium Development Goals (see Overview). A variety of reasons lie behind this responsibility: clas-sic welfare economics arguments for government intervention, political economy reasons for intervention in key social sectors, appeals to fundamental human rights. Governments demonstrate their responsibility by financing, providing, or regulating the services that contribute to health and education outcomes. The services come in many shapes and sizes: building and staffing schools, subsidizing hospitals, regulating water and electrical utility companies, building roads, providing cash transfers to individuals and households. Making these services work means that governments are meeting their responsibility.

Public spending

This responsibility is often reflected in government spending. Health and education alone account for about a third of aggregate government spending, with the average slightly lower in poorer countries and regions (table 2.1). But there are wide variations across countries, even within the same region. Health and education spending accounted for 13 percent of public spending in Sierra Leone in 1998 but 34 percent in Kenya—18 percent in Estonia in 1997 but 59 percent in Moldova in 1996. Social security and welfare spending, much of it directed to improving health and education, typically makes up another 10–20 percent of aggregate spending.[108]

Governments contribute a large share of the financing for schools and clinics. Wages and salaries on average account for 75 percent of recurrent public spending on education—and often for almost all the spending (96 percent in Kenya).[109] Most teachers and many health workers are civil service employees. Salaries aside, government subsidies can make up a large share of a facility's budget.

Public provision

In education, health, water, and electricity the public sector is a major provider (if not a monopoly) as well as a funder of services. The Indonesian government operates more than 150,000 primary schools and 10,000 junior secondary schools that cover 85 percent and 60 percent of the respective enrollments.[110] The Ugandan government operated 1,400 primary level facilities and close to 100 hospitals in 1996.[111] The Indian public sector runs almost 200,000 primary health facilities and 15,000 secondary and tertiary facilities.[112] But wide public provision does not always translate into substantial use. In Uganda government health facilities handled just 40 percent of treatments sought in facilities.[113] In India, even with the huge organization of public health facilities, the private sector accounts for 80 percent of outpatient treatments and almost 60 percent of inpatient treatments.[114]

Reasons for public responsibility

Economics gives two rationales for public responsibility. First, because of market failures, the amount of services produced and consumed would be less than optimal from society's standpoint without government intervention. Market failures can be externalities. The fact that an immunized child reduces the spread of disease in society is an incentive to immunize more children. Basic education might benefit others besides the graduate, another externality. Individuals have little incentive to build and maintain the roads that are crucial to promoting access to services, but communities and societies do. "Public goods" (goods that, once produced, cannot be denied to anyone else and whose consumption by one person does not diminish consumption by others) are an extreme form of market failure. Mosquito control in a malaria-endemic area is an example. There is no market incentive to produce public goods, so government intervention is required.

Other market failures relate to imperfect information. Different information about individuals' risk of illness can lead to a breakdown in the market for health insurance. Lack of knowledge about the benefits of hand washing or of education can lead to less than desirable investment and consumption.[115]

Table 2.1 Public expenditures on health and education: large but varied
Education and health spending as a share of government expenditures and as a share of GDP, in 2000 or latest year available (percent)

	Share of public expenditures			Share of GDP		
	Average	**Minimum**	**Maximum**	**Average**	**Minimum**	**Maximum**
East Asia and Pacific	27	12	53	6	2	11
Europe and Central Asia	31	18	59	10	4	17
Latin America and Caribbean	33	14	52	8	4	13
Middle East and North Africa	23	13	39	7	4	12
South Asia	21	16	25	5	4	8
Sub-Saharan Africa	25	13	34	7	2	12
Low-income countries	25	12	59	6	2	17
Middle-income countries	29	13	53	8	4	14
High-income countries	33	20	56	11	3	15

Note: Of the 135 countries included, 52 have data for 2000, 8 for 2001, 30 for 1999, 17 for 1998. The remaining 28 have data from earlier in the 1990s.
Source: World Development Indicators database.

These market failures call for government intervention, but they do not necessarily call for public provision: it could well be that the proper role is financing, regulation, or information dissemination.

The second economics justification for public responsibility is equity. Improving health and education outcomes for poor people, or reducing the gaps in outcomes between poor people and those who are better off, is often considered a responsibility of government. There are a variety of social justice reasons behind this. Some see this responsibility as rooted in the belief that basic education and basic health are fundamental human rights (box 2.1). The United Nations Universal Declaration of Human Rights asserts an individual's right to "a standard of living adequate for the health and well-being of himself and of his family, including food, clothing, housing and medical care" and a right to education that is compulsory and "free, at least in the elementary and fundamental stages."[116] Subsequent international accords have expanded the set of health and education rights.[117] Many national constitutions have guarantees for health and education.

BOX 2.1 *Most governments take responsibility for health and education—often appealing to human rights*

Debates on health care and education in developing countries often appeal to human rights. Rooted in the broader context of social justice, these rights are set forth in the Universal Declaration of Human Rights (1948) as well as other international conventions, such as the International Covenant on Economic and Social Rights (1966). Several international and bilateral agencies have endorsed a human rights orientation. In addition, the constitutions and laws of many countries include references to rights to education and health care (a review of constitutional rights in 165 countries with written constitutions found that 116 referenced a right to education and 73 a right to health care; 95 stipulated free education and 29 free health care for at least some services to some groups). With education and health central to rights, the

practical implications of approaches based on rights complement welfare economics.

An approach based on rights emphasizes equality in dignity and equality of opportunity. It highlights the need to look at outcomes for all individuals and groups, especially the legally and socially disadvantaged. It makes explicit a consideration that economics incorporates with difficulty: many psychological repercussions to poverty result in poor people's inability to avail themselves of health care and education services, even when such services are available.

Welfare economics provides tools for assessing priorities and possibilities for intervening when budgets are limited —and offers a metric for doing so. Several aspects of economic analysis provide instruments for implementing rights, complementing a rights-based approach.

More generally, the approaches overlap on many of their practical policy consequences. Both are skeptical that electoral politics and the market provide enough accountability for effective and equitable provision of health and education services—so there is a need for government and community involvement. An economics approach to making services work—such as the one in this Report—is informed by the guidance on participation and empowerment that international human rights instruments provide. In addition, rights reinforce poor people's claims on resources overall and on those allocated for basic services in particular—key elements of the effective "voice" of poor people discussed here.

Source: Gauri (2003).

The notion of health and education as basic human rights provides a strong basis for public responsibility, but ambiguities remain. Does a right to medical care imply that government must provide it or even finance it? The human rights to "periodic holidays with pay" or "equal work for equal pay," as mentioned in the United Nations declaration, are generally not interpreted to imply government subsidies.[118] Although free elementary education is asserted as a right, parents also have a right "to choose the kind of education that shall be given to their children"—suggesting that universal public provision is not required.[119] Social equity and fundamental human rights suggest a responsibility for government but leave open the ways of discharging that responsibility. Importantly, enshrining these notions as rights legitimizes the demands of citizens—especially poor citizens—that government take responsibility for making services work.

Market failures and social justice are normative justifications for public responsibility—they describe why governments should be involved. They do not always give much guidance on how. Why governments actually get involved provides insight on how public responsibility is discharged. Education has long been a battleground for beliefs, ideas, and values. The late 19th and early 20th centuries offer many stories of this battle, from the movement for secular primary education in France to a

public education system focused on nationalism after the Meiji restoration in Japan.[120]

Much of this involvement is high-minded: a coherent public education system probably contributes to social cohesion, particularly important in fractionalized societies.[121] Postcolonial states embraced public provision of education as a strategy for nation building. But public provision can also be the rational manifestation of a state's desire to inculcate a particular set of beliefs. Tanzania's 1967 education reforms were wrapped up with *Ujama* and African Socialism. Indonesia's mass education campaign was closely tied to nation-building and national ideology codified in *pancasila*—principles whose teaching was enforced in every school until the fall of the New Order government.

Beyond nation building and social cohesion, services operate fully in the political realm: free education and free health care are electoral rallying cries in many countries, popular with many voters. In 1997 Uganda's President Museveni campaigned on a platform of free universal primary education. The message was extremely popular—he won—and within a short time official enrollments nearly doubled (see spotlight).[122] Uganda is not unique: many politicians identify themselves with their stance toward public provision of services. But success is hard: few politicians have been able to transform these political platforms into outcomes. Services operate in the political realm in yet another way. Many politicians use jobs in the large bureaucracies associated with services to reward supporters or to build power.

Growth, though essential, is not enough

Given the responsibility to promote education and health outcomes, what can governments do? One approach is hands-off: rely solely on economic growth since higher national income is strongly associated with lower child mortality and higher primary school completion (crate 1.1 and figure 2.1). Among low-income countries, 10 percent more income per capita is associated, on average, with a 6.6 percent lower child mortality rate and a 4.8 percent higher primary school completion rate. Among middle-income countries 10 percent more income per capita is associated with 7.7 percent less mortality but little improvement in primary completion.

At low levels of income relatively small differences in per capita income can mean big differences in outcomes. Per capita income was only about $90 higher in Madagascar than in Malawi in the 1990s, but there were almost 50 fewer child deaths per 1,000 births in Madagascar in 2000.[123] The association between income and health and education outcomes works both ways: more income leads to lower mortality and more children completing primary school; better health and education can lead to higher productivity and incomes. Studies have tried to disentangle these relationships, and they typically still find income to be a robust and strong determinant of outcomes.[124]

But income is not the whole story: at any given income there are wide variations in achievement. With average incomes of just under $300 per capita in the 1990s, Vietnam had a child mortality rate of about 40 per 1,000 in 2000 and Cambodia of 120. At per capita incomes around $4,000 in the 1990s, Malaysia had a child mortality rate of about 12 per 1,000 in 2000 and Brazil of just less than 40. Similarly, Madagascar and Nigeria both had per capita incomes close to $300 in the 1990s, but by the end of the decade the primary completion rate was 26 percent in Madagascar and 67 percent in Nigeria.[125]

How much reduction in child mortality and improvement in primary school comple-

Figure 2.1   National income and outcomes are strongly associated, especially in low-income countries

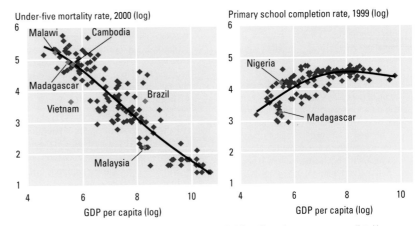

Note: The GDP per capita is based on a 1990s average, 1995 U.S. dollars. Lines show outcomes as predicted by a non-linear function of GDP per capita.
Source: GDP per capita data from World Development Indicators database; under-five mortality from UNICEF (2002); primary completion rates from Bruns, Mingat, and Rakatomalala (2003).

tion can be expected from income growth alone? Cutting child mortality by two-thirds between 1990 and 2015 (one of the Millennium Development Goals) means reducing it by 4.4 percent a year. Low-income countries would need sustained per capita income growth of 6.7 percent a year to reduce mortality by two-thirds by 2015. Senegal would have to boost per capita income from about $650 to $3,500—close to the level in Panama. Brazil would need an increase from almost $5,000 to $20,000—close to the per capita income in New Zealand.[126]

Similarly, achieving universal primary school completion through income alone would require massive economic growth. In Mauritania, where primary school completion was 46 percent in 1990, per capita income growth would need to average 6.5 percent a year. So while income and outcomes are strongly associated, especially in low-income countries, reaching the Millennium Development Goals will require dramatically high—perhaps unrealistically high—growth rates if growth is the only channel for achieving the goals. Policies that do more than increase growth are required.[127]

More public spending alone is not enough

If growth is not enough, what else can governments do to improve outcomes? One approach is to spend more. Increasing public

BOX 2.2 *The Fast-Track Initiative—providing assistance for credible national education strategies*

With more than 100 million children not in primary school, the "Fast-Track Initiative" (FTI) was launched in June 2002 to accelerate progress toward Education for All in low-income countries. Under the FTI national education plans are assessed against an indicative framework of policy benchmarks, prospects for scaling up, and allowances for flexibility and learning by doing. To ensure that education goals are embedded in an overall national strategy and consistent with countries' medium-term expenditure framework, a criterion for FTI eligibility is a national commitment to a formal Poverty Reduction Strategy.

The FTI supports countries in addressing key policy, capacity, data, and financing constraints to universal primary completion by 2015, net intake into first grade of 100 percent of girls and boys by 2010, and improved learning outcomes. An initial group of 23 countries was invited to join the initiative, and all accepted.

The FTI was inspired by the Monterrey Consensus—that better results accrue when development support is targeted to countries that accept clear accountability for results and adopt appropriate policy reforms. The FTI was conceived as a process for countries with sound education policies, embedded in an agreed-on macroeconomic framework, to receive added support from donors.

Clear impacts—and obstacles
Less than a year into the process the FTI has had some clear positive impacts. First, it has demonstrated that the new framework of mutual accountability is accepted by developing coun-

tries. With impressive speed countries have ensured that their sector plans meet the new tests for credibility and sustainability. And the donors have increased resources for FTI countries, seconded staff to an international secretariat for the initiative (in the World Bank), and agreed on FTI operating principles and guidelines.

More generally, the FTI has:

- Raised the political profile of Education for All, and increased awareness of the need for faster progress to reach education goals.
- Sharpened developing countries' focus on primary school completion and quality (not just coverage) and on the importance of getting policies right.
- Brought field-based donors into a unified policy dialogue with governments, improving coordination.
- Mobilized more resources for primary education (a 60 percent increase in official development assistance commitments to the first FTI countries).

But the experience with FTI has also highlighted some obstacles. At the country level these include difficulties in ensuring that resources reach the service delivery level; a need to consider a variety of service delivery modes—including community-run schools, NGO-run schools, and faith-based schools—and the complexities of public support to this range of providers; the need to make difficult reforms to increase efficiency and ensure sustainability; and the need for better data systems to support "real-time" tracking of education results.

Some problems for donors
Despite some progress donor procedures are not yet harmonized, and much financing remains fragmented. Some donor assistance under the FTI continues to be input-driven, subject to a "donor discount," with resources earmarked for contractors in donor countries rather than providing flexible support for core expenditures.

Too much aid still flows to historically preferred countries, rather than good performers. Although the donors have mobilized additional funding for FTI countries case by case, there remain some "donor orphans." Without pooled funding to support these countries, the FTI will not be able to deliver on the donors' commitment that "no country with a credible plan for Education for All will be thwarted for lack of external support." The momentum of FTI could easily be lost if a fundamental principle of the compact—assistance supporting effective policies—is not honored.

The FTI is a major part of international responses—including the G8 process, the Monterrey Consensus, and the New Economic Partnership for African Development—to provide momentum for universal primary completion by 2015, perhaps the most achievable of the Millennium Development Goals. Success will require that developing countries pay attention to policy reform and human and financial resources. It will also require that donors coordinate better and honor their side of the bargain by assisting performing countries.

Source: FTI secretariat.

---

spending can be a critical part of promoting improvements in health and education. For example, it may be necessary to spend more on interventions to reduce mortality or on education reforms that underpin increases in primary completion rates—and part of this spending might require international assistance (box 2.2). But the large variation in the effectiveness of using funds makes it hard to find a consistent relationship between changes in spending and outcomes—highlighting the importance of spending money well.

Just how variable is the association between public spending and outcomes? A glimpse at a handful of countries provides an indication.

- Between the 1980s and 1990s total public spending on education in Ethiopia and

Malawi increased by $8 per child of primary school age.[128] In Ethiopia primary school completion stagnated, going from 22 percent in 1990 to 24 percent in 1999, while in Malawi it rose from 30 percent to 50 percent (figure 2.2).

- Per capita public spending on health fell between $1 and $5 in Côte d'Ivoire and Haiti from the 1980s to the 1990s: child mortality worsened substantially in Côte d'Ivoire but improved in Haiti—though remaining high (figure 2.3).

- Thailand increased public spending on primary schooling more than Peru did, yet primary school completions fell in Thailand and increased in Peru.

- Public spending on health diverged in Mexico and Jordan, yet reductions in child mortality were similar.

Figure 2.2   Changes in public spending and outcomes are only weakly related: schooling

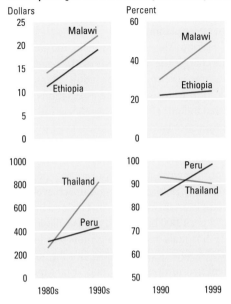

Public spending on education **Primary school completion**

Dollars / Percent charts for Malawi, Ethiopia, Thailand, Peru

Note: "Spending" refers to total annual public spending on education per child of primary school age, in 1995 U.S. dollars averaged for the 1980s and the 1990s. Primary school completion rates are calculated on the basis of 6 years in Ethiopia (primary plus two years lower secondary), 8 years in Malawi, 6 years in Thailand, and 6 years in Peru.
Source: Spending data from World Development Indicators database; primary school completion data from Bruns, Mingat, and Rakatomalala (2003).

For each country there is a story about why public spending contributed to improving outcomes or why it did not. That is the crux: the effectiveness of public spending varies tremendously.[129] In-depth studies confirm this variability—for example, an analysis of Malaysia over the late 1980s found little association between public spending on doctors and infant or maternal mortality.[130] A major improvement in the incidence of public education spending on poor people in South Africa has been slow to translate into better outcomes.[131] But an impact evaluation of the expansion of public school places in Indonesia in the 1970s found a significant positive impact on school enrollments.[132]

Another way to look at the impact of public spending is in a cross-section of countries. In general, countries that spend more public resources on health have lower child mortality, and countries that spend more on education have higher completion rates. But this association is driven largely by the fact that public spending increases with national income. After controlling for national

income, public spending and outcomes are only weakly associated (figure 2.4)—both substantively (in the sense that the correlation is small) and statistically (in the sense that the correlation is indistinguishable from zero).[133] With similar changes in spending associated with different changes in outcomes, it should come as no surprise that the cross-country association is so weak.

Why does public spending have different impacts?

Deeper analysis of the relation between public spending and child mortality finds results varying from statistical significance to insignificance—for four main reasons. First, some countries might spend more because they need to spend more to remedy urgent underlying health problems. The resulting cross-sectional association would be uninformative since more spending would appear to be associated with worse outcomes. Using statistical techniques that exploit the variation in spending that depends on factors unrelated to mortality

Figure 2.3   Changes in public spending and outcomes are only weakly related: child mortality

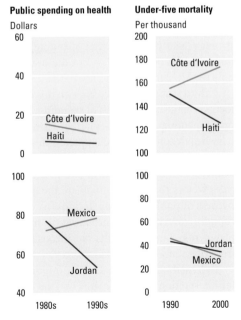

Public spending on health **Under-five mortality**

Dollars / Per thousand charts for Côte d'Ivoire, Haiti, Mexico, Jordan

Note: "Spending" refers to total annual per capita public spending on health in 1995 dollars averaged for the 1980s and the 1990s.
Source: Spending data for 1990s from World Development Indicators database. For Jordan and Côte d'Ivoire, spending data for the 1980s are from World Bank sources. For Haiti and Mexico, spending data for the 1980s are from Govindaraj, Murray, and Gnanaraj (1995). Child mortality data are from UNICEF (2002).

Figure 2.4 The association between outcomes and public spending is weak, when controlling for national income

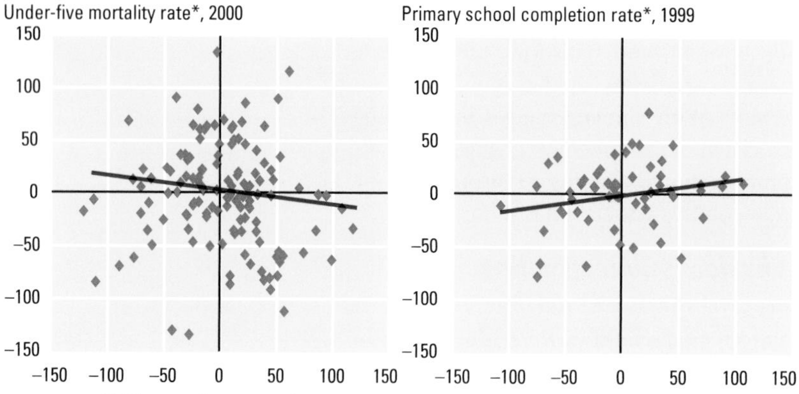

Under-five mortality rate*, 2000

Public spending per capita on health, 1990s average*

Primary school completion rate*, 1999

Public spending per child on education, 1990s average*

* Public spending, child mortality rate, and primary school completion are given as the percent deviation from rate predicted by GDP per capita.
Note: For the under-five mortality regression, the coefficient is –0.148 and the t-statistic is 1.45. For the primary completion regression, the coefficient is 0.157 and the t-statistic is 1.70.
Source: GDP per capita and public spending data, World Development Indicators database; under-five mortality, UNICEF; primary completion rate, Bruns, Mingat, and Rakatomalala (2003).

outcomes still produces an insignificant relationship.[134] Those techniques are not universally accepted, however, and it is possible that governments are adjusting what they spend in response to underlying health conditions.

Second, spending may affect different groups in society differently. Public spending could affect child mortality among poor families without having a large overall impact. Studies allowing for this effect have found a stronger association between spending and outcomes for poor people—but the result is only weakly significant and not robust.[135]

A third strand of the research on this issue focuses on the composition of spending: does more spending on primary rather than tertiary health activities have a different impact on mortality? The cross-national statistical evidence is weak.[136] A fourth strand investigates factors that might modulate the effectiveness of public spending. It finds that corruption, governance, or urbanization might play a role, but the results are inconsistent from one analysis to another.[137]

Two methodological issues are important for interpreting these analyses. First, the sample of countries in a study affects the results. A sample of a few countries that have spent a lot and achieved a lot—and a few countries that have spent little and achieved little—will yield a significant association between more spending and lower mortality. A different

sample might yield no association. The number of countries in studies that have addressed this question varies dramatically—from 22 to 116—so different results should not be surprising.[138]

Second, the specification in the analysis can change the assessment of the result. For example, controlling for adult literacy in addition to income in the associations illustrated in figure 2.4 yields an association and a significance level that are even closer to zero.

The message from these studies is not that public funding cannot be successful. It is that commitment and appropriate policies, backed by public spending, can achieve a lot. Infant mortality was high in Thailand in 1970 at 74 per 1,000 births, and the use of community hospitals and health centers was low, in part because quality was low. But the government's commitment to reduce infant mortality was strong. Health planners took stock, analyzing information on service use and from household surveys. Thailand doubled real per capita public spending on health between the early 1970s and the mid-1980s. But it also did more. It built facilities in remote areas, directed more services to poor areas and poor people, improved staff training, provided incentives for doctors to locate in remote areas, and promoted community involvement in managing health care delivery. The oversight of doctors was strengthened. And the authority for various programs was devolved to the provincial level, freeing the central Ministry of Public Health to concentrate on planning, coordination, and technical support. By 1985 infant mortality had fallen to 42 per 1,000 births, and today it is 28 per 1,000.[139] Similar stories are playing out 20 years later in other parts of the developing world.

Public spending on services fails to reach poor people

Most poor people do not get their fair share of public spending on services, let alone the larger share that might be justified on equity grounds. Public expenditure incidence analysis—matching who uses publicly financed services with how much governments spend per user—provides a snapshot of who benefits from government spending. Results typically show that the

Figure 2.5   Richer people often benefit more from public spending on health and education
Share of public spending on health and education going to the richest and poorest fifths

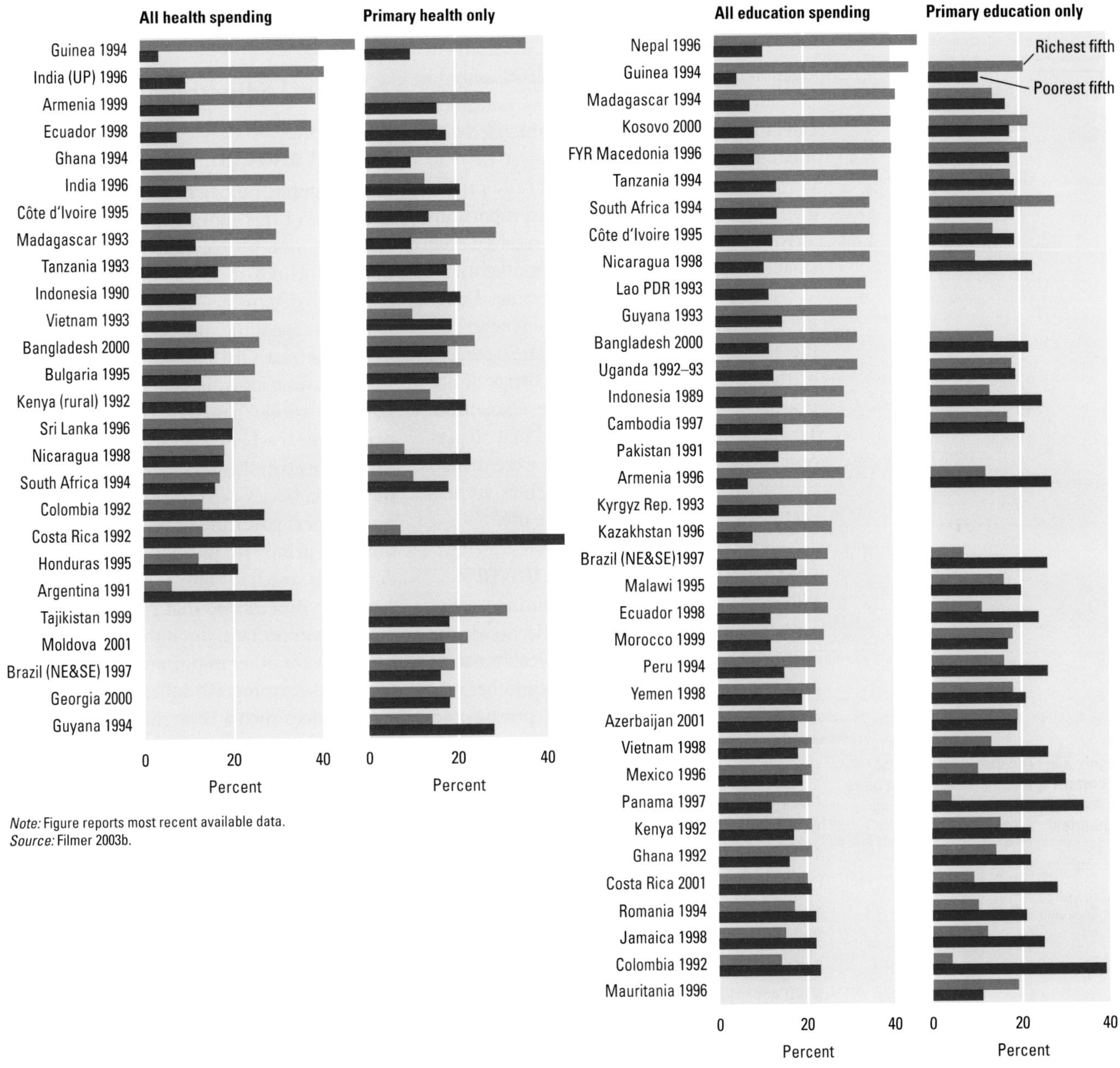

Note: Figure reports most recent available data.
Source: Filmer 2003b.

poorest fifth of the populace receives less than a fifth of education or health expenditures, while the richest fifth receives more. In Ghana for example, the poorest fifth received only 12 percent of public expenditures on health in 1994, whereas the richest fifth received 33 percent (figure 2.5).

One reason for this imbalance is that spending is skewed to services disproportionately used by richer people. Public spending on primary education tends to reach poor people. The poorest fifth of

Armenians got almost 30 percent of the benefit of public spending on primary education in 1999. But not all spending on primary services is pro-poor. While public spending on primary health care tends to be more pro-poor than overall spending, it does not always disproportionately reach the poor. The poorest fifth of the populace in Côte d'Ivoire benefited from only 14 percent of public spending on primary health facilities in 1995 (compared with 11 percent from all health spending).[140]

Orienting public spending toward services used by poor people helps, but it does not help unless the spending reaches the frontline, where it benefits poor people. A study in Uganda found that in the early 1990s only 13 percent of government primary education capitation grants made it to the intended destination, primary schools. The rest went to purposes unrelated to education or to private gain. Poor students suffered disproportionately, as schools catering to them received even smaller shares of the grants (see spotlight).[141]

The story in health is the same. Drugs intended for health clinics often never get there. In the mid-1980s more than 70 percent of the government's supply of drugs disappeared in Guinea.[142] Studies in Cameroon, Tanzania, and Uganda estimated that 30 percent of publicly supplied drugs were misappropriated—in one case as much as 40 percent were "withdrawn for private use."[143]

Private and public sectors interact

Public spending has trouble creating quality services and reaching poor people. So why be surprised that spending is only weakly associated with outcomes? But there is another reason for the weak association: private and public sectors interact, and what matters is the net impact on the use of services. Increasing public provision may simply crowd out, in whole or in part, equally effective services obtained from nongovernment providers.

This works through two channels. First, individual demand in both public and private sectors will respond to a change in the public sector. A review of the impact of price increases in public health clinics in seven countries found that a substantial percentage of visits to public providers deterred by price increases are redirected to private ones—although the magnitude of the effect varies across settings.[144] Second, private providers may respond to changes in public provision. An experiment in increasing fees in public facilities in Indonesia in the early 1990s found that the number of private dispensaries and hospitals increased substantially, and that this resulted in only small changes in health outcomes.[145]

Unless resources support services that work for poor people, they will be ineffective. The efficacy of spending is so varied that it is hard to associate a cost with achieving any target improvement in outcomes, as with the Millennium Development Goals (box 2.3).

Technical adjustments without changes in incentives are not enough

If more public money is spent on services—and more of that money is spent on services used by poor people and makes it to the intended school or clinic—how the money is used still determines its efficacy. Consider recurrent spending on education in Sub-Saharan Africa. Of 18 populous Sub-Saharan African countries with data, most spend substantially more than the recommended 66 percent on teachers (figure 2.6).[146] And this isn't just a central government phenomenon. In Nigeria wages account for about 90 percent of local government recurrent expenditures on primary education. No one would deny that teachers are a key part of the schooling process and that paying them adequately is important. But if there is no money left to pay for other important inputs, such as textbooks, learning will suffer.

Why does such a large share of education spending go to teachers? Spending on teachers is the result of balancing technical issues with political jockeying by parents, teachers, the rest of the civil service, and advocates of spending priorities outside of the education sector. Spending on other inputs often loses out to spending on teachers—who are often vocal, organized, connected, and contractually obligated to be paid. It happens where spending is fairly high—Kenya spends more than 6 percent of GDP on education—and fairly low—Tanzania spends less than 2 percent of GDP on education. The purpose is not to single out Sub-Saharan Africa—the phenomenon is widespread—or to pick on teachers. It is to suggest that fixing the problem requires dealing not just with technical or managerial questions of how much to spend on one input relative to others, but with the institutional and political contexts that generate these decisions in the first place.

Identifying what contributes to an effective classroom or appropriate medical treatment is important for decisionmaking. In well-functioning systems service provision

Figure 2.6 The dominant share of recurrent spending on education goes to teachers (selected Sub-Saharan countries)

Kenya 96%
D.R. Congo 90%
Tanzania 89%

Between 68% and 86%
Malawi
Ghana
Angola
Ethiopia
Zambia
Côte d'Ivoire
Sudan
Zimbabwe
Niger
Mozambique
Uganda
Burkina Faso
Mali
Cameroon

Madagascar 58%

Note: Data refer to primary school–level spending and primary school teachers.
Source: Bruns, Mingat, and Rakatomalala (2003).

BOX 2.3 *Why it's so hard to "cost" the Millennium Development Goals*

How much will it cost to reach the Millennium Development Goals? That question, crucial for governments and donors who have committed to the goals, is extremely difficult to answer.

What cost? For universal primary education completion, does "costing" mean putting a price tag on enrolling all primary-age children in public schools? With more than 100 million children of primary school age not in school, multiplying the number in each country by average public spending per primary student yields a total "cost" of about $10 billion. But this number overlooks a simple point: children not in school might be harder to induce to come to school, so the marginal cost of enrolling a child could be higher than the average cost. These children might have higher opportunity costs, so it might require a larger subsidy to get them into school. Or they might live in remote areas, where it would cost more to build schools or to compensate them for traveling to more central locations. In addition, this approach implicitly assumes that spending on a particular target can be earmarked separately from other spending in the sector. Though that is possible, it is not easy.

Efficiency gains. The average cost calculation also ignores the weak overall association between spending and outcomes. Additional spending will be associated with only small increases in outcomes if the additional funds are spent with the average observed efficiency (figure 2.4). That means it will take astronomically high amounts to achieve the goals. But what if the money is "well spent"?

A country-by-country simulation of spending in 47 low-income countries adjusted the proximate determinants of primary completion success—public spending as a share of GDP, the share of spending that goes to teachers, the level of teacher salaries, pupil-teacher ratio, average repetition rate. It found that average external resources of about $2.8 billion a year would be needed. (Since the simulation included domestically mobilized resources as a policy lever, the model yields the amount of external resources required).[147] The average-cost approach to enrolling out-of-school children in these 47 countries yields a total incremental cost of $3.1 billion a year.[148]

"Costing" a change in proximate determinants is useful for identifying the fiscal implications of a change in policy, but it says little about the success or failure of turning that spending into outcomes. This does not mean "if this amount of money were spent, the Millennium Development Goals will be met." It means "if the goals are met, here is what it will have cost."

Financing transitional costs. If institutional reforms are necessary for sustainable improvements in outcomes, the costs of those reforms should be counted: for example, the cost of repurposing physical infrastructure or compensating redundant staff. These costs are determined by country conditions. For example, the cost of a severance package will depend on a country's labor market, civil service regulations and norms, and other local factors. Given the uncertainty surrounding costs, it makes little sense to estimate transitional costs on a global basis.

Interdependence and double counting. Progress on each Millennium Development Goal feeds back into the others. Safe water and good sanitation contribute to better health. Good health enhances the productivity of schooling. Education promotes better health. Interventions that promote one goal promote all of them. If the cost of reaching each goal is assessed independently, and the results are totaled across goals, there is double counting.[149]

Multiple determinants. But the goals do not just depend on each other—their determinants are multiple, cutting across many sectors. Little is known about the relative contribution of each factor to outcomes or about the magnitude of potential interaction effects (see crate 1.1 in chapter 1). For example, the impact of sanitation on mortality depends on access to safe water. The effectiveness of vaccines, and thus their contribution to lowering mortality, depend on preserving the "cold chain," which depends on roads, other transport, and energy infrastructure. Precise estimates of these independent and interactive effects are not easy to come by.

In sum, costing the goals requires an estimate that distinguishes between marginal and average cost, incorporates the policy and institutional changes required to make this additional expenditure effective, does not double- or triple-count given the interdependence of the goals, and takes into account the multiple determinants of each goal. No wonder that coming up with costs of reaching the goals is so difficult.

---

can be improved through better teaching materials, more reliable availability of drugs, better training of health workers—that is, through technical improvements in the proximate determinants of successful service provision. And management reforms may reduce the frequency of shirking teachers or incompetent doctors or corrupt police. But trying to make services work in weak systems by an effective and least-cost solution—applying a codified set of actions or simply training providers—will end in frustration if politicians do not listen to citizens or if providers have no incentive to perform well.

To understand why, it is important to distinguish between institutional and managerial reforms. Reducing teacher absenteeism from 9 percent to 7 percent is a management issue; reducing teacher absenteeism from 50 percent to 9 percent is an institutional issue. Improving diagnostic recognition of specific diseases is a management issue. Reducing widespread mistreatment of routine conditions is an institutional issue.

Institutional reforms seek to strengthen the relationships of accountability among various actors so that good service provision outputs emerge—with all their proximate determinants, including active management. Institutional arrangements need to take advantage of the strengths of the market—with its strong customer responsiveness, organizational autonomy, and systemic pressures for efficiency and innovation. And the strengths of the public sector—with its ability to address equity and market failures and its power to enforce standards. This is not about reducing or avoiding key public responsibilities. It is about creating new ways to meet public responsibilities more effectively. This might include alternatives to public production, but it could just as easily include institutional changes to make public agencies perform better.

Understanding what works and why—to improve services

To produce better health, better skills, and better standards of living, service beneficiaries, providers, and the state must work together. How? Understanding what works, why, in what context—and how to spread successful approaches—is the subject of this Report. Many successful institutional innovations worldwide show clearly that services need not fail. They offer lessons to guide replication and to scale up solutions. A variety of stories illustrate the potential—and the challenge.

Citizen report cards in Bangalore, India. In the early 1990s public services in Karnataka's capital city were in bad shape. A technology boom unleashed rapid growth. Services were of low quality and corruption was rampant, affecting all income groups. To monitor the government's failure to address these problems, and to motivate change, a civil society group introduced report cards in 1994 rating user experiences with public services. The results—revealing poor quality, petty corruption, lack of access for slum dwellers, and the hidden costs of outwardly cheap services—were widely publicized by an active press.

The report cards gradually opened a dialogue between providers and user groups—and eventually got a positive response from the managers of public agencies. The state's chief minister set up a task force to improve city governance. Follow-up activities—such as an in-depth report card for hospitals—delved deeper into problems with individual services. In 1999 a report card rated some services substantially higher, though scores on corruption and access to grievance systems remained low. The initiative was so successful that the Public Affairs Centre (which conducted the survey) collaborated with local partners to prepare similar studies in other Indian cities.[150] And other countries (the Philippines, Ukraine, and Vietnam) are adopting the approach.

Participatory budget formulation in Porto Alegre, Brazil. The city of Porto Alegre, with a population of more than a million, developed an innovative model of budget formulation. Citizen associations propose projects, which are then publicly debated. The proposals are combined with technical assessments, and the procedure is repeated to determine final budget allocations. The city made substantial strides. Access to water went from 80 percent in 1989 to near universal in 1996, and access to sewerage, from less than 50 percent to 85 percent. School enrollments doubled. And with greater citizen willingness to pay for better services, city revenue increased by 50 percent. To make the process pro-poor, the poorest people had more voting power than others. The approach has proved a resounding success for the inhabitants (and for the political party, which repeatedly won elections). Several other cities have since adopted similar procedures.[151]

Different stories point to other innovations: greater transparency of school funding in Uganda, citywide reform in Johannesburg, South Africa, cash transfers to households in Mexico, statewide reform of health services in Ceará, Brazil (see spotlights). Only one of these innovations was evaluated using an experimental design (Mexico's Progresa). And not all have clear measures of change in outputs or outcomes. But all hint at ways forward.

The various stories raise questions. Why were the innovations implemented? Whom did they affect? What made them work—and what makes some other innovations fail? Can they be replicated? To examine these questions systematically—that is, to learn from such examples—the Report develops a framework that incorporates the main actors—service beneficiaries, the state, and providers—and describes how each is linked by relationships of accountability (chapters 3 to 6). It then applies these principles to specific reform agendas, exploring how those relationships play out in different sectors (chapters 7 to 11).

Kerala and Uttar Pradesh

One nation, worlds apart

States in one federal nation—following the same constitution, laws, and intergovernmental finance system, and subject to the same election cycles—Kerala and Uttar Pradesh remain worlds apart in human development. Their different worlds mean dramatic differences in the quality of life for millions—Uttar Pradesh, with 175 million people, is larger than all but six countries in the world (Kerala has 32 million people).[152] This is a story of achievement and failure, the power of public action, and the burden of official inertia.

Women born in Kerala can expect to live 20 years longer on average than women born in Uttar Pradesh. Uttar Pradesh's infant mortality rate is five times higher than Kerala's (table 1). At the start of this century, one in three girls in Uttar Pradesh had never been to school: Kerala has universal enrollment. Kerala's total fertility rate is 1.96 births per woman (lower than 2.1 in the United States and just above 1.7 in high-income European countries); Uttar Pradesh's fertility rate is 3.99 (substantially higher than the average of 2.85 for India and 3.1 for low-income countries).

Education and health services in the two states echo these differences. Studies suggest that public facilities in Kerala are likely to be well supplied, adequately maintained, and regularly staffed by teachers or physicians. Not so in Uttar Pradesh.[153] A primary health center in Kerala left unstaffed for a few days may lead to public protests at the nearest district office.[154] But a rural school in Uttar Pradesh can be nonfunctional for years and produce no civic protest.[155] Women's participation differs widely in the two states: more than 70 percent of primary school teachers in Kerala are women, only 25 percent in Uttar Pradesh.[156]

Why did Kerala succeed where Uttar Pradesh failed?

History helped. Even though its consumption-related poverty was among the highest in India, Kerala already led in human development in 1956 when it was reconstituted as a new Indian state. Longstanding social movements against caste divisions, its culture (including matrilineal inheritance in certain communities), and openness to foreign influences (including missionary-led education) all helped.

But history is not all. Much of Kerala's spectacular achievements came after the mid-1950s. Adult literacy has risen from around 50 percent in 1950 to more than 90 percent now and life expectancy at birth from 44 years to 74. The birth rate has fallen from 32 to 18. In 1956 the Malabar region of Kerala lagged substantially behind the two "native" states (Travancore and Cochin) with which it was combined to form the new Kerala state. Today, the differences have disappeared.

Public action—and neglect

Dreze and Sen (2002) suggest that Kerala's success is the result of public action that promoted extensive social opportunities and the widespread, equitable provision of schooling, health, and other basic services. They argue that Uttar Pradesh's failures can be attributed to the public neglect of the same opportunities.

- The early promotion of primary education and female literacy in Kerala was very important for social achievements later on. In Uttar Pradesh educational backwardness has imposed high penalties, including delayed demographic transition and burgeoning population growth.

- Gender equity and the agency of women appear to play a major role in Kerala's success. Uttar Pradesh has a long, well-documented tradition of oppressive gender relations and extraordinarily sharp gender inequalities in literacy and in women's participation.[157]

- Basic universal services in schooling, health care, child immunization, public

Table 1 The great divide: human development and basic services in Kerala and Uttar Pradesh
Latest available data, in percent unless otherwise stated

	Kerala	Uttar Pradesh	India
Infant mortality rate (per 1,000 live births)	16.3	86.7	67.6
Total fertility rate (per woman)	1.96	3.99	2.85
Sex ratio (women per 1,000 men)	1,058	902	933
Female school enrollment rate (age 6–17 years)	90.8	61.4	66.2
Male school enrollment rate (age 6–17 years)	91.0	77.3	77.6
Rural girls never in school (age 10–12 years)	0.0	31.7	26.6
Rural women never in school (age 15–19 years)	1.6	49.3	38.7
Immunization coverage rate (age 12–23 months)	79.7	21.2	42.0
Skilled delivery care (% of births)	94.0	22.4	42.3
Rural population in villages with:			
A primary school	90.1	75.1	79.7
A middle school	87.1	31.9	44.6
A primary health center	74.2	4.4	12.9
An all-weather road	79.1	46.0	49.2
Medical expenditure per hospitalization in public facility (Rs.)	1,417	4,261	1,902
Women reporting:			
Health care provider respected need for privacy	93.0	64.0	68.2
Health facility was clean	77.2	31.0	52.1
Skilled attendance at delivery is unnecessary	1.4	42.5	61.3
Poorest 20% of households that prefer a public health facility	55.7	9.5	32.8

Rs = Rupees
Sources: National Family and Health Survey-2, 1998–99; IIPS, 2002; Census of India, 2001; National Sample Survey 1998–99.

food distribution, and social security differ sharply in scope, access, quality, and equitable incidence. In Uttar Pradesh these services appear to have been widely neglected and there has been no particular effort to ensure results, particularly in schools.

- A more literate and better informed public in Kerala was active in politics and public affairs in a way that did not appear to have happened in Uttar Pradesh.

- Informed citizen action and political activism in Kerala—building partly on mass literacy and the emphasis placed on universal services by early communist and subsequent coalition governments—seem to have been crucial in organizing poor people. In Uttar Pradesh traditional caste and power divisions, particularly in rural areas, have persisted through more than 50 years of electoral politics—and such divisions have come to form the core of political discourse and clientelist politics.

Political incentives matter for service delivery and actual development outcomes.[158] Delivering broad, universal basic services has remained a credible political platform in Kerala in contrast to the clientelist, caste, and class-driven politics of Uttar Pradesh.

In Kerala, early governments with economic platforms emphasizing the provision of universal basic services established a political agenda that remained important in the coalition politics that followed. Political competition conditioned on promises to deliver better basic services showed up in early budget allocations (figure 1): education and health services accounted for a much higher share of public expenditures as compared to what was spent on state administration.

By contrast, in Uttar Pradesh caste and class-based divisions, and the absence of compelling political alternatives to transcend these divisions, led to poor political incentives for effective provision of universal, basic services. Political competition revolved around access to instruments of the state to deliver patronage and public employment to specific clients. Public expenditures in the early years were accordingly concentrated in state administration and remained well above expenditures on health and education. More recently, political parties have tended to underplay the program or policy content of their platforms, and instead have publicized the ethnic profile of their candidate lists to demonstrate commitment to proportional representation of ethnic groups in the bureaucratic institutions of the state.[159]

Breaking out of vicious cycles

Public action can build on history, break from it, or perpetuate it. Individuals' abilities to press their demands depend on their information, perceived rights, and literacy. Public action—by influencing information that citizens have, their legal protections, and their schooling—influences private

action, especially by the politically weak. And private action loops back to influence public action. One set of reforms can lead to further institutional evolution. A society can be caught in a vicious cycle, as in Uttar Pradesh, or be propelled by a virtuous one, as in Kerala. As Dreze and Gazdar note: "In Uttar Pradesh, the social failures of the state are quite daunting, but the potential rewards of action are correspondingly high, and the costs of continued inertia even higher."[160]

As for Kerala, despite the many economic problems that linger and the new ones that have appeared, the remarkable rescript issued in 1817 by Gowri Parvathi Bai, the 15-year-old queen of the erstwhile state of Tranvacore, certainly seems to have come true in its bold aspirations for the human development of her subjects. The rescript read:

"The state should defray the entire cost of the education of its people in order that there might be no backwardness in the spread of enlightenment among them, that by diffusion of education they might become better subjects and public servants and that the reputation of the state might be enhanced thereby."[161]

Figure 1 Kerala spent more on education and health, Uttar Pradesh on state administration

Percent of total public expenditures

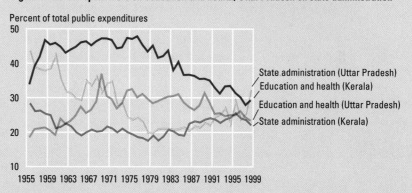

State administration (Uttar Pradesh)
Education and health (Kerala)
Education and health (Uttar Pradesh)
State administration (Kerala)

Note: Public spending on state administration does not include interest payments.
Source: Reserve Bank of India Bulletins, 1955–1998.

The framework
for service provision

The public sector has generally taken on responsibility for the delivery of services and frequently used civil service bureaucracies as the instrument. This approach has had dramatic successes and—as chapter 1 documented—far too many failures. Much remains to be done. Particularly for poor people, there are widespread challenges in providing affordable access, fixing dysfunctional facilities, improving technical quality, increasing client responsiveness, and raising productivity. As chapter 2 noted, neither economic growth, nor simply increasing public spending, nor coming up with technocratic solutions is enough to meet this challenge.

The failures in service provision have not gone unnoticed. Indeed, there is a cacophony of proposed institutional solutions: civil service reform, privatization, democratization, decentralization, contracting out, provision through NGOs, empowerment, participatory methods, social funds, community-driven development, user associations. With each of these solutions comes a bewildering variety of techniques and instruments: demand-side transfers, participatory rural appraisals, facility surveys, service score cards, participatory budgets. None is a panacea.

"One size does not fit all" is a truism but not very helpful. Everyone wanting to improve services for poor people—from the poor themselves to reform-minded professionals, advocates, political leaders, and external agencies—asks: What size fits *me?* Given the capabilities, resources, politics, and incentives that I face, what can be done? What are the actions that would improve services for poor people in my circumstances? To evaluate alternative arrangements for the provision of services requires an encompassing framework—to analyze which of the many items on the menu of service reform is right for the time, place, and circumstance.

This Report's framework starts from the specific and works to the general. Start with a child in a classroom, a pregnant woman at a clinic, someone turning a tap for water. Each is seeking a service, and the proximate determinants of success are clear. For any individual service transaction to be successful, there needs to be a frontline provider who is capable, who has access to adequate resources and inputs, and who is motivated to pursue an achievable goal. The general question: what institutional conditions support the emergence of capable, motivated frontline providers with clear objectives and adequate resources? The answer: successful services for poor people emerge from institutional relationships in which the actors are accountable to each other. (Please be patient, the rest of the Report works out exactly what that sentence means.)

This chapter does five things. It introduces the analytical framework of actors (individuals, organizations, governments, businesses) and relationships of accountability that will be used throughout the Report. It describes the characteristics of services that make creating those relationships so crucial—and so difficult. It uses the framework and the characteristics of the services to analyze why pure public sector production often fails—and why pure privatization is not the answer. It lays out how the various items on the agenda for service reform are related and how the Report will address them. And it addresses the dynamics of reform.

An analytical framework: actors and accountabilities

Language evolves through common usage, so no one is accountable when the word *accountability* acquires so many different uses and meanings. What this Report means by accountability is a relationship among actors that has five features: *delegation, finance, performance, information about performance,* and *enforceability* (figure 3.1).

Relationships of accountability can be as simple as buying a sandwich or taking a job—and as complex as running a municipal democracy.

- In buying a sandwich you ask for it (*delegation*) and pay for it (*finance*). The sandwich is made for you (*performance*). You eat the sandwich (which generates relevant *information* about its quality). And you then choose to buy or not buy a sandwich another day (*enforceability*), affecting the profits of the seller.

- In a typical employment relationship a person is given a set of tasks (*delegation*) and paid a wage (*finance*). The employee works (*performance*). The contribution of the employee is assessed (*information*). And based on that information, the employer acts to reinforce good or discourage bad performance (*enforceability*).

- In a city the citizens choose an executive to manage the tasks of the municipality (*delegation*), including tax and budget decisions (*finance*). The executive acts, often in ways that involve the executive in relationships of accountability with others (*performance*). Voters then assess the executive's performance based on their experience and *information*. And they act to control the executive—either politically or legally (*enforceability*).

There are many other vocabularies for referring to these pervasive and critical issues from a variety of disciplines (economics, political science, sociology) and practices (public administration, management). This Report makes no claims of coming up with a superior set of words. The terms here have the virtues of completeness (a name for everything the Report discusses) and consistency (the same names are used throughout). See box 3.1 for a glossary of terms used in this Report. For instance, recent work on the empowerment of poor people, extending the work of the *2000/2001 World Development Report* on poverty, suggests four elements that overlap in important ways with the analysis here: access to information, inclusion and participation, accountability, and local organizational capacity.[162] Others use the term *accountability* to refer only to the dimension of "answerability" (getting information about performance) or to "enforceability." This Report uses the term broadly.

There are two motivations for this broader approach. First, weaknesses in any aspect of accountability can cause failure. One cannot strengthen enforceability—holding providers responsible for outputs and outcomes—in isolation. If providers do not receive clear delegation, precisely specifying the desired objectives, increasing enforceability is unfair and ineffective. If providers are not given adequate resources, holding them accountable for poor outcomes is again unfair and ineffective. Second, putting finance as the first step in creating a relationship of accountability stresses that simply caring about an outcome controlled by another does not create a relationship of accountability. To be a "stakeholder" you need to put up a stake.

In the chain of service delivery the Report distinguishes four broad roles:

- *Citizens/clients.* Patients, students, parents, voters.

- *Politicians/policymakers.* Prime ministers, presidents, parliamentarians, mayors, ministers of finance, health, education.

- *Organizational providers.* Health departments, education departments, water and sanitation departments.

- *Frontline professionals.* Doctors, nurses, teachers, engineers.

In the ideal situation these actors are linked in relationships of power and accountability. Citizens exercise *voice* over politicians. Policymakers have *compacts*

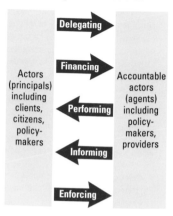

Figure 3.1 The relationships of accountability have five features

Actors (principals) including clients, citizens, policymakers

Delegating
Financing
Performing
Informing
Enforcing

Accountable actors (agents) including policymakers, providers

BOX 3.1 *A glossary for this Report*

Language is elastic—an asset reflecting the diversity of human experience, but a liability when such overused terms as *accountability* lose their meaning. This Report, in developing its service delivery framework, gives some commonly used terms (such as accountability) specific meaning and we coin a few new terms. We do not claim we have superior or better meanings, but we do try for internal consistency.

Accountability is a set of relationships among service delivery actors with five features:

- *Delegating:* Explicit or implicit understanding that a service (or goods embodying the service) will be supplied.
- *Financing.* Providing the resources to enable the service to be provided or paying for it.
- *Performing.* Supplying the actual service.
- *Having information about performance.* Obtaining relevant information and evaluating performance against expectations and formal or informal norms.
- *Enforcing.* Being able to impose sanctions for inappropriate performance or provide rewards when performance is appropriate.

This Report defines four relationships of accountability: *client power (over providers), compacts, management (by provider organizations of frontline professionals),* and *voice and politics (between citizens and politicians/policymakers).*

Actors: Individuals, households, communities, firms, governments, and other public, nongovernmental, and private organizations that finance, produce, regulate, deliver, or consume services. In economic theory the actors who hold others accountable are sometimes called *principals,* and the actors who are held accountable are called *agents.*

Client power: The relationship of accountability connecting clients to the frontline service providers, usually at the point of service delivery, based on transactions through which clients express their demand for services and can monitor supply and providers.

Clients/citizens: Service users who as citizens participate individually or in groups (e.g., labor unions) in political processes to shape and attain collective goals. As clients, individuals receive services to satisfy their household demand. All clients are citizens (in most settings) but, depending on the service, not all citizens are clients.

Clientelism: The tendency of politicians as patrons to respond to political competition by excessively favoring one group of clients over another in return for political advantage (vote banks). Providing narrow supporter groups with free public services or public employment, particularly where shirking is not sanctioned, is often the way politicians practice clientelism.

Compacts: The broad, long-term relationship of accountability connecting policymakers to organizational providers. This is usually not as specific or legally enforceable as a contract. But an explicit, verifiable contract can be one form of a compact.

Discretionary services: Locally produced services, such as classroom instruction or curative care, where the teacher or doctor must exercise significant judgment on what to deliver and how, and where clients typically have a large information deficit relative to the provider. Discretionary services that are *transaction-intensive* are hard to monitor, both for the client and for the policymaker, whether publicly or privately provided. They pose particular challenges for all the relationships of *accountability.*

Frontline professionals: The teachers, nurses, doctors, engineers, clerks, or other providers who come in direct contact with the client.

Long and short routes of accountability: Clients may seek to hold service providers accountable for performance in two ways. Client power connecting clients and providers is the direct, "short" route of accountability. When such client power is weak or not possible to use, clients must use voice and politics in their role as citizens to hold politicians accountable—and politician/policymakers must in turn use the compact to do the same with providers. The combination of the two is the roundabout, "long" route of accountability.

Management: The relationship of accountability connecting organizational providers and frontline professionals, comprising internal processes for public and private organizations to select, train, motivate, administer, and evaluate frontline professionals. These processes may be rule-bound in large bureaucracies, or idiosyncratic and ad hoc in small, private providers.

Organizational providers: Public, private nonprofit, and private for-profit entities that actually provide services. These may range from government line ministries with hundreds of thousands of employees to a private hospital chain or from a vast urban water utility to a single, community-run, village school.

Politicians/policymakers: The service delivery actors authorized by the state to discharge its legislative, regulatory, and rule-making responsibilities. Politicians may be elected or achieve their positions through nondemocratic means. They can also be policymakers (the general who is president but also runs the military, the telecom minister who administers the sale of frequencies). But more commonly policymakers are the highest nonelected officials—either from a civil service or appointed. Politicians set general directions. Policymakers implement these directions and set and enforce the conditions for public and private service providers to operate. Usually accountability subrelationships between politicians and policymakers (parodied in the TV serial "Yes Minister") are derived from the constitution, administrative law, or rules of public administration.

Service delivery framework (or chain): The four service-related actors—*citizens/clients, politicians/policymakers, organizational providers, frontline professionals*—and the four relationships of *accountability* that connect them:

- *Voice and politics:* connecting citizens and politicians.
- *Compacts:* connecting politicians/policymakers and providers.
- *Management:* connecting provider organizations with frontline professionals.
- *Client power:* connecting clients with providers.
- *Short route of accountability:* See *long and short routes of accountability.*

Strategic incrementalism: Pragmatic incremental reforms in weak institutional environments that are not likely to fully address service delivery problems but can alleviate acute service problems while at the same time creating the conditions for deeper and more favorable change—say, building capacity that can respond to service delivery challenges. This can be contrasted with, for lack of a better term, "incremental incrementalism" that merely solves one set of immediate problems but creates others. For example, working around existing government and governance structures with no strategy for how these temporary measures will affect the long term.

Transaction-intensive services: Services that require repeated, frequent client-provider contact. Transaction-intensive services may be discretionary and require constant, minute decisions (classroom teaching), making them very hard to monitor. Or the technology may not require much discretion (fire and forget) once there is client contact (immunization).

Voice and politics: The most complex relationship of accountability. It connects citizens and politicians and comprises many formal and informal processes, including voting and electoral politics, lobbying and propaganda, patronage and clientelism, media activities, access to information, and so on. Citizens delegate to politicians the functions of serving their interests and financing governments through their taxes. Politicians perform by providing services, such as law and order or communities relatively free of pathogens. Citizens enforce accountability through elections and other less definitive means, such as advocacy, legal actions, and naming and shaming campaigns.

with organizational providers. Organizations *manage* frontline providers. And clients exercise *client power* through interactions with frontline providers (figure 3.2). In low-income countries a fifth role, played by external finance agencies, affects each of these relationships (chapter 11).

Weaknesses in *any* of the relationships—or in the capacity of the actors—can result in service failures. Providers can be made directly accountable to clients (as in market transactions) by passing decisions and powers directly to citizens or communities—a "short route" of accountability. But, more typically, the public sector is involved, so two key relationships—*voice* and *compacts*—make up the main control mechanism of the citizen in a "long route" of accountability. In either case, organizations (such as health, education, and water departments) need to be able to manage frontline providers.

The four actors

Citizens and clients. Individuals and households have dual roles, as citizens and as direct clients. As citizens they participate both as individuals and through coalitions (communities, political parties, labor unions, business associations) in political processes that define collective objectives; they also strive to control and direct public action in accomplishing those objectives. As direct clients of service providers, individuals and households hope to get clean water, have their children educated, and protect the health of their family.

The role of citizens and clients as service beneficiaries does not imply that all citizens are alike or have the same views. Terms such as *civil society* and *community* are sometimes used too casually. People differ in beliefs, hopes, values, identities, and capabilities. Civil society is often not civil at all; many "communities" have little in common. Individuals and households may disagree about collective objectives and work to promote their own views, both individually and through associations, sometimes at the direct expense of others. The capability for collective action of citizens, a key element of service delivery, varies widely across societies.

Politicians and policymakers. What distinguishes the sovereign state from all other institutions is its monopoly on the legitimate use of physical force within its boundaries. From this monopoly, politicians derive the power to regulate, to legislate, to tax—to set and enforce the "rules of the game." Politicians are defined here as those who control this power and discharge the fundamental responsibilities of the state. This does not mean that electoral politics are always in play: some politicians are heads of one-party states, some have imposed their control through military force, some arrive by election. In some systems executive politicians are dominant—in others, legislative politicians.

The other actors who exercise the power of the state are policymakers. In some countries politicians are also policymakers. But in others there is a clear distinction between the highest nonelected officials of government—civil servants or appointees—and political actors. Politicians set general directions, but policymakers set the fundamental rules of the game for service providers to operate—by regulating entry, enforcing standards, and determining the conditions under which providers receive public funds.

Organizational providers. A provider organization can be a public line organization, whatever the name—ministry, department, agency, bureau (table 3.1). It can be a ministry of education that provides education services, an autonomous public enterprise (autonomous public hospitals), a

Figure 3.2 Key relationships of power

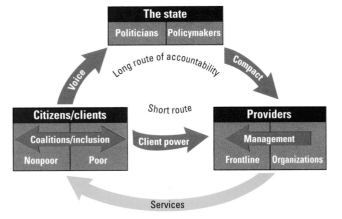

nonprofit (religious schools), or a for-profit (private hospital). It can be large (public sector ministries with tens of thousands of teachers) or small (a single community-run primary school). There can be several types of providers (public, nonprofit, and for-profit hospitals) and several providers of each type delivering the same service in the same area (many independently operated nonprofit and for-profit private hospitals).

When the organizational provider is in the public sector, one needs to be clear about the analytical distinction between the policymaker and the head of the provider organization. The policymaker sets and enforces the rules of the game for all providers—including the organizational provider. The head of the provider organization makes internal "policies" specific to the organization. Clear conceptually, the distinction is not always clear in practice, especially when the same individual plays both roles. For example, a minister of public works may be the policymaker responsible for making and enforcing the rules for all providers—but also the head of the largest organizational provider of water services, directly responsible for management. Unbundling these roles to create a clear delineation of policymaking and direct production responsibilities is one element in having clear lines of accountability.

Frontline providers.   In the end, nearly all services require a provider who comes in direct contact with clients—teachers, doctors, nurses, midwives, pharmacists, engineers, and so on.

The four relationships of accountability

Of politicians to citizens: voice and politics. This Report uses the term *voice* to express the complex relationships of accountability between citizens and politicians. Voice is about politics, but it covers much more. The voice relationship includes formal political mechanisms (political parties and elections) and informal ones (advocacy groups and public information campaigns). Delegation and finance between citizen and state are the decisions about pursuing collective objectives and mobilizing of public resources to meet those objectives. Citizens need information about how actions of the state have promoted their well-being. They also need some mechanism for enforceability, to make sure that politicians and policymakers are rewarded for good actions and penalized for bad ones. If politicians have abused their position, or even just not pursued objectives aggressively and effectively, citizens need a variety of mechanisms—not just periodic elections—to make politicians and policymakers accountable.

Table 3.1   Organizational providers take a variety of ownership and organizational structures

Ownership	Type of provider organization	Education services	Health services (ambulatory curative care)	Water services	Energy
Public sector	Ministry/department/ agency/bureau	Ministry of education schools (national, state/ province, municipal)	Ministry of health outpatient clinics	Ministry of public works	Ministry of energy
	Public sector autonomous corporation	Autonomous universities	Autonomous hospitals	State water corporations	State electricity companies
Not-for-profit sector	Community owned	Informal schools, Educo		Rural water associations	
	Not-for-profit organization	Religious schools (Catholic, Islamic), NGO-run schools (such as BRAC)	NGO-run clinics		
Private, for-profit sector	Small for-profit firms	Private, nonreligious schools	Private clinics	Informal water vendors	
	Large		Hospital chains	Private utilities	Private utilities

Note: Educo = El Salvador's Community-Managed Schools Program; NGO = Nongovernmental organization; BRAC = Bangladesh Rural Advancement Committee.

Of the organizational provider to the state: compacts. The relationships between policymakers and service providers can be thought of as *compacts*. The compact is not always as specific and legally enforceable as a contract, though a contract can be one form of a compact. Instead, it is a broad agreement about a long-term relationship. The policymaker provides resources and delegates powers and responsibility for collective objectives to the service providers. The policymaker generates information about the performance of organizations. Enforceability comes into play when the compact also specifies the rewards (and possibly the penalties) that depend on the service provider's actions and outputs. The line between "the state" and "public sector organizational provider" is not always easy to draw.

Of the frontline professionals to the organizational provider: management. In every organization, formal and informal tools of management provide frontline workers with assignments and delineated areas of responsibility, equipping them with the resources to act. In public agencies this management function is at times blurred because providers are employees of "the government." But all the standard *management* issues of selecting, training, and motivating workers in an organization apply to all organizations—private, NGO, government, whatever. All service provision organizations—whether a government ministry, a religious body, a nonprofit NGO, or a for-profit firm—have to create a relationship of accountability with their frontline providers.

Of the provider to the citizen-client: client power. Because the policymaker cannot specify all actions of providers in the compact, citizens must reveal to providers their demand for services and monitor the providers' provision of services. Clients and organizational providers interact through the individuals who provide services—teachers, doctors, engineers, repairmen—the frontline professionals and frontline workers.

BOX 3.2 *The many meanings of accountability*

Accountability is more a rubric than a single item, but it is a fruitful rubric for making useful distinctions.

Political accountability is the willingness of politicians and policymakers to justify their actions and to accept electoral, legal, or administrative penalties if their justification is found lacking. Even within "political" accountability one can have distinctions. With vertical political accountability, citizens individually or collectively hold the state to account—say, through voting or advocacy. Democracies must have some vertical accountability. With horizontal political accountability, agents of the state formally hold another agent of the state accountable—say, through the "compact" relationship between policymakers and providers.

Authoritarian states may manifest considerable horizontal accountability ("the trains run on time"), but not offer any vertical accountability. But where the relationship between clients and providers is very strong (in some instances perhaps because of the omnipresence of the ruling party, as in Cuba), service delivery may work very well without much vertical accountability.

Even for a given type of accountability there are distinctions. Formal horizontal political accountability is the formal description of institutions, and authority among agents of the state. It may differ sharply from informal horizontal political accountability, from the actual working of institutions and effective control over decisions in state organizations.

Sources: Goetz and Jenkins (2002) and Aghion and Tirole (1997).

Accountability is not the only relationship

The foregoing description is not reality, because it portrays only one direction in the relationships between actors. The reality is that actors are embedded in a complex set of relationships, and accountability is not always the most important. Through various forms of coercion, both subtle and blatant, many states' ability to impose *obligations* on citizens has proved much stronger than the ability of citizens to discipline politicians and policymakers (box 3.2). And in many cases citizens approach the state and its agents as supplicants.

Politicians often use the control over publicly provided services as a mechanism of *clientelism*—for both citizens and providers. In systems that lack accountability relationships, public service jobs (teachers, policemen) are given as political favors, which creates a relationship not of accountability but of political obligation. A recent report on education in Nepal, for instance, finds that "teachers' performance standards are nonexistent. Most teachers are aligned with one of the many associations formed on political party lines and appointment and deployment practices are often determined as a result of individual's contributions to political activities."[163]

Services are allocated in ways that reward (or punish) communities for their political support. Sometimes the ministry is the agent of the providers, not the other way around, and providers *capture* the policymaking. Providers also use their ability to control services and their superior social status to intimidate poor people. Rather than client power, there is provider power. The political scientist James Scott has argued that the pressures of "authoritarian high modernism" can mean that the state and its bureaucratic apparatus define a "thin simplification" in order to carry out services—but that the domination of this reality over citizens and their complex reality can lead to unintended consequences.

Why establishing relationships of accountability is so complex

This Report moves beyond what the public sector should do and emphasizes how public action can be made most effective. Frontline workers have to have clear objectives, adequate resources, technical capabilities, and the motivation to create valued services. This cannot be mandated. It is the result of interactions between strong actors in each of the key service provision roles. The ideal: a state that is strong, not weak. Provider organizations that have a clear vision and mission of service provision, not ones that are internally incoherent and merely process oriented. Frontline providers acting with professional autonomy and initiative, not tightly controlled automatons. And empowered citizens who demand services, not passive "recipients" who are acted on.

Strong, capable actors need to be embedded in strong relationships of accountability. But it is difficult to establish such relationships for these services. Why?

- Because there are both collective objectives and private objectives, a system that created only client power through choice (say) would meet only individual objectives, not the many public ones.
- Because of the multiple, complex objectives of public production and co-production, it is difficult to create outcome-based enforceability for providers.

Individual interests and collective objectives

A competitive market automatically creates accountability of sellers to buyers. The key information is customer satisfaction, and the key enforceability is the customer's choice of supplier. Competitive markets have proved a remarkably robust institutional arrangement for meeting individual interests. But they are not enough for services—for three reasons.

- First, the market responds only to those with purchasing power, doing nothing to ensure universal access or an equitable distribution, which societies often have as a collective objective.
- Second, the sum of the individual interests may not produce the best outcome because markets may have failures of various kinds.
- Third, other collective objectives require public action. For instance, the state and society have a strong concern about the role of schooling in the socialization of youth and may not want parents to choose for themselves.

The problem of monitoring

Locally produced services—basic education, health care, urban water supply and sanitation—have three characteristics that make it particularly difficult to structure relationships of accountability. They are discretionary and transaction-intensive. There are multiple tasks and multiple principals. And it is difficult to attribute outcomes.

Discretionary and transaction-intensive. Services are transaction-intensive, and the transactions require discretion. Teachers must continuously decide about the pace and structure of classroom activity. Have the ideas been grasped? Will another example reinforce the idea or bore the class? A doctor has to make decisions about diagnosis and treatment based on the specific case of the patient. The examples differ from other public sector activities that are discretionary but not transaction-intensive, such as setting monetary policy or regulating a monopoly—or those that are transaction-intensive but not discretionary, such as taking in bank deposits or controlling traffic.

Services may be transaction-intensive and discretionary, but some stages in service provision may be less transaction-intensive or discretionary (table 3.2). Even in the health sector, services span the range. For immunization, the appropriate action is nearly the same for each individual of a given age (easily observed). The problems in implementation, while formidable, are primarily logistical. But for curative services, providers have to respond to complaints from individuals and exercise discretion in choosing treatment.

Services that are both discretionary and transaction-intensive present challenges for any relationship of accountability—because it is difficult to know whether the provider has performed well. Administrative and bureaucratic controls that work well for logistical tasks are overwhelmed when they attempt to monitor the millions of daily interactions of teachers with students, policemen with citizens, case workers with clients, medical practitioners with patients. Rigid, scripted rules would not give enough latitude.

Multiple principals, multiple tasks. Public servants serve many masters. Power and water providers are under pressure from different segments of the market to cross-subsidize them—from producers to buy specific types of equipment, from people who want more extensive connections, and from others who want more reliable, continuous operation. The day-to-day pressure of local demand for health care can compromise efforts in disease prevention and other public health activities that are not demand-driven.[164]

Personnel in health clinics are supposed to provide immunizations, curative care to people who come to them, health education and other preventive measures to everyone (whether they come in on their own or not), keep statistics, attend training sessions and meetings, and do inspections of water and food. Police officers have to deal with everyone from lost children to dangerous criminals. This diffusion blunts the precision of incentives (box 3.3).

Attributability

The third problem in monitoring service provision is that it is often very difficult to attribute outcomes to the actions of the service providers because there are important "co-producers." As chapter 1 emphasized, health and education *outcomes* are mainly produced in households and communities. The health of individuals depends on their decisions about nutrition (constrained by income), activity levels, personal hygiene practices (often constrained by the availability of water)—and on community factors that determine exposure to pathogens. Even if people seek treatment when they are sick, the effectiveness of treatment depends in part on provider quality and individual compliance with the recommended therapies.

The difficulty in monitoring discretionary, transaction-intensive services is not unique to the public sector—it is inherent in services. Patients generally know how they feel. Studies of private practitioners in India commonly find practices that lead to short-run improvement in symptoms (such as steroid shots) but are not medically effective—or are even counterindicated.[165] Patients feel better, and this attracts repeat customers. But it does not create real accountability, because simply being pleased with the service is not sufficient information.

Table 3.2 Examples of discretionary and transaction-intensive services

Sector	Discretionary, not transaction-intensive	Discretionary and transaction-intensive	Transaction-intensive, not discretionary
Commercial banking	Setting deposit rates	Approving loans to small businesses	Taking in deposits
Social protection	Setting eligibility criteria	"Case worker" determinations	Issuing checks to the eligible
Policing	Lawmaking defining criminal behavior	Handling individual conflict situations	Directing traffic
Education	Curriculum	Classroom teaching	Providing school lunches
Health	Public information campaigns	Curative care	Vaccinations
Irrigation	Location of main canals	Allocation of water flows	Providing standpipes "in every village"
Central banks	Monetary policy	Banking regulation	Clearing house
Agricultural extension	Research priorities	Communication with farmers	

BOX 3.3 *Creating conditions of accountability: the police*

Police are delegated substantial powers—to compel and, if necessary, to use violence. What objectives should they pursue, and how could they be held accountable?

- "Client satisfaction" is not what should drive police, for who is the "client"? Certainly not the criminals, and certainly not just the victims: there are many objectives—creating a safe environment, apprehending criminals, respecting individual rights and dignity.

- Police cannot simply follow a script—they have to exercise discretion. If they went "by the book" and enforced every infraction, more important activities would grind to a halt.

- They rely on many co-producers. Without the cooperation of citizens in abiding by the law, reporting violations, helping in investigations, the job of the police would be impossible. And many determinants of crime are not under the control of the police, such as economic trends, social changes, and demographic shifts.

The recipe for inefficiency, abuse, and corruption: simply turn individuals loose with

vague objectives, lots of discretion, little performance information, few mechanisms of enforceability (either internal or external), and the public authority to compel (and often too little budget). A frequent complaint of poor people is the abuse they suffer from the police. As one Kenyan put it recently "You cannot carry much money with you these days. There are too many policemen."

There are no easy answers. "Privatizing" policing functions would face the same problems: what would be the measure of output to determine what the firm should be paid? Crime rates? They are not under police control (and they would deter reporting). Arrests? That would encourage false arrests to meet production quotas. Surveys of citizen perceptions of safety? These risk overzealous police violating the rights of the socially disadvantaged to please the minority. Penalties for abuse of authority? Police might then do too little.

Recent experience in several cities, notably New York, shows that better measurement of several important outputs is possible. Crime rates were measured by neighborhood, reported regularly as a management tool, used

to allocate police time and visibility. Crime rates fell significantly. This approach can backfire, though, if the desired outcomes are not well specified. Studies of police behavior in London and Los Angeles showed that the monitored and numerically measured activities (crime rates and citizen complaints) improved markedly. But other measures—community activities and crime rates, particularly for homicide—got worse.

So there is no general "optimal" solution. But there are solutions to particular cases, better or worse in their adaptation to local circumstance. Creating more functional police services requires creating multiple institutional channels of accountability—political (police are not simply an instrument of oppression), compacts (policymakers can hold police in check), management (organizational strategies can inculcate dedication, loyalty, restraint), and client power (citizens have mechanisms to influence police behavior directly, a free press).

Sources: Moore and others (2002); *The Economist* (2002); Burguess, Propper, and Wilson (2002); Prendergast (2001).

Many outcomes, even when observable to the patient and the doctor, are not "contractable" in the sense of being able to prove compliance to a judge or other mediator if a dispute arises.

Successes and failures of the public sector and the market

Discussions of public action often juxtapose two polar extremes for the institutional arrangements for services: traditional public production, in which all public action and resources are channeled through a public sector organization with civil servants; and market production, in which the public sector takes a minimal role (but at least establishes the basic conditions for a market, such as enforcing contracts).

This Report seeks to help the public sector meet its responsibility for health and education outcomes. The public sector can discharge its responsibility by engaging in a variety of institutional arrangements for service provision, including direct production, contracting out, demand-side transfers, and so on. Before getting to them, it helps to illustrate the weaknesses of the two

polar positions, using the five failures of services detailed in chapter 1—inaccessibility, dysfunctionality, low technical quality, lack of client responsiveness, and stagnant productivity.

Public production

Two of the most powerful innovations of the long 20th century (1870–1989) are the mutually reinforcing ideas of the nation-state, with extensive powers and responsibilities, and the civil service bureaucracy. Together they produced the consensus that governments have responsibilities for the welfare of their citizens, and that the most effective way to fulfill these responsibilities is through the direct production of services through a public sector organization with civil service employees. The contested ideologies of the 20th century—communism, capitalism, democracy—pale before the power of the twin ideas of a nation-state and a public sector bureaucracy. These ideologies were merely notions of the uses for the nation-state and its bureaucracy.

As just one example, schooling in the middle of the 19th century was almost exclusively in private hands (largely religious). Today the direct production of schooling by the public sector—with the nation-state the dominant service provider, involved in every facet of schooling from building schools, to determining the curriculum and texts, to training, hiring, assigning, and controlling teachers as civil servants—has completely triumphed as an idea, so completely that people forget it was ever contested (box 3.4).

Public bureaucracies are truly a blessing of modern life. All countries with high living standards have teachers who teach, police officers who police, judges who judge, public works that work, armies that respond to external threats. Yes, bureaucracies might be frustrating, slow, inefficient, and resistant to innovation. But the fantasy of "getting rid of the bureaucracy" would turn into a nightmare. No country has developed without state reliance on an effective public bureaucracy to discharge the key functions of the state—though not always through direct production. So why do some bureaucracies perform badly and others well? And how do countries get from badly to well?

The analytical framework of the relationships of accountability provides a way of diagnosing not just the symptoms of poor performance (inefficiency, corruption, poor performance) and not just the proximate determinants of these symptoms (lack of resources, low motivation, poor training, and little capability). It also provides a way of analyzing the deep institutional causes of poor performance.

In public sector production the direct link of client power is frequently missing, so successful public production relies on "long-route" accountability. What does that take? The policymaker must care about outcomes, including those for poor people. That concern needs to be transmitted effectively to the public agencies that receive public resources to provide the services. And the public agencies must hire technically qualified providers motivated to provide the services. When all this happens, as it often does in developed countries, public service production is reliable and effective. Indeed, some of the most admired and effective organizations in the world are public agencies.

When the long route is not working, the framework provides a way to understand the failures by identifying which relationship of accountability was the weak link—and within the relationship of accountability, which was the missing dimension.

- There are *voice* failures, when the state (controlled by politicians and policymakers) simply does not care about providing services—or does so in a strictly venal or clientelist manner. The clearest sign of this: when too little budget is devoted to services for poor people, and when that budget is allocated to meet political interests.

BOX 3.4 *The "Progressive Era": creation of modern bureaucracy*

Samuel Hays, in his study of the evolution of conservation policy in the United States in the early 20th century, expresses eloquently the political and social tensions in the shift to modern bureaucracies:

"The dynamics of conservation, with its tension between the centralizing tendencies of system and expertise on the one hand and decentralization and localism on the other, is typical of a whole series of similar tensions between centralization and decentralization within modern ... society. The poles of the continuum along which these forces were arrayed can be described briefly. On the one hand many facets of human life were bound up with relatively small scale activities focusing on the daily routines of job, home, religion, school and recreation in which a pattern of inter-personal relationships developed within relatively small geographical areas.... On the other hand, however, modern forms of social organization gave rise to larger patterns of human interaction, to ties of occupation and profession over wide areas, to corporate systems which extended into a far flung network, to impersonal—statistical—forms of understanding, to reliance on expertise and to centralized manipulation and control.... To many people the external characteristics of this process—efficiency, expertise, order—constituted the spirit of "progressivism." These new forms of organization tended to shift the location of decision-making away from the grass-roots, the smaller contexts of life, to the larger networks of human interaction. This upward shift can be seen in many specific types...: the growth of city-wide systems of executive action and representation in both school and general government to supersede the previous focus on ward representation and action; the similar upward shift in the management of schools and roads from the township to the county and state.

"Examination of the evolution of conservation political struggles, therefore, brings into sharp focus the two competing political systems.... On the one hand the spirit of science and technology, of rational system and organization, shifted the location of decision-making continually upward so as to narrow the range of influences impinging upon it and to guide that decision-making process with large, cosmopolitan considerations, technical expertness, and the objectives of those involved in the wider networks of modern society. On the other however, were a host of political impulses, often separate and conflicting, diffuse, and struggling against each other with in the larger political order. Their political activities sustained a more open political system ... in which complex and esoteric facts possessed by only a few were not permitted to dominate the process of decision-making, and the satisfaction of grassroots impulses remained a constantly viable element of the political order."

Source: Hays (1959).

• There are *compact* failures, in which the state fails to communicate clear responsibilities for outputs or outcomes to the public organization and fails to enforce any responsibility. Compact failures are also associated with management failures, in which the public sector organization fails to motivate its frontline workers.

All this is embedded in a system in which the feedback loop from client satisfaction to both frontline and organizational providers is cut.

Voice. A common cause of the failure of public service production is the apathy of the state. Governments may care about some services for ideological reasons. But when voice is weak (or divided or conflicted) and the state is freed from the constraint of satisfying its citizens, there are many possibilities for failure. The state delivers little or nothing to its poor and socially disadvantaged citizens, reserving its few services for the elite, including favored members of the government. In these circumstances alternative strategies of public sector management will be powerless to create better services.

Many analysts and advocates point out that resources devoted to services are inadequate. But those budget allocations are the result of political decisions: about the level of taxation and mobilization of resources; about the allocations of budgets across activities; about the design of programs that determine who benefits; about the allocation of expenditures across inputs (how much for wages and other things). If resources are inadequate, if they are ineffectively applied to service provision for poor people, it is often because poor people's voices are not being heard.

Nor is much information generated that would allow citizens to judge how effectively their government is providing services. Since information is power, it is often closely guarded—or never created in the first place. Politicians seldom create information about outputs and outcomes. Individuals know about the quality of the services they confront, but they have a difficult time translating that knowledge into public power. Indeed, politicians may use the selective provision of services as a clientelistic tool to "buy" political support—or, worse, to enforce state control of citizens while weakening their voice (box 3.5).

Compacts. The complex compact relationship fails in many ways. In failed or failing states (such as those the World Bank calls Low-Income Countries Under Stress, or LICUS) there is no compact because the state's control is very shallow. This happens when countries are embroiled in long civil wars (Afghanistan, El Salvador, Somalia, Sudan) or large parts of the country are beyond the reach of government (Democratic Republic of Congo).

Even in working states the compact relationship between the state and public provider agencies is often extremely weak. The delegation and specification of goals are often vague or nonexistent, and there rarely are clear responsibilities for outputs or links to outcomes. Budget allocations and staffing for agencies are determined without any direct relationship to past performance or clearly specified objectives. This means that providers are often underfunded relative to announced rhetorical, and unrealistic, targets.

Without clear delegation of responsibilities and identified objectives, there is no way of generating the relevant performance information for managing or assessing the organization. Without clear information on organizational objectives and progress, it becomes

---

BOX 3.5 *Seeking services in the Arab Republic of Egypt*

An anthropological study of urban Cairo detailing the "Avenues of Participation"—the ways residents coped with the demands of the state, and sought its favors—revealed a pattern common in many countries. First, there is a huge gap between the formal and informal realities. As a manager of a family-owned shoe factory explained:

We are caught in the middle of two totally separate systems that do not communicate with each other. One of them is the legal [formal] system. The other one is what we call the traditional system, which is much stronger than the law. That is what really controls us. (p. 205).

That gap means that, in approaching the state, individuals must rely on informal connections, personal relationships, and outright bribes to officials. There also were explicit "patron-client" relationships:

In a particular relationship I was able to observe closely that the ties between "patron" and the supposed "client" were very close and reciprocal. The "client" received loans from the politician, gifts of food and clothing for her family, publicly subsidized apartments, employment for her and her family, assistance with bureaucratic problems, and a great deal of information....At election time the client returned this service by organizing the election campaign and marshaling local political support in the district.

Source: Singerman (1995).

impossible to create enforceability. This also discourages innovation and responsiveness. There may be many isolated successes in service provision and striking examples of public servants succeeding even against the odds. But nothing in the system encourages the replication of successful innovations.

This is not to deny the enormous benefits that public provision has attained. But those benefits have often been in areas in which the compact relationship is relatively easy because the targets are numerical and provision is logistical. Strong states, even the politically repressive, have been successful in providing services. Socialist states, such as China, have had great success in the social sectors. But moving beyond the impressive logistical accomplishment and improving quality has proved much more difficult. Even weak states can launch and sustain vertical programs of logistical delivery—expanding childhood vaccinations in very troubled situations is a classic example. But going from services provided in "campaign" mode to more discretionary and quality-sensitive services has proved much more difficult.

Management.   Failures of management are also common in public production of services. Frontline workers rarely receive (explicit or implicit) incentives for successful service delivery. There are no stipulations for service quality and quantity, no measurement of effectiveness or productivity, few rewards or penalties. The provider organization monitors only inputs and compliance with processes and procedures. Even so, some states have provided some services under these conditions, but the services remain limited, low in quality, high in cost.

The problems are deep. Quick fixes that seem too good to be true probably are. One response to the corruption, absenteeism, and underperformance of providers is stricter monitoring. But if the objectives are not well known and if it is difficult to monitor behavior, it is difficult to assess performance on the basis of real, relevant output measures. So "accountability" is instead created by strict rules, intended to prevent abuse, and attempts to monitor compliance with some crudely measured proxies (attendance) or to reduce the activity to scripts that must be followed strictly. That approach can succeed for truly logistical tasks, but it can also be counterproductive. By constraining the professional autonomy of frontline providers, it may frustrate self-motivated frontline workers, driving them away and undermining the development of strong providers.

The goal is to have providers with *more* capability, *more* autonomy, and *more* discretion in providing quality services. But more autonomy requires more performance-based accountability. That is intrinsically difficult to create because of the multiple (often unobservable) objectives of public action, the demands of monitoring discretionary and transaction-intensive services, and the difficulty of attributing outputs or outcomes to actions by providers.

Take schooling (chapter 7): good teaching is a complex endeavor. The quality of a teacher cannot be assessed strictly on the basis of student scores on a standardized examination. Why not? Schooling has many other objectives. It is difficult to isolate the value added. And simply paying and promoting all teachers the same does not motivate good teaching—it can even lower morale among motivated teachers.

Perhaps good teaching can be assessed subjectively by another trained educator—a head teacher or school principal. But this creates the temptation to play favorites or, worse, to extract payments from teachers for good assessments. So the autonomy of school heads must be limited by accountability, to motivate them to reward good teachers. There must be an assessment standard for school heads. But all the problems of assessing good teaching also apply to good school heads. Indeed, that is how dysfunctional bureaucracies cascade into a morass of corruption, as upward payments from those at lower levels buy good assignments or ratings from superiors.

The market

The "market," as an idealized set of relationships of accountability, relies more or less exclusively on client power—and only on that part of client power that is based on choice, backed by purchasing power. *Customer* power is the main relationship of accountability. The market has several strengths in the provision of services—but also many weaknesses. One strength is that customers will buy where they perceive the greatest satisfaction—so organizations have incentives to be responsive to clients. Another strength is that since the organizations are autonomous, they can manage their frontline providers as they wish. Yet another is that with a variety of organizations providing services, each can be flexible with innovation and each has the incentive to adopt successful innovations (or else lose resources). Markets produce innovations and scale them up by trial and error followed by replication and imitation—for organizational innovation as well as product innovation.

But for the services in this Report, the market has three weaknesses.

- It responds exclusively to customer power, so there are no pressures for equity (much less equality) in the allocation of services (though it is not obvious that political systems lacking strong citizen voice have any greater pressures for equity).
- It will not, in general, satisfy collective objectives (simply adding up individual objectives). For instance, if one person's use of adequate sanitation affects those who live nearby, individuals may under-invest in sanitation.
- It can be effective in having customer power discipline providers only when the customer has the relevant information about provider performance. In ambulatory curative care it is easy for customers to know their waiting time and to know how they were treated. But it is very difficult for them to know whether the medical treatment they received was effective and appropriate for their condition.

From principles to instruments

This Report uses the framework of actors and their relationships of accountability and power to understand the successes and failures of centralized public service production—and to evaluate reforms and new proposed institutional arrangements for service provision. Given the failures and limitations of the traditional model of service provision—the long route—greater reliance will inevitably be placed on more direct client influence—the short route. In some extreme cases where the long route breaks down suddenly, as in the aftermath of the breakup of the Soviet Union, reliance on the short route arises by default (box 3.6). But increased reliance can be deliberate, forming the basis of a wide variety of institutional reforms, each with strong advocates.

In education people believe that schools will improve with more use of choice through vouchers, greater community control, greater school autonomy, having more information about budget flows and more aggressive testing and school-based accountability. In health people believe that care will improve through greater demand-side financing (and less public production), more use of vertical programs for specific diseases, and community control of health centers. Others emphasize solutions that cut across sectors: community-driven development, participatory budgeting, power to local governments, "new public management," and civil service reform.

All these proposals aim to improve services by changing the relationships of accountability. All recognize that, though there are many proximate causes of failure, the deep causes lie with inadequate institutional arrangements. If frontline workers (civil servants) in the existing organizations of public production are frequently absent, have little regard for clients who are poor, and lack the technical knowledge to perform their services well, this inadequate organizational capacity is the proximate cause of poor services. Too frequently those seeking improvement have focused only on internal organizational reforms—focusing on management of the frontline workers. If organizational failures are the result of deeper weaknesses in institutional arrangements (weak political commitment, unclear objectives, no enforceability), direct attacks on the proximate determinants (more money, better training, more internal information) will fail.

Different systems can underpin success. For example, countries have very different institutional arrangements in corporate finance. Crudely put, in Japan firms own banks, in Germany banks own firms, and in the United States banks and firms are separated. All three countries have very high levels

---

BOX 3.6 *Health care in Central Asia and the Caucasus: the long and short of it*

The upheavals that accompanied the breakup of the Soviet Union had serious consequences for the health sectors of the resulting states. In the Soviet era, the health system was run, virtually in its entirety, by the central government. It had its problems. It was rigidly financed on the basis of inputs rather than outputs. It was extremely biased toward hospital and specialist care. It inefficiently relied upon high-cost procedures and long hospital stays relative to other industrial countries. And it was not at all oriented toward clients. But it worked. Services were free to all, and particularly in the resource-poor republics, many in Central Asia, it contributed to levels of health status—low mortality rates and high life expectancy—much higher than in other countries at similar levels of income.

It worked because the two legs of the "long route" functioned well enough. A commitment to universal coverage of health and other social services deriving from socialist principles substituted for "voice" in the form of free political expression. "Compacts," or more specifically direct management, were enforced through means of the substantial control government had over state-employed providers. There may have been some support for this arrangement from the "short route" due to monitoring by local party leaders, but this was distinctly secondary given the strong hierarchic management capacity of government.

Then the compact collapsed. Accountability to policymakers could no longer be enforced—there was no longer funding or control from the center. Within the republics, dramatic declines in income led to similarly dramatic declines in public funding for the sector. Also, since almost everything had been produced by the state, there was no history of setting priorities according to the degree of public responsibility each activity warranted, so the budgets for even high-priority public goods were not protected. The resurgence of some vaccine-preventable diseases as well as the growth of infectious diseases (HIV/AIDS and tuberculosis especially) attest to this. The "compact" leg of the long route was gone; political structures for the "voice" leg were (and in some cases still are) yet to develop, leaving a vacuum.

All of the Commonwealth of Independent States (CIS) countries are struggling to replace the former system while suffering from the twin liabilities of declines in income and the legacy of an unsustainable degree of hospital—and staffing—intensity inherited from the former regime.

The pace and deliberateness of reform strategies have varied substantially among the CIS countries. In most there has been a marked increase in the private sector and in fees—both informal and institutionalized (particularly in Georgia and the Kyrgyz Republic)—in public facilities. Both tendencies have meant that private financing has become a large part of the health market—averaging around 40 percent but ranging from under 20 percent in Uzbekistan to over 90 percent in Georgia. Uzbekistan's retention of a large public sector reflects a more robust economy. Having natural resources to sell led to a fall in income of only 5 percent between 1990 and 2000 in contrast to more typical declines of 30 percent in Armenia, 45 percent in Azerbaijan, or the more extreme cases of 65 percent in Moldova and 70 percent in Georgia.

Even when there was no deliberate policy of privatization—the sale of public facilities to a recognized private provider—growth in the private sector was simply a matter of the market (the short route) taking over when the state became incapable of ensuring services. Similarly, the oversupply of hospital beds has fallen by an average of 40 percent from its 1990 level. Again, whether this was due to a deliberate policy (a 55 percent fall in Uzbekistan—almost all in public hands) or a simple necessity because of austerity and closures after privatization (the same 55 percent fall in Georgia) is an open question.

Reforms under consideration in the CIS countries generally involve such client-centered mechanisms as insurance (a conditional voucher) and capitation schemes, both of which allow payments to follow patients. Progress is slow, however. Institutions take time to develop and the information collection systems necessary for getting good results from insurance programs are still lacking.

The starting point for the CIS countries is very different from that of developing countries in general—too much infrastructure and resources rather than too little. However, in many ways the solutions will be similar. Substantially more reliance on the "short route" of accountability is likely, with government being a monitor and enforcer of the rules of the game regardless of who ultimately becomes the direct provider.

Source: Maria E. Bonilla-Chacin, Edmundo Murrugarra, and Moukim Temourov, "Health Care During Transition and Health Systems Reform: Evidence from the Poorest CIS Countries," Lucerne Conference of the CIS-7 Initiative, January 2003.

---

of income—so it cannot be that *any* of these institutional arrangements is incompatible with economic development. At the same time, countries with financial arrangements very similar to one of these three have failed to develop. With many proposed solutions, does anything go? No. Solutions need to conform to certain principles, but the principles need to be implemented in ways that are appropriate to the time, place, and service.

American Indians as a group are the poorest minority in America. Some tribes, such as the Pine Ridge Oglala Sioux, have severe economic problems (unemployment in 1989 was 61 percent). But others, such as the White Mountain Apache, do badly, but much better (unemployment was only 11 percent). As part of attempts to control them, their governments were imposed on them by the U.S. federal government and varied little across tribes. The imposed constitutions were reasonably well-adapted to Apache social and cultural norms, providing a reasonable fit between formal and informal structures of power. In contrast, the formal constitution was at odds with Sioux norms and led to continuing discord between formal and informal modes of exercising power, precluding the emergence of effective institutions.[166]

Many African scholars argue that the roots of the problems in Africa today lie in the legacy of colonialism. Nation-state boundaries followed colonial power rather than African realities. The struggle over how to adapt or transform the transplanted institutions continues to influence debates today.

Here is how Mamdani opens his study, *Citizen and Subject:*

> Discussions on Africa's present predicament revolve around two clear tendencies: modernist and communitarian. For modernists, the problem is that civil society is an embryonic and marginal construct; for communitarians, it is that the real flesh-and-blood communities that constitute Africa are marginalized from public life as so many "tribes." The liberal solution is to locate politics in civil society, and the Africanist solution is to put Africa's age-old communities at the center of African politics. One side calls for a regime that will champion rights, and the other stands in defense of culture. The impasse in Africa is not only at the level of practical politics. It is also a paralysis of perspective.[167]

Reforming institutions to improve services for poor people will be difficult

Because institutional reforms change power relationships among actors, they are political reforms. But politics generally does not favor reforms that improve services for poor people. Such reforms require upsetting entrenched interests, which have the advantage of inertia, history, organizational capability, and knowing exactly what is at stake. Policymakers and providers are generally more organized, informed, and influential than citizens, particularly poor citizens. But reform is possible, even against these odds.

- Pro-poor coalitions for better services increase the odds for success.
- Change agents and reform champions can shape the agenda and follow through on implementation.
- When the prospects for successful institutional reform are not propitious, strategic incrementalism may be all that is possible. But pursuing it has the danger of being merely incremental incrementalism.

Pro-poor coalitions

In most instances making services work for poor people means making services work for everybody—while ensuring that poor people have access to those services. Required is a coalition that includes poor people and significant elements of the non-poor. There is unlikely to be progress without substantial "middle-class buy-in" to proposed reforms. In the words of Wilbur Cohen, U.S. Secretary of Health, Education, and Welfare under President Lyndon Johnson in the 1960s: "Programs for poor people are poor programs."[168]

De Soto's study of rights to real estate in urban areas emphasizes that not only are poor people outside the benefits of having secure title and claim to their property, but so are nearly all of the middle class. His study of the historical evolution of property rights in the United States strongly suggested that the response to popular political pressure—not top-down technocratic design—was the key to a broad-based system of property rights.[169] Since poor people are excluded from many services, such as primary education or safe water, improvements in the system are likely to disproportionately benefit poor people.

But broad coalitions are not always sufficient because some services need to be tailored to destitute and disadvantaged groups (as in situations of ethnic or gender exclusion). A common obstacle in the access to services is that the socially disadvantaged are excluded—as a matter of policy, or because they feel excluded due to their treatment by providers, or due to actions of more powerful social groups within the community itself. The politics of services for disadvantaged groups are even more difficult, because coalitions made up exclusively of the powerless are often powerless.

Change agents—reform champions

Episodes of reform depend on reform champions, the entrepreneurs of public sector reform. They emerge from various sources. Politicians can often pursue service improvements even when the conditions are not propitious. They must act to create and sustain pressures for reform. Professional associations are often both the source of pressure for, and resistance to, major innovations. Dissatisfied with the progress in their field—education, policing, public health, sanitation—professionals emerge as champions for reform, putting pressures on politicians and policymakers for reform. For instance, the campaign of Public Services International for "Quality Public Ser-

Table 3.3   Modern institutions took a long time to develop

Institution/reform	First	Majority (of now developed countries)	Last	United Kingdom	United States
Universal male suffrage	1848 (France)	1907	1907 (Japan)	1918	1870–1965
Universal suffrage	1907 (New Zealand)	1946	1971 (Switzerland)	1928	1928–1965
Health insurance (the basis for what is now universal)	1883	1911		1911	Still no universal coverage
State pensions	1889 (Germany)	1909	1946 (Switzerland)	1908	1946

Source: Chang (2002).

vices" balances the unions' role in protecting the rights of workers with support for innovation in public service delivery.[170] Linking the efforts of these "insiders" and "technocrats" to broader coalitions of citizens is often a key element of success.

Strategic incrementalism

Sweeping or fundamental reform of institutions is rare. It requires the right conditions. A recent study emphasizes how long the development of political institutions in the now-developed countries took (table 3.3). Most "modern" institutions of "modern" political and economic governance that are recommended today emerged late in the now-developed countries (at much higher levels of income than developing countries today). And they spread slowly across countries. In the United States universal white male suffrage was not achieved until 1870, female suffrage did not come until 1925, and true universal suffrage did not come until (at least) 1965. Switzerland did not adopt female suffrage until 1971. Canada's widely discussed "single-payer" style of health insurance did not emerge until the 1970s. Institutional reform that changes the landscape usually moves at a glacial pace—but glaciers do move and carve out new landscapes when they do.

The improvement of services, always pressing, cannot wait for the right conditions. Some arrangements, such as enclave approaches to delivering services to poor people, may not be sustainable in the long run, even if they improve outcomes in the short run. Often driven by donors, these actions can undermine national relationships of accountability (chapter 11). Sometimes the desirable arrangement is to strengthen the weakest link. If the policymaker-provider link is weak, contracting out services—such as Cambodia's use of nongovernmental organizations for primary health services—may be the preferred arrangement. But incremental activities—pragmatic improvisation to make services work even in a weak institutional environment—should be used to create more favorable conditions for reform in the longer run. Temporary work-arounds cannot and should not substitute for creating the conditions for reform.

Universal primary education—what does it take?

Primary school enrollment in Uganda rose from 3.6 million students to 6.9 million between 1996 and 2001. What accounts for such a drastic increase in such a short time: Political will? Abolishing user fees? A good macroeconomic environment? Information to empower beneficiaries? All of the above.

President Yoweri Museveni's decision in 1996 to make universal primary education an issue in the presidential election campaign broke with his earlier position. He had previously emphasized that building roads and infrastructure would provide access to markets to enable people to generate income that would pay for schooling. But in a radio address in March, he promised to give access to free primary education to four children per family, up to two boys and two girls, and all orphans.

Although free primary education was only one part of Museveni's manifesto, it soon became clear that the promise had struck a chord with the electorate. Finance ministry officials recall that several of Museveni's advisors repeatedly sent them messages after campaign meetings, emphasizing how the promise had resonated with the public.

The May 1996 election was Uganda's first presidential election since the military takeover in 1986. Though the elections did not involve official multiparty competition, President Museveni faced a credible challenger, Paul Ssemogerere, the leader of the Democratic party. Ssemogerere promised to restore multiparty politics, negotiate with the rebel movement in northern Uganda, and grant greater autonomy to the Buganda region, once an independent kingdom. These stances positioned him for substantial regional support in northern and central Uganda. He also declared that he would match Museveni's promise to provide free primary education.

In December 1996, soon after a landslide victory, President Museveni announced the abolition of school fees. Since then there has been a sustained shift in Ugandan public expenditures in favor of education, especially for primary schools. Spending on education has risen as a share of government expenditures from an average of 20 percent in the three fiscal years preceding the election to an average of 26 percent in the three years following. Total enrollment in primary schools skyrocketed (figure 1).

Did emerging democracy make the difference?

The argument that free elections contributed to the success in Uganda is buttressed by three observations. Education was a salient issue for Ugandan voters. The electorate had access to information about government performance in this area. And the success of universal primary education contributed to President Museveni's continued popularity.[171]

For candidates to believe that they will be judged on whether education promises are fulfilled, education must be important for voters. Museveni's 1996 commitment to universal primary education would have been expected to draw national support, while Paul Ssemogerere's positions on the northern rebellion, Buganda autonomy, and reintroduction of political parties would have been expected to generate regional support.

Museveni's victory did not depend on a single regional base of support. He received more than 90 percent of the vote in Uganda's western region, 74 percent of the votes in Paul Ssemogerere's home region (central), and 72 percent of the vote in the eastern region.

Figure 1 Enrollments increased dramatically after 1996
Primary school enrollments in Uganda, 1996–2001

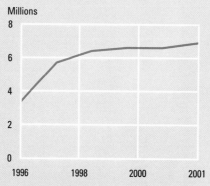

Source: Murphy, Bertoncino, and Wang (2002).

In the elections in Malawi in 1994 the winning presidential candidate also made universal primary education part of his manifesto, but voting was much more polarized along regional lines than it was in Uganda. The winner would thus have had an incentive to continue to cultivate a regional base of support, rather than to deliver on a national issue like education.

Ugandan voters had access to various sources of information about the education initiative that enabled them to evaluate how the government had made good on its 1996 election promises. Major national dailies, such as *The Monitor* and *The New Vision,* continued to give prominent coverage to universal primary education issues.

Data collected by the Afrobarometer project show that Ugandans believe that President Museveni has performed very effectively, and in rating government performance they are most satisfied with education policy. During the June 2000 survey, 93 percent of respondents reported that they were either somewhat satisfied or very satisfied with Museveni's overall performance. Eighty-seven percent of Ugandans reported that their government was handling education issues well, while the average across the 12 African countries was 59 percent.

Macroeconomic stability and budgetary institutions

Democratic politics may have given the Ugandan government an incentive to deliver on its education promise of 1996. But success in reorienting public expenditures toward primary education has also depended on stabilizing the macroeconomic environment and developing budgetary institutions.[172] Stable macroeconomic conditions have undoubtedly made it easier to forecast revenues and expenditures. Under more unstable macroeconomic conditions, African governments like Malawi have found it difficult to maintain a sustained commitment to increasing education expenditures.

Uganda's macroeconomic stability since 1992 has depended on budget reforms—from a cash budget system to the medium-term expenditure framework to the Poverty Eradication Action Plan. The framework aligns resources with budgetary priorities, while the cash budget system ensured that overall fiscal discipline is maintained if there are revenue shortfalls. The Poverty Action Fund has been particularly effective in ensuring that government spending priorities, such as primary education, receive needed funds. It seems unlikely that universal primary education would have been sustainable without these innovations in budgetary institutions.

The power of information in delivering funds for education

In 1996 a public expenditure tracking survey of local governments and primary schools revealed that only 13 percent of the per-student capitation grants made it to the schools in 1991–95.[173] In 1995 for every dollar spent on nonwage education items by the central government, only about 20 cents reached the schools, with local governments capturing most of the funding.

Poor students suffered disproportionately, because schools catering to them received even less than others. Indeed, most poor schools received nothing. Case study evidence and other data showed that the school funds were not going to other sectors either. The disbursements were rarely audited or monitored, and most schools and parents had little or no information about their entitlements to the grants. Most funds went to purposes unrelated to education or for private gain, as indicated by numerous newspaper articles about indictments of district education officers after the survey findings went public.

To respond to the problem, the central government began publishing data on monthly transfers of grants to districts in newspapers and to broadcast them on the radio. It required primary schools and district administrations to post notices on all inflows of funds. This promoted accountability by giving schools and parents access to information needed to understand and monitor the grant program.

An evaluation of the information campaign reveals a large improvement. Schools are still not receiving the entire grant (and there are delays). But the capture by interests along the way has been reduced from 80 percent in 1995 to 20 percent in 2001 (figure 2). A before-and-after assessment comparing outcomes for the same schools in 1995 and 2001—and taking into account school-specific factors, household income, teachers' education, school size, and supervision—suggests that the information campaign explains two-thirds of the massive improvement.

In 1995 schools with access to newspapers and those without suffered just as much from the leakages. And from 1995 to 2001 both groups experienced a large drop in leakage. But the reduction in capture was significantly higher for the schools with access to newspapers, which increased their funding by 12 percentage points over schools that lacked newspapers.

With an inexpensive policy action—the provision of mass information—Uganda dramatically reduced the capture of a public program aimed at increasing access to textbooks and other instructional materials. Because poor people were less able than others to claim their entitlement from the district officials before the campaign, they benefited most from it.

Figure 2 Amount of capitation grant due schools actually received by schools, 1991–2001

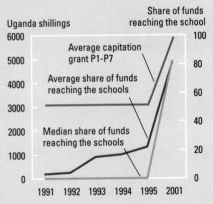

Source: Reinikka and Svensson (2001), Reinikka and Svensson (2003a).

Clients and providers

The well-being of poor people is the point of making services work. The value of public policy and expenditure is largely determined by the value the poor attach to it. When publicly provided and funded housing is left vacant,[174] when food supplies are not eaten, when free but empty public health clinics are bypassed in favor of expensive private care,[175] this money is wasted.

Improving services means making the interests of poor people matter more to providers. Engaging poor clients in an active role—as purchasers, as monitors, and as co-producers (the "short route")—can improve performance tremendously.

How can public policy help poor people acquire better services through this route? By expanding the influence of their own choices. By having the income of providers depend more on the demands of poor clients. By increasing the purchasing power of poor people. And by providing better information and a more competitive environment to improve the functioning of services. Where such choice is not feasible, governments can expand consumer power by establishing procedures to make sure complaints are acted on.

Sad to say, governments and donors frequently neglect the possible role of poor clients in sustaining better services—or treat that role merely as an instrument for achieving a technically determined outcome. Neither governments nor donors are accustomed to asking the poor for advice. Recent initiatives have begun to redress this through a variety of ways to increase participation by communities and civil society. But the potential for improvement has not yet been adequately tapped.[176]

In short, the key is to enhance the power of poor clients in service provision. This Report and this chapter try to give the term "empowerment" a precise and concrete interpretation. Specifically, the chapter discusses the potential for poor people to influence services by:

- Increasing their individual purchasing power.
- Increasing their collective power over providers by organizing in groups.
- Increasing their "capacity to aspire"[177]: allowing them to take advantage of the first two by increasing the information needed to develop their personal sense of capability and entitlement.[178]

When will strengthening the client-producer link matter most?

In the framework of chapter 3, improving client power—the short route of service delivery—can overcome various weaknesses of the long route (figure 4.1), even when services remain the responsibility of government. The clearest case is monitoring providers. Clients are usually in a better position to see what is going on than most supervisors in government hierarchies—who provide the compact and management. When the policymaker-provider link is weak because of scarce or difficult-to-manage supervisory staff, clients may be the only ones who regularly interact with providers. As discussed several times in this Report, improvements in basic education have often depended on participation by parents. Although parents cannot monitor all aspects of education, they can monitor attendance by teachers and even illiterate parents can tell if their children are learning to read and write.

Citizens as clients can also make up for shortcomings in the voice or politics relationship. If governments cannot or will not try to determine and act on the desires of the public, or if the desires of poor people are systematically ignored, there may be few options for poor communities but to develop mechanisms for getting services some other way.

The greater the differences among clients—their heterogeneity—the more that direct client power is likely to have an advantage relative to the "long route." The greater the individual differences in preferences for the type and quality of services provided, the greater the importance of discretion on the part of providers and the more difficult it is to monitor the use of this discretion centrally. Sometimes preferences differ geographically, so different levels of government may reflect this variation. But for many services, the heterogeneity of preferences applies all the way down to the individual. Take courtesy and comfort (caring) relative to technical skill (curing) in health delivery—or farmers with constraints on their time and other workers in the same community with different constraints. Certainly people differ in the amounts of water and electricity they want, given their other needs. Government structures may not be flexible enough to accommodate this variety. And where local preferences vary systematically between the poor and others, honoring poor people's preferences over those of the better-off can be a challenge.

For some collective action problems, governments may not be located at the correct level to solve them, no matter how willing they are to pursue the interests of the poor. The boundaries of the political jurisdiction may not correspond to the boundaries of the problem. So schools are often the most appropriate unit for management and operation. Sanitation services need community pressure to ensure that everyone uses fixed-point defecation, but they are often organized around communities that are larger or smaller than villages, depending on the density of population. A more active role for communities is needed in such cases.

It is important to avoid romanticizing either form of increasing client power—neither choice nor participation is sufficient for all services. Market failures and concerns for equity lead societies to want to improve or

Figure 4.1   Client power in the service delivery framework

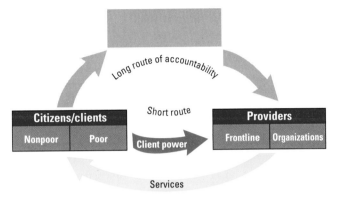

extend these services in the first place. There is no reason to believe they are all self-corrective through replicating aspects of the free market.

Similarly, some settlements constitute communities with sufficiently congruent interests among members, egalitarian norms to protect the poor, mutual trust, and the ability to mobilize information and to act collectively—that is, they have social capital.[179] But some clearly do not. How many villages and urban neighborhoods are there in the developing world? Hundreds of thousands? Millions? And how many kinds of social structures are represented? Ensuring that poor people have a say in this variety of circumstances demands that policies be examined and designed with a great deal of local knowledge and an understanding of local conflicts and inequalities. Pretending otherwise will almost certainly do real harm.

And some services, particularly for health and modern water and sanitation, need technical inputs to be successful. Patients—as individuals or health boards—are good judges of courtesy and attendance. But they are much less able to judge clinical quality or the appropriate mix of curative and preventive services. And some health problems have effects that spill over community boundaries. Large pest-control initiatives and other forms of infectious disease control may seem a low priority for any one group of citizens, yet will be effective only when all participate. Ultimately, some wide-scale government intervention is necessary. Still, emphasizing the power of clients is a welcome tonic for the top-down, technocratic orientation that has characterized much development thinking until now.

Increasing client power through choice

The most direct way to get service providers to be accountable to the client is to make whatever they get out of the transaction depend on their meeting client needs and desires. That is, money (usually) or other benefits from providing the service should follow the client—the enforceability of a relationship of accountability, discussed in chapter 3.

In market transactions, this is done by a buyer paying money to a seller. But that is not the only way. Payments by government to schools (and the pay of teachers) can depend on the number of students enrolled and continuing. The vast majority of primary education in the Netherlands is paid for by government but delivered by private schools compensated in this way. Capitation lists are the dominant method of pay for general practice medical providers in several European systems, particularly the United Kingdom. Overall consumer satisfaction can be expressed through the possibility of changing general practitioners, determining their income.

Vouchers issued to consumers are another method of linking service provider compensation to consumer choices, even though the consumer is not the original source of funds. All health insurance with some choice of provider is a form of voucher—one conditional on being sick. And intrinsically motivated providers, whose sense of self-worth depends on having a large demand for their services, try for more patients under any payment system. The essence of each of these methods is that client well-being translates directly into provider well-being—the incentives are aligned.

Many service problems can be improved by making sure that payment follows clients. Most of the evidence for this comes from studies examining the effect of fees on the behavior of private providers (who must, of course, operate this way) but it applies to all such methods. Payment can have four kinds of beneficial effects:

- Improve provider behavior.
- Increase supply and sustainability.
- Increase vigilance and a stake in receiving better service from each transaction.
- Make better choices about which services to demand.

The first two work through providers, the second two through clients.

Provider behavior

Discourtesy, social distance, abruptness of care, discrimination against women and ethnic minorities, service characteristics mismatched to individual tastes—all are associated with provider behavior. And all can improve with the purchasing power of clients. Indeed, that is why the private sector is often seen as preferable to a public sector with staff paid by salaries (box 4.1). These differences are echoed in studies from countries as diverse as Bangladesh, China, India, Lao PDR, Thailand, and Vietnam.

For courtesy, caring, and convenience the private sector usually has a distinct advantage. Private practitioners usually provide services more convenient to the client. Limited hours in public facilities (only in the morning in farm communities) is often the reason people go to a private practitioner.[180]

What accounts for the difference? Not the training but the motivation: ". . . the same government doctor who was not easily or conveniently accessible, whose medication was not satisfactory and whose manner was brusque and indifferent transformed into a perfectly nice and capable doctor when he was seeing a patient in his private practice."[181] Why? Because the doctor wants the client to return. If the staff is paid through salaries, there is no strong incentive to be accommodating. This is not lost on clients: "Anyhow, they will get their money, so they don't pay much attention."[182] Discrimination, particularly against ethnic minorities and women, and social distance are barriers to services even when the services are free, barriers that frequently yield to market forces.[183] The artificial scarcity of free services—ensuring excess demand—induces rationing by some other means (social status, personal connections, ethnicity), and poor people rarely have these other means. Groups coping with social stigma—such as prostitutes, who need to be part of the battle against HIV/AIDS—often prefer the confidentiality and more considerate behavior in private clinics.

The scarcity of commodities due to low pricing may lead to other commonly reported problems—illicit sale of materials and the demand for under-the-counter payments. Indeed, "free" public services are often very expensive. Many countries have serious diversions of pharmaceuticals from the public stock into private markets, where they instantly become expensive. In general, services that most directly resemble market goods have a greater problem of diversion and implicit privatization.

In Eastern Europe the health systems are often ranked among the most corrupt of public services (box 4.2). Under-the-table payments and pharmaceutical sales to open markets are the main elements in this assessment. If directives against such practices cannot be enforced, countervailing pressure is needed (see box 3.6). Formalizing fees and putting purchasing power in the hands of poorer clients is one possible source of such pressure.[184]

Exemptions from fees can have perverse effects by reducing this purchasing power. In Benin a measure to raise female school enrollment—waiving fees for girls—led teachers to favor the enrollment of boys and to raise informal fees for girls.[185] Of course, the problem could have been solved by abolishing fees for everyone (if the teachers could continue to be paid) or by closer monitoring and enforcement by education officials. But in a system that has problems paying teachers and weak administrative capacity, bolstering the ability of girls to pay with vouchers seems more likely to succeed.

Increase and sustain supply

Greater purchasing power may simply increase supply and overcome bottlenecks due to supply problems. In Bangladesh the Female Secondary School program awards scholarships to girls if they attend school regularly and gives secondary schools a grant based on the number of girls they enroll. Secondary school enrollment in Bangladesh is increasing, and faster for girls than for boys. It also led to the establishment, at private expense, of new schools. Desires for single-sex schools and separate toilet facilities for girls were mysteriously accommodated when girls' attendance meant more money. True,

there remain problems, such as ensuring the quality of the newly established schools, but these are secondary to getting girls to school.

The revenues that providers raise from charges at the point of collection are often the reason some services can continue at all. Much of the success of the Bamako Initiative in West Africa (see spotlight) stems from the supply of pharmaceuticals made possible by charging users for them. Bamako Initiative villages usually have drugs, other villages usually don't. Sustainability in piped water systems is almost always equivalent to financial

---

BOX 4.1 *The private sector is preferred in Andhra Pradesh, India*

A study of consumer and producer attitudes was conducted in six districts in the southern Indian state of Andhra Pradesh. The study included 72 in-depth interviews and 24 focus groups.

Private	Public
ATTITUDES OF DOCTORS	
"They speak well, inquire about our health."	"Does not talk to me, does not bother (about my feelings or the details of my problems)."
"Ask about everything from A to Z."	"Don't tell us what the problem is, first check, give us medicines and ask us to go."
"Look after everyone equally."	
"They take money . . . so give powerful medicine . . . treat better."	"They are supposed to give us Rs. 1000 and 15 kg of rice for family planning operations; they give us Rs. 500 and 10 kg rice and make us run around for the rest."
	"Anyhow they will get their money so they don't pay much attention."
CONVENIENCE	
"Treat us quickly. . . ."	"Do not attend to us immediately."
"We spend money but get cured faster."	"Have to stand in line for everything."
"I know Mr. Reddy. He is a government doctor but I go to him in the evening."	"Doctor is there from 9 a.m. to 4 p.m.—when we need to go to work."
"Can delay payment by 5–10 days. He is OK with that, he stays in the village itself."	"I have not been there, but seeing the surroundings . . . I don't feel like going."
COST	
"Recent expenses came to Rs. 500 for 3 days . . . had to shell out money immediately."	"While coming out, compounders ask us for 10–20 Rs."
"We have to be prepared to pay, you never know how much it is going to cost you."	"Anyhow, we have to buy medicines from outside."
ADVANTAGES	
"Even if I have to take a loan I will go to private place, they treat well."	"Malaria treatment—they come, examine blood, give tablets."
	"For family planning operations."
	"Polio drops."
	"In case I do not get cured in private hospital, but it is very rare."

Source: Probe Qualitative Research Team (2002).

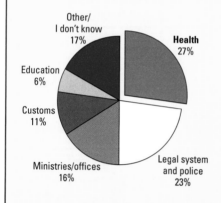
sustainability. There might be some subsidy element included in pricing, but systems to get water to a private home depend on charges for that water.

Increased client stake—and vigilance

The third argument for having money follow clients: when people buy things they make sure they get them, and they pay more attention to the quality of what they get. Money is a profound source of power for poor people. When Zambian truck drivers were expected to pay into a road fund, they took turns policing a bridge crossing to make sure overloaded trucks did not pass. Their money would have to be used to fix the bridge. Women living in slum areas of Rio de Janeiro proudly display bills they paid for water and sanitation—it proves their inclusion in society and their right to

services.[186] Farmers in southern India expect the same from irrigation services (box 4.3).

Making better choices

For some services consumer discretion is important for allocating resources efficiently. Households determine water and electricity use, scarce goods that have costs associated with them. And facing marginal costs is the only way to ensure efficient use. The alternatives: wasted water leading to shortages, unreliable service with serious consequences for the safety of the water supply, and periodic cuts in electricity familiar to most people in developing countries. Protecting the poor in network services can be achieved (assuming that meters work) with "lifeline" subsidies, in which the first few essential units are free but full marginal costs are paid beyond this level.

In health care, as in water and electricity, more is not always better. Restricting demand for curative services by pricing frees up providers, particularly public providers, to do preventive health, for which there is little private demand.[187] As the director of a prominent nongovernmental organization providing health care to the very poorest in Bangladesh puts it: "Of course you must charge at least a token amount for services, otherwise you keep seeing people with paper cuts and other minor things."[188] Similarly, crowding at outpatient clinics at public hospitals can be curtailed by charging enough that people use a cheaper level of service.

All these advantages can be obtained in ways other than charging fees at the point of service. As long as clients consider the resources used as belonging to them, the discipline of market-like mechanisms can be enforced. The Singapore Medical Savings Accounts do this by allowing people to apply funds not used for primary medical care to other purposes, such as pensions.[189] Countries with scarce administrative personnel and supervisory capacity may certainly want to enlist clients as monitors, and market mechanisms are one way of doing it.

For any of these mechanisms to work, however, there must be a real choice with real options. Otherwise, giving schools pay-

BOX 4.3 *Payment and accountability*

A conversation with farmers in Haryana state in India, who had been to see what had happened in reforming Andhra Pradesh (AP):

Q: "What did you learn when you visited AP?"

A: "That the farmers are much poorer than us, but that they pay four times as much for water"

Q: "The farmers in AP cannot be happy about that…."

A: "They are happy, because now the irrigation department is much more accountable to them … they know where the money goes and they have a say in how it is spent…."

Q: "So then, you much richer farmers would be willing to pay more?"

A: "Only if the irrigation department makes the same changes, otherwise we will refuse to pay."

Q: "Ah, but this is just because there is a particular Chief Minister who is pushing that now … once he goes it will all go back to the same old way."

A: "We also wondered about that, and so we asked the farmers in AP about that. They told us that 'no matter who is elected as CM, we will never allow the government to again give us free water.'"

Source: World Bank staff.

ments on the basis of enrollments is not far from what happens now in centrally owned and managed school systems, with all the problems we are trying to fix. Conversely, market mechanisms with a natural monopoly don't improve matters either. There is no denying that sparsely populated rural areas—where many of the world's poor people live—are much more constrained by competitive supply than urban areas. But even these markets may be "contestable" in the sense that other providers would be able to enter the market if the current provider abused monopoly power or if monopolies were periodically granted on the basis of competitive bids.

Policies to improve choice

Choice-based improvements alone cannot be a solution to the problem of bad services for the poor, though some may remain as instruments in a longer-run strategy by govern-

ment. In some cases the market would be expected to wither away as the state increases its capabilities. In the meantime, three categories of policies can make the most out of clients acting on their own behalf:

- Increasing the power of the poor over providers by providing them with finance directly.
- Increasing competition.
- Increasing information about services and providers.

Increasing the purchasing power of the poor. The big problem with services that can, in principle, be provided in markets is that poor people don't have enough money to pay for them. For market mechanisms to help the poor, their purchasing power must be increased. The voucher mechanisms discussed are a direct way of handling this for specific services. But additional mileage can come from more flexible transfers that can be used for purposes that the family chooses.

Flexible transfers can help to overcome the weakness of the citizen-policymaker link by giving poor people more direct say in what gets delivered than even the political process would give them—the transfers become *their* money. Substantial work in South Africa has shown the beneficial effects of cash pension payments on the health and well-being of all members of a family.[190] For services with large externalities, demand for the service may not be great enough, even when the service is free, so the Bolsa Escola program in Brazil paid families to send their children to school, as did the secondary school program for girls in Bangladesh, while the Education, Health, and Nutrition Program (Progresa) in Mexico paid families to use preventive health care (see spotlight).

Cash payments have problems though. First, giving unconstrained cash transfers to poor people is often not politically palatable. Second, cash payments always have to be administratively targeted, which requires determinations of eligibility. Everyone likes money, so self-targeting of cash transfers is not possible. If a government has a hard time getting goods and services into the hands of the poor, it may well have an even harder time getting cash, or cash equivalents, to them.

Increasing the scope of competition. Sometimes increasing competition merely means allowing a private sector to emerge where laws previously restricted entry. Jordan, after years of prohibition, allowed private universities in 1990. Ten years later, enrollments in these institutions accounted for one-third of all university students. Bangladesh has had a similar experience in the past decade. This increase in competition allows governments to increase enrollments without extremely regressive subsidies to public universities.

Competition can also be encouraged by allowing subsidies to the poor to be portable between public and private providers. Private providers may not exist simply because the public sector is free. Governments can increase competition by changing the form of subsidy from zero price to competitive prices, with cash or voucher payments to compensate. University education government loans, usable at any eligible institution, can increase competition, improve quality in public facilities, and reduce subsidies for all but students from poor families.

In some cases competition is not possible, at least not without substantial regulation. Health insurance markets are notoriously prone to failure, and competition within them can lead to both inefficient and inequitable outcomes, since firms can compete by excluding the sick, not by being more efficient. Network services are also hard to run without a monopoly. But in each case these markets can be contestable, capturing much of the benefit of competition.

Some readers may think that the foregoing arguments are just an attempted justification for user fees. This is wrong, for all the reasons put forth here. So, to make things as clear as possible, the pros and cons of user fees in general are laid out in box 4.4. There are times when user fees are appropriate—and some when they are not. Based on the primary goal of making services work for poor people, this Report argues against any blanket policy on user fees that encompasses all services in all country circumstances.

Increasing information to improve choices by consumers. One critical limit to well-func-tioning competitive markets is the consumer's awareness. The private sector is a mixed bag. Private "medical" providers vary from quite good doctors (including senior specialists from government hospitals in their off-hours) to totally unqualified, untrained people, some of whom are downright dangerous.[191] Private or NGO schools may cater to specific skills not provided in public schools (foreign language, religious studies, arts and music) or they may just be profiteers. An essential part of improving peoples' choices is to provide information about these providers. Many times, people simply don't know enough to choose better or worse services. And sometimes they identify good medical care with powerful medicines—which is quite wrong and potentially dangerous.

Information can be advice to families on how to choose schools or medical care-givers[192] or on how to take care of themselves. This might be supplemented with various certification programs, standard setting, and laboratory checks (say, for water purity). Scorecards of public services should also be extended to private or NGO providers. On the other side of the market, government may want to directly improve the quality of private services. Training, "partnership" arrangements, contracting, and other means of engagement can all be tried. But attempts to increase information should be subject to rigorous evaluation (chapter 6).

Increasing consumer power through participation

The accountability of providers to clients can also be achieved when people voice their concerns. In this case, enforceability is not through clients' money but through their direct interaction—encouragement and complaints. The scope for poor people to voice complaints individually is very small. In rich countries individuals get help from systems of tort law that can handle individual litigation and from government-sponsored offices of consumer protection or ombudsmen. But these are rare to nonexistent for the poor in developing countries (they don't always work so well for the poor in rich countries either).

Some problems for which voice might be expected to work are intractable. One example is corruption: the public might resent under-the-table payments, but there may be no incentive to complain if, say, a doctor is using public facilities and materials at the same time. Clients know that the service is still cheaper than if they had to go to the market, and so do not complain.[193]

There is a deeper constraint: even when there is an opportunity to redress complaints, monitoring and follow-through are public goods—the benefits accrue to the entire group while the costs are borne by a few. This is true for communities as well as individuals, but groups of people generally find it easier to elicit support from members than from individuals going it alone. So client power expressed outside market transactions will almost always be expressed through collective action.

Strengthening participation along the client-provider link can fix problems in the long route of government provision. So community groups that take on complaining, monitoring, and other means of making sure things work properly would be expected at some point to become institutionalized within government (most likely local government), or possibly to be supplanted by government as it improves. After all, collective

---

BOX 4.4 *No blanket policy on user fees*

The wide range of services and country circumstances discussed in this Report makes it impossible to claim that a particular level of user fees or none at all is appropriate in every case. User fees, as with other public policy decisions, must balance protection of the poor, efficiency in allocation, and the ability to guarantee that services can be implemented and sustained. The following flowchart summarizes the arguments and references in the text and raises most of the issues necessary in determining whether user fees of any sort are appropriate in a given case. Three points:

- First, "efficiency" is shorthand for standard principles of public economics (see any textbook) that often but not always require prices that equal social marginal cost and may include subsidies, taxes, or other interventions independent of their distributional effects. For example, infectious disease control measures will have a subsidy element because of their external effects regardless of their impact on poor people.

- Second, it is assumed that all subsidies are paid for by taxes. The net effect on poor people depends on their contribution to tax revenue (possibly substantial when taxes are based on agricultural exports) and on their share of the deadweight loss that taxes impose on the economy.

- Third, even when prices are not charged at point of service, communities may want to make contributions to capital costs by, say, helping to construct or maintain schools.

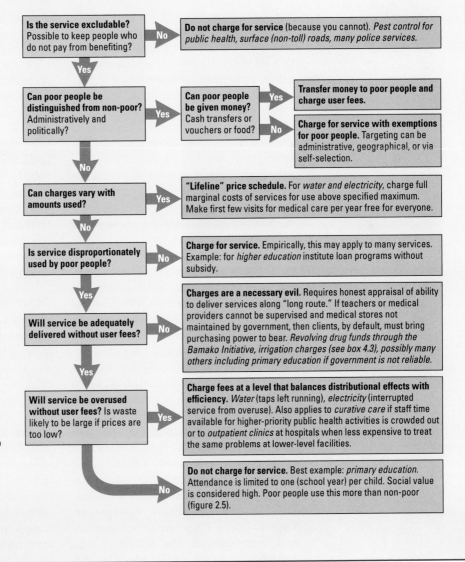

action is expensive—people, especially poor people, have more pressing things to do with their time. They will want to transfer this responsibility to permanent structures as fast as they can.[194]

But local inputs and knowledge from direct participation may be needed for some time, possibly permanently, and government can help make those inputs more effective. Education provides many of the better illustrations. Parents are in the best position to see what is happening in schools, and schools are usually the unit in which decisions are most effectively made. So giving parents power to influence school policies often has beneficial results. In the example of El Salvador's Community-Managed Schools Program (Educo—see spotlight), it was the right to hire and fire teachers and the regularity of visits from the local education committee, staffed in part by parents, that led to the increases in teacher and student attendance and in test scores.

Madhya Pradesh, India, has seen substantial improvement in test scores, completion rates, and literacy.[195] Community involvement is strong in recruiting teachers, getting new schools built, and encouraging neighbors to enroll their children. Parents have been helped by the ability to hire local, less-than-fully-trained teachers at a fraction of standard pay scales for government teachers—with better results.

This last aspect of the program complicates scaling up. The ability to avoid confrontation with public sector unions has been a great advantage. Will teachers' unions allow such recruitment to become standard?[196] Do teachers hired at low wages expect to be converted into full public servants? For now, however, the involvement of communities in Madhya Pradesh, which is much greater than in other states, has made a big difference in performance.

Other policy initiatives that can also make client voice more effective include offering more convenient venues to air complaints. Several studies have shown that the relationship between parents and teachers is important: it should be supportive, respectful, and cooperative, not punitive and confrontational. The success of local communities in improving education can

thus be compromised by too aggressive a stance. This is true for other professionals as well. In Kerala, maintaining staff at a health center became difficult when local residents made too many demands on providers' time.[197]

Beyond monitoring, communities can be the appropriate locus for more direct inputs, in effect becoming co-producers of services. Some services cannot be delivered by state agencies very well because the environment is too complex and variable—and the cost of interacting with very large numbers of poor people is too great.[198] Sanitation programs often benefit from local participation and inputs, since social relations in communities are often the best guarantors of compliance with sanitation policies and compliance must be universal if the community is to reap the health benefits.

Local perspective and knowledge are critical in transmitting needed information. The acceptability of messages on health-related habits, preventive health measures, hygiene, sexual conduct, and other sensitive issues is much greater when those messages are conveyed through informal face-to-face contact in discussions among small groups of individuals with similar backgrounds. For instance, organized discussions among informal women's groups can enhance the credibility and impact of behavior change efforts. It is possible, but unlikely, that outsiders may learn enough of local mores to influence local conversations on these subjects.[199]

Tapping local social capital

Many communities have evolved means of solving longstanding problems requiring collective action. When the benefits of cooperation are great enough, there is a way to enforce rules, and where there are no private alternatives, organizations often emerge on their own.[200] Communities have solved irrigation, forestry management, nutrition, and other problems. Recently, governments (sometimes with help from donors) have started to learn from this experience, and have funded projects and programs that rely on, and require, the formation of local user groups and committees to choose and implement development projects. Rather than give transfers of income to individuals, which can be both politically and administratively difficult, governments have channeled money through community groups. The various approaches that have been tried address two possible weaknesses in the "long route" of accountability through governments: implementation, or the "compact" by single-purpose user groups, and "voice," which allows communities to decide on projects to undertake.

A recent evaluation of six early social funds, most initiated in response to crises, found that the programs were progressive, though more between than within regions.[201] Special-purpose user groups have been more common. In water supply and sanitation particularly, there are numerous cases of better implementation through such groups. In Côte d'Ivoire, when responsibility for rural water supply shifted from central government to user groups, breakdowns and costs were reduced.[202] Some local communities have used local contractors, improving accountability and increasing efficiency through explicit contracts.[203] When governments, especially local governments, are severely hampered in delivering services, these methods have the potential to bring about marked improvements.

These programs are new—and changing as lessons emerge. Because of their potential, rigorous evaluation is a high priority. Which aspects are replicable? How can pitfalls be avoided? Some of the emerging lessons stem from the difference between groups that emerge spontaneously and those that are created from above for the purpose of channeling money.

Capture. Groups constituted as a part of projects funded by outsiders may be particularly prone to capture by elites. Local groups that evolve as a result of long-felt needs may or may not be representative of the poorest people. But when those groups are used by higher levels of government or by donors to channel formerly unheard of sums of money, even representative groups tend to change. In Indonesia, when participation was mandated by national government to go through village councils, the increased participation of some members of communities was found to have a "crowding-out" effect on others, leading to a net reduction

of participation.[204] More recent programs in Indonesia have benefited from this experience and have been designed to elicit more widespread participation (see spotlight on the Kecamatan Development Program).

A real risk comes from the speed with which groups are constituted and funds disbursed. Elites can mobilize more quickly, master the rules of submitting applications (if they can read and the majority of the community cannot), and present themselves to the community as an effective conduit for receiving such funds. In one Sahelian country a large fraction of project funds was diverted for personal gain.[205] Much of the blame lies with the speed at which donors want to disburse funds (chapter 11) and with the limits this puts on incentives and abilities to monitor the behavior of leaders. Rushing to create social capital where it does not exist can do more harm than good. If there were ever a case for patience, this is it. It is not merely the creation of participatory formats but the encouragement of the abilities of poor people themselves that will have longer-lasting effects. The policies to look for, then, may be those of education, freedom of expression, transparency, and time.

The problem of capture is not limited to groups created for investment purposes. It also affects existing community groups and local governments. Both elitism and, in many cases, gender (men as opposed to women) can determine who dominates traditional communities and local governments.[206] It is not clear that elite capture is always a problem. Wade (1988) proposes that mobilizing community action may require the leadership of the more educated, connected elite. The lessons, though, are to make sure that either the types of services funded by such methods have substantial public good characteristics (putting health and education in a sort of "gray" area) or that the right to leadership is contestable.

Developing government capacity. Some special-purpose user groups, better funded than local governments, have drawn off more capable officials to administer their funds (the same effect is seen at the national level in other donor initiatives—see chapter

11). One hypothesis is that this slows the development of local government capacity. But the opposite argument has also been made—that such groups are a catalyst for developing local government capacity. In northeast Brazil, social investment funds led villagers to organize and petition higher levels of government to, for example, guarantee a teacher to staff a school built by the community.[207]

Sustainability. Participatory water projects, underway since the 1930s and 1940s, have often improved water supply—at least for awhile. But at some point water pumps and other pieces of expensive equipment break down. Covering the capital cost (which is expensive) and obtaining the technical help (also expensive) have always been the bottleneck for water projects in poor areas. When a new infusion of capital is necessary at short notice, the community must look either to donors or to regular sources of funds, such as taxes or other general revenue. Eight or nine years after the original investment, are the donors still around? Do they have the same priorities they originally had? Can they respond quickly to small individual requests? Often not. These demands will have to be met by local government,[208] and projects have been evolving to work through them.

Such projects may have been a great deal better than relying on inadequate government structures. The argument for them is strongest where the current government system, especially the local government, is weak, with few prospects for changing any time soon.

This should, however, be a tactic that supports a longer-term strategy of developing governmental capacity—strategic incrementalism, discussed in chapter 3. Caution is required when there appears to be a tradeoff between improving services in the short run and undermining delivery capacity in the longer run. And the political consequences of participatory projects should be the subject of careful evaluations. All this complicates bringing these interventions to scale. It may be possible to replicate community efforts in many places, but whether this is the best way to make sure services are delivered to all people is one of the many open questions on the agenda.

Client power in eight sizes

To sum up, increasing client power through improved choice or direct participation will be important when people differ—are heterogeneous in their preferences—or when either of the two legs of the long route to accountability is problematic. In terms of the decision tree (figure 4.2) that determines which of the eight types of solutions is appropriate, client power matters at all three decision points.

Decision 1: Are politics pro-poor? Reliance on client power should vary with the capacity and orientation of government. Also with the question of which level of government is problematic. When governments (central, local, or both) are pro-poor, they may choose to enlist client groups as monitors or solicit their opinions regularly in sizes 3 and 4. Sizes 5 through 8, however, require ways to avoid the problems of government. All four will involve getting information to clients on their entitlements to and the performance of services.

When levels of government differ in their commitment to poor people, the role and sponsorship of user groups differ as well. If central government is a better champion of poor people, they may fund communities (if preferences vary between them) or cash transfers or vouchers (if preferences vary within them) in cases 7 and 8. If local government is better, they can provide or contract for these services. When no level of government is pro-poor, then donors, if they are inclined to be involved at all, might choose to fund community groups or organizations within civil society, being careful not to undermine the development of government capacities.

Decision 2: Does heterogeneity matter? Sizes 3, 4, 7, and 8 directly involve clients. When preferences differ by location then decentralization to local government or to community groups (depending on the capacity and pro-poor orientation of the former) makes sense. If they differ by individual, then purchasing power and compe-

Figure 4.2　Eight sizes fit all

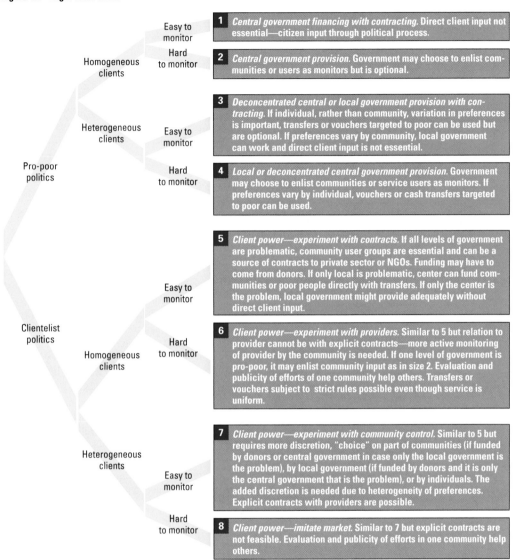

Easy to monitor

1 *Central government financing with contracting.* Direct client input not essential—citizen input through political process.

Hard to monitor

2 *Central government provision.* Government may choose to enlist communities or users as monitors but is optional.

Homogeneous clients

Heterogeneous clients

Easy to monitor

3 *Deconcentrated central or local government provision with contracting.* If individual, rather than community, variation in preferences is important, transfers or vouchers targeted to poor can be used but are optional. If preferences vary by community, local government can work and direct client input is not essential.

Hard to monitor

4 *Local or deconcentrated central government provision.* Government may choose to enlist communities or service users as monitors. If preferences vary by individual, vouchers or cash transfers targeted to poor can be used.

Pro-poor politics

Clientelist politics

5 *Client power—experiment with contracts.* If all levels of government are problematic, community user groups are essential and can be a source of contracts to private sector or NGOs. Funding may have to come from donors. If only local is problematic, center can fund communities or poor people directly with transfers. If only the center is the problem, local government might provide adequately without direct client input.

Easy to monitor

6 *Client power—experiment with providers.* Similar to 5 but relation to provider cannot be with explicit contracts—more active monitoring of provider by the community is needed. If one level of government is pro-poor, it may enlist community input as in size 2. Evaluation and publicity of efforts of one community help others. Transfers or vouchers subject to strict rules possible even though service is uniform.

Homogeneous clients

Hard to monitor

Heterogeneous clients

7 *Client power—experiment with community control.* Similar to 5 but requires more discretion, "choice" on part of communities (if funded by donors or central government in case only the local government is the problem), by local government (if funded by donors and it is only the central government that is the problem), or by individuals. The added discretion is needed due to heterogeneity of preferences. Explicit contracts with providers are possible.

Easy to monitor

Hard to monitor

8 *Client power—imitate market.* Similar to 7 but explicit contracts are not feasible. Evaluation and publicity of efforts in one community help others.

tition for individual business are preferable. Providing information to clients is critical for translating their choices into better services.

Decision 3: Is monitoring easy or hard? When monitoring is easier for clients than for governments (at any level) then client input may be required for sizes 2, 4, 6, and 8. Parents of children, patients, and net-

work service users improve services either by choice in purchasing or by active participation.

It is only in size 1, where government is perfectly capable of providing services directly, that client participation is optional. Possibly size 3 as well if government can accommodate varying needs of clients. For all other cases, the client needs to be placed more firmly at the center of service delivery.

the Bamako Initiative

Putting communities in charge of health services in Benin, Guinea, and Mali

In some of the world's poorest countries, putting communities in charge of health services, and allowing them to charge fees and manage the proceeds, increased the accountability of local health staff and improved health services for the poor.

The Bamako Initiative in Benin, Guinea, and Mali reconciled traditional community solidarity and provider payments with the objectives of the modern state.[209] How? By strengthening the power of communities over service providers. Policymakers balanced this power with sustained central involvement in subsidizing and regulating services—and in guiding community management.

The initiative improved the access, availability, affordability, and use of health services. Over the more than 10 years of implementation in these three countries, community-owned services restored access to primary and secondary health services for more than 20 million people. They raised and sustained immunization coverage. They increased the use of services among children and women in the poorest fifth of the populace. And they led to a sharper decline in mortality in rural areas than in urban areas.

Despite the various targeting mechanisms, affordability remains a problem for many of the poorest families. But even with limited inclusion of the poorest people, improvements were significant.[210]

Revitalizing health networks

In these three countries, serious disruptions to the situation of health services had occurred during the 1980s as a result of a severe economic recession and financial indebtedness. The health budget in Benin went from $3.31 per capita in 1983 to $2.69 in 1986. In Mali, rural infrastructure was almost nonexistent, and in Guinea, health services had almost totally disappeared—except in the capital city, Conakry—during the last years of the Sekou Toure regime. The vast majority of poor families in the three countries did not have access to drugs and professional health services. National immunization coverage was under 15 percent, and less

than 10 percent of families used modern curative services.

The approach focused on establishing community-managed health centers serving populations of 5,000 to 15,000 people. An analysis of the main constraints in the three countries led to emphasis on service delivery strategies focusing on the poor.[211] Priorities included:[212]

- Implementing community-owned revolving funds for drugs with local retention and management of all financial proceeds.

- Revitalizing existing health centers, expanding the network, and providing monthly outreach services to villages within 15 kilometers of facilities.

- Stepping up social mobilization and community-based communication.

- Pricing the most effective interventions below private sector prices, through subsidies from the government and donors and through internal cross-subsidies within the system. Local criteria were established for exemptions (table 1).

- Having communities participate in a biannual analysis of progress and problems in coverage with health services—and in the planning and budgeting of services.

- Tracing and tracking defaulters—and using community representatives to increase demand.

- Standardizing diagnosis and treatment and establishing regular supervision.

Scaling up incrementally

The Bamako approach was implemented gradually, with the support of UNICEF, WHO, and the World Bank, building on a variety of pilot projects.[213] Since the early 1980s, it was progressively scaled up in the three countries—from 44 health facilities in Benin to 400 in 2002, from 18 in Guinea to 367, and from 1 in Mali to 559. This raised the population with access to services within 5 kilometers to 86 percent in Benin, 60 percent in Guinea, and 40 percent in Mali, covering more than 20 million people. Importantly, a legal framework was developed to support the contractual relationship with communities, the cost-sharing arrangements, the availability of essential drugs, and community participation policies. Community associations and management committees were registered as legal entities with ability to receive public funds.

Better health outcomes for poor people

Over the 12 or so years of implementation in Benin and Guinea, and more than 7 years in Mali, health outcomes and health service use improved significantly. Under-five mor-

Table 1 Reaching out to benefit the poorest groups

Disease targeting	Geographical targeting	Cross-subsidies	Exempting the poor
Focus on the burden of diseases of the poor: malaria, diarrhea, respiratory infections, malnutrition, reproductive health	Focus on rural areas. Larger subsidies to poorer regions	• Higher markup and co-payments on diseases with lower levels of priority • High subsidies for child health services • Free immunization and oral rehydration therapy as well as promotion activities	• Exemptions left to the discretion of communities • Exempted categories include widows, orphans

Figure 1 Under-five mortality has been reduced in Mali, Benin, and Guinea, 1980–2002

Source: Krippenberg and others 2003. Calculated from Demographic and Health Survey data for Benin 1996 and 2001; Guinea 1992 and 1999; and Mali 1987, 1996, and 2001.

Figure 2 Improvements in under-five mortality among the poor in Mali

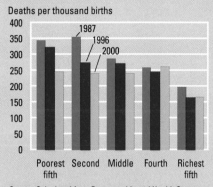

Source: Calculated from Demographic and Health Survey data 1987 and 1996 (based on births in the last five years before the survey).

tality declined significantly, even among the poorest. The poor-rich gap narrowed in the three countries (figures 1 and 2). In Guinea, the decline was steepest for the rural population and poorer groups.

Immunization levels increased in all three countries.[214] They are very high in Benin, close to 80 percent—one of the highest rates in Sub-Saharan Africa. Immunization rates are lower in Guinea and Mali, largely because of problems of access (figure 3). Coverage of other health interventions also increased. The use of health services by children under five in Benin increased from less than 0.1 visit per year to more than 1.0. In Mali exclusive breastfeeding and the use of professional services for antenatal care,[215] deliveries, and treatment of diarrhea and acute respiratory infections increased for all groups, including the poorest (figure 4).[216]

In an independent evaluation in 1996 in Benin, 75 percent of informants were satis-

fied with the quality of care, although 48 percent were not "fully" satisfied. Health care users found the availability of drugs to be high (over 80 percent said drugs were available) and the overall quality of care to be good (91 percent).

Greater access reduced travel costs, and the availability of drugs reduced the need to visit distant sources of care. Prices have been kept below those of alternative sources. In Benin the median household spending on curative care in a health center was $2 in 1989, less than half that at private providers ($5) or traditional healers ($7).[217]

Poor people still saw price as a barrier.[218] And a large proportion of the poor still do not use key health services in all three countries. In Benin and Guinea the health system allowed for exemptions, and most health centers had revenue that they could have used to subsidize the poorest, but almost none did. Management committees typically valued investment over redistribution.

Community financing—a seat at the table

The community financing of key operational costs bought communities a seat at the table. Donors and governments had to systematically negotiate new activities with community organizations. Governments in all three countries, with the support of donors, continued to subsidize health centers, particularly to support revolving drug funds in the poorest regions. In Benin and Mali today the public subsidy to health services is about the same per capita for rich and poor regions. In Guinea, however, public spending has benefited richer groups most. But all three countries face the challenge of emphasizing household behavior change and protecting the poorest and most vulnerable. Establishing mechanisms to subsidize and protect the poor remains a priority of the current reform process.

Figure 3 Evolution of national immunization coverage (DPT3), 1988–1999

Sources: World Health Organization, UNICEF, and Demographic and Health Survey data.

Figure 4 Antenatal care by medically trained persons in Mali by wealth group

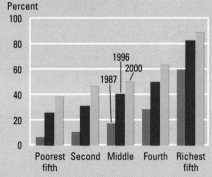

Source: Analysis of Demographic and Health Survey data.

Citizens and politicians

chapter 5

The most important political office is that of private citizen.

Louis D. Brandeis

Citizens' voice in society and participation in politics connect them to the people who represent the state—politicians and policymakers. Unlike the short route of accountability between clients and providers discussed in chapter 4, the long route of accountability involves politics. That accountability has two parts: the relationship of voice between citizens and politicians and policymakers (discussed here) and the relationship between policymakers and service providers (discussed in chapter 6).

This chapter asks several questions: Why don't politicians in well-functioning democracies deliver education, health, and infrastructure services more effectively to poor people even though they depend on poor people's votes? Why are public expenditures systematically allocated to construction projects and the salaries of bulky state administrations, often at the expense of making services like schooling work? And why, when the government does spend money on services that the poor rely on, such as primary health care, is service quality so poor? Finally, what can citizens, particularly poor citizens, do when politicians fail to make services work for them?

Empowering poor citizens by increasing their influence in policymaking and aligning their interests with those of the nonpoor can hold politicians more accountable for universal service delivery. Elections, informed voting, and other traditional voice mechanisms should be strengthened, because these processes—and the information they generate—can make political commitments more credible, helping to produce better service outcomes. Nongovernmental and civil society organizations can help to amplify the voices of the poor, coordinate coalitions to overcome their collective action problems, mediate on their behalf through redress mechanisms, and demand greater service accountability. Even when these measures have limited scope, better information—through public disclosure, citizen-based budget analysis, service benchmarking, and program impact assessments—and an active, independent media can strengthen voice.

Citizen voice and political accountability

Faced with classrooms without teachers, clinics without medicines, dry taps, unlit homes, and corrupt police, poor citizens often feel powerless.[219] Elected representatives seem answerable only to the more powerful interests in society if at all. When politicians are unaccountable to poor people as citizens, the long route of accountability—connecting citizens with providers through politicians—breaks down, voice is weak, and providers can get away with delivering inadequate services to poor clients.[220] When poor citizens are empowered, whether on their own or in alliance with others, their demand for accountability can make politicians respond in ways that compensate for weaknesses elsewhere in the service delivery chain.

Services are politically powerful

For poor people the only routine interaction with the state may be at the delivery point of services. Election platforms show that politicians are very aware that poor people's perceptions of the state are shaped by the quality of services. The 30-Baht Gold Card scheme in Thailand promised inexpensive universal healthcare and helped the Thai Rak Thai party win a landslide victory in the 2001 parliamentary elections.[221] Service delivery was important for the Labor party's successful 2001 election campaign in the United Kingdom. A Prime Minister's Delivery Unit has been set up to monitor progress.[222]

Even when services do not figure explicitly in elections, politicians often seek to enlarge their political base by providing free public services or lucrative service-related jobs to their supporters. And people are increasingly concerned about accountability for services outside the voting process. In Brazil, India, and South Africa civil society organizations are analyzing the allocation and use of public resources in the budget to understand their impact on the poor.[223] With so much political attention paid to services, why is the voice relationship often so weak?

Voice is the most complex accountability relationship in service delivery

Voice is the relationship of accountability between citizens and politicians, the range of measures through which citizens express their preferences and influence politicians (figure 5.1).[224] Accountability in this context is the willingness of politicians to justify their actions and to accept electoral, legal, or administrative penalties if the justification is found lacking. As defined in chapter 3, accountability must have the quality of *answerability* (the right to receive relevant information and explanation for actions), and *enforceability* (the right to impose sanctions if the information or rationale is deemed inappropriate).[225] One complication is that voice is not sufficient for accountability; it may lead to answerability but it does not necessarily lead to enforceability.

In principle, elections provide citizens with both answerability (the right to assess a candidate's record) and enforceability (vote the candidate in or out). In practice, democracies vary greatly on both dimensions, as do most attempts to exercise accountability. Citizen charters may spell out the service standards and obligations of public agencies toward their clients, but without redress the obligations may not be enforceable. In Malaysia the client charters introduced for public agencies in 1993 do both, giving clients the right to redress through the Public Complaints Bureau if corrective action for noncompliance is not taken.[226]

Another complication is that the voice relationship links many citizens with many politicians—all with potentially very different interests. When services fail everyone, the voice of all citizens (or even that of the non-poor alone) can put pressure on politicians to improve services for all citizens, including the poor. But when services fail primarily poor people, voice mechanisms operate in much more difficult political and social terrain. Elites can be indifferent about the plight of poor people.[227] The political environment can swamp even well-organized voice. Protest imposes large costs on the poor when their interests clash with those of the elite or those in authority.[228] It then matters whether society is homogeneous or heterogeneous and whether there is a strong sense of inclusion, trusteeship, and intrinsic motivation in the social and political leadership of the country. To expect poor people to carry the primary burden of exerting influence would be unfair—and unrealistic.

Finally, voice is only the first part of the long route of accountability. That complicates its impact on services, since the impact depends also on the compact relationship between policymakers and providers. Even strong voice may fail to make basic services work for poor people because the compact is weak. But the reverse can also be true, as was the case in the former Soviet Union.

Figure 5.1 Voice in the service delivery framework

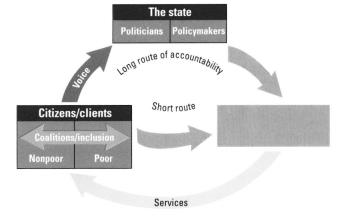

Pro-poor and clientelist service delivery environments

That voice is complex still begs the question of why, in societies where the average citizen is poor, services fail poor people. The answer has to do with whether service delivery settings are "pro-poor" or "clientelist." The distinction reflects the incentives facing politicians, whether services are designed to be universal and available to the average citizen or vulnerable to targeting to "clients" by political patrons, and, if formally targeted to the poor, whether they are in practice captured by elites (table 5.1). Pro-poor settings are those in which politicians face strong incentives to address the general interest. Clientelist political environments are those in which, even though the average citizen is poor, politicians have strong incentives to shift public spending to cater to special interests, to core supporters, or to "swing" voters.[229] When the average citizen is poor, catering to special interests at the cost of the general interest is clientelism.

The distinction between pro-poor and clientelist is clearly an oversimplification, but it provides a useful way of thinking about service delivery mechanisms. High-quality services for all are less likely if politicians cater to special interests rather than to the interests of the average citizen. Making services work for poor people is obviously more difficult in a clientelist environment than in a pro-poor environment. Less obviously, if delivery mechanisms do not account for these specific country and service differences, they are likely to fail, and the poor suffer.

The interaction of voice and accountability

When populations are heterogeneous, it matters whose voices politicians and policymakers hear and respond to. Where populations are polarized around nonservice issues—religious, ethnic, caste, or tribal background, for example—voters care more about what politicians promise on these polarizing issues than on services, giving politicians incentives to pursue other goals at the cost of effective services. Where politics is based on identities and patronage, the poor are unlikely to benefit from public services unless they have the right "identity" or are the clients of those with political power. In failed or captured states voice can become meaningless. Politicians have neither the incentives nor the capacity to listen.

Under what circumstances, then, is voice likely to lead to greater accountability? Elections can lead to improved services if the promises politicians make before elections are credible. The framework of citizen rights, the right to information, service design, the influence of the media, and administrative procedures for redress and appeal are all important for voice.[230] So too is the effectiveness of the institutions of accountability, such as parlia-

Table 5.1 Pro-poor and clientelist service environments when the average citizen is poor

	Politicians' incentives	Service delivery expenditure design	Inclusion and exclusion	Systemic service capture
Pro-poor	No strong incentives to cater to special interests, preferring instead to address general interests	Promote universal provision of broad basic services that benefit large segments of society, including poor people and the non-poor	Most poor people enjoy the same access and service quality as non-poor due to network, political, social, or altruistic reasons	None
Clientelist	Strong incentives to cater to special interests, to core supporters, or to "swing" voters	Permit targeting to narrow groups of non-poor "clients" and sometimes to poor people but with features making services vulnerable to capture by non-poor	Poor people do not enjoy the same access and service quality as the non-poor, though specific groups of poor "clients" may do so	Systemic service capture by local or national elites; ultrapopulist governments (such as "Curley effects," see box 5.2)

ments, courts, ombudsman, anticorruption commissions. And so too are higher stocks of social capital, because they help overcome the collective action problem underlying voice, particularly for poor people.[231]

What can be done to strengthen voice, particularly for poor citizens, in demanding better services? The answer depends greatly on the political setting, but in functioning democracies with elections and voting, at least three things should be done.

- Deepen understanding and awareness of why the politics of service delivery is so often clientelist and not pro-poor.

- If the politics is clientelist, consider what changes in the service delivery environment might alter political incentives and improve outcomes.

- When choosing how to deliver services, factor in, to the extent possible, the pro-poor or clientelist influence of political competition on the incentives for service delivery. Recognize and account for government failure arising from clientelism.

The politics of providing public services to poor people

In 1974 only 39 countries—one in four—were electoral democracies. By the end of 2002, this had grown dramatically to 121 governments—three in five.[232] Over the last century, the percentage of people living in democracies with competitive multiparty elections and universal suffrage has increased dramatically (figure 5.2).

Rapid democratization has brought representation and liberties, but not rapid improvements in services for poor people.[233] Most, if not all, new democracies are low-income countries with substantial poverty. Services available to poor people in these young democracies seem to be not much different from those available in nondemocracies. In some cases services are worse than those provided by ideologically committed but nonelected governments in single-party, socialist countries. Whether countries have elections or not seems not to matter for public perceptions of corruption, and since corruption worsens service delivery for poor people, by implication for public perceptions of effective services.[234]

Political incentives for basic services

If delivered effectively, basic services such as primary health care and primary education benefit the poor disproportionately. But democratically elected politicians in countries where the median voter is likely to be a poor person, or where poor people constitute the majority of voters, often seem to have little incentive to provide such basic services. And voters seem unable to strengthen incentives for politicians to ensure better public services. Why?

How politicians and voters make decisions and how politicians compete hold some answers.[235] When politicians have incentives to divert resources (including outright corruption) and to make transfers to a few clients at the expense of many, efforts to provide broad public services are undermined. How easy it is for voters to learn about the contributions of politicians to a particular service—and therefore for politicians to claim credit for the service—differs considerably by service (box 5.1). The degree of political competition is important. For example, analysis suggests that an increase in the competitiveness of elections seems to have a bigger effect on primary school enrollment than increases in education spending.[236]

Three factors therefore appear to be especially important for influencing political incentives for service delivery:

- How well voters are informed about the contribution specific politicians or political parties make to their welfare.

- Whether ideological or social polarization reduces the weight voters place on public services in evaluating politicians.

- Whether political competitors can make credible promises about public service provision before elections.

Informed voters

The incentives for transfers targeted to *informed* voters are greater when voters in general lack information about the quality of public services and the role their elected representatives play in affecting quality. The same is true if uninformed voters are easily swayed by political propaganda, or if they vote on the basis of a candidate's charisma or ethnic identity rather than record.

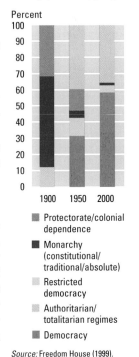

Figure 5.2 Democracy's century
World population by polity

Percent

1900   1950   2000

■ Protectorate/colonial dependence

■ Monarchy (constitutional/traditional/absolute)

■ Restricted democracy

■ Authoritarian/totalitarian regimes

■ Democracy

Source: Freedom House (1999).

Informed voting can be costly. Detailed behavioral studies show that voters tend to adopt simple rules of thumb based on very limited information about politics and public policies.[237] Most of the information voters use is likely to be essentially "free," in that it comes incidentally with the performance of social and economic roles.[238] This kind of information tends to vary widely over the electorate, depending on occupation, social setting, and cultural norms. Voters also behave myopically, giving much greater weight to events around election times or to service outputs that are immediately visible.[239]

In principle, citizens could employ voting rules requiring very little information and still motivate politicians to pursue policies in their interest—if they could coordinate their efforts.[240] It is harder for voters to coordinate rewards or penalties for basic health and education because of the difficulties in evaluating these services and attributing outcomes to politicians (see box 5.1). Transaction-intensive public services such as education and health depend on day-to-day provider behavior. Quality is hard to measure and attribute.

Information deficiencies thus lead voters to give more credit to politicians for initiating public works projects (including school construction), providing direct subsidies for essential commodities, and increasing employment in the public sector (including hiring teachers and doctors) than for ensuring that teachers show up for class and can teach—or that doctors come to clinics and heal.

If voters vote with limited information or if they are uncoordinated but can be swayed by propaganda or bribes, special-interest groups can capture policies by providing campaign finance or mobilizing votes.[241] These interest groups need not be defined along rich-poor lines. They could be organized coalitions of voters (such as farmers or public sector employees) that lobby politicians to protect their interests, pushing for targeted policies at the expense of policies that would benefit the many.

Social polarization

Social polarization can lead to voting based on social, ethnic, or religious identity rather than policy or service delivery performance. This too limits political incentives to pursue

---

B O X   5 . 1   *Why are public health and education services so difficult to get to poor people?*

When even the poorest of parents care deeply about educating their children, why is it so difficult for them to do something to ensure that the village teacher actually shows up for work regularly? A political economy perspective on public service delivery suggests that basic health and primary education are very difficult to get right because they are transaction-intensive services with outcomes that depend crucially on the judgment and behavior of providers, both difficult to monitor continually, and on household behavior.

- Learning takes place over long periods and the benefits of preventive health care are not always obvious. Compared with other, more visible public services—electricity or water connections, rural roads, law and order—monitoring basic education and health services makes large information demands on both voters and politicians.

- Poor voters may be uninformed because they are illiterate.

- Where populations are socially polarized or heterogeneous, households are less likely to have

coordinated, clear preferences in health and education services. Furthermore, successful outcomes require supportive household behavior, and very heterogeneous social and cultural household norms may make households respond differently to public interventions.

- Because of the difficulty of regularly monitoring these services and of measuring and attributing their long-term impact, it is harder for politicians to claim credit for these services than for a road or a well. And politicians who promise to improve these services may lack credibility and lose elections. For these reasons, politicians are likely to prefer infrastructure to human development, and are prone to using basic health and primary education services as patronage for clients, rather than as universal services to be provided for the general good.

So when poor people are uninformed, society is polarized along social or religious lines, and politicians lack credibility or are prone to clientelism, basic public services for poor people are the most likely to suffer.

Because of political problems of information and credibility, public antipoverty programs are more likely to take the form of private transfers, such as food subsidies, electricity subsidies, agricultural price protection, construction projects, and public sector employment. Programs of this kind are easier to capture and more amenable to targeting than basic health and education, which are more suited to universal provision.* That is why programs narrowly "targeted" to the poor may not be optimal in the sense of having the most impact on the economic well-being of poor people.

*van de Walle (1998) concludes, from a synthesis of research on public spending and the poor, that there is a well-substantiated case for "broad targeting" of the poor by allocating greater resources to universal public services such as basic health and education. In contrast, finely targeted food subsidies or other redistribution schemes may sometimes be detrimental to the interests of the poor due to the burden of administrative costs and unintended behavioral responses. See also van de Walle and Nead (1995).

public policies in the general public interest. James Curley, an Irish Roman Catholic mayor of Boston in the first half of the 20th century, fanned class and religious divisions for electoral advantage and was repeatedly reelected despite the damage his policies did to the city's growth (box 5.2).

It is this effect of social polarization on political incentives that partly accounts for the empirical evidence on the negative correlation between ethnic heterogeneity and the availability of public goods.[242] More generally, basic public services, particularly those that are not easily excludable such as primary education, can also deteriorate where there is social fragmentation—some social groups do not want to pay for public goods that benefit other groups.[243]

Credible politicians

Even when voters are informed, public policy can fall short when the promises of politicians are not credible. When candidates cannot or do not make credible promises before elections (because abandoning promises costs election winners little), incumbents are more insulated from the disciplining effects of political competition. Challengers cannot mount effective campaigns because they cannot convince voters that they will do a better job. Furthermore, if politicians are credible only to their "clients," more public resources will be allocated to these clients. This can have large implications for universal health and education services. Incumbents enjoy greater discretion to pursue goals other than those preferred by the majority of citizens who may be poor, goals such as providing narrowly targeted services to their supporters at the cost of more universal public services that benefit all.[244]

Credibility and credit go hand in hand. Credibility problems also arise when political competitors make credible promises but their term in office is too short to claim credit for policies with long maturing outcomes. Promises of jobs or public works projects can be delivered soon after an election. But promises to improve education quality and outcomes are much less credible. Similarly, voters can easily credit a

---

BOX 5.2 *The "Curley effect"*

Described as "The Rascal King," James Michael Curley dominated politics in Boston for half the 20th century, holding elected office, among others, as four-time city mayor between 1913 and 1950, besides serving two prison terms on corruption charges. Admired by working-class Irish families, Curley was noted for his railing against the Protestant Yankee establishment and for his rough-and-tumble ways.

Curley used patronage, cash, and rhetoric to shape his electorate, driving the richer Protestant citizens out of the city to ensure his political longevity. Curley's tools of patronage were public services, large construction projects, and public employment. In his first year as mayor, Curley raised the salaries of police patrolmen and school custodians but cut the salaries of higher-ranking police officers and school doctors (Beatty 1992). Miles of sidewalks were laid in Irish neighborhoods, but the cobblestones of swank Yankee neighborhoods crumbled (O'Connor 1995). Boston did not flourish under Curley: between 1910 and 1950, it had the lowest population growth rate of any U.S. city of comparable size.

Glaeser and Shleifer (2002) call this the "Curley effect"—increasing the size of one's political base, or maintaining it, through distortionary, wealth-reducing policies. They use it to shed light on the ethnic and class politics of service delivery when the net effect is to impoverish the overall community. They show how the Curley effect may apply to Detroit, USA, to contemporary Zimbabwe, and to the Labor party in the United Kingdom before its current reincarnation as New Labor.

The Curley effect demonstrates that clientelism need not benefit only rich clients. It can benefit poor clients as well, and still imply substantial losses in efficiency through the misallocation of public resources. So, clientelism results in inefficient, targeted allocations that benefit only a few, as opposed to allocations to universal public services that benefit larger segments of the same poor and not-so-poor populations.

Sources: Glaeser and Shleifer (2002), O'Connor (1995), and Beatty (1992).

---

politician for building a school or assigning teachers, but they can less easily verify that the politician is responsible when the building is maintained or supplied, or when the teacher is present and competent. If politicians cannot take credit for their efforts to improve teacher quality, teacher quality is likely to be low—and voters are unlikely to expect anything else. In Pakistan nonprofessional considerations have been common in the placement of teachers.[245] The incentives facing local politicians have been important factors in the low quality of rural schools (box 5.3).

In many countries, politicians do not campaign on their policy record, probity, or history of program involvement or on the policy record of their party. Voters then are likely to believe politicians who have shown themselves to be reliable sources of personal assistance. They might be locally influential people who have helped families by providing loans or jobs or by resolving bureaucratic difficulties. Without well-developed political parties or national leaders who are credible, promises of targeted favors are all that voters can rely on in making electoral choices.

BOX 5.3 *Better to build rural schools than to run them well in Pakistan*

Elected officials in Pakistan have demonstrated an extraordinary interest in targeting services to their supporters, but much less interest in services such as primary education that all voters can enjoy. Contributing to this outcome are three aspects of rural Pakistani politics: identity-driven politics, voting blocs that make it easy to identify core supporters, and costly elections.

Voter ignorance, poor information on political competitors, and the absence of party credibility on broad policy issues encourage politicians and voters to build personal relationships that make pre-election promises more credible. Because these relationships are personal, they tend to be based on narrow, excludable services promised and delivered to core supporters. The distance between rural communities boosts the political efficiency of targeting political benefits—it is easier to site schools,

roads, and water pipes close to supporters and far from nonsupporters.

Voting by blocs of supporters makes patronage a more effective political strategy than the provision of well-functioning services that must be provided to all. Costly elections drive politicians to provide public services to supporters who can be depended on to vote for them at low out-of-pocket cost.

Under these conditions, schools may get built for the corruption, employment, and profit opportunities that construction provides. Teachers are hired less on merit and more on how best to apportion patronage, particularly when absenteeism is not penalized. There are, in contrast, few systemic political incentives to make sure schools run well, teachers remain accountable, and children learn.

Source: World Bank (2002*l*).

Credibility can make change difficult. Problems of political credibility can cause bad policies to become entrenched. Countries often adopt poverty strategies based on subsidies for consumption and agricultural production, sometimes at the expense of broad public services such as education and health that might have resulted in lower poverty and more economic growth. India subsidizes electricity, ostensibly for poor farmers. Once political credibility is strongly linked to a particular policy such as delivering subsidized electricity, these policies continue to receive greater public resources than they would if all political promises were equally credible. Vested interests develop around suboptimal policies—rich farmers capture the power subsidy—which makes change even more difficult.

Clientelism

Clientelism is characterized by an excessive tendency for political patrons to provide private rewards to clients. Politicians allocate public spending to win elections. To do so, they can provide public goods that can improve everyone's welfare (public goods that are extensive, such as law and order, universal education, with no rivalry or excludability). Or they can target localities

(local public goods, projects limited to a jurisdiction) or individuals and specific groups (clientelism).[246]

What distinguishes clientelism? Clientelism implies a credible threat of exclusion from a stream of benefits if the voter chooses to vote for the opposition.[247] Thus an incumbent politician can use clientelism to deter core supporters from switching support. Clientelism is hard to pursue for local or extensive public goods—beneficiaries are not reliable clients because they can support the opposition and still benefit.

The Programa Nacional de Solidaridad (PRONASOL) poverty alleviation program in Mexico spent an average of 1.2 percent of GDP annually on water, electricity, nutrition, and education in poor communities between 1989 and 1994.[248] Municipalities dominated by the Institutional Revolutionary Party (PRI), the party in power, received significantly higher per capita transfers than municipalities that voted in another party (figure 5.3). An assessment of PRONASOL spending suggests that it reduced poverty by only about 3 percent. Had the budget been distributed for impact on poverty rather than party loyalty, the expected decline would have been 64 percent with perfect targeting, and it would have been 13 percent even with an untargeted, universal proportional transfer to the whole population.[249]

Even if voters want to vote for an opposition party or candidate, they might be deterred by the fear of being penalized by the withholding of funds by a central authority. So voters may end up keeping a party they may dislike in power in order to ensure funding for local public services. This is compounded by a coordination problem. Even if the majority of localities wanted to vote against the incumbent party, without certainty about what other localities planned to do, the majority would end up supporting the ruling party to avoid strategic miscoordination and the penalty of loss of funds.

Clientelism can also be the outcome of political competition when the credibility of political competitors is limited—political promises are credible only to "clients."[250] Politicians with clientelist ties can fulfill campaign promises better than politicians without them. When only clientelist promises are credible, promises of construction and government jobs become the currency of political competition at the expense of universal access to high-quality education and health care (as seen in box 5.3). Public works or jobs can be targeted to individuals and groups of voters—clear evidence of political patrons fulfilling their promises to clients. It is much more difficult to target the services of a well-run village primary school or clinic.

Cross-country evidence on public investment supports the contention that credibility and clientelism significantly influence the provision of public services. There are no variables that directly capture the credibility of pre-electoral promises or the extent of clientelism. But it is possible to argue that in young democracies political competitors are less likely to be able to make credible promises to all voters and are more likely to rely on clientelist promises, and as these democracies age, politicians are more likely to increase the number of clients since they can count on client loyalty. A study summarizing the evidence shows that targeted spending—public investment—is higher in young democracies than in old and as young democracies age, targeted spending increases.[251] Corruption falls as democracies age. These results are relevant for universal basic services since they are likely to be of lower quantity when public investment is high and of lower quality when corruption is high. Similar cross-country evidence on secondary and primary school enrollment supports the view that credibility is a significant influence on the provision of public services.[252]

Beyond the ballot box: citizen initiatives to increase accountability

When elections are not enough to make services work for poor people, political pressure builds for new approaches that enable citizens to hold politicians and policymakers more directly accountable for services. These activities do not replace the electoral process, but complement it to strengthen the long route of accountability. The emergence of such citizen initiatives and their

mobilizing potential has been accompanied by an information revolution that has dramatically simplified information exchange and citizen access to official information.

Enthusiasm for direct citizen involvement also comes from mounting frustration with the dominant mode of a national civil service delivering services that meet some technically predetermined "needs" of the population.[253] This frustration has led to greater interest in directly empowering citizens and overcoming collective action problems, driven also by the finding that civic relationships and social capital are important determinants of government efficacy.[254]

Broad range of issues and tools

The rapid growth of citizen initiatives has been described as a new accountability agenda. It involves "a more direct role for ordinary people and their associations in demanding accountability across a more diverse set of jurisdictions, using an expanded repertoire of methods, on the basis of a more exacting standard of social justice."[255] Citizens are combining electoral accountability and participation with what would traditionally have been considered the official accountability activities of the state. These initiatives address accountability at various levels. Some are aimed at strengthening voice in service delivery by enabling answerability and some at pushing further for enforceability. These initiatives, and the state's response, employ a number of old and new tools, including tools based on information technology.

These citizen initiatives cover a far-reaching array of issues, from improving law and order in Karachi[256] to preparing citizen report cards. They vary tremendously in scale, ranging from global knowledge-sharing coalitions, such as Shack/Slum Dwellers' International,[257] to community efforts in Mumbai to monitor arrivals of subsidized goods at local "fair price" shops in order to expose fraud in India's public distribution system targeted to the poor.[258] They also vary in depth and reach. On election reform, they range from generating background information on election candidates and their performance in Argentina (Poder Ciudadano[259]) to civil society efforts to implement and sustain

Figure 5.3   It paid to vote for PRI
Mexico: PRONASOL expenditures according to party in municipal government

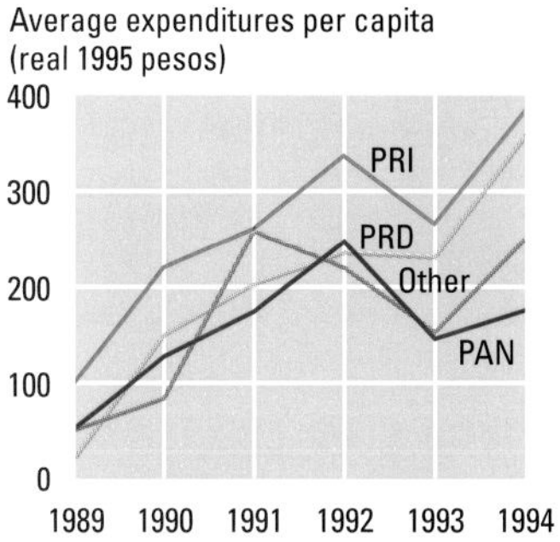

Average expenditures per capita (real 1995 pesos)

Note: PRI = Institutional Revolutionary Party; PRD = Party of the Democratic Revolution; PAN = National Action Party.
Source: Estévez, Magaloni, and Diaz-Cayeros (2002).

an Indian Supreme Court judgment making it mandatory for all election candidates to disclose their assets and any criminal record. On budget analysis, initiatives at one end seek to make national budgets accessible to citizens and at the other to promote village-level participatory audits of local public expenditures (box 5.4).

These citizen initiatives also use a broad range of tools, from door-to-door signature campaigns to cyber-activism. The rapid growth of the Internet and communication technologies has dramatically altered citizen voice nationally and internationally, though access is still limited by income and connectivity. Some innovative e-government applications are reducing corruption and delivery times and increasing service predictability and convenience. Karnataka, among India's leading states in information technology, has pioneered a computerized land records system to serve rural households (box 5.5).

Controversy and conflict of interest

Two separate trends are discernible in citizen voice initiatives: activities based on consultation, dialogue, and information sharing, and activities more direct and controversial, related to monitoring, compliance, and auditing. Some activities start with indirect objectives, build internal capacity and external trust, and then ven-

ture into more difficult areas. The impact of these initiatives varies according to how they are perceived by politicians and policymakers and the government's receptivity to change. Several studies link this receptivity to the stock of social capital.[260]

One concern with some citizen initiatives is that they can lead to conflicts of interest and reduced accountability to poor people. Facing funding uncertainties, many non-governmental organizations seek to diversify, starting from voice activities but moving on to actual service delivery. When they become advocates and providers at the same time, there can be intrinsic conflicts of interest.[261] NGOs may suffer from their own lack of accountability, internal democratic deficits, and gaps in their mandates.[262] The award of large service delivery contracts to a few big civil society organizations can exclude and spell financial difficulties for smaller organizations.[263] And if community and civic groups are captured by unscrupulous leaders, they can manipulate funding agencies and beneficiaries for their own gain.[264]

Information strategies to strengthen voice

Policies that increase information and coordination in voting, enhance the credibility of political promises, and increase the ability of civil society organizations to hold politicians

---

BOX 5.4 *Follow the public's money*

The budget, a primary statement of government priorities, is for many citizens a black box, monitored and assessed only by the traditional internal accountability relationships within government. But it can be a crucial tool for citizens to influence and monitor public policy and services. Accordingly, participatory budgeting initiatives are increasing rapidly in several countries. The challenge is to build the capacity of citizen groups, to give politicians and policymakers the incentives to listen and act on citizen feedback, and to put out budgets that are understandable and interesting to citizens.

Budget planning   The most well-known budget planning initiatives come from city municipalities in Brazil, such as Porto Alegre and Belo Horizonte. Neighborhoods indicate their spending needs at budget forums, and delegates then bring these needs to assemblies, ensuring

citizen voice in budget allocations and implementation.

Budget monitoring   The Institute for a Democratic South Africa makes information about provincial and national budget allocations accessible to citizens. Its technical experts break public budgets down to facilitate public comment. Special reports show how much money is allocated, say, to gender-related and children's issues. The most direct influence of its work is in strengthening the ability of parliamentarians to participate more effectively in budget discussions.

Budget auditing   The Mazdoor Kisan Shakti Sanghathan (MKSS), a grassroots organization in the north Indian state of Rajasthan, has turned ordinary citizens into financial auditors. Its key innovation has been the *jan sunwai* (or public

hearing), an open-air forum at which official records are presented alongside the testimony derived from interviews with local people. "Many people discovered that they had been listed as beneficiaries of anti-poverty schemes, though they had never received payment. Others were astonished to learn of large payments to local building contractors for work that was never performed" (Jenkins and Goetz 1999). Until a state right-to-information law was passed in 2000—largely a result of the protest and lobbying efforts of the MKSS—its activists had to obtain this information by appealing to sympathetic bureaucrats. A similar national law was passed in 2003.

Sources: Andrews and Shah (2003), Singh and Shah (2003), Goetz and Jenkins (2002), and Jenkins and Goetz (1999).

BOX 5.5 *Down to earth: information technology improves rural service delivery*

Karnataka state in India has pioneered Bhoomi (meaning land), a computerized land record system serving 6.7 million rural clients. Its main function is to maintain records of rights, tenancy, and cultivation—crucial for transferring or inheriting land and obtaining loans. Started in 1991 as a pilot, the Bhoomi system now has kiosks in each of the state's 177 subdistricts, servicing some 30,000 villages.

Under the old system, applicants faced long delays (3–30 days), and nearly two out of three clients paid a bribe—70 percent paid more than Rs. 100 (the official service fee was Rs. 2). There was little transparency in record maintenance—

the village accountant controlled the process, with little official or client monitoring. Even where there was no fraud, the record system could not easily handle the division of land into very small lots over generations.

Farmers can now get these records in 5–30 minutes and file for changes at a Bhoomi kiosk. The entire process takes place in the vernacular, Kannada. Clients can watch a second computer screen facing them as their request is processed. Users pay a fee of Rs. 15. In a recent evaluation, only 3 percent of users reported paying a bribe. The evaluation estimates that on average Bhoomi annually saves clients 1.32 million work

days in waiting time and (net of the higher user fee) Rs. 806 million in bribes

The resistance of village accountants had to be overcome in implementing Bhoomi. The chief minister, revenue minister, and members of the legislature championed Bhoomi, which helped. There are now plans to expand beyond land transactions. The Indian government has suggested that other states consider similar systems to improve accountability and efficiency in services that are vital to rural households.

Sources: World Bank staff and Lobo and Balakrishnan (2002).

---

and policymakers accountable are likely to improve services for poor people. Conversely, the lack of transparency in information disclosure can come at a high price. Cases during the earliest phase of the outbreak of Severe Acute Respiratory Syndrome in mid-November 2002 in China were not openly reported, which allowed a new and severe disease to become silently established in ways that made further spread almost inevitable.[265] Information campaigns have dramatically altered the behavior of politicians and policymakers, but many have also failed to induce change. Understanding when information campaigns can succeed is thus critical.

What makes for a successful information strategy?

Tracer studies of spending on Ugandan education revealed leakages as high as 90 percent. Once the information was publicized, the budgeted resources reaching schools rose dramatically.[266] Studies suggest that newspaper readership and availability in India spur state governments to respond to food crises.[267] In Buenos Aires, publishing the wildly different procurement prices paid by city hospitals for similar products led to rapid convergence of prices.[268] What did these information strategies have in common? The information was specific. Political interest in addressing the problem was high. And the information was electorally salient.

Specific information. The information identified specific government decisions, specific decisionmakers, and the effect of the decision on the voters individually or as a

group. That made benchmarking—systematic comparisons across time or space—easy. The Uganda information was not about the general quality of education or general budget support, or even about leakage from national education budgets. It was about one type of transfer—capitation grants—disaggregated to the school level, responsibility for which was easy for parents and voters to assign to the school principal. In addition, the information made clear to voters what the school should have received. The information in Buenos Aires was also specific to individual hospitals.

Government responses to food crises show how the provision of high-level information is politically enforceable by voters. First, a food crisis is a single, specific issue. Second, responsibility for it is known to rest ultimately in the state chief minister's office. Third, there are no complicated issues of quality measurement—voters know immediately that they are benefiting if they receive assistance. Benchmarking is a bit more complicated but still doable. Voters know if others less deserving receive assistance. But they do not know what effort governments should make in responding to food crises (which is different from the benchmarks in the Uganda tracer studies, where voters knew exactly how much money should have reached individual schools).[269]

Strong political or bureaucratic interest in correcting the problem. In some cases (Uganda and possibly Buenos Aires), national politicians did not benefit, and potentially lost, from leakages or inefficiencies. That is, corruption was the product of bureaucratic shirking rather than political rent-seeking. Education had become a major issue for the president of Uganda, and his reputation was on the line. He had made public promises, followed by the highly visible action of transferring more funds to local schools. His ability to fulfill those promises was being undermined by bureaucratic malfeasance. Once the malfeasance was revealed, the fear of sanctions was enough to hold individual bureaucrats accountable and produce rapid change.

In other cases, such as assistance in a food crisis, there is considerably more room for shirking. Citizens find it difficult to know how large the crisis is, what resources are available, and how efficiently and equitably the resources are distributed. This uncertainty leaves room for political inaction. But the consequences of government inaction—starvation deaths and their reports in the media—are grave enough to tarnish the chief executive's reputation, which gives the state administration a major reason to avoid them. Famines do not occur in democratic countries, even very poor ones, because the survival of the government would be threatened by the opposition and by newspapers and other media.[270] And the more citizens are informed about the crisis and the needed response, the more likely they are to hold politicians electorally accountable.

The issue is important electorally. Politicians are not interested in improving performance if voters do not care. Voters can be well informed and know who the responsible politician is, but still not hold the politician accountable because other issues loom larger. Where conflict is rife, or society is polarized, the politician's stance on conflict or polarization may dominate voter attention, allowing the politician to get away with poor performance on other issues. In Uganda, the president made education a central part of his election manifesto. In Buenos Aires, municipal politicians may have been concerned that voters would view the corruption in hospitals as indicative of deeper problems of malfeasance, in the city government and, because Buenos Aires is the capital, in other cities and the country.

Citizen report cards: information as political action

Other information strategies look directly at public service outputs (quality and quantity of services provided by government) rather than inputs (prices paid, budgets committed and delivered). The best known are the citizen report cards developed by the Public Affairs Centre in Bangalore, India.[271] Citizens are asked to rate service access and quality and to report on corruption and general grievances about public services. Citizen report cards have spread to cities in the Philippines, Ukraine, and, on a pilot basis, Vietnam. They have recently been scaled up in India to cover urban and rural services in 24 states.[272] The results have stimulated considerable media, bureaucratic, and political attention and acknowledgment of their contribution to service improvements.

Because citizen report cards focus on service outcomes, they do not provide voters with information about specific decisions that specific policymakers have made—or not made. Nor do they give voters information (at least in their first round) about service benchmarks, except to the extent that the agencies themselves have established service standards (repeat report cards do provide implicit benchmarks from the previous report card). So it can be hard for voters to assess, on the basis of one report card, whether the results justify voting against the incumbents at the next election.

Report cards seem to have had a more direct influence on the heads and senior managers of the municipal and utility agencies responsible for services, as in Bangalore. The high visibility of report cards in the press and civic forums turns them into league tables of the efficacy of municipal agencies. The reputational competition arising from the report cards is enhanced by joint agency meetings on the report cards attended by prominent social and political leaders and citizens.

But report cards clearly also perform a political function. Politicians can ignore poor public services if they believe that voters cannot penalize them for poor performance. Or if they believe that a political challenger cannot credibly promise voters better performance. An NGO conducting broad surveys and issuing report cards on public services changes the equation. Now incumbent politicians are confronted by an organized effort to improve public service delivery, which creates a latent political force that is credible because there is no obvious personal gain to members of the NGO. The information that the NGO generates and disseminates is a political challenge, both because of the demonstrated underlying ability to mobilize citizens to answer a survey and the power of that information in the hands of informed voters.

Some implications for information strategies

These examples show that pure information strategies work in fairly specific circumstances. But many information strategies are not designed around the specifics of a particular country or service. Information about broad aggregates of public sector performance—whether based on surveys, budget studies, or other methods—is less likely to be as politically relevant. Why? Because it does not provide voters with a sense of how their representatives in government have hurt or helped them.

Like report cards, such information can still be useful if voters can benchmark the information or if the very collection of the information implies some latent political organization that could challenge incumbents. But in many cases, the information collected is one-off—collected by donors and other foreign entities (posing no political threat by definition), by local survey firms (with no specific interest in social services), or by civil society organizations (which care deeply about public service performance but play no electoral role).

At the end of the day, these efforts tell citizens what they already know—that services are bad. They might tell them exactly how bad and which services are worse than others—roughly the information citizens already had, but more quantified. What citizens do not have, and what they need help in getting, is information about how bad their neighborhood's services are relative to others' and who is responsible for the difference.[273] In these cases outsiders can help in several ways:

- Supporting civil society organizations that generate and use specific information about service delivery.

- Supporting civil society organizations that show how to mobilize citizens and be a credible voice for public service provision.
- Supporting mass media development. First, improving the media's ability to ask the right questions (reporting on whether government policy succeeds or fails, including how to identify the correct benchmarks). Second, improving the media's credibility (independence from private interests that benefit from government largesse and from government influence, advertising revenue, or ownership). Reducing barriers to entry is key here. Third, improving interaction with civil society to generate information that reveals public malfeasance or nonfeasance.[274]

Decentralization to strengthen voice

Decentralizing delivery responsibilities for public services is prominent on the reform agenda in many developing countries (see chapter 10). Bolivia, India, Indonesia, Nigeria, Pakistan, and South Africa—to name a few—are all part of a worldwide movement to decentralize. A key objective, usually linked to the political motivation for decentralization, is to strengthen citizen voice by bringing services and elected politicians closer to the client.

Decentralization of service delivery to local governments

Experience with decentralization varies. In Bolivia the creation of rural local governments has been associated with dramatic shifts in public allocations away from infrastructure and into the social sectors—and a sharp fall in the geographic concentration of public investments as they get more evenly dispersed across regions.[275] But others have been less lucky, with increased regional inequalities and the capture of public resources by local elites. Since several major decentralization reforms are just beginning (Indonesia, Pakistan), there is a tremendous opportunity to rigorously evaluate the impact of different institutional designs on the quality of public goods.

What does it take for political decentralization to improve universal, basic social services? Two conditions. First, voters must be more likely to use information about the quality of local public goods in making their voting decisions. Second, local political promises to voters must be more credible than regional or national promises.

In principle, the impact of decentralization on informed voting and political credibility could go either way. On the one hand, voters may make more use of information about local public goods in their voting decisions because such information is easier to come by and outcomes are more directly affected by local government actions. And political agents may have greater credibility because of proximity to the community and reputations developed through social interaction over an extended period. On the other hand, local voters may be apathetic about local elections and have little or no information about the resource availability and capabilities of local governments. Social polarization may be more intense because of age-old differences across settled communities. With closer social relations between elected representatives and their clients, clientelist promises to a few voters may be easier to make and fulfill.

Managerial decentralization and political credibility

There has also been a push for institutionalizing greater autonomy of decisionmaking in schools, hospitals, and clinics—and encouraging greater participation of citizens through parent-teacher associations and health committees. These institutional interventions are also likely to address the credibility of elected politicians. Politicians located at the center far from the communities where services are delivered cannot credibly promise to improve service quality in such transaction-intensive services as basic health and education. At most they can commit only to providing such verifiable elements as infrastructure, equipment, and salaries.

When responsibility for delivering and monitoring primary education is completely centralized, the political incentives for improving the quality of schooling are weak. But if monitoring of providers is decentralized (to clients), voters need verify only that politicians have made resources available for schools and clinics to decide whether to reward or punish them at election time, and politicians then can be more credible.

Citizen voice in eight sizes

Whether a political system is pro-poor or clientelist is difficult to assess and address. This is obviously the case for outside actors such as donors, but also for those within a country, who are naturally influenced by the history and traditions of their particular political system, such as parliamentary democracy. But the payoffs in service delivery for assessing whether the environment is pro-poor or clientelist can be high. Even if the politics are clientelist, policy choices can be made that are likely to yield better results than the misguided application of policies that work well only in pro-poor environments.

Such choices can be combined with considerations of whether preferences are homogeneous or heterogeneous (a feature of the relationship between clients and providers, discussed in chapter 4), and whether services are easy or hard to monitor by policymakers (and therefore whether contracts between policymakers and providers can be written, as noted in chapter 3 and discussed in more detail in chapter 6). Simply put, the more people differ in their preferences, the more the decisions about service delivery should be decentralized. The harder it is for policymakers to monitor, the more clients need to be involved and the stronger client power must be.

Different combinations of these characteristics lead to different choices, some a better fit than others, so that while no one size fits all, for illustrative purposes perhaps eight sizes might (figure 5.4). None of these characteristics or choices can be precisely rendered because countries lie on a continuum. But understanding them can help in thinking about the arrangements that are the most likely to make services work for poor people. Figure 5.4 also illustrates the broad service delivery arrangements and the implied policy choices that are appropriate under different settings. The biggest problem? The appropriate choice is often not made.

In many countries, policymakers assume that for transaction-intensive and hard-to-monitor services (for example, primary education), their country or region has pro-poor politics and little heterogeneity of preferences. So they chose central government provision

Figure 5.4 Eight sizes fit all

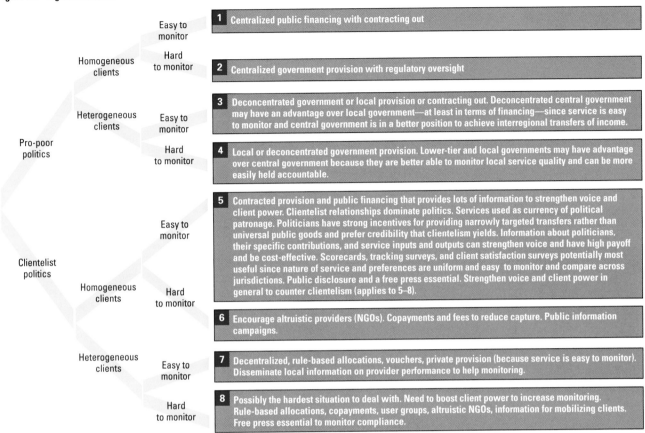

		1 Centralized public financing with contracting out
Homogeneous clients	Easy to monitor	
	Hard to monitor	**2** Centralized government provision with regulatory oversight

Pro-poor politics

Heterogeneous clients	Easy to monitor	**3** Deconcentrated government or local provision or contracting out. Deconcentrated central government may have an advantage over local government—at least in terms of financing—since service is easy to monitor and central government is in a better position to achieve interregional transfers of income.
	Hard to monitor	**4** Local or deconcentrated government provision. Lower-tier and local governments may have advantage over central government because they are better able to monitor local service quality and can be more easily held accountable.

Clientelist politics

Homogeneous clients	Easy to monitor	**5** Contracted provision and public financing that provides lots of information to strengthen voice and client power. Clientelist relationships dominate politics. Services used as currency of political patronage. Politicians have strong incentives for providing narrowly targeted transfers rather than universal public goods and prefer credibility that clientelism yields. Information about politicians, their specific contributions, and service inputs and outputs can strengthen voice and have high payoff and be cost-effective. Scorecards, tracking surveys, and client satisfaction surveys potentially most useful since nature of service and preferences are uniform and easy to monitor and compare across jurisdictions. Public disclosure and a free press essential. Strengthen voice and client power in general to counter clientelism (applies to 5–8).
	Hard to monitor	**6** Encourage altruistic providers (NGOs). Copayments and fees to reduce capture. Public information campaigns.
Heterogeneous clients	Easy to monitor	**7** Decentralized, rule-based allocations, vouchers, private provision (because service is easy to monitor). Disseminate local information on provider performance to help monitoring.
	Hard to monitor	**8** Possibly the hardest situation to deal with. Need to boost client power to increase monitoring. Rule-based allocations, copayments, user groups, altruistic NGOs, information for mobilizing clients. Free press essential to monitor compliance.

(option 2 in figure 5.4). But if the service delivery environment is actually based on clientelism, and preferences vary widely, then conditions have been misread and services fail poor people. Decentralized provision with lots of client involvement at all levels may be called for in ways that create choice and mimic the market if services are to work (option 8).

In general, services can be made to work in clientelist settings by choosing arrangements that reduce the rents from service delivery that would otherwise be captured through patronage and clientelism. These are the situations depicted in options 5 through 8. The appropriate service arrangement for hard-to-monitor services such as curative care or primary education might then be option 6 or 8 depending on whether preferences are homogenous or heterogeneous. If institutional arrangements change

and a pro-poor service delivery environment emerges, it should be possible to move to the service arrangements described in options 1 through 4. But to the extent they do not change, then trying to scale up with options 1 through 4 and make services work for poor people may be wishful thinking and a waste of resources.

Under either clientelist or pro-poor environments, having more and better information pays off in strengthening voice. Information about services that is specific, directly related to voters' concerns, and framed in a way that ensures political interest in addressing service delivery concerns is likely to be the most effective. Information from impact assessments can show what works and why. Information about politicians can boost their political credibility, strengthen incentives to provide universal public services, and avoid politically targeted goods and rent-seeking.

the Kecamatan Development Program

Choice, participation, and transparency in Indonesian villages

A new generation of community development projects in Indonesia illustrates many of the key elements of effective services. The projects transfer resources directly to local control, allowing a local decisionmaking body to choose among proposals from community groups. The three principles are: choice, participation, and transparency.

Pastoral scene—or chaotic mess

Indonesia in the New Order era of Soeharto (1967–98) has been compared to a French Impressionist painting: viewed from a distance, a beautiful pastoral scene, but viewed closely, a chaotic mess.

The government launched top-down "blueprint" development programs in fertility, health, schooling, and poverty reduction—implemented by a reasonably functional and capable bureaucracy. Viewed in the aggregate, the results were spectacular. Gross domestic product per capita grew at more than 5 percent a year. Poverty fell from nearly half the population in the 1970s to 11 percent in 1997. Infant mortality fell, fertility fell, and schooling rose dramatically.

The 1979 law establishing village governments was state of the art—on paper. With the goals of "decentralization" and "bottom-up" planning, the law established locally chosen village heads accountable to a village council. The budget planning process incorporated village-level meetings to elicit bottom-up inputs into budget priorities.

But the reality of village leadership was different. Creating multifunctional village administrative structures imposed order and uniformity at odds with existing social structures, ignoring organizations with specific functions (water) and traditional leadership (*adat*).[276] Many villages had dynamic leaders, but many others had leaders chosen essentially by the regional (province or district) government, which had veto power over candidates.[277] The village head was accountable to a council, but he also headed the council and chose many of its members. Most village heads were accountable upward—to regional governments—and not to the villagers. The bottom-up planning never really functioned: one analysis of 770 village proposals found that, at most, 3 percent were included in district budgets.[278]

Empirical results from a recent survey in 48 rural villages suggest that the government-driven organizations did not make village governance more responsive. Those who reported participating in the government-organized village groups reported being more likely to have spoken out about village problems and to have done so effectively. But this impact, by crowding out the voice of others in the village, appears to have been negative overall.

The problems with local governance were obvious in projects. The first-generation poverty alleviation programs—block grants to poor communities, under the IDT (Impres Desa Tertinggal)—used existing village structures and were judged to have had very little impact, in quantity or quality.[279] A study of all projects in villages—including those initiated by villages on their own(found that village-initiated projects were much more likely to have sustained benefits than government-initiated projects (figure 1).

The next generation of more participatory projects—two rounds of village infrastructure projects and water supply and sanitation projects—showed that greater community engagement could have real payoffs. Water projects designed to incorporate participation had much lower failure rates than conventional projects. And the costs of the village infrastructure projects were 30 to 50 percent lower than costs in projects using government construction.

Figure 1 Community-initiated projects: more likely to be maintained and in full use

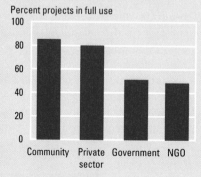

Percent projects in full use

Source: World Bank (2001g).

Scaling up with simplicity and trust

The financial and political crises that began in 1997 opened a window for action. Projects were desperately needed to help rural areas quickly. An improved design for community projects—based on the lessons of block grants under the IDT and infrastructure investments under village infrastructure projects—was being piloted. It included open menus and more emphasis on community participation and decisionmaking. The crisis also created an opportunity to act on issues of transparency, local accountability, and corruption.

The new Kecamatan Development Program (KDP) provides block grants to eligible subdistricts—or *kecamatan,* an administrative unit that includes roughly 10 to 20 villages and roughly 30,000 people, though its size varies enormously. Each subdistrict uses the funds to finance community proposals from the villages for small-scale public goods (roads, wells, bridges) or economic activities. Making the decisions about which proposals to fund is a subdistrict forum, including village delegations.

The KDP's design was based on simplicity, participation, self-reliance, transparency, and trust. These principles may sound platitudinous, but they pushed the design envelope in several directions.

- *Simplicity* meant that funds were released directly to communities, eliminating one role for regional (district and provincial) governments.

- *Participation* was encouraged, and locally chosen village and subdistrict facilitators helped groups to prepare proposals and encouraged the dissemination of information.

- *Self-reliance* reversed the usual dependence of villagers on technical staff from ministries and government, permitting villagers to hire the engineers and other technical help.

- *Transparency* meant that all financial information was publicly available, and detailed information about the use of the funds was available in each village in simple and easy-to-understand formats.
- *Trust* made it possible to move from complicated formal accounting systems for releasing funds to disbursement systems that rely on minimal documentation—but with built-in checks and oversight.

The project has so far been an implementation success, scaled up from 40 villages in 1998 to more than 15,000 in 2002. It has moved into another cycle and been replicated in urban areas. Evaluation efforts, including an innovative attempt to directly measure the impact on corruption, are examining whether the KDP has improved project performance.

This is not to suggest that the KDP is free from flaws—it is a transitional project in a transitional situation, embedded in existing institutions. There have been problems of corruption and poor technical quality, and problems of local leaders "guiding" the participatory decisionmaking. But the KDP does give villagers the structured mechanisms of decisionmaking and transparency. It also gives them recourse to force the issue of better governance. Corrupt officials have been sued. Money has been recovered. Decisions have been reversed.

Two lingering issues: First, is the KDP an idiosyncratic product of its particular time and place—or a model that can be replicated elsewhere? That versions of it are being launched in Afghanistan and the Philippines

(and perhaps elsewhere) suggests the latter. But whether it will "work" in those places is still an open question. Perhaps the principles can be implemented with the design adapted to local circumstances.

Second, are large external agencies (like the World Bank) really capable of supporting "big-time small development" projects? Perhaps yes, perhaps no. Some argue that external actors have no mandate or expertise for engaging in local governance. And preserving the traditional exclusive link of external agencies to formal public provider organizations may make them incapable of contributing to the creation of needed local accountabilities.

This or that? Three strategic choices

Community-driven development projects such as the KDP raise three strategic choices relevant to the design of service delivery.

Narrow or sharp targeting. Community funds, it is often alleged, are captured by "elites" and will not be well targeted to the poor. The KDP shows that the poor do benefit, but it is difficult to reach the poorest of the poor or to change deeply held social prejudices simply by project design (despite, for example, KDP mechanisms to enhance women's voice). Few large programs have shown greater ability to target the poor, and the very narrowly targeted programs would not elicit engagement and support.

Technical or participatory projects and service. Technical staff of the government (and of many donor agencies) are leery of

community-driven project design because it can undermine technical quality. Given the choice of a participatory bridge or an engineered bridge, most people would cross the engineered bridge. The question is how to create a well-engineered bridge that responds to community needs. Other services try to balance community control and technical quality: participation in health care does not mean that medical science can be replaced. Should KDP-like mechanisms be expanded with improved links to technical providers? Or should technical providers be strengthened and the "participatory" role be channeled not into direct control and decisionmaking but into electing local officials?

Local or regional governments. Regional governments often complain that moving resources directly to communities undermines their authority, slowing the capacity building needed for formal governance and democracy. Proponents of community development respond that deep democracy depends on the kinds of transparency, decisionmaking, open debate, and accountability that community projects build. Decentralizing decisions about budgets and programs to the provincial level—when people have not developed traditions and institutions of civic decisionmaking at the local level (or have had them suppressed)— is risky business. In a transitional environment, periodic elections alone are unlikely to be sufficient for public accountability. The development of nonelectoral mechanisms of public accountability (transparency, legal recourses, direct participation) is key.

Developing social services and building a nation

One of the richest countries in the world, Norway today is the quintessential welfare state, with universal access to basic health and education. But this welfare state evolved over two centuries, with private systems only gradually giving way to state-run institutions. Making social services available to all was seen as part of building the Norwegian nation. Though geographically close, Estonia regained its independence in 1991. It is seeking to develop its social services and build a nation in a much shorter time, and under budgetary constraints.

Norway: gradual change with top-down pressure

In 1860 the Norwegian national assembly passed two laws—the Health Act and the School Act—the first time the state took responsibility for the health and education of its people. The Health Act, which established health commissions in every municipality, was promoted by the country's social elite to improve the welfare of Norway's farming and peasant communities so that the country could compete with the more advanced nations of Europe. The elite saw educating poor rural households in personal and environmental hygiene as a key to this project, and the health commissions were charged with this task. Interestingly, members of the medical profession, which up to that point had a somewhat lower status than other professions (lawyers, priests, and the military), saw themselves as the natural leaders of the campaign. According to one doctor, appointing a lawyer to head the campaign (something that was being contemplated) "would do nothing to further the cause."[280]

But the health commissions faced significant difficulties in getting their job done. In addition to the facts that doctors were not trained in public health and their work was poorly paid, the cultural divide between the urban elites and rural farmers was an obstacle. For instance, although fertilizer was a scarce commodity, the doctors were trying to get rid of the compost heaps near people's houses because of the "rotten" air that people were obliged to breathe.

Meanwhile, many of the services were being delivered by grassroots organizations. Founded in 1896, the Norwegian Women's Public Health Association was running 14 sanatoria for patients with tuberculosis by 1920. The Association also advocated for greater public intervention in health, getting the authorities to open public baths and regularly monitor the health of infants and schoolchildren. From 1890 onwards, the health sector evolved through public-private partnerships, spurred on by pressure from grassroots and philanthropic organizations. As the state took on more responsibility for delivering universal services, a process that picked up in the 1930s, it did not have to build the institutions from scratch: it could build on institutions already built, organized, and financed by private actors and civil society.

Reforming schools

From 1739, children were required to attend school from the age of seven until they could read and undergo Lutheran confirmation. The incentives to learn to read were strong. No reading meant no confirmation, and no confirmation meant no marriage license, no land holding, no permanent job, and no chance of enlisting in the armed forces. Nevertheless, the rural population resisted sending their children to school, mainly because they found the curriculum irrelevant for farming.

As with health, formally trained teachers became the driving force behind using education to build the Norwegian nation. Teachers organized themselves in 1848 and advocated inclusion of education professionals in policymaking bodies. The School Act of 1860 shifted responsibility for running schools from the clergy to an elected school board (whose head would still be a priest). As a result of populist and agrarian pressure, local school councils were able to appoint teachers, determine their own "education plan," and introduce New Norse as the language of instruction. But a growing labor movement was demanding more universal education, so that by 1889 a common school law was passed and education finally moved from religious training to general learning and nation building.

Estonia: starting over, with few resources

At re-independence in 1991, Estonia wanted to move away from its inherited systems to modern Western European approaches that rested on progressive governmental, economic, and social reforms—partly for acceptance into the European Union. The new state had to quickly establish the mechanisms of a modern welfare system. But there was little time to establish the system's legitimacy.

The first priority in 1991 was services based on Estonian language and culture, critical for national identity. Then came the urgent need to improve efficiency and equity. But economic difficulties limited the resources for reform.

The health care system had to be completely reorganized. Unlike the situation in Norway, the administrative, legislative, and regulatory powers in Estonia were all in one place: the Ministry of Health. With little transparency and control, corruption flourished.

To address the problem, the old state-funded system was replaced by health insurance, which facilitated transparency and a steady stream of finance. A major challenge has been to convey the logic and long-term advantages of the new system. People suddenly had to pay for health care that used to be free. Drugs were sold at European prices. And, although the system has equity as a goal, the health status of a growing number of Estonians is declining, especially that of the elderly, ethnic minorities, and the unemployed. Around 6 percent of the population is not yet covered by the new national health insurance system.

On many accounts, Estonia has succeeded more than many other newly independent countries. But in seeking to find its own way of making services work, it has not had the luxury of time.

Policymakers and providers

Educated children. Good health. Clean, reliable, and convenient water. Safe neighborhoods. Lighted homes. That is what citizens, poor and rich, want from services. If policymakers take responsibility for delivering services, they must also care about these outcomes and be sure that services providers care about them, too. Chapter 5 discussed the first challenge: inducing policymakers to reflect the interests of poor people. This chapter takes up the second: inducing providers to achieve the outcomes of interest to poor people. How? By choosing appropriate providers. By aligning incentives with those outcomes. And by ensuring that policymakers do at least as well as the clients themselves in creating those incentives.

Compacts, management, and the "long route" of accountability

The "compact" introduced in chapter 3 is composed of relationships of accountability necessary for increasing the power of incentives for good performance (figure 6.1). Instructions to provider organizations must

be clear and backed with sufficient resources for adequate and regular compensation. Good information on the actions of providers and the outcomes of those actions must get to the policymaker. And remuneration must be tied as closely to these outcomes as possible. Accountability is improved by:

- Clarifying responsibilities—by separating the role of policymaker, accountable to poor citizens, from that of provider organizations, accountable to policymakers.

- Choosing the appropriate provider— civil servants, autonomous public agencies, NGOs, or private contractors. Competition can often help in this choice.

- Providing good information—an essential step. Just monitoring the performance of contracts requires more and better measures. Keeping an eye on the prize of better outcomes also requires more regular measurement. It also requires finding out what works by rigorously evaluating programs and their effects.

These steps are neither easy nor straightforward. Political pressures often make it impossible for policymakers to claim independence from the performance of service providers. Compacts for the kind of services discussed here cannot be complete or have perfectly measured outcomes. Finding enough staff, regardless of their precise employment agreements, is a real challenge for many developing countries because of international migration and, for Sub-Saharan Africa, HIV/AIDS. And finding out what works—determining the link between policies and inputs and outcomes—is difficult, not just for technical reasons. Governments, donors, and provider organizations fre-

Figure 6.1 Compact and management in the service delivery framework

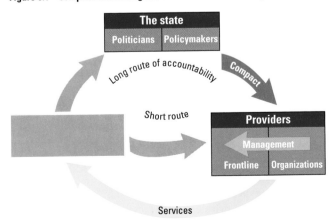

quently don't want to know—or don't want to take the risk of finding out—what doesn't work.[281]

It may be difficult to measure the outcomes of health, education, and infrastructure services, but it is possible. Improvements cannot be measured as precisely as tons of steel. But the outcomes of these services are far more amenable to measurement than many core functions of government. Mortality rates, literacy rates, and the purity of water are observable in ways that "advancing the international interests of the nation," the goal of a foreign ministry for example, are not.[282] And technical knowledge for rigorous evaluation of programs to reach the poor is certainly available.

A word on "compacts" versus "management." The focus of this chapter is the compact between the policymaker and the provider organizations, not the details of the management of frontline providers by a provider organization. Appropriate management needs to be tailored to local circumstances. Focusing on the details of management detracts from the more crucial relationship of the compact and indulges the tendency to micromanage. Here the emphasis is on the principles for designing incentives. But management cannot be ignored entirely. Much of the (very thin) literature on what works and what doesn't—on provider responses to changes in incentives—deals with management reforms, so these experiences must form the limited empirical base.

Misaligned incentives and service failures

Failures to reach poor people with effective services can usually be attributed to a misalignment between the incentives facing providers and outcomes. A private market left to itself cannot provide appropriate services to poor people. It will tend to serve clients who possess the purchasing power for a fairly narrow set of services. Modern, private medical care by skilled professionals and private education are largely used by the better off. Water is an exception, with substantial middle-class capture of public water, leaving poor people to buy from expensive private sellers. The range of services the private sector will provide on its own is limited to, well,

private goods. Private providers may be contracted by the public sector for services to poor people or for true public goods (where a private sector is impossible, even in principle). But they cannot be relied on to provide them on their own. That is why the public sector should assume responsibility for basic services, especially for poor people.

The public sector has its problems, too. Chapter 5 asked whether, in fulfilling this responsibility, policymakers have the incentive to "do the right thing." The answer is often "no." But even if policies are properly designed, it is difficult to get personnel to staff facilities in poor or remote areas. Vacancy rates for doctors in Indonesia range from near zero in Bali to as high as 60 percent in West Papua (formerly Irian Jaya), the province farthest from Java (box 6.1).

The difficulty in staffing such places varies by job. It is greatest for the most highly educated people with the best alternative employment prospects. Educated people in countries with few such people are almost always urban born and bred. In Niger 43 percent of the parents of nurses and midwives were civil servants, and 70 percent of them

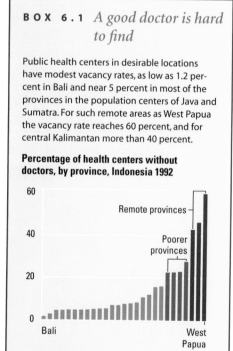

BOX 6.1 *A good doctor is hard to find*

Public health centers in desirable locations have modest vacancy rates, as low as 1.2 percent in Bali and near 5 percent in most of the provinces in the population centers of Java and Sumatra. For such remote areas as West Papua the vacancy rate reaches 60 percent, and for central Kalimantan more than 40 percent.

Percentage of health centers without doctors, by province, Indonesia 1992

Remote provinces

Poorer provinces

Bali

West Papua

Source: World Bank (1994b).

had been raised in the city.[283] It is only natural for them to want the same for their children. And it is naïve to simply say "pay them more." Doctors in Indonesia would require multiples of current pay levels to live in West Papua.[284] And giving providers too much discretion over where they serve may hurt the poor, as in rural schools in Zambia (box 6.2).

Even when people accept jobs in poor areas, their absenteeism is often astonishing (see tables 1.2 and 1.3 in chapter 1). The reasons vary, but alternative earning opportunities are a major one for professions with easily marketable skills.[285] This applies to doctors and other medical personnel and to teachers offering independent tutoring. Again, the day-to-day imperatives for people to make a living run counter to increasing services to poor people. This is particularly true where civil service pay is much less than private sector pay for the same skills.

Even when people are on the job, their performance can compromise the outcomes

for poor people. The lack of conscientiousness, the mistreatment of students and patients, and the loss of skills with time (chapter 1)—all can be attributed to a combination of the failure of incentives and a service ethos. Salaried workers with no opportunity to advance and no fear of punishment have little incentive to perform well. Chapter 4 argued that discourtesy depended on incentives, not training. If income does not come from clients, the policymaker must hold providers accountable, particularly in monitoring and rewarding good behavior.

Corruption—unauthorized private gain from public resources—is common in many services and also attributable to competing incentives. In Eastern Europe under-the-table payments to public servants and general corruption undermine the legitimacy of all government services. They are particularly costly to poor people (box 6.3). Pharmaceutical mismanagement is everywhere: thefts from public stores supply much of the private market in Côte d'Ivoire, India, Jordan, Thailand, and Zambia. Corruption responds to monetary incentives, but it also requires a lack of information on hidden activities and an inability to impose sanctions. As Captain Shotover in George Bernard Shaw's *Heartbreak House* put it, "Give me deeper darkness. Money is not made in the light." Open information can reduce both the incidence of corruption and its corrosiveness.[286]

Community pressure can also subvert the incentives to fulfill the primary responsibilities of public providers. In many places the public servant is a permanent member of the community, facing substantial social pressures to bend rules to the benefit of local preferences. Sometimes this is good—it shows the flexibility to respond to local needs. But for some services, particularly those with punitive characteristics, it can compromise the core duties of the provider. For example, forestry agents who are part of a community may be reluctant to report illegal logging by their neighbors.[287] A form of community pressure particularly harmful to the poor is the capture of services by local elites. In Northern Ghana young, inexperienced, and poorly paid facilitators for participatory projects found such pressure a major impediment.[288]

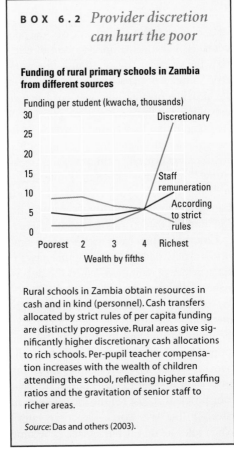

BOX 6.2 *Provider discretion can hurt the poor*

Funding of rural primary schools in Zambia from different sources

Funding per student (kwacha, thousands)

Rural schools in Zambia obtain resources in cash and in kind (personnel). Cash transfers allocated by strict rules of per capita funding are distinctly progressive. Rural areas give significantly higher discretionary cash allocations to rich schools. Per-pupil teacher compensation increases with the wealth of children attending the school, reflecting higher staffing ratios and the gravitation of senior staff to richer areas.

Source: Das and others (2003).

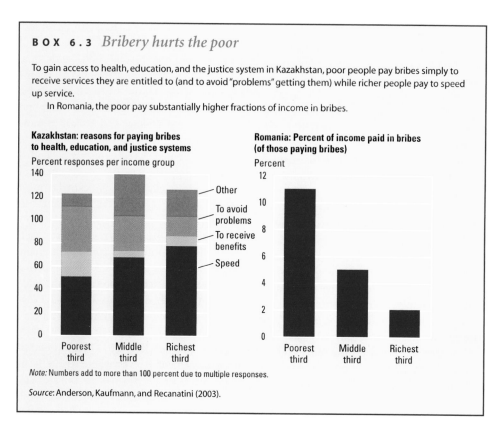

BOX 6.3 *Bribery hurts the poor*

To gain access to health, education, and the justice system in Kazakhstan, poor people pay bribes simply to receive services they are entitled to (and to avoid "problems" getting them) while richer people pay to speed up service.

In Romania, the poor pay substantially higher fractions of income in bribes.

Kazakhstan: reasons for paying bribes to health, education, and justice systems

Percent responses per income group

Other
To avoid problems
To receive benefits
Speed

Poorest third   Middle third   Richest third

Romania: Percent of income paid in bribes (of those paying bribes)

Percent

Poorest third   Middle third   Richest third

Note: Numbers add to more than 100 percent due to multiple responses.

Source: Anderson, Kaufmann, and Recanatini (2003).

Many, and usually most, providers in the public sector are dedicated people whose interests are largely compatible with the public good. But their own needs of looking after a family, ensuring their well being, having friendly relations with neighbors—all prevent them from providing sufficient services to benefit poor people. If the scale of operations needs to be increased to reach the poor, even more incentives need to be changed at the margin, whether monetary or not.[289]

Increasing accountability: separating the policymaker from the provider

The many incentives that providers face blur the focus on outcomes. Making a clear separation between the role of the policymaker and the provider organization is essential for aligning the incentives for the provider with the final outcomes that policymakers want for citizens. Who is the policymaker, and who is the provider organization? The policymaker is the person directly accountable to the citizenry, preferably the poorer citizenry. And the provider organization is responsible for delivering services. In many cases, the policymaker is the legislature or a central ministry, the provider organization a line ministry. So many of the activities of the head of the "provider organization" will look like policymaking. But these are "internal policies" of the organization to achieve the overall goals focused on here. (The literature on public management explicitly cautions against separating[290] policymaking from implementation, but that literature is concerned with management within the "provider organization" and not the separation proposed here.)

Clear separation lends itself to much simpler and less ambiguous accountability for the provider organization. When the policymaker is the provider organization, day-to-day pressures of management compromise attention to outcomes on the ground. Take the desire to find and fix problems (see the spotlight on Johannesburg). When the policymaker takes a separate role from the provider, it is easier to say "I don't care what your problem is, just tell me the vaccination rates. Or the test scores. Or crime rates." When roles are mixed, bureaucracies become insular and tend to hide mistakes.

Is this separation really necessary? Is it achieved in rich countries? Education, for example, is frequently administered through central ministries, which employ all teachers directly with little monitoring from central staff agencies (such as finance). Perhaps separation is not necessary for successful services.

But rich countries benefit from a long evolution of the relationships between the state and frontline providers. Almost all services provided directly to individuals in the now-rich countries were originally provided privately. They were eventually absorbed or consolidated by a state institution that had been separate from the existing provider organizations. The state began as an independent outside monitor and regulator of private activities. It largely retained that independence as a monitor after the same activities became public (box 6.4).

For the developing world the desire for rapid expansion of public financing and provision short-circuits this historical development. Both the monitoring and the provision are taking place simultaneously. This is not necessarily a bad thing—the poor might otherwise have to wait much longer for services to reach them. But it does show that the current institutional features of rich countries may not transfer directly to poor countries without the establishment of a complementary regulatory structure, a structure that may need to be established beforehand. Without this structure progress may be slow—possibly slower than if a not-for-profit or private sector were allowed to develop and later brought under the supervisory wing of the government.

Separating the policymaker from the provider organization also helps to increase the accountability of providers. But if the policymaker knows what services to deliver, why can't providers just be given instructions—in a contract—to do them? That is, why can't outputs just be specified and paid for accordingly?

Limits to accountability

All public services face three problems that make this solution impossible: providers face multiple principals, undertake multiple tasks, and produce outcomes that are hard to observe and hard to attribute to their actions.[291]

Multiple principals

The instructions of the policymaker to providers are not the only ones that count. Public servants have to serve many masters. Education providers are under pressure from parents of poor children (with the policymaker representing them), parents of children other than the poor, teachers' unions, potential employers, various groups in society that want (or don't want) particular items on the curriculum, and others. Power and water providers are under pressure from different segments of the market to cross-subsidize them, from producers to buy specific types of equipment, from people who want more extensive connections, and from others who want more reliable, continuous operation. The day-to-day pressure of local demand for health care can compromise efforts in disease prevention and other public health activities that are not demand-driven.[292] Whom is a provider to listen to?

BOX 6.4 *Learning to regulate*

Although the state pays for health care in most Organisation for Economic Co-operation and Development (OECD) countries, private practitioners still provide it (exceptions on the finance side include the United States; exceptions on the provision side, the United Kingdom). The state carries out the insurance function in these countries but not the services. It is the insurance market that is hampered by severe market failure. In Germany, the current system is a consolidation, begun under Bismarck in 1883, of a system of guild-based insurance schemes.

For most OECD countries, the current system of public ownership or control dates from a time after World War II when they had incomes at least as high as the upper-middle-income countries today. Before these programs were brought under public management, the state already had regulatory powers over the medical profession. The timing was fortuitous since it was only in the 20th century that technical changes in medicine made public oversight essential.

Universal public education is also fairly recent. It came out of a conflict between church and state. In the period of expansion of public facilities, the main mechanism was incorporating private schools into the public network after a system of managing individual schools had already developed.

Even the core networked services of water, electricity, gas, and railways—services now thought of as natural monopolies—began as purely private activities. In the United Kingdom early water systems were sometimes developed with duplicate pipes laid by competing firms. Only after coverage was substantial were these rationalized—and then for reasons of public health rather than duplication. German railways also began with duplicate lines. In other cases, companies worked out agreements that divided markets without the duplication experienced in the railway markets in the United States and England—for example, bus systems in many large urban areas and German natural gas transport. These were then brought under a regulatory regime but only after reaching quite high service penetration.

In each of these cases the independent regulatory capacity of the policymaker preceded the incorporation of private providers into a public system.

Source: Klein and Roger (1994).

Multiple tasks

Personnel in health clinics are supposed to provide curative care to people who come to them. They are also to provide immunizations, health education, and other preventive measures to everyone, whether they come in on their own or not. And they are to keep statistics, attend training sessions and meetings, and do inspections of water and food. Police officers have to deal with everyone from lost children to dangerous criminals. They are, at various times, investigators of crimes, social workers intervening in neighborhood and family disputes, and disseminators of information. This diffusion naturally blunts the precision of incentives.

Measuring and attributing outcomes

The most difficult problems, particularly for the social sectors, are the dual problems of measuring outcomes and attributing these outcomes to the actions of providers. Test scores may adequately reflect certain educational goals, but abstract thinking and social adaptability are not so easily measured. The alleviation of pain is a subjective judgment of the patient. Many outcomes, even when observable to the patient and the doctor, are not "contractible" in the sense that, if a dispute arises, compliance can be proved to a judge or other mediator. And attributing impacts to provider actions is difficult in almost all social services.

These problems make it impossible to have performance contracts that make payments to individual frontline providers depend on outcomes. All contracts will necessarily be incomplete, requiring at least some payment of wages independent of outputs. When the actions of the provider are specified in great detail, the results are often less than optimal because of inflexible response to local variation. The impossibility of specifying such rules ahead of time is illustrated by "work-to-rule" strikes, in which strikers bring an activity to a "grinding halt" by following rules entirely to the letter (box 6.5). The balance between control and flexibility is not easily struck.

Further, since the provider does many things, some or all of them hard to observe by the policymaker, there is the ever-present risk that payments for measured outcomes will displace hard-to-measure tasks (box 6.6). This risk has been discussed in the education literature as "teaching to the test." When teacher compensation (pay or promotion prospect) is measured by students' performance on a standard test, there will be a tendency to downplay those aspects of pedagogy not covered by the test and to concentrate on those that are. In Kenya teachers manipulated test scores by offering tutoring sessions aimed specifically at these tests. There was no improvement in other indicators of quality, such as homework assignments, teacher absences, or teaching methods.[293]

Several industrial countries, in reforming the civil service or other providers of public services, have tried to use performance contracts. The evidence of success is mixed:[294] many problems are tied to the dependence of the policymaker on information the agency provides—a problem closely related to the regulation of private firms. Some information used for performance contracts can be easily falsified or, less pejoratively, presented in too favorable a light. For example, when education reforms were instituted in the United Kingdom, truancies were redefined as excused absences.[295]

Overcoming the limits

Separating policymakers from provider organizations can help sharpen incentives to help poor people. Assigning policymakers the role of devising a compact for the provider organization and assigning provider organizations the responsibility of management can

---

BOX 6.5 *Be careful what you wish for—part 1*

"Anyone who has worked in a formal organization—even a small one strictly governed by detailed rules—knows that handbooks and written guidelines fail utterly in explaining how the institution goes about its work. Accounting for its smooth operation are nearly endless and shifting sets of implicit understandings, tacit coordinations, and practical mutualities that could never be successfully captured in a written code. This ubiquitous social fact is useful to employees and labor unions. The premise behind what are tellingly called work-to-rule strikes is a case in point. When Parisian taxi drivers want to press a point on the municipal authorities about regulations or fees, they sometimes launch a work-to-rule strike. It consists merely in following meticulously all the regulations in the Code routier and thereby bringing traffic throughout central Paris to a grinding halt. The drivers thus take tactical advantage of the fact that the circulation of traffic is possible only because drivers have mastered a set of practices that have evolved outside, and often in contravention, of the formal rules."

Source: Scott (1998).

enable the use of higher-powered incentives to align the interests of the frontline provider with those of the policymaker representing the poor, for the following three reasons. First, policymakers, balancing political pressures, can help insulate providers from the problem of satisfying masters with conflicting aims and offer unambiguous instructions. Second, provider organizations can face performance-based payments when individuals cannot. Third, managers of the provider organizations, if they have flexibility over operational decisions, can supervise staff and choose the appropriate form of remuneration that best reflects local conditions.

Insulating providers from politics

That providers have to satisfy many masters reflects the inability of government to insulate them from political pressures. While policymakers for education need to address concerns of potential employers, teachers' unions, or interest groups who want to influence curricula, there is no reason why this should affect day-to-day activities in a school, or indeed any organization of frontline providers. If the policymaking function can be separated from the provider organization, the policymaker can handle the politics of the overall objectives of education while the provider can be given more precise instructions and be held accountable to the policymaker. Poor people might legitimately delegate to policymakers curriculum development as well as the responsibility to balance their interests with those of unions.

Organizations and individuals

Individual providers will not accept performance contracts that leave them exposed to excessive risk. But the variability of aggregate performance over all providers in an organization—say, those dealing with infant mortality for a district—is very much smaller, which provides a way of sharing the risk. While a single doctor may not be able to absorb the risk to income of the bad luck of any particular patient, a district health board would. Teams—schools, school districts, health boards, city police departments—can be the recipients of performance-based incentives where teachers, nurses, and policemen cannot (see spotlight on Costa Rica and

---

BOX 6.6 *Be careful what you wish for—part 2*

The Sears Corporation lost a $48,000,000 class action suit in which its automobile repair department was accused of deliberately sabotaging customers' vehicles. The corporation was held responsible, having instructed its employees that bonuses would be paid to those branches with the most repeat business. That the intention of the instruction was to encourage courteous behavior did not impress the court.

Source: Sears Automotive Center Consumer Litigation, Action No. C-92-2227, U.S. District Court, San Francisco.

Cuba). What can be considered measurable varies by the size of the organization—larger ones being easier to hold to account.

The problem of multiple tasks is partly a problem of economies of scale as well. Some tasks can be divided into groups of complementary activities—all immunizations as a group, say, or all health education activities based on home visits (chapter 8). Then a fairly homogeneous organization can be charged with the responsibility to carry out a simpler set of tasks, with clear standards of accountability.

Reform in Johannesburg, South Africa (see spotlight), was in large part a reevaluation of the appropriate set of services to be grouped together to deliver specified outputs. Departments were reorganized so that their outputs were clearly identifiable and verifiable, with the department's CEO able to retain any savings over contract expenditures. At one extreme, commercial enterprises—such as the athletics stadium, the airport, and metro gas—were simply sold to the private sector and directly faced the forces of the market, where payment is very much dependent on outcomes.[296]

Management flexibility

Each of these potential effects depends on managers in provider organizations having the flexibility and authority to design the incentives for the frontline providers in their organizations. This allows them to adapt to local (or sectoral) variation to see whether performance pay or salaries with supervision works better. Flexibility for the manager is essential, a major part of "institutional capacity." Managers must have control over the pay scheme or the sanctions for poor performance.

Salaried systems work as long as there is the ability either to fire or to grant raises on the basis of merit. The worst case is when salaried workers face neither sanctions for poor performance nor increased pay or prestige for good performance. Civil servants in Singapore enjoy high salaries and a lot of prestige, but also work under a credible threat of being fired. A problem with some of the recent reforms in developed countries instituting contractual relations with providers is that they undermine the public service ethos. ("If I am to be treated as a mercenary, I might as well act like one.") Increased accountability through monetary incentives was partly offset by reduced accountability through internal motivation.[297] Developing countries that have instilled this sense of duty should be wary of compromising it. But they should be brutally honest with themselves before declaring this a major consideration.

Sometimes performance pay is appropriate and necessary but should be a matter for local experimentation. Several health interventions have benefited greatly by introducing performance-based incentives for workers (box 6.7). In other contexts, those incentives are precisely what is needed to obtain particular desired results. In the British National Health Service most general practitioner pay is determined on the basis of capitation payments—for how many people sign up with the doctor. But it is supplemented by specific additional payments for the provision of immunizations to counter any incentive to skimp on this priority service.

New providers for expanding supply

Where will the providers of services come from? One possibility is that competition for compacts will attract more provider organizations. The benefits from competition are reduced costs, greater effort, and better information—even when public provision is the dominant form, as long as public and other provider organizations are treated even-handedly. Three types of competition are relevant for services: competition in the market, competition for the market, and benchmarking.

Competition. Competition *in* the market simply means allowing private providers. For health and education, such providers are everywhere, and in many places larger players than the government (chapter 4). Recent technological advances have made it possible to open services formerly believed to be natural monopolies to competition. Independent power producers, for example, can be used to sell electricity to a larger grid. The cost of allowing free entry into natural monopolies is the risk of inefficient duplication of investments. Efficient regulation is necessary but complicated. If political and administrative limitations on the independence and effectiveness of regulators are severe, allowing the duplication may be the lesser of two evils.[298]

The impact of competition can go both ways: the presence of the public sector can impose indirect discipline on the private sector, both on prices and on quality. In Malaysia a credible public health system has kept price rises modest in the private sector.[299] The benefits of public provision extend beyond the numbers of patients treated publicly. Similarly, the presence of qualified medical personnel can force quality improvements in private markets.[300]

If natural monopolies exist, there can be competition *for* the market. Potential competitors bid for concessions—compacts—to provide the service. Much government pro-

---

BOX 6.7 *Incentive pay works for specific health interventions*

The Bangladesh Rural Advancement Committee (BRAC), one of the largest NGOs in Bangladesh, paid workers to teach mothers how to use oral rehydration therapy for children with diarrhea. Independent of the providers, bonuses were paid on the basis of surveys of random samples of 5–10 percent of the mothers. The greater the number of women who could explain how to make and use the rehydration solution, the higher the payment. More than half of total compensation was paid as a bonus.

The mothers' knowledge increased dramatically—to 65 percent of those taught two years after the training. Most important, the teaching techniques that the workers used changed from standard lectures to more hands-on demonstrations. Rather than have the right teaching technique specified for them from on high, workers developed the best way to achieve the measured outcome—finding out for themselves what worked in their context.

In Haiti, NGOs were given performance-based contracts, directly from the U.S. Agency for International Development, to provide preventive health care services such as immunizations, health education, prenatal care, and family planning. Again, an independent monitor, l'Institut Haitien de l'Enfance, a local survey research firm, was used to verify performance. Immunization rates increased dramatically along with several other outputs. Interestingly, some of the NGOs experimented with performance pay themselves but found lower morale and performance when workers (low paid themselves) faced such risky incomes. The NGOs, while satisfied with the high-powered incentives by which they were paid, found better ways to pay frontline providers in accordance with local circumstances.

Sources: Chowdhury (2001) and Eichler, Auxilia, and Pollock (2001).

curement in richer countries uses this model. It requires the ability to let, monitor, and enforce the explicit contracts for the winner. Recent innovations in the state of Madhya Pradesh in India allow NGOs to compete for concessions to primary schools. Payments are conditional on improved test scores based on independent measurement. One advantage the developing world has over earlier experience in Europe is that it has firms with good reputations and experience in the supply of water, power, and transport—and international courts for dispute resolution.[301] But the recent experience of Enron in India's Maharashtra State provides a reality check on over-enthusiasm for these benefits.

Benchmark or yardstick competition can be used when different providers are given parts of a larger system to run. Even when the public sector is the main provider of services, information from varying experiences can be valuable. Information on costs of production may be much cheaper to obtain by simple observation of one's own activities than from detailed technology assessments. Information on consumer preferences may be cheaper to obtain by counting customers than by conducting market research.

For road construction in Johannesburg, an explicit contract was made between the city manager and an autonomous public agency, the Johannesburg Road Agency, to build a given number of kilometers of road for a negotiated price. The basis of the negotiation was the set of historical costs in the public agencies. The manager of the autonomous agency then used both the public works department and private sector firms as contractors. Competition among the contractors determined subsequent allocations of funds. Even though it was not possible to fire personnel from the public agency, competition for funds ensured that the public agency would match the efficiency of the private firms (which it did for many contracts). There could be a gradual shift to private provision, but only on the basis of proven performance.

Limits to competition and the search for suppliers. For contracts that cannot be complete, aspects of delivery outside the contract will remain a matter of trust. For the provision of services to poor people, this trust is particularly important because there are fewer "perks" for working in poor areas—private earnings after working hours (for medical personnel and teachers) are lower, living conditions harsher.

In the long run, a public sector with a strong ethos of public service will be needed. In many places it already exists. It does no good to pretend, however, that expanding the civil service under current recruitment and incentive regimes will attract those best suited to serving poor people. In Nepal an anthropological study showed that health staff's view of their jobs often differed from the official view.[302] Many staff saw the health program solely as a source of employment. A broader set of potential providers is needed to accept the compacts.

NGOs—so much a part of the African scene and active in several other countries, such as Bangladesh—are possible candidates. They are a varied group. Many are not directly involved in service provision, and many combine service with advocacy. Those that provide services often have a great deal of autonomy, choosing where and how to deliver services. To that extent, they might be treated the same as the rest of the private sector in planning public services. The government should not be in the business of displacing them.

NGOs that have a tradition of altruistic service can frequently be lower-cost producers. In a recent study, religious NGOs providing health care in Uganda were found to offer higher-quality service than their public sector counterparts. They also paid lower wages than the private sector and very much lower than the public sector. Unlike the private sector, they were more likely to provide public health services (as opposed to simply medical care) and to charge less. And they used an extra cash grant to lower fees and provide more services, such as laboratory tests, whereas the public sector used the grant to increase pay.[303]

NGOs are often, though not always, better able to reach poor people. A substantially higher fraction of the clientele of NGOs providing health care in Zambia comes from poorer segments of society than does the clientele of government facilities or private providers.[304] But even they have a hard time reaching the very poorest. NGOs may also be in a better position, with their greater flexibility and their internal motivation, to bring services to otherwise excluded groups (box 6.8). And smaller organizations can reach niche populations that a broad-based bureaucracy may find hard to serve.

In combating AIDS, community outreach often needs to deal with prostitutes, drug users, and very sick, stigmatized people. The same difficulties in assigning public personnel to remote areas have been found in reaching these subgroups. In Brazil, however, NGOs competing for government funds were able to reach high-risk segments of society that usually avoid public programs (such as prostitutes), to distribute 2.6 million contraceptives, and to take 11,000 hotline calls. The relative independence of NGOs from the core of the public service may make it easier for them to fund their activities from public resources by granting policymakers an extra layer of deniability.

The altruistic motives of people working in NGOs can overcome the incompleteness of contracts. NGO providers are generally less likely than for-profit providers to exploit the difficulties of monitoring contract terms for their own benefit. Their altruism may partly outweigh a reluctance to locate in difficult, remote, rural areas that are hard to staff with civil servants. This possibility has led one analyst, thinking of Africa, to conclude that services to poor people may, for the time being, have to be left to such groups, particularly the church.[305]

Once again, patience is called for. Donor enthusiasm has led to a massive proliferation of NGOs, many of them not at all motivated by altruism.[306] Indeed, many appear to be run by former civil servants who have lost their jobs as a result of the downsizing of public sectors but who know how to approach donors and government contracting agencies. A rapid expansion of contracts for NGOs will tend to attract the same people, and their motives may be exactly the same as those of a for-profit firm—requiring the same monitoring and care in contract enforcement. NGOs with a track record of good performance and dedication to poor people are potentially very important elements of a strategy to extend services to the neediest people. But establishing a track record, by its very nature, does not happen as fast as donors would like. The development of trust takes time.

New challenges to supply. Although there may be ways to extend the supply of providers by promoting competition and efficient contracting with NGOs and the private sector, two recent trends in developing countries are making skilled professionals scarcer, or more expensive. First, professionals—doctors, teachers, and engineers—are increasingly part of integrated global markets and recruitment needs to compete at world wage rates. And it is not only to the rich countries that staff are emigrating. Botswana, for example, has been recruiting teachers from other, poorer English-speaking countries. The global market for services is changing rapidly due to international agreements and could lead to new sources of supply. Whether this turns out to help or hinder services in developing countries remains to be seen (see box 6.9).

Second, HIV/AIDS, particularly in Sub-Saharan Africa, has dealt a major blow to the ranks of service providers. More teachers died of AIDS in Malawi in 2000 than entered the profession (see box 1.2). Botswana's search for teachers, originally to meet a burgeoning demand for education, was given greater urgency by the country's AIDS problem. And just as demands for health service workers are increasing, their supply is being cut.

When a factor of production becomes scarcer, its use must be conserved—in one of two ways. First, techniques that are less skill-intensive can be chosen. Distance learning, while not ideal for pedagogical purposes, may need to be explored to save scarce teaching time. Similarly, it may be appropriate to use

---

B O X   6 . 8 *NGOs can be more flexible than government*

One advantage that NGOs may have over the public sector is the freedom from fixed civil service rules or standard operating procedures. In some ways this reduces accountability, but it can avoid unnecessary constraints.

A social worker in a family protection program calls on a family threatened with having a child removed for neglect. She's greeted by the mother, who says "If there is one thing I don't need in my life right now, it's one more social worker telling me what to do. You know what I really need? To get my house cleaned up."

The social worker, who happened to be a highly trained clinical psychologist, responded by saying, "Would you like to start in the kitchen?" While the two women were cleaning, they had a terrific conversation about what was going on in that family. When I told the story at a meeting, I was interrupted by the head of a university clinical psych department who said, "What that therapist did was unprofessional."

Well, all I can say is if we want effective interventions that have transformative effects on people, then we had better redefine what is professional, or allowable in the expenditure of public funds.

(from *Common Purpose* by Schorr, 1997)

In many countries there is no way for publicly employed social workers to violate the opinions of the university professor, but more independent NGOs could do so.

water systems that require less technical inputs for maintenance. Second, some kinds of services that happen to be highly skill-intensive may be reduced. Curative medical services that require trained professionals may be cut back relative to public works or public health education, more intensive in capital and unskilled labor. It is possible that these interventions (low-maintenance water systems, use of village health workers or traditional healers) may always have been under-used. Recent trends may merely have made this misallocation more costly.

Monitoring and performance

All contracts—both compacts and management relationships within provider organizations—need to be monitored with independence and objectivity. With the separation of the policymaker and the provider organization, the policymaker will want to know whether compact provisions are satisfied.

BOX 6.9 *Is the GATS a help or a hindrance?*

For a new agreement that has so far not had much impact on actual policy, the WTO's General Agreement on Trade in Services (GATS) is viewed with a surprising degree of both hope and trepidation. In the current Doha agenda negotiations, some look to the GATS to deliver much-needed reform of services from which the poor will also benefit, while others see it as a threat to regulatory sovereignty and pro-poor policies.

In principle, multilateral negotiations can foster reform in services, as in goods, by eliminating or reducing protective barriers through mutual agreement and by lending credibility to the results achieved through legally binding commitments. The expectation is that more open markets and greater predictability of policy will lead to the more efficient provision of services. That is the rationale for the GATS. We address three questions: How much market-opening has happened so far under the GATS? Does the agreement prevent recourse to the complementary policies needed to ensure that the poor have access to essential services in liberalized markets? Could the GATS process lead to liberalization before other necessary reforms, and how can this be prevented?

The GATS is certainly wide in scope. It applies to virtually all government measures affecting trade in almost all services, including educational, health, and environmental services. Moreover, in recognition of the fact that many services require proximity between consumers and suppliers, trade in services is defined to include not only cross-border supply but also foreign investment and the temporary migration of service consumers and providers. The broad reach of the GATS contrasts with the flexibility of its rules. The generally applicable rules merely require that each country that its trade-affecting measures be transparent and not discriminate among its trading partners. Thus, if a country were to prohibit all foreign supply and make this fact public, then it would have met its general obligations.

The extent of *market openness* guaranteed by a country depends on its sector-specific commitments. These promises to eliminate or limit barriers to foreign supply were mainly the outcome of negotiations—but some were volunteered, particularly in telecommunications. Most existing commitments entailed little liberalization beyond existing market conditions. Many countries committed on tourism, financial, business, and telecommunication services, but relatively few in health, education, and environmental services. Of the 145 WTO member countries, only 43 (12 developing) have made commitments in primary education, 52 (24 developing) in hospital services, and none on water distribution (which was not an explicit part of the original negotiating list of services sectors).

The most serious charge against the GATS is not its meager harvest of liberalization—after all the process has only recently begun—but that it deprives governments of the freedom to pursue pro-poor policies. It is argued that the rules of the agreement threaten public education, health, and environmental services; outlaw universal service obligations and subsidized supply; and undermine effective domestic regulation. These charges do not seem well founded for three reasons. First, services supplied in the exercise of governmental authority are excluded from the scope of the GATS, although the definition—services that are not supplied on a commercial basis or competitively—offers scope for clarification. Second, even in sectors that have been opened to full competition, the agreement does not prevent the pursuit of domestic policy objectives, including through subsidies or the imposition of universal service obligations as long as these do not discriminate against foreign suppliers. Finally, the agreement recognizes the right of members, particularly developing countries, to regulate to meet national policy objectives, and its current rules on domestic regulations are hardly intrusive.

However, the concerns noted above are not so much about what the GATS *is* but what it *may become* after the current (and any future) round of negotiations—which will aim for more liberalizing commitments and new rules in areas such as domestic regulation. Informed debate would undoubtedly help ensure that future GATS rules and commitments reflect broader development concerns and not just the dictates of domestic political economy or external negotiating pressure.

At this stage, however, the main issue is not so much what the GATS forces countries to do or what it prevents them from doing, but that it does not—indeed cannot—ensure the complementary action that is needed to deliver pro-poor liberalization. This raises a legitimate concern: *in a complex area like services, trade negotiations alone could lead to partial or inappropriately sequenced reform*. One possibility—already visible in some cases—is that less emphasis will be placed on introducing competition than on allowing a transfer of ownership of monopolies from national to foreign hands or protecting the position of foreign incumbents. Another is that market opening will be induced in countries that have not developed regulatory frameworks and mechanisms to achieve basic social policy objectives. These flaws could conceivably make the poor worse off. The problem is accentuated by the difficulty in reversing inappropriate policy choices that have been translated into legally binding external commitments.

The danger of adverse outcomes would be substantially reduced if two types of activities receive greater international support. The first is increased policy research and advice within developing countries and outside to identify the elements of successful reform—and to sift the areas where there is little reason to defer market opening from those where there is significant uncertainty and a consequent need for tempered negotiating demands. An even greater need is for enhanced technical and financial assistance to improve the regulatory environment and pro-poor policies in developing countries. The development community is already providing such support, but a stronger link could be established between any market opening negotiated internationally and assistance for the complementary reform needed to ensure successful liberalization.

Competition among providers helps, since the policymaker will not feel locked into a particular provider, obliged to ignore bad news. If the separation between the two is not achieved, an independent regulator or auditor should be assigned the monitoring activities.

Clear and observable provisions make monitoring easier. When the provisions are not so easily observed, the policymaker may want to enlist the help of other kinds of monitors. The health program in Ceará, Brazil (see spotlight), used applicants to the program who had not been selected as informal monitors.

When monitoring is difficult because of the technical nature of the service, self-monitoring by professionals may be necessary. In Bangladesh attendance by staff is much higher in larger facilities due to informal self-monitoring, among other factors.[307] Professional associations can also serve as self-monitors, establishing professional, ethical, and technical standards for medical care providers, teachers, and engineers. But the risk in self-regulation is that professional groups become effective lobbyists for their members.

A third source of monitors is the public. Even if clients are not the active monitors described in chapter 4—that is, they are not purchasers of services or direct participants in service delivery—soliciting information (as private business often does) can be useful in public services. Publicizing the results of scorecards led to a substantial improvement of many services run by the Bangalore Municipal Corporation. This practice was replicated in most states in India.

When day-to-day monitoring to assess performance is not possible, independent monitoring of the performance of services on an occasional basis can still be valuable—by bringing public information to bear on provider behavior. The Public Expenditure Tracking Survey in Uganda (see spotlight on Uganda) is an example. More regular publicity of service characteristics on several dimensions—such as absentee rates, regular delivery of pharmaceuticals, hours of operation for electricity or water—could all mobilize community concern and informal influence.

Evaluation

Generating and disseminating information are powerful ways of improving service delivery. They are also clear public goods and core responsibilities of government. Accurate information can motivate the public, particularly the poor, to demand better services—from providers and from policymakers—and arm them with facts. Knowledge of the real impact of programs helps the policymaker set priorities and design better compacts. Knowledge of the impact of different techniques of service delivery helps the provider organization better fulfill its compact. If the means to better service is the alignment of incentives with outcomes, knowing what those outcomes are and how services contribute to them is central.

Good evaluation is the research necessary to assign causality between program inputs and real outcomes. It should be directed at the full impact of programs—not just the direct outputs of specific projects. But few evaluations have been done well, even though most major donors (including the World Bank) have always made provisions for them. Evaluation, though primarily a responsibility of governments, is an area in which donors can help. It costs a small fraction of the programs examined and a small fraction of the value of the information produced, but it does require some expensive technical inputs. And since other countries will use the results, the international community should defray some of the costs.

There are impediments to collecting such information. Provider organizations often do not want to acknowledge their lack of impact (even if it does not affect their pay directly), but knowing when things are not working is essential for improvements. Further, it is necessary to know not just what works but also why—to replicate the program and increase the scale of coverage.

Provider incentives in eight sizes

Returning to the decision tree of figure 6.2 from the perspective of provider incentives, the decision concerning the difficulty of monitoring is, of course, key. When monitoring is easy—sizes 1, 3, 5, and 7—opportunities for more explicit incentives and the use of contracts should be explored. However, contracting with a private sector is often a bad idea for sizes 5 and 7. Such contracts are a common source of corruption that governments find harder to manage and citizens find harder to detect than if services were provided by government.

When monitoring is difficult—the even-numbered sizes—one goal is to improve the ability to monitor with the methods discussed in this chapter. More competition, more careful measurement of outcomes, the evaluation of the effect of inputs on outcomes, and the provision of incentives to groups of providers such as schools or districts can all help.

The boxes suggest eight sizes appropriate in different circumstances. They also indicate the relative difficulty of carrying them out—the degree of government failure associated with them. Generally speaking, the severity of the government failure increases with the size number. The degree of market failure needed to justify relatively easy policies to carry out is modest, or, equivalently, the highest-priority policies are those with large market failures or

Figure 6.2   Eight sizes fit all

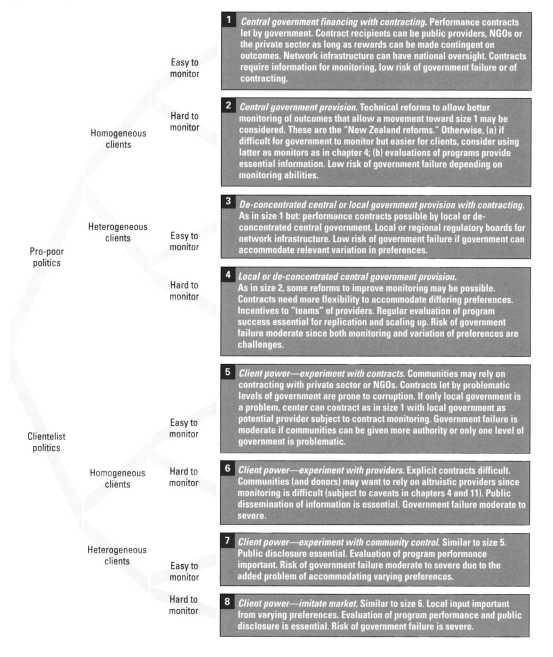

strong redistributive effects. For the hardest cases such as case 8, market failures must be quite costly to justify intervention, given the many legitimate claims on government.

Including government's ability to implement—that is, the degree of government failure to be expected—can lead to a substantial re-ranking of public policies relative to conventional analyses. For social security systems, for example, there is no particular reason on conventional economic grounds for the public sector to send out checks to pensioners. But many governments with well-developed administrative procedures do it quite well, and there is no compelling reason to change—market failures are not terrible but neither is it hard for government to do. Much of the controversy about whether rich countries should emulate New Zealand's reforms surrounds this point. New innovations in contracting with a private sector or with a government agency might improve the functioning of government somewhat. But if government is already doing tasks acceptably, the gains may be small and possibly not worth the disruption caused by the change itself.

When applied to the health sector some standard prescriptions are reinforced by these considerations while others are challenged. The provision of traditional public health services, such as pest control to prevent infectious disease, is relatively easy to carry out. But staffing and maintaining a large network of primary health centers in remote areas is often hard to do, even though the redistribution effects are potentially beneficial. It might be wiser, until government capabilities improve, to try to get poor people to government facilities, even to much maligned hospitals, than get facilities to poor people. Not only would this address a serious market failure, the absence of insurance for expensive care, but it will be easier to implement since working in less remote areas is more consistent with providers' interests and easier to monitor, with a smaller number of larger facilities.[308]

Scaling up, scaling back, and wising up

There is no "right" way to make sure services reach poor people. The appropriate technical interventions—and the institutional structures that generate them—vary enormously. Education was expanded dramatically in Chile by markets and vouchers, in Cuba by a central ministry, and in El Salvador by local school committees. Beyond trial and error, scaling up means watching what you're doing, evaluating whether it works, determining why it works or doesn't, replicating success, and evaluating the replications as well. Sometimes things work for idiosyncratic reasons—a charismatic (and literally irreplaceable) leader or a particular (and unrepeatable) crisis that solidifies support for a politically difficult innovation. So one-time successes may not be replicable. Experimentation, with real learning from the experiments, is the only way to match appropriate policies with each country's circumstances.

Scaling up also means scaling back—abandoning failures unless a good, remediable reason for failure is found. Abandoning failures is harder than it sounds. Simply admitting failure is hard enough, particularly for politicians. But with the severe resource constraints in developing countries—they are poor after all—badly performing programs are simply unaffordable. Where programs are intensive in management (and auditors and managerial talent are scarce) or intensive in trained personnel (and teachers and doctors are scarce), states need to let go of programs that are not working and find alternative ways to achieve better outcomes.

If the political will exists, the key to scaling up is information. Beyond evaluating programs and projects, a continuing focus on making services work for poor people—educated children, better health, reliable water, lighted homes, safer streets—depends on the continuing measurement of progress toward these goals. "What gets measured is what counts." This focus on outcomes helps policymakers choose the best options for serving poor people. It helps the providers know when they are doing a good job. And it helps clients judge the performance of both.

Contracts to improve health services—quickly

Cambodia began experimenting with different forms of contracting to improve health services in 1998. The lesson—thanks to good evaluation—is that contracting can help increase the coverage of some key services in a short time.

More than 25 years of conflict left Cambodia with little health infrastructure. In the late 1990s its health indicators were among the worst in Southeast Asia. Average life expectancy at birth was less than 55 years. Infant mortality was 95 per 1,000 live births. And maternal mortality was 437 per 100,000 live births.[309] The public health care system remained rudimentary: average facility use was 0.35 contacts per person per year, and patients complained of very low quality.

Then in 1998 the government contracted with nongovernmental entities to provide health services in several districts. The contracting increased access to health services—and not at the expense of equity.

Contracting primary health care services (in and out)

Intervention and control areas consisted of randomly selected rural districts, each with 100,000 to 200,000 people.[310] Contractors were chosen through a competitive process based on the quality of their technical proposal and their price. Three approaches were used.

- *Contracting out.* Contractors had full responsibility for the delivery of specified services in the district, directly employed their staff, and had full management control (two districts).

- *Contracting in.* Contractors provided only management support to civil service health staff, and recurrent operating costs were provided by the government through normal government channels (three districts).

- *Control areas.* The usual government provision was retained (four districts).

A budget supplement was provided to contracted-in and control districts.

Performance indicators were measured for all the districts by household, and health facility surveys, which were conducted in 1997 before the experiment. No district had more than 20 percent of its planned health facilities functioning. All had very poor health service coverage. And all were comparable in their socioeconomic status.

Annual per capita recurrent spending by donors and government was higher in the contracted-out districts: $2.80 in the contracted-in districts, $4.50 in contracted-out districts, compared with $2.90 in control districts.[311] These differences are large and represent slightly less than 20 percent of the health expenditures (including private and excluding capital investments from the government) in all of the districts.

Contracting for better results

All districts improved service coverage in a short time. After only 2.5 years of the four-year experiment, all districts had achieved their contractual obligations for most of the evaluation indicators.[312] The use of health services among the poorest half of the populace increased by nearly 30 percentage points in the contracted-out district (figure 1). One possible explanation is that the contracted-out districts did not charge official user fees; they also discouraged health care workers from taking "unofficial" user fees by paying significantly higher salaries to providers than in the other types of districts.

The pattern of increases is similar across a variety of service and coverage indicators (figure 2). The contracted-out districts often outperformed contracted-in districts, which outperformed control districts. But not all indicators were as responsive. The share of deliveries assisted changed by only a small amount in all three districts. And there was no difference between contracted-in and contracted-out districts in the increase in vitamin A coverage. The level of immunization in contracted districts also remained quite modest, peaking at only 40 percent.

Out-of-pocket expenditures on health care services fell dramatically in the contracted-out districts but increased slightly in contracted-in and control districts. The reduction was especially marked among the poor ($35 a year, or 70 percent), indicating better targeting and more efficient transfers of subsidies.

Even though the health ministry encouraged all districts to implement official user fees, only one contracted-in district established a formal user fee system and used the receipts from the system to reward health care workers with monthly performance and punctuality bonuses. That could account for slightly higher spending for this type of district.[313]

There are several possible reasons for these pro-poor outcomes in the contracted districts.

- The regular availability of drugs and qualified staff strengthened service provision at health centers in the villages, where most poor people are concentrated.

- The contracted nongovernmental organizations used a market-based wage and benefits package to attract and retain health care providers.

- A reduction in the private out-of-pocket cost of services and a more predictable and transparent fee structure increased the demand for health care services by the poor.

Figure 1 Percentage of illnesses treated at a health facility for people in the poorest half of the populace

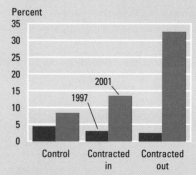

Source: Bhushan, Keller, and Schwartz (2002).

Figure 2   Coverage of selected health indicators between 1997 and 2001 in control and contracted districts of Cambodia

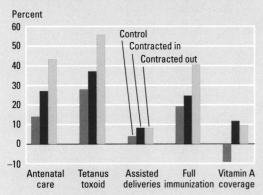

Source: Bhushan (2003).

• The availability of health services in villages reduced travel expenditures to seek health care, and NGOs enforced rules against informal payments by patients.

Agreements on deliverables— and enforceable contracts

Contracting health services to NGOs can expand the coverage for poor people. In Cambodia it took agreements on deliverables and an enforceable contract, which in turn required an independent performance verification system. Once targets for 13 key health indicators were agreed on—for poor people—progress toward achieving them was measured through independent household surveys and spot checks by government staff. Payments were linked to achieving targets, with bonuses for better-than-agreed-on performance.

Improving health services for the poor requires that health workers be adequately compensated and effectively supervised and supported. The NGOs working in contracted-out districts revised the salaries of health care providers, bringing them in line with average salaries in the private sector. In return, the NGOs required the providers to work full time in health facilities and to have no private practice.

In the contracted-in districts, the NGOs supplemented provider salaries with their own funds and, in one district, allocated a larger share of user-fee income. The control districts, left to their own devices, allowed workers to pursue private income-maximizing behavior through unofficial fees and private practice, to the detriment of the public health care services for the poorest of the poor.

Transparent and predictable fee structures are important in improving access to health services. Official user charges were introduced in only one contracted-in district, in consultation with communities, to provide incentives to health workers. To remove ambiguity about charges, a schedule of user fees was prominently displayed in all health facilities. This discouraged private practice and helped bring "under-the-table" payments formally into the system. Out-of-pocket spending on health fell in that district. No user fees were introduced in the other two contracted-in districts, or in the control districts, where out-of-pocket spending did not come down.

Contracting health services to NGOs can be difficult for policymakers to accept. But the Cambodian experience shows that it can be effective and equitable. It helped convince policymakers that the model could be adopted on a larger scale. They are extending contracting to 11 poor and remote districts, where the public provision of services is dismal.

Basic education services

An institutional arrangement for basic education should be judged by its production of high-quality learning, equitably distributed. This requires that children be in school and that they learn. This in turn rests on education systems that create relationships of accountability between citizens, politicians, policymakers, and providers, with clear objectives, adequate resources, capable and motivated providers, progress assessments, and performance-oriented managements.

Successful education systems vary widely. Some systems are centralized, others decentralized. Some have almost exclusively public schools, while others provide public support to private providers. But not just anything goes.

- The politics of schooling—particularly the effectiveness of the voice of poor people—determines both the school system's objectives and the public resources that go to education.
- The compact between policymakers and providers of schooling needs to balance the autonomy of schools and teachers with performance assessment.
- Schools (and school systems) must be enabled to manage for performance—and, particularly, to find effective ways to train and motivate teachers.
- Direct parent and community participation in schools, demand-side inducements to expand enrollments, and choice—if correctly designed—can be valuable parts of an overall plan for school improvement.

Common problems of service provision

Education systems face the common problems of service provision outlined in chapter 1—unaffordable access, dysfunctional schools, low technical quality, low client responsiveness, and stagnant productivity. But not all countries face the same problems. In many of the poorest countries there are enormous deficits in affordable access. Poor people have less access, lower attainment, and lower quality than those better off. In many countries public sector provision is close to dysfunctional and rife with corruption. The technical quality of instruction and learning outcomes are shockingly low, especially among poor people. And even the most advanced economies struggle to make education systems more productive.

Shortfalls in universal primary completion—a combined result of children who never enroll, children who do not progress, and children who drop out—reflect the failures in the system. In Madagascar only 52 percent of 15- to 19-year-olds in the poorest 20 percent of the population had ever enrolled in school, and only 4 percent completed even grade 5 (figure 7.1). In Brazil 89 percent of poor adolescents enrolled in grade 1, but only 30 percent completed grade 5 because of high dropout and repetition rates. In Turkey high retention through primary school, followed by a sharp drop in progress to the next level, suggests that systemic and institutional solutions are required to increase achievement. In Bangladesh only 60 percent of poor adolescents have completed grade 1, and only 36 percent have completed grade 5.

Unaffordable access

Despite at least 55 years of acknowledgment that universal literacy is the heart of development, and despite repeated rhetorical commitments to universal enrollment, even the

Figure 7.1   Poor children: less likely to start school, more likely to drop out
15- to 19-year-olds who have completed each grade

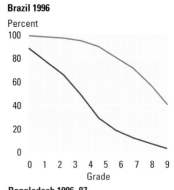

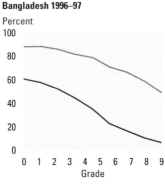

Source: Analysis of Demographic and Health Survey data.

modest goal of universal primary school completion has not been realized. Some countries have made huge strides—average completion rates in Brazil expanded from less than 50 percent in 1990 to more than 70 percent in 2000. But if countries continue at only their recent rate of progress, universal primary completion would come only after 2020 in the Middle East and North Africa, after 2030 in South Asia, and not in the foreseeable future in Sub-Saharan Africa.

In the very poorest countries the attainment deficit is spread across the population, but in most it is concentrated among children from poor households. In countries with very low attainment, like Mali, most of the population is rural, and there are substantial deficits in primary completion even among relatively wealthier and urban families. In India the rural poor (poorest 50 percent) accounted for 72 percent of the deficit in completion of grade 5 among 15- to 19-year-olds, and completion is higher among boys than girls. In the Philippines the deficit is much lower, concentrated among the rural poor and higher among boys than girls.

Dysfunctional schools

Schooling completions and learning outcomes may fall short because providers are dysfunctional. While most teachers try conscientiously to do their jobs, one recent survey found a third of all teachers in Uttar Pradesh, India, absent. Cases of malfeasance by teachers are distressingly present in many settings: teachers show up drunk, are physically abusive, or simply do nothing. This is not "low-quality" teaching—this is not teaching at all.[314]

Low technical quality

The quality of instruction can also be low because of low capability, weak motivation, and a lack of complementary inputs. In very-low-income settings learning outcomes can be dismal. The 1994 Tanzania Primary School Leavers Examination suggested that the vast majority of students had learned almost *nothing* that was tested in their seven years of schooling—more than four-fifths scored less than 13 percent correct in language or mathematics.[315] In

Bangladesh 30 percent of students who completed grade 5 were not minimally competent in reading; 70 percent were not minimally competent in writing.[316]

Evidence on learning outcomes is disappointing even in middle-income countries. For instance, in the recent Programme for International Student Assessment of the achievement of 15-year-olds in school, only 5 percent of Brazilian students reached the Organisation for Economic Co-operation and Development (OECD) median in mathematical literacy (figure 7.2). Fifty-six percent of Brazilian students were at level 1 (of 5) in reading literacy, compared with 18 percent for students in OECD countries. Only 4 percent reached proficiency levels of 4 or 5, compared with 31 percent for OECD students.[317] This is not to single out Brazil for poor performance: Brazil is widely recognized for its advances, and its willingness to participate in the study and its courage in releasing the results demonstrate a strong commitment to education outcomes (other countries have participated in examinations and then refused to disclose the results). In addition, in an earlier comparison of 11 Latin American countries Brazil was tied with Argentina for second place in the mathematics performance of 4th graders.

Low client responsiveness

When communities are not involved in establishing, supporting, or overseeing a school, the school is often seen as something alien. Villagers refer to "the government's" school, not "our" school. In *Voices of the Poor* people often complain of absent or abusive teachers and demands for illegal fees to get their children into school or to influence examination results.[318] A study of schooling in rural Nigeria found that villagers often stopped expecting anything from government schools, shouldering the burden themselves.[319]

Stagnant productivity

Creating and maintaining an institutional environment that promotes higher productivity and more learning is not easy. A recent set of studies documented that spending per pupil in real terms has increased by 50 percent or more, often two-

or threefold, in nearly all OECD and East Asian countries. Yet in none of these countries have test scores improved commensurately.[320] The obvious implication of these two facts is that measured learning achievement per dollar spent has fallen dramatically in every country examined.

For higher-quality systems, strengthen the relationships of accountability

Despite enormous differences in attainment, equity, and learning across countries, the features of school systems are strikingly similar. Public production is almost always the dominant—if not exclusive—means of government support of education. Whether in Argentina, Egypt, India, Indonesia, Paraguay, or Tanzania, public systems display age-grade organization of classrooms, replication of social structures and inequalities, and similar ways of training, hiring, compensating, and promoting teachers. Despite these surface similarities, there are widely different outcomes. Both Nigeria and Singapore retain many of the organizational elements of British education. Yet on one international achievement test in the 1980s Nigeria was among the worst performers while Singapore is frequently among the best.

That public provision has often failed to create universally available and effective schooling does not imply that the solution is a radically different approach (complete decentralization, total control by parent groups, generalized choice) or a narrow focus on proximate determinants (more textbooks, more teacher training). Universal and quality education can come from very centralized systems (France, Japan) or from very decentralized systems with considerable local accountability and flexibility (United States). Many countries have little private schooling, and some a great deal (Holland). Classroom practice is what matters. If the underlying causes of failure are not addressed, all these approaches can fail.

Chapters 3 through 6 developed a framework for analyzing service provision, looking at four relationships of accountability. In education, these are:

Figure 7.2   Fifteen-year-olds in Brazil and Mexico perform substantially worse on standardized tests than students in OECD countries

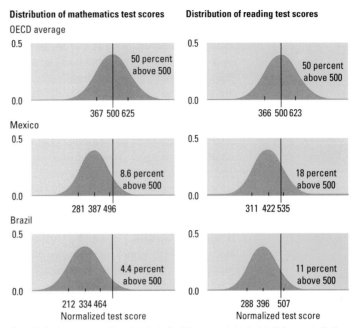

Note: Distributions are approximated on the basis of the mean and standard deviation reported in the original source.
Source: OECD (2001).

- *Voice,* or how well citizens can hold the state—politicians and policymakers—accountable for performance in discharging its responsibility for education.
- *Compacts,* or how well and how clearly the responsibilities and objectives of public engagement are communicated to the public and to private organizations that provide services (Ministries of Education, school districts).
- *Management,* or the actions that create effective frontline providers (teachers, administrators) within organizations.
- *Client power,* or how well citizens, as clients, can increase the accountability of schools and school systems.

Effective solutions are likely to be mixtures of voice, choice, direct participation, and organizational command and control, with functional responsibilities distributed among central, regional, local, and school administrations. The pieces have to fit together as a *system.* More scope for parental choice without greater information about schooling outputs will not necessarily lead to better results. Information systems that produce data on inputs but do not change the capabilities or incentives of frontline providers cannot improve quality. Schools and teachers cannot be made more accountable for results without also receiving sufficient autonomy and resources and the opportunities to build capabilities. Conversely, schools cannot be given autonomy unless they are given clear objectives and regular assessments of progress.

What successful education systems share is a working structure of accountability: clear objectives, adequate resources, and capable and motivated providers. This Report focuses on institutional reforms to achieve that system of accountability—not on the proximate determinants of success, such as curriculum design, pedagogical methods, textbooks, teacher training, school construction, or new information technologies. Institutional reforms will achieve desired outcomes by affecting proximate determinants—and proximate determinants that produce good education are the outcome of well-structured and well-functioning systems. But efforts to improve proximate determinants through internal management initiatives have usually failed. Why? Not because of a lack of knowledge of what to do. But because of lack of the sustained bureaucratic, market, parental, and political pressure needed to make things work.

The disappointing experience with teacher training shows the limit of a focus on proximate determinants (box 7.1). When teachers are not consulted in training design—often the case—poor implementation is the result. Training may not be integrated into the system, as when teachers are trained in methods inconsistent with public examinations and so are reluctant to adopt them. Teachers often have little incentive besides professional pride to adopt new methods.

If the underlying problems are not solved neither bureaucracy nor market will work well. Increasing client power, by creating mechanisms for communities and parents to improve their local school, is important. But this short-route accountability is not enough. Improving services also requires stronger mechanisms of long-route accountability—accountability of politicians and policymakers for education and improved proficiency in public administration with accountability of the education bureaucracy for outcomes. There is no quick fix in an area as complex and extensive as schooling, only the hard slog of gradual improvement through *strategic incrementalism,* which links current operational actions with long-run institutional strategies and goals.

Citizens and clients, politicians and policymakers: voice

In administration of all schools, it must be kept in mind, what is to be done is not for the sake of the pupils, but for the sake of the country.

—Mori Anori, Japanese Minister
of Education 1886–89

Politics plays a key role in establishing objectives for the education system—concerning both distribution and quality—and in mobilizing resources. The reason is that schooling, especially at the basic level, has become an important element in a child's socialization.

Those who control the state use schooling to promote beliefs they consider desirable. Nearly everywhere this means that schools promote a sense of national identity, a national language, and loyalty to the nation-state—in competition with more local or ethnic affiliations—and, in more extreme cases, a specific political indoctrination. Modern states—from Third Republic France

---

BOX 7.1 *The dismal state of teacher training in Pakistan circa 1990*

"Teacher training in this province is a mockery. We should close down the teacher training institutes and stop this nonsense. I have been teaching in a B.A./B.Ed. program for many years and see no signs that I have any impact on the students I teach."

—A university education instructor quoted in Warwick and Reimers (1995).

"Most inmates of this system [two teacher training institutes] have no respect for themselves, hence they have no respect for others. The teachers think the students are cheats, the students think the teachers have shattered their ideals. Most of them are disillusioned. They have no hopes, no aims, no ambitions. They are living from day to day, watching impersonally as the system crumbles around them."

—Nauman (1990).

A national survey of Pakistan's primary schools suggests that these anecdotal accounts are only too true. Survey data on teaching practices "provide no basis for statements that ... teacher training makes a substantial difference to how teachers teach." A 1998 study of teacher training suggests that "staff and faculty are professionally untrained, political interference is common, resources and facilities are poor and badly utilized, motivation and expectations are low and there is no system of accreditation to enforce standards." Embedded in an education system that was fundamentally unaccountable and lacked any outcome orientation, teacher training reflected worst practice.

Sources: Warwick and Reimers (1995); Kizilbash (1998), p. 45.

to Ataturk's Turkey—have also used public schools to supplant or suppress religious instruction.[321] Authoritarian states have used schooling to disseminate a single acceptable ideology—for example, Soeharto's promotion of the five principles of *pancasila*[322] in Indonesia. These examples are not the exception but the rule: countries around the world explicitly use schooling to inculcate ideas about the proper organization of society.

Voice and the objectives of schooling

Schooling has become a battleground for political conflicts. Different groups want different—often contradictory—things from schooling. Poor parents see education as an opportunity for their children to lead better lives, but they may also want education to reinforce traditional values. Elites may want universal education but often promote public spending on higher education for the benefit of their own children. Urban and business coalitions may favor more education because it increases the productivity of their workers, or industrialists may quietly oppose "too much" education because it makes workers restive. One recent study of owners and managers of modern factories in Northeast Brazil that were moving to cutting-edge business practices revealed a disturbing lack of support for expanding education. Many felt that a primary education (eight years) was helpful, but more than that was "dangerous" because it created workers who were less docile. Many commented that "too much education is a bad thing." (Tendler 2003). Politicians may want to deliver on promises of universal schooling while also using the education system to provide patronage jobs (the example of Pakistan, in box 5.3, is not unique). Teachers and their unions want high-quality universal education but also higher wages.

To get what you want, you need to know what you want. But what a society wants from its schools is not simple and cannot be decided by experts alone. A recent study of attempts to improve the quantity and quality of basic education in an Asian country in the 1990s concluded that even many pedagogically and internally sound reforms did not have a sustained impact on teaching practice or student learning. Why?

Because the educational system had no coherent, consensual focus: "For reforms to stick, there first needs to be a vision for the future with agreed long-term objectives derived from stakeholders: informed dialogue with parents, employers, religious leaders, school leavers, and others. The absence of such a shared long-term quality-of-services strategy that focused scarce resources on quality rather than quantity has left the education sector open to the imposition of ideas from outside: from donors, with agendas of questionable value to the country's situation, or from graduates returning with overseas degrees and ill-informed, though well-intentioned, agendas of their own."[323]

Democracy is not necessary for excellent schools. The huge variation in commitment to schooling across the states of India is enough to suggest that electoral democracy is also not sufficient for voice to lead to universal education (see spotlight on Kerala and Uttar Pradesh). But the absence of democracy or other means of effective citizen voice has a huge downside. While one-party states occasionally produce good results (see spotlight on Costa Rica and Cuba), many authoritarian regimes have no interest in expanding education or improving its quality. There are two risks: the system is effective but its goals are completely set by politicians and policymakers, or the system is ineffective because politicians and policymakers have goals other than effective provision of services. The results: too few resources are allocated to education, too few of those resources reach poor people, and resources are allocated ineffectively (because providers are more influential than citizens).

As more countries move to more democratic modes of choosing leaders, citizen control over the structure and content of curricula gains prominence. Having a common negotiated vision of the objectives of public support for schooling makes it easier to move to the other stages of improving the quality of schooling—mobilizing and allocating resources, communicating objectives to providers, and delegating responsibility and autonomy to schools. Without a clear vision of goals, reform is reduced to a focus on inputs and process alone.

The greater the demand for education, the sharper the vision. In Malawi, Uganda, and most recently Kenya, a commitment to universal education was a popular stance—although a difficult commitment to match with resources (see spotlight on Uganda).

Adequate resources, adequately distributed

To achieve educational goals politicians and policymakers—either autonomously or through the pressure of citizen voice—must provide adequate resources. To learn effectively, children need affordable access to infrastructure, inputs, and instruction—far from the case in many countries. A recent study of financing the global Education for All initiative compared successful and less successful countries along three dimensions:

- Revenue mobilization for primary education (overall taxation rates, the fraction of spending on schooling, the fraction of that spent on primary schooling).
- Unit cost of a year of effective schooling (teacher salaries and class size).
- Internal efficiency (years of schooling provided per primary school completer).

Even with adequate fiscal effort, reasonable costs, and internal efficiency, many countries do not generate enough resources to achieve universal completion. For these countries there is a compelling case for additional international assistance (see box 2.3).

But in many cases the resources are simply not used effectively. They are allocated to the wrong mix of inputs. Too great a share goes to higher levels of education. Or systems are inefficient in translating resources into outputs. A common problem is that teacher salaries, even at very low wages, crowd out all other inputs. A recent study found that 44 of 55 countries examined allocated more than 70 percent and half (23) allocated more than 80 percent of spending to salaries. Such levels of spending often imply either inadequate supplies to other inputs or formal or informal levies on parents. Empirical studies also show that increases in teacher salaries have little or no association with learning outcomes (discussed further below). Many studies estimate the impact of selected classroom instructional materials or school facilities to be some 10 times that of teacher salaries (this is not to say that simple "equipment-based" approaches will succeed). Another common problem is devoting resources to reduce average class sizes, which often results in inefficiently small classes—boosting unit costs and limiting access.

Public resources are politically distributed, so the effective distribution of resources *is* an issue of voice. A review of the empirical evidence suggests that the common pattern of too few resources to high-productivity inputs is so ubiquitous—figure 7.3 gives just two of many possible examples—that it is likely generated by a political economy that fails to adequately incorporate the voice of poor people. Changing this distribution of resources requires more than a technocratic adjustment—as Brazil has shown by its reforms in the 1990s.

Because poor people are almost always the last enrolled, additional spending that expands access is more favorable to poorer households than existing spending. A study in India found that even though educational expenditures on average were not more pro-poor than a uniform transfer would be, the poor benefited more than proportionately at the margin when enrollments in primary education expanded (since the better-off were already in school).[324] So education expenditures that expand access are better targeted to poor people than resources that exclusively raise quality.

But the quality-quantity tradeoff is not a simple choice between creating additional school places or improving instruction. A major problem for poor children in nearly

Figure 7.3   Increases in test scores per dollar spent on different inputs

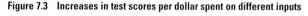

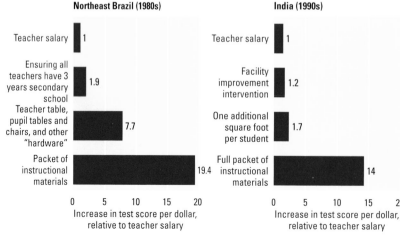

Source: Pritchett and Filmer (1999).

Table 7.1 In Madagascar, at higher levels of education unit costs are much higher and participation of the poor much lower

	Ratio of cost of a year of higher education to the cost of a year of primary school	Cumulative public spending on graduates of each level (percent of GDP)	Share of poorest 40 percent in those who complete each level (percent)	Share of poorest 40 percent in those who reach each level (percent)
No schooling	0	0	37.6	57.8
Primary (grades 1–5)	1	0.4	7.3	33.7
Lower secondary (grades 6–9)	2.75	1.25	0.5	3.1
Upper secondary (3 years)	5.5	2.56	*	*
Higher (4 years)	19.6	8.84	*	*

* indistinguishable from zero.
Sources: World Bank (2001c) and analysis of Madagascar Demographic and Health Survey.

every environment is that they drop out of school with greater frequency, in part because the quality of the schooling they receive is so low. So quality improvements need to accompany quantity improvements.

Spending on primary schooling is mildly progressive, but that on higher levels of education is not. With children from the poorest households unlikely to reach higher levels of schooling, and with greater per student spending at higher levels than at lower, children from richer households capture the bulk of educational spending. In Madagascar a single year of higher education costs 20 times that of primary schooling—and only 3 percent of children completing lower secondary school are from the poorest 40 percent of households (table 7.1). Relative cost alone is not the issue. It is whether funding across levels is equitable and efficient—or driven exclusively by elite politics.

The political conditions required for adequate budget allocations for education are not obvious. Simple answers like "democracy" are attractive—but just not true. India, democratic since independence, has wealth gaps in education attainment larger than any other country with comparable data. At least one empirical study suggests that nondemocratic countries spend more on education.[325] But there is a risk that these governments care not about the quality of education but about using schools for religious, secular, or national indoctrination. In countries with democratic elections, schooling opportunities can be limited and education resources devoted to patronage and clientelism if voice is weak and control rests with a narrow elite. Targeting resources to the desti-

tute and disadvantaged has political dangers as well. Systems that focus mainly on poor citizens, leaving the middle classes no stake, tend to be financially less sustainable and to experience less pressure for accountability—and so tend to be inefficient and unconcerned with quality.

Policymakers and organizational providers: compacts

I do not care that teachers are offended by it. I am less interested in the teacher's method of teaching than in the result she achieves. . . . There should be a test at the end to see whether the results are being achieved. . . . Let us who represent the community say here and now there should be a [test] no matter who may oppose it. . . . If we want to see that a certain standard is reached and we are paying the money we have the right to see that something is secured for that money.

Eamon de Valera, Irish Prime Minister, 1941[326]

The line separating the state as education policymaker (setting the rules of the game) and as major organizational provider (running the school system) is typically blurred. The minister of education frequently wears both hats. Often there is no interest in measuring results, so there is no way of making the public provider accountable for results.

Clarifying objectives and the roles of policymakers and providers is a first step. Without specifying desired outputs and outcomes there is no way to say whether resources are sufficient (sufficient to do what?) or used effectively (relative to what goal?). Vague oversight and vague goals reduce management to compliance with formal rules for inputs and processes. The resulting lack of clarity often results in "mission drift" and distracting struggles within the ministry of education. Lacking a clear mission, the education ministry is often accused of being captured by a teachers' union rather than representing the collective interest in schooling.

The Irish Prime Minister's insistence on testing is a common reaction to the perceived failure of schools: a temptation to define the output of the school system exclusively as test scores and then to hold schools accountable for those scores. But accountability too narrowly measured distorts the education system. Only what gets measured gets done. The strict primary completion examination brought in so confidently by the Irish government in the 1940s was gone by the 1960s, in large part because of these concerns.

The compact between policymakers and organizational providers should create an environment in which all schools have the means and motivation to provide high-quality learning. Whether there is public production or government funding of a range of providers, the compact should focus on outputs and outcomes. This requires a means of assessing a school's contribution to the collective objectives of education, and creating an environment for organizations to innovate and bring those innovations to scale—school autonomy with accountability.

The use and abuse of accountability

Creating accountability in schooling is difficult. Schooling is discretionary and transaction-intensive. It has multiple outputs that differ in measurability and in the difficulty of attribution. And it involves a complex—and not well understood—relationship between inputs and outputs. High-performance schooling conveys skills, attitudes, and values. Some steps in this process can be reduced to a detailed script. And some aspects of instruction can be replaced by technology. But face-to-face interaction and flexibility are crucial to high-quality instruction. Instructors need to be capable of exercising discretion—in assessing student mastery, providing feedback, and tailoring the instructional mode to the student and subject matter. This classroom behavior is extremely difficult to monitor.

Schooling has multiple outputs—some easily assessed, others not. Assessing mastery of simple skills through standardized testing is fairly straightforward. But it is difficult to assess how well schooling has conveyed a conceptual mastery that allows application to real-world problems. It is still more difficult to assess how well schooling has encouraged creativity. And it is even more difficult to assess how well schooling has conveyed values. Assessing success is further complicated because different actors assign different values to different objectives.

Designing an accountability system is difficult because it is difficult to attribute specific outcomes—or even outputs—to specific actors. If a 15-year-old has mastered

Table 7.2   Schools account for only a small part of variance in student learning outcomes (percent)

	Share of total variance across students			
	I **Due to differences in student performance within schools**	**II** **Due to differences across schools**	**III** **Fraction of total variation attributable to student background differences across schools**	**IV** **Share of total variation in student test performance that is (a) school specific and (b) not attributable to student background differences across schools (II minus III)**
Brazil	55	45	25	20
Russian Federation	63	37	17	20
Czech Republic	48	52	4	18
Korea, Rep. of	62	38	14	24
Mexico	46	54	32	22
Developed country average	66	34	20	14

Source: OECD (2001), Annex B1, table 2.4.

algebraic concepts, who deserves credit and in what proportion? The parents' genes? The child's nutrition? The parents' motivation and efforts? The child's peers? The child's primary school math teachers? Another teacher who motivated the child to do well in all subjects? The child's current algebra teacher?

Nearly all empirical studies of measured learning achievement agree that home background accounts for most of the explainable variation in learning outcomes, especially in primary grades. The same studies disagree widely about how much can be attributed to a child's school. The recent Programme for International Student Assessment study found wide variation in differences in student performance within or between schools (table 7.2). Half or more of the variation in performance across schools was due to variation in students' socioeconomic status, not to factors under school control. In poorer countries the effect of schools is larger—and that of parental background smaller. But, in general, identifying the school's value added is not simple.

Even for outputs easier to specify and measure, not much is known about how inputs affect them. Economists summarize this relationship under the metaphor of a "production function." Little is known about this function because instruction involves human beings—teachers and students—in all their complexity. For instance, there is ongoing, vigorous debate about the relevance of class size for student test scores. Some assert that class size is irrelevant, or nearly so. Some assert that reductions in class size have such a salutary impact on performance that they are a cost-effective means of improving performance.[327] After more than a century of widespread use of classroom instruction, intelligent, well-meaning, and methodologically sophisticated researchers are still debating such a seemingly simple issue. That shows how truly complex the research questions are—the results will vary across time, content, and context.

Assessment systems

National assessment systems are essential for monitoring educational achievement. But performance measurement is as complex as the many goals societies have for their schools. Performance measurement is *not* an attempt to reduce the output of schooling to the ability of students to answer questions on standardized examinations. The dangers of test-based school accountability have been debated for at least 140 years (box 7.2). You get what you pay for. But there are also dangers in too little attention to performance. It is important to distinguish among the three types of assessment: sample-based assessments to track performance over time, "gatekeeper" examinations that are high stakes for students, and assessments of school performance.

Tracking progress. One way to strengthen the compact between policymakers and education providers is to develop measurement and reporting systems that allow investigation of value for money. Standardized examinations are a relatively inexpensive device for monitoring progress and effectiveness. But few education systems in the developing world have disaggregated the cost of running a school, and even fewer know how that cost is associated with learning. So there is almost no reporting based on such measurements. The lack of information leads to an inability to act accordingly.

When the data are revealed, they can be surprising. One study that generated data relating expenditures and learning at the

---

BOX 7.2 *Test-based accountability—nothing new under the sun*

Test-based school accountability might seem like the latest thing. It isn't. British legislation for school funding in 1862 included a system of "payments for results." In addition to a base grant (based on number of children and attendance), schools received a grant for each student who passed a series of tests given by school inspectors in reading, writing, and arithmetic.

Proponents of the testing argued that performance-based transfers were only common sense since public money was involved. As one parliamentary proponent reasoned: paying for performance will either be cheap (because few schools meet the standard) or expensive (because many students have high performance)—but it will not be both expensive and ineffective. Educational historians claim that the pay-ments provided teachers (who at the time had little training) with clear indications of what was valued and tangible awards for achievement.

Opponents raised the same arguments made today. Teachers will "teach to the test" and ignore subjects not covered by the test (such as history and geography). Test-based accountability will lead to teaching methods that emphasize rote memorization and cramming. One educator argued that "payment for results" would "be remembered with shame."

This particular system of "payment for results" was abolished in 1890. But the debate continues today.

Sources: Based on Bowen (1981) and Good and Teller (1969).

Figure 7.4   School success depends on more than spending per student
Primary school pass rate in Mauritania

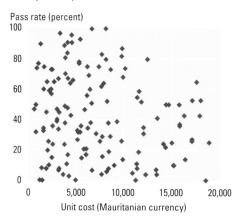

Source: Mingat (2003).

school level in Africa found little connection—Mauritanian schools with similar spending had pass rates of less than 5 percent and more than 95 percent (figure 7.4).

Needed for active management are data—on school costs, on the characteristics of students, and on school performance on cognitive achievement tests. Once implemented, these sample-based systems can be gradually scaled up to provide more census-like measurements.

Gatekeeper examinations.   In most countries examinations are seen as a fair way of allocating limited school places. One study suggests that the impact on student performance of centralized curriculum-based examinations is as large as that associated with differences in parental education or with substantially more formal education for teachers (figure 7.5). Since centralized examinations make relevant information widely available, they can be useful for generating accountability.

The impact of public examinations on the incentives of various actors points to systemic considerations. For instance, teacher training programs often attempt to instill pedagogical techniques that promote higher-order thinking skills. But when gatekeeper public examinations assess only rote memorization, teachers frequently revert to similar methods. And if public examinations have a major impact on students' life

chances, parents will exert pressure on the school system for better examination results. Where public examinations are limited and educationally inadequate, perverse pressures can worsen true educational quality in the interests of better examination scores.

School-based accountability for examination results.   School accountability is controversial—with good reason. There is empirical evidence that accountability mechanisms based on examination results lead to "teaching to the test" and to attempts to manipulate results. Evidence from locations as diverse as rural Kenya (see chapter 11 and box 7.5 later in this chapter) and urban Chicago shows that accountability raised examination scores—but also that teachers manipulated the students taking the exam, and taught to the test.

But teaching to the test is a criticism only if the test is not a reliable assessment of the skills that are the objective of public support for schooling—or if the tests divert teachers from more productive activities, such as teaching higher-order thinking. There is a tradeoff between what the test costs (in design, testing, and scoring) and how well it captures desired schooling output. Tests in some circumstances could divert teachers from more productive to less productive activities, such as "drills." But in many cases performance is so weak that even "less productive" but learning-oriented activities would be an improvement.

Figure 7.5   Centralized exams have a strong impact on student performance

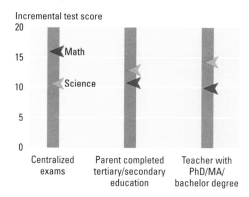

Source: Wößmann (2003).

There are three important technical design issues with school-based accountability. First, the characteristics of students, their peers, and their families are far and away the largest determinants of variation in performance. Any attempt to judge schools on their *level* of performance will therefore be judging the socioeconomic composition of the school—a "good" school might simply have wealthier students. This is true on average. Some schools serving poorer populations perform well or even very well (figure 7.6). And some schools with wealthier students are mediocre.

To focus on school value added rather than differences based on school populations, scores can be empirically adjusted for the composition of the student body (box 7.3). Or assessments can measure *changes* in student performance (which assumes that socioeconomic composition is roughly constant). Or a threshold can be set that all schools—whatever their student composition—are expected to achieve.

A second design issue in school-based accountability is statistical sampling. In many schools the number of students is small enough to result in considerable variability. That means that even schools with strong improvements over time will have years when scores are lower than in previous years—simply because of the mix and number of students. It also means that a program of rewards or punishments for performance would disproportionately reward and punish small schools relative to large schools. The third design issue is whether to reward good performance or intervene in bad performance—or both.

School autonomy

Accountability and autonomy are twins. Traditional public sector bureaucracies have little autonomy because accountability is linked to rules and procedures, which allows for little discretion. The heads of individual schools are often bound by process requirements and so have little autonomy to actively manage their schools—to define a mission, choose instructional staff, innovate, or encourage performance. Granting greater autonomy requires new forms of accountability based on outputs and out-

comes. The roles of the ministry of education can be unbundled so as to separate education policy from the operation of schools. A more explicit compact relationship can be made with organizational providers, perhaps even with multiple providers within the same jurisdiction. This structure can give clearer guidance on desired outputs and outcomes, freeing school heads and teachers to pursue defined goals.

Nicaragua created autonomous public schools guided by a school directive council comprising the school head, elected teachers, parents, and students. The school retained revenue from students, and the council could make decisions about personnel, finance, and pedagogy. The average school autonomy reported by these schools was between that reported by traditional public schools (very little) and private schools (almost complete). The degree of self-reported school autonomy was positively correlated with student performance on test scores at the primary level (though not at the secondary)—but autonomy on paper was not. In a study in Chile very little of the variation (less than 1 percent) in three measures of self-reported autonomy of teachers was *between* the four types of schools—public, private voucher, private paid, and Catholic voucher. More of the variation was between schools of the same

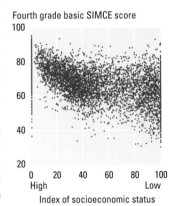

Figure 7.6 In Chile, good schools service students from every level of socioeconomic status

Fourth grade basic SIMCE score

Index of socioeconomic status

Note: The SIMCE is a standardized test in Chile.
Source: Mizala and Romaguera (2000).

B O X 7 . 3 *School-based performance awards in Chile*

Since 1996 Chile has had an award for "top-performing" schools in each region. Ninety percent of the award goes directly to teachers (in proportion to their hours of employment), and 10 percent is allocated to the schools. The awards are given every two years.

Schools are divided into comparison groups within each region of the country based on location (rural, urban), education level (primary only, secondary with primary), and socioeconomic status of parents (according to information collected as part of the examination and an official "index of vulnerability"). In 2000–01 this classification produced 104 comparison groups. In this way the performance of poor rural schools is not compared head-to-head with that of richer urban schools. Analysis suggests that this procedure diminishes the

correlation between socioeconomic status and awards.

Next, an index of school performance is calculated based on standardized tests in Spanish and mathematics in grades 4, 8, and 10. The index is weighted for average test level (37 percent) and improvement in test scores (28 percent) and includes other criteria such as "equality of opportunity" (22 percent)—based on student retention and no "discriminatory practices"—and "initiative" (6 percent)—based on regular development of group pedagogical activities.

The program has been through three rounds of selection, with 2,520 schools having received awards once, 1,084 schools twice, and 360 schools in all three rounds.

Source: Mizala and Romaguera (2002).

BOX 7.4 *Two large-scale cross-national assessments of learning*

The Third International Mathematics and Science Study (TIMSS) created a data set on student performance and characteristics and on institutional characteristics of the schooling system such as use of centralized examinations and central, local, and school decisionmaking responsibilities. Analysis of the performance of more than 266,000 students from some 6,000 schools in 39 (mostly OECD) countries yielded the following conclusions:

- Money cannot buy quality in present schooling systems.
- Incentives are the key to success.
- Schools should be allowed to decide autonomously on operational tasks.
- Schools must be made accountable.
- Teachers' incentives have to focus on improving student performance.
- Competition between schools creates incentives for improving performance.

A second study, the OECD Programme for International Student Assessment, assessed "young people's capacity to use their knowledge and skills in order to meet real-life challenges, rather than merely looking at how well they mastered a specific school curriculum." The study collected per-formance data on 265,000 students in 32 (mostly OECD) countries along with information from students and principals about themselves and schools. The conclusions for what schools can do to make a difference were:

- Students' reported use of school resources was more closely associated with performance than principals' reports of resource deficiencies.
- The ratio of students to teachers matters where it is high, while in the typical range there is a much weaker association with performance.
- Three factors of school policy are associated with better student performance: school autonomy, teacher morale and commitment, and other teacher factors such as expectations.
- Three classroom practices reported by students show a positive association with performance: the extent to which teachers emphasize performance, teacher-student relations, and the disciplinary climate of the classroom.
- Successful students are more likely to do homework.

Sources: Wößmann (2003) and OECD (2001).

---

type (between 15 and 18 percent), and most was between teachers in the same school.[328]

Teacher autonomy in classroom tasks consistently emerges as a determinant of success (box 7.4). The principles developed in chapter 6 are apt: discretion and decisionmaking power need to be delegated to those with the relevant information and professional skills. Centralized control of teacher assignment and assessment can cause bureaucratic paralysis. But making schools autonomous in curriculum design, examinations, assessment, and finance can lead to excessive variability across schools.

Innovating, evaluating, and scaling up

The goal of school autonomy and accountability is to create a system in which organizational providers have strong, sustained incentives to improve outputs. The problem is not a lack of innovation—there is a continual stream of new modes of teacher training, new teaching methods, new instructional inputs, new use of the latest technology. The problem is that there is too little systematic learning from innovation and too little replication of proven innovations.

The contrasting use of rigorous evaluations in health and education is striking. In most developed countries no drug can be used until it is proven safe and effective, and the standard of proof is the randomized double-blind clinical trial. But in schooling, instructional practices for hundreds of millions of children can be changed because a new technology appears promising. Or because a group of experts thinks so. Or because the practice has been tried in a pilot program (and subject to "Hawthorne" effects, the nonreplicable impacts that occur simply as a result of the increased attention from any innovation). Or because it has been shown to be statistically correlated with success, subject to all the dangers of improperly inferring causation. There is strikingly little use of randomized controlled experiments as a routine management practice—despite its eminent feasibility for many classroom practices (box 7.5).

A recent example of evaluating a schooling innovation illustrates the power of flexibility in design—and the power of evaluation. A remedial education program, established as a collaboration between the government and a nongovernmental organization (NGO) in two cities in India (Mumbai and Vadodara), hired local women to teach catch-up classes for students who were falling behind. The program was inexpensive—$5 a child a year. A rigorous evaluation based on the randomized design of the program found it very effective at boosting learning, especially among poorer children. The evaluation showed that, at the margin, extending the program would be about five times more cost-effective than hiring new teachers.[329] The program is implemented now in 20 Indian cities, reaching tens of thousand of children.

But "there is a particular irony to education reform . . . [as] pockets of good education practice . . . can be found almost anywhere, signifying that good education is not the result of arcane knowledge. Yet the rate of uptake of effective practices is depressingly

BOX 7.5 *Randomized experiments in Busia district, Kenya*

Since 1996 a group of researchers has been working with a Dutch nonprofit (International Christelijk Steunfonds) supporting schools in rural Kenya to estimate the impact of various interventions. Through random selection some schools were chosen to implement the interventions first, with the other schools to follow. This allowed the researchers to test a number of ideas.

Textbooks. Everybody knows that textbooks are important and that their lack is a major constraint on effective instruction. Yet the first study found "no evidence that the provision of textbooks in Kenyan primary schools led to a large positive impact on test scores, nor is there any evidence that it affected daily attendance, grade repetition, or dropout rates." Does this mean that textbooks don't matter? No. Although textbooks did not increase the performance of the *typical* (median) student, they did improve performance for students who did the best on the

pre-test. This suggests that because the textbooks in this instance were too difficult for the typical student, the books did not matter.

Teacher incentives. Everybody knows that teacher incentives are crucial since teachers are undermotivated. Yet a study on incentives for teachers based on student test scores found that "teachers responded to the program primarily by seeking to manipulate short-run test scores. . . . [T]eachers' absence rates did not decline, homework assignments did not increase, teaching methods did not change." Does this mean that teacher incentives don't matter? No. Teachers did change their behavior—they "conducted special coaching sessions and encouraged students to take the test." This suggests that you get what you pay for—whether you like it or not.

Deworming. Deworming does not feature widely in the education effectiveness literature. Yet a randomized trial of an inexpensive medical

treatment for hookworm, roundworm, whipworm, and schistosomiasis found that it reduced absenteeism by a quarter. Does this mean that health is all that matters? No. While attendance improved, test scores did not.

Three observations. First, things that everybody "knows" to be important did not work as planned, whereas the intervention with lower expectations had large impacts. Second, these results from a hundred schools in an isolated area of Kenya have been getting enormous academic attention because there are so few rigorous, randomized evaluations of schooling interventions. Third, the findings from each intervention do not reveal universal, immediately generalizable results, but they reveal that specifics matter and that learning about what works needs to be local to be useful.

Sources: Miguel and Kremer (2001); Glewwe, Ilias, and Kremer (2000); Glewwe, Kremer, and Moulin (1997).

low and effective schools are often found just a few blocks from dysfunctional ones."[330] The U.S. Agency for International Development (USAID) attempted to refocus its efforts in education in Africa from "proximate determinants" to a more systemic approach that focuses on internally driven identification and scaling up of good practices. A recent review of USAID projects based on systemic reform found, not surprisingly, that implementation was difficult because it went to the heart of the relationships of accountability among actors in education—and that was intensely political. Even so, recent work at USAID explores solutions to the challenges of linking authority, accountability, and transparency to strengthen basic education through institutional reform. There are several ways of expanding and scaling up good practice.[331] The most obvious way is to use greater school autonomy—leaving scope for school management to define a school mission, mandate, and tactics—and greater accountability to enable the monitoring of performance. The autonomy and accountability create incentives to adopt proven successful practices, to evaluate the effectiveness of homegrown initiatives, and to create a sense of pride and commitment in the school.

Accountability is, of course, difficult to define. Is it accountability within the bureaucracy (so that policymakers choose and replace principals based on performance)? Is it the direct participation of parents or school councils in choosing school management? Is it parental choice?

There are alternatives. One is to allow the most competent actors (principals, teachers) to run more than one school. This would allow the more competent to affect greater numbers of children—and reduce the sphere of influence of the less competent. A second way is to systematize a variety of standard-provision models that are easy to replicate and franchise, whether the franchise is a bureaucracy or a private provider. Franchise models should be based on local research on what capable principals currently do in a variety of real settings as well as on citizen dialogue around the emerging models. Models could also be based on statistical analysis of the maximum "output" produced by schools, using the average level of resources that schools can typically mobilize.

None of these approaches to learning about learning is possible without assessments of outputs—not just standardized exams but assessment of all the relevant outputs of schooling. Nor is any possible without enough organizational autonomy for individual schools or groups of schools to decide how best to act.

Organizational and frontline providers: management

Managing for effective services means getting people with the right skills and training in place (capacity). It means giving them the right infrastructure and inputs to work with (logistics). And it means ensuring the motivation (both extrinsic and intrinsic) of frontline workers. The typical public school is often handicapped in these endeavors in nearly every possible way. Individual school managers often cannot choose their own teachers and cannot dismiss them—even for good cause. Teacher training and capacity building are often ill-designed and poorly integrated, and so become irrelevant. Logistical issues are beyond an individual school's control—with decisions centralized and bureaucratic. Compensation structures tend to be tied to seniority and level of education or training, not to demonstrated mastery of skills. And although pay, or other extrinsic motivation, is not the only motivator for education professionals, the typical structure of working conditions and pay undermines even the intrinsic motivation of providers.

Employment relationship and structure of compensation

There is no single best approach to compensation, capacity building, and classroom autonomy. Indeed, one of the major benefits of greater autonomy is that it allows more experimentation and more flexibility in implementation and replication. With school autonomy, organizations can try different compensation schemes, training methods, and modes of parent-teacher interaction and can evaluate them relative to output and outcome objectives. If the public sector can specify what it wants from a school—a clear compact—it can leave teacher compensation to school management and let the best system win.

Teacher pay can be too low (where inflation has eroded real salaries to the point where teachers resort to alternative sources of income) or too high (where pay is several times higher than needed to attract a quality pool of teachers). But appropriate compensation involves more than the level of pay. It is the overall attractiveness of the profession and the structure of compensation that motivate performance.[332] Teacher pay is usually linked to factors that show little association with student performance—mainly seniority. Teacher earnings thus exhibit much less variance than earnings of workers in other occupations. Compensation should reward good teaching, not just longevity.

Motivation and capabilities

The schooling process is so complex—the difficulties of attribution so severe—that simple proposals of "pay for performance" for individual teachers and principals have rarely proved workable.[333] But a total lack of connection between incentives and performance allows excellent teachers working in adverse circumstances and those who never show up to be paid the same amount. This undermines the morale of good teachers and drives them out of the profession.

But motivation is affected by more than money, as a study of teachers in three types of schools in Merida, República Bolivariana de Venezuela (nonprofits, state, and national), shows. Catholic Fe y Alegría schools—which cater to low-income families—emphasize school autonomy and teacher input in decisionmaking. Even though pay is roughly the same as in state and national schools, teacher satisfaction—and student performance—are much higher (table 7.3).

Enhancing teachers' capabilities is clearly fundamental to good-quality schooling, but experience with teacher training is frequently disappointing, mainly because of too little transfer from training to classroom practice. Teachers need training that lets them do their job better. But autonomy, motivation, and assessments of providers (based on outputs and outcomes) are needed for training to improve outcomes.

Client power

Client power is a weak force in public school systems. Channeled into narrow interests, it has little impact. In nearly all

Table 7.3 Autonomy and outcome in Merida, República Bolivariana de Venezuela, in the mid-1990s

School type	Cost per student and per student hour (bolivar)	Salaries as share of operating expenses (percent)	Teacher satisfaction[a]	Student performance (average of math, reading, writing, percent)	Retention rate, grades 1–6 (percent)
State *(escuelas integrales)*	190, 24	95	3.75	40	51
National	160, 32	99	3.57	39	42
Private (Fe y Alegria)	155, 31	88	4.02	53	100

a. Rating of 5 indicates complete agreement with the statement, "I'm satisfied with my work."
Source: Navarro and de la Cruz (1998).

countries parents can choose schools for their children, within limits. But choice has little or no overall impact on school quality because there is typically no effect either on schools that lose children or on those that gain them. Even when parents abandon the public system and pay for private schools—as is happening in many countries—little systemic pressure for change is created because government resources continue to flow into public schools. Direct parental participation in schools is also typically a weak force since there is little about public schools that parents can affect. Often the school head and teachers themselves have little or no autonomy to make changes. Parent organizations are simply a means of mobilizing additional resources for the school.

There are ways to change this, to use client power to improve outcomes. One is to involve citizens directly in the assessment and operation of schools. Another is to use demand-side subsidies to increase access for poor people. A third is to make provider resources depend on client choice—to have money follow students. None is a panacea, but each can be part of a strategy for school improvement.

Direct participation: community involvement in schools

Since students, and indirectly their parents, interact daily with the education system, they have valuable information about provider performance that tends to be ignored in purely bureaucratic systems. Several successful experiences with giving parents a formal role in school governance have heightened interest in this model:

- The emergence of community-run schools in El Salvador showed that they performed as well in test scores and in student dropout rates as schools operated by the ministry of education, which catered to wealthier children (see the spotlight on Educo).

- In Cambodia a donor-financed initiative sought to improve schools by stimulating greater community engagement in schools and using direct budget transfers to schools (box 7.6).

- Evidence from Argentina supports the idea that parental participation together with school autonomy raises student performance.[334]

- NGOs can help both through direct engagement with communities and through creating and disseminating information—as in the system of school information for communities in Nepal assisted by Save the Children-UK.

BOX 7.6 *School improvement in Cambodia*

To improve school quality, the Education Quality Improvement Project in Cambodia uses a participatory approach and performance-based resource management. Operating in three provinces, the project covers 23 percent of the primary school population. Local school communities identify their needs and make proposals for change and investment. Funds are delivered directly to school clusters by the Ministry of Education.

Change management is supported by district-based "animators," who draw general lessons from the experience with the school's quality improvement grants to advise the government on how to improve its education policies. The animators are supported by a network of technical assistants at the local level, who provide pedagogical and organizational support.

The project has stimulated lively dialogue at the school, cluster, and administrative levels on how to improve schools. It has also set in motion a process of change in the administration of schooling and in teaching and learning practices. As a result, unprecedented responsibility has been devolved to school and local administrators.

Source: World Bank (2002c).

Informal and community schools exist in many settings, most often when parents take matters into their own hands and arrange for teaching outside the formal system. This is often supported by NGOs and religious organizations. A recent review of initiatives in Ethiopia points to the potential of this support for expanding access to schooling (box 7.7). The big question is how to link these efforts to the formal system so that informal schools are not a dead end.

Greater parental involvement in school management has its risks. Parents need access to relevant information and the power to effect change. Their focus should be on performance, not on micromanaging the classroom, where teachers should have professional autonomy. It is fairly straightforward for parents to assess whether the instructor is present and not abusive to students. But high-quality teaching cannot be reduced to scripted actions. Parents often have a very conservative perspective on teaching methods and will encourage teaching to the test when there are gatekeeper examinations. Ensuring that the poorest are not excluded from this process is essential—and difficult. Experience with school-based control in South Africa suggests a key role for training parent groups: without the training the more advantaged populations benefited while poorer and less powerful groups lost out.

Direct participation in schools raises the difficult issue of user fees and their relationship to community engagement. Some argue that as long as locally collected fees are retained by the school, fees are a good thing, for two reasons. First, empirical studies suggest that centrally controlled resources are almost universally devoted largely to payroll, while resources collected at the school level raise school quality by much more than equivalent resources from higher levels.[335] A study in Mali showed that paying fees left parents better off (on average) because the value of increased school quality was much larger than the fee itself.[336] Second, if communities are to feel pride in their school and empowered by their participation, then parents should be expected to make some contribution. Payment may come in-kind, such as labor for construction of the school, rather than as direct fees for use.

But these potential benefits of greater community engagement have to be weighed against the apparently large negative effects on enrollments of even very low user fees in poor countries and against the increases in inequality from relying on fees (see box 4.4). Some might argue the ideal is a compromise of a fairly apportioned fee on communities to generate ownership but with significant exemptions for poor households (subsidized from a central fund). Recent experience with such targeting (as in South Africa) suggests that it is difficult to make this work.[337]

Demand-side transfers

Many governments use scholarships or conditional transfers (households receive benefits if children are enrolled) to expand enrollments. The Education, Health, and Nutrition Program of Mexico (Progresa)

BOX 7.7 *Alternate routes to basic education in Ethiopia*

Ethiopia is a large country with a heterogeneous population. Education levels are low: only 24 percent of children complete primary school. There are very few schools in poor and remote areas: only about 30 percent of 10-year-olds in rural areas have ever attended school. But recent innovations sponsored by NGOs show other ways of getting schools to these children.

Programs run by six NGOs reveal how expanding school places is possible even in remote areas—at reasonable cost and without sacrificing quality. The NGO ActionAid proposed adapting school models used by the Bangladesh Rural Advancement Committee in Ethiopia, and since then several other NGOs have sponsored similar programs. The schools share several features:

- Compressing four years of the official curriculum into three years.
- Streamlining the curriculum to reduce repetitiveness and remove elements deemed irrelevant to local needs.
- Using instructional routines that appeal to children, such as songs or teaching in groups.
- Scheduling classes on days and times approved by the community.

- Involving community members in monitoring the attendance of teachers and students.
- Targeting class sizes of about 35 students.
- Recruiting teachers and teaching assistants from local areas and paying them less than professional teachers.
- Spending more on textbooks, other instructional materials, training, and supervision.

The results are promising. Children attending these schools continue on to higher grades. Moreover, learning does not appear to have suffered. Test scores in the second grade were about 20 percent higher than in government schools, and scores in the fourth grade were only slightly lower, even though the schools catered to children from poorer families. All this at a lower cost per student.

Issues remain, however—particularly about scaling up these programs to reach more children, the more so since some initial success was driven by a few energetic individuals.

Source: Ministry of Education Ethiopia (2000).

has drawn considerable attention because—unusual for this type of effort—it was structured to allow rigorous impact evaluations. The program has resulted in substantially higher transitions to secondary school.[338] In Bangladesh a study found that conditional transfers of rice raised enrollments. The program was also cost-effective relative to other interventions, though the government recently moved to monetize the benefits due to concerns about leakage.[339] Indonesia introduced a large scholarship program in response to the economic crisis in 1997. The program helped maintain junior secondary school enrollments.[340]

Conditional cash transfers have proved effective in expanding enrollments, but they have shortcomings. They focus on enrollment without creating incentives for improving quality. To the extent that demand-side transfers use funds that would otherwise have been devoted to school improvement, there is the risk of expanding quantity at the expense of quality. There was widespread concern that school feeding programs in India were "too successful" in attracting students. Schools were flooded with underage children not ready for learning, which put even more pressure on quality at the critical lower grades.

Resources and client choice

The Universal Declaration of Human Rights (Article 26) asserts that parents have a "right to choose the kind of education that shall be given to their children." Despite this apparent endorsement of parental choice, there is little consensus about its role.

In practice, there is a large amount of choice. A substantial fraction of schooling is carried out by a range of private providers: for-profit schools, religious and denominational schools, NGO-operated schools, and community-owned and -operated schools. In some countries the proportion of children in private schooling is rising rapidly—even without public support. In Pakistan the proportion of urban students in public schools fell from 72 percent in 1991 to 60 percent in 1996 to 56 percent in 1998—with most of the shift to private, nonreligious schools (religious schools accounted for only 1 percent). Sometimes there is government support for these schools—as for Catholic schools in Argentina or Islamic schools in Indonesia—or there is support to parents who choose private schools—as in Chile, the Czech Republic, the Netherlands, and New Zealand.

What kind of relationship should governments have with nonpublic providers? One decision is whether to allow demand-side transfers or scholarships to be used in nonpublic schools. Colombia used scholarship programs for private schools to expand enrollments for poor students. The fact that participants were chosen randomly from a pool of applicants allowed for rigorous impact evaluation, which found significant positive impacts for scholarship recipients.[341] But even though the program was both targeted and apparently effective, it was discontinued—for bureaucratic and political reasons. A second decision involves more generalized support for nonpublic schools. In general, it is hard to say anything about "choice" without provoking controversy, but here are four tries.

General subsidies to private schooling—neither disaster nor panacea. Although there is a wide-ranging and still inconclusive empirical debate about the impact of generalized choice, providing general subsidies to private schooling has never been a disaster—or a panacea. The Netherlands has had full school choice among public and denominational providers since 1920, without terrible repercussions. Chile has had choice since 1980, and while there is some controversy about whether it has produced substantial gains in measured learning outcomes (Hsiao and Urquoila 2002), no one argues it has been a disaster. New Zealand has had school choice since 1991, and in a recent assessment of 32 countries, came in third in math and sixth in reading and science literacy. The Czech Republic and Sweden have had public financing of private schools since the 1990s.

So choice is neither an ivory tower notion that could never work in practice nor an ideological Trojan horse that would destroy public schooling. It is also not a universal remedy. The successful expansion of choice has nearly always been embedded in a more general program of school reform and improvement.

Parents who exercise choice perceive themselves to be better off. But schooling transmits beliefs and values, which implies a distinction between meeting the collective goals of citizens for publicly financed schooling and satisfying the clients of schooling. Parents acting as citizens may want publicly supported schools to encourage all children to be tolerant and respectful of other people's beliefs. Yet these same parents acting as clients may want their children to receive instruction in the absolute correctness of a particular set of beliefs. A system that satisfies every individual parent's demands as a client might fail to meet the collective goals of citizens for publicly supported schools. Doubts about choice often arise from the impact of schooling on socialization.[342] But this argument cuts both ways: if socialization is chosen by an authoritarian government to repress individual or group rights, choice is all the more important.

Using taxes for private schools requires accountability. While parents should be allowed to choose their child's education and create their own accountability, using taxes for private schools requires public accountability. For choice to be effective in creating greater accountability, parents need timely, relevant information. This will not necessarily emerge spontaneously because it depends on comparable assessments across schools. Policymakers could publicize that a specific school meets minimum standards through easily visible information tools, such as symbols prominently displayed in the school. A more sophisticated approach could involve broadly disseminated census-like information on outputs and outcomes—perhaps normalized by socioeconomic status.

Making choice part of a package of reforms. The public sector always remains an important provider, and choice complements reforms to improve the public sector. Advocates of school choice emphasize the potential beneficial effects of competition—for which there is mixed evidence. But there are other elements as well. Choice as part of a package of reforms can have three benefits:

- The introduction of choice forces an unbundling of roles. To have effective choice the government must be explicit in its dual role of setting the rules for all providers and managing schools as the largest provider.

- Deciding how to regulate private providers can force a discussion of the output and outcome goals of education that can improve accountability in all schools.

- And choice often creates new acceptance of assessments for monitoring providers—which can be expanded to all schools.

Designing choice around the politics. Policy decisions about choice are intrinsically political. The United States prohibits public support to schools run by religious organizations. Cordoba, Argentina, has actively supported Catholic schools.[343] Holland explicitly supports both Catholic and Protestant schools. Rather than being based on the perceived relative effectiveness of the different schools, these policy choices seem to reflect differing public opinion at the time the decisions were taken—for example, historical concern about Catholic influence among the Protestant majority in the United States, a predominantly Catholic population in Cordoba, and a more even distribution of religions in Holland. Similarly, the suppression of Islamic schools in some countries and support for them in others, or the decision to ban private schools in Pakistan and Nigeria in the 1970s, has little to do with school effectiveness. The promotion of choice through vouchers in the Czech Republic has been seen as a reaction to the use of schools for political indoctrination.

If school choice is a political given, an effective school system can be designed around that constraint. If school choice is politically precluded, an effective school system can be designed around that as well.

Getting reform going

This chapter is about changing the relationships of accountability to produce better educational outcomes by creating the institutional conditions for the technically right things to happen. But how can institutions be changed? How do openings for reform get created and exploited? Decentralization can create opportunities. Reform champions can emerge from political, business, professional, or parental interests. And teacher groups can promote—or resist—change.

Decentralization

Decentralization can be driven by a desire to move services closer to people. But success depends on how it affects relationships of accountability. If decentralization just replaces the functions of the central ministry with a slightly lower tier of government (a province or state), but everything else about the environment remains the same—compact, management, and client power—there is little reason to expect positive change. The assumption is that decentralization works by enhancing citizens' political voice in a way that results in improved services. But this could go either way on both theoretical and empirical grounds. Decentralization is not magic. It must reach the classroom. And it will work only to the extent that it creates greater opportunities for school reform (chapter 10).

Reform champions

Getting education reform on the agenda is no mean feat, and getting reform politically supported and implemented is even more difficult. While individual parents are powerful advocates for their children, that does not necessarily translate into system improvement. Educators and progressive forces among teachers often emerge as champions of education reform because they are most acquainted with the problems inside the classroom and school. But it is much easier to mobilize educator support for certain types of education reforms (system expansion, increased resources, pedagogy improvement, technical curricular reform) than others (increased choice).[344]

Local or national politicians or technocrats can also be forces for education reform, particularly if they perceive it is strongly linked to economic performance. But it is much easier to mobilize technocratic policymaker support for certain types of edcuation reform (narrow accountability) than others (pedagogical improvement).

Teachers and teachers' unions. Effective teachers are the backbone of any educational system, but how can the power of teachers be harnessed for educational improvement? Some believe that teachers have too little power, arguing that educational reforms ignore teachers. Followed through, this view can lead to reforms that ignore classroom and school-level realities, further demoralizing teachers and undermining reforms. Others believe that teachers, especially teachers' unions, have too much power and focus exclusively on wages and working conditions (box 7.8). Both sides can marshal empirical evidence. Much of the debate stems from the joint function of teachers' unions as professional organizations, which exist to promote efficacy, advance professional knowledge, and advocate views in public policy; and as agents of collective bargaining, which emphasize resources and working conditions.

BOX 7.8 *Education reform and teachers' unions in Latin America*

Reforms to promote greater parental involvement, more school autonomy, more emphasis on results, and changes in the training, selection, assignment, and compensation of teachers are politically explosive—particularly with teachers' unions. A study of five attempts at education reforms that included many of these elements in Latin America in the 1990s found that teachers' unions opposed nearly all of them—emphatically and stridently.

"Teacher's unions in Mexico, Minas Gerais, Brazil, Bolivia, Nicaragua, and Ecuador followed similar strategies in opposing education reform. All used strikes to assert their power…against unwanted changes. The power to disrupt public life, to close down schools and ministries, to stop traffic in capital cities, to appeal to public opinion—were familiar actions to them." In April 1999 the announcement by the Bolivian Ministry of Education of its intention to transfer teacher colleges to public universities set teachers and students at those colleges "rioting in the streets, breaking windows, attacking police, throwing rocks, and setting cars on fire" (images the government used to mobilize public opinion against the unions).

Teachers' unions wanted governments to address the issues of teachers' wages and working conditions and were concerned that decentralization and school autonomy would intrude on more familiar relationships and negotiations between a centralized school administration and a centralized union.

Even when governments pushed reforms through, conflicts with the unions made implementation problematic, since successful reform requires teacher participation.

Source: Grindle (forthcoming).

In too many countries discussions between the government and teachers' unions are no different from discussions between a large company and its unions. The relationship between policymakers and teachers' organizations needs to shift from a pure bargaining game to a positive-sum game. This is easier said than done. As professional development bodies teachers' unions can reinforce professional ethics and mutual accountability. They can be used to organize teacher input on technical issues of educational reform, such as assessment, classroom autonomy, student discipline, and teacher training. If unions refuse to take on that role, preferring to concentrate on wages and working conditions, there are no firm guidelines for how reformers should cope with that.

Educación con Participación de la Comunidad en El Salvador

By contracting directly with communities, El Salvador dramatically increased the primary school enrollment of children in poor and remote areas—without reducing the quality of learning.

El Salvador was wracked by civil war throughout the 1980s. Some 80,000 people died—in a total population of roughly 5 million—and many more were wounded and disabled. Income per capita fell almost 40 percent between 1978 and 1983.[345] In 1989 the conservative Republican Alliance Party won a majority in the national assembly, with Alfredo Cristiani as president. Despite contentious negotiations, a peace accord was signed in January 1992.[346]

The war had severely damaged the education system. Communication between the central ministry and schools broke down, supervision collapsed, and many teachers, viewed by some as government "agents" and by others as agents of social opposition, abandoned their posts. By 1988 more than a third of the country's primary schools had closed.[347] And by the end of the war some 1 million children were not in school.[348]

Establishing Educo— Education with the Participation of Communities

The Ministry of Education quickly identified expanding access to basic education and raising its quality as central goals—both to rebuild national unity and to promote long-term economic development. Minister of Education Cecilia Gallardo de Cano, a reform proponent from the "modernizing" wing of the Republican Alliance Party, was intent on lessening the distrust between former combatants.

But skepticism was high. The Ministry of Education was not trusted in many parts of the country and by organized groups such as the National Association of Teachers. Expansion of the traditional education system was viewed suspiciously as a covert means of reasserting national control and building political support in opposition-dominated areas.[349]

During the war many communities had recruited local teachers and established community schools, bearing the cost themselves and paying teachers when they could. The government seized on this model of community-based schooling as the basis for a formal program that would be financially and administratively supported by the ministry: Educación con Participación de la Comunidad, or Educo, with the goal of encouraging the establishment of preschools and primary schools, or classrooms in existing schools.

Begun in 1991, Educo targeted 78 of the country's poorest rural municipalities (of 221 urban and rural municipalities). By 1993 the program was expanding to all rural areas, including many areas formerly under opposition control. But not all of the "*popular schools*" established during the war were incorporated into Educo. Some observers claimed there was selective inclusion based on political favoritism; others saw not incorporating *popular* schools into a government program as a way of sustaining spontaneous community-based education.[350]

Each Educo school (or section within a traditional school) is operated by a Community Education Association (ACE)—an elected committee made up primarily of students' parents—that enters into a one-year renewable agreement with the ministry. The agreement outlines rights, responsibilities, and financial transfers. The Ministry of Education oversees basic policy and technical design. Using the money directly transferred to them, ACEs select, hire, monitor, and retain or dismiss teachers. Teachers at Educo schools are hired on one-year renewable contracts. Parents are taught about school management and how to assist their children at home.[351]

Three-quarters of new enrollments

Educo succeeded in many respects. From a pilot phase of six ACEs in three departments, it scaled up nationally to all of the country's departments by 1993. Rural primary enrollments increased from 476,000 in 1992 to 555,000 in 1995—with over 75 percent of the new students enrolled in Educo schools (figure 1). By 2001 there were almost 260,000 students enrolled in Educo primary schools, 41 percent of all students enrolled in rural schools—and more than 100,000 children enrolled in Educo preschools, 57 percent of all children in preschool.

Even as enrollments increased rapidly, there is little evidence that learning quality suffered. A survey of 30 Educo primary schools and 101 traditional schools in 1996 found no significant differences in average math and language test scores among third graders in the two types of schools.[352] A follow-up study in 1998 found that grade promotion and repetition were similar across the two types of schools as well.[353] As the innovation matured, the institutional arrangements that it introduced took hold and ensured rapid expansion of school places and enrollments of poor children, seemingly without a substantial cost in quality.[354]

Parent visits to classrooms made much of the difference

That Educo schools served the poorest of El Salvador's students, in the poorest areas, makes these results all the more astonishing. How did they do it? Using retrospective data that allow controls for child, household, teacher, and school characteristics—

Figure 1 Students enrolled in traditional rural and in Educo primary classes

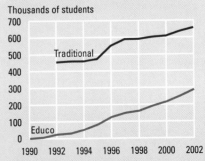

Thousands of students

Note: Figures for 2002 are estimates.
Source: El Salvador Ministry of Education.

Figure 2   Educo promoted parent involvement, which boosted test scores

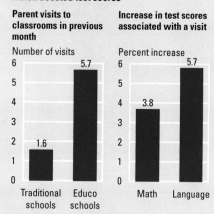

Source: Adapted from Jimenez and Sawada (1999).

and statistically adjusting for the fact that unobserved abilities of children might systematically differ between the two types of schools—researchers found that community involvement explains much of Educo's success.

Parents are more active in Educo schools. And their involvement affects learning (figure 2). Each classroom visit by parents was associated with significantly higher math and language test scores regardless of the type of school. Parents were more active informally as well: they were more likely to meet with teachers or to assist teachers in monitoring attendance or maintaining school furniture.[355]

How did Educo and parent involvement affect test scores? At least part of the story is that teachers were less likely to be absent in Educo schools (averaging 1.2 days of absence a month rather than 1.4 days). Students in Educo schools were also absent less (three fewer days a month) than students in traditional schools.[356] In addition, Educo's more flexible compensation scheme resulted in greater variability in teacher earnings, which suggests that parent associations used compensation to motivate greater effort among teachers.[357] Offering or withholding future employment itself was an incentive, and one that ACEs used. Turnover among Educo teachers was high, which suggests that job loss was not an idle threat.

Converging with traditional schools

Educo's administration has become embedded in the Ministry of Education, and Educo has developed into a major schooling model in the country. Aspects of traditional and Educo schools have been converging. Traditional schools now have more parent participation in school governance and management, and are more autonomous with supporting block financing. Similarly, the pay packages of teachers are more similar: Educo teachers receive the same salaries and benefits as teachers in traditional schools. Even so, a key distinction remains: Educo teachers are hired (and potentially fired) by parent committees while those in traditional schools are not.

Is the Educo model applicable elsewhere?

Educo's achievements might appear idiosyncratic. The end of a bloody civil war that had thrown the traditional education system into chaos opened up a unique opportunity to change the way schools were managed. Based in part on coping strategies during the civil war, El Salvador had a history of community involvement in school management. Indeed, the community associations appear to have worked better in places that had prior experience in community organization.[358] In addition, in the aftermath of the war there was an unusually large pool of educated people without jobs (coinciding with the rapid expansion of university places fueled by opening higher education to the private sector).

These factors suggest that the Educo model might not be directly replicable in a different setting. But some lessons are general. First, with political will it is possible to change the relationships between the actors in basic education. Second, schools can be transformed to work in ways that promote enrollment, participation, and learning—even for children from the poorest households. Third, getting parents to participate effectively in managing schools can help overcome some of the potential pitfalls in the provision of education services—especially monitoring schooling in remote areas. Fourth, it is possible to scale up small innovations to have a significant impact on national outcomes.

Health and nutrition services

Poor people in most countries have the worst health outcomes. They are pushed further into poverty due to ill health. And they are often excluded from support networks that enhance the social and economic benefits of good health. Unlike education, health and nutrition outcomes of poor people are produced by households—with contributions from many services. And health and nutrition services contribute to other aspects of human welfare, such as protecting people from catastrophic health spending. They should thus be judged by the way they contribute to the poor's health outcomes, to protecting citizens from impoverishing health expenditures, and to helping the poor break out of their social exclusion.

Throughout history, poor people have often paid health providers directly. But this short route from client to provider is blunted by asymmetries of information and conflicts of interest. Another problem: poor people lack the money for market transactions. A variety of market failures—disease-related externalities and fragmented insurance markets—and concerns for equity justify public intervention in financing health and nutrition services. But governments find it difficult to monitor the performance of health workers, especially those delivering highly discretionary services, such as clinical care. And since insurance-market failures affect everybody, the non-poor often capture public financing of health care.

Health services are failing poor people not because of lack of knowledge for preventing and treating illnesses but because health systems are trapped in a web of failed relationships of accountability. To break out of this trap, service delivery arrangements can be tailored for three classes of services:

- Getting highly transaction-intensive and discretionary **individual-oriented clinical** services to poor people is most challenging. To influence quality, poor clients should have greater power—through third-party payments, information, and greater oversight of health workers and facilities. Organized citizens can exert this power by contributing financial resources and co-producing and monitoring the services. But insurance market failures, asymmetries of knowledge, and conflicts of interest mean that governments need to invest in purchasing key services to protect poor households and foster a pro-poor professional ethos.

- **Population-oriented outreach** services—standardized services that can include vector control, immunization, or vitamin A supplementation—are easier for policymakers to monitor. Even governments with limited capacity can provide these services—or write contracts with public or private entities to provide them. Building coalitions to strengthen poor people's collective voice is essential to ensure adequate public resources for those services.

- For community and **family-oriented services** that **support self-care**—such as information and social support for promoting breastfeeding or safe sex—community and civil society organizations and commercial networks are often well placed to provide services close to poor households. Governments can establish partnerships and provide information and targeted subsidies.

Policymakers need to be accountable for health outcomes—which means greater investment in monitoring and evaluation mechanisms that capture disparities in health.[359]

The health of poor people

Health outcomes improved in the second half of the 20th century, a trend likely to continue in many countries. But hopes for an ever-improving trend are fading as progress slowed down in the 1990s. At the current pace most regions of the developing world will not reach the Millennium Development Goals for health by 2015 (figure 8.1). Infant mortality rates are increasing in Central Asia. Under-five mortality is on the rise in 22 countries in Sub-Saharan Africa. Stunting is rising in many African countries and remains high in South Asia. In 1995, 500,000 women died worldwide as a result of complications associated with pregnancy, mostly in developing countries. The AIDS epidemic is expanding in Africa, India, China, and Russia, along with a resurgence of tuberculosis.[360] Adult mortality rates have worsened in the Russian Federation and some of its neighbors.

The outcomes are consistently worse among the disadvantaged. In low-and middle-income countries, under-five mortality rates are 2.3 times higher among the poorest fifth of the population than among the richest fifth. Stunting rates are 3.4 times higher (figure 8.2).[361] The rich fare well in absolute terms. In Pelotas, Brazil, infant mortality for the richest 7 percent of the population in 1993 was comparable to the average for the Netherlands in 1998.[362]

Communicable diseases, malnutrition, and reproductive ailments account for most of the mortality gap between high- and low-income countries and between the rich

and poor.[363] The poor also often suffer from higher rates of noncommunicable diseases such as depression and cardiovascular diseases in North America or alcohol-related ailments in the Russian Federation. Malnutrition is a double burden: poorest groups have both high rates of malnutrition and diabetes and obesity.[364]

Improving health outcomes for the poor is a complex task. In addition to income, other household factors influence health outcomes: age, social status, religion, residence (chapter 1), ethnic background (box 8.1), and gender—particularly in South Asia. Girls in India are 30 to 50 percent more likely to die between the age of one and five than boys.[365] Maternal mortality depends mainly on health services while nutrition and under-five mortality depend on many other services, such as education, water, food security, communication, electrification, and transportation. The AIDS epidemic has particularly challenged policymakers and providers to look at links with other sectors and focus more on behavior and societal values.

Health services can work for poor people

Experience from Brazil, Chile, Costa Rica and Cuba (spotlight), Iran (box 8.2), Nepal, Matlab (Bangladesh), Tanzania, and several West African countries (spotlight) shows that health services, if delivered well, can improve outcomes for even the poorest groups. A health program in the Gadchiroli district in India reduced neonatal mortality rates by 62 percent. Midwifery services and community hospitals are linked to dramatic reductions in neonatal and maternal mortality in Sri Lanka and Malaysia. In Uganda and Thailand government efforts changed sexual behavior, reducing the prevalence of HIV. In low- and middle-income countries services promoting oral rehydration therapy led to a decrease in diarrhea-related child mortality.[366]

Health services also help protect the income of the poor. Locally managed financing schemes in Niger, contracted-out services in Cambodia, and insurance schemes targeting poor people in Thailand and Indonesia helped reduce out-of-pocket spending and extended the reach of the safety net among the poor.[367]

Figure 8.1 Reaching the MDGs in health: accelerate progress
Trends in under-five mortality by region

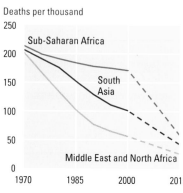

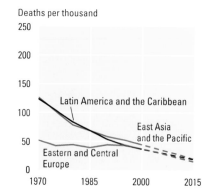

Source: World Development Indicators database (2003).

Health services, when they work, can also contribute to greater self-reliance and social inclusion of poor people. They have been used as entry points to broader development activities, as in the Democratic Republic of Congo, where community health financing schemes triggered the emergence of cooperatives to commercialize agricultural products.[368]

But those who need the most often get the least...

Despite these successes the availability of good health services tends to vary inversely with need.[369] Poor groups and regions have less access to sanitation and vector control.[370] An analysis of 30 countries shows that the use of health care interventions is consistently lower among people living on less than $1 a day than among richer groups (figures 8.3 and 8.4).

...pay the most...

Illness pushes households into poverty, through lost wages, high spending for catastrophic illnesses, and repeated treatment for other illnesses. The share of household nonfood expenditures spent on health is higher among poorer than richer groups. Patients sell assets to finance health care, as 45 percent of rural patients do in the Kyrgyz Republic.[371] Health expenses are estimated to have pushed almost 3 million Vietnamese into poverty in 1998. Out-of-pocket spending pushes poor households deeper into poverty, but it also pushes households that were not poor into extreme poverty. The poor seldom enroll in voluntary insurance schemes and rarely benefit from compulsory schemes. Even when they do, they still incur significant direct health care costs in the form of insurance premiums, copayments, and payments for noncovered services.[372]

...and lack the power to produce good health

Poor nutrition practices, careless handling of water and waste, and inadequate care for illness are major contributors to poor health. Illiteracy, women's ignorance of health issues, and lack of decisionmaking power are often the causes (figure 8.5).[373] Studies of the rich-poor gap in health outcomes show that the poor and the non-poor may respond to the same level of inputs differently.[374] In Senegal

Figure 8.2 Reaching the MDGs in health: focus on poor households
Stunting prevalence among children 3–5 years old, by wealth group

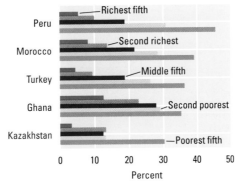

Source: Analysis of Demographic and Health Surveys, 1990–2002.

the poor are 39 percent less efficient than the rich at translating drinking water, sanitation, and health services into better health. In Mali, the poor are only 16 percent less efficient, but the gap has been widening over time: while the availability of inputs is increasing, poor households' ability to transform those inputs into health is lagging behind.

BOX 8.2 *Making health services work for poor people in the Islamic Republic of Iran*

In 1974 the infant mortality rate in Iran was 120 per 1,000 live births for rural areas and 62 in urban areas. By 2000 it stood at 28 for urban areas and 30 for rural areas. Maternal mortality rates dropped in rural areas from 370 per 100,000 to 55 between 1974 and 1996. Immunization rates, treatment of child illnesses, and antenatal care increased dramatically and are now at comparably high levels in rural and urban areas, although skilled attendance for deliveries remains lower (75 percent) in rural areas than in urban (95 percent). All this, despite the fact that 76 percent of rural children had no health insurance in 1997 and 56 percent of rural women were still illiterate.

How did this happen? In 1980, after the Iranian revolution, a new constitution bound the government to provide basic health benefits to the "disadvantaged" (*mostazafeen*). The most immediate concern was to increase access to care in rural areas. Allocations of resources for rural services increased and today are about a third of the health budget in the rural regions. By March 2002 there were 16,340 rural health houses, each covering about 1,500 people, serving

about 84 percent of rural communities. The rest were covered by mobile teams. Health centers offering emergency obstetrical care 24 hours a day (three midwives) and transport for referral were created covering about 20,000 people each.

Despite the large number of medical professionals in Iran, staffing these facilities was a challenge because personnel did not readily accept posting to rural areas. The health houses were therefore staffed by female and male health workers known as *behvarz*. Selected from the villages where they were to be stationed, with the participation of village authorities, the *behvarz* were required to have eight years of formal schooling. Their training lasted two years, was mainly local, and consisted of on-the-job training with supervisors and peer trainers. A simple health information system—the Vital Horoscope—enabled *behvarz* to identify families with child and maternal health problems and link them with health services.

Source: Mehryar, Aghajanian, and Ahmadnia (2003).

Figure 8.3   Poor people use high-impact services less

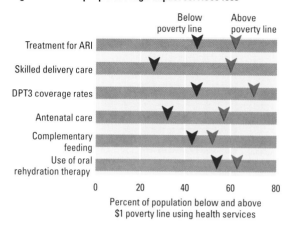

Source: Authors' calculations, based on Demographic and Health Survey data, weighted average for 30 low- and middle-income countries.

Figure 8.4   Richer groups do well in absolute terms

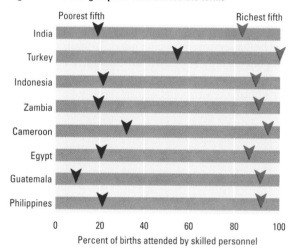

Source: Gwatkin and others (2000), Demographic and Health Survey data, weighted average for 30 low- and middle-income countries.

Market failures and government failures

Market failures and a concern for equity call for some government financing of health and nutrition services. One type of market failure is the underprovision of services to prevent or treat individual illnesses that spill over to the general populace. Another is the breakdown in insurance and credit markets, impoverishing people.[375] The concern for equity is either a social choice or based on the notion that health is a human right (see box 2.2).

Conflicts of interest and the capacity of services to do serious harm also justify government involvement in service provision. Patients find it difficult to attribute their

health status to a specific course of action. This makes them imperfect judges of health providers. Although responsiveness to patients' needs is often better in the private sector, the technical quality of private services varies broadly from very good to very bad (chapter 4). The technical complexity of clinical services confers considerable power on providers to influence the nature and quantity of services they provide—to their own financial benefit. This is well illustrated by recent increases in caesarian sections in both high- and low-income countries.[376]

Governments often aim at solving conflicts of interest through direct service provision with tight administrative control and enforcement of a public ethos. But monitoring whether services are actually delivered and of adequate quality may be difficult. These "bureaucratic" failures are particularly high for highly discretionary and transaction-intensive services such as diagnosing and treating an illness. Absenteeism rates in health clinics is high[377] (chapter 1) and although technical quality of services is often slightly better in public than in private services, quality shortcomings are still rampant in the public sector. In Tunisia in 1996 only 20 percent of pneumonia cases were managed correctly and 62 percent of cases received antibiotics inappropriately.[378]

Governments also address failed insurance markets by running "free" public hospitals. The beneficiaries of these hospital services are usually the non-poor in urban areas (chapter 2). They use their political clout to ensure that public spending for these (expensive) hospitals is maintained—often at the expense of services that could have a real effect on poor people.

Many health services are private goods, and all countries have a private health care market. Most industrial countries started with private health systems. In low- and middle-income countries out-of-pocket spending represents a large share of health spending even in countries with well-functioning public systems (figure 8.6). And in the last 20 years there has been tremendous growth in private provision (often uncontrolled) and private spending on health.[379]

Worldwide, richer groups generally resort more to the private sector, but the sit-

Figure 8.5a   Poor women do not know much about HIV

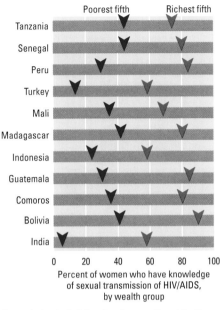

Source: Authors' calculations from Demographic and Health Survey data, 1995–2002.

Figure 8.5b   Husbands say no to contraception

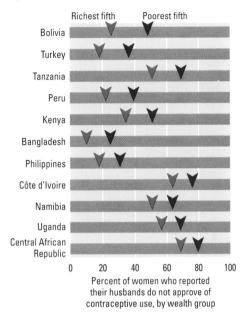

Source: Authors' calculations from Demographic and Health Survey data, 1995–2002.

uation differs by country. Richer groups also use public facilities more—which indicates that subsidies are not well targeted. The public-private mix varies by type of service (figure 8.7). The private sector is involved in many critical services, including disease control and child and reproductive health. But immunizations, family planning, and skilled delivery care are more often provided by the public sector. Even in India, poor people, who turn mainly to private providers to treat illnesses, rely on the public sector for vaccination (93 percent) and antenatal care (74 percent).[380]

The boundaries between public and private services have blurred. Many governments subsidize privately provided services—all high-income countries do and so,

Figure 8.6   A public responsibility, but private spending matters

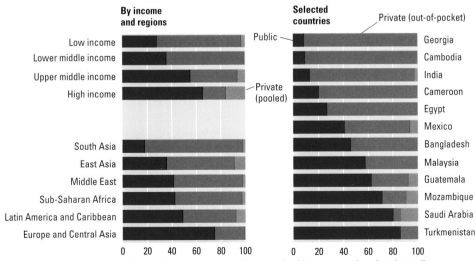

Source: WHO (World Health Organization) (1999), National Health Accounts, updated 2002.

Figure 8.7   The public-private mix differs between poor and rich, and among interventions

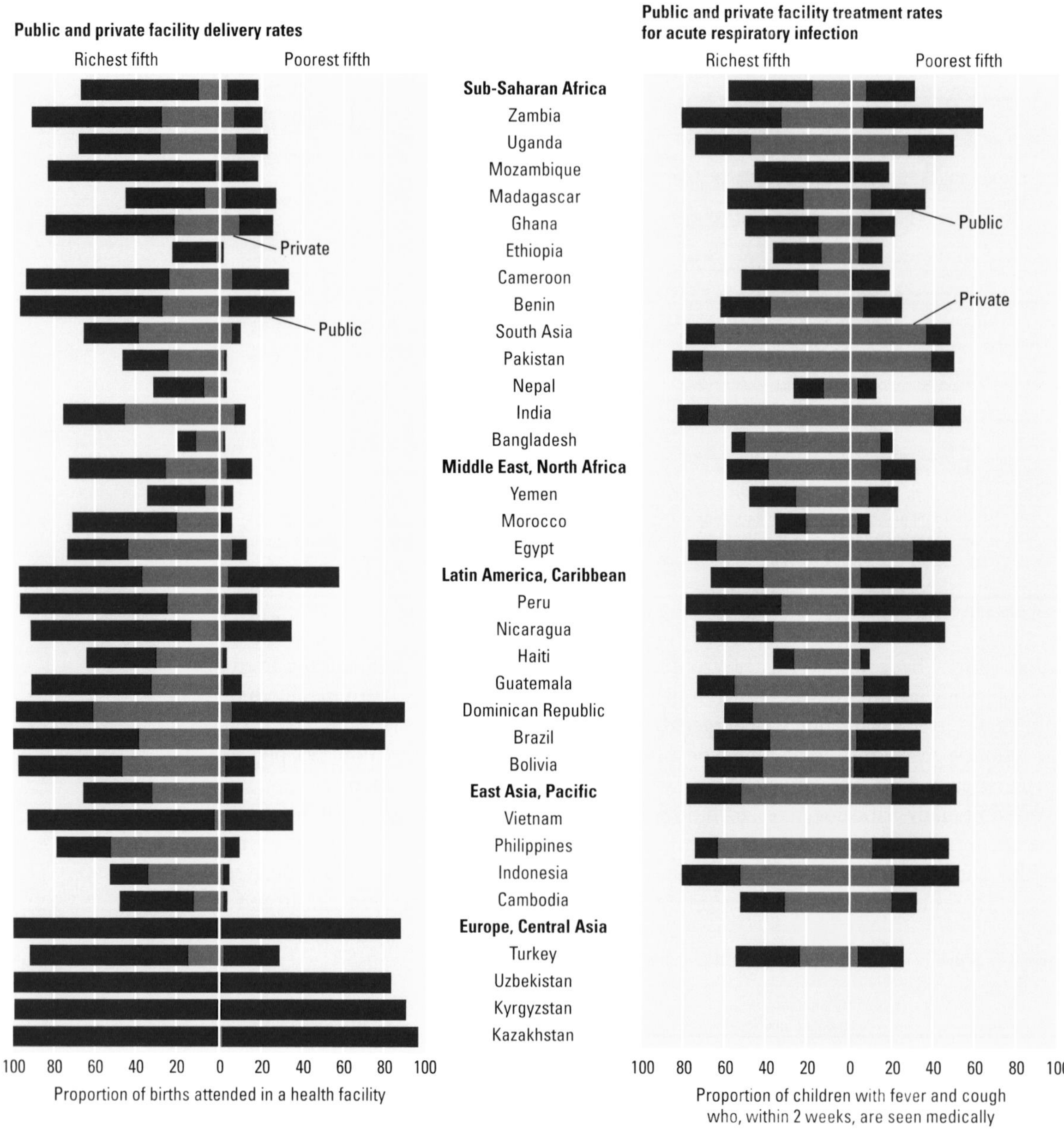

Public and private facility delivery rates

Richest fifth   Poorest fifth

Public and private facility treatment rates
for acute respiratory infection

Richest fifth   Poorest fifth

Private

Public

Public

Private

Sub-Saharan Africa
Zambia
Uganda
Mozambique
Madagascar
Ghana
Ethiopia
Cameroon
Benin
South Asia
Pakistan
Nepal
India
Bangladesh
Middle East, North Africa
Yemen
Morocco
Egypt
Latin America, Caribbean
Peru
Nicaragua
Haiti
Guatemala
Dominican Republic
Brazil
Bolivia
East Asia, Pacific
Vietnam
Philippines
Indonesia
Cambodia
Europe, Central Asia
Turkey
Uzbekistan
Kyrgyzstan
Kazakhstan

100 80 60 40 20 0 20 40 60 80 100
Proportion of births attended in a health facility

100 80 60 40 20 0 20 40 60 80 100
Proportion of children with fever and cough
who, within 2 weeks, are seen medically

Source: Authors, based on Demographic and Health Survey data 1995–2002.

increasingly, do middle- and low-income countries, as in the Thai Social Security Scheme, Poland's social insurance system, and Uganda's subsidies to not-for-profit providers. Many public facilities charge user fees, introducing a market-like transaction in the delivery of public services,[381] and poor people spend substantial sums to use them.[382]

There has also been widespread growth in informal payments to public providers in Africa, East Asia, and Eastern Europe,[383] which represents an informal marketization

of public services. Informal payments boost the cost of "free" maternity care in Bangladesh to $31 for a normal delivery—a quarter of a household's average monthly income—and to $118 for a caesarian section.[384]

Applying the framework: classes of services

Chapters 3 through 6 developed a framework for analyzing service delivery that identifies two routes for poor people to obtain services. One is the short route, where clients exert power over providers by dint of their money and ability to enforce discipline. The other is the long route of public accountability from poor clients to policymakers, and from policymakers to providers. For health services, the short route often fails because of conflicts of interest and asymmetries in information. Poor people also lack money for market transactions. But the complexity of services and the heterogeneity of health needs make it difficult to standardize service provision and to monitor performance—a major "bureaucratic" failure of the long route of accountability. Lack of voice of the poor in decisions over the use of the collective purse is another failure of the long route.

Clinical services are highly discretionary and transaction-intensive, requiring individually tailored diagnostics and treatments. So one leg of the long route, which requires the policymaker to monitor the provider, is difficult. Yet failures in the insurance market call for government involvement in high-cost services, such as inpatient services or catastrophic illnesses. But often these government-financed, high-cost services benefit primarily the non-poor. So the other leg of the long route (voice) also fails. This means that poor people have to revert to the short route of direct client purchases of a service. But the asymmetry of information between the client and the provider—and the client's lack of money—cause this route to fail too. A quandary!

The task is slightly easier for services that *support self-care* by families and communities, such as information to support changes in nutritional or sexual behavior. This service is discretionary because it has to be tailored to the family's social environment, but it requires less intensive professional transaction than services responding to individual illness. Short- and long-route failures are small.

Some professional services, despite being technical and transaction-intensive, are also well standardized and less discretionary. Such services include those that serve homogeneous needs of a population—such as vector control, immunization, supplementation with vitamin A, or screening for diabetes. These *population-oriented* services can be delivered through outreach to the poor. When health interventions have large externalities such as communicable diseases control, the short-market-like route is unlikely to work. If technology allows standardization, this delivery arrangement is then the prime choice as policymakers can monitor performance and tightly control delivery.

Technology is constantly evolving, and no intervention belongs automatically to one category (box 8.3). Service delivery approaches are continually being developed that reduce the need and difficulty of monitoring for both government and citizens. Countries have standardized highly technical interventions into less discretionary services

---

BOX 8.3 *The changing mix of cure and care: who treats what, and where?*

Throughout the 20th century, service institutions have responded—albeit slowly—to rapid changes in health technology. Countries choose combinations of "delivery modes" based on costs and international standards but also on country-specific characteristics such as geographic and density constraints, transport and infrastructure capacity, existing health infrastructure inherited from previous technological innovations, labor market characteristics, training and orientation of providers, and so forth. What is delivered as inpatient treatment, outpatient hospital, health center or home visits; and what by lay people, nurses, general practitioners, or specialists is far from being standard across countries.

- *Technological progress* triggers modifications in the nature, type, and quantity of services

required. Hospital tuberculosis treatment (the sanatorium) was replaced by outpatient clinical care—thanks to antibiotics . Screening followed by treatment—DOTS (Directly Observed Treatment Therapy)—were later standardized to allow delivery through community outreach. Similarly, new treatments for HIV and cancer cut lengthy hospitalization requirements. The care and cure functions of the hospital also evolve. Hospitals are being transformed into long-term-care centers for the elderly, while complex procedures are increasingly conducted in ambulatory clinics. Home-based nursing care is being revived.

- *At similar levels of technology countries have opted for different models with comparable lev-*

els of success. Independent practitioners developed first in Western countries and have been the cornerstone of Western systems. The hegemony of hospitals in the Western world is no older than the 20th century. In contrast, hospitals have played a much larger role in the provision of outpatient care in Eastern Europe and Central Asia, and in Latin America, Vietnam, and Sri Lanka. In Africa health systems developed through hospitals and mobile clinics since the beginning of the 20th century, with primary health care emerging only in the 1980s. Different skill levels are also used for similar interventions. Health technicians and nurses have been successfully used in Mozambique to perform caesarian sections, while other countries use general practioners or skilled obstetricians.

Figure 8.8 Making health services easier to deliver, through standardization and empowerment

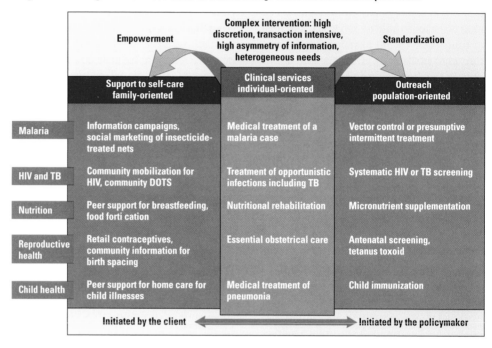

that can be initiated, controlled, and delivered by the government through reaching out to the poor. Such interventions can be addressed to population groups with similar needs. Another way is to reduce the transaction intensity of services—and the need for government monitoring—by empowering poor people to drive services that correspond to their needs and characteristics (figure 8.8).

Table 8.1 presents some of the key obstacles limiting the coverage of the poor with regard to health and nutrition services. Poor access to information and to networks distributing health-related commodities is a major impediment to the use of *community- and family-oriented support to self-care*. Rural populations often have no access to retail condoms, soap, water containers or bed nets. If they do, price remains a barrier. Fewer than 30 percent of the poorest fifth of the population have access to the media in such countries as Bolivia, India, Morocco, and Mozambique. Few poor households receive extension workers, with visits peaking at 20 percent of Indonesian and Peruvian households .

Most countries have had some success in increasing the physical access of poor communities to some *population-oriented ser-*

vices—witness the universal childhood immunization, polio eradication efforts, and the elimination of onchocerciasis. Egypt and Mexico have successful itinerant clinics. But sustaining these efforts for the poor is problematic. Low demand and poor quality reduce effectiveness of family planning services in India. Governments can control and monitor such services easily, but they often underinvest in them. In transition countries in Europe and Asia, moving from publicly provided services to social insurance led to confusion about the government's role in health, which led to the neglect of these services and the subsequent re-emergence of communicable diseases.

Low-income countries have difficulty ensuring physical access to *clinical services* for a large part of their population. In Chad only 20 percent of the poorest fifth live less than one hour from a health facility. Middle-income countries have more trouble ensuring affordable and quality care to excluded, vulnerable, and difficult-to-reach segments of the population. Inequitable risk pooling still leaves the poor exposed to the financial risk of illness in most of these countries. Studies report large inefficiencies in the way health facilities are run. In Turkey, a study found that only 54 of 573 general hospi-

Table 8.1   Selected examples of obstacles for the delivery of health and nutrition services to the poor

Dimensions of performance of health services	Community- and family-oriented support to self-care	Individual-oriented clinical services	Population-oriented outreach
General			
Knowledge *Demand*	Low literacy and low knowledge of caring practices among the poor, particularly women	High demand, but large asymmetry of information between people with low literacy levels and providers; low access to technical information	Low demand for key services (e.g., immunization in India)
Empowerment	Intrahousehold allocation unfavorable to women or children, particularly in South Asia	No control over socially powerful providers; no inclusion of the poor in risk pooling schemes	Low decisionmaking power of women in public life, particularly in the Middle East
Affordability	Low affordability of safe water, food, radio, magazines, bed nets, condoms, etc.	Low affordability of insurance premiums as well as service fees and impoverishment due to catastrophic illnesses	High transport and opportunity costs for the poor even when services are free
Social and cultural access	Social and cultural factors affect nutritional and caring practices	Social distance from providers: social class and ethnic minorities, castes in India, Western-educated providers in Africa	Information on benefits of services not tailored to local values and social norms
Physical access	Poor access to safe water, commercial networks, and media	Low geographical access to facilities in Africa mainly, but also in poor areas of other regions	Increased access and demand through mobile strategies but large dropout rates
Availability of human resources	Norm setters, opinion leaders, community elders, peers may resist change	Major poor region–rich region and rural-urban imbalance in qualified human resources	Health workers' training and remuneration modes do not provide incentives to deliver those services
Availability of consumables	Deficient markets: no bed nets, condoms, contraceptives, etc., in retail	Fake, dangerous drugs mainly in Sub-Saharan Africa and East Asia	Often not very sensitive to market dynamics
Organizational quality	Inappropriate information channels: e.g., information on HIV and condoms in clinics instead of schools or bars	Poor facilities amenities, inconvenient opening hours, poor attitude of staff	Often mainly supply driven, even centrally planned, with little involvement of recipients
Technical quality	Noncomparable standardized information, diffusion of erroneous information	Broad variations in quality of care in private services, poor use of drugs, overprescription	Standardization allows quality assurance, but supervision can be inadequate leading to quality shortcomings
Input/technical efficiency	Technical efficiency of provision of information/community support often not known	Poor input mix: inappropriate investment/recurrent balance, lack of nonsalary recurrent inputs	Integration in clinical services is not effective if use of clinical services is low and there are no incentives
Resource management	Low level of multisectoral coordination	Leakages of drugs, and funds; absenteeism of personnel, moonlighting/informal practices of public servants	Vertical program approaches may have opportunity costs by diverting resources away from other services and creating skewed incentives
Governance *Supply*	Capture of subsidies by richer groups	Lack of transparency in financing of health facilities, large capture by richer groups	Financing often dependent on donors in low-income countries

Adapted from Claeson and others (2003).

tals—public and private—could be considered to be operating efficiently.[385]

With a broad variety of situations and problems, the key issue is to find a balance in the public-private mix to minimize the consequences of both market and government failures in financing and providing services. Increased resources for health services will translate into better results for the poor only if used to address the country-specific obstacles to service delivery (box 8.4). This clearly requires defining the accountabilities of those involved and ensuring that there are sufficient resources, information, and enforcement mechanisms to make the relationships work. The mix of client power and government action will need to differ according to the nature of services, the country, its institutions, and its government.[386]

BOX 8.4   *Buying results to reach the Millennium Development Goals*

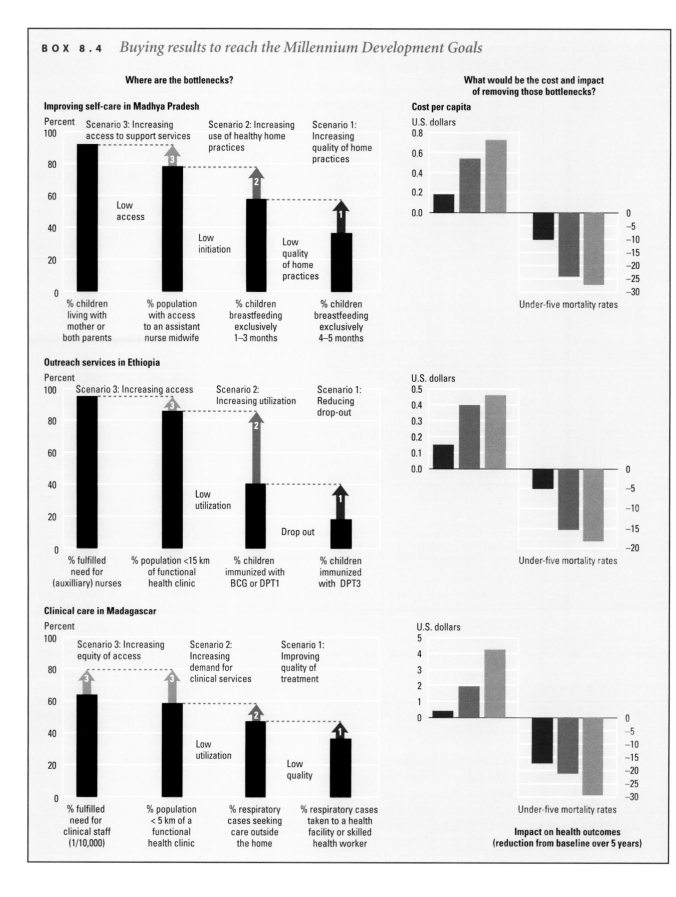

Where are the bottlenecks?

Improving self-care in Madhya Pradesh

Percent

Scenario 3: Increasing access to support services

Scenario 2: Increasing use of healthy home practices

Scenario 1: Increasing quality of home practices

Low access

Low initiation

Low quality of home practices

% children living with mother or both parents

% population with access to an assistant nurse midwife

% children breastfeeding exclusively 1–3 months

% children breastfeeding exclusively 4–5 months

Outreach services in Ethiopia

Percent

Scenario 3: Increasing access

Scenario 2: Increasing utilization

Scenario 1: Reducing drop-out

Low utilization

Drop out

% fulfilled need for (auxilliary) nurses

% population <15 km of functional health clinic

% children immunized with BCG or DPT1

% children immunized with DPT3

Clinical care in Madagascar

Percent

Scenario 3: Increasing equity of access

Scenario 2: Increasing demand for clinical services

Scenario 1: Improving quality of treatment

Low utilization

Low quality

% fulfilled need for clinical staff (1/10,000)

% population < 5 km of a functional health clinic

% respiratory cases seeking care outside the home

% respiratory cases taken to a health facility or skilled health worker

What would be the cost and impact of removing those bottlenecks?

Cost per capita

U.S. dollars

Under-five mortality rates

U.S. dollars

Under-five mortality rates

U.S. dollars

Under-five mortality rates

Impact on health outcomes (reduction from baseline over 5 years)

BOX 8.4 *Buying results to reach the Millennium Development Goals (continued)*

Budgeting approaches often don't link the money spent with the expected results. The impact of public funds invested in health services and their contribution to the Millennium Development Goals are thus difficult to assess. Budgeting the contribution of health and nutrition services to goals should address three questions:

1. *What are the major bottlenecks hampering the delivery of health services, and what is the potential for improvement?*

The analysis of the determinants of the baseline coverage of interventions in terms of availability of critical resources (human and material), physical accessibility, demand (utilization of the services), and continuity and quality of health services helps identify the main constraints to the increase in coverage.

In Madagascar the bottlenecks of clinical care are mainly low quality, utilization, and human resource availability. Increasing the demand for clinical services (scenario 2) especially the use of health facilities or skilled health workers for the treatment of severe respiratory infections (scenario 1) could raise the effective coverage of this intervention to almost 60 percent. The potential for improving the availability of health staff in poor rural areas (scenario 3) is limited, and this

determines a real-life "coverage frontier" (at 80 percent). In Ethiopia the coverage with at least one dose of DPT (diphtheria-pertussis-tetanus vaccine) in relation to the geographical access is the main bottleneck, while the dropout between the first and third dose of DPT constitutes another obstacle to adequate coverage with outreach services. Increasing the use of immunization services through information and communication (scenario 2) as well as defaulter tracking (scenario 1) can increase the adequate coverage to over 80 percent. In Madhya Pradesh in India, late initiation and non-exclusiveness of breastfeeding (BF) are the main bottlenecks identified in self-care. Increasing the use (early initiation of BF, scenario 2) and quality (exclusiveness of BF, scenario 1) of healthy home practices through information and the creation of a supportive environment can increase effective coverage to nearly 80 percent.

2. *How much money is needed for the expected results?*

Once coverage bottlenecks and the potential for improvement (coverage frontiers) have been identified for each mode of health services delivery, the cost of the strategies can be calculated using country-specific data. This allows the

preparation of investment and recurrent budgets that specifically support strategies most likely to improve efficiency of demand (scenario 1), support increased demand (scenario 2), or increase access to health services and availability of health staff (scenario 3). This enables Ministries of Health and Finance to determine the spending needed to support the goals and to encourage policymakers to ensure funding of priority activities that address the major coverage bottlenecks.

3. *How much can be achieved in health outcomes by removing the bottlenecks?*

The increase in coverage in specific interventions achievable through well-targeted strategies and budgets such as those defined above can be converted into measures of improved health outcomes using various epidemiological models. Preliminary analysis can show the reduction in under-five mortality rate that can be expected from removing the bottlenecks of clinical care, outreach services, and self-care in Madagascar, Ethiopia, and Madhya Pradesh, India.

Source: UNICEF and World Bank (2003).

Strengthening client power

These are our people. This is our money, you cannot touch it.

> President of Benin's Health Committees, responding to the Ministry of Health's attempt to centralize community-owned health funds and return them to the Treasury

Strengthening client power can improve services for the poor by substituting for or correcting the weaknesses of the long route of accountability. Throughout the world, poor people are engaged as purchasers, co-producers, and monitors of health services. For poor clients to have more control over health providers means:

- Making the income of health service providers depend more on demand from poor clients.

- Increasing the purchasing power of the poor.

- Fostering the involvement of poor people in co-producing and monitoring services.

- Expanding consumer power to use complaint and redress mechanisms.

Paying for services confers power

The poor often first use the commercial sector to purchase key commodities for improving health. In Colombia and Mexico community cooperatives distribute insecticide-treated bed nets. In more than 40 countries social marketing programs have relied on market incentives. They have increased the use of bed nets, condoms, contraceptives, soap, and locally produced disinfectant for water treatment (which has reduced the risk of diarrhea by 44 to 85 percent).[387]

Modest copayments can also provide an entry ticket to clinical services for poor people by reducing capture of supposedly free services by richer groups (box 4.4). Controlled studies in several countries[388] find improvements in the use of services among poor people after copayments increased the transparency and accountability of providers to poor clients (figure 8.9). But to be pro-poor copayments need to be retained locally and tied to performance, and they need to contribute to the income of providers rather than compensate for inadequate public funds (chapter 4).

Figure 8.9   Community-managed health services increase utilization and reduce spending
Randomized control study of three districts in Niger, 1992–94

Percent increase in number of curative consultations

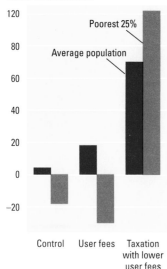

Percent change in health expenditures per episode

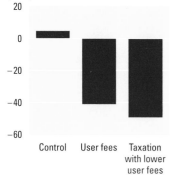

Source: Diop, Yazbeck, and Bitran (1995).

Yet for many services the purchasing power of poor people remains insufficient to overcome price barriers (table 8.2). Marketing programs for condoms are unlikely to be pro-poor in the early stages, and a focus on cost recovery excludes the poorest.[389] Governments can then provide subsidies, as is often done for food to address malnutrition. The subsidies may need to be very high to substantially increase use among poor people, as demonstrated in the programs to distribute free condoms to sex workers[390] and to offer bed nets as part of antenatal care.[391] Market segmentation, tier pricing, and product differentiation can be helpful. In Malawi, highly subsidized bed nets for pregnant women differ in color and shape from regular market-priced nets.[392] Cross-subsidizing preventive and maternal and child health services using the margins on fees for adult clinical care made the first more affordable in Bolivia.[393]

Direct transfers to client households—demand-side subsidies—can also boost client power. Vouchers have a good record in promoting use of some well-defined services. Food stamps can increase food consumption.[394] In Honduras and Nicaragua families receive financial stipends under the condition that they use key preventive health services.[395] Financial support through vouchers for consultations reduced sexually transmitted diseases for sex workers (box 8.5). And poverty funds ensured third-party payments for the poor in China.[396] How the subsidies are managed matters, however. In Tanzania, the poor pregnant women targeted by the bed net program almost never used the vouchers, probably because the subsidies were too low.[397]

A problem with subsidies is how well they reach the poor. Thailand's low-income insurance scheme has used demand-side subsidies—health cards—for clinical services, but about a third of the beneficiaries were not poor and half the poor did not benefit.[398] Demand-side subsidies also have limits if provided in isolation. Even well-targeted food-related transfer programs seldom have measurable impacts on malnutrition unless accompanied by programs to promote breastfeeding, complementary feeding, hygiene, and care of childhood illnesses. In Mexico the success of the Education, Health, and Nutrition Program (Progresa—see spotlight) was made possible by a parallel program of itinerant health teams.[399]

Coproducing health services

Self-care is a particularly important type of service co-production, relied on by poor and rich alike, and more common in industrial countries than the use of professional services. Support to families and communities can help poor communities reduce malnutrition, as in East Asia where community-based programs were linked to service delivery structures, often village outlets for primary health care. Government employees were trained as facilitators of nutrition-relevant actions coordinated and managed by volunteers selected by local communities. In Honduras the strongly community-owned AIN-C program reduced severe malnutrition by 31 percent. Civil society organizations can serve as intermediaries between clients and providers. Women's support groups have helped spread the practice of exclusive breastfeeding in Africa and Latin America. Other successes include greater use of oral rehydration solutions, better environmental health, and better AIDS interventions.[400]

Communities are often involved in building health facilities. But they have also taken over provision and management of professional health services, as in the more than 500 community-led health clinics in Peru, which cover more than 2 million people.[401] Cooperative pharmacies have sprung up in Haiti, Nigeria, and Singapore. The availability of high-quality drugs has been improved

Table 8.2   Affordability remains a problem for the poor
Ratio (in percent) of average annualized price of health services to income

	Russia	South Africa	Brazil	Tanzania
Poorest	11.9	34.6	20.6	4.4
Second poorest	5.3	20.3	11.6	2.7
Middle	3.3	13.3	7.2	2.0
Second richest	2.1	9.2	4.1	1.3
Richest	0.8	3.2	1.2	0.5

Sources: Authors' calculation based on Living Standards and Development Survey from Brazil (1996); South Africa (1993); Tanzania (1993–94); Uganda (1999); and Russia Longitudinal Monitoring Survey (1998).

through client-controlled revolving funds in Mongolia, Vietnam, and West Africa and through Ethiopia's special pharmacies. Particularly resilient to crisis, these efforts can be a source of stability and sustainability. In the Democratic Republic of Congo *zones de santé* continued to provide immunization through community-managed services after more than two decades, without state or donor support.[402]

Client financial and managerial control over health staff—the power to hire and fire—can help ensure that services are actually delivered. In Mali user associations hire and pay professional health staff serving more than 6 million people (spotlight on the Bamako Initiative). There, as in Peru, provider attendance is high, with strong local ownership of community centers. But the approach can have problems. The relationship between communities and health personnel can become antagonistic, requiring state intervention to arbitrate disputes. And the right of local health boards to hire and fire staff may mean little in countries facing severe human resource shortages. In Zambia during the health reform most districts hired the staff already working in the health facilities. In Mali the shortage of nurses made recruitment difficult, loosening the control of clients over frontline providers.[403]

Solidarity mechanisms to protect socially and economically disadvantaged groups by pooling financial resources can strengthen communities in their negotiations with health care providers. Micro-insurance schemes for health have been linked to such traditional modes of self-organization as rotating savings—as with *abotas* in Guinea-Bissau and traditional community schemes in the Philippines.[404] In Germany and the Republic of Korea, small, not-for-profit insurance societies became independent purchasers of health services, contracting with public and private providers.[405] The proximity of these schemes to their insured members allows effective monitoring. But the risk pool's small size makes them very vulnerable. Reinsurance can help,[406] but the added complexity can lead to the same managerial and governance problems in large-scale public

provision. The transparency of direct community control is lost. Scaling up would then be the kiss of death.

Information and monitoring

One of the strongest levers for strengthening client power is information, a critical instrument for changing self care behaviors. Under government leadership in Thailand, messages on AIDS were broadcast every hour during the peak of the epidemic. But behavior change is possible only when grounded in an understanding of cultural norms and the links between behavior and disease—and when local actors are involved. Community-based nutrition programs have often improved nutritional status through information exchanges, as in Tamil Nadu, India. In addition to giving women greater control over resources, the microcredit programs of the Bangladesh Rural Action Committee also increased knowledge.[407]

Clients can exert more leverage on providers by participating in decisionmaking and by monitoring some aspects of service delivery. Community monitoring of health service performance in Bolivia and Vietnam raises community awareness of key demand-side barriers and helps ensure that services meet community needs. Civil society representatives are also part of health boards in New Zealand. These approaches increase the transparency of management. But these health boards also remain vulnerable to capture by local elites unless institutional mechanisms ensure the representation of disadvantaged clients (chapter 5).[408]

BOX 8.5 *Vouchers for sex workers in Nicaragua*

A voucher program has been operating in Managua, Nicaragua, since 1995, with the objective of increasing the use of reproductive health services by female sex workers. The vouchers entitle the sex workers to free services at selected for-profit, NGO, and public clinics. The clinic turns the voucher in to the voucher agency, which reimburses the provider at an agreed-upon fee per voucher. The incidence of sexually transmitted diseases among sex workers who used the vouchers dropped by 65 percent in the first three years of the program. Vouchers are now available to the clients of sex workers and their partners.

Source: Gorter and others (1999).

BOX 8.6 *Making health insurance work for poor people*

Copayments are not always regressive (see chapter 4), and prepayment and insurance are not inherently pro-poor. In Tanzania's Community Financing Funds, poorer groups' copayments subsidized care for wealthier insured groups. The poor enroll in voluntary health schemes in small numbers, as in Cameroon, Ghana, and Rwanda—and in smaller proportions than richer groups, as in the Democratic Republic of Congo, Guinea, and Senegal. Employment-based social insurance systems have been observed to benefit richer groups most in Latin America and Africa. A review of Asian community financing schemes concluded that equity was low. Matching grants for insurance premiums are often captured by the local elites, as in Thailand during the early days of the health card. The grants sometimes simply lead richer groups to substitute private care for public services.

One way for governments to provide income protection to the poor is through progressive taxation or payroll-based social insurance, with egalitarian benefits. But this is often difficult to implement in developing and transition countries with weak taxation capacity (in China the proportion of gross domestic product collected by the state fell from 30 percent in 1980 to 10 percent in 1999). Taxes in low-income countries are also often regressive.

An alternative is for governments to subsidize insurance for the poor, using income-related sliding scales for premiums and copayments. Income-related contributions were successful in promoting equity in Israel and in the Gomoshasthaya Kendra community financing scheme in Bangladesh. Governments can also develop specific schemes for the poor, as was successfully done in Indonesia and Thailand. Both approaches require some means testing and the adequate and timely compensation of providers. And leakages are to be expected.

Source: Preker and others (2001).

Since ancient times, city councils have been involved in curtailing the spread of plague, cholera, and leprosy. But the state as the main actor in health emerged only in the 20th century, starting in centrally planned systems—the Soviet Union and others—and then spreading to Western Europe after World War II, with the government as unchallenged leader of the formal health system. Many developing countries have followed, with health services being part of the social contract between the (often) newly independent states and their citizens. The model was not always successful—witness the remaining health gaps between poor and rich in middle- and low-income countries. But some countries—Brazil, Malaysia, Sri Lanka, and Costa Rica (chapter 1)—have done better than others in making the long route of accountability work for poor people by:

- Channeling collective resources to poor people through multiple allocation mechanisms that combine targeting diseases of the poor, poor regions, service delivery providers close to poor people, and vulnerable groups and individuals.
- Developing coalitions that bring poor people into the policymaking process through both elections and advocacy by civil society.
- Establishing accountability for progress on outcomes, particularly among poor people through increased information and citizen monitoring of health services.

Enforcement and regulation

Legal and other dispute mechanisms—ombudsman services, the judicial system, and pressures on professional associations—can enforce provider accountability. But there is little proof that such mechanisms work in favor of the poor. A study in the United States in 2000 found that 97 percent of people with negligent injury did not sue. Better-off clients went to court, while poor clients did not. In India women from lower castes were less likely to use consumers' courts. Seventy-six percent of Indian doctors believed the Consumer Protection Act to be only moderately effective because of weak enforcement and resistance from professionals. Sanctions are often a weak threat, because health providers tend to protect one another, and accountability channels do not favor poor clients. Rampant corruption in the legal system of many countries also works against poor people.[409]

Strengthening poor citizens' voice

Simply don't vote for your mayor . . . if he doesn't provide you access to your health program.
Managers of the Health Agent Program
that reduced infant mortality
in Ceará, Brazil

Which services and for whom?

How do we know if voice works for poor people? There is no conclusive evidence that either one of the main resource-generation mechanisms for health services emanating from collective action—social insurance (Bismark model) or general taxation (Beveridge model)—works better for the poor.[410] To be pro-poor they both require some level of cross-subsidy—through either differential premiums or progressive taxes. More than prepayment, third-party payment—whether through insurance or other solidarity funds—is what makes the difference for poor people (box 8.6).

There is also no clear answer on whether providing universal access to a limited set of

Table 8.3   How do we know whether poor people's voices have been heard?

Key questions	Evidence	Problems
Is there a constitutional or legislative commitment to guarantee some level of health service to all?	• Most countries have constitutions that express some commitment to universal access or rights to health care. Few have an expressed commitment to the poorest segments of society. Rights-based arguments such as the Special Session For Children of the United Nations General Assembly can provide legal grounds for claiming access to services. • With the exception of Mexico, Turkey, and the United States, all OECD countries today offer their populations universal protection against the cost of illness.	• Lack of prioritization or targeting gives the non-poor incentives to seek more services or shift from private to public providers. • The distribution of health resources is influenced by more vocal and often urban populations and is concentrated in a highly visible urban hospital infrastructure, as in Nepal. With the exception of a few countries (e.g., Costa Rica, Malaysia), public spending on health care often disproportionately benefits the non-poor (chapter 2).
Are the diseases that affect the poor priorities for public action?	• Cost-effective packages of services addressing the overall burden of disease often overlap with the diseases that affect the poor most.	• Cost-effective health interventions have also been captured to a large extent by richer groups. • Epidemiological profile often polarized between rich and poor.
Are services that are close to the poor given priority?	• Benefit incidence studies show primary health care to be significantly more pro-poor than hospital-level care.	• Primary care also benefits richer groups more in many countries.
Do disadvantaged areas benefit as much or more than richer areas?	• Population and needs-based funding increase the health funding for poor groups. Brazil led richer states such as Parana to have their share reduced to the benefit of poorer states in the Northeast.	• The wealthiest areas often receive larger government subsidies than poorer regions, as documented in Bangladesh, the Kyrgyz Republic, Mauritania, Mozambique, Pakistan, and Peru. • Political resistance to equalization.
Do children, women, and the elderly benefit from public services?	• Thailand's exemption policy for children and the elderly has been largely successful. Mozambique's exemption for treatment of illnesses in children at the primary care level has been partially successful: 65 percent of children were exempted.	• Poor children and poor women may not be reached. And services leave out poor male adults, whose welfare indirectly affects the welfare of children and women.
Do individual households benefit from specific protection measures?	• Exemptions can be effective when funds are available to compensate providers, as in the insurance fund in the Kyrgyz Republic or the Type B scheme in Thailand. Ghana's program of fee exemptions for the poor was initially successful, then faltered when providers were not compensated.	• Exemptions have a poor track record of serving the poor, often benefiting civil servants and their families. • Assessment of individual targeting left to individual providers, which generates a conflict of interest.

Sources: Pearson and Belli (2003) and Soucat and Rani (2003a).

services or targeting poor people is the way to go. The debate is often not in these terms. Most Organisation for Economic Co-operation and Development (OECD) countries use both approaches. Many middle-income countries are moving gradually, developing multiple programs to protect children, women, and the poor, as in Colombia, Indonesia, Iran, and Turkey. These programs may eventually merge into a national system of universal coverage, as happened in industrial countries and recently in Thailand. Geographical, age, and individual targeting—despite leakages—often reach the poor. But a combination of mechanisms seems necessary, and each country has to assess whether mechanisms in place are successful (table 8.3).

Decentralization has often been implemented with the hope that it would better align spending with local needs, reducing the information asymmetry between citizens and politicians. But decentralization has had mixed results in health.[411] It has not always meant increased resources for poor areas. Transferring the provision function to local governments has often overwhelmed them, leaving them with little capacity and incentives to develop the policy function and encourage citizen oversight. The transfer of ownership of assets—hospitals and clinics—to local government has also created incentives for rent-seeking by local elites. In Uganda allocations to health services declined when districts received responsibility for service delivery, personnel management, and allocation of health resources. Spending on primary health care fell from 33 percent to 16 percent during 1995–98, and the use of maternal and child health services declined significantly[412] (chapter 10).

Pro-poor coalitions

With widespread capture of health services by the non-poor, building pro-poor coalitions to influence health spending is critical. The democratic process conveys what poor citizens value in health and health care. The extent of health benefits and the financing of health services are an electoral issue in industrial countries—and, increasingly, everywhere. In Thailand access to health services was a key plank in the political platform of the Thai Rak Thai party, and its proposal for universal health insurance, with a single 30-baht copayment, was eventually implemented.[413] Eliminating hunger was a major theme in the recent elections in Brazil.

Beyond the ballot box, poor citizens can communicate their preferences through national consultations, such as those for poverty reduction strategy papers (chapter 11). A review of the consultation process for 25 poverty reduction strategy papers shows that the poor care about health services, especially access, price, and social distance. In the state of Oregon in the United States, tradeoffs in benefit coverage are discussed in consultations with the public. In the Netherlands the Dunning Report, proposing criteria for rationing health services, relied heavily on citizen consultations. Citizen involvement in budgeting is now an avenue for more voice in health service delivery, as in Porto Alegre, Brazil (chapter 5).[414]

Advocacy by civil society organizations can put the interests of groups forgotten or discriminated against on the agenda, as in the campaign and court action to ban the use of quinacrine for chemical sterilization in India. Such organizations can build coalitions for the interests of the disadvantaged. Pressure through self-help groups and NGOs has triggered a productive dialogue on the public response to AIDS in the Philippines and South Africa.

Yet despite years of endorsement of participation, most health systems still resist greater involvement by civil society in influencing health care allocations. Reforms in the health sector often engender opposition by powerful unions and professional associations, which have a much stronger power base than poor citizens and can fight to maintain the status quo, as in New Zealand.

An altruistic vision can nonetheless motivate coalitions between providers and citizens for better services. Associations of rural doctors in Thailand and midwives in Guatemala have promoted alternative modes of health service delivery that better reach the poor.

Information and monitoring to increase accountability for outcomes

Creating policymaker accountability to citizens for delivering health services is a difficult task. A patient dying while waiting in line at a public hospital makes front-page news. But the thousands of children who die of treatable or vaccine-preventable diseases do not get equal time. Politicians find it easier to claim success for building a hospital and providing employment to nurses and doctors than for reducing malnutrition among a nomadic group. Yet with a web of market and government failures affecting those services, policymakers are uniquely placed to create a vision conducive to better outcomes. They need to be accountable for equitably distributed health outcomes, protecting citizens against impoverishing health expenditures and helping the poor escape their social exclusion, and not for the provision of growing quantities of services.

Better informed and educated citizens can make politicians more accountable. Civil society organizations can bridge the asymmetry of information between poor citizens and policymakers. They can bring community participation into research, to ensure that the perspectives of poor people influence policy. Monitoring the performance of government policies, with report cards as in Bangalore and Ukraine (chapter 5), can work well, particularly when income-disaggregated data are available.

Civil society can also serve as a watchdog. A Belgian health publication set in motion six royal decrees of protective legislation by drawing attention to health hazards. In Bolivia a census-based, impact-oriented approach combines pragmatism with quantitative and qualitative approaches.[415] But generating information to support pro-poor coalitions is a challenge. Epidemiological surveys may neglect the needs of peripheral social groups, such as minority groups or those affected by less common diseases.

Compacts: provider incentives to serve the poor

As long as men are liable to die and are desirous to live, a physician will be well paid.

Jean de La Bruyère, 1645–1696

Even when policymakers truly care about health services for poor people, it is not easy to translate policy into reality. Making the compact between policymakers and providers work for the poor implies that governments:

- Benchmark performance for services they can monitor easily;
- Foster autonomous providers for clinical services;
- Establish a strong monitoring function.

Buying results

Widespread deficiencies in the technical quality and ethics of frontline providers serving the poor—whether public or private—reveal an incentive problem.[416] The solution lies in some form of compact between the policymaker and provider to align the provider's incentives—already acknowledged by La Bruyère in the 17th century—with the policymaker's wishes. How countries can create incentives to make autonomous or dispersed health service providers accountable for outputs and outcomes depends on the nature of services and the capacity to create accountability for public objectives through purchasing and regulation.[417]

Outcome-based contracts are difficult to implement because health outcomes are often slow to change, difficult and expensive to measure, and affected by multiple factors other than health services. Such contracts are especially difficult to write when outcomes are linked to a variety of services, both professional and nonprofessional, as in efforts to reduce under-five mortality or HIV prevalence. But the experience of Madagascar and Senegal with nutrition programs for the poor shows that it is possible, at least for malnutrition (box 8.7).

Less difficult to implement are output-based contracts that specify criteria for disbursing public subsidies—on the basis of increasing immunization rates, for example. Output-based contracting is particularly successful for easily monitorable, single-product,

---

BOX 8.7 *The government as active purchaser of health outcomes through strategic contracting*

Community nutrition projects in Madagascar and Senegal contracted out nutritional services. Transaction costs for introducing and maintaining the contracts were 13 percent of total project costs in Madagascar and 17 percent in Senegal. Both projects were well targeted to the poor communities.

Activities included growth monitoring, health and nutrition education services for mothers, food supplementation for malnourished children, and referrals to health centers and home visits when necessary. In Madagascar the project also had a social fund for income-generating activities, and in Senegal an effort to improve access to water.

The frontline providers in Madagascar included women from the targeted neighborhoods selected by the communities and supervised by physicians hired by the projects. Open tendering was used to select the supervising NGOs in Madagascar. Contractual agreements specified the services to be provided and the number of beneficiaries to be served, monitored monthly by the user community and the project.

Childhood malnutrition declined significantly in both projects. An evaluation in Senegal after 17 months of project implementation showed almost zero prevalence of severe malnutrition among children aged 6–11 months and a reduction in moderate malnutrition from 28 percent to 24 percent among children aged 6–35 months.

Source: Marek and others (1999).

---

population-oriented services that can be standardized. Explicit contracts have proven effective in serving poor, hard-to-reach groups.[418] Output-based fees for services can be paid to providers when quantity and quality can be defined, thus contributing to improvements in productivity. In Bangladesh NGO field health workers were paid on the basis of their clients' knowledge of oral rehydration therapy.

Implicit contracts with focus on specific outputs can also work, as demonstrated by the universal childhood immunization campaigns of the 1980s, and the Vitamin A supplementation and itinerant health teams in Egypt, Indonesia, and Mexico.[419] Malawi and Uzbekistan have achieved immunization coverage of more than 90 percent among the poor with very low per capita spending. But Bolivia, Guatemala, and Turkey, with higher levels of spending, are much less successful in providing equitable coverage (figure 8.10).

Performance-based contracts, whether directly with health providers or with purchasers or insurers, need to align money with intent, taking into account the variations in effort required to produce a given output in poor and disadvantaged regions and in better-off communities.[420] Costs of services can be much higher in remote rural areas, and broad variations have been found in the cost of immunization between regions in the same country.[421]

Figure 8.10 High spending does not ensure more equitable immunization

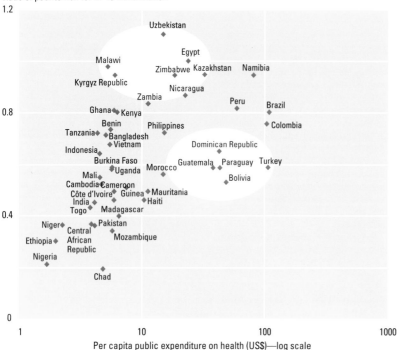

Ratio of poor to rich for DPT3 immunization

Per capita public expenditure on health (US$)—log scale

Source: Authors' calculations using Demographic and Health Survey data and World Bank data.

Performance benchmarks for more discretionary or multitask services, such as clinical care, are more difficult to establish. Which services for whom, when, where, how, and how much are difficult to specify in advance. Effort and quality are not readily verifiable. Providers have more gaming space.[422] Targeted payments to increase cervical smears in the United Kingdom led to a short-term increase in the number of smears. But in the long term providers reorganized their activities so that they would continue to receive the payments without delivering the services.[423]

Clinical service contracts also take considerable capacity to write and enforce.[424] Purchasing based on output—per visit, per case, per hospital day—causes the quantity of clinical services provided to rise (sometimes mainly among better-off groups) and the costs to escalate. Health reforms often try to contain costs by establishing fixed-price contracts—capitated payments, or prospective global budgets—using caps to keep costs down and shifting risks to the provider. But this leaves to frontline

providers the responsibility for rationing services, opening the possibility for cream-skimming. Providers can lower their standard of care, deny service, or insist on additional informal fees (box 8.8).

Equitable service distribution then requires providers to have both the technical capacity to inform the rationing process and a pro-poor ethos to make this process benefit the poor—a combination often difficult to achieve. High- and middle-income countries are therefore increasingly delegating the undertaking of clinical service contracts to an autonomous—often parastatal—social insurance organization that negotiates agreements for services to be provided. They rely on more sophisticated contracts and monitoring systems using complex payment methods: for example, case-based payments in Georgia or diagnostically related groups in Hungary.

Identifying poor target groups and monitoring results are also more difficult for clinical care, because needs are more difficult to define. Cambodia's contract, which included specific provisions to increase clinical services for the poor, had mixed results (spotlight on Cambodia). Incentives for treating those most in need can be strengthened by calibrating payments to providers on the basis of impact on health outcomes, with higher payments for emergency obstetric care, as in Burkina Faso, or with higher payments for treating the poor, as in the Kyrgyz Republic (box 8.9). To exempt the poor from fees, how-

---

BOX 8.8 *The risks of capitation payments*

In 1999 in Poland, Mrs. K. contributed a health premium amounting to 7.5 percent of her salary, but was not able to see a public-private insurance doctor "free of charge" even once. Several times she tried to get an appointment with the doctor in the outpatient clinic where she signed in. But she was told every time that "there are no tickets" for that day. In the end she went to the private internal medicine doctor and paid out of pocket.[425]

Source: World Bank (2001d).

ever, providers need to receive timely and adequate compensation.

Contractual arrangements often need to combine soft capacity-building components to meet unserved needs with rewards for performance. Experience with performance-based contracts for immunization as part of the Global Alliance for Vaccines and Immunizations shows that zero-based contracts and the threat of resource withdrawal were not very effective in raising coverage.[426] Variations across communities can be taken into account through a two-tier allocation system. The first tier can be allocated to a local government on a capitation basis—as in Argentina, Brazil, Ethiopia, and Poland—and the second tier to an insurance fund or a purchasing agency in charge of maximizing the efficiency of resources and purchasing an appropriate mix and quantity of clinical services—as in Korea and New Zealand (figure 8.11).

The impact on the poor of the changes in provider payments from input-based to more complex output-based is not conclusive, and there has been little evaluation. But the separation of policymaking from purchasing and service provision creates clearer channels of accountability. Autonomous providers have more flexibility in ensuring the appropriate input mix including hiring and firing, as in Kenya and Zambia.[427] Purchasing bodies are more independent actors, subject to a double line of accountability because they are often financed by governments and households through insurance systems. Governments need to be involved in these agencies to define which services the poor need most, price the subsidy support needed by the poor, and limit providers' conflicts of interest.

Selecting providers

There is no presumption that one type of provider—public, for-profit, or not-for-profit—is likely to be better than any other. Public health facilities can be remarkably efficient, as in Malaysia, or largely ineffective, as in middle-income Gabon, where immunization levels have stalled at under 30 percent. Nor are NGOs necessarily pro-poor. When contracted by governments, NGOs also tend to get closer to the public

BOX 8.9 *Modulated payments for providers according to income criteria*

The Kyrgyz Republic created an insurance fund to purchase services from health facilities, compensating them for increased use of services and providing greater financial access to the poor. Facilities charge fees to patients and claim payments from the insurance funds under a sliding scale based on five categories of patients: self-referred, uninsured, insured, partly exempt, and fully exempt. Facilities get higher compensation for clients from the partly exempt and exempt categories, who pay lower fees. Sixty-eight percent of poor patients preferred the copayment system over the previous theoretically free system, which often required "informal" payments. Under the new payment mechanism, many informal payments were replaced by formal copayments. The very poor have access to treatment through a reserve fund.

Source: Kutzin (2003).

sector. An autonomous parastatal hospital in France that enjoys large financial and management flexibility and an NGO hospital under government contract in Canada are not very different.

For population-oriented services that can be standardized, governments can generally write contracts for public or private providers. Policymakers can specify the service

Figure 8.11 Citizens exert power on both providers and purchasers

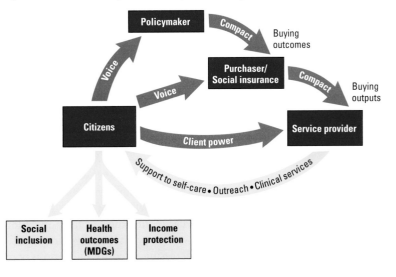

characteristics and monitor and enforce the contract. Government providers deliver high immunization rates in Tajikistan or Tunisia—but in Cambodia and Haiti so do contracted NGOs. As contractors NGOs can extend service outreach and test new approaches to service delivery.[428]

To support self-care, private services— whether for-profit or not-for-profit—often are most appropriate. Private for-profit providers can be very efficient in providing information and distributing commodities—witness the success of social marketing. For information and social support, grassroots organizations, small private providers, and community-based organizations often do the job better than rigid public organizations. Governments can contract some key services such as information. Yet public services can sometimes be more pro-poor than NGO services. In Ceará, Brazil, "many NGOs delivered services in clinics while the public service sent its workers into households"[429] (see spotlight).

For clinical services the contrast is sharper. Public provision works well when there is a strong public ethos, the politics are pro-poor, and rules are enforced. For-profit providers—qualified or not—are usually in tune with demand, but the inherent conflicts of interest require external control. In Lebanon and elsewhere, expansion of the private sector did not benefit the poor much.[430] In India, private providers serving poor groups are often less than qualified. Governments can then exert control only if they have sophisticated regulation and purchasing functions. When these do not exist, partnerships between government and civil society organizations can compensate by strengthening clients' power over clinical providers.

Because not-for-profit organizations often benefit from strong intrinsic motivation and professional ethos, government can also write open-ended contracts with them and still expect that providers will do the right thing. Service delivery by NGOs can help repair the link between policymakers and providers for clinical services with significant benefits for the poor. In Guatemala, about a third of the population is now served by NGO providers, significantly increasing access for indigenous poor

populations although management and quality problems have been observed.[431]

Regulation and enforcement

Governments can also use market regulation to counter conflicts of interest. In Hungary accreditation mechanisms have been quite successful in establishing quality criteria for providers. To reduce supplier-induced over-supply and compensate for the lack of investment in poorer settings, most countries use certificates of needs (in United States), planning boards (Australia), or health maps (Spain and most of Africa). But most low-income countries do not regulate their pharmaceutical market successfully, though Cambodia has had some success. When regulation fails, a combination of user education and provider training can yield the greatest benefits.[432] Government involvement through national tendering, price capping, or tariff reduction has also influenced the prices of pharmaceuticals.[433] Overall the enforcement of regulatory controls is often weak, focusing mainly on personnel licensing. The same political and institutional failures hampering health service delivery affect the legislative, administrative, and judicial services needed to make regulation work.

Expanding access to professional health care providers—particularly midwifery, surgical skills for reducing maternal mortality, and clinical skills for reducing neonatal deaths—is a priority to reach the Millennium Development Goals. In many countries the imbalance between rural and urban areas in terms of skilled health workers is extreme. In Turkey, there is one doctor per 266 people in the richest region and one per 2,609 in the poorest. In Ghana and Senegal more than half the physicians are concentrated in the capital city, where fewer than 20 percent of people live. Health workers lack opportunities in rural areas where turnover is high. Rural workers are less likely to be female and educated. Lack of services (school, water) and access to training/education are major incentives to leave rural areas. Undifferentiated salary structures are disincentives to work in areas where the poor live, because it is difficult to supplement low salaries with alternative income from activities such as private practice, teaching, and consulting.[434]

BOX 8.10 *The human resource crisis in health services*

When the international community set out in 1955 to eradicate malaria, Africa was left out because it lacked adequately trained personnel. Today, Africa still lacks such personnel, and yet it must deal with multiple disease-control efforts. In Burkina Faso, the average number of physicians per 100,000 people was 3.4 in the 1990s compared with 303 for nine industrial countries. In Zambia the already low number of physicians, at 8.3 per 100,000 people in the 1960s, declined to 6.9 in the 1990s. To meet the requirements of the priority health interventions recommended by the World Health Organization, Chad would require a sevenfold increase in health personnel.

High rates of absenteeism reflect disenchantment with working conditions. Studies of health professionals in Ghana, India, Mozambique, Tanzania, and Uganda show that the health work force—nurses and physicians in particular—feel overworked and underappreciated. In Guinea, Mauritania, Poland, and Russia health staff wages have declined in real terms.

There has been considerable emigration of health professionals from developing countries. More than 600 South African doctors are registered in New Zealand, at a cost to South African taxpayers of roughly $37 million. An estimated 61 percent of Ghanaian doctors trained between 1985 and 1994 left the country. Nurses are leaving too: in 2001 the United Kingdom approved 22,462 work permits for nurses from developing countries.

To retain internationally marketable health staff, poor countries will have to offer internationally competitive wages and benefits. That requires replacing inflexible civil service policies with more flexible approaches. Training specifically oriented to national markets can also help. Countries that emulate the training standards of industrial countries tend to be more vulnerable to poaching (Ghana). There is evidence from Ethiopia and the Gambia that community nurses and health officers with curricula not internationally certified are less likely to migrate.

Human resources constraints for clinical care

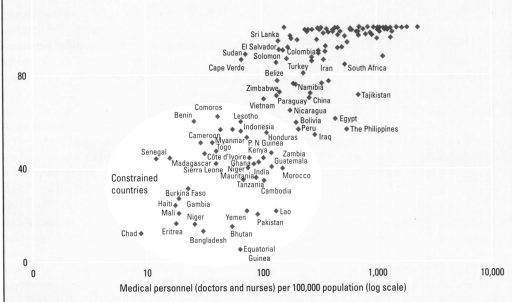

Sources: Liese and others (2003), Commission on Macroeconomics and Health (2001), Ferrinho and Van Lerberghe (2003), and Reinikka and Svensson (2003b).

Chile, Mexico, and Thailand[435] have used financial and nonfinancial incentives to encourage qualified staff to work in rural areas. In Indonesia doctors were also allowed to supply private services during or after duty hours. Other countries have tried to establish new credentials, as for health officers in Ethiopia, and trained community workers in India and Brazil (spotlight on Ceará). Another approach includes progressively upgrading the skills of traditional providers, such as community midwives in Malaysia, or encouraging the hiring and training of health workers from underserved areas or social groups as done in Indonesia and Iran. In the Bangladesh Rural Advancement Committee (BRAC) community workers are trained to seek out the extremely poor in need of urgent medical care. But success requires careful design and evaluation. In El Salvador low-skilled health promoters posted in rural villages did little to improve health or health-seeking behavior.[436] The global crisis in the labor market for clinical services also requires innovative strategies to get professional services to rural areas and the poor (box 8.10).

The complexity and dispersed nature of clinical health services and the potential for conflicts of interest make self-monitoring by providers critical for effective service delivery. Historically, peer regulation has been the common response to a conflict of interest. But because of state dominance in many countries, professional bodies are fairly weak. Provider-driven changes in the organization of service provision can yield substantial benefits for clients, as in initiatives such as Health Workers for Change.[437] The German health system is largely self-regulated. Professional associations in Zimbabwe maintain professional ethics and standards among public and private nurses.[438] Associations of midwives in Guatemala and New Zealand develop and promote a pro-poor ethos (box 8.11).

Information and monitoring

Decentralization, devolution, and output-based contracting of services increase the importance of timely and accurate information for monitoring performance. National and international statistics do not yet capture the range of practices or the performance of all health care providers. Most ministries of health know little about the private sector, which makes it hard to develop partnerships or contracts, although countries are attempting to conduct provider surveys as in Poland.[439] Information on access, quality, and efficiency is scarce and often noncomparable. And because many factors outside the health sector affect health status, cross-sectoral monitoring and planning are also required, as Thailand's National Economic and Social Development Board does regularly.

Monitoring of average outcomes or service utilization patterns often does not reveal where change is occurring. Changes in fertility rates and contraceptive use in most Sub-Saharan countries in the 1990s have been concentrated in the urban, richest population segments. In Tanzania the declining use of skilled delivery care between 1993 and 1999 can be attributed mainly to declining use among the poorest groups. When collecting information on income is difficult, alternative indicators can be used, such as ethnicity, caste, region, gender, linguistic group, or religion. Countries as different as Colombia, Indonesia, Iran, Mexico, and the Philippines use community maps to identify high-risk individuals and households in need of home visits and special attention.[440]

Six sizes fit all?

Which accountability mechanisms should be emphasized to ensure that health resources go where they should? There is no single path. The many things that influence the short and long routes of accountability call for different responses. For health and nutrition services, one size does not fit all. What works varies by country and type of service. A strong command-and-control approach can achieve much if policymakers have a solid mandate or the ideological drive to make tough choices about which health services to deliver and to whom—as in Cuba,[441] Malaysia, or Iran. Greater inclusion of poor people in the political debate can influence policymakers, as in Brazil where the pro-poor orientation of health policies has improved over the past 10 years (spotlight on Ceará). But when the mandate is less clear and implementation levers are weak, the short route of accountability through client partnerships with private and community-based providers gives poor people more control over services.

B O X   8 . 1 1   *Developing a professional ethos in midwifery*

In the words of a professor of midwifery, "Midwives should be able to take on a more enabled, 'for women' role. This then has implications for regulation, which should be 'self regulated' to a point—but should also have input to that process from women themselves, and from fellow professionals.... Midwives should be very involved in the process, ... but if they are the only ones involved, the danger is that a 'for midwife' culture develops, protecting midwives and perpetuating problems.... The formal process can also be backed up by a less formal process (i.e. peer review) to ensure lots of midwife to midwife contact and learning. This 'with-women/for-women' stance can then form a foundation for what 'professionalism' looks like for midwifery....

We need to be able to form a contract, ... and follow up on it, all the time respecting woman's individuality and the culture in which she lives. This all implies enough education to do this well, and enough power to influence the system. This is what I would describe as 'professional.'"

Sources: ICM (2003) and Davies (2001).

Figure 8.12   Six sizes fit all

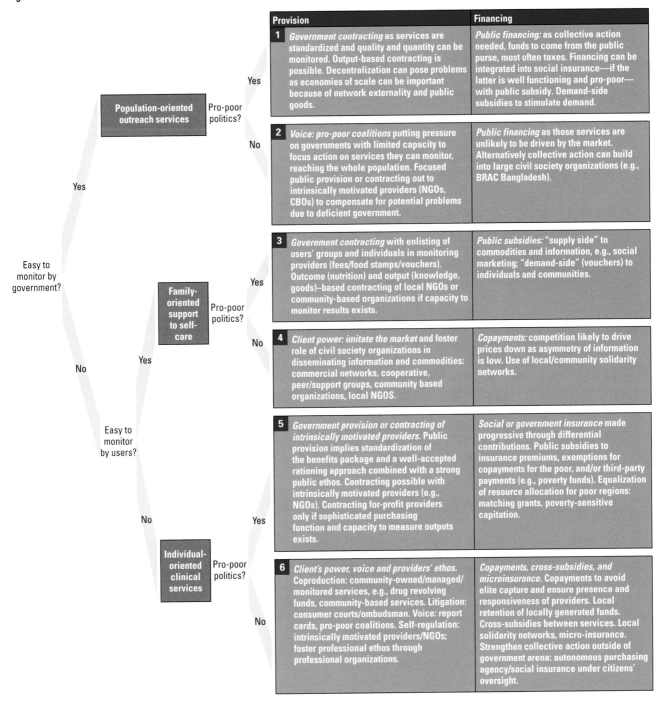

Provision	Financing
1 *Government contracting* as services are standardized and quality and quantity can be monitored. Output-based contracting is possible. Decentralization can pose problems as economies of scale can be important because of network externality and public goods.	*Public financing:* as collective action needed, funds to come from the public purse, most often taxes. Financing can be integrated into social insurance—if the latter is well functioning and pro-poor—with public subsidy. Demand-side subsidies to stimulate demand.
2 *Voice: pro-poor coalitions* putting pressure on governments with limited capacity to focus action on services they can monitor, reaching the whole population. Focused public provision or contracting out to intrinsically motivated providers (NGOs, CBOs) to compensate for potential problems due to deficient government.	*Public financing* as those services are unlikely to be driven by the market. Alternatively collective action can build into large civil society organizations (e.g., BRAC Bangladesh).
3 *Government contracting* with enlisting of users' groups and individuals in monitoring providers (fees/food stamps/vouchers). Outcome (nutrition) and output (knowledge, goods)–based contracting of local NGOs or community-based organizations if capacity to monitor results exists.	*Public subsidies:* "supply side" to commodities and information, e.g., social marketing; "demand-side" (vouchers) to individuals and communities.
4 *Client power: imitate the market* and foster role of civil society organizations in disseminating information and commodities: commercial networks, cooperative, peer/support groups, community based organizations, local NGOS.	*Copayments:* competition likely to drive prices down as asymmetry of information is low. Use of local/community solidarity networks.
5 *Government provision or contracting of intrinsically motivated providers.* Public provision implies standardization of the benefits package and a well-accepted rationing approach combined with a strong public ethos. Contracting possible with intrinsically motivated providers (e.g., NGOs). Contracting for-profit providers only if sophisticated purchasing function and capacity to measure outputs exists.	*Social or government insurance* made progressive through differential contributions. Public subsidies to insurance premiums, exemptions for copayments for the poor, and/or third-party payments (e.g., poverty funds). Equalization of resource allocation for poor regions: matching grants, poverty-sensitive capitation.
6 *Client's power, voice and providers' ethos.* Coproduction: community-owned/managed/monitored services, e.g., drug revolving funds, community-based services. Litigation: consumer courts/ombudsman. Voice: report cards, pro-poor coalitions. Self-regulation: intrinsically motivated providers/NGOs; foster professional ethos through professional organizations.	*Copayments, cross-subsidies, and microinsurance.* Copayments to avoid elite capture and ensure presence and responsiveness of providers. Local retention of locally generated funds. Cross-subsidies between services. Local solidarity networks, micro-insurance. Strengthen collective action outside of government arena: autonomous purchasing agency/social insurance under citizens' oversight.

So if one size does not fit all, can six sizes? Figure 8.12 attempts to capture some typical situations that could provide guidance. Situations vary according to the homogeneity of the health needs, the nature of services, and the characteristics of the political process.

When the long route of accountability works well for poor people—their concerns are included in the political process—public action benefits them. Governments can provide or contract out standardized population-oriented services (1), and provide demand-side subsidies to poor families for those and for appropriate self-care (3). Needs for clinical care can be made homogeneous through a technocratic rationing of services based on equal benefits. In this case an integrated service delivery approach—or a universal single payer system—can be appropriate, as in Cuba, Finland, and Vietnam (5).

But these conditions are far from universal. Needs for self-care or clinical services are rarely homogeneous. This heterogeneity can be accommodated in a pro-poor context through decentralization and flexible output-based and outcome-based contracting combined with equalization of subsidies between rich and poor regions (3 and 5). Subsidies for clinical services can be provided to local medical schemes (as in Germany and Poland), to specific schemes for poor people (as in France, Indonesia, and Thailand), or directly to poor groups (poverty funds in China) (5).

The long route of accountability may also not be working—either because richer groups capture the political process or because the bureaucratic process—compact—does not deliver. In these cases more investment in the long route through taxation and strengthened government actions is unlikely to do much for the poor. Instead, more needs to be invested in making poor citizens' voice heard by fostering civil society groups, and building pro-poor coalitions for services requiring collective action. Governments with limited capacity can then be pressured to focus on contracting population-oriented services, in partnership with intrinsically motivated providers—community or civil society organizations—to make sure the services are delivered (2).

Serving heterogeneous needs where the long route of accountability is not working is common in developing countries and requires enlisting poor people as monitors, investing in client's power. Commercial and media networks, cooperatives, and community-driven development activities are then best used to support self-care (4). Micro-insurance schemes, and community co-managed health services and drug funds are especially relevant for clinical care (6). But this power is not enough to avoid conflicts of interest. Litigation can be of limited help. More importantly, altruistically motivated providers, such as not-for-profits, can help foster a stronger pro-poor ethos supported by professional self regulation (6).

None of the solutions is fast or easy. But success is clearly possible, as hundreds of examples have shown. "It does not matter how slowly you go so long as you do not stop" (Confucius, 551–479 BC).

Good health at (initially) low income

Costa Rica and Cuba have both attained very low levels of infant mortality in the last 50 years. For Costa Rica, this is easily explained by rapid income growth and attention to traditional public health and, in recent years, to innovative approaches to publicly funded health care. Cuba, on the other hand, has maintained lower levels of infant mortality than many industrial countries and has eliminated diseases common to developing countries while remaining very poor. The achievements came with a community-based health system with numerous health workers, highly motivated staff, and close monitoring and evaluation of outcomes. Can Cuba's model survive the economic reversals of the 1990s and pressure for a more open and free society?

Costa Rica and Cuba both have very similar, low infant mortality rates—almost as low as Canada's though at much lower incomes (figure 1).[442] Their routes to this happy circumstance, however, have been quite different

In 1945, infant mortality—measured in deaths of infants under one year per 1,000 live births—was 100 in Costa Rica and 40 in Cuba, respectively. Up to 1960 Costa Rica made progress largely due to economic growth and aggressive public health programs.[443] Hookworm was eliminated with a program starting in 1942, and public health campaigns accelerated after the revolution of 1948. As a result, malaria, tuberculosis, and most diseases that were preventable by vaccines at that time were also eliminated by 1960. In stark contrast, Cuba's admittedly low level of infant mortality stagnated under a particularly corrupt political regime.

Since 1960, progress in Costa Rica has been rapid but not too difficult to explain. Costa Rica's real income per capita increased by 25 percent from 1960 to 1970—the same rate, coincidentally, that infant mortality declined. Income growth of 40 percent by 1980 along with the universalization of coverage for health care saw a further decrease of 60 percent in infant

Figure 1 Infant mortality in Cuba: low in the 1950s, even lower by 2000

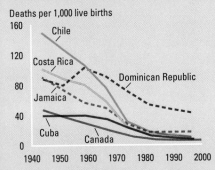

Deaths per 1,000 live births

Note: 1945 refers to years 1945–1949, 1950 to 1950–1954.
Source: 1945, 1950 from *United Nations Demographic Yearbook 1961.* Data for 1960–2000 are from UNICEF.

mortality. After recessions in the 1980s, growth has resumed and progress on health status continues. One way to attain good health from initially low income is surely to stop having a low income.

The Cuban puzzle— good health without growth

The puzzle is Cuba. How has Cuba managed to maintain an infant mortality rate at least as low as that of any developing country in the Western Hemisphere and quite a few industrial counties as well? The sustained focus of the political leadership on health for more than 40 years surely played a big part. After the revolution, universal and equitable health care was one of the government's top three goals. The government sees good health as a key performance indicator for itself.

Despite low infant mortality before the revolution, rural areas lagged far behind urban areas. The new government, committed to changing this, concentrated on providing health care to rural areas. It required all new medical school graduates to serve for one year in rural areas. It also increased the number of rural health facilities. In 1961 the government nationalized mutual-aid cooperatives and private hospitals, which left the public sector as the sole provider of health services—a feature of the system that remains today. At that time many of the country's medical professionals left the country (as many as two-thirds by one estimate).

In the mid- to late 1960s there were two major innovations in the health system. First was the establishment of policlinics— the basic unit of health services—each staffed by several specialists and nurses and serving a population of 25,000–30,000. This was combined with campaigns to immunize many more people, control vectors (such as mosquitoes), and promote good health practices.

Second was the creation of a community health program, with specialists tending patients in clinics as well as at home, school, or work.

In the mid-1980s this community-based approach was intensified with the Family Doctor Program. The goal: to place a doctor trained in primary health care and a nurse in every neighborhood (serving about 150 families). By 2001 there were more than 30,000 doctors—a ratio of one family doctor for every 365 Cubans.[444] Services are free, although nonhospitalized patients are required to co-pay for medicines.

While this approach clearly contributes to better health outcomes, it is also expensive. Indeed, Cuba spends substantially more of its gross domestic product on health than other Latin American countries: 6.6 percent in 2002. (Average public spending on health is 3.3 percent in Latin America and the Caribbean, but some other countries also spend substantial amounts—Costa Rica 4.4 percent and Panama 5.2 percent).[445]

Specifying what you want—and keeping track of what's going on

The Cuban health model rests on three pillars: giving clear instructions to providers, motivating staff, and monitoring and evaluating the system.[446] Clear guidelines are provided through national specialist advisory groups—which draw up standards and technical procedures (and evaluate the performance of physicians and specialists)— and regulations that standardize activities in the national hospital care system.

Health staff in Cuba typically are highly motivated. Medical training emphasizes the altruism of medical service—often culminating in service of one or two years abroad. This is volunteer service, but there are strong social pressures for it. Serving in poor rural areas in Cuba remains a right of passage for many newly trained doctors. Television programs lauding health workers engaged in international solidarity missions raise their profile and contribute to a sense of pride in Cuba's doctors.

Cuba also keeps close track of what's going on in health facilities. Monitoring is strong, with information flowing in many directions. The main elements are:

- An integrated national health statistics system that collects data routinely from service providers. Indicators of particular concern, such as infant mortality, are collected with high frequency—some even daily.

- Regular inspection of, and supervision visits to, health facilities.

- Annual evaluations of health technicians on the technical and scientific results of their work. In addition, a randomly selected sample undergoes external evaluation.

- Annual reports by the Ministry of Public Health and the provincial and municipal health directorates to the People's Power Assembly.

Monitoring and evaluation go beyond statistical and expert assessments. Public dissemination of health indicators, at the end of each year, draws citizens into the process. In addition, citizens can complain about providers. Their complaints can go through the health system—such as the policlinic that coordinates the local health facilities, the municipal health council, or hospital administrators. Or they can go through political channels—say, to the local representative of the People's Power Assembly, which is required to respond. Despite this monitoring, there is limited direct citizen control: participation in administrative and health councils does not entail much more than setting broad targets.[447] Likewise, citizens play only a small role in setting priorities within the health sector, and between health and other sectors.

Can Cuba sustain the system?

The 1990s were difficult for Cuba. The collapse of the socialist system in Europe and in the Soviet Union and the tightening of the economic embargo by the United States led to a severe economic contraction. Cuba lost the trading partners that had provided most of its imports of medicines, food, fuel, and equipment used in agriculture and mining. Between 1988 and 1993 imports of medicines fell by more than 60 percent. By 1994 agricultural production had fallen by almost half. Drug shortages persist today.[448]

Government spending on social services, particularly health care, was protected, with public spending on health exceeding 10 percent of GDP in 2000. But in real terms, spending had gone down. Health outcome indicators worsened in the early and mid-1990s, recovering only somewhat by the end of the decade.

As health infrastructure suffered, so did transport services. Public transport had all but disappeared by the early 1990s, and fuel shortages limited the use of private cars. Cubans resorted to walking miles to work, and the use of bicycles skyrocketed.[449]

The economic reversal also appears to be weakening motivation among staff. Physicians are paid relatively well, earning almost 15 percent more than the average national wage.[450] But their pay is in local currency, with purchasing power declining steadily over the past decade. The legalization of a separate "dollar economy" has made occupations that pay in dollars highly prized. Stories of doctors shirking their formal duties to join this parallel economy—driving taxicabs, for example— are common.[451]

Time will tell whether an approach that relies on a publicly paid doctor for every 150 families can be sustained in times of economic hardship—and with competition from an economy that relies more on the dollar.

Drinking water, sanitation, and electricity

Drinking water, sanitation, sewage disposal, electricity, rural roads, and urban transport influence human development outcomes (crate 1.1). As with education and health services, the impact of infrastructure services on human development is direct (e.g., reducing water-related diseases, which rank among the top killers of children). The impact is also indirect, through economic growth.[452] But like education and health, these services are failing poor people.

Focusing on water, sanitation, and electricity services, this chapter uses the Report's service delivery framework to find out why and to show how things might be improved. The reform lessons from these services, representing both network and non-network services, are also likely to apply to other infrastructure services.

For networked services, such as urban water and electricity, regulating providers and ensuring that poor people have access to affordable services are the main reasons for government intervention. This brings the long route of accountability into play. But poor citizens have a weak voice because water and electricity are particularly vulnerable to patronage politics. Providers end up being more accountable to policymakers than to clients, which breaks the long route of accountability.

The solution is to separate the policymakers from the providers—and to make providers more responsive to clients. Dispersing ownership through decentralization and private participation, promoting competition through benchmarking, ensuring alternative access by using independent providers, and charging for services are ways of separating policymakers from providers and strengthening compacts, client power, and voice.

In rural network and non-network settings, community and self-provision dominate. The policymaker as standard setter and capacity builder in support of the client is missing. To avoid ensuing problems, such as arsenic in Bangladesh's rural drinking water, policymakers need to support clients in ensuring service quality and access.

Externalities in sanitation in rural, non-network settings are best contained within the village or community. So supply-side support at the household level should be complemented with interventions at the community level—be it information about hygiene or subsidization of latrines—that are designed to spur household demand and create community peer pressure for behavior that internalizes the externalities. In urban settings, where demand for sanitation services may be greater, property rights and facilitating private response can support collective efforts.

The state of water and sanitation services

About 2 of every 10 people in the developing world were without access to safe water in 2000; 5 of 10 lived without adequate sanitation; and 9 of 10 lived without their wastewater treated in any way.[453] There have been gains, but despite the many global commitments, notably the U.N. Decade for Water and Sanitation, access to water and sanitation lags far behind the milestones set in the 1980s. Nor do aggregate trends in the 1990s give comfort (figure 9.1). The share of people with access to these services in Africa and Asia—where the world's poor are concentrated—has fallen, remained constant, or increased only slowly.

Innumerable city and town studies confirm the UN-Habitat Report's key message

Figure 9.1 Little progress in access to improved water and sanitation, 1990 and 2000

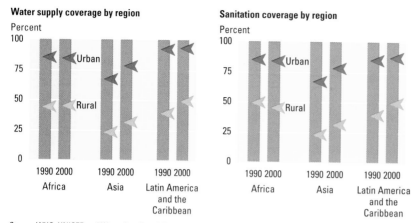

Source: WHO, UNICEF, and Water Supply and Sanitation Collaborative Council (2000).

that water and sanitation services are too often failing communities.[454] Full-pressure, "24-7" water supply remains a pipe dream in many cities. Because a quarter to half (and more) of urban water supply remains unaccounted for, many cities are turned into leaking buckets (figure 9.2). The limited number of network access points must be widely shared, which dramatically increases waiting times and often simply overwhelms the system. Rural infrastructure often goes to seed: more than a third of existing rural infrastructure in South Asia is estimated to be dysfunctional.[455]

Poor people bear a disproportionate share of the impact of inefficient water and sanitation services. Fewer poor people are connected to a network. When they do have access, the installation has to be shared among many more people (figure 9.3). And the prices they pay are among the highest, generally more than those paid by more affluent households connected to the piped system (figure 9.4). The price differential is partly a result of inefficiencies—the inequitable practice of subsidizing piped water, lack of scale economies for independent providers, or worse, providers taking advantage of poor people's lack of choice. But some of the price differential can also reflect the flexibility and convenience of services offered by independent providers—no connection charges or access to quantities of water that are more affordable for poor people.

Infrastructure and the accountability framework for service delivery

Countries are trying different approaches to address failing water, sanitation, and electricity services. These include decentralizing to local governments, private sector participation, regulatory reform, community-driven development, and small independent providers. Some approaches try to make services work for poor people through targeted interventions. Others seek to improve services overall—on the premise that making services work for all is necessary for making them work for poor people. The same approach has worked in one setting and failed in another, and different approaches have worked in seemingly the same setting. What is needed is a way to think about the institutional and political characteristics of infrastructure services to understand what works where and why.

Accountability in infrastructure services

Chapters 3–6 of this Report develop a framework for analyzing how well the actors in service delivery—clients and citizens, politicians and policymakers, and service providers—

Figure 9.2 24-hour water: a pipe dream

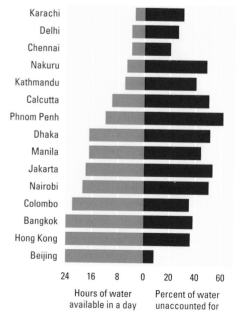

Source: Human Settlements Program (2003).

Figure 9.3 Water and sanitation by poorest and richest fifths

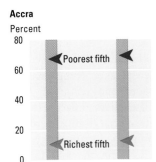

Accra

Percent

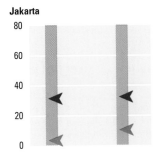

Jakarta

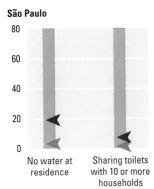

São Paulo

No water at residence / Sharing toilets with 10 or more households

Source: Human Settlements Program (2003).

Short route of accountability. In a simple market transaction, the buyer holds the seller accountable for the product bought, rewards the seller by repeating business, or penalizes the seller by choosing another provider. This accountability is "short" because the client can hold the provider directly accountable, without any intermediaries. Small, independent providers in water and sanitation and their clients are usually in such a market relationship.

In Dar-es-Salaam, Tanzania, a cholera outbreak in 1996 forced the sewerage and sanitation department to loosen its monopoly on cesspit cleaning and allow private providers in. There is now an emerging competitive private market for cesspit cleaning—households can choose a provider based on price and (easy-to-monitor) performance. Besides allowing entry and implementing regulations on sewage disposal, the city's role has been small.[456] But service and market conditions that automatically give clients power—through choice, ease of monitoring, and market enforceability—are not always present for infrastructure services. So the route of accountability has to be long.

Long route of accountability. Governments worldwide deem it their responsibility to provide, finance, regulate, and in other ways influence infrastructure services. They do it for two good reasons: market failures and equity concerns. First, networked infrastructure services exhibit

hold each other accountable within four relationships (figure 9.5):

- *Client power* connects service users with providers.
- *Voice* connects *citizens* with *politicians* and *policymakers* through the political process.
- *Compacts* connect policymakers through implicit or explicit contracts with *providers* responsible for services.
- And *management* connects provider organizations with frontline across-the-counter providers.

Figure 9.4 Alternative sources of water: poor people pay more
Price of water per liter, U.S. dollars

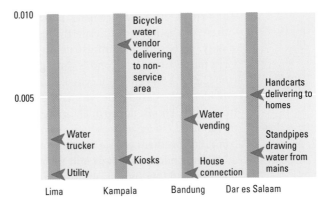

Lima / Kampala / Bandung / Dar es Salaam

Source: Human Settlements Program (2003).

Figure 9.5   Accountability in infrastructure services

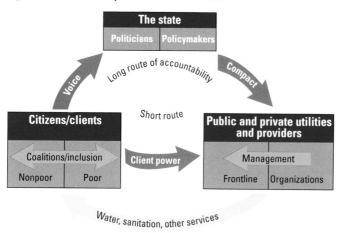

Board, a corporation owned and operated by government.

The short and long routes of accountability need to work together. Indeed, even for cesspit services in Dar-es-Salaam, government regulation was necessary to ensure that the small private operators complemented the public provider and complied with sewage disposal guidelines. Effective solutions are likely to be a strategic mixture of the short and long routes of accountability as a system in which the clients, the policymaker, and the provider are linked in accountability relationships that make services work for poor people.

economies of scale, or network externalities, that make it technically more efficient to have a single distributor of the service. In sanitation the externalities come literally from spillovers. Yes, households in Dar-es-Salaam were willing to pay for improved sanitation with larger health benefits to the city. But free-rider problems, where one person's behavior hurts others with impunity—as in the case of runoff from open defecation in many parts of Asia and Africa—require community or government intervention. Second, societies care about equity, and governments often redistribute resources—such as a lifeline water subsidy—to ensure the minimum equitable service access that markets cannot.

Network externalities, collective action problems, and distributional goals thus provide powerful reasons for the government to be involved. The arrangements then are no longer primarily between the client and the provider, and new accountability relationships become important. The first of these arrangements is voice—citizens delegating to politicians the responsibility to ensure the infrastructure services they want. The second is through the compacts between policymakers and providers—to design the service delivery framework, choose a provider, and ensure that it meets citizen expectations. Voice and compacts together become the "long route" of accountability. In Bangladesh the prime minister and her power minister are, in principle, accountable to citizens for the performance of the Power Development

Why infrastructure services fail poor people: patronage

Because the family has been without daytime water for the past decade, the children have never seen water come out of their home faucets. . . . The faucet flows only between midnight and 4 a.m. in most of Baryo Kapitolyo. MWSS, you know that. Did you care?

> Dahli Aspillera, a citizen of Manila, on the eve of the privatization of Manila's public water agency, Metro-Manila Waterworks and Sewerage System (MWSS), in 1997

Where water, sanitation, and electricity are publicly managed, the accountability to citizens is achieved when the state ensures that utilities, boards, and government departments provide efficient and equitable services for all citizens, including the poor. When the state is unsuccessful and the voice relationship is not effective, the long route of accountability has failed.

In 1997 the MWSS was typical of service utilities, boards, and government departments that consider politicians and policymakers as their real clients. Politicians—responding to equity concerns or, more likely, to short-term political gain—often keep prices for infrastructure services well below those for cost recovery. This makes service providers dependent on politically motivated budget transfers for survival—or when transfers are not forthcoming, on service cutbacks that attract no penalties from policymakers.

State-owned water and electricity providers then cease to function as autonomous service providers.[457] They become

BOX 9.1 *Clientelism in service delivery*

Patronage weakening accountability in the citizen-provider chain

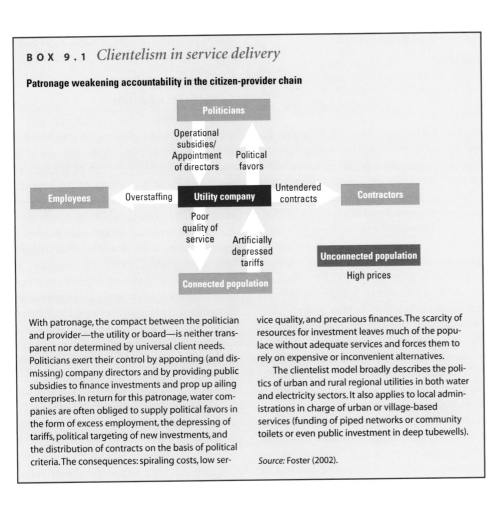

With patronage, the compact between the politician and provider—the utility or board—is neither transparent nor determined by universal client needs. Politicians exert their control by appointing (and dismissing) company directors and by providing public subsidies to finance investments and prop up ailing enterprises. In return for this patronage, water companies are often obliged to supply political favors in the form of excess employment, the depressing of tariffs, political targeting of new investments, and the distribution of contracts on the basis of political criteria. The consequences: spiraling costs, low service quality, and precarious finances. The scarcity of resources for investment leaves much of the populace without adequate services and forces them to rely on expensive or inconvenient alternatives.

The clientelist model broadly describes the politics of urban and rural regional utilities in both water and electricity sectors. It also applies to local administrations in charge of urban or village-based services (funding of piped networks or community toilets or even public investment in deep tubewells).

Source: Foster (2002).

extensions of policymakers. The policymaker and provider begin to fuse into one role. When this happens, policymakers can no longer hold providers accountable for delivering to all citizens, services deteriorate, and poor citizens as clients are left powerless.

The dynamics of this relationship can be even more debilitating for poor clients. Over time providers become a strong political force, influencing the policymaker. In effect, providers capture the policymaking process, exerting pressures through organized labor or their ability to control service delivery for the politician. With deteriorating service levels, policymakers and providers ration access. This has an important implication when lumpy investments are needed to gain access to services—whether through an electricity grid, a village water network, or even a stand-alone system, such as tubewells. Citizens or their groups respond to rationed access by supporting politicians who favor them as their clients over politicians who push for universal access. This strengthens the ability of politicians to use patronage. The accountability linking clients, politicians, policymakers, and providers is displaced by patron-client relationships—clientelism—on both legs of the long route of accountability (box 9.1).[458]

In such settings, the breakdown in voice for poor citizens is reinforced by their loss of client power. Dahli Aspillera's question—did you care?—reflects both a sense that the client cannot penalize the provider for poor service and a deeper reality that the long route of accountability has failed the *citizen*. If failure of voice is at the root of weak service delivery in water, sanitation, and electricity, what are the options for reform?

Urban water networks

Who is the Water Board accountable to?

Question asked of the Managing Director
of the Hyderabad Water Board by a consumer,
Hyderabad, September 2002

In cities and towns, where scale economies prevail, water systems have major network suppliers—generally a public sector provider, such as the Lagos water board in Nigeria, or a small municipal water department, as in Chapai Nawabganj in Bangladesh. Some of these providers belong to local governments—as in the case of the Johannesburg water utility; some to a state government—as is common in India; and some—like MWSS in Manila—to central governments. For all, the relevant questions are whether there is a clear delineation of roles between the policymaker and the provider—and whom the provider is accountable to, the policymaker or the client? When voice and politics fail, the distinction between the two is blurred, and the provider is accountable to the policymaker.

Four reform strategies can potentially separate policymakers and providers: decentralizing assets, using private participation in operations, charging for services, and relying on independent providers to give clients choice. The first two aim to influence compacts, the second two to strengthen client power. All are politically difficult to implement. That is not surprising, since strong political forces—not technocratic failures—blur the roles of policymakers and providers. The issue is whether these strategies can provide incentives to remove patronage and compensate for the weak voice of poor people.

Strengthening the compact: decentralizing assets

Devolving responsibilities to different tiers of policymakers and separating powers between them can create the right incentives to improve service delivery. First, by having service and political boundaries better coincide, decentralization can strengthen voice and accountability. Second, when the center is in charge of both regulatory and service delivery responsibilities, it has few incentives to hold itself accountable. Devolving services to another tier of policymaker triggers incentives more compatible with having the center (or an upper-tier government) oversee the regulatory framework. Finally, devolution creates an opportunity to benchmark performance and use fiscal resources and reputation as rewards to support efficient service provision. The contestability for resources in this context requires a tier with fiscal capacity and without service provision responsibilities—appropriate for the center (or a state in a federal system).

Devolving responsibilities to local governments has had mixed results in water and sanitation, often leading to the loss of scale economies, eroding commercial viability by excessive fragmentation, and even constitutional conflicts between municipalities and upper-tier governments.[459] The historical experience of industrial countries offers lessons for addressing these problems (box 9.2).

BOX 9.2 *Decentralization and the water industry—in history*

In France water assets have historically been devolved to the commune—the lowest tier of government. Clusters of communes have integrated the industry by delegating water and sanitation services "upward" to private or semi-public companies. The functional boundaries of the companies cut across several communes, which continue to own the assets but contract out the management of services.

In the United States water and sanitation assets are also devolved to local governments. Where local governments have been carved up into small political jurisdictions and individual water works are impractical, privately owned companies have emerged to provide regional services covering several local governments.

Examples include Elizabeth and Hackensack, both in New Jersey.

Interestingly, for France and some areas in the United States, the limited capacity of the smaller local governments provided the incentives for private companies to serve clusters of political jurisdictions. In both France and the United States the multijurisdictional coverage prevents the water provider from being captured by any one local body—thus maintaining the separation from local policymakers.

The approach was different in England and the Netherlands. At the outset of the 20th century in both countries, oversight and direct provision of water services were in the hands of local authorities. In the Netherlands these were under company structures, mostly owned and run by municipalities, but many were under private operation if not ownership. In England the national government consolidated the local water systems into regional bodies, moving from 1,400 in World War II to 187 in 1974 and 10 in the 1980s, all eventually privatized. In the Netherlands, also under central government mandate, the municipal companies were converted to regional companies to support the expansion of services to rural areas. But the companies remained under the ownership of municipalities and provinces.

Sources: Lorrain (1992); Seidenstat, Haarmeyer, and Hakim (2002); Jacobson and Tarr (1996).

Fragmentation and the loss of scale economies can be partly addressed by permitting interjurisdictional agreements. In the French *syndicat* model, municipal jurisdictions can cede the right to provide water and sanitation services to a company jointly owned by several local authorities. Bolivia's water law explicitly allows for multi-municipal companies. Colombia empowered its regulator to enforce mergers of nonviable local water agencies, but ironically exempted the smallest of the municipalities that would have benefited most from this rule. Brazil's state companies were created through voluntary agreements with municipalities, financed by central funds.

These examples suggest an important approach for aligning general decentralization with sectoral priorities. When authority is being decentralized, a window usually opens for central government to influence the restructuring of local services. Decentralization gives the center the ability to negotiate the restructuring of devolved assets through fiscal incentives—say, by deciding to retain the liabilities while devolving only the assets.

Where devolution has already happened, the center can provide incentives such as fiscal grants to subnational governments that are dependent on milestones of institutional reform. Australia's federal government provided grants to states to reform the water sector. The South African government is also using central fiscal incentives to support municipal restructuring and to influence reform of urban services, including water and sanitation. India's federal government is exploring a similar policy instrument—the City Challenge Fund—to create incentives for general urban reform, including municipal services.

Such fiscal incentives are more effective if allocated competitively to local tiers of government. But this requires information so the center can compare the performance of different local governments, promoting competition and accountability. It also requires that the policy and legal framework enable local governments to have the flexibility to reform service delivery—to form regional companies and use contracting, for example. Countries such as Pakistan and South Africa that have recently embarked on decentralization have adopted such legislation.

The bottom line: upper-tier governments can influence the design of compacts at the local level through legislation and incentives. However, as demonstrated by experience in Latin America, decentralization processes have not always been designed with sufficient care to allow these kinds of benefits to be reaped. The success of managing service reforms during decentralization will depend on whether broader decentralization policies can ensure that local politicians and policymakers bear the consequences of policy decisions. Ensuring that decentralization can separate policymakers and providers at the local level requires that it also separate roles and responsibilities of the different tiers of government (chapter 10). Without that separation, decentralization may simply transfer patronage to local levels.

Strengthening the compact: using private participation in operations

Over the past decade, private participation has grown significantly in water, sanitation, and electricity in different forms and across many regions (box 9.3). In general, private participation in infrastructure has been advocated for many reasons, including accessing management expertise and private investment and introducing incentives in the operations of infrastructure services. Private participation is also a direct way of separating policymakers and service providers through two aspects of the accountability chain—compacts and voice.

In the design of compacts, private providers generally require explicit contracts that define up front the service responsibilities of the provider and the policymaker, the regulatory and tariff parameters, and issues of access by poor households. In addition, the process of contracting private providers can strengthen the voice channel, particularly if advocacy groups and public information mechanisms are involved in the process. Indeed, service delivery standards and services for poor people are often explicit in the policy debate on private participation in water and sanitation.

In many industrial countries the involvement of the private sector in service delivery enabled governments to develop the

BOX 9.3 *Trends in private participation: water, sewerage, and electricity*

Investment commitments in projects with private participation in developing countries, 1990–2001

Water and sewerage projects
2001 U.S. dollars (billions)

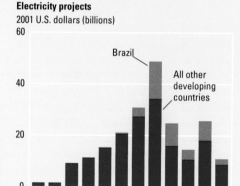

Electricity projects
2001 U.S. dollars (billions)

Cumulative investment, water and sewerage projects (total $40 billion)

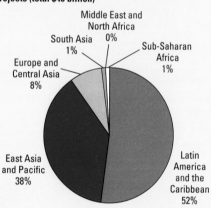

Cumulative investment, electricity projects (total $213 billion)

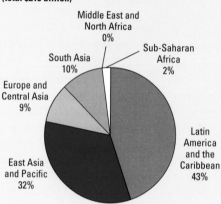

Water and sewerage projects by type (total 202 projects)

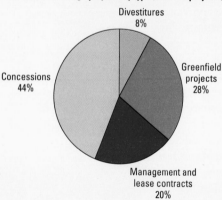

Electricity projects by type (total 832 projects)

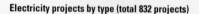
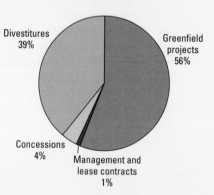

Private investment has been far higher in electricity than in water and sanitation. Not surprisingly, the decline in private investment in the late nineties was more pronounced in electricity. In both sectors, the impact of "large deals" and country specific changes are visible—reflected also in the geographic concentration—East Asia and Latin America—of pri-

vate investment. Finally, in electricity privatization dominates; in water, management contract and concessions—public ownership—remains the norm.

Source: World Bank, PPI Project Database.

BOX 9.4 *Private participation—in history*

England. In London private companies supplied water for more than 400 years with little government restriction on entry. Companies competed against each other, invested in service and quality innovations, and increased household connections. By the 19th century London's extensive water system helped make that city "one of the best housed and healthiest cities in Europe, with a death rate lower than birth rate by about 1800, at a time when most European cities were devourers of men." Ninety-five percent of London residents received piped supply from the private companies, and a majority had direct home connection.

Technological change led to significant price competition, industry consolidation, and higher prices. And the improved water supply increased demand for flush toilets, which created problems of sewage removal. Parliament responded with regulation, and by 1908 the private system was nationalized. (In the 1980s England shifted back to private provision.)

Holland. Between 1853 and 1920 the water sector was dominated by private water supply

companies, which were then progressively taken over by municipalities and operated as public utilities. The amalgamation was promoted by central regulation and facilitated by municipal politics. A major motivation was to use the companies to deliver services more regionally to rural areas. By the time the public sector took over, principles of economic management of water services had become well embedded in the political system. Arms-length management of public utilities by municipalities became the norm.

United States. Between 1800 and 1900, U.S. cities experienced a tremendous growth of water works. Initially dominated by private owners, half of them were public by 1900. The shift to public ownership emerged because of contracting problems between municipalities and companies over water for fire fighting. The difficulties of establishing contracts when cities were growing rapidly, and several urban conflagrations, offered opportunities for both private companies and governments to evade performance targets or force renegotiations of contracts. A lack of metering and direct charg-

ing led to conflicts over fiscal transfers from municipalities to companies. Not surprisingly, public ownership increased, and with it the public system inherited the tradition of managing and regulating water as an economic good.

France. Starting with private provision of water at the local government level and maintaining it from the mid-1600s onward, France evolved toward public ownership and private provision through different types of management and lease contracts. The reasons: scale issues (small local authorities), the history of the French legal system, and the role of voice in controlling policymakers. The issue of fire fighting did not come up in France, perhaps because cities were built with vastly different materials and densities.

Sources: Tynan (2002), Schwartz and Maarten (2002), Crocker and Mastens (2002), and Lorrain (1992).

capacity and political setting to regulate, price, and manage water in public and private contexts (box 9.4). But in today's developing countries private participation is being flung into a context of institutional rigidity, not necessarily conducive to the organic growth of formal private participation. Using private provision to drive a wedge into patronage makes managing private participation intensely political—but potentially powerful for increasing accountability.

The proof of this potential is already evident. Formal private participation in water and sanitation has led to greater demand for accountability—this, despite accounting for a small part of total investment in water and sanitation. During the 1990s private investment accounted for only 15 percent of total investment in water and sanitation, covering less than 10 percent of the world's population. Even in Latin America, where private provision has made the greatest inroads in the water sector, it only covers 15 percent of the continent's urban population.[460] In addition, in contrast to electricity, for example, public ownership and not divestiture of assets remains the norm in the sector.

Ulitmately, like decentralization, private provision offers an opportunity to influence the relationships of accountability. And like decentralization, its success depends on design and implementation (box 9.5). Experience so far suggests that regulation and information—two interlinked parts of overall sector reform—are important in successfully implementing private sector participation in water, sanitation, and electricity sectors and in promoting greater voice in service delivery.

Regulation. A regulatory system in this Report's framework is best defined along the dimensions of accountability between the policymaker and the provider—delegation of responsibilities and finance, information about the performance of the provider, and enforcement (chapter 3). The regulator could be responsible for specific elements of the accountability chain—just providing information on performance or also ensuring enforcement. Sometimes the policymaker is the regulator, and sometimes a dedicated third party has this responsibility. Sometimes even an association of providers can self-regulate. Whichever method is followed, the regulatory

---

B O X   9 . 5   *Private participation in water and sanitation can save poor people's lives, and money*

In the 1990s Argentina embarked on one of the largest privatization campaigns in the world as part of a structural reform plan. The program included local water companies covering approximately 30 percent of the country's municipalities. Child mortality fell by 5–7 percent in areas that privatized their water services. The largest gains were seen in the poorest municipalities, where child mortality fell by 24 percent. Overall, privatization of water services prevented approximately 375 deaths of young children each year.

Aggregate data from other sources on the distribution of new water connection by income quintile from three countries in Latin America confirm the results of the pro-poor impact of private sector services. As the data show, 25–30 percent of the network expansion was targeted at the lowest 20 percent of the income profile.

Distribution of new connections following private sector participation in water and sanitation services

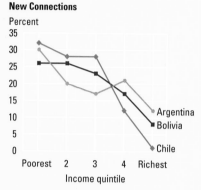

Source: Foster (2002).

Responding to the need for alternatives for reaching poor people, one of the Manila concessionaires has developed a system for water delivery in densely populated, hard-to-reach slum areas. In the Bayan Tubig ("Water for the Community") program, the use of appropriate technological standards, client participation in maintenance, and community-based organizations in intermediation and mapping of the network reduced water costs for poor families by up to 25 percent. To increase affordability, the concessionaire has introduced an interest-free repayment scheme over a period of 6 to 24 months. Between 1991 and 2001, the program provided water connections to more than 50,000 households—this despite the fact that the contract of one of the Manila concessionaires is under review.

Source: Galiani, Gertler, and Schargrodsky (2002); Water and Sanitation Program (WSP-AF) (2003).

---

process has to separate policymaker and provider and preserve its own independence.

Organizing regulation: one size does not fit all. Where voice is strong and supported by an effective legal system, the policymakers and the judiciary do the regulating. In France, where the compact for water is between municipal policymakers and a private company, regulation is done primarily through municipal monitoring of contracts, with some support from central authorities.

In countries without a tradition of separating policymakers and providers and with discretionary policymaking, credible regulation requires a third party—an agency—to set or interpret regulatory rules. Several formal safeguards can support the independence of a regulatory agency from political influence.[461] Some examples: earmarking funds for the regulatory agency, hiring staff from the market without being restricted by civil service rules (competence and capacity are important elements of gaining credibility and independence), ensuring that the hiring and firing of regulators are protected from the political interference of the executive and legislative branches, and not linking the terms of staff to electoral cycles.

A multi-tiered governmental structure offers additional scope for protecting the independence of a regulator by placing it at the national level, or at the state level if policymaking and provision are done at the local level. Another option in a multi-tiered government is to use local regulation but have the appeals process at a different level. In the United States the Constitution provides an overall framework for property rights while state regulatory commissions oversee the operations of privately owned local utilities. Local governments regulate public utilities directly.

Regulation and sector reform. The accountability framework clarifies the conditions under which a regulator will be effective in supporting sector reforms. Just as accountability is blurred if any one of its relationships is broken (see chapter 3), the effectiveness of a regulator is abridged if delegation of responsibilities and finance between the state and the provider is incomplete. That is the case in the electricity sector in some states in India. In other words, an independent regulator is needed to enforce the separation between policymaker and provider, but if the separation is not initiated through general reform to begin with, the regulator may well be ineffective. A regulator cannot substitute for broader sector reforms.

At the same time an effective regulator can help sustain sector reform. A recent study of about 1,000 concessions in Latin America showed that even a moderately well-functioning regulator can temper opportunistic renegotiations of contracts.[462] The study concludes that where a regulatory body exists in a country, the probability of a renegotiation is 17 percent; where none exists, the probability is 60 percent.

Regulating the public sector. Sector regulation is often discussed in the context of private sector participation. But issues of monopoly behavior and service performance are also relevant for public sector provision—perhaps even more, because the contracts between the policymaker and the public provider are often not explicit. Independent regulation of public providers is therefore equally important. But unless public providers have operational flexibility and are brought under explicit compacts—and unless all the relationships of accountability are applied—it is not clear how regulation of the public providers would have an impact on service standards. In particular, because most of the instruments of modern regulation are based on financial incentives, in the absence of user charges regulation of public providers would be ineffective. In Chile public sector regulation was introduced in the context of sector reforms, which included greater provider autonomy in operations and economic pricing of water. This helped catalyze regulatory capacity in the public sector—an important asset, now that Chile has privatized water services.

The role of information. With private provision more needs to be done to deliver on the demand for greater voice—informing communities about the why and how of private sector contracting. A public opinion poll in Peru found support for privatization of electricity among only 21 percent of the citizens. But when informed that privatization was to be undertaken through a transparent process and tariff increases would be regulated, support increased to 60 percent.[463] In Manila the concession process was preceded by a widespread public campaign by President Ramos, who convened "Water Summits" to bring together different stakeholders.[464] In South Africa Johannesburg's water management contract was also undertaken after significant—and often difficult—consultation with

communities, labor unions, and other interest groups. Neither process was flawless, but both opened the door to greater accountability. An open process is needed to broaden the participation of communities in the policy debate on private provision—otherwise narrow interest groups can capture the information and representation.

Community involvement is also essential in the regulatory process—but it has not been sufficiently encouraged. A review of urban water utilities in Latin America and Africa concludes that giving consumers little information about the process of reform and tariff setting—and limiting their opportunity for comment before taking regulatory decisions—weaken the regulatory process and the credibility of reform, and make tariff changes—however justified—difficult to implement.[465]

Organizing consumers is, however, not an easy task. There are major free-rider (and related financing) problems in developing countries that prevent consumers from organizing themselves to a degree where they can be an articulate voice in the regulatory process. The problem is even more severe for poor consumers. In industrialized countries, relatively well-developed consumer associations perform this role reasonably effectively. Where competent and effective consumer associations are absent, the asymmetry between consumers and providers becomes more acute, and the regulator risks being captured by the provider.

Examples exist of regulatory bodies engaging communities—especially poor communities—more actively. In Jamaica the regulator reaches out to communities through local churches; in some cases in Brazil special consultative or advisory bodies have been created; and in Peru regulators have made extensive use of the radio to engage and communicate with communities.[466] But these are few examples only—much more needs to be learned about how to organize and access communities in the regulation of services.

Managing private participation also requires information on how private players are performing relative to their contract and the performance of other public and private providers. This information, which is critical for regulators, also strengthens the relationship between citizens, politicians, and policymakers. For private provision to have a catalytic impact on the sector, information is essential on the performance of both the public and private sectors. But too little information has been available on the performance of the public sector and through few credible sources. Leveling the playing field between public and private providers—as discussed later—and benchmarking their performance are essential in getting the best out of private participation in the sector.

Overall, the impact of private sector participation is best leveraged within a broader reform context—greater separation of policymakers and providers for all public providers; greater participation of communities in the process of private participation and in the regulatory framework; and greater use of benchmarking of both public and private providers. The Australian approach is instructive. An enabling framework and a national competition law level the playing field for all public and private providers. Sectoral legislation provides guidelines for service provision. The central government provides fiscal incentives to support change at the state level. A variety of delivery approaches are supported—corporatization (Melbourne), management contract (Adelaide), vertically integrated public utility (Sydney), multi-utility (Canberra). Regulation differs between states and is backed by independent regulatory agencies as well as benchmarking done through an association of water providers.

BOX 9.6 *Charging for water—in history*

Treating water as an economic good and charging for services enabled France and the Netherlands to use private provision to jump-start the sector's development. In France the private sector remains the major service provider of water and sanitation services. In the Netherlands the system shifted from the private to the public sector. But in both countries charging users for water remained the norm, which enabled providers to sustain service delivery at arm's length from local government and gave them greater incentives to be responsive to the needs of the clients.

Sources: Lorrain (1992); Blokland, Braadbaart, and Schwartz (1999).

Strengthening client power: charging for services

User charges provide operational autonomy for the provider, support client power, and elicit greater accountability from the state (box 9.6). Without access to enough revenues from the clients, service providers depend on the policymaker for fiscal resources to maintain service provision. In addition, if the seller is not dependent on the buyer for at least some part of revenues, the provider will have little incentive to respond to the client. At the same time, given the politics of water pricing, implementing user charges can quickly elicit a consumer response—as in Johannesburg, Manila, and very visibly in Cochabamba, Bolivia.

Implementing user charges. Drawing on the power of user charges to leverage accountability in service delivery requires, as discussed earlier, effective regulation to address monopoly provision. But more importantly, the critical policy issue is how to increase tariffs. There are two implementation issues: the first is synchronizing tariffs with quality improvements, and the second is ensuring that there is a safety net to safeguard basic affordability.

In many countries, bringing the tariffs to cost-recovery levels would require significant adjustment and rebalancing of tariffs among residential, business, and industrial customers. In Indian cities the charges on residential users are less than a tenth of the operating and maintenance costs. Industrial users pay ten times more but are below the benchmark for operating and maintenance costs in two-thirds of the metropolitan cities and 80 percent of smaller cities.[467] Even if there is a willingness to charge, how can the transition to prices be managed?

Charging cannot be assessed independent of the broader policy framework and the credibility of service providers. Policymakers are obviously concerned that services will not improve enough to justify the price increases. Central to a price increase is what comes first—the increases or service improvement? Guinea entered a lease contract for water services in its major towns and cities in 1989. During the first six years of the contract, the government subsidized a declining share of the private operator's costs while tariffs were adjusted gradually toward cost recovery, which avoided a major tariff shock. This jump-started the move to cost recovery and better service delivery. It also gave the reform credibility in a region that had little experience with private provision.[468] For various reasons the lease contract expired in 1999 and was not renewed, but the pricing strategy remains relevant for other countries.

Similarly, subsidies to poor people could be better targeted and designed, which would enable user charges to be implemented overall. Chile has a nationally funded household water subsidy. Colombia uses geographic targeting. South Africa has a national lifeline tariff system that guarantees each household 6 kiloliters of water a month.[469] Given the substantial divergence between piped water prices and the high cost of the inferior alternatives that many of the poorest are forced to use, there is often a strong case for giving highest priority to connection subsidies rather than subsidizing the use of water by those who already enjoy access to the piped network. Connection subsidies also have the advantage that they are easier to target (since lacking access to service is already a strong indicator of poverty) and cheaper to administer (since relatively large one-time payments are involved). Generally it is more efficient to subsidize the connection costs for low-income households, but there are alternative options for designing connection and consumption charges that benefit poor people.

Ultimately, tariff adjustment and subsidy mechanisms are technocratic tools that can be designed and applied in many ways. What is critical is to turn payments for services into a political tool for reducing patronage and strengthening client power of poor people.

Strengthening client power: relying on independent providers

As the example of pit operators in Dar-es-Salaam suggests, small independent providers are a common feature in providing water and sanitation services across income groups. Their organization varies from household vendors of water, small network providers, and private entrepreneurs to cooperatives. In some cases they are the primary suppliers, and in others they supplement the formal provider. In some cases they are part

of a competitive market, and in others they are controlled by a few groups.

Enhancing the role of independent providers as part of the short route of accountability is a key policy challenge. How can this be achieved?[470] By recognizing independent providers and giving them legal status, by ensuring that network providers are not given exclusive supply, by enabling greater partnership between formal public and private network providers and small independents, by ensuring that the regulatory framework for network providers gives the flexibility to enable contracting with independent providers, by enabling small-scale provider associations and working with these umbrella bodies to introduce appropriate levels of regulation, and by enabling poor people to gain access to multiple independent providers while keeping their regulation more focused on health and issues related to groundwater depletion.

Of particular concern is the effect of bringing in a formal private provider in an area dominated by independent providers. This issue was not addressed in the design of the Cochabamba contract—where the private provider was given exclusivity rights—and it contributed to the contract's cancellation.[471] In reality, if coverage targets are defined in such a way that they can be met with the services of small independent providers, the operator will have an incentive to encourage their involvement.

Rural areas: network and non-network systems

Rural settings are complex in their settlement patterns, ranging from dense settlements in South Asia to dispersed communities in many African countries. Suppliers include household systems in Bangladesh, water vendors in Laos, and community-managed local piped water systems in Ghana. Across all situations, the client-provider link is the norm. Understanding why the long route of accountability is needed to support this client power, and how this can be done, are the main service delivery challenges in rural areas.

Community-managed networks

In countries as diverse as India and Kenya, water boards or engineering departments have traditionally been responsible for delivering water services to rural communities. Top-down in their approach, with little skill in community mobilization, and backed by fiscal support from central government, the boards scaled up physical investment. But they had little success in ensuring sustainable operations and maintenance. Indeed, these boards face the same problems of state capture inherent in the patronage model of service delivery.

Given the failures of top-down institutions, some countries are shifting to community-managed systems—often supported by donors, as in India and Ghana. Communities are involved in the design and management of their water systems, paying for operations and maintenance costs. Governments, generally central governments, pay a significant part of the capital costs. Donor-funded project management units, backed by not-for-profit organizations, often form the technical and organizational backbone of these systems.

The client-based model puts the client at the center of the accountability relationship, but many challenges remain in scaling it up.[472]

- Communities require technical support in the medium to long run to manage water systems, and donor-funded project management units are not well suited for this.
- Communities pay for current operating costs, but replenishing capital investments and covering higher tariffs—to pay for rising power costs, for example—are not easily managed through group contributions.
- Communities are not homogeneous—problems of exclusion and elite capture can be the same as in government systems. And different communities may have differing abilities to form cohesive groups.
- Efficient technologies that require scale economies are not selected because of the focus on village-level associations.

Supporting client provision

Three approaches—local governments, regional utilities, and independent providers—provide examples of institutional mechanisms for supporting community-based systems. They are all "works in progress," and learning from them will offer insights on how to advance rural community-based systems of delivery.

Local governments can form the institutional and financial support for expanding community-based systems. With access to a tax base, local governments can provide resources to cover periodic capital expenditure, provide temporary fiscal support to communities to adjust to economic shocks, and facilitate access to technical assistance. Uganda and South Africa provide examples of arrangements in which local governments are part of a larger fiscal decentralization program with own resources and greater autonomy. Local governments thus strengthened can support community-based programs. Even in India, where local *panchayats* do not have as much autonomy, the relations between local governments and user groups are evolving. Where neighboring small towns have effective providers, these can be contracted in by rural local governments to support their communities.

In Côte d'Ivoire a national utility run by a private partner has responsibilities for urban centers and smaller towns. The national utility uses cross subsidies—with the capital city providing the fiscal surplus—to support the smaller urban centers. Expansion of its responsibilities to rural areas is now being tried. The early lessons have not been successful but the approach is still evolving.[473]

Finally, communities can contract with a third party or an independent provider to manage local network systems. In China formal cooperatives (rural companies) run on commercial principles with very high cost recovery.[474] In several African countries village entrepreneurs manage water systems under contract. In East Asia small independent providers are being organized to take on operational responsibility on a concession basis. In each case, the process is organized through group consultation and endorsement. While small systems can be contracted by community organizations, villagewide systems may again require the support of policymakers at the local level.

Self-provision.   Households managing wells and hand pumps are common in large parts of rural Asia and Africa. Nowhere is self-provision more dramatically showcased than in Bangladesh, where shallow aquifers and the market provision of hand pumps enabled households to directly manage water services and replace pathogen-contaminated surface water with groundwater. Service delivery improved—less waiting time, no quantity limits, and the convenience of household connection. And the health impact, which included a decline in diarrhea-related deaths, was remarkable.

Missing was any attempt to monitor water quality. Finding arsenic in the groundwater caught everyone by surprise. The government had withdrawn from the rural water sector, assuming that access was now fully addressed by the private market and household efforts directly. In addition, in a unitary system of government, there was no local government to respond to the crisis. In rural Bangladesh today, a policymaker is needed to support communities, manage externalities, and understand the technological choices for addressing the arsenic crisis (box 9.7). More broadly, for a collective good such as the monitoring of water quality, a partnership between clients and providers will not suffice; policymakers are needed to support communities

Sanitation

Policy issues in sanitation need to be discussed in the context of the private and public goods dimensions of the sector. To the extent it is primarily a client-provider relationship, households invest in sanitation systems and contract independent providers for the removal of excreta. To the extent the public goods dimensions are dominant, policymakers need to support collective action to change behavior at the household and community levels, and organize common infrastructure for excreta removal.

Access to sanitation services has often been seen as an issue of subsidizing latrines and prescribing latrine technology. This supply-driven approach, emphasizing the fiscal and engineering aspects of sanitation, has failed. In response, some countries have been shifting toward "complete sanitation"—focusing on community and household behavior and sanitation practices.[475] This involves breaking the fecal-oral chain by encouraging households to change behavior—shifting away from open defecation, washing hands, keeping food and water covered, using safe water, focusing on

---

BOX 9.7 *Fighting arsenic by listening to rural communities*

The arsenic contamination of shallow aquifers may be undoing the success of rural drinking water provision in Bangladesh. While the number of individuals showing symptoms of arsenic poisoning is still low—despite the high concentration of arsenic in the water—between 25 and 30 million people may be at risk in the future.

The first response to the crisis by government and many donors was denial. This was followed by an effort to test all water sources and hand pumps. There were various technological and logistical problems—which is not surprising in view of the fact that arsenic contamination of this scale has not been faced anywhere in the world. These problems were further complicated by a lack of coordination and blurring of roles among government, donors, and nongovernmental organizations (NGOs).

The efforts so far have revealed that surface water does not contain arsenic and that not all aquifers are contaminated. Government, donors, and NGOs are advocating several options: shifting to alternative water sources, including some surface sources; sharing of uncontaminated tubewells in villages; sinking deep tubewells in public areas; and promoting household filtering technologies. The latter, if successful, would preserve the use of shallow tubewells—decentralized, household means of water access—that have defined the "water miracle" of Bangladesh. In all of this, little effort was made to understand the preferences of rural households.

A WSP-BRAC (Water and Sanitation Program–Bangladesh Rural Advancement Committee) team undertook a comprehensive survey of household preferences for different approaches to arsenic mitigation in selected areas of rural Bangladesh. The results reveal that communities place a high premium on convenience. Unless the alternatives are as convenient as the current hand pumps, the shift to dug wells, well-sharing, and other mechanism may not work. Indeed they have not yet been successful as solutions.

Communities strongly indicated a preference and willingness to pay for centralized, community-based filtering systems, such as local piped-water systems with a central filtering point for chemical and biological contaminants. The piped water network systems introduced in the Bogra area by the Rural Development Academy suggest the potential of such systems in Bangladesh. This has been confirmed by preliminary data, which show the cost effectiveness of piped water in settlements that have 300 or more households. If implemented broadly, this approach would dramatically change the nature of water institutions in rural Bangladesh—a change that communities are willing to undertake.

Source: Ahmad and others (2002).

children's hygiene behavior and maintaining a clean environment. The use of hygienic latrines is a result of this process of changing behavior.

Because the health impact of a household's sanitation practices is affected not only by the household's behavior but also by the practices of the community, there is a collective action problem. The provider's role in ensuring information and social support to households through community structures becomes critical. Success depends on making people see themselves as a community, where every member's behavior affects the other—a daunting challenge and perhaps the reason why sanitation has always lagged behind demand for water.

A participatory focus in rural areas

Because communities need to manage sanitation collectively, innovative participatory approaches are required to generate demand for it, especially in dispersed settlements. The shift from open to fixed-point defecation may be motivated by health, safety, and privacy concerns—issues of importance to women, who bear much of the burden of poor sanitation practices. In the approach practiced by Village Education Resource Center (VERC) and WaterAid in Bangladesh, an external group triggers community-wide recognition of the need for better sanitation practices. The community then takes responsibility for self-regulation—motivating households to strive for complete sanitation. In East and South Asia this has even led to innovations in latrine technology and micro-credit financing for investments in latrines and associated infrastructure.

Subsidies. The community focus also changes the approach to latrine subsidies. In Bangladesh, villages in the VERC/WaterAid project did not require any external subsidy. To assist low-income households, higher-income households provided resources. Once communities focused on the need for collective responsibility, assisting individual households to reach community goals was more readily accepted. In Vietnam the participatory approach was supported by a subsidy targeted at poorer households.

But even if a subsidy is required, the fiscal contribution could be delivered to the community, rewarding collective action, self-regulation, and the elimination of open defecation. Take one of India's largest states—Maharashtra state, with 97 million people. It subsidized latrine construction by households below the poverty line only to discover that close to 45 percent of the latrines were not being used. So it shifted its subsidy to a competitive scheme (the Gadge Baba scheme) that rewarded communities for good sanitation practices, using an information campaign to define the principles of sanitation and publicizing the names of winning villages. Reputation, recognition, and community rewards became the catalyst. Over a short period an estimated 100,000 household latrines were built, and for every rupee of state resources, local spending on sanitation and related infrastructure increased by 35 rupees.

Local compacts.   Making the shift to better sanitation practices is the first objective—but sustaining the shift is equally important. The local externalities and the need to understand and draw on local conditions and knowledge suggest that local governments are the appropriate policymaker tier. In Vietnam and West Bengal, India, local governments have supported community participation and ensured its continuity by financing the work of the service provider, usually a not-for-profit organization. In Vietnam some local governments have used a program similar to Maharashtra state's Gadge Baba scheme to acknowledge village and individual achievements.

Responding to demand in urban areas

Households in urban settlements with high population densities often show a greater demand for better sanitation facilities. The condominial systems in São Paulo, Brazil, and the community sanitation systems of Orangi in Karachi, Pakistan, and Parivartan in Ahmedabad, India, suggest that informal urban communities may be willing to manage and pay for efficient systems of sanitation and waste disposal. Small independent providers serving households directly, as in Dar-es-Salaam, show that urban households do invest in sanitation. So what are the impediments to expanding these approaches?

The answer may lie outside the realm of water and sanitation—and in the regulatory domain of urban centers. First, the formal recognition of informal communities by governments and the provision of some form of tenure have strongly influenced community willingness to invest in household infrastructure and to work collectively on community infrastructure (La Paz in Bolivia, Ahmedabad in India). Research on garbage collection in informal settlements in Indonesia provides empirical evidence of the negative relationship between incomplete property rights and community investment in local public goods.[476] It suggests that improving tenure security increases the probability of garbage collection by 32–44 percent.

Second, in dense urban areas the municipal government's willingness to allocate some public land to sanitation systems has enabled communities to develop community facilities, contracting them with a third party to maintain and operate them (Pune in India). Use is restricted to the community through a monthly charge collected by the community and paid to the operator.

Third, municipal laws need to support flexible standards and ensure that communities and households can make arrangements with independent providers. Laws that permit exclusive service provision need to be replaced by laws that permit different approaches and standards.

A concluding caveat is, however, necessary on the discussion about sanitation. Historical evidence suggests that demand for water and sanitation follows a sequencing—water first, followed by sanitation and then demand for waste water treatment. Experience also suggests that this sequencing is influenced by many factors of which service delivery arrangements in the sector is only one. In this context, policymakers must remain realistic and patient about how far they can catalyze the demand for sanitation through external interventions. Unless embedded in a demand-responsive approach, throwing subsidies at latrines will not resolve the challenge of scaling up sanitation.

Electricity

Like water, electricity has urban and rural components—and issues of managing grid and off-grid systems. In the grid setting, the issues of separating the policymaker from the provider, charging for services, using private providers, and developing effective regulatory systems are similar to water network issues (box 9.8).[477] A key difference is unbundling (rather than decentralizing) services.

For electricity in rural settings, the extension of the grid network provides lessons for managing non-network systems in water. And the emerging use of off-grid electricity systems can draw on lessons from community-managed water in rural settings.

Grid systems. The experience from Latin America, Eastern Europe, and South Asia suggests that unbundling the electricity chain into generation, transmission, and

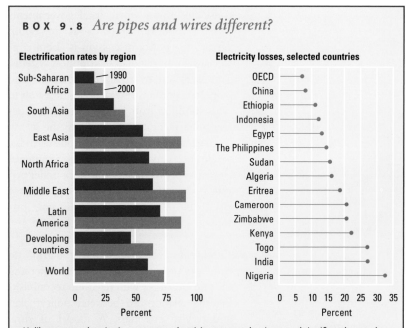

BOX 9.8 *Are pipes and wires different?*

Unlike water and sanitation coverage, electricity coverage has increased significantly over the past decade. But like water and sanitation, electricity faces daunting challenges in South Asia and Africa and rural areas across most regions in the world. And as in the case of water and sanitation, increased electricity coverage does not automatically imply efficient service delivery. The problems of theft, intermittent supply, shared access—captured broadly under the heading of electricity losses—make wires no different from pipes in the context of creating accountability in service delivery.

Source: International Energy Agency (2002).

distribution components is critical to reforms in the sector—but only if the market is large enough to support multiple electricity generators, and hence genuine competition.[478] Unbundling provides scope for competition in the relevant sectors, primarily generation. Separating the components also creates scope for getting better information about the cost structure of each part of the chain. The competition and the information add to client power.

But transmission and distribution functions are monopolies, and without effective regulation it may be difficult to ensure the separation of policymaker and provider, and even reduce the scope to introduce competition in generation. Unless distribution is transferred to different types of ownership, a national or regional government as a sole owner will not have much incentive to separate its policymaking responsibilities from the operations of the distribution system.

Privatizing distribution is a common policy approach, but decentralizing electricity assets to local governments is not generally considered. Even where local governments own distribution systems—as in South Africa—the policy discussion is about consolidating into regional distribution systems. This is driven by economies of scale and scope, and perhaps also by policy decisions to cross-subsidize from urban to rural settings and to keep the cross subsidy in the sector. Interestingly, in Mumbai and Kolkata, India, where electricity is under local governments, electricity provision has long been under private operation. Even in Delhi—in effect a city-state—power distribution is now private.

Rural grid. The extension of the grid into rural areas offer insights for rural water and off-grid electricity with regard to reestablishing the relationship between policymaker and service providers. A model of rural cooperatives has emerged in the United States and is being adapted in Bangladesh and the Philippines. A regional or national provider organization contracts with community cooperatives to be village-level distributors. In Bangladesh the Rural Electricity Board (REB) supports the village cooperatives through technical assistance and fiscal transfers for a part of the capital costs. This would be similar to using regional water utilities to support community-managed water systems. Importantly, the owner of the distribution is not the policymaker but the clients. Unbundling the national REB into regional REBs, with some form of benchmarking, could support the clients in breaking a possible monopolistic relationship between the REB and the cooperatives.

Rural off-grid. Rural provider organizations—or local governments—can also support off-grid systems in villages, in many cases using renewable energy to generate power. Donors have traditionally advocated solar household systems—not unlike the technology push in latrines. But today's renewable systems can support villagewide grids—similar to villagewide piped water systems—to provide AC electricity for household appliances of various types. Depending on local conditions the systems can also be wind-powered, solar, tidal, bio-gas, or hybrid, with fossil-fueled generators as backup.

Moving the reform agenda forward

India is revolting and the Thames stinks.
Slogan in London, 1857
The result: Chadwick and the sanitary revolution in the United Kingdom.[479]

Given the weak voice relationship between citizens and politicians in the water, sanitation, and electricity sectors, deep institutional reform often comes from broader stresses in the economic, political, and institutional machinery of a country. In London pollution was such a cause. In Johannesburg the city's bankruptcy was the impetus. In cities in Africa and Latin America a core impulse for reform of urban water and sanitation is the combination of sector problems and a macroeconomic crisis.[480]

Society's view of economic development is also important. In Australia, Chile, and Peru, growth-driven economic development strategy provided the impetus for improving the performance of water and power markets. So the possibilities for sector reform seem greatest when there is a confluence of natural challenge, fiscal crisis, and institutional reform-mindedness.[479] Opportunities for reform may well arrive only by chance, when broader changes in turn catalyze sectoral reforms. What are the potential interim measures? Can incremental change be strategic?

For urban networks, change will require separating the delivery functions from those of benchmarking and regulation. Keeping the latter with an upper-tier government—central or regional—while dispersing ownership of water and sanitation assets to lower-tier governments and the private sector could create this separation. Without ownership responsibilities, the upper-tier policymaker would have greater incentives to use fiscal instruments, benchmarking, and regulation to promote improvements in service provision. Such incentives are less inherent in a model where the regulator, provider, and owner are one and the same. Charging users for services strengthens this separation by directly involving clients in the service chain through the short route of accountability.

Where the introduction of private sector participation is tempered by politics or other factors, strategic change may have to come first through changes in ownership and relationships of accountability between tiers of the public sector. Interestingly, the history of some industrialized countries suggests that local ownership can trigger a more credible path to private sector participation, especially if local governments are effective in strengthening voice.

Where local governments exist and water and sanitation services have been devolved to local governments, the challenge of improved service delivery would lie in making decentralization work. Where local governments do not exist, the lever of decentralized ownership would be lost, but benchmarking and regulation of the public sector would remain. But for such a strategy to be effective, charging for water would become even more critical. It would enable providers to achieve some independence in operations, but more importantly it would give clients a role in sus-

taining the separation and ensuring that the regulation of public providers is effective. In this context, introducing private players in a few of the utilities would enhance the effectiveness of benchmarking the public providers.

Where this broader approach of making services work for all is not possible, a targeted approach for serving poor people using small independent providers is still an option. Indeed, increasingly independent providers may, at the margin, emerge as a critical lever for making services work for poor people.

For rural systems—community-managed systems and self-provision—the challenge is to seek mechanisms for the policymaker to support client power, using local governments, regional utilities, and independent providers. This is similar to the model of the rural electricity cooperatives supported by a provider organization that provides a technical and fiscal hub. Where local governments provide this hub, the voice channel is direct; where utilities are the support mechanism, the voice channel is indirect. Where these options are not possible, the approach—however unsatisfactory—of targeted community projects remains.

For sanitation, the focus is on collective action—to change behavior and mobilize communities to invest in community infrastructure. To support this, compacts between policymakers and NGOs may be more appropriate. In urban areas, where greater demand for sanitation services may exist, policymakers can support client power by allowing independent providers to function and by supporting tenure in informal settlements. A more incremental version would be similar to that in the rural water sector—with a public provider organization supporting NGO delivery in targeted areas.

But if the failure of voice is why infrastructure services have failed poor people, targeted intervention cannot form the basis of institutional reform. Reforming the relationships of accountability would remain the policy challenge.

Accountability in city services

In 1999 the Transformation Lekgotla, the political body directed to address the financial and institutional crisis of Johannesburg, South Africa, appointed a new city management team. The team's task was clear: not to fix street lights but to fix the institutions that fix street lights.[482] The solution was a three-year plan—"iGoli 2002"—to reconfigure city services.[483]

By most developing world standards Johannesburg is not a poor city. But it faces serious development and service delivery challenges. Apartheid made sure that exclusive white suburbs were well serviced, forcing black residents into sprawling underdeveloped slums. Poverty, unemployment, and homelessness are all worsened by the deeper problem of inequality.

The Johannesburg Metropolitan Municipality was democratically elected in 1995 to address the service imbalances. It quickly found itself in a fiscal and institutional crisis.

Johannesburg was not one institution but five, with an overarching Metropolitan Council and four primary-level councils. Each could decide its priorities and approve its budget. But responsibilities for key services were split between the two levels, and the operating budgets of the councils had to balance only in aggregate. That meant each council could blissfully spend on the assumption that its shortfalls would be offset by surpluses in another.

The arrangement was a recipe for disaster. Each municipality went on a spending spree, and ambitious infrastructure plans were rolled out without the finance. Deteriorating revenues—due to a service-payment boycott culture left over from anti-apartheid struggles, poverty, and poor credit control—made the situation worse. The city was forced to delve into its reserves, but these could go only so far, and by late 1997 major creditors could no longer be paid. At the peak of the crisis, the city had an operating deficit of R314 million.

Johannesburg was in serious trouble. Having decentralized responsibilities, the national government followed the intergovernmental rules and would not bail the city out. So Johannesburg had to dig itself out of its own crisis.

Two years of harsh cutbacks followed. Blaming officials for the crisis, politicians took a much tighter rein over day-to-day decisions, ending management discretion.

They slashed capital and operating budgets, and even expenditures needed to maintain minimum service levels. They froze posts, causing huge increases in workloads as despairing officials began to drift away. And they began to explore public-private partnerships.

The city of gold—iGoli 2002

The new city management team realized that Johannesburg needed a new system of accountability for service delivery within a dramatically different institutional architecture. To address fragmentation and the severe moral hazard, the city had to be reunified. Political debate focused on two models of metropolitan coordination:

- Defining more clearly the rules of budgeting, fiscal transfers, and service delivery between the metropolitan and municipal tiers, strengthening both.

- Creating a one-tier metropolitan government.[484]

Johannesburg chose a hybrid. It centralized political authority, treasury management, and spatial planning under one metropolitan government. But it organized service delivery through decentralized structures. This meant merging five separate councils into one overarching municipality, creating integrated service delivery structures with new incentives.

Accountability in service delivery

Under one metropolitan council, iGoli 2002 split the institution for policy formulation and regulation from the institutions for implementation. On one side, a core administration remained responsible for strategic planning, contract administration, and such corporate services as finance, planning, and communication. On the other, two sets of operating entities were established: 11 new regional administrations for libraries, health, recreation, and other community services; and financially ring-fenced, semi-

independent, single-purpose entities to overhaul larger municipal services.

These operating entities were the major innovation of iGoli 2002.

- Three utilities were established for user charge–based services—water and sanitation, electricity, and waste management.

- Two agencies were established—for parks and cemeteries, and for roads and storm water—where expenditure would still have to be covered by tax revenue.

- Smaller corporatized units were set up for facilities like the zoo and the civic theater.

All were established as new companies, with the council as sole shareholder.

Two key units would guide and oversee the new entities: a corporate planning unit to do citywide strategic planning, and a contract management unit to regulate the operating utilities through a range of new instruments, including licensing agreements and annual service level agreements.

One size does not fit all

Since the operating entities are not bound by overarching administrative rules, they have scope to differentiate. Each could set up different management structures, reporting lines, delegations, job descriptions, performance management systems, and operating procedures. Each could configure its internal accountability to suit a specific service delivery environment. Three examples:

- The water and sanitation departments were merged into one department and under the Company's Law converted into a city-owned utility with a board of directors. The assets and workers of the departments were transferred to the utility, which was put under a five-year management contract with a private company.

- The roads department was converted into a city-owned agency with a professional board and divided into two departments—for planning and for contracts. The contracts department operated against specific outcomes set by the planning department, with the threat that failing to meet benchmarks could lead to contracting tasks out to the private sector.

- The gas company was sold to the private sector.

The reforms gave operating entities management independence. For example, salaries have been adjusted to attract top-flight skills, and new systems have been procured for everything from human resource management to remote water-pressure metering—increasing productivity and service efficiency. And they have introduced innovative staff development programs and performance-linked pay schemes.

The entities operate at arm's length from the council, but accountability has been strengthened because the primary mechanism is no longer the impossible-to-digest committee report on everyday operational matters. Now councilors focus on strategic oversight, and officials are responsible for outcomes clearly defined in service-level agreements. Reporting goes through structured channels, either to the contract management unit or to company boards of directors, which include external specialists capable of probing service results.

The operating entities have also set up user forums allowing communities to communicate needs, raise complaints, and even participate actively in service provision. Officials are much more sensitive to ever-changing service delivery challenges.

These management improvements are already translating into better service delivery. Waste collection has been extended to poorer neighborhoods for the first time. Fleets of new buses now serve outlying communities. In addition, expenditure on water infrastructure has increased and water services have expanded. Results are

Figure 1   Getting back to an operating surplus—thanks to iGoli 2002

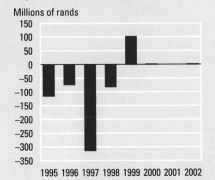

Millions of rands

Source: Allan, Gotz, and Joseph (2001).

also apparent in the city's financial standing, with dramatic improvement in both operating and capital budgets (figure 1).

Engaging other stakeholders

Labor: Despite protracted negotiations with organized labor, iGoli 2002 did not get its endorsement. According to labor groups, the city's crisis was not a result of a failure of institutional design. Instead it was a result of "a lack of skills and experience, and management's unwillingness to [establish] functional organizations and . . . financially unsound decisions."[485]

National government: The team negotiated a R500 million restructuring grant with the National Treasury to support iGoli 2002 in exchange for a commitment to timely and steadfast implementation of its key elements. It is a key accountability mechanism between the national and city governments and has become an incentive scheme to catalyze citywide restructuring throughout the country.

Capital markets: On the strength of the reforms, management sought a new credit rating, aiming to win back the confidence of the city's banking community. As the city shifted from a large deficit to a balanced budget, capital expenditure financed by the markets went from R300 million to well over R1 billion in two years.

Risks and prospects

Will Johannesburg maintain the separation between policymaking, providers, and regulators? The roles of client and contractor are still evolving. Some implementation capacity remains within the core administration. As in the past, managers occasionally get hauled into councilors' offices to explain their actions. There are also unresolved governance debates, with the council arguing for a greater councilor representation on the boards of operating entities.

Five factors will be critical in sustaining the commitment to the principles of iGoli 2002:

- Keeping the monitoring and regulatory unit of the operating entities within the city administration; they are not legally and administratively independent.

- Maintaining the contract management unit's operational autonomy and capacity—and thus the independence of the operating entities.

- Benchmarking service delivery standards, monitoring these over time, and making the information available.

- Ensuring that fiscal and financial decentralization remains binding. Municipalities relying primarily on their own revenue sources to fulfill their democratic duties without national guarantees are more likely to be accountable to their citizens. The current intergovernmental system has devolved authority and accountability to the cities; this needs to remain.

- Both councilors and officials consistently adhering to a clear, courageous, and far-sighted strategy. Sustaining momentum will require greater citizen voice at all levels. The decentralized operating entities and the administrative regions have mechanisms for engaging citizens. Using them will be critical for sustaining iGoli 2002.

Public sector underpinnings of service reform

chapter 10

For Forms of Government let fools contest;
What'er is best administer'd is best.

Alexander Pope, *Essay on Man.*

For basic services in education, health, and infrastructure to work for poor people, governments have to be involved. Whether they fulfill this responsibility by providing, financing, regulating, or monitoring services or providing information about them, the basic functioning of government should underpin, not undermine, effective services.

When governments do not run well, they cannot sustain the institutional arrangements and accountability relationships that yield good services. Looking at all that governments do, the biggest payoffs to service delivery are likely to come from a few key actions: spending wisely and predictably in line with priorities and coordinated across sectors; managing decentralization to reap the benefits of being closer to the client; developing and deploying administrative capacity to take sound decisions at the top and to implement them well; curtailing corruption; and learning from success and failure.

Public sector reforms take time and skillful political navigation. Agreeing on desirable goals is easy. Managing the transition is hard. When starting capacities are low, the road to improved performance may need to be covered in small steps—what this Report calls strategic incrementalism. Reforming basic incentives that strengthen accountability and raise performance closer to formal standards is the place to start. As incentives become better aligned and internalized and as administrative capacity grows, more advanced reforms can be deployed to support deeper institutional change and scaling up. Throughout this process reforms should be guided by the lessons of success and failure.

Strengthening the foundations of government

Governments are essential to making basic services work for poor people, but a government village school does not ensure that children learn, or a maternity clinic that mothers can give birth safely. Both need timely budget transfers, reliable electricity, a connecting road, probity in procurement, and competent public servants. To sustain services that work, broader structures at the foundation of government must also work.

Whether providing, financing, regulating, or monitoring services, governments focused on outcomes for poor people must strengthen the compact relationship between policymakers and providers along the long route of accountability.[486] For basic services in education, health, and infrastructure, policymakers must deal with multiple compact relationships with providers across sectors, space, and time (figure 10.1). Just as an ensemble makes great music when it is well coordinated and not because it has a few virtuoso musicians, strengthening the long route is easier when the *general* business of government runs well across the entire gamut of government activities, and not just in a few

Figure 10.1 Strengthening public sector foundations for service delivery requires coordinating multiple compact relationships

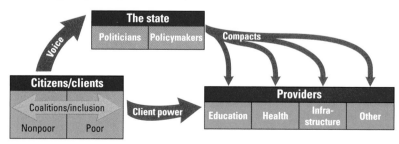

sectors or agencies. The more sound the basic functioning of government, the stronger the foundations for service reforms.

In managing the cross-cutting activities of governments, the three institutional structures likely to influence service delivery the most are budgets, decentralization, and public administration. These are crucial tasks for a government that wants to make services work for people: making budget allocations and implementing them; organizing and monitoring the tiers of government that provide, finance, regulate, or monitor services; and managing public employees involved in service delivery.

Spending wisely

When services fail poor people, a good place to start looking for the underlying problem is almost always how the government spends money. If politicians and policymakers spend more than they can sustain, services deteriorate. If budgets are misallocated, basic services remain underfunded and frontline providers are handicapped. And if funds are misappropriated, service quality, quantity, and access suffer. The budget is the critical link on the long route of accountability connecting citizens to providers through politicians and policymakers.

Public expenditure management—formulating, implementing, and reporting annual budgets—is a challenging task, particularly when capacities are limited and the long route of accountability is weak. Chapter 5 discusses how citizen budget initiatives can increase voice. This chapter discusses how politicians and policymakers can strengthen the compact using public expenditure management to systematically achieve three desirable outcomes that can underpin effective services: aggregate fiscal discipline, allocative efficiency and equity, and operational impact.[487]

Aggregate fiscal discipline

With no effective mechanism for resolving the competing budget claims of politicians, line ministries, and subnational governments, public expenditures will exceed available funds. The resulting unsustainable fiscal deficits can translate into high infla-

tion, high interest rates, and burgeoning current account deficits. Despite the simple logic of this argument—and sometimes driven by external shocks—countries slip into macroeconomic crises that inevitably lead to belt-tightening. Countries in crisis may have no option but to curtail basic services, even if the service delivery chain normally works well. Argentina is just the most recent example (box 10.1).

Countries can instill fiscal discipline by strengthening budget formulation by the finance ministry. Constitutional or legislative restraints can rein in legislatures and ministries. Brazil and Chile have laws on fiscal responsibility that limit budget deficits. In Colombia, Peru, the Philippines, and Uruguay the constitution constrains or prohibits amendments to increase budgets. Sound public expenditure management requires reliable revenue projections and comprehensive budgets that do not hide guarantees and other contingent liabilities. When budgets are not comprehensive, the consequences can be harsh, as Thailand found in 1997 when contingent liabilities from the banking and finance sectors blindsided the government and triggered a regionwide financial crisis.

Allocative efficiency and equity

For basic services in education, health, and infrastructure to work for poor people, governments have to be involved, as chapter 2

BOX 10.1 *The impact of Argentina's crisis on health and education services*

After three years of recession, the economic and financial crisis in Argentina came to a head at the end of 2001. The social impact of the crisis has been devastating. Poverty rates have jumped 40 percent. There is growing evidence of deterioration in service quality, access, and use of social services. Roughly 12 percent of people with formal health insurance discontinued or reduced their coverage, increasing the burden on already strapped public hospitals, the traditional provider for the uninsured. Difficulties with federal transfers have led to serious shortages in medical supplies throughout the public hospital network. The pressure for maintaining funding for high-cost curative care has further cut into the already low resources allocated to primary care. Maternal and child health is likely to be at risk. Epidemiological surveillance data report an increase in some endemic diseases.

Education has been similarly hit, with salary delays and work stoppages in several provinces. During 2002 roughly a third of provinces experienced school closings of 20–80 days over a school year of 180 days. Many provinces were forced to concentrate their falling resources on wages, sharply reducing financing for school lunches, infrastructure, and other investments.

Source: World Bank staff.

Table 10.1   Fallible markets, fallible governments, or both?

		Government failure	
		High	**Low**
Market failure	**High**	Ambiguous, hard-to-monitor situations in which government failure may swamp market failure and so public financing for efficiency or equity reasons may not work for poor people (government primary teachers fail to show up for work, public clinical care goes only to the non-poor). Public expenditures should be directed to increasing client power through demand-side subsidies, co-payments, client monitoring, provider peer monitoring, and information; strengthening voice (through decentralization, delivery arrangements that yield more information, participatory budget analysis); and supporting altruistic providers. Market and community-led delivery should be used to strengthen public institutions over time.	Market failures keep services from benefiting poor people. Depending on the nature of the market failure, public actions could range from public provision or financing (subsidies) to regulation or information disclosure that does not crowd out private responses or that at least takes them into account.
	Low	Private provision and financing with appropriate public regulation or education	Private provision with appropriate regulation, and equity-driven public interventions informed by potential private responses

makes clear. This requires sound budgeting. Good, results-oriented budget allocations are both an outcome of the long route of accountability and a source of its strength, particularly for the link between policymakers and providers. How should governments allocate budgets to improve education and health outcomes? First, the efficiency rationale for government intervention: are there market failures due to public goods or externalities? Or is redistribution for equity the goal? Second, given the rationale, what is the appropriate instrument—public provision or financing, or regulation, or educating the public? Third, what are the fiscal costs over time, and how do their expected benefits compare with those for expenditures on other things that government should finance? In considering these issues, politicians and policymakers need to pay particular attention to what is known about the multisectoral determinants of health and education outcomes in their country (see crate 1.1). Reducing infant mortality may have as much to do with how the water ministry (clean water) or the education ministry (female literacy) gets and uses its budget as with how the health ministry does.

There are many pitfalls in considering the rationale and instruments for government interventions. Focusing on market failures alone (information asymmetry, missing insurance markets) presumes that government implementation failures are inconsequential. Where this is actually true, public provision or financing is appropriate (table 10.1). But where government failures outweigh market failures, ignoring them can lead to large public expenditures that benefit only the non-poor or to services so defective that their opportunity costs outweigh their benefits for most poor people. In difficult-to-monitor clinical care, if primary rural health clinics lack professional staff and medicines and the political environment is not pro-poor, public provision or even subsidies for private provision may not work for poor people. Better alternatives might be funding demand-side health subsidies or district hospitals where monitoring is easier and peer pressure for doctors can work. Where monitoring is easy, as in immunization campaigns, contracting for private provision may be a good solution.

Similarly, ignoring the likely private response to public interventions (such as the crowding out of private providers or household income effects of government subsidies) can lead to ineffective public expenditures. Equity-seeking public expenditures can end up helping the non-poor if analysis suggesting that services or money never reach poor people is ignored in policy design.

These questions about rationale and instruments cannot be answered without detailed information about the sector, the service, the nature and depth of market and government failures, who benefits (expenditure incidence), and private responses to public interventions. This information needs to be developed through in-depth analytical work (in itself a public good that governments and their external partners should fund). Determining true costs and impacts for allocation decisions is not easy, particularly when self-serving line agencies have strong incentives to manipulate or withhold information from the ministry of finance. This information asymmetry can lead to perverse practices (such as line ministries back-loading costs to later years) that reduce the transparency of the budget and its alignment with overall priorities and the practicalities of what works.

In recent years several countries have approached these problems of transparency and results orientation in budget formulation through medium-term expenditure frameworks. These multiyear frameworks make tradeoffs more transparent across sectors and time and synchronize medium-term priority setting with the annual budget cycle. They offer the promise of better budget management, though early implementation suggests that realizing these gains takes quite a bit of time, effort, and parallel improvements in budget execution and reporting.[488]

Properly implemented, a medium-term expenditure framework can reduce incentives for bureaucratic gaming and reveal the true costs of the political choices being made in the budget. It can usefully address the information asymmetry between the ministry of finance and line agencies, because its forward-estimate system requires line ministries to cost their programs over the medium term—essentially a rolling three- or four-year budget. A properly functioning forward-estimate system can induce line agencies to set aside funding for recurrent costs and improve the delivery of services suffering from inadequate maintenance, such as primary schools.

As the capacity to manage grows, a medium-term expenditure framework can offer other advantages. Sector-specific expenditure frameworks can be developed and linked to the overall framework, increasing confidence that the budget is becoming more results-oriented (chapter 8 discusses this approach to health budgeting in Mali). With a multiyear framework poli-cymakers can focus on new programs, since allocations for existing programs, decided in previous years, would only need updating. Finance ministries can more transparently require line ministries to propose cuts in ongoing activities to pay for new programs. Line ministries would have an incentive to know the least effective programs at any point in time, creating demand for systematic monitoring and impact assessment capacity and for client feedback.

For all their advantages however, medium-term expenditure frameworks are not a magic bullet. Aggregate and sectoral outcomes and capacity development reveal a mixed picture. Some applications are maturing slowly (in Albania, South Africa, Uganda), some are still coming together (Rwanda, Tanzania), and some are struggling (Bolivia, Burkina Faso, Cameroon, Ghana, Malawi).[489] In Malawi's development budget for 1996–97, health was allocated at 21 percent of the total but it received only 4 percent.[490] Implementing medium-term expenditure frameworks is difficult, perhaps taking a dozen years or more, as the experience of early adopters such as Uganda demonstrates. A solid foundation of budget execution and reporting seems key, but is also difficult to achieve. Implementing a medium-term expenditure framework can help build the basics, as can participatory budgeting initiatives discussed in chapter 5. Other success factors include carefully matching implementation to capacity, keeping budget projections and estimates realistic, distinguishing between collective ministerial responsibility in the cabinet and the interests of individual ministries, and engaging line ministries in the strategic phase prior to considering detailed estimates, when the rationale and instruments for public intervention can be carefully thought through.

Operational impact

Ultimately, even the best budget allocations are only as good as their impact on desired outcomes for poor people. After controlling for national income, comparative studies show that public spending per capita and outcomes are only weakly associated (chapter 2). Similar changes in spending are associated with different changes in outcomes, and different changes in spending are associated with similar changes in outcomes. This is not to suggest that public funding cannot be successful—countries like Thailand have sharply reduced infant mortality rates through commitment, good policies, and spending. But it does mean that unless public expenditures are results-oriented they will be ineffective. There has been a major push in recent years to make policymakers and providers accountable not only for how they spend money but also for what they achieve—for intermediate outputs and final outcomes. Countries are using several instruments: single-sector and multisector program approaches, alignment of overall national strategies with budgets, tools for verifying where the money goes, and stronger oversight controls to reduce fraud and misuse of public funds.

Programmatic approaches. Individual investment projects can fall short of their objectives if they ignore linkages or trade-offs over time and space or with other sectors. Chapter 11 discusses sectorwide approaches as a way of enhancing development impact, building stronger donor partnerships, improving the management of sector resources, and scaling up successes. Used in countries as diverse as Bangladesh, Bolivia, Brazil, Burkina Faso, Ethiopia, Ghana, Mali, Mozambique, Pakistan, Tanzania, and Zambia, sectorwide approaches show that over time strategies and objectives are better articulated, and management information, monitoring, evaluation, and resource planning systems better established, in sectors that use such approaches than in those that do not.

Poverty reduction strategies. A country's poverty reduction strategy can link public expenditures explicitly to service delivery for the poor, build country ownership, and strengthen citizen voice through consultations with civil society. In 1999 low-income countries began preparing Poverty Reduction Strategy Papers (PRSPs) as the basis for concessional lending from the World Bank

and the International Monetary Fund and for debt relief under the enhanced Heavily Indebted Poor Countries (HIPC) Debt Initiative.[491] Many countries and donors have stressed better public expenditure management as a means of tracking pro-poor spending and increasing donor and recipient accountability for external assistance. A recent review of the pro-poor expenditure tracking capacities of budget management systems among HIPCs suggests that they have far to go.[492] While recognizing that improvements in public expenditure management will take time,[493] both domestic stakeholders and donors have highlighted the need for developing and implementing detailed plans for improvement.

Ideally, poverty strategies should be fully integrated into the budget, but this is still a new approach and success has varied. For some countries integration has been a primary goal (Albania). Tanzania and Uganda have integrated poverty strategies with their medium-term expenditure frameworks, adding focus, legitimacy, and stability to both. But other countries have assigned responsibility for preparing their poverty strategy to a ministry not directly concerned with public expenditure planning. In Ghana, it was initially assigned to the planning ministry, though more recently the planning portfolio has been folded into the finance minister's portfolio.

Public expenditure tracking surveys. In judging operational impact—the quality and quantity of service delivery, and where, how, and to what effect allocated funds are spent—public expenditure tracking surveys can follow the flow of funds through tiers of government to determine whether the funds actually reach the schools or clinics they are destined for. Tracking surveys not only highlight the uses and abuses of public funds, but also give insights into capture, cost efficiency, decentralization, and accountability.[494] Even when little financial information is available, tracking surveys can show what money is supposed to reach a community and how much actually does. Made public, this information can strengthen voice and client power relationships (box 10.2).

Financial management. Auditing helps a government hold itself accountable for the way policymakers and providers spend money. Audits have traditionally focused on basic financial controls and cash flows. This focus reflects the control culture in public finance and the long-established view that accountability for fund use supports the disciplined use of resources as intended by budgets. In recent years, however, accounting and auditing processes have been challenged to examine expenditure performance as well as conformance. The new performance orientation of audits is particularly relevant to operational efficiency concerns in budgets and suggests an expanded notion of accountability. Public financial managers now need to consider their roles as contributors to final outcomes as well as controllers.[495]

Procurement. The cost and quality of government programs are critically affected by the procurement process through which budgets are spent. Procurement inevitably encompasses an intricate set of rules and procedures, each capable of retarding or promoting transparency, contestability, accountability, and efficiency. Leakages, primarily through fraud and corruption, can mean substandard equipment and infrastructure, lack of essential medical supplies, insufficient textbooks, unnecessary low-priority goods, and poor-quality public services. Inefficient procedures create higher costs for suppliers, which are passed through as higher program costs. Improving procurement requires extensive analysis of its rules, procedures, and institutional arrangements. To support streamlining, several countries have turned to information and communications technology. Brazil, Chile, Mexico, the Philippines, and the Republic of Korea, among others, have developed strong e-procurement systems that lower costs and increase transparency, competition, and efficiency.[496]

Decentralizing to improve services

In countries big and small central governments are transferring responsibilities to lower tiers of government, motivated in part by the desire to bring politicians and policymakers closer to clients and to make services more effective. The world's two largest coun-

---

BOX 10.2 *The case of the missing money: public expenditure tracking surveys*

In the early 1990s the Ugandan government dramatically increased spending on primary education. But school enrollments stagnated. Could it be that the money was not reaching schools? To answer this question, a public expenditure tracking survey started collecting data in 1996 on government transfers to schools. It found that 87 percent of the nonwage resources intended for the schools was diverted to other uses. This information was made public and prompted a vigorous response from the national government, which, along with parents, put pressure on school principals to plug the leaks (see spotlight on Uganda). Follow-up studies have shown that the situation has improved.

Tracking surveys can find problems in unexpected places. A survey in Peru tracking a participatory food supplement program (Vaso de Leche, or "Glass of Milk") revealed that less than a third of each dollar transferred from the central government reached intended beneficiaries. Most of the leakage occurred below the municipal level—in the Mothers Committees and households. The results challenged the belief underlying the program that local community organizations were always more accountable than public agencies. Authorities have decided to merge all nutri-

tion programs into a social fund that will transform Vaso de Leche into a conditional, multipurpose, cash-transfer program with stronger accountability.

These and other tracking surveys in Chad, Ghana, Honduras, Mozambique, Papua New Guinea, Rwanda, Senegal, Tanzania, and Zambia suggest several lessons. They confirm that budget execution is a major problem and show that procedural clarity and due process are often missing. They find that poor resource management is often a result of too much discretion in resource allocation when there is limited information, weak controls, and strong vested interests. Tracking surveys reveal insights into the actual (rather than the formal) operation of schools and health clinics and allow comparisons of public, private, and nongovernmental providers. Tracking surveys are highly cost-effective if the leaks they detect are plugged. But they need an authorizing environment: unless there is a solid political commitment for more transparency, government agencies may be reluctant to open their books. The challenge is to institutionalize tracking surveys within a country's own financial control regime.

Source: World Bank staff.

---

tries, China and India, have embraced decentralization. China's phenomenal industrial growth took place within an institutional framework of decentralization, and India's constitution was amended in 1992 to promote local government.[497] But the extent of decentralization varies considerably and is probably less than generally imagined: even in developed countries the average subnational share of expenditures was just above 30 percent in recent years (figure 10.2).

Subnational authorities can be efficient providers and regulators of local services under the right institutional incentives and with clarity about who does what—and with what.[498] But greater autonomy can also increase opportunistic behavior and create moral hazard, resulting in costs that diminish accountability and the benefits of decentralization.[499] Good design, sound management, and constant adaptation by both central and subnational authorities are needed to make decentralization work.

Figure 10.2 Subnational shares of expenditures vary considerably

By country, latest available year

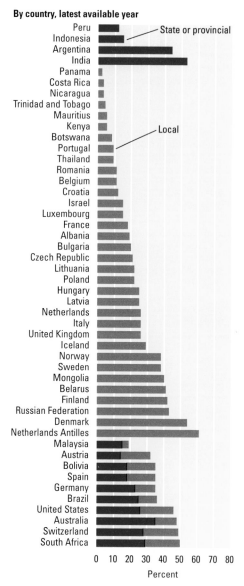

By region, latest available year

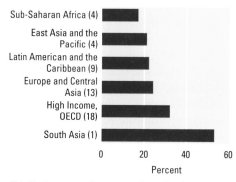

Note: Simple averages of most recent observations for countries with available data. Numbers in parentheses indicate number of countries represented. South Asia refers only to India.

Source: IMF, Government Finance Statistics; World Bank staff.

Decentralization and service delivery

Decentralization is not magic. Allocating more responsibilities to subnational governments does not itself transform service delivery. This depends on whether decentralization is motivated by political, fiscal, or service reform objectives.

Decentralization is often primarily a political act aimed at greater regional autonomy. Decentralization of services is a by-product (box 10.3). Indonesia decentralized responsibility for many services in 1999–2000, including schooling, as part of a larger move to greater regional autonomy. In such cases decentralization is a fact of life educators must cope with—not a deliberate educational reform. New arrangements can always create opportunities for reform, however. Using those opportunities effectively depends on two conditions. First, there must be relevant information about performance across jurisdictions so that citizens can bring justified pressure to bear on politicians and policymakers if their area is lagging. Second, there must be an environment in which local jurisdictions can experiment and evaluate new approaches.

Decentralization may also be driven by fiscal concerns to align responsibility for services with the level of government best able to manage and mobilize resources for them. One danger is that the central government uses this as an excuse to off-load expenditure responsibilities onto jurisdictions that cannot have recourse to potentially inflationary financing. While this could lead to a greater willingness to pay more local taxes (because citizens perceive a direct link between taxes and service quality), there is no reason to believe that this is automatic. Fiscally motivated decentralization is particularly worrisome where special equalization efforts for lagging regions or safety nets for poor families must be sustained by the center.

Decentralization can also be driven by a desire to move services administratively closer to the people. But success depends on how decentralization affects relationships of accountability. If decentralization just replaces the functions of the central ministry with a slightly lower tier of government (a province or state), but everything else about service delivery remains the same, there is little reason to expect positive change. The assumption is that decentralization works by enhancing citizens' voice in a way that leads to improved services. But on both theoretical and empirical grounds this could go either way. The crucial question always is whether decentralization increases accountability relative to its alternatives. If local governments are no more vulnerable to capture than the center is, decentralization is likely to improve both efficiency and equity.[500]

The impact of decentralization on services is further complicated when, as is usually the case, political, fiscal, and administrative goals are not followed simultaneously or in a supportive sequence. Decentralization in eight Latin American countries suggests that political objectives were often the trigger, but paths diverged thereafter (box 10.4). Only some countries moved on to fiscal and administrative decentralization as primary objectives. Such variation, inevitable as countries adapt, makes it hard to predict the course of decentralization and to measure its costs and benefits.[501] Given its many paths, the record of service improvements is mixed—including some notable successes (decentralizing education in Central America, devolution in Bolivia, municipal reforms in South Africa), some reversals (in the Russian Federation and parts of Latin America), and some cases too new to assess (initiatives in Indonesia and Pakistan).[502]

BOX 10.3 *Decentralization as a political imperative: Ethiopia*

In Ethiopia decentralization has been a response to pressures from regional and ethnic groups for greater political participation. When the Ethiopian People's Revolutionary Democratic Front (EPRDF) defeated the Mengistu dictatorship in 1991, the new government faced a complex political landscape. Ethnicity was extremely politicized, and the struggle against Mengistu had been spearheaded by organizations promoting ethnic nationalism in Ethiopia's diverse population. The single-party EPRDF government needed to establish control over the entire country, legitimize its authority, and include other groups in the political system.

The 1994 constitution transformed Ethiopia into an ethnicity-based federation and decentralized administrative responsibilities to nine regions. The accompanying education reforms were laid out in the "Education and Training Policy of 1994." Regions were given responsibility for planning, designing, implementing, and monitoring the primary education curriculum and teacher training. The syllabus remained centrally controlled, with input from the regions. Previously, Amharic had been the sole language of instruction, but the new policy gave all children the right to receive primary education in their mother tongue. At least 18 languages are now being used as the medium of instruction, although Amharic remains the national language.

Politically motivated decentralization carries implications that are critical for the impact of reform. The education policies adopted along with political decentralization may well be good ideas for improving the quality of instruction and learning. But if improving quality is not a central objective of decentralizing Ethiopian education, the resulting lack of commitment to ensuring that outcome could become the most difficult obstacle to overcome.

Source: Pritchett and Farooqui (2003).

Decentralization and accountability for services

Decentralization must reach the clinic, the classroom, and local water and electricity utilities in ways that create opportunities for strengthening accountability between citizens, politicians/policymakers, and providers. Depending on its degree—deconcentration, delegation, and devolution—and its implementation, decentralization offers opportunities for strengthening different parts of the

---

BOX 10.4 *Many roads to decentralization: Latin America*

Decentralization in Latin America shows how objectives changed over time in each country and shaped outcomes and the path of decentralization. Where decentralization was driven mainly by political objectives (as in Ecuador, Peru, and Venezuela), the transfer of resources was often significant, but the transfer of responsibilities was more difficult to pursue. Where political decentralization was joined and driven by sophisticated but misaligned regional fiscal autonomy (as in Argentina and Brazil), cyclical economic and political crises erupted because of the inability of the center to impose fiscal discipline on subnational governments. In Colombia, though decentralization was initially driven by political motives, fiscal and administrative adjustments ran deeper, and cyclical adjustments in the fiscal and administrative systems were common.

This experience in Latin America shows that the transfer of political, fiscal, and administrative power does not necessarily occur simultaneously or in a supportive sequence. In fact, only in Bolivia's reform effort in 1994 were these powers transferred together. Chile democratized in 1990, introduced popular participation but not regional elections and devolution, and in the mid-1990s further deepened the administrative delegation that had marked its earlier military regime. Of these countries Chile may now be best placed to attempt deeper administrative and political devolution because of the growth of local capacity and the absence of the regional fiscal crises that struck many of its neighbors on their road to decentralization.

Source: Frank, Starnfeld, and Zimmerman (2003).

Figure 10.3 Decentralization and the service delivery framework

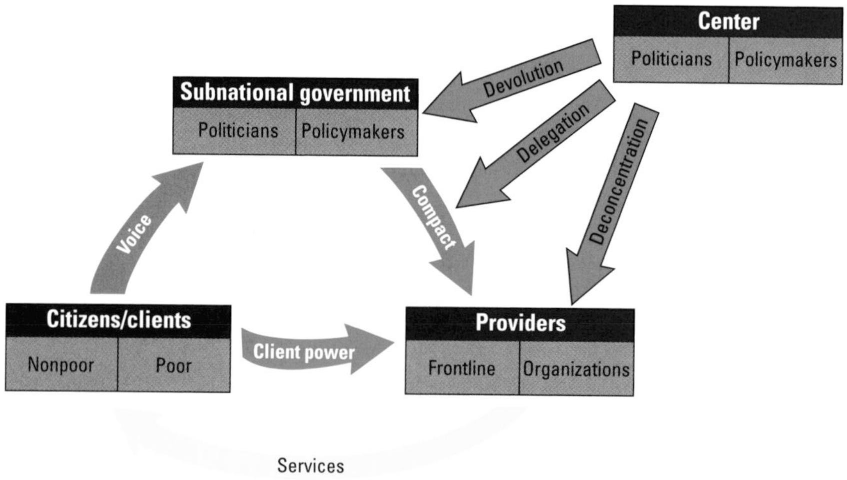

service delivery chain (figure 10.3). *Deconcentration* affects primarily the compact relationship between central policymakers and their local frontline providers and may have little influence on local voice. At the other end, *devolution* implies the handing over of greater power and resources to local politicians and therefore greater scope for strengthening local voice, their compact with local providers, and local client power. *Delegation* falls in between. The degree of decentralization thus impacts differently on the short and long routes of accountability (table 10.2). In practice, decentralization inevitably involves a mix of deconcentration, delegation, and devolution.

Particularly when local taxing and spending powers and central financing are well matched, decentralization can create checks and balances that can motivate both central and subnational governments to make local services work. But accountability may not improve, and the potential gains of decentralization may be lost, if the fiscal and other incentives underlying the center-subnational relationship are misaligned so that checks and balances do not work. A study of the transfer of responsibility for secondary schools to provinces in Argentina in 1994–98 found that while average test scores improved, the gains were much lower when schools were transferred to severely mismanaged provinces (as measured by provincial fiscal deficits).[503]

To allow decentralization to reach local classrooms, clinics, hospitals, and public works departments in a way that increases accountability and makes services work bet-

ter, three areas are key: subnational finance, the division of administrative responsibilities between center and subnational governments, and local capacity.

Getting fiscal incentives right

A subnational government will have weaker incentives to deliver cost-effective services that meet minimum standards if it can manipulate funding (from the center or from market borrowing) to shift its liabilities to the center (called a soft budget constraint).[504] Subnational liabilities can be contractual, fiscal deficits, or public goods that are underprovided. A soft budget constraint weakens accountability, creates moral hazard, and threatens macroeconomic stability by creating contingent liabilities for the center that it may find hard to refuse to pay. Underdeveloped capital markets and elections that do not penalize local politicians for cost and deficit shifting are part of the problem. A hard budget constraint strengthens accountability but requires a sound intergovernmental fiscal system. The center, having devolved responsibility and resources, is prodded by a hard budget constraint to support effective subnational management and service delivery, thereby avoiding fiscal problems and unhappy citizens.

Getting the intergovernmental fiscal system right. Standard welfare economics suggests the efficiency and equity grounds for assigning expenditure responsibilities, revenues, and grants to lower tiers of government.[505] Service decisions and expenditures should be

Table 10.2   Decentralization is never simple
Key political, fiscal, and administrative features of decentralization and the accountability for service delivery

Degree of decentralization	Political features	Fiscal features	Administrative features
Deconcentration (minimal change)	• No elected local government • Local leadership vested in local officials, such as a governor or mayor, but appointed by and accountable to the center • Voice relationships are remote and possibly weak	• Local government is a service delivery arm of the center and has little or no discretion over how or where services are provided • Funds come from the center through individual central ministry or department budgets • No independent revenue sources	• Provider staff working at local level are employees of center, and accountable to center, usually through their ministries; weak local capacity is compensated for by central employees • Accountability remains distant: the *short route of accountability* may be weak if provider monitoring is weak and citizens may have to rely on a weak *long route* stretching to politicians at the center; a strong *compact* between policymakers and providers can compensate to some extent
Delegation (intermediate change)	• Local government may be led by locally elected politicians, but it is still accountable, fully or partially, to the center • *Voice* relationships are more local and proximate, but can be overruled by center	• Spending priorities are set centrally, as well as program norms and standards; local government has some management authority over allocation of resources to meet local circumstances • Funding is provided by the center through transfers, usually a combination of block and conditional grants • No independent revenue sources	• Providers could be employees of central or local government, but pay and employment conditions are typically set by center • Local government has some authority over hiring and location of staff, but less likely to have authority over firing • Both *long* and *short routes of accountability* potentially stronger; greater local knowledge can allow better matching and monitoring of supply with local preferences, strengthening both the *compact* and *client power*
Devolution (substantial change)	• Local government is led by locally elected politicians expected to be accountable to the local electorate • *Voice* relationships can be very strong, but also subject to capture by elites, social polarization, uninformed voting, and clientelism	• Subject to meeting nationally set minimum standards, local government can set spending priorities and determine how best to meet service obligations • Funding can come from local revenues and revenue-sharing arrangements and transfers from center • A hard budget constraint is imperative for creating incentives for accountable service delivery	• Providers are employees of local government • Local government has full discretion over salary levels, staffing numbers and allocation, and authority to hire and fire • Standards and procedures for hiring and managing staff may still be established within an overarching civil service framework covering local governments generally • Potentially strongest *long* and *short routes of accountability*, but now also more influenced by local social norms and vulnerable to local capacity constraints and politics

Note: See the glossary in chapter 3 of this Report for definitions of accountability terms (in italics).
Source: Based on Evans (2003).

devolved to the lowest tier of government that can internalize the costs and benefits of the service—the so-called subsidiarity principle. The principle suggests that subnational governments should administer basic health and education services. But setting minimum standards (for quantity, quality, and access) and financing minimum access should be central responsibilities on grounds of interjurisdictional equity. In practice, things get more complicated. Expenditures are often not assigned carefully to subnational governments.[506] Central governments delay transfers. Shared expenditure responsibilities are the trickiest to handle and can lead to free-rider problems and deficit- and cost-shifting behavior that softens the budget constraint.

To increase responsiveness to local citizens, subnational governments need a local tax instrument and the freedom to set rates.

Also important are simple, transparent, formula-based transfers from the center that are predictable over several years. If made contingent on service outputs, lump-sum grants can ensure a minimum level of service delivery for poor people, equalize fiscal capacity across jurisdictions, and create performance incentives. Ideally, expenditures, revenue assignments, and transfers should be designed jointly so that once they are set, any additional expenditure demands could be met through taxes rather than grants.[507] The more these principles are violated, the greater the informality around transfers, and the lower their predictability and stability, the softer the budget constraint gets.[508]

Getting subnational borrowing right. Capital markets, where sufficiently developed, can bolster subnational accountability.

Where markets are underdeveloped and market discipline is weak, a prior question is whether subnational governments should borrow at all. Effective fiscal decentralization should certainly precede financial decentralization to avoid giving the signal that the center is underwriting subnational debts.[509] Allowing subnational borrowing from public financial institutions can unintentionally send this signal. In Argentina, Brazil, India, and Ukraine, specialized development banks and institutions have provided a backdoor route to central subsidies when transfers would have been simpler and more transparent.

Getting subnational regulation right. Governments find it hard not to bail out lower-tier governments when financial profligacy threatens basic services, risks spreading to other jurisdictions, or threatens monetary policy or the country's credit rating. This has led to the imposition of top-down regulation, either administrative controls or rule-based debt restrictions that mimic the market. Regulation, because it is vulnerable to political bargaining, usually needs to be supplemented by checks and balances on the center itself so that its stance remains credible. In South Africa these are provided by the constitution, the constitutional court, and international capital markets.[510] Subnational bankruptcy arrangements can help. A control board (that can be invoked only by an independent court) to finance minimum, nationally set service levels can protect the center from having to step in. Where bailouts are unavoidable, the center can use the opportunity to make regulation more effective. A comprehensive fiscal monitoring and evaluation system that works consistently across jurisdictions can help greatly in implementing no-bailout and regulation strategies.

Getting administrative responsibilities right

Political and fiscal considerations generally claim far greater attention than administrative decentralization does.[511] In many instances decentralization has proceeded without explicit staffing strategies, and a central civil service typically coexists with subnational and local governments.

Though the 1992 landmark amendments to the Indian constitution require each state to create urban and rural local governments and assign functions and revenues, virtually all staff at the local level remain state employees. In contrast, Indonesia recently adopted a "big-bang" approach, moving quickly to transfer roughly 2.1 million civil servants to subnational district governments.[512] Uganda, in shifting from deconcentration to devolution in the 1990s, established district service commissions with the authority to hire and fire personnel—though in practice central policy and administrative rules have tightly controlled the process so that it has resembled delegation more than devolution. That may change as local capacities grow. Pakistan's recent three-tier devolution envisages the creation of district and subdistrict cadres: district health and education cadres have been created in some provinces, but administrative decentralization still has a long way to go.

National pay scales, rigid collective bargaining agreements, and disagreements with national labor unions can severely circumscribe the flexibility that subnational governments have in rationalizing employment, as seen in many Asian, African, and Latin American countries.[513] Centralized labor negotiations and bargaining agreements can act as unfunded mandates that undo fiscal decentralization (as in South Africa). Engaging public sector workers and unions in discussions about different aspects of decentralization can increase local flexibility and improve provider compacts. At the same time, administrative devolution needs to strike a balance between autonomy and uniformity to allow for desirable features such as interjurisdictional mobility for highly skilled staff in short supply. It is important to align the structure of the civil service with the assignment of service responsibilities to different tiers—misalignment confuses incentives, weakens accountability, and creates conflicts of interest instead of checks and balances. In practice this is not easy, and it takes time.

The twin tasks of devolving administration and building local capacity can be daunting even under ideal conditions of budget and stakeholder support. When budgets are constrained and support is mixed, public administration reform is inevitably drawn out, falling behind political and fiscal decentralization. So the earlier the start in building local capacities, the smoother the process of decentralization is likely to be.

Building local capacity with autonomy

Decentralize or build local capacity: which first? In an ideal world subnational governments would be made fully accountable before they were given authority and autonomy. Decentralization in the absence of adequate local capacity was once considered undesirable,[514] but that view is changing as experience shows that local capacities expand best as decentralized systems mature, even though sequencing remains difficult. The challenge is to balance political, fiscal, and administrative considerations even when capacity mismatches occur. Where local institutions already exist, even informal ones, the challenge is to define their responsibilities and legal status and move the informal closer to the formal. Where local institutions do not exist, the challenge is to construct the underlying legal and political framework for new institutions.

Fostering capacity is best done in partnership between the center and subnational governments, with the center providing incentives for subnational governments to match demand-driven capacity growth with supply-side assistance and financing (box 10.5). In this partnership the functions of central staff also change, from line management to policy formulation, technical advice, and monitoring. Central staff require incentives and training to do their new jobs effectively.

Pulling the pieces together

Decentralization fails or succeeds in the interplay of its fiscal, administrative, and local capacity attributes. The center's role is crucial for all three elements and, more broadly, for the design and implementation of decentralization. When there is a soft budget constraint and the relationships of voice and client power are weak, subnational governments will have little incentive to develop local capacity and perform well, which will make local capture by elites more likely. Ultimately, the center is both regulator and facilitator of decentralization. Its challenge is to balance these roles as it makes and manages the policy framework for the public sector and for service delivery.

Making, managing, and implementing good policies

When the policy decisions of politicians and policymakers at the center of government—senior decisionmakers and veto holders in the executive, council of ministers, or cabinet—are uncoordinated, inconsistent, or badly implemented, the long route of accountability and service delivery are likely to suffer. Breakdowns in policy management can include a range of failures (box 10.6). Sure signs of breakdown? When political policy decisions are not implemented, partially implemented, or reversed.[515] A study of two African nations revealed that more than

---

BOX 10.5 *Building local capacity: the role of the center*

Devolution is difficult when subnational governments lack skills and institutional capacity. The central government can provide training in top-down ways. Or it can create an enabling environment, using its finance and regulatory powers to help subnational governments define their needs (making the process demand-driven), to deploy training from many sources (local or national private sector), to learn by doing as decentralization proceeds, and to establish learning networks among jurisdictions. This second approach is more consistent with devolution and more likely to produce capacity tailored to the many cross-sector responsibilities of subnational governments. It also avoids the pitfalls of a supply-driven approach.

The center may need to provide capacity support, through both a demand-driven grant facility (for example, to help subnational governments contract local and other expertise) and a supply window (for example, mobile teams with financial management, technical, and community mobilization skills). Fiscal support through block grants or challenge funds can work on a competitive or matching basis to support local governments that achieve performance benchmarks (implementing a budgeting system, attaining service targets). Monitoring and evaluation capacity can also be facilitated by performance-based incentive grants. Monitoring efforts should feed into stronger public communication and outreach efforts so that subnational governments can benefit from better client feedback.

Successful capacity building requires a phased strategy, starting with the stabilization of core responsibilities. Next comes a transformation phase with restructuring plans based on a critical examination of service responsibilities and priorities, institutional arrangements, and financial and human resources. Finally, a consolidation phase seeks to internalize capacity growth based on constant learning by doing and adaptation. This is inevitably a drawn-out process marked by the constant need to balance greater autonomy and capacity.

Source: World Bank staff.

> **BOX 10.6** *"Yes, Minister"*
>
> Breakdowns in policy management cover a wide spectrum:
>
> - Failure to set major policy priorities, to understand tradeoffs and make tough choices between conflicting objectives, or to translate priorities into concrete operational decisions, most typically through the budget process.
> - A policy vacuum, because of government discontinuity or weak or poorly articulated policies.
> - Lack of trust between politicians and policymakers, leading to frequent end runs around formal decision structures.
> - Unclear organizational roles or conflicting agendas among line ministries, com-
>
> bined with a failure to consult all ministries with a stake in a particular decision.
>
> - Failure to consult external stakeholders, anticipate opposition, and build electoral support through the relationship of voice.
> - Poorly drafted and inadequately costed submissions (particularly ignoring downstream expenditures), and proposals not vetted thoroughly for their legality and consistency with previous policies.
> - Parallel groups, often invisible and unaccountable, influencing policy from outside formal government.
>
> *Source:* Beschel and Manning (2000).

two-thirds of cabinet decisions were never implemented.[516] In Zambia genuine support for reforms introduced by the multiparty democratic government in the early 1990s never extended beyond a few cabinet ministers. As a result, special interest groups, who had not been consulted, slowed implementation to a crawl.[517] Such missteps are possible at each stage of the policy management process (figure 10.4).

Getting good policies in education, health, and infrastructure

Policy management is particularly difficult in health, education, and infrastructure because outcomes such as reduced infant mortality have multiple determinants that cross sectors and jurisdictions (see crate 1.1); costs come early and impacts much later; and the spillover effects of services are

strong. Policy management in these sectors is often an outcome of well-informed bargaining between competing domestic interests, so accounting for domestic political concerns is important. By contrast, macroeconomic management tends to be the preserve of a few relatively insulated technocrats, with the central bank and finance ministry as key veto players, crises having to be dealt with expeditiously, and domestic political concerns often not included in decisionmaking.[518]

How a cabinet secretariat or presidential staff that links politicians with policymakers plays its role can be crucial to the efficacy of policy management in these sectors. Members of these staffs, which often include elite advisory groups that provide high-quality policy advice, can be vital gatekeepers. They can use contestability—or the careful evaluation of alternatives—to sharpen policy advice. In Thailand the National Economic and Social Development Board in the prime minister's office provides independent fiscal analysis of social sector initiatives and has promoted a coordinated and participatory institutional response to Thailand's HIV/AIDS crisis. Cabinet committees, consisting of subsets of ministers, their representatives, policymakers, and sometimes outside experts, can be particularly effective for intersectoral coordination and implementation and for identifying contending views and resolving them before the formal decision process.

Research on cabinet functioning suggests the conditions that favor high-quality policy management in dealing with complex multi-

Figure 10.4 The anatomy of policy mismanagement at the top

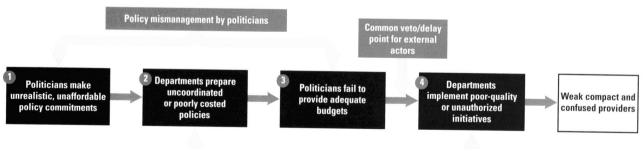

Source: Adapted from Blondel and Manning (2002).

sectoral issues: discipline (decisions are realistic and can be implemented), transparency (systematic procedures that cannot be manipulated by individual members and that emphasize collective responsibility), stability (no flip-flopping), contestability (consideration of alternatives), and structured choice (only core issues come before the cabinet).[519] Of these conditions, discipline seems most important. Practices vary. In the Netherlands all items requiring cabinet approval are specified in the rules of business, and in Finland almost every government decision requires cabinet approval. In Australia the Cabinet Expenditure Review Committee ensures collective responsibility and contestability for spending proposals—ministers have every incentive to test the new spending proposals of their colleagues so as to maximize the pool of uncommitted budget funds available for their own proposals.

More realistic fiscal forecasting and discussion rules that allow sensible tradeoffs to emerge between key service sectors may be needed to avoid overcommitment at early stages of the policy management process. A cabinet office that can negotiate feasible policy and legislative programs with line departments, analyze policy proposals, and coordinate without itself developing policy (to avoid conflicts of interest) can thereafter help ensure delivery on policy and budget proposals on these commitments. In establishing budgets, a multiyear budget framework may help ensure adequate funding and reduce budget instability if supported by politicians and the requisite implementation capacity. Communication, outreach, and consultation can forestall opposition and improve implementation plans. Finally, the compact may need to be strengthened so that neglect, incompetence, misapplication, or malfeasance does not prevent executive decisions from being implemented or cause those that are implemented to be flawed.

Making strategic choices in public administration and management

Choosing how to implement good policies is as important as making them. Countries have experimented in the past two decades with different public administration approaches to improving the performance and

accountability of public officials and agencies. Analysis suggests that the basic drivers of performance are merit-based recruitment and promotion, adequate compensation, and reasonable autonomy from political interference.[520] As a result of the different approaches, the share of public employment in total employment varies widely: for the period 1997–99 it averaged 38 percent in transition economies (16 countries), 24 percent in industrial countries (20), and 21 percent in developing countries (23).[521] General government employment in education and health and in central and subnational government also varies considerably (figure 10.5). The differences reflect the different roles of the state and public administration in individual countries, institutions that have historic roots and cannot be changed overnight.

Figure 10.5   Working to keep citizens educated, healthy, and safe
General government employment, mid- to late-1990s

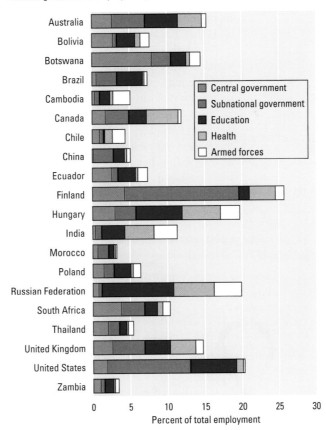

Note: General government excludes employment in state-owned enterprises. Central and subnational government totals exclude health, education, and police personnel. Armed forces excludes police.
Source: World Bank (2002e).

The New Public Management philosophy has dominated the debate on public administration reforms in recent years. Implemented principally in Australia, New Zealand, and the United Kingdom, it recognizes the government's special role in service provision, financing, or regulation, and the resulting incentive problems. It seeks to strengthen accountability by exchanging management flexibility for internal contracting among policymakers and between policymakers and providers. New Public Management also seeks to provide a more transparent accounting system and tighter, private sector–like financial management controls. In its extreme form civil servants have no tenure, and their term in office and promotion depend on successful completion of contract-specified deliverables. Experience in developing countries has been mixed, with some improvements in efficiency and uneven effects on equity.[522] In the weak institutional settings of many developing countries, New Public Management reforms may impose high transaction costs that may outweigh efficiency gains.

As the experience with New Public Management suggests, often the problem in implementing public sector reforms is not deciding on reform objectives but on how to get there. In Bolivia agencies were given management flexibility in the early 1990s, but there were no central controls to enforce accountability. Public administration problems remained.[523] The Bolivian experience highlights the "catch-22": central controls are necessary when the policymaker-provider relationship is weak and agencies lack competence and effective internal controls. But as long as external controls are in place, line agencies lack the incentive to acquire competency and establish internal controls.

The answer? Choosing and sequencing public sector reforms carefully, in line with initial capacities, to create firmer ground for further reform. Pragmatic, incremental reforms in weak institutional environments—strategic incrementalism—can alleviate, if not fully resolve, accountability problems while creating the conditions for deeper change by modifying incentives and building capacity to respond to the next stage of reforms. Thailand is considering a "hurdle" approach to reforming its centralized budget system. Line agencies would clear a series of hurdles to qualify at each level for greater budget autonomy. In this incremental approach to budget reform, the dismantling of external controls has to be synchronized with the building of internal controls.[524] Other countries can follow a more traditional but still sequenced path of budget reforms, differentiating between short- and medium-term measures and building information channels for accountability as the reforms unfold—another form of strategic incrementalism (figure 10.6).

Formality in public sector institutions. Many aspects of government performance rest on an ingrained institutional discipline or formality. Actual behavior follows written rules, or actual budget outcomes bear a close resemblance to the legislatively agreed budget.[525] Informality emerges in weak institutional settings where incentives and procedures do not match formal rules, rewards, and procedures.[526]

This formality gap is most evident in personnel and budget problems. Teacher absenteeism in many countries exposes the stark differences between explicit rules on recruitment, promotion, pay determination, and monitoring and the actual, informal arrangement of connections and patronage that determine who gets hired and even whether they have to show up at all. Lateral entry to the civil service, intended to provide flexibility and contestability, becomes a window for patronage and nepotism when official posts

Figure 10.6   No straight roads to success: sequencing budget reforms

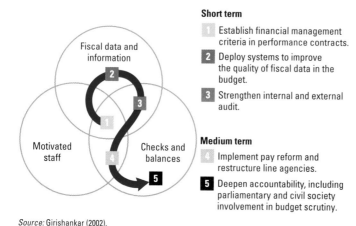

Short term

1 Establish financial management criteria in performance contracts.

2 Deploy systems to improve the quality of fiscal data in the budget.

3 Strengthen internal and external audit.

Medium term

4 Implement pay reform and restructure line agencies.

5 Deepen accountability, including parliamentary and civil society involvement in budget scrutiny.

Source: Girishankar (2002).

are bought and sold by politicians for private profit.[527] Checks and balances on policymakers are misused when reformers who arouse opposition are transferred capriciously.[528] In budget management as well a formal process of policy choices disciplined by budget rules can differ greatly from the informal process in which the budget is made and remade constantly during execution. As noted earlier, several African countries suffer from this formality gap in implementing their medium-term expenditure frameworks.

What are the practical implications of formality in public sector performance? The experience of countries with public management reforms suggests that the presence or absence of formality should influence the direction of reform, even if the objectives are the same. Where there is no strong tradition of merit-based civil service employment, the direction of reform has been to set up checks and balances to legally define entry to the civil service and the responsibilities of civil servants, and to build a distinct and unified corps. Security and stability of tenure and objectivity in promotion are used to protect against political interference. Where formality is the norm, the ambition has been to move in the opposite direction—to reduce the security of tenure and seniority in promotions and increase individual performance contracting, lateral entry, and rewards for results. This experience points to an important formality threshold in making reform choices.

First-stage and second-stage reforms. This threshold suggests a useful distinction between first-stage or basic reforms and second-stage or more advanced reforms (figure 10.7). First-stage reforms provide incentives to achieve or strengthen formality when the starting point is a weak institutional setting. Second-stage reforms build on a foundation of formality in stronger institutional environments (table 10.3 suggests illustrative examples of such reforms). In budget management the basics include hardening the budget constraint as a more top-down approach to budget formulation and strengthening implementation of input-oriented line item budgeting. Disseminating performance information internally and to

citizens can give budget management a basic performance orientation (though well short of performance contracting). In personnel management first-stage reforms might include enhancing job security to strengthen protection from political interference.

Second-stage reforms build on a culture of following rules and offer more choices. In budget management second-stage reforms include a much stronger orientation toward results and performance auditing, building on good budget execution capacities in government. In personnel management second-stage reforms include reducing job security, harmonizing individual rewards with performance targets, and aligning broader terms and conditions with those in the private sector. But a greater contract orientation is not the only way to go. Countries such as Canada and Germany have adopted a process of continuous adaptation of their existing systems that relies on granting greater flexibility to achieve stronger results.

Curbing corruption in service delivery

Many reforms to improve public sector performance and its results orientation cut across multiple sectors. Curbing corruption is one. Service delivery is weakened by corruption, and poor people suffer its consequences more than others do.

Understanding the economic and social costs of corruption

Corruption—the abuse of public office for private gain—is a symptom of weak relationships in the service chain. Both grand

Figure 10.7 **From weak basics to strong foundations in public sector institutional reforms**

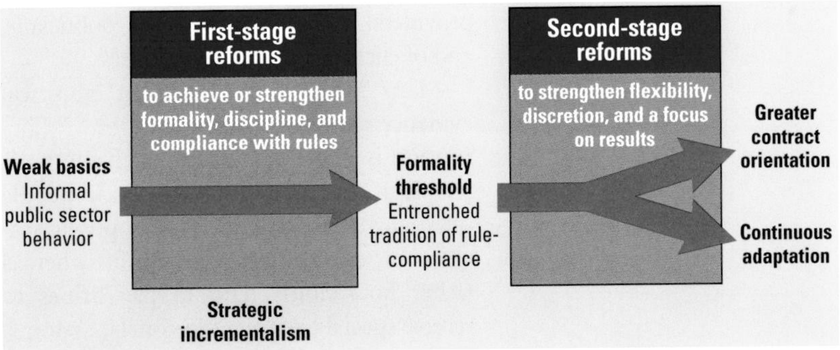

Source: Adapted from World Bank (2002e).

Table 10.3   Walk before you run

	Objective	First-stage reforms	Second-stage reforms
Budget management reforms	*Greater efficiency and impact*	Introduce input-oriented line-item budgeting with some performance information	Change budget formulation and format to link the budget to program performance and out-year plans
	Aggregate cost management	Harden budget constraints and focus on implementation and reporting	Use block or frame budgeting
	Accounting reforms	Strengthen cash accounting	Introduce double-entry bookkeeping and accrual accounting
	Auditing reforms	Strengthen traditional financial and compliance audit and introduce some performance auditing	Institutionalize performance auditing in a supreme audit institution and in internal audit
Personnel management reforms	*Career management*	Enhance job security and protection from political interference	Decrease tenure and link to continuous performance assessment
	Unity of the civil service	Create a legally defined cadre with common terms and conditions	Devolve and diversify pay arrangements to provide flexibility to employers
	Individual incentives	Apply standard merit promotion and reward rules consistently	Establish annual performance targets
	Openness	Encourage career development within a closed system and avoid nepotism	Move toward "position-based" systems and encourage lateral entry

Source: Adapted from World Bank (2002e).

corruption (involving politicians, senior officials, and state capture) and petty corruption (involving lower-level officials, administrative procedures, and routine public services) weaken services. The avenues for corruption in education, health, and infrastructure are many; they include absenteeism, patronage, construction kickbacks, procurement fraud, sale of lucrative official positions, false certification, misuse of facilities, unwarranted services (unjustified caesarian deliveries, private payments to government teachers for after-school tuition), and bribes at the point of service.[529] Bribes are the most common face of corruption for poor people, as payments to providers to evade approved procedures or to perform stated duties. Once entrenched, corruption reduces the ability and incentives of policymakers to monitor providers, of citizens to monitor politicians, and of clients to monitor providers.

Many recent studies present empirical evidence on the costs of corruption.[530] Corruption is a regressive tax, penalizing poor people more than others.[531] Poor people often pay bribes to receive basic public services in education and health, whereas richer households tend to pay bribes to receive special treatment in courts, customs, and tax authorities. Household surveys show that the poor are the least likely to know how to get redress when officials abuse their position. Transaction-intensive discretionary services that are hard to monitor offer particularly broad scope for corruption because providers have a strong information advantage over clients.

Corruption in its broader sense of the capture of public resources and decision-making affects public spending decisions. The loss of revenue, diversion of public funds, and evasion of taxes associated with such corruption mean that governments have less to spend on education, health, and infrastructure. Studies have found that corruption is negatively associated with the share of public expenditures on health and education[532] and with health and education outcomes. Politicians may prefer to spend less on ensuring that primary health and education services work and more on new construction and infrastructure, which offer greater opportunities for corruption.[533] And corruption is empirically associated with lower economic growth rates.

Dealing with corruption

There has been rapid growth in diagnostic tools to measure corruption, assess service delivery, and make informed judgments about entry points for reform.[534] Diagnostic surveys, already implemented in some 20 countries, usually consist of three separate but linked instruments covering households, firms, and public officials. This allows triangulation of perspectives on the extent, incidence, locus, and causes of corruption.[535] Public expenditure tracking surveys and quantitative service delivery surveys of specific facilities can yield useful information on the contours of corruption and identify entry points for reform. Service delivery surveys can measure staff incentives and efficiency, providing information on the determinants of service quality and qualitative data on corruption. Together, they can provide a cross-check on the causes and consequences of corruption and provide information that strengthens the voice relationship and client power.

Corruption in service delivery is a symptom of an underlying systemic malaise. Dealing piecemeal with corruption risks treating the symptom and not the malaise. Curtailing corruption requires a multipronged strategy that addresses a number of concerns—political accountability, institutional restraints, citizen voice, effective media, public disclosure laws, competition, and good public sector performance (figure 10.8). A multipronged strategy is difficult anywhere, but particularly where corruption is widespread and the institutional setting is weak. Anticorruption diagnostics can shed light on the patterns and root causes of corruption, thereby helping to sort reform priorities and suggest suitable entry points. In transition economies that are building new public institutions while massively redistributing state assets, opportunities arise for both administrative corruption and state capture.[536] Where administrative corruption is high but state capture at the center is not, strengthening accountability

Figure 10.8   Many forces at play in curbing corruption in service delivery

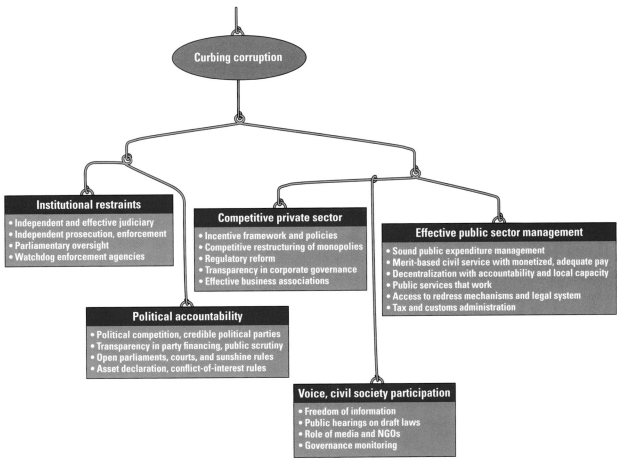

Source: World Bank (2000a).

within public administration and deploying expenditure tracking surveys and other tools for financial accountability might be the place to start. But where state capture at the center is high, political accountability and decentralization might be the better entry points.

An independent, well-functioning judiciary is vital for combating corruption and often offers a viable entry point. In enforcing laws and providing checks and balances on the power of policymakers and providers, courts directly strengthen voice. In many countries, however, courts are themselves a corrupt arm of government. Even if judges are above reproach, lawyers, court clerks, and other court officials on the take can add to the web of corruption. The ingredients of reform are many—freedom of information, greater transparency and sunshine laws, self-regulation through reform-minded bar associations and law societies, updating of antiquated laws and court procedures, and the independence, competence, and integrity of judicial personnel—but they are complicated to assemble and need time to take root. Experience suggests that important progress can be made if reforms focus on incentives, institutional relationships, and information access rather than only on formal court rules, procedures, and court expansion. Anti-corruption legislation that matches the enforcement capacity of the country, independent supreme audit organizations, and legislative oversight can help.

Managing transitions: overcoming reform hurdles

Public sector reforms can arouse stiff opposition from groups that benefit from existing relationships. How can this opposition be softened? And how to explain the dilemma of "considerable reform in political landscapes seeded with the potential for failure"—exemplified, for example, by contentious education reforms in Latin America.[537] There is no easy answer, but a major factor is how politicians and policymakers manage the numerous transitions in public sector and service delivery reforms, engaging with citizens and frontline providers to promote change. Experience suggests that dealing with the political economy of such transitions may be the hardest task for reformers. While each country's experience is unique, some general principles provide a starting point (box 10.7). But knowing what to push and what to hold back is an art not easy to learn or teach.

Policy managers must choose appropriately between first- and second-stage reforms. Even reforms such as implementing the budget require considerable leadership, capacity, and coordination across many parts of government. Choosing second-stage reforms in a weak institutional setting can be doubly difficult. Not only is

---

BOX 10.7 *Managing the thorny politics of pro-poor service delivery reforms*

Reform means change and therefore opposition, often political. This is particularly the case for reform of basic services in which governments are involved as providers, financiers, or regulators, and for which the long route of accountability therefore comes into play.

Institutional reforms in education, health, and infrastructure service delivery are particularly complex. Multiple actors, long timetables, early costs, and late benefits create many known and unknown veto players and risks. Support for expanding access is easy to organize (new jobs, new contracts, new patronage), but improving quality is hard.

Reforms can be implemented more easily in pro-poor settings because of the consensus on social equity. Managing politics then often implies curbing unsustainable populism, promoting universal public services, and building coalitions among the poor and the middle class so that there is broad support for reforms.

But in clientelist settings consensus on reforms may be difficult to reach among politicians, policymakers, and potential veto players (government bureaucracies, business associations, labor unions, nongovernmental organizations). Vested interests and patron-client relationships may have co-opted many institutions. Reformers must then create political room by more purposefully managing the politics of reform.

Though each situation is different, experience suggests some basics:

- *Setting the terms of the debate, controlling the agenda, and taking the high road,* including getting ahead of the opposition, using information disclosure and

the media to empower supporters, and seeking strategic entry points.

- *Striking sensible tradeoffs* between comprehensive and incremental reforms, seeking early wins for stakeholders, and supporting reform champions and cross-agency teams that can bring along others of like mind.

- *Welcoming policy contestability* as inevitable, but using it to mobilize stakeholders, build coalitions, and gain electoral credibility.

- *Ensuring broad, sustainable support* as early as possible, and avoiding a backlash by aiming at universal services that benefit all users, including the poor, rather than special groups.

- *Marginalizing opponents* before, during, and after implementation, particularly those with veto power, and exploiting splits in their ranks to move beyond the static arithmetic of winners and losers.

Managing the politics of reform is often a top-down technocratic process led by central design teams and lacking participation, transparency, and occasionally even legitimacy. This is usually a mistake. Without good feedback it is difficult to master changing areas of conflict. Making services work for poor people requires strengthening their voice in order to strengthen accountability. This reduces, in a positive way, the room for maneuver by reformers. Inclusive decisionmaking and implementation processes are both a means and an end in the management of the politics of pro-poor service reforms.

Sources: Grindle (forthcoming), Nelson (2000), Weyland (1997), and Olson (1971).

there likely to be significant opposition (second-stage reforms represent a greater departure from the status quo than first-stage reforms) but supporters may favor the reforms for the wrong reasons (anticipating the possibility of private gain when complex reforms fail in an informal institutional environment). So a mismatch of reforms and initial conditions can lead to the subversion of the reforms from outside and inside.

Even if reformers recognize the need to start with first-stage reforms, there is the problem of reform traction.[538] Embarking on reform is less of a challenge where traction is high—reformers have considerable leverage in society and politics, are good communicators who have sold their vision to the majority of the population, and the institutions to be reformed are amenable to change and salvageable. But in settings where traction is low, reformers must deal with their slippery grip on reforms, which can make it hard to shape the implementation of even first-stage reforms.

How then should reformers in low-traction settings initiate and implement reforms? The answers, clearly country-specific, go beyond the simple principles enunciated in box 10.7. Above all, initiating reforms in low-traction settings is a matter of opportunity and patience. To take advantage of opportunities as they arise, reformers need to build alliances with key stakeholders in advance. They need to encourage diversity and experimentation and to learn quickly and systematically from the results. And they need to create their own opportunities; building on what traction does exist in their settings.

Evaluating and learning

Monitoring and evaluation give meaning to the accountability relationships between service clients, policymakers, and providers. Traditionally, governments have associated monitoring and evaluation with individual areas of the core public sector—the audit system, discussion of audited financial statements by the legislature—but these have tended to remain unconnected and myopic. What has been missing is the feedback on outcomes and consequences of actions at each stage of the service delivery chain connecting policymakers, providers, and clients. A results-based monitoring and evaluation system that joins information from more traditional monitoring efforts with information from the service delivery framework can provide guidance on the institutional reforms needed to improve service delivery. It can be particularly useful to embed an evaluation regime within a poverty reduction strategy so that it is possible to see what the strategy is doing for services for poor people.

The technology of monitoring and evaluation is widely known and usually specific to the service and delivery mechanism.[539] What is more important to focus on are the underlying incentives for monitoring and evaluation, and how demand for information can be made to drive the supply. Three issues stand out: the institutional framework for monitoring and evaluation, the role of systematic program assessment and its links back into policymaking, and the importance of dissemination.

Creating a new information system that results in greater transparency, accountability, and visibility will alter political power equations. It can challenge conventional wisdom on program performance, drive new resource allocation decisions, and call into question the leadership of those responsible. Box 10.8 highlights the importance of understanding the institutional and political dimensions of a results-based monitoring and evaluation system and how demand for monitoring and evaluation should drive the supply, rather than the other way around. Efforts to improve statistical systems, for example, have often focused on fixing supply problems by strengthening national statistical systems to collect, process, and disseminate data rather than on understanding the sources of demand. This has led in some cases to an oversupply of information: in Tanzania, for example, health information systems abound, but it is still difficult to obtain accurate estimates of service delivery coverage.

Without some understanding of how information is used, those who collect it may see the process as time consuming and unrewarding, leading to poor compliance and low quality. As decentralization proceeds in many countries, it is important to

---

BOX 10.8 *Ready for results?*

- Are champions of results-based monitoring and evaluation evident within the country?
- What reforms are underway or planned to which a results-based monitoring and evaluation initiative might be linked?
- Who will use results-based monitoring and evaluation information to assess service delivery performance?
- What management framework within the government will oversee the introduction and operation of a results-based monitoring and evaluation system?
- Are there links between budget and resource allocation procedures and existing monitoring and evaluation information?
- Who regularly collects and analyzes monitoring and evaluation information to assess government performance, either inside or outside the government?
- Where can local capacity be found in public management, surveying, evaluation, and data management to support the supply of and the demand for results-based monitoring and evaluation?
- Are there proposed or existing donor-supported initiatives, such as a PRSP, to which a results-based monitoring and evaluation initiative might be linked?

Source: Based on Kusek, Rist, and White (2003).

---

build decentralized monitoring and evaluation capacity so that central and local systems are complementary.

As emphasized elsewhere in this Report, systematic program evaluation can be a powerful tool for showing what works and what does not. Given the complexity of public sector reforms and the difficulty of choosing entry points and appropriate sequencing, governments are constantly trying new policy and program approaches. Some of them work well, many produce mediocre results, and many fail. But unless there is systematic evaluation of reforms, there is no way to be sure that they worked because of the policy or program or because of other reasons.[540] And unless the results play a major part in the design of subsequent delivery mechanisms, there is no way to be sure that governments can succeed when they decide to scale up.

Finally, as chapter 5 and the rest of the Report emphasize, wide dissemination of the results of monitoring and evaluation activities is crucial to improvements in service delivery. If not widely disseminated inside and outside government through mechanisms tailored to specific audiences, the results of monitoring and evaluation activities may not live up to their potential for improving service delivery.

170,000 community health agents reaching 80 million Brazilians

One of Brazil's poorest states, Ceará reduced infant mortality dramatically in the late 1980s and 1990s. A major effort of the local government motivated health workers, municipalities, local communities, and families to work for better health.

In the 1980s the socioeconomic indicators in Ceará, a state of about 7 million people in northeast Brazil, were among the worst in the country. The infant mortality rate was around 100 per 1,000 live births. Fewer than 30 percent of municipalities had a nurse. And essential health services reached only 20–40 percent of the population. In 1986 the state government began a massive effort to reduce infant deaths. It succeeded. By 2001 infant mortality was down to 25 per 1,000 live births.

Sending health workers to poor households

The Ceará state government began in 1987 to recruit, train, and deploy community health agents. By the early 1990s health agents were visiting 850,000 families a month, the first public service to regularly reach nearly all local communities.

The monthly family visits and family records improved oral rehydration therapy, breastfeeding, immunization, antenatal care, and growth monitoring—as well as treatment of pneumonia, diarrhea, and other diseases.

By 2001 more than 170,000 community health agents covered 80 million Brazilians (figure 1). In 1994 the teams of community health agents were gradually expanded to include a doctor, a nurse, a nurse's aid, and five to six community health agents for every 800 families.

This Family Health Program was based on the success of the São Paulo, Porto Alegre, and Niterói municipalities with "family physicians." It added follow-up of at-risk families and home care for chronic diseases to the existing services. The family physicians and nurses' aides also provide curative care and referrals to hospitals. By 2002, 150,000 Family Health teams were reaching 45 million people.

Health outcomes, 1987–2001

Some of the decreases in infant mortality and malnutrition can be attributed to the increased coverage of immunization, oral rehydration therapy, and breastfeeding (figure 2). Socioeconomic inequalities in coverage were also reduced, and the greatest improvements were made among the poorest of the population.[541] Output measures—such as immunization, oral rehydration therapy, breastfeeding, and child weighing—have also improved.

Anecdotal evidence points to impacts in other states. Implementing the Family Health Program in the town of Camaragibe brought infant mortality down from 65 per 1,000 live births in 1993 to 17 at the end of the 1990s, and in Palmas the incidence of diarrhea fell by half, with antenatal care coverage doubling between 1997 and 1998.[542]

Balancing decentralization with a results orientation

Mobilizing actors

Using matching funds to motivate municipalities to implement new programs, Ceará state policymakers struck a balance between decentralizing responsibilities to the municipalities and keeping a results focus through state control over key aspects of the program.

Strategies were also developed to strengthen community leverage over health providers and to strengthen community voice. The widely publicized selection of a large number of community health agents from the communities helped to "socialize" the program. Community organizations were involved in the second round of assessments for the Municipal Seal of Approval—a program to give incentives to municipalities to improve outcomes (box 1).

Financing

Several financing mechanisms covered annual program costs of roughly $1.50 per beneficiary. In line with the 1988 constitution and 2001 health funding laws, municipalities can retain tax revenues but must spend 25 percent on education and 10 percent on health. The salaries of community health agents ($60 a month), and the costs of supervision and drugs are paid directly by the state. Municipalities are required to cover only the salaries of nurse-supervisors ($300 a month), but many voluntarily support other costs.

The national government offers matching block grants to municipalities for education and health as an incentive to implement priority programs. The grants for minimum basic health care amount to 10

Figure 1   The number of community health agents increased dramatically

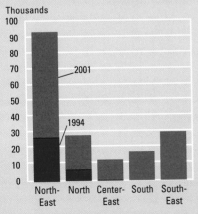

Thousands

2001

1994

North-East   North   Center-East   South   South-East

Source: Brazil Ministry of Health (2001).

Figure 2   Changes in health and nutrition indicators in Ceará 1987–94 and 1997–2001

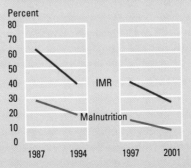

Percent

IMR

Malnutrition

1987   1994   1997   2001

Source: 1987 to 1994 from Victora and others (2000a); 1997 to 2001 from Fuentes and Niimi (2002).

BOX 1 *The Ceará Municipal Seal of Approval*

In 1990 Brazil enacted the Statute for Children and Adolescents, one of the world's most advanced laws on child rights, introducing local rights councils and guardianship councils to help define, implement, and monitor public policies for children.

In 1997 Ceará introduced Municipal Seals of Approval with support from UNICEF. The seals were awarded to municipalities based on performance indicators of child survival and development and on administrative management of health, education, and child protection.

No monetary award is attached to the seals, but the municipality may display the seal on official stationary and in health centers, schools, and other official services. Mayors, showing interest in the seal, like being viewed as "child friendly" and good managers.

mayors," and scorecards of municipal indicators. The Seal of Approval required that municipalities have better-than-average health indicators for the group in which the municipality was classified, based on socioeconomic criteria. Color-coded maps facilitated monitoring and recorded the evolution of indicators.

---

reals per person per year, 2,400 reals per health agent per year for municipalities implementing the Community Health Worker Program, and 28,000 to 54,000 reals per year per team when the municipalities implement the Family Health Program.

Monitoring and information dissemination

To encourage municipalities to participate, Ceará state officials tried to create a strong "image" program. Citizens were informed of its benefits, and they lobbied mayors to join the program. Implementation was phased in, beginning with municipalities that demonstrated interest and readiness, stimulating competition among municipalities.

Innovative social mobilization strategies expanded public awareness of the Seal of Approval and broadened understanding of the social indicators needed for certification. These included compact discs to guide radio coverage, elections of "child

Enforcement through hiring and firing

Although the program was decentralized to municipalities, a special team attached to the state governor had control over the hiring and firing of the community health workers, and over a special fund created for the program.

Many community health agents were recruited from the community through a high-profile selection process that contributed to a sense of ownership and empowered communities to demand better services from the mayors. Candidates not selected become public monitors of the performance of the community health agents.

Donors and service reform

Timeo danaos et dona ferentes.—I fear the Greeks even when they bear gifts.

Laocoön on the Trojan Horse

In many developing countries, external donors support service reform. In middle-income or large low-income countries, they mostly pilot innovations or implement demonstration projects. If chosen strategically and evaluated properly, these projects can be powerful. In other low-income countries the story is quite different. Donors supply 20 percent or more of public resources in more than 60 low-income countries. And they supply more than 40 percent of public resources in at least 30 poor countries—such as Bolivia, Madagascar, Nepal, and Tanzania. For these countries aid flows are obviously important for service delivery.

The international community has come a long way in understanding what makes aid more effective, focusing on the selection of recipient countries.[543] This chapter suggests that, along with country selectivity, the way donors provide their aid matters a lot.

Donors still underestimate how difficult it is to influence reform without undercutting domestic accountabilities. Too aware of failures in the key relationships of accountability in recipient countries, donors often bypass them. This can produce good isolated projects, but it can also weaken the aid recipient's internal systems and accountability relationships (chapters 3 to 6). This chapter suggests that:

- Donors need to pay more attention to the problems in influencing service reform in recipient countries.
- They should strengthen the critical relationships among policymakers, providers, and clients. In circumventing those relationships, they can undermine the delivery of services.

- Donors should support recipient institutions by evaluating innovations systematically, by harmonizing and realigning their financial assistance and knowledge transfers with the recipient's service delivery (particularly where aid's share of spending is large), and by focusing on outcomes and results.
- In good country environments where there are genuine reformers, donors should also integrate their support in the recipient's development strategy, budget, and service delivery system.
- In low-income countries coming out of conflict or with weak institutions, donors should support urgent social and other services, while identifying mechanisms that build transparent public institutions in the longer term. Pooling of aid will reduce transaction costs.

This is all fine, but the multiple objectives of foreign aid create incentives for donors to control their interventions directly rather than to align them with the recipient's service delivery systems. Because of these incentives, reforming aid will not be easy. Yet for service reform to succeed, donors have to attach an even higher priority to aid effectiveness and development outcomes.

Aid and accountabilities

Aid differs in important ways from domestically financed services. The beneficiaries and financiers are not just distinct—they live in different countries, with different political constituencies.[544] This geographical and political separation—between beneficiaries in the recipient country and taxpayers in the donor country—breaks the normal performance feedback loop in service delivery (figure 11.1). For example,

Figure 11.1   The feedback loop between beneficiaries and donor country taxpayers is broken

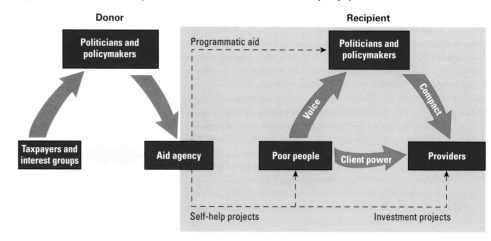

beneficiaries in a recipient country may be able to observe the performance of aid agencies. But they cannot reward or punish the policymakers responsible for this performance in donor countries. The broken feedback loop induces greater incentive biases in aid than in domestic programs. So aid effectiveness is determined not only by the performance of the recipient but also by the incentives embedded in the institutional environment of aid agencies. Understanding these incentives is central to any reform of aid to support service delivery better.

The divergence and distance between constituencies and clients may be important—but there is more. Even if donor constituencies adopted client feedback as a paramount criterion for aid, there would still be difficulties in exercising external influence without undermining local accountability relationships. To illustrate the inherent problem of external actors, consider enterprise finance. When financiers or venture capitalists want to influence an enterprise they are investing in, they become an equity holder and perhaps request a seat on the company's board. Clearly it would be politically infeasible for donors to request seats in the recipient's cabinet. Yet the influence that donors exercise on the recipient's public spending often resembles that of an equity financier.

Strengthen—don't weaken—the compact

When aid flows are substantial relative to the recipient's resources, donors affect the com-

pacts between policymakers and provider organizations (chapter 6) in many ways. By influencing spending patterns and budgetary processes, donors interfere directly with the design of the compact. And by going straight to provider organizations, donors sidestep the policymaker as well as the compact.

Donors affect the recipient's spending patterns and budgetary processes in many ways:[545]

- Donors may support only capital spending (construction) and expect the government to supply complementary inputs (staffing, maintenance). Governments often fail to finance the complementary inputs.

- Donors may fund projects that governments are not interested in. This contradicts ownership, though it can work where a good pilot project encourages a new approach through its demonstration effect—or where a one-time intervention is needed.

- Donors may give aid to a priority sector and assume that government spending from its own resources remains unchanged. This runs into fungibility because governments attempt to smooth spending by adjusting their own allocations.[546]

- Donors may set targets for the share of spending in particular sectors as conditions for aid flows. Consider the current donor preference for social sectors, which appears to have increased both recipients' public spending on these sectors and the social sector's share of aid (from 14 percent of the aid flows in 1991 to 34 percent in 2000).[547] But strong donor preferences can leave other important areas underfunded or set perverse incentives in the privileged sector. In Zambia protecting social spending led to deep cuts in rural infrastructure spending—possibly creating more rural poverty.[548]

To avoid such distortions, donors can discuss priorities with policymakers and work to shape public expenditure during the annual budget cycle. But the recipient has to have a budget process that functions fairly well.

Many donors see a need to align aid with the recipient's compact between policymakers and providers. But there are other tendencies as well. Global funds, which are private-public partnerships at the global level, have chosen to provide funding on a project basis directly to service providers in poor countries.[549] The new health-related global funds also develop policies for global procurement and distribution of commodities, such as mosquito nets, vaccines, and essential medicines.

In many ways, the delivery of global funds—from a global source of finance directly to the local provider—reflects the need for donors to demonstrate that the funds are additional to what otherwise would have been given. But it might also reflect dissatisfaction with the functioning of the recipient's relationships of accountability and with aid agencies. But it is not clear that this is a sustainable solution to the institutional problems. Evidence from Uganda indicates that global funds can pit the recipient's policymakers—in charge of the overall spending program—against its provider organizations, who directly lobby for off-budget funds at the international level (box 11.1). Parallel financing mechanisms can also undermine efforts to rationalize expenditures, reform government systems, and increase transparency at the country level.

Donors interact directly with provider organizations at various levels. Some aid agencies choose to work with line ministries. Others choose to engage providers under local governments. And others go directly to frontline providers, such as health clinics or schools. Sectoral ministries independently lobby donors for funding. From the donor perspective competition among ministries, departments, and other organizations permits a better selection process—because hopeful recipients will do their best to reveal as much information as possible to attract donors. The result: recipients' policymakers lose control of the expenditure program, because the finance is off-budget and the activities bypass the compact. Incoherent spending allocations and uneven coverage of services ensue.

Similar competition can occur among donors, making incentive problems worse. When the recipient agency knows that if one donor threatens to withdraw due to the recipient agency's poor performance other donors will step in, few incentives exist for improving its performance.[550]

Some donors, including the World Bank, even circumvent provider organizations by setting up autonomous or semi-autonomous project implementation units for their interventions. Advocates of project implementation units recognize that the arrangements can undermine local capacity building, create salary distortions, and weaken the compact between the policymaker and the provider organization. But they argue that the better results outweigh the costs. A study of about 100 World Bank projects in the Latin America and Caribbean Region shows otherwise: that project implementation units have no

---

BOX 11.1 *The debate over global funds: Uganda*

It is like a hungry boy who sees ripe mangoes hanging abundantly from a tree, but he is not allowed to pick the fruits. The Ministry of Health remains needy, while donor money hangs around. As part of the budget and medium-term expenditure framework, the Ministry of Finance sets a limit to the amount of money that can be spent on health—as it does for all sectors—refusing to earmark excess funds for health from global funds. The Ministry of Finance argues that there are a whole host of important things that poor people need and that there are not enough resources around to provide all of them.

But health officials insist that the Ministry of Finance is constructing ceilings below floors and that it costs much more to deliver health services than the budget allocation it receives. The Ministry of Finance counters by saying that the country's attractiveness to donors depends on its reputation for sound macroeconomic management. Global funds risk undermining this by providing resources outside the normal budget process. It is not government's intention to turn away additional resources, finance officials say, but it is important that such resources be channeled through the regular budget process.

Source: Adapted from *The New Vision*, Uganda's main daily newspaper.

significant positive impact on project outcomes, while the likely sustainability of results clearly suffered.[551] A parallel study in the Eastern Europe and Central Asia Region produced similar findings.[552]

In Bangladesh donors responded to a crisis by setting up a separate project management unit for the Bangladesh Arsenic Mitigation Water Supply Project—to speedily address arsenic contamination in drinking water (chapter 9). The unit bypassed the traditional water engineering departments, deemed too inflexible to respond to the emergency. Two years later it has fallen far short of expectations. The government is expected to close the project shortly, arguing that the unit, having bypassed government, was unable to deliver on the ground.

To staff project implementation units, donors tend to hire the most highly skilled civil servants, often at salaries many times what they could earn from the government.[553] In Kenya a World Bank agricultural project paid eight local staff between $3,000 and $6,000 a month, many times the $250 available to a senior economist in the civil service.[554] Another study found that of 20 Kenyan government economists receiving master's degree training in a donor-funded program between 1977 and 1985, 15 were working for aid agencies or nongovernmental organizations (NGOs)—or for their projects by 1994. The study concluded: "elite external master's degrees are, in effect, passports out of the public sector."[555] In countries with many donors, salaries are likely to be bid up even more, as donors compete for qualified staff.

A better choice to improve aid effectiveness is to phase these units out and to work with the recipient's provider organizations, building their capacity. And it should take place within the compact between the recipient's policymakers and service providers. But this requires changes in incentives in aid agencies (see the last section of this chapter).

Let provider organizations manage

Donors affect management of provider organizations in recipient countries in at least three ways: by the fragmentation of aid in a large number of donor projects, by the choice of activities, and by the choice of inputs.

The costs of aid fragmentation

The problem with aid fragmentation is not that individual projects are misconceived—it is that there are too many projects for any to work efficiently. When a project's fixed costs are high and there are returns to scale, fragmented aid can be wasteful. Furthermore, when donors each have only a small share of the total aid in a recipient country, their stake in the country's development, including capacity building, may be reduced relative to their concern for the success of their own projects. Fragmentation also imposes high transactions costs on recipients, with large amounts of officials' time taken up by donor requirements.

Little systematic evidence is available on fragmentation and its effect on the management of provider organizations. One source, though limited, is the Development Gateway database, with records on about 340,000 aid projects and programs across the developing world.[556] Using the database to quantify the extent of donor fragmentation yields a mean index value for donor fragmentation across recipients of 0.87.[557] (Index values increase with the number of donors active in the country and with greater parity among donors. Low values indicate a smaller number of donors, or that some donors dominate.[558]) For example, Tanzania has a high index value of 0.92, with more than 80 aid agencies having funded 7,000 projects over time. A similar index computed from another data set—annual aid disbursements—suggests that donor fragmentation is on the rise (figure 11.2).[559]

High fragmentation indices could reflect donor specialization in different sectors, so that fragmentation would be low in each sector. But mean levels of the index are only slightly lower within individual sectors: 0.85 for education, 0.77 for health, and 0.78 for water projects. High fragmentation values for most recipients show that donors do not specialize very much, either by sector or by country. Most donors are active in many sectors, in most countries: a typical recipient nation in 2000 received aid from about 15 bilaterals and 10 multilaterals (table 11.1).

How does donor fragmentation affect the recipient's provider organizations? As mentioned, little systematic evidence is

Figure 11.2   Donor fragmentation: on the rise

Donor fragmentation index

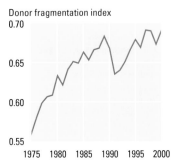

Note: The higher the index, the greater the degree of donor fragmentation.
Source: Knack and Rahman (2003).

available. One study finds an association between rising fragmentation and declining bureaucratic quality in high-aid countries and in Sub-Saharan Africa, controlling for changes in per capita income and other variables (figure 11.3).[560] This finding suggests that donors with a small share of the aid in a country may focus more on delivering successful projects, even at the expense of government capacity—for example, by hiring the most qualified government administrators to run their projects. This collective action problem may be less severe where there is a dominant donor, who has a greater incentive to take a broader and longer-term view of the country's development.

High fragmentation means high transaction costs for recipients. Tanzanian government officials have to prepare about 2,000 reports of different kinds to donors and receive more than 1,000 donor delegations each year. These requirements tax rather than build provider organizations' limited capacities, diverting efforts toward satisfying donor obligations rather than reporting to domestic policymakers. Recognizing the adverse effects, donor agencies have recently initiated measures to curb compliance costs and streamline operational policies, procedures and practices, focusing on financial management, procurement, environmental assessment, and reporting and monitoring.

High fragmentation may have an even stronger impact in low-income countries with weak policies and institutional environments. This is because the domestic capacity to implement reforms is typically highly constrained—both the political capital of reformers and the technical capacity of the administration. Fragmented donor interventions create pressure on existing capacity, by demanding both political and administrative efforts to implement change across a wide variety of areas at the same time. Aid flows are often at low per capita levels, so a large number of projects may also mean that the average value of each project is small, leading to high overhead and transaction costs.

But change has been slow. The emphasis has so far been to find common international standards and principles at the aid agency level, rather than to adapt donor

Table 11.1 So many donors . . .

	Type of aid donor	
	Bilateral donors only	Bilateral and multilateral donors
Number of recipients with 1–9 donors	3	13
Number of recipients with 10–19 donors	93	27
Number of recipients with 20–29 donors	22	69
Number of recipients with 30–39 donors	0	40
Average number of donors per recipient	14	26
Median number of donors per recipient	16	23

Note: The number of donors was calculated by using figures for total official development assistance (ODA) in 2000, provided by the OECD DAC. The number of recipients takes into consideration only the independent countries according to the list of member states of the United Nations.
Source: Acharya, de Lima, and Moore (2003), from OECD DAC data.

behavior to the procedures used by the recipient's service providers in their reporting to domestic policymakers. Exceptions are beginning to emerge, including Tanzania, Bolivia, Vietnam, and Ethiopia, where donors are planning to help the government develop a harmonization program rather than limit it to the donor community.

Donor influence on choice of activities and inputs

Donors also influence the choice of activities within a sector. They tend to be generous with training. In Malawi training accounts for a staggering $4.5 million, or 10 percent of donor spending on health care a year.[561] It is hard to believe that the return on this investment matches the cost or that the government would spend this much on training if it had the choice. And the real cost appears to be even higher: staff may be absent from work for long periods on training courses. Training opportunities are often a form of incentive for staff. If so, the funds would likely be better used if the sponsoring donors provided them directly to supplement salaries through the budget. The $4.5 million spent on training health workers in Malawi would translate on average to a 50 percent increase in salary for all health care staff.

The input mix in aid-financed public spending often differs from that in recipient spending. For example, donors provide far

Figure 11.3   Bureaucratic quality declines with donor fragmentation in Sub-Saharan Africa

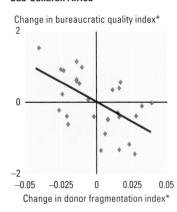

Change in bureaucratic quality index*

Change in donor fragmentation index*

*After controlling for the effect of initial level of bureaucratic quality, growth of per capita income, growth of population, and level of aid in relation to GDP (averaged over the period).
Note: The scatter plot shows the partial relationship between the change in bureaucratic quality (1982–2001) and donor fragmentation (based on project counts).
Source: Knack and Rahman (2003).

more technical assistance (and project vehicles) than the recipient would buy if it had the money. In Malawi technical assistance accounts for 24 percent of donor spending on health.[562] A major obstacle to addressing this issue is the shortage of data. Many recipient budgetary systems have much better data on the input mix for domestically financed expenditures than they do on donor projects, which are sometimes treated as single lines in the budget. Donor officials have weak incentives to provide full information to recipient governments. Public expenditure reviews, often critical of government spending, let donors off lightly. To improve scrutiny, better data are urgently needed.

Increase client power

Client power—the relationship between beneficiary and service provider—tends to be weak in many developing countries. This has long presented donors with a dilemma. Should they help strengthen the links between users and existing providers? Or should they find a way around the recipient's service delivery system to ensure that aid-funded services reach poor people? This becomes even more complicated in heavily HIV/AIDS-affected countries, those coming out of conflict, and those with weak and corrupt public institutions. Official donor agencies have followed the example of their nongovernmental counterparts, approaching communities and user groups directly, through sharply increased funding for social funds and self-help projects. Three main problems surface in these activities: an undermining of government and other local capacity, weakened prospects of sustainability, and the capture of benefits by elites (chapter 4).

In principle, social funds and self-help projects could operate within the recipient's service delivery system. They could also serve as entry points for the policy dialogue with policymakers and providers and hence build local government capacity rather than undermine it. But like many other projects, they tend to be operated directly by donors with little integration.

Most assessments of social funds and self-help projects focus on poverty targeting. Overall, the evidence suggests that centralized systems do better at identifying poor communities than at identifying poor households or poor individuals.[563] The effectiveness of targeting varies widely, which suggests the importance of unobserved attributes of communities. Some studies show that public service delivery—measured by access to infrastructure or outcomes—improved through community involvement,[564] and others, that performance could be better.[565]

Yet social funds and self-help interventions continue to face serious challenges of sustainability. One challenge arises from the cultural and social context of communities and their capacity for collective action. It is not clear that the self-help approach can benefit fractured, heterogeneous communities that have little capacity for collective action. Alternative methods of service delivery may suit such poor communities better. But there is little factual evidence on this because evaluations typically do not compare social funds and self-help projects with conventional service delivery mechanisms. Nor do they take into account the negative side effects. The sustainability of self-help projects can be in jeopardy if line ministries or local governments ignore them once they are completed. Unless communities can ensure continuing support for recurrent costs and staff, they may not be able to sustain their project.

Donors need to disburse funds fast and to show visible results quickly to supporters or taxpayers. A recent study in a Sahelian country, also applicable elsewhere, shows that these needs may be incompatible with reducing poverty.[566] When donors are impatient, when they compete with similar agencies for good projects, when they do not have the capacity to monitor activities on the ground, they may choose particular groups to work with—risking the capture of donor funds by elites. Impatient donors may even make the patient donors attach greater weight to quick results, undermining the prospects for poverty reduction. This becomes a serious problem when malevolent elites capture donor funds for private gain. But that need not be the case (box 11.2).

Social funds and self-help projects should be designed for each context, with best-practice templates as initial guides only. Rapid expansion of such projects by donors with little experience may not be feasible. Rather than implementing numerous enclave operations in a single recipient country, donors could pool support openly and transparently to achieve better results in scaling up and preventing elite capture—even when bypassing the policymaker-provider relationship in a failed state or low-income country under stress.[567] Where conditions are right, the pooling of aid should not stop with the donors—it should extend to national and local governments and other providers, private for-profit and not-for-profit.

Donors can also promote other initiatives to enhance client power. They can encourage citizen monitoring of service providers, such as report cards and public expenditure tracking surveys (chapters 5 and 10, and see spotlight on Uganda). They can help monitor the use of services and support benefit-incidence analyses to identify the groups missing out. Keep in mind, however, that involving providers in the design of the monitoring process is critical to ensuring buy-in for the results.

Promote voice

Promoting citizen voice through formal political mechanisms or through informal advocacy groups or public information campaigns is one of the most difficult endeavors for donors. Yet donors attempt to do it in many ways—a testament to the importance of voice in service reform. The attempts include imposing conditions and setting performance criteria on aid flows where voice is weak, providing direct support to democratic governance, and actively promoting transparency and participatory processes.

By imposing conditions donors try to replace the weak voice of citizens in disciplining policymakers (chapter 5). Yet donor conditions are fundamentally different from citizen voice, which is diffuse, after-the-fact, and a long-term process. In the 1980s structural adjustment loans extended conditions in projects to a wide spectrum of government economic policies, processes, and public spending. There is ample evidence today that conditions based on promises do not work well, because they undermine ownership of the reform program.[568]

When policymakers are not encouraged to develop their own positions on, say, privatization of water supply or other services, but rely on donor conditions in taking action, they can more easily deny responsibility for a later failure. It is not the quantity of aid that makes the recipient's policies good or institutional reforms happen. Empirical studies show that aid finance is ineffective in inducing policy reform in a bad policy environment.[569] What works

---

BOX 11.2 *Social Investment Fund: Jamaica*

There are more questions than answers on how self-help projects really work. Do they improve participation and targeting? Do they build capacity for collective action? One way to answer these questions is to analyze how the process works in a particular political, social, and cultural setting.

A case study of the Jamaica Social Investment Fund integrates quantitative and qualitative data from five pairs of randomly selected communities. Each pair has similar social and economic characteristics, but only one of the pair participated in the social fund. The fund typically uses NGOs to mobilize communities to participate. The NGOs work closely with local elites, such as pastors and teachers. Project selection is not generally participatory but is driven by this small, motivated group. Once construction of a service facility commences, however, the group is often able to

motivate a larger group to contribute to the project. And once completed, the service facility is generally viewed as belonging to the community and there seems to be wide satisfaction with the outcome. But it also appears that the positive social benefits from a community-based intervention may be difficult to sustain in the long term, particularly in communities beset by deep divisions.

Quantitative data on 500 randomly chosen households from the same five pairs of communities mirror these qualitative findings. Within-community "preference targeting" is poor, with three of the five participating communities not obtaining the project preferred by a majority. By the end of construction, however, 80 percent of the community members expressed satisfaction with the outcome. More educated and networked individuals dominate the selection process and are more likely to have their priori-

ties met. The Social Investment Fund also appears to have improved trust and capacity for collective action, but the gains are greater for more educated and networked individuals. So the process might be characterized as "benevolent capture": elites dominate the process but in a way that eventually benefits the community. Both participating and nonparticipating communities show more community-based decisionmaking, indicative of a broad-based effort to promote participatory development.

The Jamaica Social Investment Fund shows that self-help does not necessarily "empower the poor" and can be either supply or demand driven. But community involvement does seem to make service delivery more effective by increasing ownership and participation and by improving the capacity for collective action.

Source: Rao (2003) and Rao and Ibáñez (2003).

better is choosing recipients more carefully, based on performance (country selectivity), and setting conditions that reward reforms completed rather than those promised.[570]

Traditional conditionality does not work well. How can donors then allocate aid so that it provides a strong incentive for the recipient to promote citizen voice and undertake service reform and thus increases aid effectiveness? In principle, there is broad agreement today that, instead of conditions, the aid compact needs to contain verifiable indicators that can measure performance. But, in practice, the use of performance indicators has not yet changed the incentives underpinning the relationship between recipients and donors.[571]

Few performance indicators used today measure outcomes; most still measure inputs and processes. So far the link between these operational performance indicators and the outcome targets articulated in poverty reduction strategies remains vague. And there are few transparent mechanisms

to allow donors to signal the conditions for a recipient to expect an increase or reduction in aid. Initiatives to improve the measurement of results are under way, but it will take time to establish an effective link between the volume of aid and performance.

There is also tension between the monitoring and incentive functions of performance indicators. Donors, preoccupied with fiduciary concerns, tend to keep a close watch on the programs they support—hence the focus on short-term process undertakings rather than genuine outcome measures as triggers for performance evaluation.[572] But this can lead instead to micromanagement, exactly what the new system of performance-based conditions is intended to avoid. This tension, if unresolved, makes aid compacts incoherent.

Many bilateral donors go further and support electoral participation and democracy directly and use aid to induce and reward such reforms (box 11.3). For example, donors rewarded Ghana for holding free elections in 1992, despite the excessive public spending prior to the elections that resulted in poor macroeconomic performance.

Donors also support informal mechanisms to strengthen citizen voice. One is to promote participatory processes in the development of poverty reduction strategies and budgetary processes (box 11.4). But aid agencies and recipient governments sometimes have different views on what form the participation should take. Aid agencies seldom hold a dialogue with parliamentarians, stressing instead the extragovernmental aspects of participation, involving a wide range of civil society. Members of parliament sometimes view the donor emphasis on civil society as undermining the legitimacy of elected representatives, particularly in emerging democracies. They also question the legitimacy of NGOs selected to speak for "the people."

Donors have encouraged many low-income countries to open policy debates and discussions when preparing poverty reduction strategies. Governments are working to bring the views of a wider range of stakeholders into discussions. Madagascar, Rwanda, and Vietnam now have more timely information, make greater use of

---

BOX 11.3 *Donors support democratic governance*

Most bilateral donors explicitly include promoting democracy among the goals of their aid programs. The U.S. Agency for International Development alone spends more than $700 million a year on programs—supporting free elections, fostering civil society organizations, and strengthening parliaments, judiciaries, and political parties. Election assistance is the highest-profile component of democracy promotion. Particularly in postconflict situations, numerous bilateral donors, international organizations—such as the United Nations, the Organization of American States, and the Organization of Security and Cooperation in Europe—and private organizations send observer missions and provide assistance to election administrators. More than 80 international groups observed the 1996 elections in Nicaragua. Aid for promoting democracy has increased from 0.5 percent of total official development assistance in 1991 to 5 percent in 2000.

The donor approach to democratic governance—democracy, participation, human rights, and the rule of law—has striking similarities to the rest of aid: a heroic short-term effort to get countries through a sudden takeoff to democracy. Rather than try to reproduce certain types of institutions,

donors could more actively nurture core political processes and values, such as representation, accountability, tolerance, and openness. Legislative aid programs have often failed due to donors' lack of knowledge about the political and personal dynamics of the institutions they are trying to reshape, their determination to apply models that do not fit the local situation, and their focus on technical solutions (such as new rules for staffers or Internet access) for deeply political problems.

To overcome some of these problems, the Swedish International Development Agency (SIDA) has initiated a new type of analysis of the underlying interests and power relationships as part of a program to support political institutions in Burkina Faso, Ethiopia, Kenya, and Mali. In electoral assistance SIDA has moved to longer-term programs and closer donor collaboration in South Africa and Zambia. In Cambodia it supports a "national issues forum" to air public debates on topics like corruption and trafficking in women and children on television and radio across the country.

Sources: Carothers (1999), Ottaway and Chung (1999), Knack (2001), and SIDA.

local languages, and use participation more than consultation. There is also evidence that these processes are influencing a shift toward broader consultation on government decisions beyond the poverty reduction strategy. But major challenges remain in regularizing greater openness in government decisionmaking.

Poverty reduction strategies seek to promote stronger citizen voice, with an effective link to public spending. But they also seek to change the relationship between recipients and donors by stressing the recipient's ownership of the reform agenda. There are often tradeoffs when one instrument is used to achieve multiple goals. Countries preparing the early poverty reduction policy papers (PRSP) faced many challenges in managing the participatory process and linking their strategy to the budget, while adhering to tight timetables for debt relief for which a PRSP was a condition. Experience in many countries suggests that when a government presents a national development strategy, supported by broad ownership and well-defined sector priorities, this contributes in no small measure to attracting broad donor support. Moreover, it also offers a framework to better align and harmonize donor support.

Align aid delivery with service delivery

For donors that want to align their aid delivery with service delivery in recipient countries, this Report has three important messages.

- First, evaluate interventions and aid projects for impact. More systematic evaluations of, say, an intervention's effects on student learning or health status are critical for scaling up in both middle- and low-income countries. Evaluation linked to early steps toward rebuilding state capacity is important in situations where donors are working through alternative service providers due to conflict or state failure.

- Second, to reduce the costs of aid fragmentation and to build capacity, work with other donors to harmonize and align policies, procedures, and practices

---

BOX 11.4 *Donors support transparent budget processes: Tanzania*

Since 1997 Tanzania has conducted an annual public expenditure review, led by the government with the participation of donors and a wide range of civil society. A primary objective is to review the government's forward expenditure plans in its medium-term expenditure framework, to discuss the program with donors, and to confirm the external financing. From its inception the initiative also had the objective of developing a public consultative process to engage a wide range of domestic constituencies on the government's performance and forward plans. The working group overseeing the process is led by the Ministry of Finance but includes members from donors and a range of nongovernmental bodies.

Several features of the process show how donor accountability requirements can be met in a way that promotes a sustainable domestic system of accountability:

- Not tying the consultations to a single donor or financing instrument. Individual donors can use the process in their own monitoring and review procedures.

- Grounding the review process in the domestic policymaking and budgetary cycle, rather than in donor review procedures that open the possibility for domestic constituencies to use the process increasingly for their own purposes of legislative scrutiny, feedback, public comment, and lobbying.

- Expanding the scope of the review over time, from immediate donor concerns—how donor interests have been addressed in budget plans or how donor finance features in the framework—to broader concerns of policy and performance, such as the government's overall strategy and how it is reflected in budget plans, performance record, and efforts to strengthen service delivery. The review also provides a national forum for attending to various sectors and lower levels of government.

- Having domestic players take on a greater role over successive budget cycles, both in government and among constituencies outside the executive, including the legislature and civil society groups.

Source: World Bank staff.

---

around the recipient's own systems. Where country systems are weak, they need to be strengthened to meet good practice standards, not bypassed and substituted with ring-fenced donor systems and procedures. This is crucial for aid effectiveness in low-income countries that receive a substantial part of their public resources as foreign aid. But it is also relevant in middle-income countries in sectors where donors are especially active, as in social protection in Latin America and elsewhere.

- Third, harmonization and realignment are best done at the country level and by strengthening the recipient's existing institutions. In countries with fairly good expenditure management and genuine service reforms—where donors and recipients trust each other—budget support should be considered a viable tool. Resource pooling can also be effective in scaling up service delivery and reducing transaction costs in low-income countries that are under stress—for example, due to past or current conflict.[573]

Innovate and evaluate

Large public sector organizations—in both donor and recipient countries—focus on inputs and process evaluation rather than outputs and outcomes (box 11.5). The incentive to do this in aid agencies is even stronger because of the broken feedback loop between taxpayers in the donor country and beneficiaries in the recipient country (figure 11.1). Outcome and impact evaluations are seldom built into aid projects. Special attention is required to counter the tendency of aid agencies to be input-oriented and to increase the share of interventions subject to rigorous impact evaluation. Outcome-oriented international targets, such as the Millennium Development Goals, can add to the incentives for aid agencies to overcome their focus on inputs.

A major difficulty in assessing the impacts of any public program is that beneficiaries are rarely selected randomly. Indeed, most programs are purposely targeted to specific groups or regions. Isolating the impacts from the circumstances that led to participation is then tortuous. Yet not

doing so may produce misleading results. Schemes that select participants randomly provide the best opportunities for unbiased impact evaluation. An example is the Education, Health, and Nutrition Program of Mexico (Progresa), a large government transfer program (see spotlight). Strong evidence of its high impact led to an expansion of the program in Mexico and the adoption of similar programs elsewhere. Another example is the secondary school voucher program in Colombia, which assigned beneficiaries by lottery, making it feasible to compare those receiving vouchers with those who did not.[574] A randomly assigned pilot program for treating intestinal worms in Kenyan schoolchildren has been similarly evaluated.[575]

In many operational settings, however, randomization cannot be applied, and other methods must be found to create a matched comparison. Even when data on beneficiaries before and after implementation exist, determining the real effects of a program or policy change requires data on matched comparison groups to get at the counterfactual of what would have happened without the policy. For some schemes that do not have baseline data, it is possible to construct an adequate control group from the postintervention data. But baseline data are needed for others, such as rural roads with far-reaching impacts on poverty, health, and education outcomes.[576]

Not every program can be evaluated for impact, so governments and donors should select programs for evaluation carefully, focusing on areas where new knowledge is needed. Interventions rolled out in phases because of budget and other constraints offer good opportunities for effective impact evaluation. Similarly, when a pilot is required before a large-scale rollout, an impact evaluation will generate important information for decisionmakers.

Harmonizing donor support around recipient systems

Harmonizing is easier where the recipient has a well-functioning national development strategy and budget process that can serve as the common framework. But these are not prerequisites—for even in their

---

BOX 11.5 *Why aid agencies focus on inputs*

The disruption in the feedback loop between donor country taxpayers and recipient beneficiaries, combined with the complexity of measuring performance, results in a focus on inputs in aid agencies. Budgets, contracts, and expenditures on projects are easier to monitor and assign than are the outputs and impacts that the aid projects produce.

Elected policymakers in donor countries impose administrative procedures on aid agencies to restrict their discretionary decisionmaking. In addition, bureaucracies tend to develop their own procedures, which increases the complexity. In this sense aid agencies are like any other large public organization. Extensive consultations with nongovernmental organizations diffuse the risk of political pressure in donor countries—and complex tender and contract procedures defuse criticism by aid service suppliers. With such an incentive structure, aid agencies allocate comparatively few resources to verify

the results of aid projects or to mainstream rigorous impact evaluation. The input bias and the need to handle political problems or pressures tilt staffing toward generalists and administrators.

Yet most aid projects include a formal evaluation requirement. Process evaluations—such as audits, monitoring, and verifications that the intended action took place—are often conducted well. Outcome evaluations are seldom built in, and if done at all are contracted later to consultants. If evaluations are a small part of these consultants' foreign aid market, they also tend toward input bias and may avoid revealing results that can affect their main market. Consultants may not consciously misreport; the market pressure is usually more subtle. Contractors who work mainly for aid agencies often become generalists themselves.

Source: Martens and others (2002).

absence harmonization and pooling of aid can offer significant benefits and reduce transaction costs.[577] In low-income countries coming out of conflict or in situations of very weak public institutions, a "budget within the budget"—with separate accountability mechanisms for donors—or an independent service agency funded by donors, or a consortium of nongovernmental providers chosen jointly through a transparent process can be relevant options.[578] Both arrangements can be linked to public sector reform efforts, which emerge over time. But to be effective, harmonization requires a radical realignment of procedures and operational policies in donor agencies, as the health project in Bolivia shows (box 11.6).

For donor-financed services shifting responsibility—and hence accountability—toward the recipient would reduce duplication, waste, and transaction costs. It would also keep donors from crowding into a few fashionable sectors—and thus lessen concerns about absorptive capacity. And it would build capacity, improve collective learning, and create stronger incentives for monitoring and evaluating impacts and results.

A common refrain is that recipients need to improve their financial management and public procurement practices before donors can align their support around the recipient's systems. But reality is more nuanced. First, donors need to ask whether relying on country systems is riskier than the alternative of ring-fencing. Currently, developing-country borrowers must produce 8,000 audit reports every year for multilateral development banks—5,500 of such reports for the World Bank. Such a fragmentation of activities cannot increase accountability. Second, even if it is riskier, this needs to be set against the more sustainable benefits of helping to build the recipient's institutions and systems. Third, donors need to avoid the trap of making a given level of capacity a condition for aligning or pooling aid, when in many cases the pooling launches efforts that can get capacity closer to where it needs to be. That said, there will still be cases in which donors judge (rather than scientifically determine) that it would be inappropriate to pool, given the fiduciary risks.

Sectorwide approaches

Since the mid-1990s many countries have worked to integrate government and donor activities within a sector. In the *ideal* approach, outlined in early documents on sectorwide approaches, the government and its partners would agree on a predictable resource envelope and on a policy environment consistent with the national budget and economic strategy.[579] They would then agree on how to assign resources within this envelope. Procedures for disbursement would be harmonized, and funds would be pooled. All activities would reflect a shared view of the priorities and costs of activities. Differences would be resolved by compromises in the design of programs, not in the activities undertaken. There would be no detectable difference between the approach taken on government-funded and that taken on donor-funded activities; indeed, that distinction would wither away.

Sectorwide approaches have been established in several sectors in many low-income countries—health, education, agriculture, transport, energy, and water.[580] Efforts so far are only partial realizations of the ideal. To some extent determining what constitutes a sectorwide approach is still an arbitrary decision. There has been progress toward pooling funds in recent

---

BOX 11.6 *A case for harmonization in Bolivia*

In Bolivia three donors in the health sector agreed to cofinance construction of a building. But the fact that each donor had its own procurement procedures made it difficult to find a common approach. The donors could not pool their contribution in a common fund because the agencies' rules prohibited channeling money to another agency. None of the agencies could accept the procedures of the others, and two of the agencies were unwilling to adopt Bolivian rules.

A thematic approach was considered first. One donor would pay for the design, another the construction works, and the third would contribute paint, air conditioning, electrical apparatus, and lavatories. Then, for practical and administrative reasons and to avoid blaming the other agencies if something went wrong, it was suggested that each donor would pay for

particular floors, procuring the materials and hiring builders according to its own standards and procedures. The idea was that one donor agency would finish the first two floors, after which the second would build the third floor, and the third would finish the building.

After long debates, one of the donors withdrew from the project. Of the remaining two, the one contributing the smaller amount accepted the rules of the donor putting up the bulk of the funds. Only one contractor would be hired, not the three previously envisaged, and just one engineer would supervise construction. One agency would oversee the entire process. The process took two years, and the foundation stone has yet to be laid.

Source: World Bank (2002i).

years, however. For the 24 programs tracked by the Strategic Partnership with Africa in 2002, 41 percent of assistance came through projects (down from 56 percent two years earlier), 13 percent through NGOs, 11 percent as common basket, and 35 percent as budget support. In Ghana's health program the pooling arrangements started with "one donor and minimal funding" but later reached 40 percent of program resources.[581]

Preparing and implementing sectorwide approaches can be a long, drawn-out process. It can also weaken rather than strengthen the recipient's compact between its policymakers and provider organizations by taking the sector out of the domestic decisionmaking process, particularly the budgetary process, financial management and public procurement.[582] Four lessons have emerged from sectorwide approaches:

- An institutional analysis of the sector is recommended beforehand, including the sector's relation to the rest of the public sector.
- If the capacity constraint is in the lead ministry rather than the country, new personnel can sometimes be found quickly, as in the Ugandan education and health sectors.[583]
- Procedures need to be designed with capacity limitations in mind, particularly at decentralized levels. This will often involve encouraging public transparency and bottom-up monitoring to bolster simple but rigorously enforced upward-reporting requirements. Procurement procedures—often a major difficulty—need to balance rigor with simplicity.
- Capacity constraints are not a reason to delay a sectorwide approach. Few countries achieve the ideal, but most can benefit from some aspects of the process.

Assessments of sectorwide approaches have reached mixed findings. Ratings by the Strategic Partnership with Africa in 2002 show an average implementation rating for programs of between 0.42 and 0.58, depending on the sector (on a scale where 0 is poor, 0.33 fair, 0.66 good, and 1 very good). But it is possible that these relatively poor ratings

also reflect the ambitious agenda for sectorwide approaches. A tentative conclusion is that sectorwide approaches are an important part of a poverty reduction strategy, not an alternative, and the full benefits will not be realized until financing mechanisms become more flexible.

Budget support

The focus on budget support was sharpened by the debt relief for heavily indebted poor countries, allocating relief to priority sectors through the recipient's budget. Budget support restores the compact between policymakers and providers. It allows contestability in public spending. And it reduces the costs from fragmentation and separate project implementation units. Providing funds to the general budget also offers a better framework for discussing intersectoral allocations. Advocates of more funding to one sector have to show that the sector has higher returns than others at the margin.[584] If funds go to sectors that demonstrably reduce poverty—directly or indirectly—donors should be flexible about budget allocations.

Budget support, like basket funding for a sectorwide approach, raises questions of fiduciary risk. But there is no clear evidence that the risk is greater for budget support than for project aid.[585] Needed are transparent systems for procurement and public information to ensure that the movement of funds through the system can be publicly observed and that charges paid for services are clearly defined. Donors can contribute best by promoting these systems in the recipient country. The Utstein group of donors—the United Kingdom, the Netherlands, Norway, and Germany—has been developing monitoring arrangements along these lines. The European Union links part of its budget support to performance, using a small set of indicators (box 11.7).

What does all this suggest? That aid will work best where it is provided flexibly to recipients with sound overall strategies and well-designed sectoral programs. Flexible aid can catalyze processes within governments to produce sound strategies, rational spending programs, and effective services.

Knowledge transfers

Donor competition for new ideas can be good for the recipient. It can also create confusion, particularly in low-income countries that have weak capacity. One solution is to pool knowledge transfers and joint analytical work at the country level, including impact evaluations of interventions and programs. All analytical work supported by donors should draw on in-country capacity, including universities, government, and the private sector (box 11.8).

Poor institutions—post-conflict and "failed" states

In poor institutional environments—as in post-conflict countries or "failed" states—donors may not be able to rely on conventional channels of service provision because policymakers and providers lack the capacity or the intent to use resources well.[586] Whatever the short-term or even medium-term delivery vehicle, aid should contribute in the longer term to rebuilding an effective service delivery system and public sector. The temptation to avoid the government is understandable. But without some clear and shared donor strategy for rebuilding a responsive and effective state, the proliferation of nongovernmental and community-based organizations—and self-help and social fund initiatives—will lack breadth of impact and sustainability. Civil society organizations cannot design national policies or standards. Nor can they substitute in the long term for the citizen-policymaker relationship.

The options for donors range from selectively supporting existing programs, such as immunization programs operated by the government or private providers, to establishing an independent service authority with a temporary mandate to deliver or regulate basic services.[587] In between are self-help projects and social funds. An independent service authority and a social fund are ways to deliver services in difficult circumstances, perhaps by wholesaling to a local consortium of NGOs, religious organizations, and private firms. Such organizations require institutional autonomy to

---

BOX 11.7 *Linking budget support to performance*

The European Commission is explicitly linking part of its budget support to performance. The amount to be disbursed is based on progress in social service delivery, notably health and education, and in public expenditure management. Progress is measured by a small number of performance indicators agreed to by the recipient and the European Commission. Indicators are typically drawn from the recipient's poverty reduction strategy. For the first set of countries, the most frequently used indicators are:

- Planned and actual expenditures in the social sectors.
- Differences in unit costs of key inputs between the public sector and the market.
- Use of primary and antenatal health care services.
- Immunization rates.
- Births assisted by medical personnel.
- Enrollment rates for boys and girls.
- Cost of primary education (private and public).

After a joint evaluation by government and donors, a score is calculated for each indicator: one point if the agreed objective is attained, half a point if there is evidence of "considerable positive development," and zero if there is no progress. The budget support provided is the maximum amount available multiplied by the (unweighted) average performance score (ranging from zero to one). The approach is not mechanical but also takes into account external factors.

The performance-based system highlights the quality of data. According to the European Commission, the system is not an end but a means: getting policymakers and the public in developing countries to pay more attention to results than to declarations of intentions and conditions set by donors.

So far, 30 percent of the European Commission's budget support is linked to performance indicators. This is deliberate, motivated by the desire to introduce a new approach gradually and to balance performance rewards and the recipient's need for predictable budget finance.

Source: European Commission.

---

ensure high standards of accountability directly to donors. To deliver on such standards, hiring may have to be outside the public sector. Again, donors should coordinate and pool their support to reduce waste and duplication, financing both recurrent and capital expenditures.

Donors face the challenge of finding a balance between short- to medium-term institutional failures and the long-term creation of an effective state that can deliver on its public responsibilities. Donors have sought to address short-term service needs through national and international NGOs, social funds, United Nations agencies, or a combination of these providers. What needs to be given equal emphasis is the identification of country-specific paths for strengthening capacity and reduction in patronage and corruption. Nongovernmental channels for service delivery can thus play a very important role but should be seen as a transitional strategy to strengthen state capacity in the long term.

Even in the weakest states donors and domestic stakeholders would benefit from

---

B O X   1 1 . 8 *Pooling knowledge transfers*

To improve access to infrastructure services for poor people, several donors have pooled funds to augment and disseminate knowledge on infrastructure services. These facilities, administered by the World Bank, provide a source of knowledge and advice that is "fire-walled" from the Bank's lending activities. Donors in the pool are Canada, Japan, the Netherlands, Sweden, Switzerland, the United Kingdom, and the United Nations Development Programme.

The Energy Sector Management Advisory Program, a global technical assistance program, focuses on energy in economic development, with the objectives of contributing to poverty alleviation and economic development, improving living conditions, and preserving the environment. It focuses on:

- Market-oriented energy sector reform and restructuring

- Access to efficient and affordable energy
- Environmentally sustainable energy production, transportation, distribution, and use.

The Water and Sanitation Program assists central governments, municipal agencies, local authorities, NGOs, community organizations, private service providers, and external agencies in helping poor people gain sustained access to better water and sanitation services. It focuses on:

- Policy, strategy, and institutional reform advisory services
- Innovative solutions to problems, including pilot and demonstration projects
- Strategically selected investment support services, including networking and knowledge sharing.

With its strong field presence in Africa, South and East Asia, and the Andes, the program has a well-established network of sector specialists who can respond quickly to the changing demands of clients.

The Public-Private Infrastructure Advisory Facility is a technical assistance facility helping developing countries to improve their infrastructure through private sector involvement. It pursues its mission through:

- Technical assistance to governments on strategies for tapping the full potential of private involvement in infrastructure
- Identifying, disseminating, and promoting best practices related to private involvement in infrastructure.

Source: World Bank staff.

---

pooling efforts for a better results. Harmonization of aid may not be feasible through budget support, but agreement on a common framework and implementation arrangements for service delivery will help avoid too heavy a burden on limited domestic capacity. Further, it is important to share lessons and to recognize that aid may be less effective when modalities that work in good policy environments are transferred to other situations. The flexibility of "eight sizes fit all" includes a strong emphasis on country context.

Why reforming aid is so difficult

The unintended negative effects of donor behavior are not a recent discovery. *World Development Report 1990: Poverty* (World Bank (1990)) discussed the role of aid in poverty reduction, drawing attention to many similar problems. Why has there not been more reform? Why, for instance, are donors so reluctant to channel aid as part of the recipient's budget?

Simplifying donor policies, procedures, and practices and directing aid flexibly through sectorwide approaches or the budget process would lower the high transaction costs in low-income countries and allow recipients to pursue their objectives more efficiently. That could be done if

donors were driven solely by the motive to reduce poverty—and if recipients were perceived to be committed to the same goal. But the world is more complex. Incentives in aid agencies and the political economy of aid in donor countries work against this:

- Aid agencies want to be able to identify their own contributions, often through distinct "projects," to facilitate feedback to taxpayers and sustain political support for aid flows. A new hospital is easier to showcase than the outcome of policy reform or budget support.

- Aid agencies, facing disbursement pressures, need to show quick results to taxpayers—and NGOs, to their contributors. This is easier when donors are in charge of interventions.

- Politicians and policymakers in donor countries cannot dismiss the interest groups that support them, groups that may place a high priority on funding likeminded groups in developing countries.

- Many donors limit the market for aid services and supplies to their own nationals (tied aid). Foreign aid sustains a large consultancy industry in OECD countries—estimated at $4 billion a year for Sub-Saharan Africa, or 30 percent of aid to the continent.

- Preferences for spending differ among donors and between donors and recipients. Donors often are most comfortable with service delivery systems of the type operating in their own country. For instance, British and Nordic advisers are familiar with a clinic-based free health service and so prefer to support those systems in low-income countries too.

- Fiduciary concerns and incentives in aid agencies cause donors to focus on monitoring inputs and processes. Again, the monitoring is easier in project aid where the donor controls the design and implementation of each intervention.

- Donors may want to persuade aid recipients of the value of a different approach through a pilot project, to show success.

- Bilateral donors distribute their aid budgets across a large number of recipients and sectors, to increase the visibility of their programs or to leverage or reward diplomatic support from recipient nations.[588] More specialization among sectors or recipients, however efficient, could expose a donor to charges that it is neglecting, say, a global health crisis or a regional humanitarian crisis. Such considerations help explain why the typical bilateral donor in 2000 provided official development aid (ODA) to about 115 independent nations. Even omitting recipients that received less than $100,000, the mean number of ODA recipients for each of the 22 major bilateral donors was 95.

These multiple objectives create incentives for donors to finance and directly control their aid interventions. That creates problems for recipient countries: donors often do not know (or don't care) what other donors and the recipient are doing, which results in duplication, waste, and gaps in services.[589] These days donors tend to favor social sector projects over other public expenditures. If they do not pay attention to what the others are doing, they may concentrate too much on higher-priority sectors, leaving sectors with a lower priority, such as rural roads in Zambia, short of funds. Or there may be gaps in the priority areas simply because nobody is looking at the big picture. But priorities among donors vary, and their approaches change over time.[590] So there is some scope—and hope—for improvement.

Bibliographic note

This Report draws on a wide range of World Bank documents and on numerous outside sources. Background papers and notes were prepared by Abdelwahid El Abassi, A. Aghajanian, S. Ahmadnia, Harold H. Alderman, James Anderson, Matthew Andrews, Aida Atienza, Suresh Balakrishnan, Nabhojit Basu, Paolo Carlo Belli, Surjit Bhalla, Gerry Bloom, Ronelle Burger, J. Edgardo L. Campos, Indu Bushan, Yero Boye Camara, Jonathan Caseley, Prema Clarke, Dave Coady, Alberto Diaz-Cayeros, Richard Crook, Monica Das Gupta, Antara Dutta, Dan Erikson, Paulo Ferrinho, Angela Ferriol, Varun Gauri, Anne Marie Goetz, Kelly Hallman, Maija Halonen, Susanne Hesselbarth, Rob Jenkins, Anuradha Joshi, Henry Katter, Daniel Kaufmann, Philip Keefer, Peyvand Khaleghian, Stuti Khemani, Stephen Knack, Rudolf Knippenberg, Kenneth Leonard, Bernard Liese, Angela Lisulo, Annie Lord, John Mackinnon, Beatriz Magaloni, Nick Manning, James Manor, Melkiory Masatu, A. Mehryar, Anne Mills, Mick Moore, Joyce Msuya, Fatoumata Traore Nafo, Joseph Naimoli, Andrew Nickson, Rami Osseni, C. Torres Parodi, Harry Patrinos, Mark Pearson, Victoria Perez, Janelle Plummer, Benjamin Powis, Didio Quintana, Carole Radoki, Aminur Rahman, Francesca Recanatini, John Roberts, James Robinson, F. Halsey Rogers, Pauline Rose, Suraj Saigal, R. Sarwal, Parmesh Shah, Maureen Sibbons, Janmejay Singh, Hilary Standing, David Stasavage, Jonas Gahr Støre, Denise Vaillancourt, Servaas van der Berg, Wim van Lerberghe, Ayesha Vawda, Emiliana Vegas, and Peter Wolf.

Background papers for the Report are available either on the World Wide Web via **http://econ.worldbank.org/wdr/wdr2004/** or through the World Development Report office. The views expressed in these papers are not necessarily those of the World Bank or of this Report.

Many people inside and outside the World Bank gave comments to the team. Valuable comments and contributions were provided by Christopher Adam, James Adams, Orville Adams, Olosodji Adeyi, Shafiul Azam Ahmed, Asad Alam, Aya Aoki, Omar Azfar, Raja Rehan Arshad, Yvette Atkins, Melvin Ayogu, Raja Bentaouet Kattan, Peter Berman, Paul Berminghan, Markus Berndt, John Besant Jones, Robert Beschel, David Bevan, Anil Bhandari, Helena Bjuremalm, John Briscoe, Colin Bruce, Barbara Bruns, Donald A. P. Bundy, Pronita Chakravarty, Vandana Chandra, Mae Chu Chang, Robert Chase, Marian Claeson, Paul Collier, Michael Crawford, Jishnu Das, Angelique de Plana, Jean-Jacques Dethier, Annette Dixon, Paula Donovan, William Dorotinsky, Mark Dumol, Ibrahim Elbadawi, Poul Engberg-Pedersen, Gunnar Eskeland, Antonio Estache, Barbara Evans, Shahrokh Fardoust, Armin Fidler, Ariel Fiszbein, Jonas Frank, Ahmad Galal, Marito Garcia, Varun Gauri, Alan Gelb, Ejaz Ghani, Elizabeth Gibbons, Indermit Gill, Daniele Giusti, Philip S. Goldman, Mark Gradstein, Vincent Greaney, Daniela Gressani, Charles Griffin, Merilee S. Grindle, Jan Willem Gunning, Christopher Hall, Kirk Hamilton, Clive Harris, Robert Hecht, John Hellbrunn, Susanne Hesselbarth, Norman Hicks, Dale Hill, James Keith Hinchliffe, Karla Hoff, Mary Kathryn Hollifield, Robert Holzmann, Timothy Irwin, Jaime Jaramillo-Vallejo, Abhas Kumar Jha, Anne Johansen, Olga Jonas, Ruth Kagia, Satu Kähkönen, Jeffrey A. Katz, Philip Keefer, Damoni Kitabire, Homi Kharas, Stuti Khemani, Jeni Klugman, Steve Knack, Valerie Kozel, Dan Kress, Jody Kusek, Karen Lashman, Frannie Leautier, Danny Leipziger, Brian Levy, Samuel Lieberman, Soe Lin, Magnus Lindelöw, Marlaine Lockheed, Elizabeth Laura Lule, Mattias Lundberg, Akiko Maeda, Wahiduddin Mahmud, Nick Manning, Bertin Martens, Om Prakash Mathur, Subodh Mathur, Aaditya Mattoo, Elizabeth McAllister, Judith McGuire, Oey Astra Meesook, Vandana Mehra, Alain Mingat, Mick Moore, Christopher Murray, David Nabarro, Raj R. Nallari, Deepa Narayan, W. Paatii Ofosu-Amaah, Peter O'Neill, Elisabeth Page, Elisabeth Pape, Puspa Pathak, Harry Patrinos, Judith Pearce, Ronald F. Perkinson, David Peters, Guy Pfeffermann, Tomas Philipson, Janelle Plummer, Alexander Preker, Robert Prouty, Firas Raad, Anand Rajaram, Mamphela Ramphele, Vijayendra Rao, Ray Rist, Peter Roberts, F. Halsey Rogers, David Rosenblatt, Alex Ross, James Sackey, Mauricio Santamaria, Sarosh Sattar, William Savedoff, Eugen Scanteie, Norbert Schady, George Schieber, Ruth Ingeborg Schipper-Tops, Supriya Sen, Nemat Talaat Shafik, Monica Singh, John Snow, Lyn Squire, Lynn Stephen, Mark Sundberg, M. Helen Sutch, Jakob Svensson, Jee-Peng Tan, Judith Tendler, Gregory Toulmin, Emmanuel Tumusiime-Mutebile, Brian van Arkadie, Caroline van den Berg, Dominique van de Walle, Rudolf van Puymbroeck, Hema Visnawathan, Adam Wagstaff, Jeffrey Waite, Wendy Wakeman, Christine Wallich, Maitree Wasuntinwongse, Hugh Waters, Dana Weist, Michel Welmond, Richard Westin, Howard White, Mark Williams, James D. Wolfensohn, Michael Woolcock, Alan Wright, Ian P. Wright, Salman Zaheer, Abdo Yazbeck, and Jürgen Zattler.

Other valuable assistance was provided by Mary Bitekerezo, Soucha Borlo, Johanna Cornwell and staff of the World Bank libraries, John Garrison, Phillip Hay, Rachel Winter Jones, Agnes Kaye, Emily Khine, Zenaida Kranzer, Angela Lisulo, Precinia Lizarondo, Joaquin Lopez, Jr., Jimena Luna, Karolina Ordon, Carolyn Reynolds. The Water and Sanitation Program (WSP) of South Asia provided support for the consultation in Bangladesh and access to on going research and policy work of the WSP.

Despite efforts to compile a comprehensive list, some who contributed may have been inadvertently omitted. The team apologizes for any oversights and reiterates its gratitude to all who contributed to this Report.

Endnotes

1. Taking the world as a whole hides the fact that Sub-Saharan Africa is off track in reaching the income poverty goal.

2. Walker, Schwarlander, and Bryce (2002).

3. Devarajan, Miller, and Swanson (2002).

4. Peters and others (2003), p. 218.

5. Reinikka and Svensson (2001).

6. Chaudhury and Hammer (2003).

7. Jaffré, Olivier, and de Sardan (2002).

8. PROBE Team in association with Centre for Development Economics (1999); Rosskam (2003).

9. Analysis of Demographic and Health Survey data (see table 1.1 of the Report). U.K. Department of International Development (2002).

10. Bhushan, Keller, and Schwartz (2002).

11. Ahmad (1999).

12. World Bank (2002n).

13. Behrman and Hoddinott (2001) and Gertler and Boyce (2001).

14. Spotlights on Educo and Bamako Initiative.

15. Glaeser and Shleifer (2002).

16. Diaz-Cayeros and Magaloni (2002).

17. Spotlight on Costa Rica and Cuba.

18. Besley and Burgess (2002).

19. Spotlight on Kerala and Uttar Pradesh.

20. When asked why he did not complain, one villager replied, "I could meet with an accident on the road. I could be put in the brick kiln oven. My bones could be broken." (Spotlight on Kerala and Uttar Pradesh).

21. Spotlight on Johannesburg.

22. International Labor Organization (ILO) (2002).

23. Scott (1998).

24. Reinikka and Svensson (2003b).

25. Chomitz and others (1998).

26. Computerization of land registration in Karnataka, India, reduced the transaction time to 30 minutes and eliminated the payment of bribes, which had risen to 25 to 50 times the registration fee.

27. Koenig, Foo, and Joshi (2000).

28. Jimenez and Sawada (1999).

29. Hsieh and Urquiola (2003).

30. Gauri and Vawda (2003).

31. Angrist and others (2002).

32. Interview by John Briscoe.

33. World Bank (1998a) and World Bank (2002a).

34. Even a recommendation to apply interventions that pass a social benefit-cost analysis test will not be enough. Social benefit-cost analysis is concerned with valuing an intervention's outputs and inputs at the right set of shadow prices (Bell and Devarajan (1987) and Dreze and Stern (1987)). Yet the problem is that the inputs often do not translate to the desired output because of weak incentives. The same point applies to recommendations of using "cost-effective" interventions in health (World Bank (1993).

35. Spotlight on Cambodia.

36. Schick (1998).

37. Realizing that the central education system has led to underrepresentation of students from low-income families, one of the prestigious French grandes écoles, L'Institut d'Etudes Politiques de Paris ("Sciences Po") has begun to use separate admissions criteria for students from poor neighborhoods.

38. Leonard (2002).

39. Another reason is that most project managers are not interested in investing in knowledge that might show their program to have been a failure.

40. This account from the *New York Times,* excerpted from Brooke (1993), describes the unprecedented joint effort by politicians, health workers, and communities to put in place a program to substantially reduce infant mortality in the state of Ceará in Brazil. The infant mortality rate for children born in Ceará between 1981 and 1985 was 142 deaths per 1,000 births, for children born between 1986 and 1990 the rate had fallen to 91, almost a 40 percent reduction. Infant mortality in the poorest fifth of the population fell from 154 to 113—almost 30 percent. The decline in infant mortality in neighboring states of Northeast Brazil was 20 percent over the same period (Analysis of Demographic and Health Survey data).

41. Department for International Development and Water and Environmental Health at London and Loughborough (1998). In Ethiopia more than 70 percent of households use an open spring or river as their main source of drinking water, and about 80 percent of households have no toilet facilities (Analysis of Demographic and Health Survey data).

42. Kunfaa and Dogbe (2002).

43. Lewis, Eskeland, and Traa-Valerezo (1999).

44. Mtemeli (1994).

45. See also Gwatkin and Others (2000) and Wagstaff (2000).

46. See also Filmer and Pritchett (1999a) and Filmer (2000).

47. UNESCO (2002).

48. UNICEF (2001).

49. The multiple determinants of child health are discussed in Wagstaff and others (2002).

50. See Deaton (1997).

51. For more on this approach see Filmer and Pritchett (2001).

52. For example, see World Bank (2001k).

53. Papua New Guinea Office of National Planning (1999).

54. Gibson (2000) based on a survey undertaken in 1996. Average distance may be lower today since a subsequent education reform expanded the number of elementary and primary schools.

55. International Forum for Rural Transport and Development, 2002 input to WDR team.

56. Estimates for 2000 from WHO UNICEF Joint Monitoring Programme for Water Supply and Sanitation (2001). "Improved" water source is defined as sources that provide adequate quality and quantity of water (i.e., a household connection or a protected well and not an unprotected well or bottled water). "Improved" sanitation covers flush toilets and private latrines.

57. "Improved" water source is at best a crude proxy for access to safe water. For example, in Bangladesh access to water through tube-wells—an "improved" source—is extremely high although the water so accessed is frequently contaminated with arsenic (see chapter 9).

58. Filmer, Lieberman, and Ariasingam (2002). An evaluation of the enrollment and labor market outcomes of the program are in Duflo (2001).

59. See the discussion in Alderman and Lavy (1996).

60. Based on World Bank (2002s).

61. Radoki (2003).

62. Leonard, Mliga, and Mariam (2002).

63. Yip and Berman (2001).

64. Leonard, Mliga, and Mariam (2002).

65. Samrasinghe and Akin (1994) and Akin and Hutchinson (1999).

66. Pakistan Institute for Environment Development Action and Project Management Team (1994).

67. Alderman and Lavy (1996) and Lloyd and others (2001).

68. Chaudhury and Hammer (2003).

69. NRI and World Bank (2003).

70. Chomitz and others (1998).

71. PROBE Team in association with Centre for Development Economics (1999).

72. Schleicher, Siniscalco, and Postlewaite (1995).

73. World Bank (2001e).

74. Thomas, Lavy, and Strauss (1996).

75. Alderman and Lavy (1996).

76. Thomas, Lavy, and Strauss (1996).

77. Schleicher, Siniscalco, and Postlewaite (1995).

78. PROBE Team in association with Centre for Development Economics (1999).

79. Schleicher, Siniscalco, and Postlewaite (1995).

80. World Bank (2002m).

81. GfK Praha—Institute for Market Research (2001).

82. World Bank (2000c).

83. McPake and others (2000) and Levy-Bruhl and others (1997).

84. Di Tella and Savedoff (2001a).

85. Narayan and others (2000a).

86. Knippenberg and others (1997).

87. King and Ozler (2002).

88. Lewis, La Forgia, and Sulvetta (1996).

89. WHO (World Health Organization) (1998).

90. Langsten and Hill (1995).

91. Rowe and others (2001).

92. Lakshman and Nichter (2001).

93. For example, see Bruns, Mingat, and Rakatomalala (2003) or Pritchett and Filmer (1999).

94. Millot and Lane (2002).

95. World Bank (1998b).

96. Waitzkin (1991).

97. Betancourt and Gleason (2000) and Koenig, Foo, and Joshi (2000).

98. Lewis, Eskeland, and Traa-Valerezo (1999).

99. Jaffré and Prual (1994).

100. WHO (World Health Organization) and World Bank (2002).

101. Schneider and Palmer (2002).

102. Narayan and others (2000b).

103. Haddad and Fournier (1995).

104. Davis and Patrinos (2002).

105. Rao and Walton (forthcoming).

106. Dutta (2003).

107. This spotlight is based on Coady (2003) and Levy and Rodríguez (2002).

108. Percentages from World Development Indicators database.

109. Bruns, Mingat, and Rakatomalala (2003).

110. Indonesia: Ministry of National Education (2002); Indonesia: Ministry of Religious Affairs (2002); and Filmer, Lieberman, and Ariasingam (2002).

111. Hutchinson (2001).

112. 137,000 health subcenters, 28,000 dispensaries, 23,000 primary health centers, 3500 urban family welfare centers, 3000 community health centers, and an additional 12,000 secondary and tertiary hospitals (Peters and others (2003)). The populations of Uganda, Indonesia, and India are 22 million, 210 million, and 1,015 million, respectively.

113. Hutchinson (2001).

114. Peters and others (2003).

115. A comprehensive exposition of these ideas is in Stiglitz (2000).

116. Articles 25 and 26 of the Universal Declaration of Human Rights (http://www.un.org/Overview/rights.html).

117. See, for example, WHO (World Health Organization) (2002).

118. Articles 23 and 24 of the Universal Declaration of Human Rights. (http://www.un.org/Overview/rights.html).

119. Hunt (2002).

120. See discussions in Green (1990), Pritchett (2002), and Kremer and Sarychev (2000).

121. For example, see the theoretical discussion in Gradstein and Justman (2002) and empirical exploration in Ritzen, Wang, and Duthilleul (2002).

122. Appleton (2001).

123. In Madagascar GDP per capita was about $250 averaged over the 1990s and mortality 156 in 2000. In Burundi GDP per

capita was about $160 averaged over the 1990s and mortality 190 in 2000. These two countries fall very close to the cross-country regression line between income and mortality. These data on child mortality are from UNICEF (2002).

124. See in particular: Barro (1991), Bhargava and others (2001), Bils and Klenow (2000), Pritchett and Summers (1996), and Savedoff and Schultz (2000).

125. Dollar amounts in this paragraph are in 2001 U.S. dollars and refer to averages for the 1990s.

126. Dollar amounts are in 2001 U.S. dollars.

127. Moreover, these cross-national estimates likely overstate the association between income and outcomes as they do not take into account specific country attributes. The growth rates discussed here are at best underestimates of those necessary.

128. Dollar amounts in this list are expressed in 1995 U.S. dollars.

129. Between 1980 and 2000 annual average growth of GDP per capita was: Ethiopia –0.55 percent; Malawi 0.25 percent; Thailand 0.046 percent; Peru –0.41 percent; Mexico 0.74 percent; Jordan –0.57 percent; Côte d'Ivoire –0.017 percent; Haiti –0.025 percent (based on World Development Indicators database).

130. Hammer, Nabi, and Cercone (1995).

131. van der Berg and Burger (2003).

132. Duflo (2001). Filmer, Hammer, and Pritchett (2000) discuss the within-country evidence further.

133. The result holds for other outcomes as well. For example, the Organisation for Economic Co-operation and Development's *Program for International Student Assessment* found that more spending on education was associated with better test results in a sample of largely upper income countries (Organization for Economic Cooperation and Development (2001)). However, the association becomes almost zero (and insignificant from it) once GDP per capita is controlled for.

134. Filmer and Pritchett (1999b).

135. Bidani and Ravallion (1997) and Wagstaff (2002).

136. Gupta, Verhoeven, and Tiongson (2002).

137. Rajkumar and Swaroop (2002); Gupta, Verhoeven, and Tiongson (2002) find corruption to be important, but Jayasuriya and Wodon (2002) do not.

138. For example, the number of countries, and country coverage, in cross-national studies of spending and mortality are: 98 in Filmer and Pritchett (1999b); 22 in Anand and Ravallion (1993); 76 and 56 in Jayasuriya and Wodon (2002); 22 in Gupta, Verhoeven, and Tiongson (2002); 32 in Gupta, Verhoeven, and Tiongson (forthcoming);116 in Gupta, Davoodi, and Tiongson (2002); 32 in Wagstaff (2002); 35 in Bidani and Ravallion (1997). There is a parallel, although somewhat less developed literature on education outcomes and spending: for example, Wößmann (2003); Gupta, Verhoeven, and Tiongson (2002).

139. This discussion is based on Lieberman (2003).

140. Such expenditure incidence studies of health and education spending provide a valuable description, but they cannot tell the full story. First, they provide a cross-sectional snapshot that is not the same as who would benefit from the marginal resources devoted to the sector. Second, while the data are often based on the best available they are limited—especially when it comes to assessing the costs of each unit of the service provided. Third, the studies implicitly assume that the value of the expenditure is equal across

all users. Fourth, they do not include the incidence of raising funds—that is, a fairly regressive pattern of spending might still be pro-poor if it is financed through a very progressive tax system. Fifth, it is hard to know what a "good" allocation is without comparing it to other types of social spending.

141. Reinikka and Svensson (2001).

142. Foster (1990).

143. World Bank (1994a).

144. Filmer, Hammer, and Pritchett (2000).

145. Gertler and Molyneaux (1995).

146. Sixty-six percent is the amount recommended by Bruns, Mingat, and Rakatomalala (2003) based on a review of countries that have made substantial progress toward universal completion.

147. Bruns, Mingat, and Rakatomalala (2003).

148. Devarajan, Miller, and Swanson (2002) use a similar approach to costing the first Millennium Development Goal, halving income poverty between 1990 and 2015.

149. Devarajan, Miller, and Swanson (2002) avoid some of the double counting by calculating the cost of the health, education, and environmental goals independently of the income poverty goal and then calculating the cost of the income poverty goal independently of all the others.

150. This account is drawn from Paul (2002).

151. Drawn from Community Driven Development (2002).

152. This spotlight relates to Uttar Pradesh as it existed before its hill districts were separated out into a new state, Uttaranchal, in late 2000.

153. Ramachandran (1996) and Dreze and Gazdar (1996).

154. Mencher (1980), Nag (1989), and Antia (1994).

155. Dreze and Gazdar (1996) and PROBE Team in association with Centre for Development Economics (1999)

156. See Shah and Rani (2003).

157. Dreze and Sen (2002).

158. Keefer and Khemani (2003), Shah and Rani (2003).

159. Chandran (1999).

160. Dreze and Gazdar (1996), p. 111.

161. Ramachandran (1996), p. 268. The Tranvancore rescript was issued 55 years before the similar Meiji Educational Law of 1872 in Japan.

162. Narayan (2002).

163. World Bank (2001h).

164. Hammer and Jack (2001) and Gertler and Hammer (1997b).

165. Das and Hammer (2003).

166. Cornell and Kalt (1995); Cornell and Kalt (1997); Cornell and Kalt (2000)

167. Mamdani (1996).

168. Cohen (1957).

169. de Soto (2000).

170. Public Services International and Education International (2000).

171. Stasavage (2003).

172. Tumusiime-Mutebile (2003).

173. Reinikka and Svensson (2001), Reinikka and Svensson (2003a).

174. Shreenivasan (2002).

175. Akin, Guilkey, and Denton (1995) and Peters and others (2003).

176. Pritchett and Woolcock (2002).

177. Appadurai (2001).

178. In the literature this is known as equalizing their agency (Rao and Walton (forthcoming). Empowerment also refers to poor peoples' abilities to influence the political power structure, but that is the subject of chapter 5, "Citizens and Politicians."

179. Conning and Kevane (2002) discuss this in the context of community-based targeting programs. See also Mansuri and Rao (2003).

180. This does not apply to technical quality, which can be quite low—and more variable—in the private sector.

181. Probe Qualitative Research Team (2002).

182. Ibid Probe Qualitative Research Team (2002). See also Leonard (2002).

183. Becker (1971).

184. Lewis (2000).

185. Tan, Soucat, and Mingat (2000).

186. Wolfensohn (1997).

187. Gertler and Hammer (1997b).

188. Personal communication with Dr. Zafrullah Chowdhury of Gonoshasthaya Kendra.

189. Nichols, Prescott, and Phua (1997).

190. Case (2001).

191. Das and Hammer (2003).

192. Werner, Thuman, and Maxwell (1992).

193. Shleifer and Vishny (1993) call this corruption with theft.

194. Goetz and Gaventa (2001).

195. Glinskaya and Jalan (2003).

196. Grindle (forthcoming).

197. Chandran (1999).

198. Ostrom (1990).

199. Scott (1998), and Mackey (2002).

200. Wade (1987) and Blomquist and Ostrom (1958).

201. *World Bank Economic Review,* Special Issue (2002)

202. Hino (1993).

203. Water and Sanitation Program (2001).

204. Alatas, Pritchett, and Wetteberg (2003).

205. Platteau and Gaspart (2003).

206. Agarwal (2001).

207. World Bank (1998c).

208. Mansuri and Rao (2003) and Kleemeier (2000).

209. Mehrotra and Jarrett (2002).

210. Gilson and others (2001).

211. Gilson and others (2001).

212. Knippenberg and others (1997).

213. In the early 1980s, successes in delivering primary care services were first analyzed based on the experiences of the Narangwal, Lampang and Bohol projects in Asia, as well as the Danfa, Kintampo, Kisantu, Kasongo and Institute of Child Health Nigeria projects in West Africa. These best practices were translated into a coherent set of service delivery strategies, management systems, and instruments in the Pahou pilot project in Benin (1982–86).

214. Ministry of Health Guinea (2002).

215. Ministère de la Santé de Bénin (2003).

216. Zhao, Soucat, and Traore (2003).

217. Soucat, Gandaho, and Levy-Bruhl (1997).

218. Gilson (1997) and Gilson and others (2000).

219. Narayan and Pettesch (2002) and Narayan and others (2000a).

220. See Glossary for explanations of terms related to the service delivery framework.

221. See http://www.hinso.moph.go.th/30baht_English/index.htm.

222. See http://www.cabinet-office.gov.uk/pmdu/.

223. International Budget Project (2000).

224. Hirschman (1970) shaped understanding of "voice" as directed protest, both in its electoral (voting) and nonelectoral (advocacy, lobbying, naming/shaming, participation in policymaking) sense.

225. Goetz and Jenkins (2002) and Schedler (1999). The many meanings given to accountability—an overused term—often blur. So, "vertical" accountability (citizens individually or collectively holding the state to account, as in elections) is sometimes distinguished from "horizontal" accountability *within* government (a minister or senior civil servant formally holding another civil servant accountable). Authoritarian states may manifest horizontal accountability, but not offer much vertical accountability.

226. Shah (2003a); also see http://www.mampu.gov.my/Circulars/Clients_Charter.htm.

227. Hossain and Moore (2002).

228. Jenkins and Goetz (2002) discuss civil engagement with India's public distribution system for basic goods targeted to poor people. When the system was exploited as a source of patronage, civil society groups advocating more efficient delivery had no traction for their equity-led agenda, and the poor suffered.

229. For a review of clientelism and how core and swing voting can impact services, see Diaz-Cayeros and Magaloni (2003).

230. Joshi and Moore (2000) discuss the role of the right to guaranteed work in the Maharashtra Employment Guarantee Scheme in India and its implications for the mobilization and voice of the poor. Jenkins and Goetz (1999) examine the role of the right to information in the state of Rajasthan in India.

231. Putnam, Leonardi, and Nanetti (1992) and Boix and Posner (1998).

232. Freedom House (2002). Democracies are defined as political systems whose leaders are elected in competitive multi-party and multi-candidate processes in which opposition parties have a legitimate chance of attaining power or participating in power.

233. See Moore and Putzel (2001) for a discussion of democracy and poverty outcomes.

234. Keefer (2002).

235. This draws on Keefer and Khemani (2003).

236. Keefer (2003), based on countries with available education expenditure data from among the 117 countries in the Database of Political Institutions, 1975–95 (Beck and others (2001)).

237. See various articles in Ferejohn and Kuklinsky (1990).

238. Fiorina (1990).

239. See the literature on political cycles in developing countries, including Shi and Svensson (2003), Khemani (forthcoming), Block (2002), and Schuknecht (1996).

240. Fiorina and Shepsle (1990) and Chappell and Keech (1990).

241. Grossman and Helpman (1999).

242. Easterly and Levine (1997); Alesina, Baqir, and Easterly (1999); Betancourt and Gleason (2000).

243. Alesina, Baqir, and Easterly (1999).

244. Ferejohn (1974) and Persson and Tabellini (2000).

245. Gazdar (2000).

246. Diaz-Cayeros and Magaloni (2003).

247. Medina and Stokes (2002).

248. Diaz-Cayeros and Magaloni (2003).

249. Miguel (1998), as noted by and consistent with the findings of Diaz-Cayeros and Magaloni (2003).

250. Keefer (2002) and Robinson and Verdier (2002).

251. Keefer (2002).

252. Keefer and Khemani (2003).

253. Alatas, Pritchett, and Wetteberg (2003).

254. Putnam, Leonardi, and Nanetti (1992).

255. Goetz and Jenkins (2002); see also Narayan (2002).

256. Masud (2002).

257. See http://www.sdinet.org/ and Appadurai (2001).

258. Jenkins and Goetz (2002).

259. See http://www.poderciudadano.org.ar/.

260. Boix and Posner (1998).

261. NGOs can make huge contributions to human development by stepping in to provide local community-based services where there is little public presence. But these NGOs may lack a credible voice in reforming public services because they may be perceived as having a vested interest in the existing service delivery arrangements.

262. Goetz and Gaventa (2001).

263. Manor (2002).

264. Platteau (2003) and Crook (2002).

265. World Health Organization (2003).

266. See spotlight on Uganda in this Report.

267. Besley and Burgess (2002)

268. National Democratic Institute for International Affairs and World Bank (1998); Di Tella and Schargrodsky (forthcoming)

269. It is not possible, of course, to know whether the actual outcomes in better-informed states were socially superior. It could just as easily be the case that state governments in which media coverage of food crises was widespread devoted more resources to assistance than they should have, including providing assistance not only to those who needed it but also to those who didn't but were core or swing supporters and voters.

270. Sen (2002) and Dreze and Sen (1991).

271. Paul (2002) and Balakrishnan (2002).

272. For information on the Millennial Surveys, see http://www.pacindia.org.

273. Deichmann and Lall (2003).

274. For a recent discussion of the role of the media in development, see World Bank (2002q).

275. Faguet (2001).

276. Wetterberg and Guggenheim (forthcoming).

277. Evers (2003).

278. Evers (2003).

279. Molyneaux and Gertler (1999) and Alatas (1999).

280. Schiotz (2002).

281. Pritchett (forthcoming).

282. Wilson (1989).

283. Jaffré and Prual (1993).

284. Chomitz and others (1998).

285. Chaudhury and Hammer (2003).

286. Shleifer and Vishny (1993).

287. Vasan (2002).

288. Botchway (2001).

289. Lazear (2000).

290. Boston (1996) and Stewart (1996).

291. Dixit (2000) and Holmstrom and Milgrom (1991).

292. Hammer and Jack (2001) and Gertler and Hammer (1997a).

293. Glewwe, Ilias, and Kremer (2000).

294. Dixit (2000) and Burguess, Propper, and Wilson (2002).

295. Fitz-Gibbon (1996).

296. The City of Johannesburg Council (2001).

297. Frey (1997).

298. Irwin (2003).

299. Hammer, Nabi, and Cercone (1995).

300. Hammer and Jack (2001).

301. Klein and Roger (1994).

302. Aitken (1994).

303. Reinikka and Svensson (2003b).

304. World Bank (2001l).

305. Leonard (2002).

306. Bierschenk, Olivier de Sardan, and Chauveau (1997); Bebbington (1997); Meyer (1995); Chabal and Daloz (1999); Platteau and Gaspart (2003).

307. Chaudhury and Hammer (2003).

308. This is discussed in greater detail in Filmer, Hammer, and Pritchett (2000), Filmer, Hammer, and Pritchett (2002).

309. Cambodia National Institute of Statistics and ORC Macro (2001).

310. The operations research was funded by the Asian Development Bank.

311. Bhushan, Keller, and Schwartz (2002).

312. There is only one instance, that of vitamin A coverage, in which one district had not increased coverage at the time of the mid-term evaluation.

313. Soeters and Griffiths (2003).

314. PROBE Team in association with Centre for Development Economics (1999).

315. Galabawa, Senkoro, and Lwaitama (2000).

316. Greaney, Khandker, and Alam (1999). In reading, "minimally competent" means able to answer three of five questions based on a literal passage; in writing, "minimally competent" means able to write a short (12-word) passage based on a picture.

317. And testing 15-year-olds still in school *overstates* Brazil's performance relative to that of OECD countries because larger numbers of Brazilian teens have already dropped out.

318. Narayan and Pettesch (2002).

319. Daramola and others (1998).

320. Gundlach and Wößman (2001) and Gundlach, Wößman, and Gmelin (2001). The key empirical insight of these studies is that the evolution of learning achievement can be inferred for the countries that do not themselves maintain comparability over time by linking their performance relative to that of the United States at a point in time based on the internationally comparable exams and then linking those to the U.S. National Assessment of Education Progress results, which are comparable over time.

321. Lewis (1961).

322. The five briefly: Belief in one supreme God; just and civilized humanity; the unity of Indonesia democracy is the wisdom of the deliberation; social justice for the whole of the Indonesian people.

323. Sweeting (2001).

324. Lanjouw and Ravallion (1999).

325. Lott (1999).

326. Cited in Madaus and Greaney (1985).

327. Much of the debate is about how to properly isolate the causal impact of variations in class size, mostly from nonexperimental data. This is a problem because if class size is consciously chosen in ways that cause a correlation between performance and class size—say, by school administrators who make classes with disruptive children (who would cause low performance) smaller (so the teacher can better handle the situation) or by students, who, given choice within a school will choose teachers with better reputations—then the observed, nonexperimental data might show a negative or zero correlation between class size and performance even though a truly *exogenous* shift in class size would improve performance. There is evidence of a reasonably large effect of class size from a randomized experiment in Tennessee, and "quasi-experimental" evidence from Israel (Angrist and Lavy (1999)), South Africa (Case and Deaton (1999)), and Bolivia (Urquiola (2001)). But critics of this evidence argue that reported results are "hit and miss"—in that, if class size effects are measured in two subjects in three grades, there are class size effects in some grades and subjects and not others—with no particular pattern; that the literature is subject to enormous "publication bias" in that statistically significant results are much more likely to be written up and published, even if they are in fact rare; and that randomized experiments in which the teachers know the purpose of the experiment are not in fact a clean test, as teachers will attempt to perform well to justify smaller class sizes (Hoxby 2000). Hanushek (2002) continues to emphasize the huge literature in which there is a *general* lack of a correlation—with "better" studies less likely to find effects—and points to the "big picture" evidence unlikely to be affected by the "endogeneity arguments"—the time series in the United States and OECD countries in which class sizes have fallen substantially while scores have stagnated, and the lack of cross-national evidence. Hoxby (2000) produces quasi-experimental evidence from the United States (Vermont) showing no class size effects and argues her results are more typical and representative than others.

328. Vegas (2002).

329. Banerjee and others (2003).

330. Crouch and Healey (1997).

331. Sillers (2002).

332. For instance, empirical studies that run standard wage (or earnings) regressions with a few characteristics (age, gender, education) and include a dummy variable (or interaction terms) for teachers provide a purely statistical answer to the question, "Does the wage regression over- or underpredict wages (or earnings) of teachers?" But even this answer is without a clear interpretation and these studies do not, in themselves, answer the question, "Are teachers underpaid?' (Psacharopoulos, Valenzuela, and Arends (1996); Liang (1999); Filmer (2002); Vegas, Pritchett, and Experton (1999). In some situations in which these regressions suggested that teachers were "underpaid" the annual output of teachers colleges exceeded available positions by several-fold (suggesting teacher pay was adequate), while in others where the regressions suggested teachers were "overpaid" there were few new teachers and wages were being increased (suggesting teacher pay was inadequate).

333. Murnane and Cohen (1986).

334. Eskeland and Filmer (2002).

335. King, James, and Suriyadi (1996) and Pritchett and Filmer (1999).

336. Birdsall and Orivel (1996).

337. Case (2001).

338. See Progresa spotlight.

339. Wodon (1999).

340. Cameron (2001).

341. Angrist and others (2002).

342. Carnoy (1997) and Ladd (2002).

343. World Bank (1996).

344. Grindle (forthcoming).

345. World Bank (2002s).

346. Eriksson, Kreimer, and Arnold (2000).

347. This assessment of the position of teachers and school closings is from Reimers (1997).

348. Action learning program on participatory processes for PRSP (2003).

349. Action learning program on participatory processes for PRSP (2003).

350. For an example of this critique see Davies (2000) and a discussion in Reimers (1997).

351. Initial studies suggested that few of these "Parent School" programs took hold. But they were made an official program—with financial support—in the past five years, and they appear to have expanded since then.

352. Jimenez and Sawada (1999).

353. Jimenez and Sawada (2002).

354. Indeed, one early assessment based on a survey of 140 schools in 1993 found little difference between different types of schools (Reimers (1997)).

355. El Salvador Evaluation Team (1997).

356. Jimenez and Sawada (1999).

357. Sawada (1999).

358. Reimers (1997).

359. A detailed bibliography for this chapter can be found in Soucat and Rani (2003a).

360. UNAIDS and WHO (2003).

361. Gwatkin and others (2000).

362. Victora and others (2000a).

363. Gwatkin and Guillot (2000) and Bonilla-Chacin and Hammer (2003).

364. Haddad and Gillespie (2001) and Wang, Monteiro, and Popkin (2002).

365. Das Gupta (1987) and Claeson and others (2000).

366. Victora and others (2000a); Mehryar, Aghajanian, and Ahmadnia (2003); Suwal (2001); Bhuiya and others (2001); Schellenberg and others (2001); Bang and others (1999); Pathmanathan and others (2003); Rojanapithayakorn and Hanenberg (1996); Victora and others (2000b).

367. Diop, Yazbeck, and Bitran (1995); Soeters and Griffiths (2003); Bhushan, Keller, and Schwartz (2002); Saadah, Pradhan, and Sparrow (2001).

368. Evans (1996) and Moens (1990).

369. Hart (1971).

370. Das Gupta, Khaleghian, and Sarwal (2003).

371. As studies from Madagascar, Ghana, Georgia and the Kyrgyz Republic show Makinen and others (2000), Pannarunothai and

Mills (1997), Peters and others (2003). Castro-Leal and others (2000), Chawla (2001), Lewis (2000).

372. As as studies in China, Egypt, Lebanon, Peru, and Vietnam show. Carrin and others (1999), Cotteril and Chakaraborty (2000), Preker and others (2001), Wagstaff and van Doorslaer (forthcoming).

373. Cebu Study Team (1991) and Glewwe (1999).

374. Wagstaff, van Doorslaer, and Watanabe (2001).

375. Schieber and Maeda (1997).

376. Cai and others (1998).

377. Chaudhury and Hammer (2003).

378. WHO (World Health Organization) (1998).

379. Bennet and McPake (1997).

380. Waters and Aselsson (2002), Soucat and Rani (2003c), and Peters and others (2003).

381. Bloom and Standing (2001).

382. Peters and others (2003).

383. Lewis (2000).

384. Nahar and Costello (1998).

385. World Bank (2003b)

386. Soucat and Rani (2003b) and Schieber and Maeda (1997).

387. Mills and others (2002) and Macy and Quick (2002).

388. Gilson and others (2000); Soucat, Gandaho, and Levy-Bruhl (1997); Diop, Yazbeck, and Bitran (1995); Litvack and Bodart (1993).

389. Price (2001).

390. Rojanapithayakorn and Hanenberg (1996).

391. UNICEF (2002).

392. Population Services International (2003).

393. Mintz, Savedoff, and Pancorvo (2000); Cuellar, Newbrander, and Timmons (2000); Soucat, Gandaho, and Levy-Bruhl (1997); Diop, Yazbeck, and Bitran (1995).

394. Castañeda (1999),

395. Mesoamerica Nutrition Program Targeting Study Group (2002).

396. Institute For Health Sciences and World Bank (2001).

397. Marchant and others (2002).

398. Jongudomsuk, Thammatuch-aree, and Chittinanda (2002).

399. World Bank (2002j) and Gertler and Boyce (2001).

400. Van Lerberghe and Ferrinho (2003).

401. Cotlear (2000).

402. Porignon and others (1998).

403. Maiga, Nafo F., and El Abassi (1999).

404. Criel (1998).

405. Barnighausen and Sauerborn (2002) and Baris (2003).

406. Dror and Preker (2003).

407. Domenighetti and others (1988); Ainsworth, Beyrer, and Soucat (2003); Lamboray (2000); Haddad and Gillespie (2001); Hadi (2001).

408. Platteau and Gaspart (2003).

409. Studdert and others (2000) and Bhat (1996).

410. Jonsson and Musgrove (1997).

411. Janovsky (2002).

412. Akin, Hutchinson, and Strumpf (2001).

413. Pannarunothai and others (2000).

414. Van Lerberghe and Ferrinho (2003).

415. Perry and others (1999).

416. We focus here on how governments can buy health services outputs and outcomes, in contrast to the purchasing of inputs—

ancillary or security services, consumables, equipment—which is part of the management function as per the framework presented in chapter 3.

417. Manning (1998).

418. Nieves, La Forgia, and Ribera (2000); Eichler, Auxilia, and Pollock (2001); Chowdhury (2001).

419. World Bank (2002j).

420. Naimoli and Vaillancourt (2003).

421. Brenzel and Claquin (1994).

422. Holmstrom and Milgrom (1991) and Mills and Bromberg (1998).

423. Hughes (1993).

424. Mills, Broomberg, and Hongoro (1997); Commission on Macroeconomics and Health (2002); Taylor (2003).

425. World Bank (2001d).

426. Save the Children (2002).

427. Hanson and others (2002) and McPake (1996).

428. Hanson (2000) and Brinkerhoff and McEuen (1999),

429. Tendler (1998).

430. Van Lerberghe and others (1997) and Tangcharoensathien and Nittayaramphong (1994).

431. as in Bolivia, Cambodia, and Matlab (Bangladesh), Nieves, La Forgia, and Ribera (2000); Mintz, Savedoff, and Pancorvo (2000); Bhuiya, Rob, and Quaderi (1998); Bhushan (2003).

432. Mills and others (2002).

433. as in Vietnam World Bank (2001j).

434. Lindelow, Ward, and Zorzi (2003) and Mozambique Health Facility Survey, Ferrinho and Van Lerberghe (2003).

435. Nitayaramphong, Srivanichakom, and Pongsupap (2000).

436. Lewis, Eskeland, and Traa-Valerezo (1999).

437. Onyango-Ouma and others (2001).

438. Ferrinho and Van Lerberghe (2003).

439. World Bank (2001d).

440. Cochi and others (1998).

441. Ferriol and others (2003).

442. United Nations (1961).

443. The references to Costa Rica are based on Lisulo (2003).

444. Erikson, Lord, and Wolf (2003). This corresponds to 2.75 family doctors per 1,000 people—in the Latin America and Caribbean region as a whole there are 1.5 doctors (of any kind) per thousand people (World Development Indicators 2002.

445. Ferriol and others (2003) and World Bank (2002s).

446. Ferriol and others (2003).

447. Ferriol and others (2003).

448. Uriarte (2002).

449. Uriarte (2002).

450. Ferriol and others (2003).

451. Erikson, Lord, and Wolf (2003) and Uriarte (2002).

452. See the World Bank (1994c) for a full discussion of economic infrastructure.

453. International Monetary Fund and World Bank (2003).

454. Human Settlements Program (2003).

455. Parker and Skytta (2000).

456. Water and Sanitation Program (WSP-AF) (2003).

457. Schleifer and Vishny (1994).

458. Savedoff and Spiller (1999).

459. Foster (2002).

460. Foster (2002).

461. Smith (1997a), Smith (1997b), Irwin, personal communication.

462. Guasch (2003).

463. Apoyo Opinión y Mercado S.A. (2002).

464. Dumol (2000).

465. Shirley (2002).

466. Smith (2003).

467. Raghupati and Foster (2003).

468. Brook and Locussol (2001).

469. Gómez-Lobos and Contreras (2000); David Savage, personal communication.

470. Plummer (2003).

471. Nickson and Vargas (2002).

472. Parker and Skytta (2000) and World Bank (2002o).

473. Tremolet (2002).

474. Iyer (2002).

475. Term suggested by Peter Kolsky based on his work in this area.

476. Hoy and Jimenez (2003).

477. World Bank (2001i).

478. von der Fehr and Millan (2001).

479. Briscoe (1997).

480. Shirley (2002).

481. Briscoe (1997).

482. Allan, Gotz, and Joseph (2001).

483. iGoli means "city of gold."

484. Ahmad (1996).

485. Allan, Gotz, and Joseph (2001).

486. See the *Glossary* in this Report for explanations of terms relating to the service delivery framework.

487. This draws on Andrews and Campos (2003). See also Campos and Pradhan (1997).

488. See Holmes (2002), Roberts (2002), and Le Houerou and Taliercio (2002) for reviews.

489. Holmes (2002).

490. Le Houerou and Taliercio (2002).

491. IMF and IDA (2002).

492. IMF (2002).

493. See Shah (2003b) for a discussion of the importance of public expenditure management in PRSPs and the large challenges in governance reforms that the early PRSPs show.

494. Dehn, Reinikka, and Svensson (forthcoming).

495. Andrews (2001).

496. See Talero (2001). For a country perspective, see Chile's comprehensive 2002–04 e-procurement strategic plan, ChileCompra (2002), and other materials on the same website. See http://wbln0018.worldbank.org/OCS/egovforum.nsf/Main/ccp for an e-procurement profile of Australia, Brazil, Canada, Chile, Denmark, Mexico, and the United States.

497. See Bardhan (2002) for a recent review.

498. Litvack, Ahmad, and Bird (1998) and Burki, Perry, and Dillinger (1999).

499. Prud'homme (1995) and Rodden, Eskeland, and Litvack (2003).

500. Bardhan and Mookherjee (2002).

501. von Braun and Grote (2000).

502. See Grindle (forthcoming) on education and Burki, Perry, and Dillinger (1999) more generally on Latin America; Faguet (2001) for Bolivia; Ahmad (1999) on South Africa; World Bank (2001a) on transition economies; World Bank (2002f) on Indonesia; and World Bank (2002k) and Lundberg (2002) on Pakistan.

503. Galiani and Schargrodsky (2002).

504. Rodden, Eskeland, and Litvack (2003). An expectation of a bailout reflects a soft budget constraint.

505. Musgrave (1959).

506. Political expediency led the Indonesian parliament to hastily pass laws in 1999 to implement a "big-bang," rapid decentralization, but left the expenditure law unclear on expenditure assignments. The laws are now being revised; see World Bank (2002d).

507. In Indonesia, the 1999 expenditure law was passed independently of the law governing revenue assignments; see World Bank (2002d).

508. Khemani (2003).

509. Ahmad (1999). Financial decentralization (ability to borrow) is usually subsumed into fiscal decentralization. Separating them conceptually can shed more light on the interactions between them.

510. Ahmad (2003).

511. See Evans (2003) for a recent review of staffing practices in decentralization in Benin, India, Indonesia, Mexico, Pakistan, the Philippines, Poland, and Uganda.

512. Much of the government's service delivery had already been deconcentrated, so even though reporting arrangements changed, most employees moved physically just from one office to another within the same city.

513. Grindle (forthcoming).

514. Bahl and Linn (1992).

515. Blondel and Manning (2002).

516. Schacter, Haid, and Koenen-Grant (1999); Koenen-Grant and Garnett (1996).

517. Devarajan, Dollar, and Holmgren (2001).

518. Collier and Pattillo (2000).

519. Beschel and Manning (2000).

520. Evans and Rausch (forthcoming)

521. International Labour Organization (2001).

522. There is an ongoing debate on whether New Public Management should be attempted in developing countries: Schick (1996), Bale and Dale (1998), Schick (1998), Batley (1999), Manning (2001).

523. World Bank (2000b).

524. Dixon (2002).

525. Schick (1998).

526. This draws on Manning and Parison (2003) and World Bank (2002e).

527. Wade (1982); Wade (1985).

528. Even in countries with a strong civil service tradition, the problem of political interference can be pernicious, as the huge problem in India of ad hoc transfers of civil servants to "punishment postings" demonstrates; see Sundaram (2001).

529. Azfar (2002).

530. For a recent list of these studies, see, for example, World Bank (2000a) and Abed and Gupta (2002).

531. Anderson, Kaufmann, and Recanatini (2003).

532. Mauro (1998).

533. Rajkumar and Swaroop (2002), Abed and Gupta (2002), Azfar and Gurgur (2001), and Di Tella and Savedoff (2001b).

534. See Kaufmann, Pradhan, and Ryterman (1998) for a discussion of the early diagnostic approach.

535. Anderson, Kaufmann, and Recanatini (2003) highlight the findings of these diagnostic surveys for service delivery.

536. World Bank (2000a).

537. Grindle (forthcoming).

538. World Bank (2002e).

539. For example, see chapter 3 of World Bank (2002b) for guidance on designing a poverty monitoring system.

540. Kremer (2002).

541. Victora and others (2000a).

542. Davey (2000).

543. World Bank (1998a), Burnside and Dollar (2000a), Burnside and Dollar (2000b), and Collier and Dollar (2002).

544. Martens and others (2002) and Ostrom and others (2001).

545. Mackinnon (2003).

546. The literature on fungibility—including Devarajan and Swaroop (1998); Devarajan, Rajkumar, and Swaroop (1999); and Feyziogly, Swaroop, and Zhu (1998)—finds that only a portion of aid stays in the sector: when the government receives sector-specific aid, it shifts its own resources partially to other sectors. Fungibility suggests that donors should take a more holistic approach to recipients' public spending.

547. Development Assistance Committee (DAC) of the Organisation for Economic Co-operation and Development (OECD).

548. World Bank (2001l).

549. For example, the Global Fund to Fight AIDS, Tuberculosis and Malaria; the Global Alliance for Vaccinations and Immunizations; the Global Vaccine Fund; and the Global Environment Facility. For details on health-related global funds see Kalter (2003).

550. Ostrom and others (2001).

551. Boyce and Haddad (2001).

552. World Bank (2001f).

553. Bräutigam (2000).

554. World Bank (1998a).

555. Cohen and Wheeler (1997).

556. Data for the Development Gateway are provided by the OECD DAC and other donor sources over several decades. Unfortunately, the database has no indication of the number of projects ongoing at any given time.

557. A Herfindahl index of donor concentration is first calculated by summing the squared shares of aid over all donor agencies operating in the recipient country (O'Connell and Saludo (2001)). This index, which ranges from 0 to 1, is then subtracted from 1 to form an index of donor fragmentation, with high values indicating greater fragmentation (Knack and Rahman (2003)).

558. Index values do not necessarily rise with aid levels or number of projects: doubling each donor's aid or number of projects but keeping the number of donors and their activity shares constant leaves the index values unchanged.

559. Data are from the OECD DAC. The trend may overstate the worsening of donor fragmentation to the extent pooling of donor funds has also increased, because the index calculated on the basis of disbursements does not distinguish pooled funds from non-pooled funds.

560. Knack and Rahman (2003). The Bureaucratic Quality Indexes are subjective assessments from the International Country Risk Guide (ICRG). High ratings reflect the "strength and expertise to govern without drastic changes in policy or interruptions in government services." Ratings are strongly correlated with more detailed, independent assessments of "Weberian" bureaucratic structure and stability (Evans and Rauch (1999)), available for a subset of countries covered by the ICRG.

561. Picazo (2002).

562. Picazo (2002).

563. Mansuri and Rao (2003).

564. Chase (2002), Newman and others (2002), Paxson and Schady (2002), and Van Domelen (2002).

565. World Bank (2002p).

566. Platteau and Gaspart (2003).

567. World Bank (2002r).

568. Gunning (2001).

569. Collier (1997), Kapur and Webb (2000), Devarajan, Dollar, and Holmgren (2001), Dollar and Svensson (2000).

570. Svensson (2003).

571. Adam and Gunning (2002).

572. Adam and Gunning (2002).

573. World Bank (2002r).

574. Angrist and others (2002).

575. Miguel and Kremer (2001).

576. van de Walle (2002) and van de Walle and Cratty (2003).

577. Riddel (1999).

578. World Bank (2002r).

579. Harrold and Associates (1995).

580. There have been a number of reviews of the sectorwide approach, including Brown (2000a), Conway (2000), Foster (2000), Foster, Brown, and Conway (2000), Jones (1997), Jones and Lawson (2001), and ; World Bank (2001b).

581. Fozzard and Foster (2001) and Kanbur and Sandler (1999).

582. Adam and Gunning (2002).

583. Brown (2000b).

584. Mackinnon (2003).

585. The perception—rather than the reality—of fiduciary risk may reduce political support for foreign aid in the donor country. But that is a political issue in rich countries, not a service-delivery issue in poor countries.

586. World Bank (2002r).

587. World Bank (2002r).

588. Most bilateral donors give more aid to countries that vote similarly to them in the United Nations General Assembly, where each nation regardless of size has one vote (Alesina and Dollar (2000) and Wang (1999)).

589. Halonen (2003).

590. See, for example, Tarp and Hjertholm (2000).

References

The word processed describes informally reproduced works that may not be commonly available through libraries.

Abed, George T., and Sanjeev Gupta. 2002. *Governance, Corruption, & Economic Performance.* Washington, D.C.: International Monetary Fund.

Acharya, Arnab, Fuzzo de Lima, and Mick Moore. 2003. "The Proliferators: Transactions Costs and the Value of Aid." Institute of Development Studies: Brighton, U.K. Processed.

Action learning program on participatory processes for PRSP. 2003. "Reform Of Basic Education in El Salvador." World Bank: Washington, D.C. Available on line at http://www.worldbank.org/participation/web/webfiles/eseducation.htm. Processed.

Adam, Christopher S., and Jan Willem Gunning. 2002. "Redesigning the Aid Contract: Donors' Use of Performance Indicators in Uganda." *World Development* 30(12):2045–56.

Agarwal, Bina. 2001. "Participatory Exclusions, Community Forestry, and Gender: An Analysis for South Asia and a Conceptual Framework." *World Development* 29(10):1623–48.

Aghion, Phillipe, and Jean Tirole. 1997. "Formal and Real Authority in Organizations." *Journal of Political Economy* 105(1):1–29.

Ahmad, Junaid. 1996. "The Structure of Urban Governance in South African Cities." *International Tax and Public Finance* 3(2):193–213.

———. 1999. "Decentralizing Borrowing Powers." World Bank PREM Note 15. Washington, D.C.

———. 2003. "Creating Incentives for Fiscal Discipline in the New South Africa." In Jonathan Rodden, Gunnar Eskeland, and Jennie Litback, eds., *Decentralization and Hard Budget Constraints.* Cambridge: MIT Press.

Ahmad, Junaid, B. N. Goldar, M. Jakariya, and Smita Misra. 2002. "Fighting Arsenic, Listening to Rural Communities: Findings from a Study on Willingness to Pay for Arsenic-free, Safe Drinking Water in Rural Bangladesh." World Bank, Water and Sanitation Program-South Asia: Dhaka, Bangladesh. Available on line at http://www.wsp.org/pdfs/sa_arsenic_learning.pdf.

Ainsworth, Martha, Chris Beyrer, and Agnes Soucat. 2003. "AIDS and Public Policy: The Lessons and Challenges of 'Success' in Thailand." *Health Policy* 64:13–37.

Aitken, Jean-Marion. 1994. "Voices from the Inside: Managing District Health Services in Nepal." *International Journal of Health Planning and Management* 9(4):309–40.

Akin, John, Paul Hutchinson, and Koleman Strumpf. 2001. "Decentralization and Government Provision of Public Goods: The Public Health Sector in Uganda." Abt. Associates Inc.; MEASURE Evaluation Project Working Paper 01-35. Bethesda, Md.

Akin, John S., David K. Guilkey, and E. Hazel Denton. 1995. "Quality of Services and Demand for Health Care in Nigeria: A Multinomial Probit Estimation." *Social Science and Medicine* 40(11): 1527–37.

Akin, John S., and Paul Hutchinson. 1999. "Health-Care Facility Choice and the Phenomenon of Bypassing." *Health Policy and Planning* 14(2):135–151.

Alatas, Vivi. 1999. "Analyzing Indonesia's Poverty Profile." PhD's thesis. Princeton University.

Alatas, Vivi, Lant Pritchett, and Anna Wetteberg. 2003. "Voice Lessons: Local Government Organizations, Social Organizations, and the Quality of Local Governance." Kennedy School of Government, Harvard University: Cambrige, Mass. Processed.

Alderman, Harold, and Victor Lavy. 1996. "Household Responses to Public Health Services: Cost and Quality Tradeoffs." *World Bank Research Observer* 11(1):3–22.

Alesina, Alberto, Reza Baqir, and William Easterly. 1999. "Public Goods and Ethnic Divisions." *Quarterly Journal of Economics* 114:1243–1284.

Alesina, Alberto, and David Dollar. 2000. "Who Gives Foreign Aid to Whom and Why?" *Journal of Economic Growth* 5(1):33–63.

Allan, Kevin, Graeme Gotz, and Carmel Joseph. 2001. *Johannesburg, An African City in Change.* Johannesburg: Zebra Press.

Anand, Sudhir, and Martin Ravallion. 1993. "Human Development in Poor Countries: On the Role of Private Incomes and Public Services." *Journal of Economic Perspectives* 7(1):133–150.

Anderson, James, Daniel Kaufmann, and Francesca Recanatini. 2003. "Service Delivery, Poverty, and Corruption—Common Threads from Diagnostic Surveys." Background paper for the WDR 2004.

Andrews, Matthew. 2001. "Adjusting External Audits to Facilitate Results-Oriented Government." *The International Journal of Government Auditors* 28(2):10–13.

Andrews, Matthew, and J. Edgardo Campos. 2003. "The Management of Public Expenditures and Its Implications for Service Delivery." Background paper for the WDR 2004.

Andrews, Matthew, and Anwar Shah. 2003. "Towards Citizen-oriented Local-level Budgets in Developing Countries." In Anwar Shah, eds., *Ensuring Accountability When there is No Bottom Line.* Washington, D.C.: World Bank.

Angrist, J. D., and Victor Lavy. 1999. "Using Maimonides' Rule to Estimate the Effect of Class Size on Scholastic Achievement." *Quarterly Journal of Economics* 114(2):533–75.

Angrist, Joshua, Eric Bettinger, Erik Bloom, Elizabeth M. King, and Michael Kremer. 2002. "Vouchers for Private Schooling in Colombia: Evidence from a Randomized Natural Experiment." *American Economic Review* 92(5):1535–58.

Antia, N. H. 1994. *Kerala Shows the Way to Health, International Congress on Kerala Studies, Abstracts, Volume 2.* Thiruvananthapuram: A.K.G. Centre for Research and Studies.

Apoyo Opinión y Mercado S.A. 2002. "Sentimientos Encontrados." *Opinión Data: Resumen de Encuestas a la Opinión Pública* 21(2):1–1.

Appadurai, Arjun. 2001. "Deep Democracy: Urban Governmentality and the Horizon of Politics." University of Chicago: Chicago. Processed.

Appleton, Simon. 2001. "What Can We Expect from Universal Primary Education?" In Ritva Reinikka and Paul Collier, eds., *Uganda's Recovery: The Role of Farms, Firms, and Government.* Washington, D.C.: World Bank.

Azfar, Omar. 2002. "Corruption and the Delivery of Health and Education Services." University of Maryland, IRIS: College Park, Md. Processed.

Azfar, Omar, and Tugrul Gurgur. 2001. "Does Corruption Affect Health and Education Outcomes in the Philippines?" University of Maryland, IRIS: College Park, Md. Processed.

Bahl, Roy, and Johannes Linn. 1992. *Urban Public Finance in Developing Countries.* New York: Oxford University Press for the World Bank.

Balakrishnan, Suresh. 2002. "Citizen Report Cards and Basic Services for the Poor." Public Affairs Centre: Bangalore, India. Processed.

Bale, Malcolm, and Tony Dale. 1998. "Public Sector Reform in New Zealand and Its Relevance to Developing Countries." *World Bank Research Observer* 13(1):103–121.

Banerjee, Abhijit, Shawn Cole, Esther Duflo, and Leigh Linden. 2003. "Improving the Quality of Education in India: Evidence from Three Randomized Experiments." Massachusetts Institute of Technology, Department of Economics: Cambridge, Mass. Processed.

Bang, A. T., R. A. Bang, S. B. Baitule, M. H. Reddy, and M. D. Deshmukh. 1999. "Effect of Home-Based Neonatal Care and Management Septics on Neonatal Mortality: Field Trial in Rural India." *Lancet* 354(9194):1955–61.

Bardhan, Pranab. 2002. "Decentralization of Governance and Development." *Journal of Economic Perspectives* 16(4):185–205.

Bardhan, Pranab, and Dilip Mookherjee. 2002. "Decentralizing Anti-Poverty Program Delivery in Developing Countries." University of California, Berkeley, Institute of International Studies: Berkeley, C.A. Processed.

Baris, E. 2003. "Resource Allocation and Purchasing in East Asia and Pacific Region." World Bank: Washington, D.C. Processed.

Barnighausen, T., and R. Sauerborn. 2002. "One Hundred and Eighteen Years of the German Health Insurance System: Are there Any Lessons for Middle- and Low-Income Countries?" *Social Science and Medicine* 54(10):1559–87.

Barro, Robert J. 1991. "Economic Growth in a Cross-Section of Countries." *Quarterly Journal of Economics* 106(2):407–443.

Batley, Richard. 1999. "The Role of Government in Adjusting Countries: An Overview of Findings." International Development Department, University of Birmingham. Monograph.

Beatty, Jack. 1992. *The Rascal King: The Life and Times of James Michael Curley, 1874-1958.* Reading, Mass.: Addison-Wesley.

Bebbington, A. 1997. "New States, New NGOs? Crises and Transitions among Rural Development NGOs in the Andean Region." *World Development* 25(11):1755–65.

Beck, Thorsten, George Clarke, Alberto Groff, Philip Keefer, and Patrick Walsh. 2001. "New Tools in Comparative Political Economy: The Database of Political Institutions." *World Bank Economic Review* 15(1):165–176.

Becker, Gary. 1971. *The Economics of Discrimination.* Chicago: University of Chicago Press.

Behrman, Jere R., and John Hoddinott. 2001. "An Evaluation of the Impact of PROGRESA on Preschool Child Height." IFPRI FCND Discussion Paper 104. Washington, D.C. Available on line at www.ifpri.org.

Bell, Clive, and Shantayanan Devarajan. 1987. "Intertemporally Consistent Shadow Prices in an Open Economy: Estimates for Cyprus." *Journal of Public Economics* 32(3):263–85.

Bennet, S., and B. Mills A. McPake. 1997. *Private Health Providers in Developing Countries. Serving the Public Interest?* Lodon and New Jersey: Zed Books.

Beschel, Robert P. Jr., and Nick Manning. 2000. "The 'Brain' of Government: Central Mechanisms for Policy Formulation and Coordination." In Salvatore Schiavo-Campo and Pachampet Sundaram, eds., *To Serve and to Preserve: Improving Public Administration in a Competitive World.* Manila: Asian Development Bank.

Besley, Timothy, and Robin Burgess. 2002. "The Political Economy of Government Responsiveness: Theory and Evidence from India." *Quarterly Journal of Economics* 117(4):1415–51.

Betancourt, Roger, and Suzanne Gleason. 2000. "The Allocation of Publicly-Provided Goods to Rural Households in India: On Some Consequences of Caste, Religion and Democracy." *World Development* 28(12):2169–82.

Bhargava, Alok, Dean T. Jamison, L. J. Lau, and Christopher J. Murray. 2001. "Modeling the Effects of Health on Economic Growth." *Journal of Health Economics* 20(3):423–440.

Bhat, R. 1996. "Regulation of the Private Health Sector in India." *International Journal of Health Planning and Management* 11:253–74.

Bhuiya, A., M. Chowdhury, F. Ahmed, and A. Adams. 2001. "Bangladesh: An Intervention Study of Factors Underlying Increasing Equity in Child Survival." In T. Evans, M. Whitehead, F. Diderichsen, A. Bhuiya, and M. Wirth, eds., *Challenging Inequities in Health: From Ethics to Action.* New York: Oxford University Press.

Bhuiya, A., U. Rob, and M. R. Quaderi. 1998. "Ensuring Community Participation in MCH-FP Activities in Rural Bangladesh Lessons Learned from a Pilot Project." International Centre for Diarrhoeal Disease Research and Population Council: Dhaka, Bangladesh.

Bhushan, Indu. 2003. "Contracting Health Services in Cambodia." Background note for the WDR 2004.

Bhushan, Indu, Sheryl Keller, and Brad Schwartz. 2002. "Achieving the Twin Objectives of Efficiency and Equity: Contracting for Health

Services in Cambodia." Asian Development Bank, Policy Brief Series 6. Manila.

Bidani, Benu, and Martin Ravallion. 1997. "Decomposing Social Indicators Using Distributional Data." *Journal of Econometrics* 77(1):125–139.

Bierschenk, T., J. P. Olivier de Sardan, and J. P. Chauveau. 1997. *Courtiers Locaux en Développement. Les villages Africaines en Quête de Projets.* Paris: Karthala.

Bils, Mark, and Peter J. Klenow. 2000. "Does Schooling Cause Growth?" *American Economic Review* 90(5):1160–1183.

Birdsall, Nancy, and Francois Orivel. 1996. "Demand for Primary Schooling in Rural Mali: Should User Fees Be Increased?" *Education Economics* 4(3):279–96.

Block, Steven A. 2002. "Political Business Cycles, Democratization, and Economic Reform: The Case of Africa." *Journal of Development Economics* 67(1):205–28.

Blokland, M., O. Braadbaart, and K. Schwartz. eds. 1999. *Private Business, Public Owners, Government Share Holding in Water Enterprises.* The Hague: Ministry of Housing, Spatial Planning, and the Environment, Government of the Netherlands and the Water Supply and Sanitation Collaborative Council.

Blomquist, William, and Elinor Ostrom. 1958. "Institutional Capacity and the Resolutions of a Commons Dilemma." *Policy Studies Review* 5(2):383–93.

Blondel, Jean, and Nicholas Manning. 2002. "Do Ministers Do What They Say? Ministerial Unreliability, Collegial and Hierarchical Governments." *Political Studies* 50:455–76.

Bloom, G., and H. Standing. 2001. "Pluralism and Marketization in the Health Sector: Meeting Health Needs in Contexts of Social Change in Low and Middle-Income Countries." University of Sussex, Institute of Development Studies Working Paper 136. Brighton, U.K.

Boix, Carles, and Daniel N. Posner. 1998. "Social Capital: Explaining its Origins and Effects on Government Performance." *British Journal of Political Science* 28, 4(October):686–693.

Bonilla-Chacin, Maria E., and Jeffrey Hammer. 2003. "Life and Deaths among the Poorest." World Bank: Washington, D.C. Processed.

Bonilla-Chacin, Maria E., Edmundo Murrugarra, and Moukim Temourov. 2003. "Health Care during Transition and Health Systems Reforms: Evidence from the Poorest CIS Countries." Paper presented at the *Initiative of the CIS-7* Conference. Lucerne. January 20.

Boston, Jonathan. 1996. "Separation of Policy and Operations in Government: The New Zealand Experience." In International Governance Network, eds., *Policy and Operations.* Ottawa: Canadian Centre for Management Development.

Botchway, Karl. 2001. "Paradox of Empowerment: Reflections on a Case Study from Northern Ghana." *World Development* 29(1):135–53.

Bowen, James. 1981. *A History of Western Education. The Modern West: Europe and the New World.* London: Methuen.

Boyce, Daniel, and Afef Haddad. 2001. "Thematic Review on Project Implementation Units: An Analysis of Ongoing and Completed Projects in Latin America and the Caribbean." World Bank, A study carried out on behalf of the Latin American and Caribbean Region Quality Enhancement Team: Washington, D.C.

Bräutigam, Deborah. 2000. "Aid Dependence and Governance." Expert Group on Development Issues Study (EDGI) 2000:1. Stockholm, Sweden.

Brazil Ministry of Health. 2001. "Evolution of Numbers of Community Health Agents 1994-2001." Brazil Ministry of Health: Brasilia.

Brenzel, Logan, and Pierre Claquin. 1994. "Immunization Programs and Their Costs." *Social Science and Medicine* 39(4):527–36.

Brinkerhoff, Derick, and Mark McEuen. 1999. "New NGO Partners for Health Sector Reform in Central Asia: Family Group Practice Associations in Kazakhstan and Kyrgyzstan." Special Initiatives Report 19. Bethesda, Md.

Briscoe, John. 1997. "Lessons for the Water Sector." World Bank: Washington, D.C. Processed.

Brook, Penelope, and Alain Locussol. 2001. "Easing Tariff Increases, Financing the Transition to Cost-Recovering Water Tariffs in Guinea." In Penelope Brook and Suzanne M. Smith, eds., *Contracting for Public Devices: Output-Based Aid and Its Applications.* Washington, D.C.: World Bank.

Brooke, James. 1993. "Brazilian State Leads Way in Saving Children." *The New York Times,* May 14. Page: A.

Brown, Adrienne. 2000a. "Current Issues in Sector-Wide Approaches for Health Development: Mozambique Case Study." World Health Organization WHO/ISS 4. Geneva.

————. 2000b. "Current Issues in Sector-Wide Approaches for Health Development: Uganda Study." World Health Organization who/iss 3. Geneva.

Bruns, Barbara, Alain Mingat, and Ramahatra Rakatomalala. 2003. "A Chance for Every Child: Achieving Universal Primary Education by 2015." World Bank: Washington, D.C.

Burguess, Simon, Carol Propper, and Deborah Wilson. 2002. "Does Performance Monitoring Work?: A Review of the Evidence from the UK Public Sector, Excluding Health Care." University of Bristol, Department of Economics, CMPO Working Paper Series 02/49. Bristol, U.K.

Burki, Shaid Javed, Guillermo Perry, and William Dillinger. 1999. "Beyond the Center: Decentralizing the State." World Bank: Washington, D.C.

Burnside, Craig, and David Dollar. 2000a. "Aid, Growth, the Incentive Regime and Poverty Reduction." In Christopher L. Gilbert and David Vines, eds., *The World Bank Structure and Policies.* Cambridge, U.K.: Cambridge University Press.

————. 2000b. "Aid, Policies and Growth." *American Economic Review* 90(4):847–868.

Cai, W. W., J. S. Marks, C. H. Chen, Y. X. Zhuang, L. Morris, and J. R. Harris. 1998. "Increased Caesarean Sections Rates and Emerging Patterns of Health Insurance in Shanghai, China." *American Journal of Public Health* 88:777–80.

Cambodia National Institute of Statistics, Ministry of Health, and ORC Macro. 2001. "Cambodia Demographic and Health Survey 2000." Cambodia National Institute of Statistics, Ministry of Health: Phnom Penh, Cambodia.

Cameron, Lisa. 2001. "The Impact of the Indonesian Financial Crisis on Children, An Analysis Using the 100 Villages Data." *Bulletin of Indonesian Economic Studies* 37(1):7–41.

Campos, J. Edgardo, and Sanjay Pradhan. 1997. "Evaluating Public Expenditure Management Systems: An Experimental Methodology with an Application to the Australia and New Zealand Reforms." *Journal of Policy Analysis and Management* 16(3):423–45.

Carnoy, Martin. 1997. "Is Privatization through Education Vouchers Really the Answer? A Comment." *World Bank Research Observer* 12(1):105–16.

Carothers, Thomas. 1999. *Aiding Democracy Abroad. The Learning Curve.* Washington, D.C.: Carnegie Endowment for International Peace.

Carrin, G, A. Ron, Y. Hui, W. Hong, Z. Tuohong, Z. Licheng, Z. Shuo, Y. Yide, Ch. Jiaying, J. Qicheng, Z. Zhaoyang, Y. Jun, and L. Xuesheng. 1999. "The Reform of the Rural Cooperative Medical System in the People's Republic of China: Interim Experience in 14 Pilot Counties." *Social Science and Medicine* 48(7):961–72.

Case, A., and A. Deaton. 1999. "School Inputs and Educational Outcomes in South Africa." *Quarterly Journal of Economics* 114(3):1047–84.

Case, Anne. 2001. "Does Money Protect Health Status? Evidence from South African Pensions." National Bureau of Economic Research Working Paper 8495. Cambridge, Mass.

Castañeda, Tarsicio. 1999. "The Design, Implementation and Impact of Food Stamp Programs in Developing Countries." World Bank, Human Development Network. Washington, D.C.

Castro-Leal, Florencia, Julie Dayton, Lionel Demery, and Kalpana Menhra. 2000. "Public Spending on Health Care in Africa: Do the Poor Benefit?" *Bulletin of the World Health Organization* 78(1):66–74.

Cebu Study Team. 1991. "Underlying and Proximate Determinants of Child Health: The Cebu Longitudinal Health and Nutrition Study." *American Journal of Epidemiology* **1**33(2):185–201.

Chabal, Patrick, and Jean-Pascal Daloz. 1999. *Africa Works: Disorder as Political Instrument.* Oxford, U.K.: James Currey.

Chandran, Ashok. 1999. "Effectiveness of Public Action in Rural Health Service Delivery: A Case Study from Kerala." Masters's thesis. London School of Economics, Development Studies Institute.

Chang, Ha-Joon. 2002. *Kicking away the Ladder: Development Strategy in a Historical Perspective.* London: Anthem Press.

Chappell, Henry W., and William Keech. 1990. "Citizen Information, Rationality, and the Politics of Macroeconomic Policy." In John Ferejohn and James H. Kuklinsky, eds., *Information and Democratic Processes.* Urbana: University of Illinois Press.

Chase, Robert. 2002. "Supporting Communities in Transition: The Impact of Armenian Social Investment Fund." *World Bank Economic Review* 16(2):219–40.

Chaudhury, Nazmul, and Jeffrey Hammer. 2003. "Ghost Doctors: Absenteeism in Bangladeshi Health Facilities." Background paper for the WDR 2004.

Chaudhury, Nazmul, Jeffrey S. Hammer, Michael Kremer, Karthik Muralidharan, and F. Halsey Rogers. 2003. "Teacher and Health Care Provider Absenteeism : A Multi-Country Study." World Bank: Washington, D.C.

Chawla, Mukesh. 2001. "How Well Does the Health Sector in Georgia Serve the Poor: An Examination of Public and Out-of-Pocket Expenditures on Health." World Bank, prepared for the Health Systems Development Thematic Group (training material series): Washington, D.C.

ChileCompra. 2002. "Chile Public Procurement System: Strategic Plan 2002-2004." Gobierno de Chile, Ministerio de Hacienda: Santiago, Chile.

Chomitz, Kenneth, Gunawan Setiadi, Azrul Azwar, and Nusye Ismail Widiyarti. 1998. "What Do Doctors Want?: Developing Incentives for Doctors to Serve in Indonesia's Rural and Remote Areas." World Bank Policy Research Working Paper 1888. Washington, D.C.

Chowdhury, Sadia. 2001. "Educating Mothers for Health: Output-Based Incentives for Teaching Oral Rehydration in Bangladesh." In J. Penelope and Suzanne M. Smith, eds., *Contracting for Public Services: Output Based Aid and Its Applications.* Washington, D.C.: World Bank.

Claeson, M., E. R. Bos, T. Mawji, and I. Pathmanathan. 2000. "Reducing Child Mortality in India in the New Millenium." *Bulletin of the World Health Organization* 78(10):1192–99.

Claeson, M., C. Griffin, T. Johnston, A. Soucat, A. Wagstaff, and A. Yazbec. 2003. "Health, Nutrition, and Population." In Jeni Klugman, eds., *A Sourcebook for Poverty Reduction Strategies Vol. II: Macreconomics and Sectoral Approaches.* Washington, D.C.: World Bank.

Coady, David. 2003. "Alleviating Structural Poverty in Developing Countries: The Approach of PROGRESA in Mexico." Background paper for the WDR 2004.

Cochi, S. L., C. A. De Quadros, S. Dittman, S. O. Foster, J. Z. Galvez Tan, F. C. Grant, J. M. Olivé, H. A. Pigman, C. E. Taylor, and K. Wang. 1998. "Group Report: What Are the Societal and Political Criteria for Disease Eradication?" In W. R. Dowdle and D. R. Hopkins, eds., *The Eradication of Infectious Diseases.* Berlin: John Wiley & Sons: West Sussex.

Cohen, John M., and John R. Wheeler. 1997. "Building Sustainable Professional Capacity in African Public Sectors: Retention Constraints in Kenya." *Public Administration and Development* 17:307–24.

Cohen, Wilbur J. 1957. *Retirement Policies under Social Security: A Legislative History of Retirement Ages, the Retirement Test, and Disability Benefits.* Berkeley: University of California Press.

Collier, Paul. 1997. "The Failure of Conditionality." In C Gwin and J. M. Nelson, eds., *Perspectives on Aid and Development.* Washington, D.C.: Overseas Development Council.

Collier, Paul, and David Dollar. 2002. "Aid Allocation and Poverty Reduction." *European Economic Review* 46(8):1475–1500.

Collier, Paul, and Catherine Pattillo. 2000. *Reducing the Risk of Investment in Africa.* Basingstone: Macmillan.

Commission on Macroeconomics and Health. 2001. *Macroeconomics and Health: Investing in Health for Economic Development.* Geneva: World Health Organization.

————. 2002. "Mobilizing Domestic Resources for Health." World Health Organization, report of working group 3 on Macro-Economics and Health chaired by Kesi Botchewey and Alan Tait: Geneva.

Community Driven Development. 2002. "Sourcebook for Community Driven Development in Sub-Saharan Africa." Community Driven Development, Environment and Socially Sustainable

Development Network: Washington, D.C. Available on line at http://essd.worldbank.org/CDDWk2000.nsf/GWeb/cdd_concepts.

Conning, Jonathan, and Michael Kevane. 2002. "Community-Based Targeting Mechanisms for Social Safety Nets: A Critical Review." *World Development* 30(3):375–94.

Conway, Tim. 2000. "Current Issues in Sector-Wide Approaches for Health Development: Cambodia Case Study." World Health Organization WHO/GPE/00.2. Geneva.

Coombe, Carol. 2000. "Managing the Impact of HIV/AIDS on the Education Sector." The Center for the Study of AIDS, University of Pretoria: Pretoria, South Africa. Processed.

Cornell, Stephen, and Joseph Kalt. 1995. "Where Does Economic Development Really Come From? Constitutional Rule among the Contemporary Sioux and Apache." *Economic Inquiry* 33(3):402–426.

———. 1997. "Successful Economic Development and Heterogeneity of Governmental Form on American Indian Reservations." In Merilee S. Grindle, eds., *Getting Good Government: Capacity Building in the Public Sectors of Developing Countries.* Cambridge, Mass.: Harvard University Press.

———. 2000. "Where's the Glue? Institutional and Cultural Foundations of American Indian Economic Development." *Journal of Socio Economics* 29(5):443–70.

Cotlear, D. 2000. "Peru: Reforming Health Care for the Poor." World Bank, Human Development Department (LCSHD) Paper Serie 57. Washington DC.

Cotteril, P., and S. Chakaraborty. 2000. "Lebanon Provider Payment Case Study." World Bank, HNP network, background paper to the Resource Allocation and Purchasing Research Project: World Bank.

Criel, B. 1998. *District-Based Health Insurance in Sub-Saharan Africa. Part I: From Theory to Practice.* Antwerp: ITG Press.

Crocker, Keith, and Scott E. Mastens. 2002. "Prospects for Private Water Provision in Developing Countries: Lessons from 19th Century America." In Mary Shirley, eds., *Thirsting for Efficiency: The Economics and Politics of Urban Water System Reform.* Amsterdam, New York: World Bank, Pergamon.

Crook, Richard. 2002. "Urban Service Partnerships: "Street Level Bureaucrats" and Environmental Sanitation in Kumasi and Accra, Ghana: Coping with Organizational Change in the Public Bureaucracy." Paper presented at the *the WDR Conference on Making Services Work for Poor People* Conference. Eynsham Hall, Oxfordshire. November.

Crouch, Luis, and Henry F. Healey. 1997. "Education Reform Support. Volume One: Overview and Bibliography." Office of Sustainable Development, Bureau for Africa, United States Agency for International Development (USAID), Publication Series, Paper 47. Washington, D.C.

Cuellar, Carlos J., William Newbrander, and Barbara K. Timmons. 2000. "The PROSALUD Model for Expanding Access to Health Services." World Bank, HNP Network: Washington D.C.

Daramola, A. G., Hawa A. Biu, S. Ogoh Alubo, Agi S. P. I. Shebu, Uchenna M. Nzewi, and Paul Francis. 1998. *Hard Lessons: Primary Schools, Community, and Social Capital in Nigeria.* Washington, D.C.: World Bank.

Das Gupta, Monica. 1987. "Selective Discrimination against Female Children in Rural Pubjab, India." *Population and Development Review* 13(1):77–100.

Das Gupta, Monica, P. Khaleghian, and R. Sarwal. 2003. "Governance of Communicable Disease Control Services: A Case Study and Lessons from India." Background paper for the WDR 2004.

Das, Jishnu, Stefan Dercon, Promila Krishnan, and James Habyarimana. 2003. "Rules versus Discretion: Public and Private Funding in Zambian Education." World Bank: Washington, D.C. Processed.

Das, Jishnu, and Jeffrey Hammer. 2003. "Money for Nothing: The Dire Straits of Indian Health Care." World Bank: Washington, D.C. Processed.

Davey, Shelia. eds. 2000. *Health a Key to Prosperity - Success Stories in Developing Countries.* Geneva: World Health Organization.

Davies, Betty Ann. 2001. "Reforming Birth and the (Re) making Midwifery in North America." In R. Devries, van Teijlingen Benoit C., and S. Wrede, eds., *Birth by Design: Pregnancy, Maternity Care, and Midwifery in North America and Europe.* London: Routledge.

Davies, Ian. 2000. "The Debate Over Popular Education in El Salvador." Edgewood College, Madison W.I.: LASA, Miami, Florida, March 2000. Available on line at http://forlang.edgewood.edu/ian/Education.htm. Processed.

Davis, Shelton H., and Harry Anthony Patrinos. 2002. "Investing in Latin America's Indigenous Peoples: The Human and Social Capital Dimensions." World Bank: Washington, D.C. Processed.

de Soto, Hernando. 2000. *The Mystery of Capital: Why Capitalism Triumphs in the West and Fails Everywhere Else.* New York: Perseus Book Group.

Deaton, Angus. 1997. *The Analysis of Household Surveys: A Microeconometric Approach to Development Policy.* Baltimore and London: Johns Hopkins University Press for The World Bank.

Dehn, Jan, Ritva Reinikka, and Jakob Svensson. Forthcoming. "Survey Tools for Assessing Service Delivery." In Francois Bourguinon and Luiz Pereira da Silva (eds.) *Evaluating the Poverty and Distributional Impact of Economic Policies.* New York: Oxford University Press.

Deichmann, Uwe, and Somnik V. Lall. 2003. "Are you satisfied? Citizen Feedback and Delivery of Urban Services." World Bank: Washington, D.C. Processed.

Department for International Development and Water and Environmental Health at London and Loughborough. 1998. "Guidance Manual on Water Supply and Sanitation Programmes." WEIDC for DIFD: London. Available on line at http://www.lboro.ac.uk/well/resources/books-and-manuals/guidance-manual/guidance-manual.htm.

Devarajan, Shantayanan. 2002. "Growth Is Not Enough." Word Bank: Washington, D.C. Processed.

Devarajan, Shantayanan, David Dollar, and Torgny Holmgren. 2001. *Aid and Reform in Africa Lessons from Ten Case Studies.* Washington, D.C.: World Bank.

Devarajan, Shantayanan, Margaret J. Miller, and Eric L. Swanson. 2002. "Goals for Development: History, Prospects, and Costs." World Bank Policy Research Working Paper 2819. Washington, D.C.

Devarajan, Shantayanan, Andrew Sunil Rajkumar, and Vinaya Swaroop. 1999. "What Does Aid to Africa Finance?" World Bank Policy Research Working Paper 2092. Washington, D.C.

Devarajan, Shantayanan, and Vinaya Swaroop. 1998. "The Implications of Foreign Aid Fungibility for Development Assistance." World Bank Policy Research Working Paper Series 2022. Washington, D.C.

Di Tella, Rafael, and William D. Savedoff. eds. 2001a. *Diagnosis Corruption: Fraud in Latin America's Public Hospitals* . Washington, D.C.: The Inter-American Development Bank.

Di Tella, Raphael, and William Savedoff. 2001b. *The Corruption That Compromises Health: Studies of Public Hospitals in Latin America.* Washington, D.C.: Inter-American Development Bank.

Di Tella, Raphael, and Ernesto Schargrodsky. Forthcoming. "The Role of Wages and Auditing during a Crackdown on Corruption in the City of Buenos Aires." *Journal of Law and Economics.*

Diaz-Cayeros, Alberto, and Beatriz Magaloni. 2002. "Public Services Mediated by the Political Process." Stanford University: Stanford, C.A. Processed.

————. 2003. "The Politics of Public Spending: Part I - The Logic of Vote Buying. Part II -The Programa Nacional de Solidaridad (PRONASOL) in Mexico." Background paper for the WDR 2004.

Diop, F., A. Yazbeck, and R. Bitran. 1995. "The Impact of Alternative Cost Recovery Schemes on Access and Equity in Niger." *Health Policy and Planning* 10(3):223–40.

Dixit, Avinash. 2000. "Incentives and Organizations in the Public Sector: An Interpretive Review." *Journal of Human Resources* 37(4):696–772.

Dixon, Geoffrey. 2002. "Thailand's 'Hurdle' Approach to Budget Reform." World Bank PREM Note 73. Washington, D.C.

Dollar, David, and Jakob Svensson. 2000. "What Explains the Success or Failure of Structural Adjustment Programmes?" *Economic Journal* 110(466):894–917.

Domenighetti, Gianfranco, Pierangelo Luraschi, Antoine Casabianca, Felix Gutzwiller, Alberto Spinelli, Ennio Pedrinis, and Francesca Repetto. 1988. "Effect of Information Campaign by the Mass Media on Hysterectomy Rates." *The Lancet* 2:1470–3.

Dreze, Jean, and Haris Gazdar. 1996. "Uttar Pradesh: The Burden of Inertia." In Jean Dreze and Amartya Sen, eds., *Indian Development: Selected Regional Perspectives.* New York: Oxford University Press.

Dreze, Jean, and Amartya Sen. 2002. *India: Development and Participation.* Oxford: Oxford University Press.

————. eds. 1991. *The Political Economy of Hunger: Famine Prevention.* Oxford: Clarendon Press.

Dreze, Jean, and Nicholas Stern. 1987. "The Theory of Cost-Benefit Analysis." In A. J. Auerbach and M. Feldstein, eds., *Handbook in Public Economics Vol. 2.* Amsterdam, New York: North-Holland.

Dror, D. M., and A. Preker. 2003. *Social Re-insurance - A New Approach to Sustain Community Health Financing.* Geneva: International Labor Organization.

Duflo, Esther. 2001. "Schooling and Labor Market Consequences of School Construction in Indonesia: Evidence from an Unusual Policy Experiment." *American Economic Review* 91(4):795–813.

Dumol, Mark. 2000. *The Manila Water Concession: A Key Government Official's Diary of the World's Largest Water Privatization.* Washington, D.C.: World Bank.

Dutta, Antara. 2003. "Public Service Delivery: The PROBE and Its Impact." Background paper for the WDR 2004.

Easterly, William, and Ross Levine. 1997. "Africa's Growth Tragedy: Policies and Ethnic Divisions." *Quarterly Journal of Economics* 112(4):1203–50.

Eichler, Rena, Paul Auxilia, and John Pollock. 2001. "Output-Based Health Care: Paying for Performance in Haiti." World Bank, Viewpoint, Note 236. Washington, D.C.

El Salvador Evaluation Team. 1997. "El Salvador's EDUCO Program: A First Report on Parents' Participation in School-Based Management." World Bank Working Paper Series on Impact Evaluation of Education Reforms 4. Washington, D.C. Available on line at http://www.worldbank.org/research/projects/impact.htm.

Erikson, Dan, Annie Lord, and Peter Wolf. 2003. "Cuba's Social Services: A Review of Education, Health, and Sanitation." Background paper for the WDR 2004.

Eriksson, Joh, Alcira Kreimer, and Margaret Arnold. 2000. "El Salvador: Post-Conflict Reconstruction." World Bank Operation Evaluation Department, Country Case Study Series: Washington, D.C.

Eskeland, Gunnar S., and Deon Filmer. 2002. "Autonomy, Participation, and Learning in Argentine Schools." World Bank Policy Research Working Paper 2766. Washington, D.C.

Estévez, Federico, Beatriz Magaloni, and Alberto Diaz-Cayeros. 2002. "The Erosion of One-party Rule: Clientelism, Portfolio Diversification, and Electoral Strategy." Paper presented at the *the 2002 Annual Meetings of the American Political Science Association* Conference. Boston. August.

Evans, A. 2003. "Decentralization: A Review of Staffing Practices in Eight Countries." World Bank: Washington, D.C. Processed.

Evans, Peter. 1996. "Government Action, Social Capital and Development: Reviewing the Evidence on Synergy." *World Development* 24(6):1119–32.

Evans, Peter B., and James E. Rauch. 1999. "Bureaucratic Structure and Bureaucratic Performance in Less Developed Countries." *Journal of Public Economics* 75(1):49–71.

Evans, Peter B., and James Rausch. Forthcoming. "Bureaucracy and Growth: A Cross-National Analysis of the Effects of 'Weberian' State Structures on Economic Growth." *Journal of Public Economics.*

Evers, Pieter. 2003. "Village Governments and Their Communities." World Bank/Bappenas Local Level Institutions Study: Jakarta. Processed.

Faguet, Jean-Paul. 2001. "Does Decentralization Increase Government Responsiveness to Local Needs? Evidence from Bolivia." World Bank Policy Research Working Paper 2516. Washington, D.C.

Ferejohn, John. 1974. *Pork Barrel Politics: Rivers and Harbors Legislation, 1947-1968.* Standford C.A.: Stanford University Press.

Ferejohn, John, and James H. Kuklinsky. eds. 1990. *Information and Democratic Processes.* Urbana: University of Illinois Press.

Ferrinho, P., and W. Van Lerberghe. 2003. "Managing Health Professionals in the Context of Limited Resources: a Fine Line Between Corruption and the Need for Moonlighting." Background paper for the WDR 2004.

Ferriol, Angela, Victoria Perez, Didio Quintana, and Aida Atienza. 2003. "Servicios de Educacion, Salud, Agua y Saneamiento en Cuba." Background paper for the WDR 2004.

Feyziogly, Tarhan, Vinaya Swaroop, and Min Zhu. 1998. "A Panel Data Analysis of the Fungibility of Foreign Aid." *World Bank Economic Review* 12(1):29–58.

Filmer, Deon. 2000. "The Structure of Social Disparities in Education: Gender and Wealth." World Bank Policy Research Working Paper 2268. Washington, D.C.

————. 2002. "Teacher Pay in Indonesia." World Bank: Washington, D.C. Processed.

————. 2003a. "Determinants of Health and Education Outcomes." Background note for the WDR 2004.

————. 2003b. "The Incidence of Public Expenditures on Health and Education." Background paper for the WDR 2004.

Filmer, Deon, Jeffrey S. Hammer, and Lant H. Pritchett. 2000. "Weak Links in the Chain: A Diagnosis of Health Policy in Poor Countries." *World Bank Research Observer* 15(2):199–224.

————. 2002. "Weak Links in the Chain II: A Prescription for Health Policy in Poor Countries." *World Bank Research Observer* 17(1):47–66.

Filmer, Deon, Samuel Lieberman, and David Ariasingam. 2002. "Indonesia and Education for All." World Bank, Development Research Group and Human Development Unit of East Asia Region: Washington, D.C. Processed.

Filmer, Deon, and Lant Pritchett. 1999a. "The Effect of Household Wealth on Educational Attainment: Evidence from 35 Countries." *Population and Development Review* 25(1):85–120.

Filmer, Deon, and Lant H. Pritchett. 1999b. "The Impact of Public Spending on Health: Does Money Matter?" *Social Science and Medicine* 49(10):1309–23.

————. 2001. "Estimating Wealth Effects without Expenditure Data—or Tears: An Application to Educational Enrollments in States of India." *Demography* 38(1):115–132.

Fiorina, Morris P. 1990. "Information and Rationality in Elections." In John Ferejohn and James H. Kuklinsky, eds., *Information and Democratic Processes.* Urbana: University of Illinois Press.

Fiorina, Morris P., and Kenneth Shepsle. 1990. "A Positive Theory of Negative Voting." In John Ferejohn and James H. Kuklinsky, eds., *Information and Democratic Processes.* Urbana: University of Illinois Press.

Fitz-Gibbon, Carol Taylor. 1996. *Monitoring Education: Indicators, Quality and Effectiveness.* London: Cassell.

Foster, Mick. 2000. "New Approaches to Development Cooperation: What Can We Learn from Experience with Implementing Sector-Wide Approaches?" Overseas Development Institute Working Paper 140. London. Available on line at http://www.odi.org.uk/pppg/publications/working_papers/140.html.

Foster, Mick, Adrienne Brown, and Tim Conway. 2000. "Sector Health Approaches for Health Development: A Review of Experience." World Health Organization WHO/GPE/00.1. Geneva.

Foster, S. D. 1990. "Improving the Supply and Use of Essential Drugs in Sub-Saharan Africa." World Bank Policy Research Working Paper 456. Washington, D.C.

Foster, Vivien. 2002. "Ten Years of Water Service Reform in Latin America: Towards an Anglo-French Model." In Paul Seidenstat, David Haarmeyer, and Simon Hakim, eds., *Reinventing Water and Wastewater Systems: Global Lessons for Improving Management.* New York: John Wiley and Sons, Inc.

Fozzard, Adrian, and Mick Foster. 2001. "Changing Approaches to Public Expenditure Management in Low-Income Aid Dependent Countries." United Nations University, World Institute for Development Economic Research Discussion Paper 107. Helsinki.

Frank, Jonas, Federico Starnfeld, and Janos Zimmerman. Forthcoming. "*Linea de Referencia: El Proceso de Descentralización en Argentina, Bolivia, Brasil, Chile, Colombia, Ecuador, Perú y Venezuela.*" Quito: GTZ/CONAM.

Freedom House. 1999. "Democracy' s Century: A Survey of Global Political Change in the 20th Century." Freedom House: New York.

————. 2002. "Freedom in the World 2002." Freedom House: New York.

Frey, Bruno S. 1997. "The Cost of Price Incentives: An Empirical Analysis of Motivation Crowding-Out." *American Economic Review* 87(4):746–55.

Fuentes, Patricio, and Reiko Niimi. 2002. "Motivating Municipal Action for Children: The Municipal Seal of Approval in Ceará, Brazil." *Environment and Urbanisation* 14(2):123–133.

Gachuhi, D. 1999. "The Impact of HIV/AIDS on Education Systems in the Eastern and Southern Africa Region and the Response of Education Systems to HIV/AIDS: Life Skills Programs." Paper presented at the *Sub-Saharan Africa Conference on EFA 2000* Conference. Johannesburg, South Africa. December 21.

Galabawa, J. C. J., F. E. M. K. Senkoro, and A. F. Lwaitama. 2000. *The Quality of Education in Tanzania.* Dar-es-Salaam: Institute of Kiswahili Research.

Galiani, Sebastian, Paul Gertler, and Ernesto Schargrodsky. 2002. "Water for Life: The Impact of the Privatization of Water Services on Child Mortality." Stanford University, Center for Research on Economic Development and Policy Reform Working Paper 154. Stanford.

Galiani, Sebastian, and Ernesto Schargrodsky. 2002. "School Decentralization and Education Quality: The Role of Fiscal Deficits." Universidad de San Andres: Buenos Aires, Argentina. Processed.

Gauri, Varun. 2003. "A Rights-Based Approach to Health Care and Education." Background note for the WDR 2004.

Gauri, Varun, and Ayesha Vawda. 2003. "Vouchers for Basic Education in Developing Countries: A Principal-Agent Perspective." Background paper for the WDR 2004.

Gazdar, Haris. 2000. "State, Community, and Public Schooling—A Political Economy of Universal Education in Pakistan." London School of Economics: London, U.K. Processed.

Gertler, Paul. 2000. "Final Report: The Impact of PROGRESA on Health." International Food Policy Research Institute: Washington, D.C. Available on line at http://www.ifpri.org/.

Gertler, Paul, and Simone Boyce. 2001. "An Experiment in Incentive Based Welfare: The Impact of Mexico's PROGRESA on Health." University of California at Berkeley: Berkeley, C.A. Available on line at http://faculty.haas.berkeley.edu/gertler/. Processed.

Gertler, Paul, and Jeffrey S. Hammer. 1997a. "Financing and Allocating Public Expenditures in the Health Sector." In G. Scheiber and D. Chollet, eds., *Health Reform in Developing Countries.* Washington, D.C.: World Bank.

—————. 1997b. "Strategies for Pricing Publicly Provided Health Services." In George J. Schieber, eds., *Innovations in Health Care Financing: Proceedings of a World Bank Conference.* Washington, D.C.: World Bank.

Gertler, Paul, and John Molyneaux. 1995. "Experimental Evidence on the Effect of Raising User Fees for Publicly Delivered Health Care Services: Utilization, Health Outcomes and Private Provider Response." RAND: Santa Monica, CA. Processed.

GfK Praha—Institute for Market Research. 2001. "Corruption Climate—Central and Eastern Europe: Results of and International Research Project on Corruption in 11 Central and Eastern European Countries." GfK Praha: Prague.

Gibson, John. 2000. "Who's Not in School? Economic Barriers to Universal Primary Education in Papua New Guinea." *Pacific Economic Bulletin* 15(2):46–58.

Gilson, L. 1997. "The Lessons of User Fee Experience in Africa." *Health Policy and Planning* 12(4):273–85.

Gilson, L., D. Kalyalya, F. Kuchler, S. Lake, H. Oranga, and M. Ouendo. 2000. "The Equity Impacts of Community Financing Activities in Three African Countries." *International Journal of Health Planning and Management* 15(4):291–317.

—————. 2001. "Strategies for Promoting Equity: Experience with Community Financing in Three African Countries." *Health Policy* 58(1):37–67.

Girishankar, Navin. 2002. "Institutional Underpinnings of Public Expenditure Management in Malawi: Current Practice, Change Prospects, and Critical Pathways." World Bank: Washington, D.C. Processed.

Glaeser, Edward L., and Andrei Shleifer. 2002. "The Curley Effect." National Bureau of Economic Research Working Paper 8942. Cambridge, Mass.

Glewwe, Paul. 1999. "Why Does Mother's Schooling Raise Child Health in Developing Countries? Evidence from Morocco." *Journal of Human Resources* 34(1):124–59.

Glewwe, Paul, Nauman Ilias, and Michael Kremer. 2000. "Teacher Incentives." University of Minesota, Competitions Economics Inc., and Harvard University: Minesota, W.I. and Cambridge, Mass. Processed.

Glewwe, Paul, M. Kremer, and Sylvie Moulin. 1997. "Textbooks and Test Scores: Evidence from a Prospective Evaluation in Kenya." Harvard University: Cambridge, Mass. Processed.

Glinskaya, Elena, and Jyotsna Jalan. 2003. "Improving Primary School Education in India: An Impact Assesment of DPEP—Phase I." World Bank: Washington, D.C. Processed.

Goetz, Anne-Marie, and John Gaventa. 2001. "Bringing Citizen Voice and Client Focus into Service Delivery." Institute of Development Studies Working Paper 138. Brighton, U.K.

Goetz, Anne-Marie, and Rob Jenkins. 2002. "Voice, Accountability and Human Development: The Emergence of a New Agenda." Background Paper for the HDR 2002, Occasional Paper 2002/4. New York.

Gómez-Lobos, Andrés, and Dante Contreras. 2000. "Subsidy Policies for the Utility Industries: A Comparison of the Chilean and Colombian Water Subsidy Schemes." Universidad de Chile, Departamento de Economía: Santiago de Chile. Processed.

Good, Harry G., and James D. Teller. 1969. *A History of Western Education.* London: Macmillan.

Gorter, A., P. Sandiford, Z. Segura, and C. Villabela. 1999. "Improved Health Care for Sex Workers: A Voucher Program for Female Sex Workers in Nicaragua." *Research for Sex Work 2*

Govindaraj, Ramesh, Christopher J. L. Murray, and Chellaraj Gnanaraj. 1995. "Health Expenditures in Latin America and the Caribbean." World Bank Technical Paper 274. Washington, D.C.

Gradstein, Mark, and Moshe Justman. 2002. "Education, Social Cohesion, and Economic Growth." *American Economic Review* 92(4):1192–1204.

Greaney, Vincent, Shahidur R. Khandker, and Mahmudul Alam. 1999. *Bangladesh: Assessing Basic Learning Skills.* Dhaka, Bangladesh: University Press.

Green, Andy. 1990. *Education and State Formation: The Rise of Education Systems in England, France, and the USA.* New York: St. Martin's Press.

Grindle, Merilee S. Forthcoming. *Despite the Odds: Contentious Politics and Education.* Princeton N.J.: Princeton University Press.

Grossman, Gene, and Elhanan Helpman. 1999. "Competing for Endorsements." *American Economic Review* **89**(3):501–24.

Guasch, J. Luis. 2003. "Concessions of Infrastructure Services: Incidence and Determinants of Renegotiation—An Empirical Evaluation and Guidelines for Optimal Concession Design." World Bank and University of California, San Diego: Washington, D.C. and San Diego, C.A. Processed.

Gundlach, Erich, and Ludger Wößman. 2001. "The Fading Productivity of Schooling in East Asia." *Journal of Asian Economies* 12(3):401–17.

Gundlach, Erich, Ludger Wößman, and Jens Gmelin. 2001. "The Decline of Schooling Productivity in OECD Countries." *Economic Journal* 111(471):C135–C147.

Gunning, Jan Willem. 2001. "Rethinking Aid." In Boris Pleskovic and Nicholas Stern, eds., *Annual World Bank Conference on Development Economics.* Washington, D.C.: World Bank.

Gupta, Sanjeev, Hamid R. Davoodi, and Erwin R. Tiongson. 2002. "Corruption and the Provision of Health Care and Education Services." In George T. Abed and Sanjeev Gupta, eds., *Governance, Corruption and Economic Performance.* Washington, D.C.: The International Monetary Fund.

Gupta, Sanjeev, Marijn Verhoeven, and Erwin R. Tiongson. Forthcoming. "Public Spending on Health Care and the Poor." *Health Economics.*

—————. 2002. "The Effectiveness of Government Spending on Education and Health Care in Developing and Transition Economics." *European Journal of Political Economy* 18(4):717–737.

Gwatkin, D., and M. Guillot. 2000. "The Burden of Disease among the Global Poor: The Current Situation, Future Trends, and Implications for Strategy." World Bank: Washington DC.

Gwatkin, D., S. Rutstein, K. Johnson, R. Pande, and A. Wagstaff. 2000. "Socioeconomic Differences in Health, Nutrition and Population." World Bank, Health, Nutrition and Population Discussion Paper. Washington D.C.

Gwatkin, Davidson, and Others. 2000. "Theme Section: Poverty and Health." *Bulletin of the World Health Organization* 78(1):2–96.

Habyarimana, James, Jishnu Das, Stefan Dercon, and Pramila Krishnan. 2003. "Sense and Absence: Absenteeism and Learning in Zambian Schools." World Bank: Washington, D.C. Processed.

Haddad, L., and S. Gillespie. 2001. "Attacking the Double Burden of Malnutrition in Asia and the Pacific." Asian Development Bank and International Food Policy Research Institute: Manila and Washington, D.C.

Haddad, Salim, and Pierre Fournier. 1995. "Quality, Cost and Utilization of Health Services in Developing Countries. A Longitudinal Study in Zaire." *Social Science and Medicine* 40(6):743–53.

Hadi, A. 2001. "Promoting Health Knowledge through Micro-Credit Programmes: Experience of BRAC in Bangladesh." *Health Promotion International* 16(3):219–28.

Halonen, Maija. 2003. "Coordination Failure in Foreign Aid." Background paper for the WDR 2004.

Hammer, Jeffrey S., and William G. Jack. 2001. "The Design of Incentives for Health Care Providers in Developing Countries: Contracts, Competition and Cost Control." World Bank Policy Research Working Paper 2547. Washington, D.C.

Hammer, Jeffrey S., Ijaz Nabi, and James Cercone. 1995. "The Distributional Impact of Social Sector Expenditures in Malaysia." In D. van de Walle and K. Nead, eds., *Public Spending and the Poor: Theory and Evidence.* Baltimore: Johns Hopkins University Press.

Hanson, K., J. Kamwanga, B. McPake, and F. Ssengooba. 2002. "Towards Improving Hospital Performance in Uganda and Zambia: Reflections and Opportunities for Autonomy." *Health Policy* 61(1):73–94.

Hanson, Kara. 2000. "Implementing Health Sector Reforms in Africa: A Review of Eight Country Experiences." UNICEF; Division of Evaluation, Policy and Planning: Paris.

Hanushek, Eric A. 2002. "Evidence, Politics, and the Class Size Debate." In Mishel Lawrence and Richard Rothstein, eds., *The Class Size Debate.* Washington, D.C.: Economic Policy Institute.

Harrold, Peter, and Associates. 1995. "The Broad Sector Approach to Investment Lending: Sector Investment Programs." World Bank Discussion Paper 302. Washington, D.C.

Hart, Julian. 1971. "The Inverse Care Law." *The Lancet* 360(9328): 405–12.

Hays, Samuel P. 1959. *Conservation and the Gospel of Efficiency: The Progressive Conservation Movement 1890-1920.* Cambridge, Mass.: Harvard University Press.

Hino, T. 1993. "Community Participation in 'Programme de Restructuration de L'Hydraulique Villageoise' in Côte d'Ivoire." Africa Country Department 11. World Bank: Washington, D.C.

Hirschman, Albert O. 1970. *Exit, Voice, and Loyalty: Responses to Declines in Firms, Organizations, and States.* Cambridge. Mass.: Harvard University Press.

Holmes, Malcolm. 2002. "MTEF Synthesis Summary." Overseas Development Institute: London, U.K. Processed.

Holmstrom, Bengt, and Paul Milgrom. 1991. "Multitask Principal-Agent Analysis: Incentive Contracts, Asset Ownership and Job Design." *Journal of Law, Economics and Organization* 7(special issue):24–52.

Hossain, Naomi, and Mick Moore. 2002. "Arguing for the Poor: Elites and Poverty in Developing Countries." Institute of Development Studies Working Paper 148. Brighton, U.K.

Hoxby, C. M. 2000. "The Effects of Class size on Student Achievement: New Evidence from Population Variation." *Quarterly Journal of Economics* 115(4):1239–85.

Hoy, Michael, and Emmanuel Jimenez. 2003. "The Impact on the Urban Environment of Incomplete Property Rights." World Bank: Washington, D.C. Processed.

Hsieh, Chang, and Miguel Urquiola. 2003. "When Schools Compete, How Do They Compete? An Assessment of Chile's Nationwide School Voucher Program." Princeton University and World Bank: Princeton, N.J. and Washington, D.C. Processed.

Hughes, D. 1993. "General Practitioners and the New Contract: Promoting Better Health Through Financial Incentives." *Health Policy* 25:39–50.

Human Settlements Program, International Institute for Environment and Development. 2003. "Local Action for Global Water Goals: Addressing Inadequate Water and Sanitation in Urban Areas, (or the State of the World's Cities: Water and Sanitation)." International Institute for Environment and Development for UN-HABITAT: London, U.K. Processed.

Hunt, Paul. 2002. "The International Human Rights Treaty Obligations of States Parties in the Context of Service Provision." UN Committee on the Rights of the Child: Geneva.

Hutchinson, Paul. 2001. "Combating Illness." In Ritva Reinikka and Paul Collier, eds., *Uganda's Recovery: The Role of Farms, Firms, and Government.* Washington, D.C.: World Bank.

ICM. 2003. "Draft Statement on the Philosophy and Model of Midwifery Care." ICM: Hague, Netherlands. Processed.

IMF. 2002. "Actions to Strengthen the Tracking of Poverty-Reducing Public Spending in Heavily Indebted Poor Countries." International Monetary Fund: Washington, D.C.

IMF, and IDA. 2002. "Review of the Poverty Reduction Strategy Paper (PRSP) Approach: Early Experience with Interim PRSPs and Full PRSPs." International Monetary Fund: Washington, D.C.

Indonesia: Ministry of National Education. 2002. "Indonesia Education at a Glance". Jakarta, Indonesia: Ministry of National Education. Available on line at http://www.depdiknas.go.id/statistik.htm.

Indonesia: Ministry of Religious Affairs. 2002. "Project Lensa". Jakarta, Indonesia: Ministry of Religious Affairs. Available on line at www.depag.net.

Institute For Health Sciences, Kunming Medical College, and World Bank. 2001. "Report on Maternal and Child Health Poverty Alleviation Fund Study in China." Institute for Health Sciences, Kunming Medical College (HIS, KMC) and World Bank. Processed.

International Budget Project. 2000. "A Taste of Success: Examples of the Budget Work of NGOs." International Budget Project of the Center on Budget and Policy Priorities: Washington, D.C.

International Energy Agency. 2002. "Energy and Poverty." In International Energy Agency, eds., *World Energy Outlook 2002.* Paris: International Energy Agency.

International Labor Organization (ILO). 2002. "Social Dialogue in the Health Services: Institutions, Capacity and Effectiveness." International Labor Organization: Geneva. Available on line at http://www.ilo.org/public/english/dialogue/sector/techmeet/jmhs02/jmhs-r.pdf.

International Labour Organization. 2001. "The Impact of Decentralization and Privatization on Municipal Services." International Labor Organization: Geneva.

International Monetary Fund, and World Bank. 2003. "Progress Report and Critical Steps in Scaling Up: Education for All, Health, HIV/AIDS, Water and Sanitation." Development Committee (Joint Ministerial Committee of the Boards of Governors of the Bank and the Fund on the Transfers of Real Resources to Developing Countries): Washington, D.C.

Irwin, Timothy. 2003. "Free-Entry Competition in Infrastructure as a Response to Poor Governance." World Bank: Washington, D.C. Processed.

Iyer, Parameswaran. 2002. "Willingness to Charge and Willingness to Pay: The World Bank-assisted China rural Water Supply and Sanitation Program." *Water and Sanitation Program, Field Note*

Jacobson, Charles D., and Joel A. Tarr. 1996. "No Single Path: Ownership and Financing of Infrastructure in the 19th and 20th Centuries." In Ashoka Mody, eds., *Infrastructure Delivery: Private Initiative and the Public Good.* Washington, D.C.: World Bank.

Jaffré, Y., J.-P. Olivier, and Olivier de Sardan. eds. 2002. *Les Dysfonctionnements des Systèmes de Soins. Rapport du Volet Socio-anthropologique. Enquêtes sur l'Accès aux Soins dans 5 Capitales d'Afrique de l'Ouest.* Marseille: UNICEF-Coopération Francaise.

Jaffré, Y., and A. Prual. 1993. "Le Corps des Sages Femmes, Entre Identités Sociales et Professionnelles." *Sciences Sociales et Sante* XI(2):63–80.

Jaffré, Yannick, and Alain Prual. 1994. "Midwives in Niger: An Uncomfortable Position between Social Behaviors and Health Care Constraints." *Social Science and Medicine* 38(8):1069–1073.

Janovsky, K. 2002. "Review of Experiences in Health Services Decentralization." World Health Organization: Geneva.

Jayasuriya, Ruwan, and Quentin Wodon. 2002. "Explaining Country Efficiency in Improving Health and Education Indicators: The Role of Urbanization." World Bank: Washington, D.C. Processed.

Jenkins, Rob, and Anne-Marie Goetz. 1999. "Accounts and Accountability: Theoretical Implications of the Right-to-Information Movement in India." *Third World Quarterly* 20(3):603–22.

———. 2002. "Civil Society Engagement and India's Public Distribution System: Lessons from the Rationing Kruti Samiti in Mumbai." Paper presented at the the *WDR Conference on Making Services Work for Poor People* Conference. Eynsham Hall, Oxfordshire. November.

Jimenez, Emmanuel, and Yasuyuki Sawada. 1999. "Do Community-Managed Schools Work? An Evaluation of El Salvador's EDUCO Program." *World Bank Economic Review* 13(3):415–441.

———. 2002. "Does Community Management Help Keep Kids in Schools? Evidence using Panel Data from El Salvador's EDUCO Program." World Bank: Washington, D.C. Processed.

Jones, Stephen. 1997. "Sector Investment Programs in Africa: Issues and Experience." World Bank Technical Paper 374. Washington, D.C.

Jones, Stephen, and Andrew Lawson. 2001. "Moving from Projects to Programmatic Aid." World Bank Operation Evaluation Department, OED Working Paper Series 5. Washington, D.C.

Jongudomsuk, Pongpisut, Jadej Thammatuch-aree, and Prae Chittinanda. 2002. "Pro-Poor Health Financing Schemes in Thailand: A Review of Country Experience and Lessons Learned." Bureau of Health and Planning, MOPH, Thailand: Bangkok. Processed.

Jonsson, Bengt, and Phillip Musgrove. 1997. "Government Financing of Health Care." In G. Schieber, eds., *Innovations in Health Care.* Washington, D.C.: World Bank Discussion Paper 365.

Joshi, Anuradha, and Mick Moore. 2000. "The Mobilization Potential of Anti-Poverty Programmes." Institute of Development Studies Discussion Paper 374. Brighton, U.K.

Kalter, Henry. 2003. "Global Health Funds." Background paper for the WDR 2004.

Kanbur, Ravi, and Todd Sandler. 1999. "The Future of Development Assistance: Common Pools and International Public Goods." Overseas Development Council, Policy Essay 25. Baltimore.

Kapur, Devesh, and Richard Webb. 2000. "Governance-Related Conditionalities of the International Financial Institutions." United Nations and Center for International Development Harvard University; G-24 Discussion Paper 6. New York and Boston.

Kaufmann, Daniel, Sanjay Pradhan, and Randy S. Ryterman. 1998. "New Frontiers in Diagnosing and Combating Corruption." World Bank PREM Note 7. Washington, D.C.

Keefer, Philip. 2002. "Clientelism, Credibility, and Democracy." World Bank: Washington, D.C. Processed.

———. 2003. "Personal Communication." World Bank: Washington, D.C. Processed.

Keefer, Philip, and Stuti Khemani. 2003. "The Political Economy of Social Service Provision." Background paper for the WDR 2004.

Kelly, Michael J. 1999. "The Impact of HIV/AIDS on Schooling in Zambia." Paper presented at the *XIth International Conference on AIDS and STDs in Africa* Conference.

———. 2000. "Planning for Education in the Context of HIV/AIDS." UNESCO, International Institute for Educational Planning: Paris.

Khemani, Stuti. Forthcoming. "Political Cycles in a Developing Economy: Effect of Elections in the Indian States." *Journal of Development Economics.*

———. 2003. "Partisan politics and Intergovernmental Transfers in India." World Bank: Washington, D.C. Processed.

King, Elizabeth, Estelle James, and A. Suriyadi. 1996. "Finance, Management and Costs of Public and Private Schools in Indonesia." *Economics of Education Review* 15(4):387–98.

King, Elizabeth, and Berk Ozler. 2002. "What's Decentralization Got To Do with Learning? Endogenous School Quality and Student Performance in Nicaragua." World Bank, Development Research Group: Washington, D.C. Available on line at http://www.worldbank.org/research/projects/impact.htm. Processed.

Kizilbash, Hamid H. 1998. "Teaching Teachers to Teach." In Pervez Hoodbhoy, eds., *Education and the State: Fifty Years of Pakistan.* Karachi: Oxford University Press.

Kleemeier, Elizabeth. 2000. "The Impact of Participation on Sustainability: An Analysis of the Malawi Rural Piped Scheme Program." *World Development* 28(5):929–44.

Klein, Michael, and Neil Roger. 1994. "Back to the Future: The Potential in Infrastructure Privatisation." In Richard O'Brien, eds., *Finance and the International Economy.* Oxford, U.K.: Oxford University Press.

Knack, Stephen. 2001. "Does Foreign Aid Promote Democracy?" University of Maryland, IRIS Center Working Paper 238. College Park, Md.

Knack, Stephen, and Aminur Rahman. 2003. "Aid Intensity, Donor Fragmentation and the Quality of Governance." Background paper for the WDR 2004.

Knippenberg, Rudolf, Eusebe Alihonou, Agnes Soucat, Kayode Oyegbite, Maria Calivis, Ian Hopwood, Reiko Niimi, Mamadou Pathe Diallo, Mamadou Conde, and Samuel Ofosu-Amaah. 1997. "Implementation of the Bamako Initiative: strategies in Benin and Guinea." *International Journal of Health Planning and Management* 12 Suppl 1:S29–S47.

Koenen-Grant, Julie, and Harry Garnett. 1996. "Improving Policy Formulation in Zambia." Implementing Policy Change Project Case Study 2. Washington, D.C.

Koenig, Michael A., Gillian H. C. Foo, and Ketan Joshi. 2000. "Quality of Care within the Indian Family Welfare Programme: A Review of Recent Evidence." *Studies in Family Planning* 31(1):1–18.

Kremer, Michael. 2002. "Innovations and Donor Assistance." University of Maryland, IRIS: College Park, Md. Processed.

Kremer, Michael, and Andrei Sarychev. 2000. "Why Do Governments Operate Schools?" Harvard University: Cambridge, Mass. Available on line at http://post.economics.harvard.edu/faculty/kremer/papers.html. Processed.

Kunfaa, Ernest Y., and Tony Dogbe. 2002. "Empty Pockets." In Deepa Narayan and Patti Petesch, eds., *Voices of the Poor: From Many Lands.* New York: World Bank and Oxford University Press.

Kusek, Jody, Ray Rist, and Elyzabeth White. 2003. "How Will We Know the Millennium Development Goal Results When We See Them?" World Bank: Washington, D.C. Processed.

Kutzin, Joseph. 2003. "Health Expenditures, Reforms and Policy Priorities for the Kyrgyz Republic." MANAS Health Policy, Policy Research Paper 24. Bishkek,Kyrgyztan.

Ladd, Helen F. 2002. "School Vouchers: A Critical View." *Journal of Economic Perspectives* 16(4):3–24.

Lakshman, M, and Mark Nichter. 2001. "Contamination of Medicine Injection Paraphernalia Used by Registered Medical Practitioners in South India: An Ethnographic Study." *Social Science and Medicine* 51:11–28.

Lamboray, Jean Louis. 2000. "HIV and Health Reform in Phayao: From Crisis to Opportunity." UNAIDS: Geneva. Available on line at http://www.unaids.org/publications/documents/care/general/una0004e.pdf.

Langsten, Ray, and Kenneth Hill. 1995. "Treatment of Childhood Diarrhea in Rural Egypt." *Social Science and Medicine* 40(7):989–1001.

Lanjouw, Peter, and Martin Ravallion. 1999. "Benefit Incidence, Public Spending Reforms and the Timing of Program Capture." *The World Bank Economic Review* 13(2):257–73.

Lazear, Edward P. 2000. "The Future of Personnel Economics." *Economic Journal* 110(467):F611–39.

Le Houerou, Philippe, and Robert Taliercio. 2002. "Medium Term Expenditure Frameworks: From Concept to Practice. Preliminary Lessons from Africa." World Bank, Africa Region Working Paper 28. Washington, D.C.

Leonard, Kenneth L. 2002. "When Both States and Markets Fail: Asymmetric Information and the Role of NGOs in African Health Care." *International Review of Law and Economics* 22(1):61–80.

Leonard, Kenneth L., Gilbert R. Mliga, and Damen Haile Mariam. 2002. "Bypassing Health Centers in Tanzania: Revealed Preferences for Observable and Unobservable Quality." *Journal of African Economies* 11(4):441–71.

Levy, Santiago, and Evelyne Rodríguez. 2002. "El Programa de Educación, Salud y Alimentación de México, Progresa." Instituto Mexicano del Seguro Social y Secretaría de Hacienda y Crédito Público: Ciudad de Mexico, Mexico. Processed.

Levy-Bruhl, Daniel, Agnes Soucat, Raimi Osseni, Jean-Michel Ndiaye, Boubacar Dieng, Bethune Xavier De, Alpha Telli Diallo, Mamadou Conde, Mohamed Cisse, Yarou Moussa, Kandjoura Drame, and Rudolf Knippenberg. 1997. "The Bamako Initiative in Benin and Guinea: Improving the Effectiveness of Primary Health Care." *International Journal of Health Planning and Management* 12 Suppl 1:S49–S79.

Lewis, Bernard. 1961. *The Emergence of Modern Turkey.* Oxford, U.K.: Oxford University Press.

Lewis, Maureen. 2000. *Who is Paying for Health Care in Eastern Europe and Central Asia?* Washington, D.C.: World Bank, Europe and Central Asia Region, Human Development Unit.

Lewis, Maureen, Gunnar S. Eskeland, and Ximena Traa-Valerezo. 1999. "Challenging El Salvador's Rural Health Care Strategy." World Bank Policy Research Working Paper 2164. Washington D.C.

Lewis, Maureen A., Gerald M. La Forgia, and Margaret B. Sulvetta. 1996. "Measuring Public Hospital Costs: Empirical Evidence from the Dominican Republic." *Social Science and Medicine* 43(2):221–34.

Liang, Xiaoyan. 1999. "Teacher Pay in 12 Latin American Countries: How Does Teacher Pay Compare to other Professions, What Determines Teacher Pay, and Who are the Teachers?" World Bank, Human Development Department, LCSHD Paper Series 49. Washington, D.C.

Lieberman, Samuel. 2003. "The Role of Government in Influencing Child Health, Saving Lives." Background paper for "Working Together to Accelerate Progress Towards the Health and Nutrition Millennium Development Goals". World Bank: Washington, D.C. Processed.

Liese, B., and and others. 2003. "Human Resources Crisis in Health Services in Sub-Saharan Africa." Background paper for the WDR 2004.

Lindelow, M., P. Ward, and N. Zorzi. 2003. "Expenditure Tracking and Service Delivery Survey: The Health Sector in Mozambique. Report on Preliminary Findings." World Bank: Washington, D.C. Processed.

Lisulo, Angela. 2003. "Costa Rica: Health Policies." Background paper for the WDR 2004.

Litvack, J. I., and C. Bodart. 1993. "User Fees Plus Quality Equals Improved Access to Health Care: Results of a Field Experiment in Cameroon." *Social Science and Medicine* 37(3):369–83.

Litvack, Jennie, Junaid Ahmad, and Richard Bird. 1998. "Rethinking Decentralization in Developing Countries." World Bank Sector Studies Series September 1998. Washington, D.C.

Lloyd, Cynthia B., Sahar El Tawila, Wesley H. Clark, and Barbara S. Mensch. 2001. "Determinants of Educational Attainment among Adolescents in Egypt: Does School Quality Make a Difference?" Population Council Policy Research Division Working Papers 150. New York.

Lobo, Albert, and Suresh Balakrishnan. 2002. "Report Card on Service of Bhoomi Kiosks." Public Affairs Centre: Bangalore, India. Processed.

Lorrain, Dominique. 1992. "The French Model of Urban Services." *West European Politics* 15(2):77–92.

Lott, John R. Jr. 1999. "Public Schooling, Indoctrination, and Totalitarianism." *Journal of Political Economy* 107(6):S127–S157.

Lundberg, Paul. 2002. "A Comparison of Decentralization in Pakistan and Nepal." Paper presented at the the *2nd International Conference on Decentralization* Conference. Manila. June 25.

Mackey, Jo Ann. 2002. "Using a Health Belief Model in Teaching Preventive Health Care Principles to Israeli RN's." Paper presented at the *CITA Conference* Conference. University of Massachusetts. November.

Mackinnon, John. 2003. "How Does Aid Affect the Quality of Public Expenditure? What We Know and What We Do not Know." Background paper for the WDR 2004.

Macy, J., and R. Quick. 2002. "The Safe Water System - A Household-Based Water Quality Intervention Program for the Developing World." *Water Conditioning and Purification Magazine* 44(4):—.

Madaus, G. F., and V. Greaney. 1985. "The Irish Experience in Competency Testing: Implications for American Education." *American Journal of Education* 93(2):268–94.

Maiga, Z., Traore Nafo F., and A. El Abassi. 1999. "La Reforme du Secteur Sante au Mali." *Studies in Health Services Organisation & Policy* 12:132–132.

Makinen, M., H. Waters, M. Rauch, N. Almagambetova, R. Bitran, L. Gilson, D. McIntyre, S. Pannarunothai, A. L. Prieto, G. Ubilla, and S. Ram. 2000. "Inequalities in Health Care Use and Expenditures: Empirical Data from Eight Developing Countries and Countries in Transition." *Bulletin of the World Health Organization* 78(1):55–65.

Mamdani, Mahmood. 1996. *Citizen and Subject: Contemporary Africa and the Legacy of Late Colonialism.* Princeton, N.J.: Princeton University Press.

Manning, N. 1998. "Unbundling the State Autonomous agencies and Service Delivery." World Bank: Washington, D.C. Processed.

Manning, Nick. 2001. "The legacy of the New Public Management in Developing Countries." *International Review of Administrative Sciences* 67:297–312.

Manning, Nick, and Neil Parison. 2003. "Building on Strengths: Lessons from Comparative Public Administration Reforms." Higher School of Economics and World Bank: Moscow. Processed.

Manor, James. 2002. "Partnerships between Governments and Civil Society for Service Delivery in Less Developed Countries: Cause for Concern." Paper presented at the the *WDR Conference on Making Services Work for Poor People* Conference. Eynsham Hall, Oxfordshire. November.

Mansuri, Ghazala, and Vijayendra Rao. 2003. "Evaluating Community Driven Development: A Critical Review of the Research." World Bank: Washington, D.C. Processed.

Marchant, T. J., Armstrong Schellenberg J.R.M., T. Edgar, R. Nathan, S. Abdulla, O. Musaka, H. Mponda, and C. Lengeler. 2002. "Socially Marketed Insecticide-Treated Nets Improve Malaria and Anaemia in Pregnancy in Southern Tanzania." *Tropical Medicine and International Health* 7(2):149–58.

Marek, T., I. Diallo, B. Ndiaye, and J. Rakotosalama. 1999. "Successful Contracting of Preventions Services: Fighting Malnutrition in Senegal and Madagascar." *Health Policy and Planning* 14(4): 382–89.

Martens, Bertin, Uwe Mummert, Peter Murrell, and Paul Seabright. 2002. *The Institutional Economics of Foreign Aid.* Cambridge, U.K.: Cambridge University Press.

Masud, Mohammad O. 2002. "Co-producing Citizen Security: The Citizen-Police Liaison Committee in Karachi." Institute of Development Studies Working Paper 172. Brighton, U.K.

Mauro, Paulo. 1998. "Corruption and the Composition of Government Expenditures." *Journal of Public Economics* 69:263–79.

Mayer, Elizabeth Ann. 1997. "Only Very Few Girls Even Start to Go to School in Yemen." *Women's International Network News* 23(3): 52–52.

McPake, B. 1996. "Public Autonomous Hospitals in Sub-Saharan Africa: Trends and Issues." *Health Policy* 35(2):155–77.

McPake, Barbara, Delius Asiimwe, Francis Mwesigye, Matthius Ofumbi, Pieter Streefland, and Asaph Turinde. 2000. "Coping Strategies of Health Workers in Uganda." In Paulo Ferrinho and Wim Van Lerberghe, eds., *Providing Health Care Under Adverse Conditions: Health Personnel Performance and Individual Coping Strategies (Studies in Health Services and Organization, 16).* Antwerp, Belgium: ITG Press.

Medina, Luis Fernando, and Susan Stokes. 2002. "Clientelism as Political Monopoly." Paper presented at the the *2002 Annual Meetings of the American Political Science Association* Conference. Boston. August 29.

Mehrotra, S., and S. W. Jarrett. 2002. "Improving Basic Health Service Delivery in Low-Income Countries: 'Voice' to the Poor." *Social Science and Medicine* 54(11):1685–90.

Mehryar, A. H., A. Aghajanian, and S. Ahmadnia. 2003. "Primary Health Care and Rural Poverty Eradication in the Islamic Republic of Iran." Background paper for the WDR 2004.

Mencher, Joan. 1980. "The Lessons and Non-lessons of Kerala: Agricultural Labourers and Poverty." *Economic and Political Weekly* 15(41-43):1784–802.

Mesoamerica Nutrition Program Targeting Study Group. 2002. "Targeting Performance of Three Large Scale, Nutrition Oriented Social Programs in Central America and Mexico." *Food Nutrition Bulletin* 23(2):162–74.

Meyer, C. A. 1995. "Opportunism and NGOs Entrepreneurship and Green North-South Transfers." *World Development* 23(8):1277–89.

Miguel, Edward, and Michael Kremer. 2001. "Worms: Education and Health Externalities in Kenya." National Bureau of Economic Research Working Paper Series 8481. Cambridge, Mass.

Miguel, Szekely. 1998. *The Economics of Poverty, Inequality, and Wealth Accumulation in Mexico.* New York: St. Martin's Press.

Millot, Benoit, and Julia Lane. 2002. "The Efficient Use of Time in Education." *Education Economics* 10(2):209–28.

Mills, A., and J. Bromberg. 1998. "Experiences of Contracting: An Overview of the Literature." World Health Organization 33. Geneva.

Mills, A., J. Broomberg, and C. Hongoro. 1997. "Improving the Efficiency of District Hospitals: Is Contracting an Option?" *Tropical Medicine and International Health* 2:116–26.

Mills, A., R. Brugha, K. Hanson, and B. McPake. 2002. "Approaches for Improving Delivery in the Non-State Sector: What Is the Evidence on What Works, Where and Why?" Paper presented at the *Making Services Work for the Poor* Conference. Eynsham Hall, Oxfordshire. November 4.

Mingat, Alain. 2003. "Management of Education Systems in Sub-Saharan African Countries: A Diagnostic and Ways towards Improvement in the Context of the EFA-FTI." World Bank: Washington, D.C. Processed.

Ministère de la Santé Bénin. 2003. "Revue des Dépenses Publiques dans le Secteur de la Santé." Ministère de la Santé Bénin: Porto-Novo.

Ministry of Education Ethiopia. 2000. "Alternate Routes to Basic Primary Education." Ministry of Education: Addis Ababa.

Ministry of Health Guinea. 2002. "Guinea, A Country Status Report on Health and Poverty, Health, Nutrition, and Population Inputs for the PRSP and HIPC Process." Ministry of Health Guinea: Conakry.

Mintz, Patricia, William D. Savedoff, and Jorge Pancorvo. 2000. "Bolivia: PROSALUD and the Insurance Program for Mothers and Children (SNMN)." World Bank: Washington, D.C.

Mizala, Alejandra, and Pilar Romaguera. 2000. "School Performance and Choice." *Journal of Human Resources* 35(2):392–417.

————. 2002. "Evaluacion del Desempeño e Incentivos en la Educación Chilena." *Cuadernos de Economía* 39(118):353–94.

Moens, F. 1990. "Design, Implementation and Evaluation of Community Financing Schemes for Hospital Care in Developing Countries: A Prepaid Health Plan in Bwamanda Health Zone, Zire." *Social Science and Medicine* 30(12):1319–27.

Molyneaux, Jack, and Paul Gertler. 1999. "Evaluating the Impact of IDT." The RAND Corporation: Santa Monica, C.A. Processed.

Moore, Mark H., David Thacher, Andrea Dodge, and Tobias Moore. 2002. "Recognizing Public Value in Policing: The Challenge of Measuring Police Performance." Policy Executive Research Forum: Washington, D.C.

Moore, Mick, and James Putzel. 2001. "Thinking Strategically about Politics and Poverty." Institute of Development Studies Working Paper 101. Brighton, U.K.

Mtemeli, D. N. 1994. "An Investigation into Why Women in Mutasa District Prefer to Deliver at Home and Not in Health Institutions." Provincial Medical Direction: Manicaland, Zimbabwe. Processed.

Murnane, Richard J., and David K. Cohen. 1986. "Merit Pay and the Evaluation Problem: Why Most Merit Pay Plans Fail and a Few Survive." *Harvard Educational Review* 56(1):1–17.

Murphy, Paud, Carla Bertoncino, and Lianqin Wang. 2002. "Achieving Universal Primary Education in Uganda: The 'Big-Bang' Approach." World Bank, Human Development Network, Education Notes: Washington, D.C.

Musgrave, Richard. 1959. *The Theory of Public Finance: A Study in Public Economy.* New York: McGraw-Hill.

Nag, Moni. 1989. "Political Awareness as a Factor in Accessibility of Health Services: A Case Study of Rural Kerala and West Bengal." *Economic and Political Weekly* 24(8):417–26.

Nahar, S., and A. Costello. 1998. "The Hidden Cost of 'Free' Maternity Care in Dhaka, Bangladesh." *Health Policy and Planning* 13(4):417–22.

Naimoli, Joseph, and Denise Vaillancourt. 2003. "Performance-Based Management in an Evolving Decentralized Public Health System in West Africa: The Case of Burkina Faso." Background paper for the WDR 2004.

Narayan, Deepa. eds. 2002. *Empowerment and Poverty Reduction: A Sourcebook.* Washington, D.C.: World Bank.

Narayan, Deepa, Robert Chambers, Meera Kaul Shah, and Patti Petesch. 2000a. *Crying out for Change: Voices of the Poor.* New York: Oxford University Press for the World Bank.

Narayan, Deepa, Raj Patel, Kai Schafft, Anne Rademacher, and Sarah Koch-Schulte. 2000b. *Voices of the Poor: Can Anyone Hear Us?* New York: Oxford University Press.

Narayan, Deepa, and Patti Pettesch. eds. 2002. *From Many Lands: Voices of the Poor.* Washington, D.C.: World Bank and Oxford University Press.

National Democratic Institute for International Affairs, and World Bank. 1998. "Promoviendo Transparencia y Gobernabilidad: Experiencias en la República Argentina, Colombia y los Estados Unidos." National Democratic Institute for International Affairs and World Bank: Buenos Aires.

Nauman, Huma. 1990. "Primary Teacher Certificate Program in NWFP: A Study." Project BRIDGES, HIID: Cambridge, Mass.

Navarro, Juan Carlos, and Rafael de la Cruz. 1998. "Federal State and Nonprofit Schools in Venezuela." In William D. Savedoff, eds., *Organization Matters: Agency Problems in Health and Education in Latin America.* Washington, D.C.: Inter American Development Bank.

Nelson, Joan. 2000. *The Politics of Social Sector Reforms.* Washington, D.C.: Overseas Development Council.

Newman, John, Menno Pradhan, Laura B. Rawlings, Geert Ridder, Ramiro Coa, and Jose Luis Evia. 2002. "An Impact Evaluation of Education, Health and Water Supply Investments by the Bolivian Social Investment Fund." *World Bank Economic Review* 16(2):241–74.

Nichols, Len M., Nicholas Prescott, and Kai Hong Phua. 1997. "Medical Savings Accounts for Developing Countries." In George J. Schieber, eds., *Innovations in Health Care Financing: Proceedings of a World Bank Conference.* Washington, D.C.: World Bank.

Nickson, Andrew, and Claudia Vargas. 2002. "The Limitations of Water Regulation: The Failure of the Cochabamba Concession in Bolivia." *Bulletin of Latin American Research* 21(1):99–120.

Nieves, I., Gerard M. La Forgia, and Jaume Ribera. 2000. "Guatemala: Large-Scale Government Contracting of NGO's to Extend Basic Health Services to Poor Populations in Guatemala." World Bank. Washington DC. Available on line at www.worldbank.org.

Nitayaramphong, S., S. Srivanichakom, and Y. Pongsupap. 2000. "Strategies to Respond to Health Manpower Needs in Rural Thailand." *Studies in Health Services Organisation & Policy* 16:55–72.

NRI and World Bank. 2003. "Public Expenditure and Service Delivery in Papua New Guinea: Draft." World Bank: Washington, D.C.

O'Connell, Stephen A., and Charles C. Saludo. 2001. "Aid Intensity in Africa." *World Development* 29(9):1527–52.

O'Connor, Thomas H. 1995. *The Boston Irish: A Political History.* Boston: Northeastern University Press.

OECD. 2001. "Knowledge and Skills for Life: First Results from PISA 2000." OECD: Paris.

Olson, Mancur. 1971. *The Logic of Collective Action: Public Goods and the Theory of Groups.* Cambridge, Mass.: Harvard University Press.

Onyango-Ouma, Washington, Rose Laisser, Musiba Mbilima, Margaret Araoye, Patricia Pittman, Irene Agyepong, Mairo Zakari, Sharon Fonn, Marcel Tanner, and Carol Vlassof. 2001. "An Evaluation of Health Workers for Change in Seven Settings: A Useful Management and Health System Development Tool." *Health Policy and Planning* 16(Sup. 1):24–32.

Organization for Economic Cooperation and Development. 2001. "Knowledge and Skills for Life: First Results from PISA 2000." Organisation for Economic Cooperation and Development: Paris.

Ostrom, Elinor. 1990. *Governing the Commons.* New York: Cambridge University Press.

Ostrom, Elinor, Clark Gibson, Sujai Shivakumar, and Krister Anderson. 2001. "Aid Incentives and Sustainability: An Institutional Analysis of Development Cooperation." SIDA Studies in Evaluation 02/01. Stockholm, Sweden.

Ottaway, M, and T. Chung. 1999. "Debating Democracy Assistance: Toward a New Paradigm." *Journal of Democracy* 10(4):99–128.

Pakistan Institute for Environment Development Action, and Project Management Team. 1994. "The State of the Public Sector Primary Health Care Services, District Sheikhupura, Punjab, Pakistan." Bamako Initiative technical report series, UNICEF 31.

Pannarunothai, S., and A. Mills. 1997. "The Poor Pay More: Health-Related Inequality in Thailand." *Social Science and Medicine* 44(12):1781–90.

Pannarunothai, S., S. Srithamrongsawat, M. Kongpan, and P. Thumvanna. 2000. "Financing Reforms for the Thai Health Card Scheme." *Health Policy and Planning* 15(3):303–11.

Papua New Guinea Office of National Planning. 1999. "Papua New Guinea Human Development Report 1998." Government of Papua New Guinea and United Nations Development Program: Port Moresby, Papua New Guinea.

Parker, Ronald, and Tauno Skytta. 2000. "Rural Water Projects: Lessons from OED Evaluations." World Bank Operations Evaluation Department, Working Paper Series 3. Washington, D.C.

Pathmanathan, Indra, Jerker Liljestrand, Jo M. Martins, Lalini Rajapaksa, Craig Lissner, Amala de Silva, Swarna Selvaraju, and Prabha Joginder Singh. 2003. *Investing Effectively in Maternal Health in Malaysia and Sri Lanka.* Washington D.C.: World Bank.

Paul, Samuel. 2002. *Holding the State to Account: Citizen Monitoring in Action.* Bangalore: Books for Change.

Paxson, Christina, and Norbert A. Schady. 2002. "The Allocation and Impact of Social Funds: Spending on School Infrastructure in Peru." *World Bank Economic Review* 16(2):297–319.

Pearson, Mark, and Paolo Carlo Belli. 2003. "The Impact of Resource Allocation Mechanisms, and Priority Setting Policies to Improve Services for the Poor." Background paper for the WDR 2004.

Perry, H., N. Robinson, D. Chavez, O. Taja, C. Hilari, D. Shanklin, and J. Wyon. 1999. "Attaining Health for All through Community Partnerships: Principles of the Census-Based, Impact-Oriented (CBIO) Approach to Primary Health Care Developed in Bolivia, South America." *Social Science and Medicine* 48(8):1053–67.

Persson, Torsten, and Guido Tabellini. 2000. *Political Economics: Explaining Public Policy.* Cambridge, Mass.: MIT Press.

Peters, David H., Abdo S. Yazbeck, Adam Wagstaff, G. N. V. Ramana, Lant Pritchett, and Rashmi R. Sharma. 2003. *Better Health Systems for India's Poor: Findings, Analysis and Options.* Washington, D.C.: World Bank.

Picazo, Oscar F. 2002. "Better Health Outcomes from Limited Resources: Focusing on Priority Services in Malawi." World Bank, Africa Region Human Development Working Paper Series. Washington, D.C.

Platteau, Jean-Philippe. 2003. "Rushing to Help the Poor Through Participation May Be Self-Defeating." Paper presented at the the *WDR Conference on Making Services Work for Poor People* Conference. Berlin, Germany. July.

Platteau, Jean-Philippe, and Frederic Gaspart. 2003. "The 'Elite Capture' Problem in Participatory Development." Centre for Research on the Economics of Development, University of Namur: Namur, Belgium. Processed.

Plummer, Janelle. 2003. "Independent Providers in Water and Sanitation." World Bank, draft note prepared for the Water and Sanitation Program: Washington, D.C. Processed.

Population Services International. 2003. "Profiles." Population Services International: Washington D.C. Available on line at http://www.psi.org/resources/profiles.html.

Porignon, D., E. M. Soron'Gane, T. E. Lokombe, D. K. Isu, P. Hennart, and W. Van Lerberghe. 1998. "How Robust Are District Health Systems? Coping with Crisis and Disasters in Rutshuru, Democratic Republic of Congo." *Tropical Medicine and International Health* 3(7):559–65.

Preker, A. S., G. Carrin, D. Dror, M. Jakab, W. Hsiao, and D. Arhin. 2001. "Role of Communities in Resource Mobilization and Risk Sharing: A Synthesis Report." World Bank, HNP Discussion Paper. Washington DC.

Prendergast, Carnice. 2001. "Selection and Oversight in the Public Sector, with the Los Angeles Police Department as an Example." National Bureau of Economic Research Working Paper 8664. Cambridge, Mass.

Price, N. 2001. "The Performance of Social Marketing in Reaching the Poor and Vulnerable in AIDS Control Programmes." *Health Policy and Planning* 16(3):231–39.

Pritchett, Lant. Forthcoming. "It Pays to Be Ignorant." *Journal of Policy Reform.*

Pritchett, Lant, and Duriya Farooqui. 2003. "The Economics of Education Reeducated." Kennedy School of Government and Center for Global Development: Cambridge, Mass. Processed.

Pritchett, Lant, and Deon Filmer. 1999. "What Education Production Functions Really Show: A Positive Theory of Education Expenditure." *Economics of Education Review* 18(2):223–39.

Pritchett, Lant, and Michael Woolcock. 2002. "Solutions When the Solution is the Problem: Arraying the Disarray in Development." Center for Global Development Working Paper 10. Washington, D.C.

Pritchett, Lant H. 2002. "When Will They Ever Learn? Why All Governments Produce Schooling." John F. Kennedy School of Government, Harvard University: Cambridge, Mass. Processed.

Pritchett, Lant H., and Lawrence H. Summers. 1996. "Wealthier is Healthier." *The Journal of Human Resources* 31(4):841–68.

Probe Qualitative Research Team. 2002. "Healthcare Seeking Behavior in Andhra Pradesh." Probe Qualitative Research: Bombay.

PROBE Team in association with Centre for Development Economics. 1999. *Public Report on Basic Education in India.* New Delhi: Oxford University Press.

Prud'homme, Remy. 1995. "The Dangers of Decentralization." *World Bank Research Observer* 10(2):201–20.

Psacharopoulos, Georges, Jorge Valenzuela, and Mary Arends. 1996. "Teacher Salaries in Latin America: A Review." *Economics of Education Review* 15(4):401–6.

Public Services International, and Education International. 2000. "Improving the Effectiveness of the Public Sector—If Not Us, Who?" Public Services International and Education International: Paris and Brussels. Available on line at http://www.world-psi.org.

Putnam, Robert, Robert Leonardi, and Raffaella Nanetti. 1992. *Making Democracy Work: Civic Traditions in Modern Italy.* Princeton N.J.: Princeton University Press.

Radoki, Carole. 2003. "What Are the Most Effective Strategies for Understanding and Channeling the Preferences of Service Users to Make Public Services More Responsive." Background paper for the WDR 2004.

Raghupati, Usha, and Vivien Foster. 2003. "A Scorecard for India, Tariffs and Subsidies in South Asia." World Bank, PPIAF and Water and Sanitation Program Paper 2. Washington, D.C.

Rajkumar, Andrew Sunil, and Vinaya Swaroop. 2002. "Public Spending and Outcomes: Does Governance Matter?" World Bank Policy Research Working Paper 2840. Washington, D.C. Available on line at http://econ.worldbank.org/view.php?type=5&id=15176.

Ramachandran, V. K. 1996. "On Kerala's Development Achievements." In Jean Dreze and Amartya Sen, eds., *Indian Development: Selected Regional Perspectives.* New York: Oxford University Press.

Rao, Vijayendra. 2003. "Experiments in Participatory Econometrics: Improving the Connection Between Economic Analysis and the Real World." *Economic and Political Weekly,* May 18.

Rao, Vijayendra, and Ana Maria Ibáñez. 2003. "The Social Impact of Social Funds in Jamaica: A Mixed-Methods Analysis of Participation, Targeting and Collective Action in Community Driven Development." World Bank Policy Research Working Paper 2970. Washington, D.C.

Rao, Vijayendra, and Michael Walton. Forthcoming. "Culture and Public Action: An Introduction." In Vijayendra Rao and Michael Walton (eds.) *Culture and Public Action.* Stanford University Press.

Reimers, Fernando. 1997. "The Role of the Community in Expanding Educational Opportunities: The EDUCO Schools in El Salvador." In James Lynch, Celia Modgil, and Sohan Modgil, eds., *Education and Development: Tradition and Innovation: Volume Two—Equity and Excellence in Education for Development.* London: Cassel.

Reinikka, Ritva, and Jakob Svensson. 2001. "Explaining Leakage in Public Funds." World Bank, Policy Research Woking Paper 2709. Washington, D.C.

————. 2003a. "The Power of Information: Evidence from an Information Campaign to Reduce Capture." World Bank: Washington, D.C. Processed.

————. 2003b. "Working for God? Evaluating Service Delivery of Religious Not-for-Profit Health Care Providers in Uganda." Policy Research Working Paper Series 3058. Washington, D.C.

Riddel, Roger C. 1999. "The End of Foreign Aid to Africa? Concerns about Donor Policies." *African Affairs* 98:309–35.

Ritzen, Jo, Lianqin Wang, and Yael Duthilleul. 2002. "Education as an Agent of Social Cohesion." World Bank, Human Development Network: Washington, D.C. Processed.

Roberts, John. 2002. "Results-Oriented Public Expenditure Management:Lessons from Country Case Studies." Overseas Development Institute: London, U.K. Processed.

Robinson, James, and Thierry Verdier. 2002. "The Political Economy of Clientelism." Centre for Economic Policy Research Discussion Paper Series 3205. London.

Rodden, Jonathan, Gunnar Eskeland, and Jennie Litvack. eds. 2003. *Decentralization and Hard Budget Constraints.* Cambridge, Mass.: MIT Press.

Rojanapithayakorn, W., and R. Hanenberg. 1996. "The 100% Condom Program in Thailand." *AIDS* 10(1):1–7.

Rosskam, Ellen. 2003. "No Pills, No Bandages, Nothing." International Labor Organization: Geneva. Processed.

Rowe, Alexander K., Faustin Onikpo, Marcel Lama, Francois. Cokou, and Michael S. Deming. 2001. "Management of Childhood Illness at Health Facilities in Benin: Problems and Their Causes." *American Journal of Public Health* 91(10):1625–35.

Saadah, F., M. Pradhan, and R. Sparrow. 2001. "The Effectiveness of the Health Card as an Instrument to Ensure Access to Medical Care for the Poor during the Crisis." World Bank: Washington, D.C. Processed.

Samrasinghe, Daya, and John Akin. 1994. "Health Strategy and Financing Study: Final Report." Sri Lanka, Ministry of Health and Women's Affairs: Columbo.

Save the Children. 2002. "New Products into Old Systems: The Initial Impact of the Global Alliance for Vaccines and Immunizations (GAVI) at Country Level." Save the Children and London School of Hygiene and Tropical Medicine: London. Available on line at http://www.savethechildren.org.uk/development/latest/Gavi_report_cover.pdf.

Savedoff, William, and Pablo Spiller. 1999. *Spilled Water: Institutional Commitment in the Provision of Water Services.* Washington, D.C.: Inter-American Development Bank.

Savedoff, William D., and T. Paul Schultz. eds. 2000. *Wealth from Health.* Washington, D.C.: Inter-American Development Bank.

Sawada, Yasuyuki. 1999. "Community Participation, Teacher Effort, and Educational Outcome: The Case of El Salvador's EDUCO Program." William Davidson Institute Working Papers 307. University of Michigan. Available on line at http://eres.bus.umich.edu/web/dwpauth.html.

Schacter, Mark, Phillip Haid, and Julie Koenen-Grant. 1999. *Cabinet Decision-Making: Lessons from Canada; Lessons from Africa.* Ottawa: Institute on Governance.

Schedler, Andreas. 1999. "Conceptualizing Accountability." In Andreas Schedler, Larry Diamond, and Marc F. Plattner, eds., *The Self-Restraining State: Power and Accountability in New Democracies.* Boulder and London: Lynne Rienner.

Schellenberg, J. R., S. Abdulla, R. Nathan, O. Musaka, T. J. Marchant, N. Kikumbih, A. K. Mushi, H. Mponda, H. Minja, H. Mshinda, M. Tanner, and C. Engeler. 2001. "Effect of Large-Scale Social Marketing of Insecticide-treated Nets on Child Survival in Rural Tanzania." *The Lancet* 357(9264):1241–7.

Schick, Allen. 1996. *The Spirit of Reform: Managing the New Zealand State Sector in a Time of Change.* Wellington: State Services Commission and the Treasury.

————. 1998. "Why Most Developing Countries Should Not Try New Zealand's Reforms." *World Bank Research Observer* 13(1): 123–31.

Schieber, G, and A. Maeda. 1997. "A Curmudgeon's Guide to Financing Health Care in Developing Countries." In George J. Schieber, eds., *Innovations in Health Care Financing: Proceedings of a World Bank Conference.* Washington, D.C.: World Bank.

Schiotz, Ania. 2002. "Hygiene in Nineteenth-Century Norway." Institut for Allmenn- og Samfunnsmedisin, University of Oslo: Oslo, Norway. Processed.

Schleicher, Andreas, Maria Teresa Siniscalco, and Neville Postlewaite. 1995. "The Conditions of Primary Schools: A Pilot Study in the Least Developed Countries." UNESCO and UNICEF: Paris. Processed.

Schleifer, Andrei, and Robert W. Vishny. 1994. "Politicians and Firms." *Quaterly Journal of Economics* 109(4):995–1025.

Schneider, Helen, and Natasha Palmer. 2002. "Getting to the Truth? Researching User Views of Primary Health Care." *Health Policy and Planning* 17(1):32–41.

Schorr, Lisbeth B. 1997. *Common Purpose: Strengthening Families and Neighborhoods to Rebuild America.* New York: Doubleday.

Schuknecht, Ludger. 1996. "Political Business Cycles and Fiscal Policies in Developing Countries." *Kyklos* 49(2):155–70.

Schultz, T. Paul. 2001. "School Subsidies for the Poor: Evaluating the Mexican PROGRESA Program." Yale University Economic Growth Center Discussion Paper 834. New Haven, Conn. Available on line at http://www.econ.yale.edu/~egcenter/EGCdiscussion3.htm.

Schwartz, Klaas, and Blokland Maarten. 2002. "Government-Owned Public Limited Companies in the Dutch Water Sector." In Paul Seidenstat, David Haarmeyer, and Simon Hakim, eds., *Reinventing Water and Wastewater Systems: Global Lessons for Improving Management.* New York: John Wiley and Sons, Inc.

Scott, James C. 1998. *Seeing Like a State: How Certain Schemes to Improve the Human Condition Have Failed.* New Haven: Yale University Press.

Seidenstat, Paul, David Haarmeyer, and Simon Hakim. eds. 2002. *Reinventing Water and Wastewater Systems: Global Lessons for Improving Management.* New York: John Wiley and Sons, Inc.

Sen, Amartya. 2002. "Why Half the Planet is Hungry." *Observer of London,* June 16.

Shah, Anwar. 2003a. "On Getting the Giant to Kneel: Approaches to a Change in the Bureaucratic Culture: A Primer on Results-oriented Management and Evaluation." In Anwar Shah, eds., *Ensuring Accountability When There is No Bottom Line.* Washington, D.C.: World Bank.

Shah, Shekhar. 2003b. "Walk Before you Run: Governance and Public Sector Reforms in Poverty Reduction Strategies." Background paper for the WDR 2004.

Shah, Shekhar, and Manju Rani. 2003. "Worlds Apart: Why are Kerala and Uttar Pradesh so Different in Human Development?" Background paper for the WDR 2004.

Shi, Min, and Jakob Svensson. 2003. "Political Budget Cycles in Developed and Developing Countries." World Bank: Washington, D.C. Processed.

Shirley, Mary. eds. 2002. *Thirsting for Efficiency: The Economics and Politics of Urban Water System Reform.* Oxford, U.K.: Elsevier Press.

Shleifer, Andrei, and Rober W. Vishny. 1993. "Corruption." *Quarterly Journal of Economics* 108(3):599–617.

Shreenivasan, Jain. 2002. "Last Word: Development Scam." *The Week,* February 10.

Sillers, Son. 2002. "Strengthening Basic Education through Institutional Reform: Linking Authority, Accountability, and Transparency." USAID Issues Paper 1. Washington, D.C.

Singerman, Diane. 1995. *Avenues of Participation: Family, Politics and Networks in Urban Cairo.* Princeton, N.J.: Princeton University Press.

Singh, Janmejay, and Parmesh Shah. 2003. "Making Services Work for Poor People: The Role of Participatory Public Expenditure Management." Background note for the WDR 2004.

Smith, Warrick. 1997a. "Utility Regulators: Decisionmaking Structures, Resources and the Start-up Strategy." World Bank, Finance, Private Sector and Infrastructure Network Viewpoint 129. Washington, D.C.

————. 1997b. "Utility Regulators: Roles and Responsibilities." World Bank, Finance, Private Sector and Infrastructure Network Viewpoint 128. Washington, D.C.

————. 2003. "Regulating Infrastructure for the Poor: Regulatory System Design." In Penelope Brook and Tymothy Irwin, eds., *Infrastructure for Poor People—Public Policy For Private Provision.* Washington, D.C.: World Bank.

Soeters, Robert, and Fred Griffiths. 2003. "Improving Government Health Services through Contract Management: A Case from Cambodia." *Health Policy and Planning* 18(1):74–83.

Soucat, Agnes, T. Gandaho, and D. Levy-Bruhl. 1997. "Health Seeking Behavior and Household Health Expenditures in Benin and Guinea: the Equity Implications of the Bamako Initiative." *International Journal of Health Planning and Management* 12(Supp. 1):S137–S164.

Soucat, Agnes, and Manju Rani. 2003a. "Making Health and Nutrition Services Work for Poor People." Background note for the WDR 2004.

————. 2003b. "Reaching the Poor with or without Qualified Professionals: A Review of Obstacles to and Levers for Reaching the Poor with Health and Nutrition Services." Background paper for the WDR 2004.

————. 2003c. "Who Do the Poor Really Get Their Services From: Myths and Reality of the Public-Private Mix." Background paper for the WDR 2004.

Stasavage, David. 2003. "On the Role of Democracy in Uganda's Move to Universal Primary Education." Background paper for the WDR 2004.

Stewart, John. 1996. "A Dogma of Our Times - The Separation of Policy-Making and Implementation." *Public Money and Management* July–September: 33–40.

Stiglitz, Joseph E. 2000. *Economics of the Public Sector.* New York: W.W. Norton.

Studdert, D. M., E. J. Thomas, H. R. Burstin, B. I. Zbar, E. J. Orav, and T. A. Breannd. 2000. "Negligent Care and Malpractice Claiming Behavior in Utah and Colorado." *Medical Care* 38(3):250–60.

Sundaram, Pachampet. 2001. "Transfers and Postings in India." World Bank: Washington, D.C. Processed.

Suwal, J. V. 2001. "The Main Determinants of Infant Mortality in Nepal." *Social Science and Medicine* 53(12):1667–81.

Svensson, Jakob. 2003. "Why Conditional Aid Doesn't Work and What Can Be Done about It." *Journal of Development Economics* 70(2):381–402.

Sweeting, E. M. 2001. "Basic Education Projects in Indonesia since 1990: A Study in Sustainability." World Bank: Washington, D.C. Processed.

Talero, Eduardo. 2001. "Electronic Government Procurement: Concepts and Country Experiences." World Bank, Operational Policy and Services: Washington, D.C. Processed.

Tan, Jee-Peng, Agnes Soucat, and Alain Mingat. 2000. "Enhancing Human Development in the HIPC/PRSP Context: Progress in the Africa Region During 2000." World Bank, Africa Region, Human Development Sector: Washington, D.C.

Tangcharoensathien, V, and S Nittayaramphong. 1994. "Thailand: Private Health Care Out of Control?" *Health Policy and Planning* 9(1):31–40.

Tarp, Finn, and Peter Hjertholm. eds. 2000. *Foreign Aid and Development: Lessons Learnt and Directions for the Future.* London, New York: Routledge.

Taylor, J. 2003. "Contracting for Health Services." In A. Preker and A. Harding, eds., *Private Participation in Health Services.* Washington D.C.: World Bank.

Tendler, Judith. 1998. *Good Government in the Tropics.* Baltimore: John Hopkins University Press.

The City of Johannesburg Council. 2001. *Johannesburg: An African City in Change.* Cape Town: Zebra Press.

The Economist. 2002. "Kenya's election: Waiting for the Newish Man." *The Economist,* December 19.

Thomas, Duncan, Victor Lavy, and John Strauss. 1996. "Public Policy and Anthropometric Outcomes in Côte D'Ivoire." *Journal of Public Economics* 61(3):155–192.

Torres Parodi, C. 2003. "Health and Ethnicity." Background note for the WDR 2004.

Tremolet, Sophie. 2002. "Rural Water Service." World Bank Private Sector Finance Viewpoint 249. Washington, D.C.

Tumusiime-Mutebile, Emmanuel. 2003. "Uganda's Experience with the Medium-term Expenditure Framework." Ministry of Finance, Planning, and Economic Development: Kampala, Uganda. Processed.

Tynan, Nicola. 2002. "London's Private Water Supply, 1582-1902." In Paul Seidenstat, David Haarmeyer, and Simon Hakim, eds., *Reinventing Water and Wastewater Systems: Global Lessons for Improving Management.* New York: John Wiley and Sons, Inc.

U.K. Department of International Development. 2002. "Transport's Role in Achieving the Millenium Development Goals." U.K. Department of International Development, Transport Resource Center: London, U.K.

UNAIDS. 2000. "Report on the Global HIV/AIDS Epidemic." UNAIDS: Geneva.

UNAIDS, and WHO. 2003. "Aids Epidemic Update." Joint United Nations Programme on HIV/AIDS (UNAIDS) and World Health Organization (WHO): Switzerland.

UNESCO. 2002. "EFA Global Monitoring Report, 2002: Is the World on Track?" UNESCO: Paris. Available on line at http://www.unesco. org/education/efa/monitoring/monitoring_2002.shtml.

UNICEF. 2001. "Progress since the World Summit for Children: A Statistical Review." UNICEF: New York. Available on line at http://www.unicef.org/pubsgen/wethechildren-stats/.

UNICEF. 2002. "Accelerating Early Child Survival and Development in High Under-Five Mortality Areas in the Context of Health Reform and Poverty Reduction: A Results Based Approach, Proposal for CIDA." UNICEF: New York.

UNICEF. 2002. "End of Decade Databases: Child Mortality". Geneva, UNICEF. Available on line at http://www.childinfo.org/cmr/revis/db2.htm.

UNICEF-World Bank 2003. Marginal Budgeting for Bottlenecks: How to reach the impact frontier of health and nutrition services and accelerate progress towards the Millennium Development Goals. A budgeting model and an application to low-income countries (forthcoming).

United Nations. 1961. "United Nations Demographic Yearbook". The United Nations. Monograph.

Uriarte, Miren. 2002. "Cuba Social Policy at the Crossroads:Maintaining Priorities, Transforming Practice." Oxfam America: Boston.

Urquiola, Miguel. 2001. "Identifying Class Size Effects in Developing Countries: Evidence from Rural Schools in Bolivia." World Bank Policy Research Working Paper 2711. Washington, D.C.

van de Walle, Dominique. 1998. "Targeting Revisited." *World Bank Research Observer* 13(2, August):231–248.

————. 2002. "Choosing Rural Road Investments to Help Reduce Poverty." *World Development* 30(4):575–89.

van de Walle, Dominique, and Dorothyjean Cratty. 2003. "Impact Evaluation of a Rural Road Rehabilitation Project." World Bank: Washington, D.C. Processed.

van de Walle, Dominique, and Kimberly Nead. eds. 1995. *Public Spending and the Poor: Theory and Evidence.* Baltimore: Johns Hopkins University Press.

van der Berg, Servaas, and Ronelle Burger. 2003. "The Stories behind the Numbers: An Investigation of Efforts to Deliver Services to South Africa's Poor." Background paper for the WDR 2004.

Van Domelen, Julie. 2002. "Social Funds: Evidence on Targeting, Impacts and Sustainability." *Journal of International Development* 14(5):627–42.

Van Lerberghe, W., W. Ammar, R. el Rashidi, M. Awar, A. Sales, and A. Mechbal. 1997. "Reform Follows Failure: II. Pressure for Change in the Lebanese Health Sector." *Health Policy and Planning* 12(4):312–19.

Van Lerberghe, W., and P. Ferrinho. 2003. "Civil Society Organizations and the Poor: The Unfulfilled Expectations." Background paper for the WDR 2004.

Vasan, Sudha. 2002. "Ethnography of the Forest Guard: Contrasting Discourses, Conflicting Roles and Policy Implementation." *Economic and Political Weekly,* October 5.

Vegas, Emiliana. 2002. "School Choice, Student Performance, and Teacher and School Characteristics: The Chilean Case." World Bank Policy Research Working Paper 2833. Washington, D.C.

Vegas, Emiliana, Lant Pritchett, and William Experton. 1999. "Cómo Atraer y Retener Docentes Calificados en la Argentina: Impacto del Nivel y la Estructura de la Remuneración." World Bank Department of Human Development, LCSHD Paper Series 38. Washington, D.C.

Victora, Cesar, J. Patrick Vaughan, Fernando C. Barros, Anamaria C. Silva, and Elaine Tomasi. 2000a. "Explaining Trends in Inequities: Evidence from Brazilian Child Health Studies." *The Lancet* 356(9235):1093–98.

Victora, Cesar G., Jennifer Bryce, Oliver Fontaine, and Roeland Monasch. 2000b. "Reducing Deaths from Diarrhoea through Oral Rehydration Therapy." *Bulletin of the World Health Organization* 78(10):1246–55.

von Braun, Joachim, and Ulrike Grote. 2000. "Does Decentralization Serve the Poor?" Paper presented at the *IMF Conference on Fiscal Decentralization* Conference. Washington, D.C. November 21.

von der Fehr, Nils-Henrik M., and Jose Jaime Millan. 2001. "Sustainability of Power Sector Reform in Latin America: An Analytical Framework." Inter American Development Bank Working Paper. Washington, D.C. Available on line at www.iadb.org.

Wade, Robert. 1982. "System of Administrative and Political Corruption: Canal Irrigation in South India." *Journal of Development Studies* 18(April 1982):287–328.

———. 1985. "The Market for Public Office: Why the Indian State Is Not Better at Development?" *World Development* 13:467–97.

———. 1987. "Management of Common Property Resources: Finding a Cooperative Solution." *World Bank Research Observer* 2(2):219–34.

———. 1988. *Village Republics: Economic Conditions for Collective Action in South India.* Cambridge, U.K.: Cambridge University Press.

Wagstaff, Adam. 2000. "Socioeconomic Inequalities in Child Mortality: Comparisons across Nine Developing Countries." *Bulletin of the World Health Organization* 78(1):19–29.

———. 2002. "Child Health on a Dollar a Day: Some Tentative Cross-Country Comparisons." World Bank, Development Research Group: Washington, D.C. Processed.

Wagstaff, Adam, Jennifer Bryce, Flavia Bustreo, Mariam Claeson, Niklas Danielsson, and WHO-World Bank Child Health and Poverty Working Group. 2002. "Child Health: Reaching the Poor." World Bank: Washington, D.C. Processed.

Wagstaff, Adam, and E. van Doorslaer. Forthcoming. "Catastrophe and Impoverishment in Paying for Health Care: With Applications to Vietnam: 1993–1998." *Health Economics.*

Wagstaff, Adam, Eddy van Doorslaer, and Naoko Watanabe. 2001. "On Decomposing the Causes of Health Sector Inequalities with an Application to Malnutrition Inequalities in Vietnam." World Bank Policy Research Working Paper 2714. Washington, D.C.

Waitzkin, Howard. B. 1991. *The Politics of Medical Encounters: How Patients and Doctors Deal with Social Problems.* New Haven, Conn.: Yale University Press.

Walker, N., B. Schwarlander, and J. Bryce. 2002. "Meeting International Goals in Child Survival and HIV/AIDS." *The Lancet* 360(9329):284–89.

Wang, T. Y. 1999. "U.S. Foreign Aid and UN Voting: An Analysis of Important Issues." *International Studies Quarterly* 43:199–210.

Wang, Youfa, C. Monteiro, and B. M. Popkin. 2002. "Trends of Overweight and Underweight in Children and Adolescents in the United States, Brazil, China and Russia." *American Journal of Clinical Nutrition* 75:971–77.

Warwick, Donald P., and Fernanda Reimers. 1995. *Hope or Despair: Learning in Pakistan's Primary Schools.* Westport, Conn.: Praeger.

Water and Sanitation Program. 2001. "Community Contracting in Rural Water and Sanitation: The Swajal Project, Uttar Pradesh, India." Water and Sanitation Program: New Delhi.

Water and Sanitation Program (WSP-AF). 2003. "Building Partnerships to Deliver Water supply and Sanitation Services to Low-income Communities, Good-Practice from Sub-Saharan Africa." World Bank, Water and Sanitation Program (WSP-AF): Washington, D.C. Processed.

Water Supply and Sanitation Collaborative Council. 2000. "Global Water Supply and Sanitation Assessment." Water Supply and Sanitation Collaborative Council: Geneva. Available on line at www.wsscc.org.

Waters, Hatt, and Aselsson. 2002. "Working for the Private Sector for Child Health." The World Health Organization and The World Bank. Prepared for the USAID-sponsored SARA Project.: Washington D.C.

Werner, David, Carol Thuman, and Jane Maxwell. 1992. *Where There is no Doctor: A Village Health Care Handbook.* Palo Alto, Calif.: rev. ed., Hesperian Foundation.

Wetterberg, Anna, and Scott Guggenheim. Forthcoming. "Capitalizing on Local Capacity: Institutional Change in the Kecamatan Development Program." In A. J. Bebbington, M. Woolcock, and S. Guggenheim (eds.) *Practical Theory, Reflective Action: Social Capital and Development Projects at the World Bank.* New York: Oxford University Press.

Weyland, Kurt. 1997. "'Growth with Equity' in Chile's New Democracy?" *Latin America Research Review* 32(1):37–67.

WHO (World Health Organization). 1999. "World Health Report". The World Health Organization. Monograph.

———. 2002. "25 Questions and Answers on Health and Human Rights." Health and Human Rights Publication Series 1. Geneva, Switzerland.

WHO (World Health Organization), and World Bank. 2002. "Dying for Change: Poor People's Experience of Health and Ill-Health." World Health Organization and World Bank: Geneva and Washington, D.C.

WHO (World Health Organization), Division of Child Health and Development. 1998. "CHD 1996-97 Report." World Health Organization: Geneva. Available on line at http://www.who.int/child-adolescent-health/publications/puboverview.htm#progress.

WHO UNICEF Joint Monitoring Programme for Water Supply and Sanitation. 2001. "Global Water Supply and Sanitation Assessment 2000 Report." World Health Organization and United Nations Children's Fund: Geneva and New York. Available on line at http://www.who.int/water_sanitation_health/Globassessment/GlobalTOC.htm.

Wilson, James Q. 1989. *Bureaucracy: What Government Agencies Do and Why they Do It.* New York: Basic Books.

Wodon, Q. 1999. "Cost-Benefit Analysis of Food for Education in Bangladesh." World Bank, Background paper for the 1998 Bangladesh Poverty Assesment: Washington, D.C. Processed.

Wolfensohn, James D. 1997. "The Challenge of Inclusion." World Bank, Annual Meeting Address, Hong Kong SAR, China.

World Bank. 1990. *World Development Report 1990: Poverty.* New York: Oxford University Press.

———. 1993. *World Development Report 1993: Investing in Health.* New York: Oxford University Press.

———. 1994a. "Better Health in Africa: Experience and Lessons Learned." World Bank: Washington, D.C.

———. 1994b. "Indonesia's Health Work Force: Issues and Options." World Bank: Washington, D.C.

———. 1994c. "World Development Report 1994: Infrastructure for Development." Oxford University Press: New York.

———. 1996. "Argentina Cordoba - Public Sector Assessment: Proposals for Reform Volume II Annexes." World Bank: Washington, D.C.

———. 1998a. *Assessing Aid: What Works, What Doesn't, and Why.* New York: Oxford University Press.

———. 1998b. "Basic Education in Indonesia: From Crisis to Recovery." World Bank: Washington, D.C. Available on line at http://www-wds.worldbank.org/servlet/WDS_IBank_Servlet?pcont=details&eid=000094946_99031910544076.

———. 1998c. "Public Expenditure for Poverty Alleviation in Northeast Brazil: Promoting Growth and Improving Services." World Bank: Washington, D.C.

———. 2000a. "Anticorruption in Transition: A Contribution to the Policy Debate, The World Bank." World Bank: Washington, D.C.

———. 2000b. "Bolivia: From Patronage to a Professional State, Institutional and Governance Review." World Bank: Washington, D.C.

———. 2000c. "Making Transition Work for Everyone: Poverty and Inequality in Europe and Central Asia." World Bank: Washington, D.C.

———. 2001a. "Decentralization in the Transition Economies: Challenges and the Road Ahead." World Bank: Washington, D.C.

———. 2001b. *Education and Health in Sub-Saharan Africa: A Review of Sector-Wide Approaches.* Washington, D.C.: World Bank.

———. 2001c. "Education and Training in Madagascar: Towards a Policy Agenda for Economic Growth and Poverty Reduction." World Bank, Human Development 4 (AFTH4): Washington, D.C.

———. 2001d. "Evaluating the Impact of Health Care Reforms in Poland: The Challenges of Systemic Changes in a Transforming Environment." World Bank ECA Region: Washington, D.C.

———. 2001e. "Honduras: Public Expenditure Management for Poverty Reduction and Fiscal Sustainability." World Bank: Washington, D.C.

———. 2001f. "Implementation of World Bank-finance Projects. A Note on Eastern Europe and Central Asia Experience with Projects Implementation Units." World Bank: Washington, D.C.

———. 2001g. "Indonesia Poverty Report." World Bank: Washington, D.C.

———. 2001h. "Nepal: Priorities and Strategies for Education Reform." World Bank, Human Development Unit, South Asia Region: Washington, D.C.

———. 2001i. "Reform of the Electrical Power Sector in India. Report on Fact-Finding Mission (August 2001)." World Bank, Energy and Infrastructure Unit, South Asia Regional Office, Energy and Water Department: Washington, D.C.

———. 2001j. "Vietnam, Growing Healthy: A Review of Vietnam's Health Sector." World Bank, Human Development Sector Unit, Vietnam Country Unit, East Asia and Pacific Region: Washington, D.C.

———. 2001k. *World Development Report 2000/2001: Attacking Poverty.* New York: Oxford University Press.

———. 2001l. "Zambia Public Expenditure Review: Public Expenditure, Growth and Poverty: A Synthesis." World Bank: Washington, D.C.

———. 2002a. *A Case for Aid: Building a Consensus for Development Assistance.* Washington, D.C.: World Bank.

———. 2002b. *A Sourcebook for Poverty Reduction Strategies. Vol. 1.* Washington, D.C.: World Bank.

———. 2002c. "Achieving Education for All in Post-Conflict Cambodia." Education Notes . Washington, D.C. Available on line at www.worldbank.org/education.

———. 2002d. "Bangladesh: The Experience and Perceptions of Public Officials." World Bank: Washington, D.C. Processed.

———. 2002e. "Building on Strengths: Lessons from Comparative Public Administration Reforms." World Bank: Washington, D.C. Processed.

———. 2002f. "Decentralizing Indonesia: A Regional Public Expenditure Review, Overview Report." East Asia, The World Bank: Washington, D.C. Processed.

———. 2002g. "EdStats: Gender-disaggregated Education Profiles." World Bank: Washington, D.C. Available on line at http://sima/edstats/td.asp.

———. 2002h. "Education and HIV/AIDS: A Window of Hope." World Bank: Washington, D.C.

———. 2002i. "Evaluation of the Comprehensive Development Framework (CDF): Synthesis Report." World Bank: Washington, D.C. Processed.

———. 2002j. "Mexico: Second Basic Health Project: Implementation Completion Report." World Bank: Washington, D.C.

———. 2002k. "Pakistan Development Policy Review: A New Dawn?" World Bank: Washington, D.C.

———. 2002l. "Pakistan Poverty Assessment. Poverty in Pakistan: Vulnerabilities, Social Gaps, and Rural Dynamics." World Bank: Washington, D.C.

———. 2002m. "Poverty in Pakistan: Vulnerabilities, Social Gaps, and Rural Dynamics." World Bank: Washington, D.C.

———. 2002n. "Romania: Local Social Services Delivery Study." World Bank: Washington, D.C.

———. 2002o. "Rural Water Projects: Lessons Learned." World Bank Operations Evaluation Report 215. Washington, D.C.

———. 2002p. *Social Funds: Assessing Effectiveness.* Washington, D.C.: World Bank.

———. 2002q. "The Right to Tell: The Role of Mass Media in Economic Development." World Bank: Washington, D.C.

———. 2002r. "World Bank Group Work in Low-Income Countries Under Stress." World Bank: Washington, D.C.

———. 2002s. *World Development Indicators.* Washington, D.C.: World Bank.

———. 2003a. "Global Economic Prospects and the Developing Countries: Investing to Unlock Global Opportunities." World Bank: Washington, D.C.

———. 2003b. "Turkey-reforming the Health Sector for Improved Access and Efficiency." World Bank, Human Development Sector Unit: Washington, D.C.

World Health Organization. 2003. "Severe Acute Respiratory Syndrome (SARS): Status of the Outbreak and Lessons for the Immediate Future." World Health Organization: Geneva.

Wößmann, Ludger. 2003. "Schooling Resources, Educational Institutions, and Student Performance: The International Evidence." *Oxford Bulletin of Economics and Statistics* 65(2):117–170.

Yip, Winnie, and Peter Berman. 2001. "Targeted Health Insurance in a Low Income Country and its Impact on Access and Equity in Access: Egypt's School Health Insurance." *Health Economics* 10(3):207–20.

Zhao, Feng, Agnes Soucat, and Niagale Traore. 2003. "The Poor in Mali: Outcomes and Household Determinants of Child Health." World Bank, Africa Region. Washington, D.C.

Background papers for the WDR 2004

Anderson, James, Daniel Kaufmann, and Francesca Recanatini. "Service Delivery, Poverty, and Corruption - Common Threads from Diagnostic Surveys."

Andrews, Matthew, and J. Edgardo Campos. "The Management of Public Expenditures and Its Implications for Service Delivery."

Bhalla, Surjit, Suraj Saigal, and Nabhojit Basu. "Girl's Education is it—Nothing else Matters."

Chaudhury, Nazmul, and Jeffrey Hammer. "Ghost Doctors: Absenteeism in Bangladeshi Health Facilities."

Clarke, Prema. "Education Reform in the Education Guarantee Scheme in Madhya Pradesh, India and the Fundescola Program in Brazil."

Coady, David. "Alleviating Structural Poverty in Developing Countries: The Approach of PROGRESA in Mexico."

Das Gupta, Monica, P. Khaleghian, and R. Sarwal. "Governance of Communicable Disease Control Services: A Case Study and Lessons from India."

Diaz-Cayeros, Alberto, and Beatriz Magaloni . "The Politics of Public Spending: Part I - The Logic of Vote Buying. Part II -The Programa Nacional de Solidaridad (PRONASOL) in Mexico."

Dutta, Antara. "Public Service Delivery: The PROBE and Its Impact."

Erikson, Dan, Annie Lord, and Peter Wolf. "Cuba's Social Services: A Review of Education, Health, and Sanitation."

Ferrinho, P., and W. Van Lerberghe. "Managing Health Professionals in the Context of Limited Resources: a Fine Line Between Corruption and the Need for Moonlighting."

Ferriol, Angela, Victoria Perez, Didio Quintana, and Aida Atienza. "Servicios de Educacion, Salud, Agua y Saneamiento en Cuba."

Filmer, Deon. "The Incidence of Public Expenditures on Health and Education."

Gauri, Varun, and Ayesha Vawda. "Vouchers for Basic Education in Developing Countries: A Principal-Agent Perspective."

Halonen, Maija. "Coordination Failure in Foreign Aid."

Kalter, Henry. "Global Health Funds."

Keefer, Philip, and Stuti Khemani. "The Political Economy of Social Service Provision."

Khaleghian, Peyvand. "Decentralization and Public Services: The Case of Immunization."

Knack, Stephen, and Aminur Rahman. "Aid Intensity, Donor Fragmentation and the Quality of Governance."

Knippenberg, Rudolf, Fatoumata Traore Nafo, Raimi Osseni, Yero Boye Camara, Abdelwahid El Abassi, Agnes Soucat. "Increasing client's power to scale up health services for the poor: The Bamako Initiative in West Africa."

Leonard, L. Kenneth and Melkiory Masatu. "Report on Basic Findings in Outpatient Facility Evaluations in Arusha Municipality, Arumer District and Monduli District, Arusha Region, Tanzania."

Liese, B., and and others. "Human Resources Crisis in Health Services in Sub-Saharan Africa."

Lisulo, Angela. "Costa Rica: Health Policies."

Mackinnon, John. "How Does Aid Affect the Quality of Public Expenditure? What We Know and What We Do not Know."

Mehryar, A. H., A. Aghajanian, and S. Ahmadnia. "Primary Health Care and Rural Poverty Eradication in the Islamic Republic of Iran."

Msuya, Joyce. "Horizontal and Vertical Delivery of Health Services: What are The Trade Offs?"

Naimoli, Joseph, and Denise Vaillancourt. "Performance-based Management in an Evolving Decentralized Public Health System in West Africa: The Case of Burkina Faso."

Patrinos, Harry. "A Review of Demand-Side Financing Initiatives in Education."

Pearson, Mark, and Paolo Carlo Belli. 2003. "The Impact of Resource Allocation Mechanisms, and Priority Setting Policies to Improve Services for the Poor."

Radoki, Carole. "What Are the Most Effective Strategies for Understanding and Channeling the Preferences of Service Users to Make Public Services More Responsive."

Roberts, John "Managing Public Expenditure for Development Results and Poverty Reduction."

Robinson, James A. "Politician-Proof Policy."

Saigal, Suraj. "Literature Review on Service Delivery in India."

Shah, Shekhar, and Manju Rani. "Worlds Apart: Why are Kerala and Uttar Pradesh Do Different in Human Development?"

Shah, Shekhar. "Walk Before you Run: Governance and Public Sector Reforms in Poverty Reduction Strategies."

Soucat, Agnes, and Manju Rani. "Reaching the Poor with or without Qualified Professionals: A Review of Obstacles to and Levers for Reaching the Poor with Health and Nutrition Services."

Soucat, Agnes, and Manju Rani. "Who Do the Poor Really Get Their Services From: Myths and Reality of the Public-Private Mix."

Stasavage, David. "On the Role of Democracy in Uganda's Move to Universal Primary Education."

StØre, Jonas Gahr. "The Provision of Social Services and the Emerging Welfare State. A Norwegian Perspective."

van der Berg, Servaas, and Ronelle Burger. "The Stories behind the Numbers: An Investigation of Efforts to Deliver Services to South Africa's Poor."

Van Lerberghe, W., and P. Ferrinho. "Civil Society and Health."

Vegas, Emiliana "Do Changes in Teacher Contracts and Compensation Affect Student Performance? Evidence from Togo."

Background notes for the WDR 2004

Alderman, Harold H. "Impact of Nutrition On Other Health Outcomes;"

Bhushan, Indu. "Contracting Health Services in Cambodia."

Filmer, Deon. "Determinants of Health and Education Outcomes."

Gauri, Varun. "A Rights-Based Approach to Health Care and Education."

Hallman, Kelly. "Health and Nutrition Impacts of Arsenic Contamination in Bangladesh."

Hesselbarth, Susanne. Federal Ministry for Economic Cooperation and Development. "Program of Action 2015: Alliances against Poverty Chances and Challenges for the Water Sector."

Singh, Janmejay, and Parmesh Shah. "Making Services Work for Poor People: The Role of Participatory Public Expenditure Management."

Soucat, Agnes, and Manju Rani. "Making Health and Nutrition Services Work for Poor People."

Torres Parodi, C. "Health and Ethnicity."

Consultation papers

Caseley, Jonathan. "Understanding Service Delivery Reform and Organizational Performance in an Indian State."

Cotton, Andrew. "Sanitation: A Problem of Scale."

Crook, Richard. Urban Service Partnerships: "Street Level Bureaucrats" and Environmental Sanitation in Kumasi and Accra, Ghana: Coping with Organizational Change in the Public Bureaucracy."

Grindle, Merilee S. "First in the Queue? Mainstreaming The Poor in Service Delivery."

Jenkins, Rob and Anne Marie Goetz. "Civil Society Engagement and India's Public Distribution System: Lessons form The Rationing Kruti Samiti in Mumbai."

Manor, James. "Partnerships between Governments and Civil Society for Service Delivery in Less Developed Countries: Cause for Concern."

McPake, Barbara. "What Can Be Done About the Private Health Sector in Low-Income Countries."

Moore, Mick. "Organisations that Reach the Poor: Why Coproduction Matters."

Nickson, Andrew. "The Role of The Non-State Sector in Urban Water Supply."

Platteau, Jean-Philippe. "Rushing to Help the Poor Through Participation May Be Self-Defeating."

Plummer, Janelle. "Developing Inclusive Public-Private Partnerships: The Role of Small-Scale Independent Providers in the Delivery of Water and Sanitation Services."

Powis, Benjamin. "Who Uses User Groups?"

Rakodi, Carole. "What are the most Effective Strategies for Understanding and Channelling the Preferences of Service Users to Make Public Services more Responsive?."

Rose, Pauline. "Is The Non-State Education Sector Serving The Needs of The Poor?: Evidence From East and Southern Africa"

Sibbons, Maureen. "Making Education Services Work for Poor People."

Standing, Hilary and Gerry Bloom. "Beyond Public and Private? Unorganized Markets in Health Care Delivery."

Introduction to Selected World Development Indicators

This year's edition presents comparative socioeconomic data for more than 134 economies in six tables. An additional table provides data on basic indicators for 74 economies with sparse data or with populations of less than 1.5 million. Data are for the most recent year available and, for some indicators, an earlier year is provided for comparison purposes.

The first two tables present data on the size of economies and several indicators on non-income poverty that are included in the Millennium Development Goals. Four additional tables cover data on special topics related to the main WDR themes on health, education, service delivery, and foreign aid.

The indicators presented here are a selection from more than 800 included in *World Development Indicators 2003*. Published annually, *World Development Indicators* reflects a comprehensive view of the development process. Its opening chapter reports on the Millennium Development Goals which grew out of agreements and resolutions of world conferences organized by the United Nations (UN) in the past decade, and reaffirmed at the Millennium Summit in September 2000 by member countries of the UN. The other five main sections recognize the contribution of a wide range of factors: human capital development, environmental sustainability, macroeconomic performance, private sector development, and the global links that influence the external environment for development. *World Development Indicators* is complemented by a separately published database that gives access to over 1,000 data tables and 800 time-series indicators for 225 economies and regions. This database is available through an electronic subscription (*WDI Online*) or as a CD-ROM.

Data sources and methodology

Socioeconomic and environmental data presented here are drawn from several sources: primary data collected by the World Bank, member country statistical publications, research institutes, and international organizations such as the United Nations and its specialized agencies, the International Monetary Fund (IMF), and the Organisation for Economic Co-operation and Development (OECD). Although international standards of coverage, definition, and classification apply to most statistics reported by countries and international agencies, there are inevitably differences in timeliness and reliability arising from differences in the capabilities and resources devoted to basic data collection and compilation. For some topics, competing sources of data require review by World Bank staff to ensure that the most reliable data available are presented. In some instances, where available data are deemed too weak to provide reliable measures of levels and trends or do not adequately adhere to international standards, the data are not shown.

The data presented are generally consistent with those in *World Development Indicators 2003*. However, data have been revised and updated wherever new information has become available. Differences may also reflect revisions to historical series and changes in methodology. Thus data of different vintages may be published in different editions of World Bank publications. Readers are advised not to compile data series from different publications or different editions of the same publication. Consistent time-series data are available on *World Development Indicators 2003* CD-ROM and through *WDI Online*.

All dollar figures are in current U.S. dollars unless otherwise stated. The various methods used to convert from national currency figures are described in the *Technical Notes*.

Because the World Bank's primary business is providing lending and policy advice to its low- and middle-income members, the issues covered in these tables focus mainly on these economies. Where available, information on the high-income economies is also provided for comparison. Readers may wish to refer to national statistical publications and publications of the OECD and the European Union for more information on the high-income economies.

Classification of economies and summary measures

The summary measures at the bottom of each table include economies classified by income per capita and by region. GNI per capita is used to determine the following income classifications: low-income, $735 or less in 2002; middle-income, $736 to $9,075; and high-income, $9,076 and above. A further division at GNI per capita $2,935 is made between lower-middle-income and upper-middle-income economies. See the table on classification of economies in this volume for a list of economies in each group (including those with populations of less than 1.5 million).

Summary measures are either totals (indicated by **t** if the aggregates include estimates for missing data and non-reporting countries, or by an **s** for simple sums of the data available), weighted averages (**w**), or median values (**m**) calculated for groups of economies. Data for the countries excluded from the main tables (those presented in Table 7) have been included in the summary measures, where data are available, or by assuming that they follow the trend of reporting countries. This gives a more consistent aggregated measure by standardizing country coverage for each period shown. Where missing information accounts for a third or more of the overall estimate, however, the group measure is reported as not available. The *Technical Notes* provides further information on aggregation methods. Weights used to construct the aggregates are listed in the technical notes for each table.

From time to time an economy's classification is revised because of changes in the above cutoff values or in the economy's measured level of GNI per capita. When such changes occur, aggregates based on those classifications are recalculated for the past period so that a consistent time series is maintained.

Terminology and country coverage

The term *country* does not imply political independence but may refer to any territory for which authorities report separate social or economic statistics. Data are shown for economies as they were constituted in 2002, and historical data are revised to reflect current political arrangements. Throughout the tables, exceptions are noted.

Technical notes

Because data quality and intercountry comparisons are often problematic, readers are encouraged to consult the *Technical notes,* the table on *Classification of economies by region and income,* and the footnotes to the tables. For more extensive documentation see *World Development Indicators 2003.*

Readers may find more information on the *WDI 2003,* and orders can be made online, by phone, or fax as follows:

For more information and to order online: **http://www. worldbank.org/data/wdi2003/index.htm** To order by phone or fax: **1-800-645-7247** or 703-661-1580; Fax 703-661-1501

To order by mail: The World Bank, P.O. Box 960, Herndon, VA 20172-0960, U.S.A.

Classification of economies by region and income, FY2004

East Asia and Pacific		Latin America and Caribbean		Sub-Saharan Africa		High income OECD
American Samoa	UMC	Argentina	UMC	Angola	LIC	Australia
Cambodia	LIC	Belize	UMC	Benin	LIC	Austria
China	LMC	Bolivia	LMC	Botswana	UMC	Belgium
Fiji	LMC	Brazil	LMC	Burkina Faso	LIC	Canada
Indonesia	LIC	Chile	UMC	Burundi	LIC	Denmark
Kiribati	LMC	Colombia	LMC	Cameroon	LIC	Finland
Korea, Dem. Rep.	LIC	Costa Rica	UMC	Cape Verde	LMC	France
Lao PDR	LIC	Cuba	LMC	Central African Rep.	LIC	Germany
Malaysia	UMC	Dominica	UMC	Chad	LIC	Greece
Marshall Islands	LMC	Dominican Rep.	LMC	Comoros	LIC	Iceland
Micronesia, Fed. Sts.	LMC	Ecuador	LMC	Congo, Dem. Rep.	LIC	Ireland
Mongolia	LIC	El Salvador	LMC	Congo, Rep.	LIC	Italy
Myanmar	LIC	Grenada	UMC	Côte d'Ivoire	LIC	Japan
N. Mariana Islands	UMC	Guatemala	LMC	Equatorial Guinea	LIC	Korea, Rep.
Palau	UMC	Guyana	LMC	Eritrea	LIC	Luxembourg
Papua New Guinea	LIC	Haiti	LIC	Ethiopia	LIC	Netherlands
Philippines	LMC	Honduras	LMC	Gabon	UMC	New Zealand
Samoa	LMC	Jamaica	LMC	Gambia, The	LIC	Norway
Solomon Islands	LIC	Mexico	UMC	Ghana	LIC	Portugal
Thailand	LMC	Nicaragua	LIC	Guinea	LIC	Spain
Timor-Leste	LIC	Panama	UMC	Guinea-Bissau	LIC	Sweden
Tonga	LMC	Paraguay	LMC	Kenya	LIC	Switzerland
Vanuatu	LMC	Peru	LMC	Lesotho	LIC	United Kingdom
Vietnam	LIC	St. Kitts & Nevis	UMC	Liberia	LIC	United States
		St. Lucia	UMC	Madagascar	LIC	
Europe and Central Asia		St. Vincent & Grenadines	LMC	Malawi	LIC	**Other high income**
Albania	LMC	Suriname	LMC	Mali	LIC	Andorra
Armenia	LMC	Trinidad & Tobago	UMC	Mauritania	LIC	Antigua & Barbuda
Azerbaijan	LIC	Uruguay	UMC	Mauritius	UMC	Aruba
Belarus	LMC	Venezuela, RB	UMC	Mayotte	UMC	Bahamas, The
Bosnia & Herzegovina	LMC			Mozambique	LIC	Bahrain
Bulgaria	LMC	**Middle East and North Africa**		Namibia	LMC	Barbados
Croatia	UMC	Algeria	LMC	Niger	LIC	Bermuda
Czech Rep.	UMC	Djibouti	LMC	Nigeria	LIC	Brunei
Estonia	UMC	Egypt, Arab Rep.	LMC	Rwanda	LIC	Cayman Islands
Georgia	LIC	Iran, Islamic Rep.	LMC	São Tomé & Principe	LIC	Channel Islands
Hungary	UMC	Iraq	LMC	Senegal	LIC	Cyprus
Kazakhstan	LMC	Jordan	LMC	Seychelles	UMC	Faeroe Islands
Kyrgyz Rep.	LIC	Lebanon	UMC	Sierra Leone	LIC	French Polynesia
Latvia	UMC	Libya	UMC	Somalia	LIC	Greenland
Lithuania	UMC	Morocco	LMC	South Africa	LMC	Guam
Macedonia, FYR	LMC	Oman	UMC	Sudan	LIC	Hong Kong, China
Moldova	LIC	Saudi Arabia	UMC	Swaziland	LMC	Isle of Man
Poland	UMC	Syrian Arab Rep.	LMC	Tanzania	LIC	Israel
Romania	LMC	Tunisia	LMC	Togo	LIC	Kuwait
Russian Fed.	LMC	West Bank & Gaza	LMC	Uganda	LIC	Liechtenstein
Serbia & Montenegro	LMC	Yemen, Rep.	LIC	Zambia	LIC	Macao, China
Slovak Rep.	UMC			Zimbabwe	LIC	Malta
Tajikistan	LIC	**South Asia**				Monaco
Turkey	LMC	Afghanistan	LIC			Netherlands Antilles
Turkmenistan	LMC	Bangladesh	LIC			New Caledonia
Ukraine	LMC	Bhutan	LIC			Puerto Rico
Uzbekistan	LIC	India	LIC			Qatar
		Maldives	LMC			San Marino
		Nepal	LIC			Singapore
		Pakistan	LIC			Slovenia
		Sri Lanka	LMC			Taiwan, China
						United Arab Emirates
						Virgin Islands (U.S.)

This table classifies all World Bank member economies, and all other economies with populations of more than 30,000. Economies are divided among income groups according to 2002 GNI per capita, calculated using the World Bank Atlas method. The groups are: low income (LIC), $735 or less; lower middle income (LMC), $736–2,935; upper middle income (UMC), $2,936–9,075; and high income, $9,076 or more.

Source: World Bank data.

Table 1 Size of the economy

	Population	Surface area	Population density	Gross national income [a]		PPP gross national income [b]		Gross domestic product	
	millions	thousand sq. km	people per sq. km of land area	$ billions	Per capita $	$ billions	Per capita $	% growth	Per capita % growth
	2002	2002	2002	2002	2002	2002	2002	2001–2002	2001–2002
Albania	3	29	117	4.4	1,380	13	4,040	4.7	3.7
Algeria	31	2,382	13	53.8	1,720	167 [c]	5,330 [c]	4.1	2.5
Angola	14	1,247	11	9.2	660	24 [c]	1,730 [c]	17.1	13.8
Argentina	38	2,780	14	154.1	4,060	377	9,930	–10.9	–12.0
Armenia	3	30	109	2.4	790	9	3,060	12.9	13.5
Australia	20	7,741	3	386.6	19,740	528	26,960	3.5	2.5
Austria	8	84	98	190.4	23,390	230	28,240	1.0	0.9
Azerbaijan	8	87	95	5.8	710	24	2,920	10.6	9.7
Bangladesh	136	144	1,042	48.5	360	234	1,720	4.4	2.6
Belarus	10	208	48	13.5	1,360	53	5,330	4.7	5.1
Belgium	10	33	314	239.9	23,250	282	27,350	0.7	0.4
Benin	7	113	60	2.5	380	7	1,020	5.3	2.6
Bolivia	9	1,099	8	7.9	900	20	2,300	2.5	0.4
Bosnia & Herzegovina	4	51	81	5.2	1,270	24	5,800	3.9	2.4
Botswana	2	582	3	5.1	2,980	13	7,770	3.5	2.5
Brazil	174	8,547	21	497.4	2,850	1,266	7,250	1.5	0.3
Bulgaria	8	111	71	14.1	1,790	54	6,840	4.3	4.9
Burkina Faso	12	274	43	2.6	220	12 [c]	1,010 [c]	5.6	3.1
Burundi	7	28	275	0.7	100	4 [c]	610 [c]	3.6	1.7
Cambodia	12	181	71	3.5	280	20	1,590	4.5	2.6
Cameroon	16	475	33	8.7	560	25	1,640	4.4	2.2
Canada	31	9,971	3	700.5	22,300	882 [c]	28,070 [c]	3.3	2.2
Central African Rep.	4	623	6	1.0	260	5 [c]	1,190 [c]	4.2	2.6
Chad	8	1,284	6	1.8	220	8	1,000	10.9	7.8
Chile	16	757	21	66.3	4,260	143	9,180	2.1	0.9
China	1,281	9,598 [d]	137	1,209.5	940	5,625 [e]	4,390 [e]	8.0	7.2
Hong Kong, China	7	..	..	167.6	24,750	182	26,810	2.3	1.5
Colombia	44	1,139	42	80.1	1,830	257	5,870	1.5	–0.1
Congo, Dem. Rep.	54	2,345	24	5.0	90	31	580	3.0	0.2
Congo, Rep.	3	342	9	2.2	700	2	700	3.5	0.7
Costa Rica	4	51	77	16.2	4,100	33	8,260	2.8	1.0
Côte d'Ivoire	17	322	53	10.3	610	24	1,430	–0.9	–3.0
Croatia	4	57	78	20.3	4,640	43	9,760	5.2	5.3
Czech Rep.	10	79	132	56.7	5,560	148	14,500	2.0	2.1
Denmark	5	43	127	162.7	30,290	158	29,450	1.6	1.3
Dominican Rep.	9	49	178	20.0	2,320	51	5,870	4.1	2.5
Ecuador	13	284	47	19.0	1,450	41	3,130	3.0	1.2
Egypt, Arab Rep.	66	1,001	67	97.6	1,470	246	3,710	3.0	1.1
El Salvador	7	21	315	13.5	2,080	30	4,570	2.3	0.4
Eritrea	4	118	43	0.7	160	4	950	9.2	6.5
Estonia	1	45	32	5.6	4,130	15	11,120	5.8	6.2
Ethiopia	67	1,104	67	6.4	100	48	720	5.0	2.7
Finland	5	338	17	122.2	23,510	132	25,440	1.6	1.4
France	59	552	108	1,342.7 [f]	22,010 [f]	1,556	26,180	1.0	0.6
Georgia	5	70	74	3.3	650	11	2,210	5.4	6.4
Germany	82	357	231	1,870.4	22,670	2,163	26,220	0.2	0.0
Ghana	20	239	88	5.4	270	40 [c]	2,000 [c]	4.5	2.6
Greece	11	132	82	123.9	11,660	194	18,240	4.0	3.6
Guatemala	12	109	111	20.9	1,750	47	3,880	2.0	–0.6
Guinea	8	246	32	3.1	410	15	1,990	4.3	2.1
Haiti	8	28	301	3.7	440	13 [c]	1,580 [c]	–0.9	–2.7
Honduras	7	112	60	6.2	920	17	2,450	2.0	–0.6
Hungary	10	93	110	53.7	5,280	130	12,810	3.3	3.5
India	1,048	3,287	353	501.5	480	2,691	2,570	4.4	2.8
Indonesia	212	1,905	117	149.9	710	632	2,990	3.7	2.3
Iran, Islamic Rep.	66	1,648	40	112.1	1,710	415	6,340	5.9	4.2
Ireland	4	70	56	92.6	23,870	109	28,040	3.6	2.6
Israel	6	21	315	..	.. [g]	..	..	..	..
Italy	58	301	197	1,097.9	18,960	1,467	25,320	0.4	0.4
Jamaica	3	11	241	7.4	2,820	9	3,550	1.0	0.1
Japan	127	378	349	4,265.6	33,550	3,315	26,070	–0.7	–0.8
Jordan	5	89	58	9.1	1,760	21	4,070	4.9	2.0
Kazakhstan	15	2,725	5	22.3	1,510	81	5,480	9.5	10.2
Kenya	31	580	55	11.3	360	31	990	1.8	–0.2
Korea, Rep.	48	99	483	473.0	9,930	785	16,480	6.3	5.7
Kuwait	2	18	118	..	.. [g]	..	..	..	..
Kyrgyz Rep.	5	200	26	1.5	290	8	1,520	–0.5	–1.5
Lao PDR	6	237	24	1.7	310	9 [c]	1,610 [c]	5.0	2.6
Latvia	2	65	38	8.1	3,480	21	8,940	6.1	7.2
Lebanon	4	10	434	17.7	3,990	20	4,470	1.0	–0.3
Lesotho	2	30	69	1.0	470	6 [c]	2,710 [c]	3.8	2.6
Lithuania	3	65	54	12.7	3,660	34	9,880	6.7	6.9
Macedonia, FYR	2	26	80	3.5	1,700	13	6,210	0.3	0.1
Madagascar	16	587	28	3.9	240	12	720	–11.9	–14.4
Malawi	11	118	114	1.7	160	6	570	1.8	–0.3

Note: For data comparability and coverage, see the technical notes. Figures in italics are for years other than those specified.

Table 1 Size of the economy—continued

	Population	Surface area	Population density	Gross national income [a]		PPP gross national income [b]		Gross domestic product	
	millions	thousand sq. km	people per sq. km of land area	$ billions	Per capita $	$ billions	Per capita $	% growth	Per capita % growth
	2002	2002	2002	2002	2002	2002	2002	2001–2002	2001–2002
Malaysia	24	330	74	86.0	3,540	201	8,280	4.2	2.1
Mali	11	1,240	9	2.8	240	10	840	9.6	7.1
Mauritania	3	1,026	3	1.0	340	..	..	5.1	2.2
Mexico	101	1,958	53	596.7	5,910	862	8,540	0.7	-0.8
Moldova	4	34	129	1.7 [h]	460 [h]	7	1,560	7.2	7.6
Mongolia	2	1,567	2	1.1	440	4	1,650	3.7	2.6
Morocco	30	447	66	35.4	1,190	109	3,690	4.5	2.9
Mozambique	18	802	24	3.9	210 [i]	..	..	9.9	7.7
Myanmar	49	677	74	..	..	..	..	..	..
Namibia	2	824	2	3.3	1,780	12 [c]	6,650 [c]	3.0	1.2
Nepal	24	147	169	5.6	230	33	1,350	-0.6	-2.8
Netherlands	16	42	477	386.8	23,960	443	27,470	0.1	-0.6
New Zealand	4	271	14	53.1	13,710	77	20,020	3.8	3.2
Nicaragua	5	130	44	..	.. [i]	..	..	..	..
Niger	12	1,267	9	2.0	170	9 [c]	770 [c]	3.0	-0.2
Nigeria	133	924	146	38.7	290	103	780	-0.9	-3.1
Norway	5	324	15	171.8	37,850	163	35,840	2.0	1.4
Pakistan	145	796	188	59.2	410	281	1,940	4.4	1.9
Panama	3	76	40	11.8	4,020	17 [c]	5,870 [c]	0.8	-0.7
Papua New Guinea	5	463	12	2.8	530	11 [c]	2,080 [c]	-2.5	-4.7
Paraguay	6	407	14	6.4	1,170	25 [c]	4,450 [c]	-2.2	-4.3
Peru	27	1,285	21	54.7	2,050	128	4,800	5.2	3.7
Philippines	80	300	268	81.5	1,020	342	4,280	4.6	2.4
Poland	39	323	127	176.6	4,570	391	10,130	1.2	1.2
Portugal	10	92	110	108.7	10,840	174	17,350	0.4	0.3
Romania	22	238	97	41.3	1,850	141	6,290	4.3	4.5
Russian Fed.	144	17,075	9	307.9	2,140	1,127	7,820	4.3	4.8
Rwanda	8	26	331	1.9	230 [i]	10	1,210	9.4	6.3
Saudi Arabia	22	2,150	10	..	.. [j]	..	..	..	..
Senegal	10	197	52	4.7	470	15	1,510	2.4	0.0
Serbia & Montenegro	11	102	108	11.6 [k]	1,400 [k]	..	..	..	..
Sierra Leone	5	72	73	0.7	140	3	490	6.3	4.2
Singapore	4	1	6,826	86.1	20,690	96	23,090	2.2	1.4
Slovak Rep.	5	49	112	21.4	3,950	66	12,190	4.4	4.3
Slovenia	2	20	99	19.6	9,810	35	17,690	2.9	2.9
South Africa	44	1,221	36	113.5	2,600	430 [c]	9,870 [c]	3.0	2.2
Spain	41	506	82	594.1	14,430	842	20,460	1.8	1.6
Sri Lanka	19	66	293	15.9	840	64	3,390	3.0	1.7
Sweden	9	450	22	221.5	24,820	224	25,080	1.9	1.5
Switzerland	7	41	183	274.2	37,930	226	31,250	-0.2	-0.2
Syrian Arab Rep.	17	185	93	19.2	1,130	55	3,250	3.1	0.6
Tajikistan	6	143	45	1.1	180	6	900	9.1	7.9
Tanzania	35	945	40	9.6 [l]	280 [l]	19	550	5.8	3.6
Thailand	62	513	121	122.2	1,980	411	6,680	5.2	4.5
Togo	5	57	88	1.3	270	7	1,430	3.0	0.5
Tunisia	10	164	63	19.6	2,000	61	6,280	1.9	0.7
Turkey	70	775	90	174.0	2,500	426	6,120	7.8	6.1
Turkmenistan	6	488	12	6.7	1,200	25	4,570	14.9	12.6
Uganda	23	241	119	5.9	250	31 [c]	1,320 [c]	6.3	3.6
Ukraine	49	604	84	37.7	770	226	4,650	4.5	5.3
United Kingdom	59	243	244	1,486.2	25,250	1,523	25,870	1.5	1.4
United States	288	9,629	31	10,110.1	35,060	10,110	35,060	2.3	1.2
Uruguay	3	176	19	14.8	4,370	41	12,010	-10.8	-11.3
Uzbekistan	25	447	61	11.5	450	40	1,590	4.2	2.9
Venezuela, RB	25	912	28	102.6	4,090	127	5,080	-8.9	-10.6
Vietnam	81	332	247	34.9	430	180	2,240	7.1	5.8
Yemen, Rep.	19	528	35	9.4	490	14	750	4.2	1.1
Zambia	10	753	14	3.5	330	8	770	3.0	1.3
Zimbabwe	13	391	34	.. [i]	..	28	2,120	-5.6	-6.6
World	6,201 s	133,875 s	48 w	31,483.9 t	5,080 w	46,952 t	7,570 w	1.7 w	0.5 w
Low income	2,495	33,612	77	1,071.7	430	5,092	2,040	4.1	2.3
Middle income	2,742	67,898	41	5,033.3	1,840	15,431	5,630	3.2	2.2
Lower middle income	2,411	54,970	45	3,352.4	1,390	12,378	5,130	4.8	3.9
Upper middle income	331	12,928	26	1,667.9	5,040	3,050	9,220	-1.5	-2.7
Low & middle income	5,237	101,510	53	6,101.7	1,170	20,474	3,910	3.3	2.0
East Asia & Pacific	1,838	16,302	116	1,740.5	950	7,640	4,160	6.7	5.8
Europe & Central Asia	476	24,217	20	1,030.2	2,160	3,188	6,690	4.7	4.6
Latin America & Carib.	527	20,450	26	1,726.5	3,280	3,556	6,750	-0.5	-1.9
Middle East & N. Africa	306	11,135	28	670.0	2,230	1,657	5,410	..	..
South Asia	1,401	5,140	293	640.5	460	3,352	2,390	4.3	2.6
Sub-Saharan Africa	688	24,267	29	306.5	450	1,116	1,620	3.2	0.9
High income	965	32,365	31	25,383.7	26,310	26,622	27,590	1.3	0.8

a. Calculated using the World Bank Atlas method. b. PPP is purchasing power parity; see the technical notes. c. The estimate is based on regression; others are extrapolated from the latest International Comparison Programme benchmark estimates. d. Includes Taiwan, China; Macao, China; and Hong Kong, China. e. Estimate based on bilateral comparison between China, and USA (Ruoen and Kai, 1995). f. GNI and GNI per capita estimates include the French overseas departments of French Guiana, Guadeloupe, Martinique, and Reunion. g. Estimated to be high income (9,076 or more). h. Data excludes Transnistria. i. Estimated to be low income ($735 or less). j. Estimated to be upper middle income ($2,935–9,075). k. Data excludes Kosovo. l. Data refer to mainland Tanzania only.

Table 2 Millennium Development Goals: eradicating poverty and improving lives

	Eradicate extreme poverty and hunger			Achieve universal primary education		Promote gender equality		Reduce child mortality		Improve maternal health		
	Share of poorest quintile in national income or consumption %	Prevalence of child malnutrition % of children under 5		Primary completion rate (%)		Ratio of female to male enrollments in primary and secondary school (%) [a]		Under-five mortality rate per 1,000		Maternal mortality ratio per 100,000 live births modeled estimates	Births attended by skilled health staff % of total	
	1987–2001 [b]	1990	2001	1990	2001	1990	2000	1990	2001	1995	1990	2000
Albania	..	..	14	101	..	90	102	42	25	31	..	99
Algeria	7.0 c	9	6	82	..	80	98	69	49	150	..	92
Angola	..	20	..	..	28	..	84	260	260	1,300	..	23
Argentina	..	..	..	..	96	..	103	28	19	85	..	..
Armenia	6.7 c	..	3	..	..	..	106	58	35	29	..	98
Australia	5.9 d	..	..	..	..	96	100	10	6	6	100	100
Austria	7.0 d	..	..	..	..	90	97	9	5	11	..	..
Azerbaijan	7.4 c	..	17	47	100	94	101	106	96	37	..	88
Bangladesh	9.0 c	66	48	50	70	72	103	144	77	600	7	12
Belarus	8.4 c	..	..	97	..	..	101	21	20	33	..	100
Belgium	8.3 d	..	..	..	..	97	106	9	6	8	..	..
Benin	..	..	23	23	39	..	62	185	158	880	38	..
Bolivia	4.0 c	11	8	55	72	89	97	122	77	550	43	59
Bosnia & Herzegovina	..	..	4	..	88	..	..	22	18	15	43	100
Botswana	2.2 c	..	13	114	..	107	102	58	110	480	..	99
Brazil	2.2 d	7	..	48	71	..	103	60	36	260	79	99
Bulgaria	6.7 c	..	..	90	..	94	97	19	16	23	..	99
Burkina Faso	4.5 c	..	34	19	25	61	70	210	197	1,400	30	27
Burundi	5.1 c	..	45	46	43	82	79	190	190	1,900	20	25
Cambodia	6.9 c	..	45	71	70	..	83	115	138	590	47	34
Cameroon	4.6 c	15	22	57	43	82	81	139	155	720	58	56
Canada	7.3 d	..	..	..	..	94	101	8	7	6	..	..
Central African Rep.	2.0 c	..	..	28	19	61	..	180	180	1,200	66	44
Chad	..	..	28	19	19	..	56	203	200	1,500	15	16
Chile	3.2 d	..	1	94	99	98	88	19	12	33	..	..
China	5.9 d	17	10	99	..	81	98	49	39	60	..	70
Hong Kong, China	5.3	..	..	..	..	..	..	..	..	..	..	..
Colombia	3.0 d	10	7	72	85	104	104	36	23	120	100	100
Congo, Dem. Rep.	..	..	..	48	40	69	80	205	205	940	94	86
Congo, Rep.	..	..	..	61	44	88	89	110	108	1,100	..	70
Costa Rica	4.4 d	3	..	73	89	96	101	17	11	35	..	98
Côte d'Ivoire	7.1 c	..	21	44	40	..	71	155	175	1,200	50	47
Croatia	8.3 c	..	..	86	..	97	..	13	8	18	..	100
Czech Rep.	10.3 d	1	..	89	..	94	101	12	5	14	..	..
Denmark	8.3 d	..	..	..	..	96	103	9	4	15	..	..
Dominican Rep.	5.1 d	10	5	..	82	..	106	65	47	110	92	69
Ecuador	5.4 c	..	14	99	96	97	100	57	30	210	56	61
Egypt, Arab Rep.	8.6 c	10	4	77	..	78	94	104	41	170	37	90
El Salvador	3.3 d	15	12	61	80	100	98	60	39	180	90	90
Eritrea	..	..	..	22	35	82	77	155	111	1,100	..	..
Estonia	7.0 d	..	..	93	..	99	99	17	12	80	..	..
Ethiopia	2.4 d	48	47	22	24	68	68	193	172	1,800	8	10
Finland	10.1 d	..	..	..	..	105	106	7	5	6	..	..
France	7.2 d	..	..	..	..	98	100	9	6	20	..	..
Georgia	6.0 c	..	3	..	90	94	102	29	29	22	..	96
Germany	5.7 d	..	..	..	..	94	99	9	5	12	..	..
Ghana	5.6 c	30	25	63	64	..	88	126	100	590	55	44
Greece	7.1 d	..	..	..	..	93	101	11	5	2	..	..
Guatemala	3.8 d	..	24	43	52	..	92	82	58	270	30	41
Guinea	6.4 c	..	33	16	34	43	57	240	169	1,200	..	35
Haiti	..	27	17	28	70	..	..	150	123	1,100	..	24
Honduras	2.0 d	18	17	66	67	103	..	61	38	220	78	..
Hungary	10.0 c	2	..	93	..	96	100	17	9	23	..	..
India	8.1 c	64	..	70	76	68	78	123	93	440	..	..
Indonesia	8.4 c	..	25	92	91	91	98	91	45	470	44	42
Iran, Islamic Rep.	5.1 c	..	11	94	..	80	95	72	42	130	47	56
Ireland	6.7 d	..	..	..	..	99	..	9	6	9	78	..
Israel	6.9 d	..	..	..	..	99	100	12	6	8	..	..
Italy	6.0 d	..	..	..	..	95	98	10	6	11	..	..
Jamaica	6.7 c	5	4	90	94	97	101	20	20	120	92	95
Japan	10.6 d	..	..	..	..	96	101	6	5	12	100	..
Jordan	7.6 c	6	..	102	104	93	101	43	33	41	87	..
Kazakhstan	8.2 c	..	4	..	..	..	98	52	99	80	..	98
Kenya	5.6 c	..	22	87	63	..	97	97	122	1,300	50	44
Korea, Rep.	7.9 d	..	..	96	96	93	100	9	5	20	98	..
Kuwait	..	..	..	56	..	97	101	16	10	25	..	98
Kyrgyz Rep.	9.1 c	..	..	..	100	100	99	81	61	80	..	98
Lao PDR	7.6 c	..	40	44	69	75	82	163	100	650	..	21
Latvia	7.6 d	..	..	76	..	96	101	18	21	70	95	95
Lebanon	..	..	..	..	..	..	102	37	32	130	..	..
Lesotho	1.4 c	16	18	75	68	124	107	148	132	530	40	60
Lithuania	7.9 c	..	..	88	..	93	99	14	9	27	88	97
Macedonia, FYR	8.4 c	..	6	89	..	94	98	33	26	17	50	56
Madagascar	6.4 c	41	..	34	26	..	97	168	136	580	..	46
Malawi	4.9 c	28	25	33	64	79	94	241	183	580	..	56

Note: For data comparability and coverage, see the technical notes. Figures in italics are for years other than those specified.

	Eradicate extreme poverty and hunger — Share of poorest quintile in national income or consumption % 1987–2001[b]	Prevalence of child malnutrition % of children under 5 — 1990	2001	Achieve universal primary education — Primary completion rate (%) 1990	2001	Promote gender equality — Ratio of female to male enrollments in primary and secondary school (%)[a] 1990	2000	Reduce child mortality — Under-five mortality rate per 1,000 1990	2001	Improve maternal health — Maternal mortality ratio per 100,000 live births modeled estimates 1995	Births attended by skilled health staff % of total 1990	2000
Malaysia	4.4 d	25	..	91	..	98	105	21	8	39	..	96
Mali	4.6 c	..	..	11	23	57	66	254	231	630	40	57
Mauritania	6.4 c	48	32	34	46	67	93	183	183	870	..	..
Mexico	3.4 d	17	8	89	100	96	101	46	29	65	..	..
Moldova	7.1 c	..	..	67	79	103	102	37	32	65	100	97
Mongolia	5.6 c	12	13	..	82	107	112	107	76	65	..	..
Morocco	6.5 c	10	..	47	..	67	83	85	44	390	94	..
Mozambique	6.5 c	..	..	30	36	73	75	235	197	980	..	76
Myanmar	..	32	..	..	..	95	98	130	109	170	..	12
Namibia	1.4 d	26	..	70	..	111	104	84	67	370	..	..
Nepal	7.6 c	..	48	51	65	53	82	145	91	830	100	100
Netherlands	7.3 d	..	..	..	..	93	97	8	6	10	..	..
New Zealand	6.4 d	..	..	..	..	96	103	11	6	15	..	61
Nicaragua	2.3 c	..	12	45	65	..	105	66	43	250	..	..
Niger	2.6 c	43	40	18	20	54	67	320	265	920	31	42
Nigeria	4.4 c	35	31	72	67	76	..	190	183	1,100	100	..
Norway	9.7 d	..	..	..	..	97	101	9	4	9	40	20
Pakistan	8.8 c	40	..	44	59	47	61	128	109	200	..	90
Panama	3.6 c	6	..	87	94	96	100	34	25	100	40	..
Papua New Guinea	4.5 c	..	..	53	..	77	90	101	94	390	71	71
Paraguay	1.9 d	4	..	65	78	95	99	37	30	170	78	..
Peru	4.4 d	11	7	85	98	93	97	75	39	240	..	56
Philippines	5.4 c	34	32	89	..	..	103	66	38	240	..	..
Poland	7.8 c	..	..	100	..	96	98	22	9	12	98	100
Portugal	5.8 d	..	..	..	..	99	102	15	6	12	..	98
Romania	8.2 c	6	..	96	..	95	100	36	21	60	..	99
Russian Fed.	4.9 c	..	..	..	96	..	..	21	21	75	22	31
Rwanda	.. c	29	24	34	28	98	97	178	183	2,300	88	91
Saudi Arabia	..	..	..	60	..	82	94	44	28	23	42	51
Senegal	6.4 c	22	18	45	41	69	84	148	138	1,200	..	93
Serbia & Montenegro	..	..	2	72	96	96	..	26	19	15	..	42
Sierra Leone	1.1 c	29	27	..	32	67	77	323	316	2,100	..	100
Singapore	5.0 d	..	..	..	..	89	..	8	4	9	..	..
Slovak Rep.	8.8 d	..	..	96	..	98	101	14	9	14	100	..
Slovenia	9.1 d	..	..	99	..	97	..	10	5	17	..	84
South Africa	2.0 c	..	..	76	..	103	100	60	71	340	..	..
Spain	7.5 d	..	..	..	..	99	103	9	6	8	85	..
Sri Lanka	8.0 c	..	33	100	111	99	102	23	19	60	..	..
Sweden	9.1 d	..	..	..	..	97	115	7	3	8	..	..
Switzerland	6.9 d	..	..	..	..	92	96	8	6	8	64	..
Syrian Arab Rep.	..	..	..	98	..	82	92	44	28	200	..	77
Tajikistan	8.0 c	..	..	..	95	..	87	127	116	120	44	35
Tanzania	6.8 c	29	29	65	60	97	99	163	165	1,100	71	..
Thailand	6.1 c	..	..	93	90	94	95	40	28	44	32	51
Togo	..	25	25	41	63	59	70	152	141	980	80	90
Tunisia	5.7 c	10	4	75	..	82	100	52	27	70	77	81
Turkey	6.1 c	..	8	90	..	77	84	74	43	55	..	97
Turkmenistan	6.1 c	..	12	..	..	..	..	98	87	65	38	..
Uganda	7.1 c	23	23	49	65	..	89	165	124	1,100	..	99
Ukraine	8.8 c	..	3	58	..	..	92	22	20	45	100	99
United Kingdom	6.1 d	..	..	..	..	97	111	9	7	10	99	99
United States	5.2 d	..	..	..	..	95	100	11	8	12	..	100
Uruguay	4.5 d,e	6	..	95	98	..	105	24	16	50	..	96
Uzbekistan	9.2 c	..	..	..	100	..	..	65	68	60	97	95
Venezuela, RB	3.0 d	8	4	91	78	101	105	27	22	43	95	70
Vietnam	8.0 c	45	34	..	101	..	..	50	38	95	..	22
Yemen, Rep.	7.4 c	30	..	..	58	..	50	142	107	850	41	..
Zambia	3.3 c	25	..	91	73	..	92	192	202	870	62	84
Zimbabwe	4.6 c	12	13	97	..	96	94	80	123	610	..	..
World		.. w	.. w	.. w	.. w	84 w	92 w	93 w	81 w	.. w	.. w	.. w
Low income		..	..	68	..	74	78	141	121		43	..
Middle income		18	10	94	..	84	98	51	38		..	..
Lower middle income		..	..	95	..	82	97	54	41		..	..
Upper middle income		..	..	90	..	96	100	34	23		..	70
Low & middle income		19	15	83	..	80	90	101	88		..	..
East Asia & Pacific		..	..	98	..	83	97	59	44		..	..
Europe & Central Asia		..	..	..	..	..	102	44	38		..	..
Latin America & Carib.		..	..	81	..	79	95	53	34		..	..
Middle East & N. Africa		64	..	70	74	68	79	77	54		39	42
South Asia		..	..	57	..	79	82	129	99		..	..
Sub-Saharan Africa		..	..	..	..	96	101	178	171		..	..
High income		..	..	..	..	..	..	10	7		..	..

a. Break in series between 1997 and 1998 due to change from International Standard Classification of Education 1976 (ISCED76) to ISCED97. b. Data are for the most recent year available. c. Refers to expenditure shares by percentiles of population; ranked by per capita expenditure. d. Refers to income shares by percentiles of population; ranked by per capita income. e. Data refer to urban only.

Table 3 Expenditures on education and health

	Public expenditure per student [a]			Recurrent spending on primary teacher salaries [b]	Incidence of education expenditure		Health expenditure			Incidence of health expenditure	
	Primary % of GDP per capita 2000	Secondary % of GDP per capita 2000	Tertiary % of GDP per capita 2000	% of total recurrent spending on primary education 2000	lowest quintile 1991–2001[c]	highest quintile 1991–2001[c]	Public % of GDP 2000	Private % of GDP 2000	Total per capita $ 1997–2000	lowest quintile 1991–2001[c]	highest quintile 1991–2001[e]
Albania	..	..	..	82.5	..	..	2.1	1.3	41	..	..
Algeria	..	..	..	..	..	..	3.0	0.6	64	..	..
Angola	..	..	..	81.0	..	..	2.0	1.6	24	..	..
Argentina	12.5	16.4	17.7	..	..	..	4.7	3.9	658	..	..
Armenia	4.0	22.2	17.9	47.1	7	29	3.2	4.3	38	33	6
Australia	15.9	13.9	24.9	..	..	..	6.0	2.3	1,698	13	39
Austria	25.1	30.5	51.0	..	..	..	5.6	2.4	1,872	..	..
Azerbaijan	24.8	0.9	13.1	84.2	18	22	0.6	0.2	8	..	..
Bangladesh	7.3	14.1	38.9	75.0	12	32	1.4	2.4	14	16	26
Belarus	..	..	..	..	..	..	4.7	1.0	57	..	..
Belgium	17.0	..	..	..	..	..	6.2	2.5	1,936	..	..
Benin	10.3	12.1	108.2	73.6	..	..	1.6	1.6	11	..	..
Bolivia	13.3	11.0	45.2	80.6	..	..	4.9	1.8	67	..	..
Bosnia & Herzegovina	..	..	..	..	..	..	3.1	1.4	50	..	..
Botswana	..	..	..	..	..	..	3.8	2.2	191	..	..
Brazil	12.5	12.6	72.8	..	18[d]	25[d]	3.4	4.9	267	..	..
Bulgaria	15.2	17.1	14.5	..	..	..	3.0	0.9	59	..	..
Burkina Faso	..	..	..	69.3	..	..	3.0	1.2	8	13	25
Burundi	10.9	66.6	923.6	77.9	..	..	1.6	1.5	3	..	..
Cambodia	3.2	15.0	48.6	80.0	15	29	2.0	6.1	19	..	..
Cameroon	8.3	24.6	69.6	67.5	..	..	1.1	3.2	24	..	..
Canada	..	..	46.1	..	..	..	6.6	2.5	2,058	..	..
Central African Rep.	..	..	..	71.5	..	..	1.4	1.5	8	..	..
Chad	9.5	28.5	423.7	65.8	..	..	2.5	0.6	6	..	..
Chile	13.9	15.2	21.9	..	..	..	3.1	4.1	336	..	..
China	6.1	12.1	85.8	..	..	..	1.9	3.4	45	..	..
Hong Kong, China	..	..	..	..	..	..	..	..	..	..	..
Colombia	..	..	..	..	23	14	5.4	4.2	186	..	..
Congo, Dem. Rep.	..	..	..	89.7	..	..	1.1	0.4	9	27	13
Congo, Rep.	9.9	..	..	79.7	..	..	1.5	0.7	22	..	..
Costa Rica	14.9	19.4	55.7	..	21	20	4.4	2.0	273	..	..
Côte d'Ivoire	14.7	35.7	139.6	..	13	35	1.0	1.7	16	27	13
Croatia	..	..	..	77.5	..	..	8.0	2.0	434	11	32
Czech Rep.	12.5	23.2	33.9	..	..	..	6.6	0.6	358	..	..
Denmark	23.4	37.2	65.1	..	..	..	6.8	1.5	2,512	..	..
Dominican Rep	..	..	..	..	..	..	1.8	4.5	151	..	..
Ecuador	4.3	8.9	..	..	12	25	1.2	1.2	26	..	..
Egypt, Arab Rep.	..	..	39.4	..	..	..	1.8	2.0	51	8	38
El Salvador	2.0	26.4	10.4	..	..	..	3.8	5.0	184	..	..
Eritrea	..	..	..	70.4	..	..	2.8	1.5	9	..	..
Estonia	24.5	30.8	33.0	..	..	..	4.7	1.4	218	..	..
Ethiopia	..	..	..	79.5	..	..	1.8	2.8	5	..	..
Finland	17.3	25.5	39.7	..	..	..	5.0	1.6	1,559	..	..
France	18.0	29.3	30.3	..	..	..	7.2	2.3	2,057	..	..
Georgia	..	..	..	84.0	..	..	0.7	6.4	41	..	..
Germany	17.8	20.5	42.5	..	..	..	8.0	2.6	2,422	..	..
Ghana	..	..	..	82.3	16	21	2.2	2.0	11	..	..
Greece	16.0	17.9	26.7	..	..	..	4.6	3.7	884	12	33
Guatemala	4.9	12.1	..	..	..	..	2.3	2.4	79	..	..
Guinea	9.5	..	..	65.3	5	44	1.9	1.5	13	..	..
Haiti	..	..	..	90.0	..	..	2.4	2.5	21	4	48
Honduras	..	..	..	88.0	..	..	4.3	2.5	62	..	..
Hungary	17.7	18.7	30.5	..	..	..	5.1	1.7	315	21	12
India	7.2	23.1	..	76.8	..	..	0.9	4.0	23	..	..
Indonesia	3.2	8.7	..	80.1	15	29	0.6	2.1	19	10	32
Iran, Islamic Rep.	10.3	11.8	81.6	..	..	..	2.5	3.0	258	12	29
Ireland	13.3	15.2	27.8	..	..	..	5.1	1.6	1,692	..	..
Israel	21.2	22.5	31.6	..	..	..	8.3	2.6	2,021	..	..
Italy	21.2	27.1	26.0	..	..	..	6.0	2.1	1,498	..	..
Jamaica	16.2	26.8	80.0	..	22	15	2.6	2.9	165	..	..
Japan	21.3	..	..	..	..	..	6.0	1.8	2,908	..	..
Jordan	13.7	16.1	31.1	..	..	..	4.2	3.9	137	..	..
Kazakhstan	..	..	..	..	..	..	2.7	1.0	44	..	..
Kenya	0.4	1.2	496.9	95.8	8	26	1.8	6.5	28	..	..
Korea, Rep.	18.3	16.8	8.0	..	17	21	2.6	3.4	584	14[e]	24[e]
Kuwait	..	..	..	..	..	..	2.6	0.4	586	..	..
Kyrgyz Rep.	..	18.3	32.2	78.2	14	27	2.2	2.2	12	..	..
Lao PDR	6.5	8.7	145.3	80.4	12	34	1.3	2.1	11	..	..
Latvia	23.6	25.2	22.5	..	..	..	3.5	2.4	174	..	..
Lebanon	10.5	..	9.3	..	..	..	2.5	9.9	499	..	..
Lesotho	27.0	76.3	962.7	70.1	..	..	5.2	1.1	28	..	..
Lithuania	61.4	..	40.4	..	..	..	4.3	1.7	185	..	..
Macedonia, FYR	..	30.6	44.8	..	9	40	5.1	0.9	106	..	..
Madagascar	3.9	..	76.2	57.6	8	41	2.5	1.0	9	12	30
Malawi	..	..	..	86.0	16	25	3.6	4.0	11	..	..

Note: For data comparability and coverage, see the technical notes. Figures in italics are for years other than those specified.

Table 3 Expenditures on education and health—continued

	Public expenditure per student [a]			Recurrent spending on primary teacher salaries [b]	Incidence of education expenditure		Health expenditure			Incidence of health expenditure	
	Primary % of GDP per capita 2000	Secondary % of GDP per capita 2000	Tertiary % of GDP per capita 2000	% of total recurrent spending on primary education 2000	lowest quintile 1991–2001 [c]	highest quintile 1991–2001 [c]	Public % of GDP 2000	Private % of GDP 2000	Total per capita $ 1997–2000	lowest quintile 1991–2001 [c]	highest quintile 1991–2001 [c]
Malaysia	11.2	19.9	86.1	..	..	..	1.5	1.0	101	..	..
Mali	13.7	..	241.4	68.9	..	..	2.2	2.7	10	..	..
Mauritania	11.7	36.4	..	81.8	..	..	3.4	0.9	14	..	..
Mexico	11.7	13.8	45.2	..	19	21	2.5	2.9	311	..	..
Moldova	1.3	28.7	19.3	32.2	..	..	2.9	0.6	11	..	..
Mongolia	..	40.6	26.8	85.0	..	..	4.6	2.0	23	..	..
Morocco	20.5	49.9	102.7	..	12	24	1.3	3.2	50	..	..
Mozambique	..	..	..	73.9	..	..	2.7	1.6	9	..	..
Myanmar	1.6	1.9	19.4	..	..	..	0.4	1.8	153	..	..
Namibia	20.7	34.0	147.1	..	..	..	4.2	2.9	136	..	..
Nepal	14.2	15.6	98.7	80.0	11	46	0.9	..	..	..	..
Netherlands	15.4	21.8	43.0	..	..	..	5.5	2.6	1,900	..	..
New Zealand	19.9	22.3	25.5	..	..	..	6.2	1.8	1,062	..	..
Nicaragua	20.5	..	..	67.3	11	35	2.3	2.1	43	18	18
Niger	22.3	81.0	441.0	74.1	..	..	1.8	2.1	5	..	..
Nigeria	..	..	..	90.9	..	..	0.5	1.7	8	..	..
Norway	29.2	..	46.5	..	..	..	6.6	1.2	2,832	..	..
Pakistan	..	..	..	80.7	14	29	0.9	3.2	18	..	..
Panama	15.8	24.4	47.7	..	12	21	5.3	2.3	268	..	..
Papua New Guinea	11.1	18.0	40.4	..	..	..	3.6	0.5	31	..	..
Paraguay	..	18.1	..	..	..	..	3.0	4.9	112	..	..
Peru	8.0	10.6	22.0	..	15	22	2.8	2.0	100	..	..
Philippines	14.3	12.5	23.2	..	..	..	1.6	1.8	33	..	..
Poland	26.5	12.0	20.2	..	..	..	4.2	1.8	246	..	..
Portugal	20.5	29.4	28.2	..	..	..	5.8	2.4	862	..	..
Romania	..	..	..	..	22	17	1.9	1.0	48	..	..
Russian Fed.	..	20.5	15.8	..	..	..	3.8	1.5	92	..	..
Rwanda	6.9	..	571.6	91.4	..	..	2.7	2.5	12	..	..
Saudi Arabia	..	..	86.9	..	..	..	4.2	1.1	448	..	..
Senegal	13.6	33.1	244.6	63.4	..	..	2.6	2.0	22	..	..
Serbia & Montenegro	..	..	..	..	..	..	2.9	2.7	50	..	..
Sierra Leone	..	..	..	66.9	..	..	2.6	1.7	6	..	..
Singapore	..	..	..	..	..	..	1.2	2.3	814	..	..
Slovak Rep.	10.8	19.2	30.8	..	..	..	5.3	0.6	210	..	..
Slovenia	..	..	..	..	..	..	6.8	1.8	788	..	..
South Africa	14.0	17.9	61.3	..	14	35	3.7	5.1	255	16	17
Spain	18.8	25.5	19.8	..	..	..	5.4	2.3	1,073	..	..
Sri Lanka	..	..	..	..	..	..	1.8	1.8	31	20	20
Sweden	23.5	28.3	53.5	..	..	..	6.5	1.9	2,179	..	..
Switzerland	23.2	28.2	55.8	..	..	..	5.9	4.8	3,573	..	..
Syrian Arab Rep.	12.9	23.3	..	..	..	..	1.6	0.9	30	..	..
Tajikistan	..	..	9.9	..	..	..	0.9	2.3	6	..	..
Tanzania	..	..	..	88.8	14	37	2.8	3.1	12	17	29
Thailand	12.5	12.8	38.2	..	..	..	2.1	1.6	71	..	..
Togo	11.6	23.1	295.3	74.8	..	..	1.5	1.3	8	..	..
Tunisia	16.2	28.4	89.8	..	..	..	2.9	2.6	110	..	..
Turkey	17.6	11.8	72.1	..	..	..	3.6	1.4	150	..	..
Turkmenistan	..	..	..	73.8	..	..	4.6	0.8	52	..	..
Uganda	..	..	..	73.8	13	32	1.5	2.4	10	..	..
Ukraine	..	21.2	28.2	..	..	..	2.9	1.2	26	..	..
United Kingdom	14.0	14.9	26.3	..	..	..	5.9	1.4	1,747	..	..
United States	17.9	22.4	..	..	..	..	5.8	7.2	4,499	..	..
Uruguay	8.2	12.0	21.3	..	..	..	5.1	5.8	653	..	..
Uzbekistan	..	..	..	73.0	..	..	2.6	2.6	29	..	..
Venezuela, RB	..	..	..	..	..	..	2.7	2.0	233	..	..
Vietnam	..	..	..	55.0	18	21	1.3	3.9	21	12	29
Yemen, Rep.	..	..	..	73.3	19	22	2.1	2.8	20	..	..
Zambia	..	..	..	78.3	..	..	3.5	2.1	18	..	..
Zimbabwe	13.2	20.1	200.9	75.0	..	..	3.1	4.2	43.0	..	..
World	.. m	.. m	.. m				5.4 w	3.9 w	482 w		
Low income	..	..	..				1.1	3.2	21		
Middle income	..	..	..				3.0	2.9	115		
Lower middle income	..	..	..				2.7	3.1	85		
Upper middle income	12.4	..	..				3.5	2.5	330		
Low & middle income	..	..	..				2.7	2.9	71		
East Asia & Pacific	7.6	..	40.1				1.8	2.9	44		
Europe & Central Asia	..	..	..				4.0	1.5	108		
Latin America & Carib.	..	..	..				3.3	3.7	262		
Middle East & N. Africa	..	..	..				2.9	1.7	170		
South Asia	7.3	..	..				1.0	3.7	21		
Sub-Saharan Africa	..	..	..				2.5	3.4	29		
High income							6.0	4.2	2,735		

a. Break in series between 1997 and 1998 due to change from ISCED76 to ISCED97. b. Source: Bruns, Barbara, Alain Mingat and Ramahatra Rakotomalala, 2003, "Achieving Universal Primary Education by 2015: A Chance for Every Child" (2003). Washington D.C., The World Bank, Table A.2. c. Data are for the most recent year available. d. Includes northeast and southeast Brazil only. e. Data refer to rural only.

Table 4 Service indicators

	Primary teacher absence rate	Primary pupil-teacher ratio	Trained teachers in primary education	Health personnel absence rate	Child immunization rate		Tuberculosis treatment success rate	Physicians	Hospital beds	Inpatient admission rate	Access to an improved water source	Access to improved sanitation facilities
	% of total	pupils per teacher	% of total	% of total	% of children under age one		% of registered cases	per 1,000 people	per 1,000 people	% of population	% of population	% of population
					Measles 2001	DPT 2001	1999	1995–2000 a	1995–2000 a	1995–2000 a	2000	2000
	2002–2003	2000	2000									
Albania	..	22	..	..	95	97	..	1.3	3.2	..	97	91
Algeria	..	28	93.7	..	83	89	87	1.0	2.1	..	89	92
Angola	..	35	..	..	72	41	..	0.1	..	..	38	44
Argentina	..	22	..	..	94	82	59	2.7	3.3	..	..	..
Armenia	..	..	..	..	93	94	88	3.2	0.7	8	..	..
Australia	..	..	..	..	93	92	84	2.5	7.9	16	100	100
Austria	..	13	..	..	79	84	77	3.1	8.6	30	100	100
Azerbaijan	..	19	99.9	..	99	98	88	3.6	9.7	6	78	81
Bangladesh	..	57	65.0	35	76	83	81	0.2	..	..	97	48
Belarus	..	17	100.0	..	99	99	..	4.4	12.2	26	100	..
Belgium	..	12	..	..	83	96	..	3.9	7.3	20	..	..
Benin	..	54	65.0	..	65	76	77	0.1	..	..	63	23
Bolivia	..	24	74.2	..	79	81	74	1.3	1.7	..	83	70
Bosnia & Herzegovina	..	..	..	..	92	91	90	1.4	1.8	..	..	..
Botswana	..	27	89.2	..	83	87	71	..	..	..	95	66
Brazil	..	26	..	..	99	97	11	1.3	3.1	0	87	76
Bulgaria	..	18	..	..	96	96	..	3.4	7.4	..	100	100
Burkina Faso	..	47	80.4	..	46	41	61	0.0	1.4	2	42	29
Burundi	..	50	..	..	75	74	..	..	..	..	78	88
Cambodia	..	53	95.9	..	59	60	93	0.3	..	..	30	17
Cameroon	..	63	..	..	62	43	75	0.1	..	..	58	79
Canada	..	15	..	..	96	97	..	2.1	3.9	10	100	100
Central African Rep.	..	74	..	..	29	23	..	0.0	..	..	70	25
Chad	..	71	37.2	..	36	27	..	..	..	..	27	29
Chile	..	25	..	..	97	97	83	1.1	2.7	..	93	96
China	..	20	..	..	79	79	96	1.7	2.4	4	75	38
Hong Kong, China	..	..	..	..	..	..	78	1.3	..	..	..	..
Colombia	..	26	..	..	75	74	82	1.2	1.5	..	91	86
Congo, Dem. Rep.	..	26	..	..	46	40	69	0.1	..	..	45	21
Congo, Rep.	..	51	64.6	..	35	31	61	0.3	..	..	51	14
Costa Rica	..	25	..	..	82	88	81	0.9	1.7	9	95	93
Côte d'Ivoire	..	48	99.1	..	61	57	63	0.1	..	..	81	52
Croatia	..	18	..	..	94	94	..	2.3	..	..	..	..
Czech Rep.	..	18	..	..	97	98	78	3.1	8.8	21	..	..
Denmark	..	10	..	..	94	97	..	3.4	4.5	20	100	..
Dominican Rep.	..	40	..	..	98	62	81	2.2	1.5	..	86	67
Ecuador	16	23	..	..	99	90	75	1.7	1.6	..	85	86
Egypt, Arab Rep.	..	22	..	..	97	99	87	1.6	2.1	3	97	98
El Salvador	..	26	..	..	99	99	78	1.1	1.6	..	77	82
Eritrea	..	45	70.5	..	88	93	44	0.0	..	..	46	13
Estonia	..	14	..	..	95	94	63	3.0	7.4	18	..	..
Ethiopia	..	55	70.4	..	52	56	76	..	..	..	24	12
Finland	..	16	..	..	96	99	..	3.1	7.5	27	100	100
France	..	19	..	..	84	98	..	3.0	8.2	23	..	..
Georgia	..	16	..	..	73	86	61	4.4	4.8	5	79	100
Germany	..	15	..	..	89	97	..	3.6	9.1	24	..	..
Ghana	..	33	68.6	..	81	80	55	0.1	..	..	73	72
Greece	..	13	..	..	88	88	..	4.4	4.9	15	..	..
Guatemala	..	33	..	..	90	82	81	0.9	1.0	..	92	81
Guinea	..	44	..	..	52	43	..	0.1	..	..	48	58
Haiti	..	..	..	..	53	43	70	0.2	0.7	..	46	28
Honduras	..	34	..	..	95	95	88	0.8	1.1	..	88	75
Hungary	..	11	..	..	99	99	..	3.2	8.2	24	99	99
India	23 b	40	..	43	56	64	82	..	..	..	84	28
Indonesia	18	22	..	42	59	60	50	..	..	..	78	55
Iran, Islamic Rep.	..	25	96.5	..	96	95	82	0.9	1.6	..	92	83
Ireland	..	22	..	..	73	84	..	2.3	9.7	15	..	..
Israel	..	12	..	..	94	95	..	3.8	6.0	..	..	..
Italy	..	11	..	..	70	95	71	6.0	4.9	18	..	..
Jamaica	..	36	..	..	85	90	74	1.4	2.1	..	92	99
Japan	..	20	..	..	96	85	76	1.9	16.5	10	..	..
Jordan	..	..	..	..	99	99	88	1.7	1.8	11	96	99
Kazakhstan	..	19	..	..	96	96	79	3.5	8.5	15	91	99
Kenya	..	30	96.6	..	76	76	78	0.1	..	..	57	87
Korea, Rep.	..	32	..	..	97	99	..	1.3	6.1	6	92	63
Kuwait	..	14	100.0	..	99	98	..	1.9	2.8	..	..	..
Kyrgyz Rep.	..	24	48.4	..	99	99	83	3.0	9.5	21	77	100
Lao PDR	..	30	76.2	..	50	40	84	0.2	..	..	37	30
Latvia	..	15	..	..	98	97	74	2.8	10.3	21	..	..
Lebanon	..	17	..	..	94	93	96	2.1	2.7	17	100	99
Lesotho	..	48	74.2	..	77	85	69	0.1	..	..	78	49
Lithuania	..	16	..	..	97	95	84	4.0	9.2	24	67	67
Macedonia, FYR	..	22	..	..	92	90	..	2.2	4.9	9	..	..
Madagascar	..	50	..	..	55	55	..	0.1	..	..	47	42
Malawi	..	56	51.2	..	82	90	71	..	1.3	..	57	76

Note: For data comparability and coverage, see the technical notes. Figures in italics are for years other than those specified.

Table 4 Service indicators—continued

	Primary teacher absence rate	Primary pupil-teacher ratio	Trained teachers in primary education	Health personnel absence rate	Child immunization rate		Tuberculosis treatment success rate	Physicians	Hospital beds	Inpatient admission rate	Access to an improved water source	Access to improved sanitation facilities
	% of total	pupils per teacher	% of total	% of total	% of children under age one		% of registered cases	per 1,000 people	per 1,000 people	% of population	% of population	% of population
					Measles 2001	DPT 2001						
	2002–2003	2000	2000				1999	1995–2000 [a]	1995–2000 [a]	1995–2000 [a]	2000	2000
Malaysia	..	18	..	..	92	97	90	0.7	2.0	..	65	69
Mali	..	63	..	..	37	51	68	0.1	0.2	1	37	33
Mauritania	..	42	..	..	58	61	..	0.1	..	..	88	74
Mexico	..	27	..	..	97	97	80	1.8	1.1	6	92	99
Moldova	..	20	..	..	81	90	..	3.5	12.1	19	60	30
Mongolia	..	32	92.9	..	95	95	86	2.4	..	..	80	68
Morocco	..	28	..	..	96	96	88	0.5	1.0	3	57	43
Mozambique	..	64	61.8	..	92	80	71	..	..	..	72	64
Myanmar	..	32	85.4	..	73	72	81	0.3	..	..	77	41
Namibia	..	32	36.0	..	58	63	50	0.3	..	..	88	28
Nepal	..	37	44.5	..	71	72	87	0.0	0.2	..	100	100
Netherlands	..	10	..	..	96	97	79	3.2	10.8	10	..	..
New Zealand	..	16	..	..	85	90	..	2.2	6.2	13	77	85
Nicaragua	..	36	..	..	99	92	81	0.9	1.5	..	59	20
Niger	..	42	84.1	..	51	31	60	0.0	0.1	28	62	54
Nigeria	..	..	..	..	40	26	75	..	..	..	100	..
Norway	..	..	..	..	93	95	77	2.9	14.6	17	90	62
Pakistan	..	..	..	..	54	56	70	0.6	..	..	90	92
Panama	..	25	79.0	..	97	98	80	1.7	2.2	..	42	82
Papua New Guinea	15	36	..	19	58	56	66	0.1	..	..	78	94
Paraguay	..	20	..	..	77	66	..	1.1	1.3	..	80	71
Peru	13	25	..	26	97	85	93	0.9	1.5	1	86	83
Philippines	..	35	..	..	75	70	87	1.2	..	..	..	..
Poland	..	11	..	..	97	98	69	2.2	4.9	16	..	..
Portugal	..	13	..	..	87	96	85	3.2	4.0	12	58	53
Romania	..	20	..	..	98	99	78	1.8	7.6	18	99	..
Russian Fed.	..	17	..	..	98	96	65	4.2	12.1	22	41	8
Rwanda	..	51	..	..	78	86	67	..	..	..	95	100
Saudi Arabia	..	12	..	..	94	97	66	1.7	2.3	11	78	70
Senegal	..	51	100.0	..	48	52	..	0.1	0.4	..	98	100
Serbia & Montenegro	..	20	100.0	..	90	93	..	2.0	5.3	..	57	66
Sierra Leone	..	44	78.9	..	37	44	75	0.1	..	..	100	100
Singapore	..	..	..	..	89	92	95	1.6	..	..	100	100
Slovak Rep.	..	19	..	..	99	99	79	3.5	7.1	20	100	..
Slovenia	..	14	..	..	98	92	88	2.3	5.7	..	86	87
South Africa	..	33	67.9	..	72	81	60	0.6	..	..	..	..
Spain	..	14	..	..	94	95	..	3.3	4.1	12	77	94
Sri Lanka	..	..	..	..	99	99	84	0.4	..	..	100	100
Sweden	..	11	..	..	94	99	..	2.9	3.6	18	100	100
Switzerland	..	14	..	..	81	95	..	3.5	17.9	15	100	100
Syrian Arab Rep.	..	24	92.2	..	93	92	84	1.3	1.4	..	80	90
Tajikistan	..	22	..	..	86	83	..	2.0	..	..	60	90
Tanzania	..	40	44.1	..	83	85	78	0.0	..	..	68	90
Thailand	..	21	..	..	94	96	77	0.4	2.0	..	84	96
Togo	..	34	80.0	..	58	64	76	0.1	1.7	..	54	34
Tunisia	..	23	..	..	92	96	91	0.7	1.7	..	80	84
Turkey	..	..	..	..	90	88	..	1.3	2.6	8	82	90
Turkmenistan	..	..	..	..	98	95	..	3.0	..	..	..	..
Uganda	26	59	45.0	35	61	60	61	..	..	..	52	79
Ukraine	..	20	..	..	99	99	..	3.0	11.8	20	98	99
United Kingdom	..	18	..	..	85	94	..	1.8	4.1	15	100	100
United States	..	15	..	..	91	94	76	2.8	3.6	12	100	100
Uruguay	..	21	..	..	94	94	83	3.7	4.4	..	98	94
Uzbekistan	..	..	..	..	99	97	79	3.1	8.3	..	85	89
Venezuela, RB	..	..	..	..	49	70	82	2.4	1.5	..	83	68
Vietnam	..	28	84.9	..	97	98	92	0.5	1.7	8	77	47
Yemen, Rep.	..	30	..	..	79	76	83	0.2	0.6	..	69	38
Zambia	17	45	100.0	..	85	78	..	0.1	..	..	64	78
Zimbabwe	..	37	..	..	68	75	73	0.1	..	..	83	62
World		27 m	.. m		72 w	73 w		.. w	.. w	9 w	81 w	55 w
Low income		39	78.9		59	61		..	..		76	43
Middle income		21	..		86	85		1.9	3.3	6	82	60
Lower middle income		21	..		85	84		1.9	3.3	6	81	58
Upper middle income		21			91	92		1.8	3.3	11	..	..
Low & middle income		29			71	71		..	..		79	51
East Asia & Pacific		21			76	77		1.7	2.4	4	76	46
Europe & Central Asia		..			95	94		3.1	8.9	18	91	..
Latin America & Carib.		26			91	89		1.5	2.2	2	86	77
Middle East & N. Africa		24			92	92		..	..		88	85
South Asia		42	66.5		58	65		..	..		84	34
Sub-Saharan Africa		47	78.9		58	53		..	..		58	53
High income		17	..		90	94		3.0	7.4	15	..	..

a. Data are for the most recent year available. b. Average for 14 states.

Table 5 Foreign aid recipient indicators

	Net official development assistance or official aid ($ millions)		Aid per capita ($)		Aid dependency ratios								Donor fragmentation index
					Aid as % of GNI		Aid as % of gross capital formation		Aid as % of imports of goods and services		Aid as % of central government expenditure		
	1996	2001	1996	2001	1996	2001	1996	2001	1996	2001	1996	2001	
Albania	228	269	72	85	8.3	6.3	54.7	33.6	20.3	15.0	28.5	..	0.9
Algeria	304	182	11	6	0.7	0.3	2.6	1.3	2.5	1.4	2.2	1.1	0.7
Angola	473	268	40	20	8.1	3.4	18.1	8.3	7.9	3.2	..	..	0.9
Argentina	135	151	4	4	0.1	0.1	0.3	0.4	0.3	0.4	..	..	0.9
Armenia	293	212	90	69	18.3	9.7	91.8	53.8	31.8	20.9	..	..	0.7
Australia	..	..	..	..	..	..	..	..	..	..	..	..	..
Austria													
Azerbaijan	96	226	12	28	3.1	4.2	10.5	18.9	5.3	8.9	18.1	16.4	0.8
Bangladesh	1,236	1,024	10	8	3.0	2.1	15.2	9.4	15.8	9.8	..	21.4	0.9
Belarus	77	39	8	4	0.5	0.3	2.2	1.4	1.0	0.4	1.6	1.1	0.8
Belgium													
Benin	288	273	51	42	13.3	11.6	76.3	60.1	36.1	36.0	..	..	0.9
Bolivia	832	729	110	86	11.6	9.4	69.2	70.5	42.3	31.3	48.9	34.2	0.9
Bosnia & Herzegovina	845	639	239	157	33.5	12.7	73.6	111.1	33.8	23.8	..	..	0.9
Botswana	75	29	48	17	1.6	0.6	6.2	2.5	2.9	1.0	4.3	..	0.9
Brazil	288	349	2	2	0.0	0.1	0.2	0.3	0.3	0.4	..	..	0.8
Bulgaria	182	346	22	44	1.9	2.6	22.6	12.5	2.8	3.7	3.8	7.4	0.7
Burkina Faso	420	389	41	34	16.9	15.7	61.8	61.7	55.0	57.4	..	..	0.8
Burundi	111	131	18	19	12.5	19.3	102.3	274.3	69.9	80.7	44.6	39.8	0.9
Cambodia	422	409	38	33	13.6	12.4	51.8	66.9	30.5	20.1	..	..	0.9
Cameroon	412	398	30	26	4.8	4.9	29.5	26.0	16.7	13.3	..	31.1	0.8
Canada	..	..	..	..	..	..	..	..	..	..	..	..	..
Central African Rep.	170	76	49	20	16.2	7.9	369.9	56.0	70.7	49.5	..	..	0.8
Chad	296	179	43	23	18.8	11.3	123.7	26.9	57.1	18.1	..	..	0.9
Chile	196	58	14	4	0.3	0.1	1.1	0.4	0.8	0.2	1.4	0.4	0.8
China	2,646	1,460	2	1	0.3	0.1	0.8	0.3	1.5	0.5	4.1	2.2	0.7
Hong Kong, China	13	4	2	1	0.0	0.0	0.0	0.0	0.0	0.0	..	..	0.6
Colombia	189	380	5	9	0.2	0.5	0.9	3.1	1.0	2.0	1.3	1.9	0.7
Congo, Dem. Rep.	166	251	4	5	3.1	5.3	10.3	95.1	9.0	18.1	..	..	0.9
Congo, Rep.	429	75	160	24	26.4	3.8	62.7	10.0	17.6	3.4	56.8	10.5	0.7
Costa Rica	−10	2	−3	1	−0.1	0.0	−0.5	0.1	−0.2	0.0	−0.4	0.1	0.9
Côte d'Ivoire	965	187	67	11	8.6	1.9	65.6	18.2	19.3	4.3	35.6	10.6	0.7
Croatia	133	113	29	26	0.7	0.6	3.1	2.3	1.3	1.0	1.5	1.3	0.9
Czech Rep.	129	314	12	31	0.2	0.6	0.6	1.8	0.4	0.7	0.6	1.4	0.8
Denmark	..	..	..	..	..	..	..	..	..	..	..	..	..
Dominican Rep.	100	105	13	12	0.8	0.5	3.9	2.1	1.3	0.9	4.8	2.0	0.8
Ecuador	253	171	22	13	0.2	0.9	0.8	3.2	4.1	2.1	..	..	0.9
Egypt, Arab Rep.	2,199	1,255	37	19	3.2	1.3	19.6	8.2	11.6	5.6	10.0	..	0.7
El Salvador	302	234	52	37	2.9	1.7	19.3	10.7	8.2	3.7	..	66.9	0.8
Eritrea	159	280	43	67	24.6	40.9	71.6	115.2	27.3	52.3	..	..	0.9
Estonia	59	69	42	50	1.4	1.3	4.9	4.5	1.7	1.2	4.0	4.1	0.8
Ethiopia	818	1,080	14	16	13.7	17.5	80.6	95.9	55.9	53.6	..	39.3	0.9
Finland	..	..	..	..	..	..	..	..	..	..	..	..	..
France	..	..	..	..	..	..	..	..	..	..	..	..	..
Georgia	310	290	58	55	10.3	9.0	93.3	48.9	..	21.5	..	82.7	0.7
Germany	..	..	..	..	..	..	..	..	..	..	..	..	..
Ghana	651	652	37	33	9.6	12.6	32.2	51.2	25.5	19.2	..	..	0.9
Greece	..	..	..	..	..	..	..	..	..	..	..	..	..
Guatemala	194	225	19	19	1.2	1.1	9.7	7.1	5.1	3.5	..	..	0.8
Guinea	299	272	44	36	7.9	9.2	44.6	41.3	28.4	27.4	..	32.6	0.9
Haiti	370	166	50	20	12.8	4.4	45.2	14.4	46.8	13.2	140.8	54.2	0.8
Honduras	359	678	62	103	9.4	10.8	28.2	34.7	14.1	18.3	..	..	0.9
Hungary	204	418	20	41	0.5	0.8	1.7	3.0	0.9	1.1	1.0	1.9	0.8
India	1,897	1,705	2	2	0.5	0.4	2.3	1.6	3.2	2.2	3.3	2.0	0.8
Indonesia	1,123	1,501	6	7	0.5	1.1	1.6	4.9	1.7	2.5	3.4	4.3	0.7
Iran, Islamic Rep.	169	115	3	2	0.2	0.1	0.8	0.3	0.9	0.5	0.5	0.2	0.7
Ireland	..	..	..	..	..	..	..	..	..	..	..	..	..
Israel	2,217	172	389	27	2.3	0.8	9.4	3.7	5.2	0.3	4.7	0.3	0.1
Italy	..	..	..	..	..	..	..	..	..	..	..	..	..
Jamaica	58	54	23	21	0.9	0.7	3.1	2.3	1.4	1.0	2.2	1.8	0.9
Japan	..	..	..	..	..	..	..	..	..	..	..	..	..
Jordan	507	432	117	86	7.6	4.9	24.0	18.9	8.7	6.7	21.6	15.1	0.8
Kazakhstan	125	148	8	10	0.6	0.7	3.7	2.6	1.6	1.3	..	4.6	0.7
Kenya	597	453	22	15	6.6	4.0	38.4	31.1	16.1	10.8	22.3	..	0.9
Korea, Rep.	−149	−111	−3	−2	0.0	0.0	−0.1	−0.1	−0.1	−0.1	−0.2	..	0.5
Kuwait	3	4	1	2	0.0	0.0	0.1	0.0	0.0	0.0	0.0	0.1	0.8
Kyrgyz Rep.	231	188	50	38	12.9	12.9	50.1	68.5	21.4	29.2	56.5	69.5	0.8
Lao PDR	332	243	69	45	17.8	14.6	61.2	62.9	42.5	40.6	..	..	0.8
Latvia	72	106	29	45	1.4	1.4	7.5	5.1	2.3	2.4	4.5	4.8	0.9
Lebanon	232	241	57	55	1.7	1.4	6.0	8.6	2.9	..	4.7	3.3	0.8
Lesotho	104	54	55	26	8.2	5.5	18.9	18.4	8.9	6.9	21.9	..	0.9
Lithuania	91	130	25	37	1.2	1.1	4.7	5.0	1.8	1.8	4.6	4.1	0.8
Macedonia, FYR	106	248	53	122	2.4	7.3	11.9	39.4	5.7	12.4	..	..	0.9
Madagascar	357	354	26	22	9.3	7.8	76.7	49.6	30.5	188.8	51.4	48.7	0.9
Malawi	492	402	52	38	20.5	23.4	174.9	210.2	42.8	38.3	..	..	0.9

Note: For data comparability and coverage, see the technical notes. Figures in italics are for years other than those specified.

Table 5   Foreign aid recipient indicators—continued

	Net official development assistance or official aid ($ millions)		Aid per capita ($)		Aid dependency ratios								Donor fragmentation index
					Aid as % of GNI		Aid as % of gross capital formation		Aid as % of imports of goods and services		Aid as % of central government expenditure		
	1996	2001	1996	2001	1996	2001	1996	2001	1996	2001	1996	2001	
Malaysia	−457	27	−22	1	−0.5	0.0	−1.1	0.1	−0.5	0.0	−2.1	..	0.3
Mali	491	350	50	32	19.1	13.9	81.9	62.7	49.1	28.4	..	..	0.8
Mauritania	272	262	116	95	25.7	26.6	131.3	97.4	43.7	56.6	..	..	0.8
Mexico	287	75	3	1	0.1	0.0	0.4	0.1	0.2	0.0	0.6	−0.1	0.8
Moldova	36	119	8	28	2.1	7.5	8.9	40.2	2.8	9.7	7.6	35.4	0.8
Mongolia	201	212	87	88	19.4	20.5	71.8	67.5	33.5	28.7	90.8	65.9	0.7
Morocco	650	517	24	18	1.8	1.6	9.1	6.1	5.3	3.8	..	5.9	0.8
Mozambique	888	935	55	52	33.2	28.2	149.7	70.8	74.9	20.3	..	..	0.9
Myanmar	43	127	1	3	..	..	..	..	1.8	4.1	0.3	0.3	0.7
Namibia	188	109	116	61	5.3	3.4	23.3	14.4	8.0	5.1	14.8	12.3	0.9
Nepal	391	388	19	16	8.6	6.7	31.8	28.8	23.8	19.1	51.0	39.4	0.9
Netherlands	..	..	..	..	..	..	..	..	..	..	..	..	..
New Zealand	..	..	..	..	..	..	..	..	..	..	..	..	..
Nicaragua	934	928	205	178	58.4	..	180.0	..	57.2	41.3	137.9	84.7	0.9
Niger	255	249	27	22	13.0	12.9	132.7	111.0	51.2	47.9	..	..	0.8
Nigeria	190	185	2	1	0.6	0.5	3.8	2.2	1.3	1.1	..	..	0.9
Norway	..	..	..	..	..	..	..	..	..	..	..	..	..
Pakistan	884	1,938	7	14	1.4	3.4	7.3	20.7	5.1	13.1	6.2	16.2	0.8
Panama	49	28	18	10	0.6	0.2	1.8	0.8	0.5	0.3	2.2	0.6	0.8
Papua New Guinea	381	203	82	39	7.6	7.2	32.2	33.8	13.9	11.0	27.1	20.2	0.5
Paraguay	89	61	18	11	0.9	0.9	3.9	3.6	1.7	2.0	5.9	4.8	0.6
Peru	329	451	14	17	0.6	0.9	2.6	4.5	2.6	4.0	3.3	4.6	0.7
Philippines	901	577	13	7	1.0	0.8	4.5	4.6	2.0	1.5	5.9	4.2	0.5
Poland	1,167	966	30	25	0.9	0.5	4.1	2.5	2.7	1.6	2.1	1.5	0.8
Portugal	..	..	..	..	..	..	..	..	..	..	..	..	..
Romania	233	648	10	29	0.7	1.6	2.6	7.4	1.8	3.8	2.1	5.3	0.8
Russian Fed.	1,282	1,110	9	8	0.3	0.4	1.2	1.6	1.3	1.3	..	1.5	0.6
Rwanda	467	291	82	37	34.1	17.3	234.9	92.7	120.6	62.0	..	..	0.9
Saudi Arabia	23	27	1	1	0.0	0.0	0.1	0.1	0.0	0.1	..	..	0.7
Senegal	580	419	68	43	12.7	9.2	67.5	45.0	32.0	21.7	58.8	41.6	0.8
Serbia & Montenegro [a]	70	1,306	7	123	..	11.3	..	89.2	1.6	25.0	..	..	0.9
Sierra Leone	184	334	40	65	20.0	45.8	195.2	563.9	51.2	110.1	132.3	52.5	0.8
Singapore	15	1	4	0	0.0	0.0	0.0	0.0	0.0	0.0	0.1	0.0	0.7
Slovak Rep.	98	164	18	30	0.5	0.8	1.3	2.5	0.7	0.9	1.1	2.1	0.9
Slovenia	82	126	41	63	0.4	0.7	1.9	2.6	0.8	1.1	1.1	1.7	0.8
South Africa	364	428	9	10	0.3	0.4	1.5	2.5	1.0	1.2	0.8	1.3	0.9
Spain	..	..	..	..	..	..	..	..	..	..	..	..	..
Sri Lanka	487	330	28	18	3.6	2.1	14.4	9.6	7.5	4.4	12.6	8.0	0.7
Sweden	..	..	..	..	..	..	..	..	..	..	..	..	..
Switzerland	..	..	..	..	..	..	..	..	..	..	..	..	..
Syrian Arab Rep.	219	153	15	9	1.6	0.8	6.6	3.7	3.1	2.1	1.6	1.3	0.7
Tajikistan	103	159	17	25	10.5	15.5	44.0	124.0	11.7	18.4	..	129.1	0.8
Tanzania	877	1,233	29	36	13.8	13.3	81.2	77.7	38.6	53.5	..	..	0.9
Thailand	830	281	14	5	0.5	0.2	1.1	1.0	0.9	0.4	2.8	1.2	0.2
Togo	157	47	39	10	10.9	3.8	57.1	17.9	18.7	6.8	..	..	0.8
Tunisia	124	378	14	39	0.7	2.0	2.5	6.9	1.3	3.3	1.9	3.6	0.7
Turkey	238	167	4	2	0.1	0.1	0.5	0.7	0.4	0.3	0.5	0.2	0.7
Turkmenistan	24	72	5	13	1.0	1.2	..	3.3	1.2	2.3	..	..	0.6
Uganda	676	783	34	34	11.3	14.1	69.6	68.9	40.5	48.3	..	64.6	0.9
Ukraine	398	519	8	11	0.9	1.4	3.9	6.4	1.8	2.4	..	4.7	0.7
United Kingdom	..	..	..	..	..	..	..	..	..	..	..	..	..
United States	..	..	..	..	..	..	..	..	..	..	..	..	..
Uruguay	35	15	11	5	0.1	0.1	1.1	0.6	0.8	0.3	0.6	0.3	0.8
Uzbekistan	88	153	4	6	0.6	1.4	2.2	6.6	1.8	4.5	..	..	0.7
Venezuela, RB	38	45	2	2	0.1	0.0	0.3	0.2	0.2	0.2	0.3	0.1	0.8
Vietnam	939	1,435	13	18	3.9	4.4	13.6	14.1	7.3	7.7	16.5	18.0	0.7
Yemen, Rep.	247	426	16	24	4.8	5.0	18.6	25.9	7.0	9.1	10.8	23.0	0.9
Zambia	610	374	66	36	19.9	10.7	145.1	51.2	35.8	20.9	..	..	0.9
Zimbabwe	371	159	31.8	12	4.5	1.8	23.4	22.5	10.5	7.3	12.5	..	0.9
World	62,264 s	58,244 s	11 w	10 w	0.2 w	0.2 w	0.9 w	0.9 w	0.8 w	0.6 w	.. w	.. w	
Low income	24,618	24,611	11	10	2.6	2.5	10.4	10.9	9.4	8.4	..	..	
Middle income	22,401	21,006	9	8	0.4	0.4	1.7	1.7	1.6	1.3	..	..	
Lower middle income	18,557	17,145	8	7	0.5	0.5	1.9	1.9	2.3	1.8	..	..	
Upper middle income	3,175	3,336	10	10	0.3	0.2	1.0	0.9	0.6	0.5	..	..	
Low & middle income	58,925	57,208	12	11	1.0	0.9	3.9	3.9	3.6	2.9	..	..	
East Asia & Pacific	8,039	7,394	5	4	0.6	0.5	1.4	1.3	1.6	1.2	..	..	
Europe & Central Asia	8,670	9,783	18	21	0.8	1.0	3.3	4.4	2.4	2.3	..	..	
Latin America & Carib.	7,430	5,985	15	12	0.4	0.3	1.8	1.6	1.9	1.2	..	..	
Middle East & N. Africa	5,884	4,836	22	16	1.0	0.7	5.0	3.3	3.6	2.7	..	..	
South Asia	5,169	5,871	4	4	1.0	1.0	4.7	4.3	5.5	5.1	..	..	
Sub-Saharan Africa	16,552	13,933	28	21	5.2	4.6	27.3	24.6	14.2	11.0	..	..	
High income	3,339	1,036	4	1	0.0	0.0	0.1	0.0	0.1	0.0	..	..	

Note: Regional aggregates include data for economies not specified elsewhere. World and income group totals include aid not allocated by country or region. The 2001 data exclude aid from the World Food Programme.

a. Aid to the states of the former Socialist Federal Republic of Yugoslavia that is not otherwise specified is included in regional and income group aggregates.

Table 6 Aid flows from Development Assistance Committee members

Net flows to part I countries

	Net official development assistance										Untied aid [a]	
	$ millions		% of GNI		annual average % change in volume [b]	Per capita of donor country [b]		% of general government disbursements		% of bilateral ODA commitments	
					1995–96 to 2000–2001	$	$				
	1996	2001	1996	2001		1996	2001	1996	2001	1996	2001
Australia	1,074	873	0.27	0.25	0.6	46	49	0.76	0.74	78.1	59.3
Austria	557	533	0.24	0.29	0.2	51	66	0.46	0.57	..	..
Belgium	913	867	0.34	0.37	3.5	67	85	0.68	0.82	..	89.8
Canada	1,795	1,533	0.32	0.22	−2.6	59	51	0.68	0.57	31.5	31.7
Denmark	1,772	1,634	1.04	1.03	4.4	265	306	1.72	2.00	61.3	93.3
Finland	408	389	0.33	0.32	5.0	61	75	0.59	0.72	60.2	87.5
France	7,451	4,198	0.48	0.32	−6.6	95	72	0.93	0.66	38.7	66.6
Germany	7,601	4,990	0.32	0.27	−1.2	67	62	0.67	0.59	60.0	84.6
Greece	184	202	0.15	0.17	24.3	14	19	0.33	0.40	..	17.3
Ireland	179	287	0.31	0.33	11.9	43	74	0.67	0.92	..	100.0
Italy	2,416	1,627	0.20	0.15	−2.3	34	28	0.38	0.32	..	7.8
Japan	9,439	9,847	0.20	0.23	3.0	73	89	0.58	0.64	98.9	81.1
Luxembourg	82	141	0.44	0.82	18.1	156	325	1.05	1.89	94.4	..
Netherlands	3,246	3,172	0.81	0.82	5.0	161	195	1.73	1.97	82.2	91.2
New Zealand	122	112	0.21	0.25	5.6	22	30	0.49	0.61	..	..
Norway	1,311	1,346	0.84	0.83	1.7	278	299	1.82	1.95	88.4	98.9
Portugal	218	268	0.21	0.25	6.7	18	26	0.47	0.58	100.0	57.7
Spain	1,251	1,737	0.22	0.30	7.3	25	43	0.50	0.79	0.0	68.9
Sweden	1,999	1,666	0.84	0.81	4.4	173	207	1.27	1.52	78.9	86.5
Switzerland	1,026	908	0.34	0.34	3.0	108	123	..	..	92.9	96.1
United Kingdom	3,199	4,579	0.27	0.32	5.8	58	80	0.66	0.84	86.1	93.9
United States	9,377	11,429	0.12	0.11	3.2	38	39	0.37	0.36	28.4	..
Total or average	**55,622**	**52,336**	**0.25**	**0.22**	**1.8**	**59**	**63**	**0.63**	**0.61**	**71.3**	**79.1**

Net flows to part II countries

	Net official development aid						
	$ millions		% of GNI		annual average % change in volume [b]	Per capita of donor country [b]	
					1995–96 to 2000–2001	$	$
	1996	2001	1996	2001		1996	2001
Australia	10	5	0.00	0.00	2.8	0	0
Austria	226	212	0.10	0.11	0.7	21	26
Belgium	70	88	0.03	0.04	7.0	5	9
Canada	181	152	0.03	0.02	−5.4	6	5
Denmark	120	181	0.07	0.11	10.3	18	34
Finland	57	61	0.05	0.05	3.6	9	12
France	711	1,334	0.05	0.10	22.4	9	23
Germany	1,329	687	0.06	0.04	−20.0	12	8
Greece	2	9	0.00	0.01	66.2	0	1
Ireland	1	0	0.00	0.00	−61.8	0	0
Italy	294	281	0.02	0.03	7.0	4	5
Japan	184	84	0.00	0.00	−35.9	1	1
Luxembourg	2	9	0.01	0.05	12.5	4	20
Netherlands	13	214	0.00	0.06	16.8	1	13
New Zealand	0	0	0.00	0.00	−1.4	0	0
Norway	50	32	0.03	0.02	−11.0	11	7
Portugal	18	28	0.02	0.03	10.8	1	3
Spain	98	14	0.02	0.00	−31.5	2	0
Sweden	178	119	0.07	0.06	−0.5	15	15
Switzerland	97	63	0.03	0.02	−3.7	10	9
United Kingdom	362	461	0.03	0.03	1.8	7	8
United States	1,694	1,542	0.02	0.02	4.6	7	5
Total or average	**5,696**	**5,574**	**0.03**	**0.02**	**0.2**	**6**	**7**

a. Excluding administrative costs and technical cooperation. b. At 2000 exchange rates and prices.

Table 7 Key indicators for other economies

	Population	Surface area	Gross national income				Gross domestic product		Life expectancy at birth	Reduce child mortality	Education	
	Thousands	Thousands sq. km	$ millions	Per capita $	$ millions	PPP Per capita $	% growth	Per capita % growth	years	Under-five mortality rate per 1,000	Primary completion rate % of relevant age group	Adult illiteracy rate % ages 15 and above
	2002	2002	2002 [a]	2002 [a]	2002 [b]	2002 [b]	2001–2002	2001–2002	2001	2001	1995–2001 [c]	2001
Afghanistan	27,963 [d]	652	..	.. [e]	..	.. [f]	..	..	43	257	8	..
American Samoa	70	0.2	..	..	..	..	..	..	..	..	..	..
Andorra	70	0.5	..	..	..	..	..	..	..	7	..	..
Antigua & Barbuda	69	0.4	647	9,390	686	9,960	2.7	2.1	..	14	..	..
Aruba	90	0.2	..	.. [g]	..	..	..	..	..	..	..	5
Bahamas, The	314	13.9	4,533	14,860	4,867	15,900	..	..	70	16	..	5
Bahrain	672	0.7	7,246	11,130	10,350	15,900	..	..	73	16	91	12
Barbados	269	0.4	2,614	9,750	4,173	15,560	..	..	75	14	..	0 [h]
Belize	253	23.0	750	2,960	1,352	5,340	3.7	1.2	74	40	82	7
Bermuda	60	0.1	..	.. [g]	..	..	..	..	..	..	..	..
Bhutan	851	47.0	505	590	..	..	7.7	4.8	63	95	59	..
Brunei	351	5.8	..	.. [g]	..	..	..	..	76	6	..	8
Cape Verde	458	4.0	590	1,290	2,164 [i]	4,720 [i]	4.0	1.4	69	38	117	25
Cayman Islands	35	0.3	..	.. [g]	..	..	..	..	..	..	..	..
Channel Islands	149	0.2	..	..	..	..	..	..	79	..	..	..
Comoros	586	2.2	228	390	959	1,640	3.0	0.5	61	79	..	44
Cuba	11,263	110.9	..	..	..	..	..	..	77	9	..	3
Cyprus	765	9.3	9,372	12,320	13,798 [i]	18,040 [i]	2.0	1.4	78	6	..	3
Djibouti	657	23.2	590	900	1,361	2,070	1.6	–0.3	45	143	30	35
Dominica	72	0.8	228	3,180	348	4,840	–2.8	–2.7	76	15	103	..
Equatorial Guinea	481	28.1	327	700	2,689	5,590	0.2	–2.4	51	153	..	16
Faeroe Islands	50	1.4	..	.. [g]	..	..	..	..	..	..	..	..
Fiji	823	18.3	1,775	2,160	4,371	5,310	4.4	3.6	69	21	..	7
French Polynesia	240	4.0	3,794	16,150	5,725	24,360	..	..	73	12	..	..
Gabon	1,291	267.7	4,028	3,120	6,870	5,320	3.0	0.6	53	90	80	..
Gambia, The	1,376	11.3	392	280	2,316 [i]	1,680 [i]	–0.6	–3.1	53	126	70	62
Greenland	60	341.7	..	.. [g]	..	..	..	..	73	25	106	..
Grenada	102	0.3	356	3,500	644	6,330	–0.5	–1.8	73	9	..	..
Guam	159	0.6	..	.. [g]	..	..	..	..	78	..	..	..
Guinea-Bissau	1,253	36.1	193	150	935	750	–4.2	–6.3	45	211	31	60
Guyana	772	215.0	651	840	2,919	3,780	0.3	–0.4	63	72	89	1
Iceland	284	103.0	7,944	27,970	8,118	28,590	0.0	–0.7	80	4	..	..
Iraq	24,256	438.3	..	.. [j]	..	..	..	..	62	133	..	60
Isle of Man	80	0.6	..	.. [f]	..	..	..	..	..	..	..	..
Kiribati	95	0.7	77	810	..	..	2.8	0.7	62	69	..	..
Korea, Dem. Rep.	22,519	120.5	..	.. [e]	..	..	..	..	61	55	..	..
Liberia	3,295	111.4	489	150	..	..	4.2	1.6	47	235	..	45
Libya	5,534	1,759.5	..	.. [f]	..	..	..	..	72	19	..	19
Liechtenstein	30	0.2	..	.. [g]	..	..	..	..	..	11	..	..
Luxembourg	444	2.6	17,221 [k]	38,830 [k]	22,644	51,060	0.8	0.2	77	5	..	6
Macao, China	443	..	6,329 [k]	14,380 [k]	8,349 [i]	18,970 [i]	..	..	79	..	..	6
Maldives	287	0.3	598	2,090	..	..	2.3	0.0	69	77	..	3
Malta	397	0.3	3,632	9,200	6,634	16,790	..	..	78	5	..	8
Marshall Islands	53	0.2	125	2,350	..	..	4.0	..	65	66	..	..
Mauritius	1,212	2.0	4,669	3,850	12,764	10,530	4.4	3.3	72	19	111	15
Mayotte	145	0.4	..	.. [f]	..	..	..	..	..	..	..	..
Micronesia, Fed. Sts.	122	0.7	242	1,980	..	..	2.0	0.2	68	24	..	..
Monaco	30	0.0	..	.. [g]	..	..	..	..	..	5	..	3
Netherlands Antilles	220	0.8	..	..	..	..	..	..	73	..	..	..
New Caledonia	220	18.6	2,989	14,050	4,670	21,960	..	..	..	10	..	..
N. Mariana Islands	80	0.5	..	.. [g]	..	..	..	..	..	..	..	..
Oman	2,539	309.5	19,137	7,720	32,788	12,910	2.2	–0.3	74	13	76	27
Palau	20	0.5	142	7,140	..	..	3.0	..	..	29	..	..
Puerto Rico	3,869	9.0	42,052	10,950	60,679	15,800	..	..	76	..	..	6
Qatar	610	11.0	..	.. [g]	..	..	..	..	75	16	44	18
Samoa	176	2.8	250	1,420	942	5,350	1.3	0.0	69	25	99	1
San Marino	30	0.1	..	.. [g]	..	..	..	..	..	6	..	..
São Tomé & Principe	154	1.0	45	290	..	..	3.0	0.9	65	74	84	..
Seychelles	84	0.5	538	6,530	..	..	–2.4	–3.8	73	17	..	..
Solomon Islands	443	28.9	254	570	672 [i]	1,520 [i]	–4.0	–6.7	69	24	..	..
Somalia	9,391	637.7	..	.. [e]	..	..	..	..	47	225	..	..
St. Kitts & Nevis	46	0.4	293	6,370	450	9,780	–4.3	–6.3	71	24	110	..
St. Lucia	159	0.6	609	3,840	792	5,000	–0.5	–1.6	72	19	106	..
St. Vincent & Grenadines	117	0.4	329	2,820	595	5,100	0.7	0.0	73	25	84	..
Sudan	32,365	2,505.8	11,471	350	54,561	1,690	10.6	8.3	58	107	46	41
Suriname	423	163.3	828	1,960	..	..	2.7	2.0	70	32	..	20
Swaziland	1,088	17.4	1,285	1,180	4,928	4,530	1.8	–0.1	45	149	81	20
Timor-Leste	..	14.9	402	.. [e]	..	..	..	..	..	124	54	..
Tonga	101	0.8	143	1,410	641	6,340	1.6	1.1	71	20	..	..
Trinidad & Tobago	1,318	5.1	8,553	6,490	11,446	8,680	2.7	2.0	72	20	81	2
United Arab Emirates	3,049	83.6	..	.. [g]	..	..	..	..	75	9	80	23
Vanuatu	206	12.2	221	1,080	569	2,770	–0.3	–2.4	68	42	..	..
Virgin Islands (U.S.)	110	0.3	..	.. [g]	..	..	..	..	78	11	..	..
West Bank & Gaza	3,212	..	2,982	930	..	..	–19.1	–22.2	72	25	..	..

a. Preliminary World Bank estimates calculated using the World Bank Atlas method. b. Purchasing power parity; see the technical notes. c. Data are for the most recent year available. d. Estimate does not account for recent refugee flows. e. Estimated to be low income ($735 or less). f. Estimated to be upper middle income ($2,936 to $9,075). g. Estimated to be high income ($9,076 or more). h. Less than 0.5. i. The estimate is based on regression; others are extrapolated from the latest International Comparison Programme benchmark estimates. j. Estimated to be lower middle income ($736 to $2,935). k. Refers to GDP and GDP per capita.

Technical notes

These technical notes discuss the sources and methods used to compile the indicators included in this edition of Selected World Development Indicators. The notes follow the order in which the indicators appear in the tables.

Sources

The data published in the Selected World Development Indicators are taken from *World Development Indicators 2003*. Where possible, however, revisions reported since the closing date of that edition have been incorporated. In addition, newly released estimates of population and gross national income (GNI) per capita for 2002 are included in table 1.

The World Bank draws on a variety of sources for the statistics published in the *World Development Indicators*. Data on external debt are reported directly to the World Bank by developing member countries through the Debtor Reporting System. Other data are drawn mainly from the United Nations and its specialized agencies, from the International Monetary Fund (IMF), and from country reports to the World Bank. Bank staff estimates are also used to improve currentness or consistency. For most countries, national accounts estimates are obtained from member governments through World Bank economic missions. In some instances these are adjusted by staff to ensure conformity with international definitions and concepts. Most social data from national sources are drawn from regular administrative files, special surveys, or periodic censuses.

For more detailed notes about the data, please refer to the World Bank's *World Development Indicators 2003*.

Data consistency and reliability

Considerable effort has been made to standardize the data, but full comparability cannot be assured, and care must be taken in interpreting the indicators. Many factors affect data availability, comparability, and reliability: statistical systems in many developing economies are still weak; statistical methods, coverage, practices, and definitions differ widely; and cross-country and intertemporal comparisons involve complex technical and conceptual problems that cannot be unequivocally resolved. Data coverage may not be complete for economies experiencing problems, such as those deriving from internal or external conflicts, affecting the collecting and reporting of data. For these reasons, although the data are drawn from the sources thought to be most authoritative, they should be construed only as indicating trends and characterizing major differences among economies rather than offering precise quantitative measures of those differences. Also, national statistical agencies tend to revise their historical data, particularly for recent years. Thus, data of different vintages may be published in different editions of

World Bank publications. Readers are advised not to compile such data from different editions. Consistent time series are available from the *World Development Indicators 2003* CD-ROM.

Ratios and growth rates

For ease of reference, the tables usually show ratios and rates of growth rather than the simple underlying values. Values in their original form are available from the *World Development Indicators 2003* CD-ROM. Unless otherwise noted, growth rates are computed using the least-squares regression method (see *Statistical methods* below). Because this method takes into account all available observations during a period, the resulting growth rates reflect general trends that are not unduly influenced by exceptional values. To exclude the effects of inflation, constant price economic indicators are used in calculating growth rates. Data in italics are for a year or period other than that specified in the column heading—up to two years before or after for economic indicators and up to three years for social indicators, because the latter tend to be collected less regularly and change less dramatically over short periods.

Constant price series

An economy's growth is measured by the increase in value added produced by the individuals and enterprises operating in that economy. Thus, measuring real growth requires estimates of GDP and its components valued in constant prices. The World Bank collects constant price national accounts series in national currencies and recorded in the country's original base year. To obtain comparable series of constant price data, it rescales GDP and value added by industrial origin to a common reference year, currently 1995. This process gives rise to a discrepancy between the rescaled GDP and the sum of the rescaled components. Because allocating the discrepancy would give rise to distortions in the growth rate, it is left unallocated.

Summary measures

The summary measures for regions and income groups, presented at the end of most tables, are calculated by simple addition when they are expressed in levels. Aggregate growth rates and ratios are usually computed as weighted averages. The summary measures for social indicators are weighted by population or subgroups of population, except for infant mortality, which is weighted by the number of births. See the notes on specific indicators for more information.

For summary measures that cover many years, calculations are based on a uniform group of economies so that the composition of the aggregate does not change over time. Group measures are compiled only if the data available for a given year account for at least two-thirds of the full group, as defined for the 1995 benchmark year. As long as this criterion is met, economies for which data are missing are assumed to behave like those that provide estimates. Readers should keep in mind that the summary measures are estimates of representative aggregates for each topic and that nothing meaningful can be deduced about behavior at the country level by working back from group indicators. In addition, the estimation process may result in discrepancies between subgroup and overall totals.

Table 1. Size of the economy

Population is based on the de facto definition of population, which counts all residents regardless of legal status or citizenship—except for refugees not permanently settled in the country of asylum, who are generally considered part of the population of their country of origin. The values shown are midyear estimates for 2002. Population estimates are usually based on national censuses, but the frequency and quality of these vary by country. Errors and undercounting occur even in high-income countries; in developing countries such errors may be substantial because of limits in the transport, communications, and other resources required to conduct a full census. Intercensal estimates are usually interpolation or extrapolations based on demographic models.

Surface area is a country's total area, including areas under inland bodies of water and some coastal waterways.

Population density is midyear population divided by land area in square kilometers. Land area is a country's total area excluding areas under inland bodies of water and coastal waterways.

Gross national income (GNI—formerly gross national product or GNP), the broadest measure of national income, is the sum of value added by all resident producers plus any product taxes (less subsidies) not included in the valuation of output plus net receipts of primary income (compensation of employees and property income) from abroad. Data are converted from national currency to current U.S. dollars using the World Bank Atlas method. This involves using a three-year average of exchange rates to smooth the effects of transitory exchange rate fluctuations. (See the section on statistical methods below for further discussion of the Atlas method).

GNI per capita is gross national income divided by midyear population. GNI per capita in U.S. dollars is converted using the World Bank Atlas method. The World Bank uses GNI per capita in U.S. dollars to classify economies for analytical purposes and to determine borrowing eligibility.

PPP Gross national income, which is GNI converted to international dollars using purchasing power parity (PPP) conversion factors, is included because nominal exchange rates do not always reflect international differences in relative prices. At the PPP rate, one international dollar has the same purchasing power over domestic GNI that the U.S. dollar has over U.S. GNI. PPP rates allow a standard comparison of real price levels between countries, just as conventional price indexes allow comparison of real values over time. The PPP conversion factors used here are derived from price surveys covering 118 countries conducted by the International Comparison Programme. For Organisation for Economic Co-operation and Development countries data come from the most recent round of surveys, completed in 2000; the rest are either from the 1996 survey, or data from the 1993 or earlier round, which have been extrapolated to the 1996 benchmark. Estimates for countries not included in the surveys are derived from statistical models using available data.

PPP GNI per capita is PPP GNI divided by midyear population.

Gross domestic product (GDP) per capita growth is based on GDP measured in constant prices. GDP is the sum of value added by all resident producers plus any product taxes (less subsidies) not included in the valuation of output. Growth in GDP is considered a broad measure of growth of an economy. GDP in constant prices can be estimated by measuring the total quantity of goods and services produced in a period, valuing them at an agreed set of base year prices, and subtracting the cost of intermediate inputs, also in constant prices. Growth is calculated from constant price GDP data in local currency.

Table 2. Millennium Development Goals: eradicating poverty and improving lives

Share of the poorest quintile in national consumption is the share of consumption (or, in some cases, income) that accrues to the poorest 20 percent of the population. Data on personal or household income or consumption come from nationally representative household surveys. The data in the table refer to different years between 1987 and 2001. Footnotes to the data indicate whether the ranking are based on per capital income or consumption. Each distribution is based on percentiles of population-rather than of households-with households ranked by income or expenditure per person.

Prevalence of child malnutrition is the percentage of children under five whose weight for age is less than minus two standard deviations from the median for the international reference population ages 0–59 months. The reference population, adopted by the World Health Organization in 1983, is based on children from the United States, who are assumed to be well nourished. Estimates of child malnutrition are from national survey data. The proportion of children who are underweight is the most common indicator of malnutrition. Being underweight, even mildly, increases the risk of death and inhibits cognitive development in children.

Moreover, it perpetuates the problem from one generation to the next, as malnourished women are more likely to have low-birth-weight babies.

Primary completion rate is the total number of students successfully completing (or graduating from) the last year of primary school in a given year, divided by the total number of children of official graduation age in the population. The primary completion rate reflects the primary cycle as nationally defined, ranging from three to four years of primary education (in a very small number of countries) to five or six years (in most countries) and seven or eight years (in a relatively small number of countries). For any country it is therefore consistent with the gross and net enrollment ratios. The numerator may include coverage children who have repeated one or more grades of primary school but are now graduating successfully as well as who entered school early. The denominator is the number of children of official graduation age, which could cause the primary completion rate to exceed 100 percent. There are other limitations that contribute to completion rates exceeding 100 percent, such as the use of estimates for population, different times of the year that the school and population surveys are conducted, and other discrepancies in the numbers used in the calculation

Ratio of female to male enrollments in primary and secondary school is the ratio of the number of female students enrolled in primary and secondary school to the number of male students. Eliminating gender disparities in education would help to increase the status and capabilities of women. This indicator is an imperfect measure of the relative accessibility of schooling for girls. With a target date of 2005, this is the first of the targets to fall due. School enrollment data are reported to the UNESCO Institute for Statistics by national education authorities. Primary education provides children with basic reading, writing, and mathematics skills along with an elementary understanding of such subjects as history, geography, natural science, social science, art, and music. Secondary education completes the provision of basic education that began at the primary level, and aims at laying foundations for lifelong learning and human development, by offering more subject-or skill-oriented instruction using more specialized teachers.

Under-five mortality rate is the probability that a newborn baby will die before reaching age five, if subject to current age-specific mortality rates. The probability is expressed as a rate per 1,000. The main sources of mortality date are vital registration systems and direct or indirect estimates based on sample surveys or censuses. To produce harmonized estimates of under-five mortality rates that make use of all available information in a transparent way, a methodology that fits a regression line to the relationship between mortality rates and their reference dates using weighted least squares was developed and adopted by both UNICEF and the World Bank.

Maternal mortality ratio is the number of women who die from pregnancy-related causes during pregnancy and childbirth, per 100,000 live births. The data shown here have been collected in various years and adjusted to a common 1995 base year. The values are modeled estimates based on an exercise carried out by the World Health Organization (WHO) and United Nations Children's Fund(UNICEF). In this exercise maternal mortality was estimated with a regression model using information on fertility, birth attendants, and HIV prevalence. This cannot be assumed to provide an accurate estimate of maternal mortality in any country in the table.

Births attended by skilled health staff are the percentage of deliveries attended by personnel trained to give the necessary supervision, care, and advice to women during pregnancy, labor, and the postpartum period, to conduct deliveries on their own, and to care for newborns. The share of births attended by skilled health staff is an indicator of a health system's ability to provide adequate care for a pregnant women. Good antenatal and postnatal care improves maternal health and reduces maternal and infant mortality. But data may not reflect such improvements because health information system are often weak, material deaths are underreported, and rates of maternal mortality are difficult to measure.

Table 3. Expenditures on education and health

Public expenditure per student is the public current spending on education divided by the number of students by level, as a percentage of gross domestic product (GDP) per capita. Data on education are compiled by the UNESCO Institute for Statistics from official responses to surveys and from reports provided by education authorities in each country. The data on education spending in the table refer solely to public spending—government spending on public education plus subsidies for private education. The data generally exclude foreign aid for education. They may also exclude spending by religious schools, which play a significant role in many developing countries. Data for some countries and for some years refer to spending by the ministry of education only (excluding education expenditures by other ministries and departments and local authorities).

Recurrent spending on primary teacher salaries is the total amount spent on primary as a percent of total recurrent spending on primary education (the latter including spending on personnel other than teachers). The data refer to the primary education level of the education system only. For countries with a five or six year primary system, the data are for the official primary cycle. For countries with primary systems either longer than 6 years, or shorter than 5 years, the data are an estimate of a hypothetical 6-year equivalent system (although based on actual enrollment, teacher, spending data, etc. through grade 6 in that country). The data are estimates for 2000 based on the latest years for which data are available. The data are derived from Bruns, Mingat, and Rakatomalala (2003). Incidence of education expenditures (lowest and highest quintiles).

Incidence of education and health expenditures (lowest and highest quintiles). Average expenditure incidence studies relate household data on the use of public services by different quintiles of the population to average spending on those services by the government. Results from these studies provide a cross-sectional snapshot of who benefits from public spending on services. Note that this is not necessarily the same as who would benefit from the marginal resources devoted to the sector. The data are accompanied by several caveats. First, while the data are often based on the best sources available, they are often limited when it comes to assessing the unit costs of services. Second, cross-country comparability is hampered by the fact that studies differ in the detail to which they differentiate average spending: for example some use a uniform estimate, some estimate separate unit costs for urban and rural areas, some for different provinces, and so on. Third, since the value of spending might differ for different populations (for example spending on urban dwellers might go much further towards providing quality services than an equal amount spent on people in remote rural areas) the label "expenditure incidence" is distinguished from "benefit incidence". Fourth, the results do not include the incidence of raising funds. A fairly regressive pattern of spending might still be pro-poor if it is financed through a very progressive tax system. Fifth, it is hard to know what a "good" allocation is without comparing it to other types of social spending. Details on the sources for these results, as well as a disaggregation by types of expenditures, are available in Filmer (2003) WDR Background Note.

Public health expenditure consists of recurrent and capital spending from government (central and local) budgets, external borrowings and grants (including donations from international agencies and nongovernmental organizations), and social (or compulsory) health insurance funds. The data in the table are the product of an effort by the World Health Organization (WHO), the Organization for Economic Co-operation and Development (OECD), and the World Bank to collect all available information on health expenditures from national and local government budgets, national accounts, household surveys, insurance publications, international donors, and existing tabulations.

Private health expenditure includes direct household (out-of-pocket) spending, private insurance, spending by non-profit institutions serving households (other than social insurance), and direct service payments by private corporations. The data in the table are the product of an effort by the World Health Organization (WHO), the Organization for Economic Co-operation and Development (OECD), and the World Bank to collect all available infor-

mation on health expenditures from national and local government budgets, national accounts, household surveys, insurance publications, international donors, and existing tabulations.

Total health expenditure is the sum of public and private health expenditure. It covers the provision of health services (preventive and curative), family planning activities, nutrition activities, and emergency aid designated for health but does not include provision of water and sanitation. The data in the table are the product of an effort by the World Health Organization (WHO), the Organization for Economic Co-operation and Development (OECD), and the World Bank to collect all available information on health expenditures from national and local government budgets, national accounts, household surveys, insurance publications, international donors, and existing tabulations.

Table 4. Service indicators

Primary teacher absence rate is the percentage of primary school teachers who were absent from a random sample of schools during surprise visits.

Absenteeism of public servants from their jobs has long been discussed as an impediment to effective public service delivery in developing countries, yet there has been relatively little systematic empirical evidence on this issue. As background research for this World Development Report, several country studies were conducted. A multi-county study Bangladesh, Ecuador, India (20 States), Indonesia, Peru, and Uganda (Chaudhury and others 2003). Additional studies with virtually identical methodologies were conducted in Papua New Guinea (NRI and World Bank 2003) and Zambia (Habyarimana and others 2003).

The common survey methodology was built around unannounced visits to a nationally representative random sample of primary schools and primary health care centers. The study used clustered random sampling: after stratifying each country (or Indian state) geographically, districts were randomly selected on a population-weighted basis, and then facilities were randomly selected in each district. Enumerators visited each facility and, after verifying workers' schedules, recorded which of them were absent.

The figures in the table are preliminary calculations, based on data from surveys conducted mostly in late 2002 and early 2003. Further research will refine the calculations, in some cases drawing on data from additional visits to each facility. In addition, these facility surveys have collected a wealth of information now being used to probe the causes of teacher and health personnel absence in the different countries.

Note that these studies did not measure "absenteeism," which is a term that is usually used to imply unjustifiable or unexplained absence, but instead reported on rates of "absence." That is, they reported the number of staff who were supposed to be on duty but were in fact absent from the facility - without regard to the reasons for absence. Many personnel were doubtless absent for valid reasons, such as authorized leave or official duties. Nevertheless, we report the absence rates for two reasons: first, because the reasons for absence given by facility directors were typically not verifiable; and second, because even authorized absences reduce the quantity and quality of public services in these primary schools and primary health centers.

Primary pupil-teacher ratio is the number of pupils enrolled in primary school divided by the number of primary school teachers (regardless of their teaching assignment). The comparability of pupil-teacher ratios across countries is affected by the definition of teachers and by differences in class size by grade and in the number of hours taught. Moreover, the underlying enrollment levels are subject to a variety of reporting errors. They are based on data collected during annual school surveys, which are typically conducted at the beginning of the school year. They do not reflect actual number of attendance. And school administrators may report exaggerated enrollments, especially if there is a financial incentive to do so. While the pupil-teacher ratio is often used to compare the quality of schooling across countries, it is often weakly related to the value added of schooling systems (Behrman and Rosenzweig 1994). The data are from the UNESCO Institute for Statistics, which compiles international data on education in cooperation with national commissions and national statistical services.

Trained teachers in primary school: are the percentage of primary school teachers who have received the minimum organized teacher training (preservice or in service) required for teaching. The share of trained teachers in primary schools measures the quality of the teaching staff. It does not take account of competencies acquired by teachers through their professional experience or self-instruction, or of such factors as work experience, teaching methods and materials, or classroom conditions, all of which may affect the quality of teaching. Since the training teachers receive varies greatly, care should be taken in comparing across countries. The data are from the UNESCO Institute for Statistics, which compiles international data on education in cooperation with national commissions and national statistical services.

Health personnel absence rate is the percentage of medical personnel at primary health clinics who were absent from a random sample of schools during surprise visits. (See the technical notes on the primary teacher absence rate for further information).

Child immunization rate is the percentage of children under one year of age receiving vaccination coverage for four diseases—measles and diphtheria, pertussis (whooping cough), and tetanus (DPT). A child is considered adequately immunized against measles after receiving one dose of vaccine, and against DPT after receiving three doses.

Tuberculosis treatment success rate is the percentage of new, registered smear-positive (infectious) cases that were cured or in which a full course of treatment was completed. Data on the success rate of tuberculosis treatment are provided for countries that have implemented the recommended control strategy: directly observed treatment, short course (DOTS). Countries that have not adopted DOTS or have only recently done so are omitted because of lack of data or poor comparability or reliability of reported results.

Physicians are graduates of any faculty or school of medicine who are working in the country in any medical field (practice, teaching, research). Data are from the WHO and OECD, supplemented by country data.

Hospital beds include inpatient beds available in public, private, general, and specialized hospitals and rehabilitation centers. In most cases beds for both acute and chronic care are included. Data are from the WHO and OECD, supplemented by country data.

Inpatient admission rate is the percentage of the population admitted to hospitals during a year. Data are from the WHO and OECD, supplemented by country data.

Access to an improved water source refers to the percentage of the population with reasonable access to an adequate amount of water from an improved source, such as a household connection, public standpipe, borehole, protected well or spring, or rainwater collection. Unimproved sources include vendors, tanker trucks, and unprotected wells and springs. Reasonable access is defined as the availability of at least 20 liters a person a day from a source within one kilometer of the dwelling. The data are based on surveys and estimates provided by governments to the Joint Monitoring Programme of the WHO and United Nations Children's Fund (UNICEF). The coverage rates for water are based on information from service users on the facilities their households actually use rather than on information from service providers, who may include nonfunctioning systems. Access to drinking water from an improved source does not ensure that the water is safe or adequate, as these characteristics are not tested at the time of the surveys.

Access to improved sanitation facilities refers to the percentage of the population with at least adequate access to excreta disposal facilities (private or shared but not public) that can effectively prevent human, animal, and insect contact with excreta. Improved facilities range from simple but protected pit latrines to flush toilets with a sewerage connection. To be effective, facilities must be correctly constructed and properly maintained. The data are based on surveys and estimates provided by governments to the Joint Monitoring Programme of the WHO and United Nations Children's Fund (UNICEF). The coverage rates for sanitation are based on information from service users on the facilities their households actually use rather than on information from service providers, who may include nonfunctioning systems.

Table 5. Foreign aid recipient indicators

Net official development assistance or official aid cover net concessional flows to developing countries, transition economies of Eastern Europe and the former Soviet Union and to certain advanced developing countries and territories as determined by the Development Assistance Committee (DAC) of the OECD. The flows are from members of the DAC, multilateral development agencies, and certain Arab countries. Data on aid are compiled by DAC and published in its annual statistical report, *Geographical Distribution of Financial Flows to Aid Recipients,* and in the DAC chairman's annual report, *Development Co-operation.* The 2001 data exclude aid from the World Food Programme because the organization implemented an annual program budget in 2002, and the 2001 data are not yet consistent with the DAC reporting system.

Aid dependency ratios Net official aid or official development assistance as a percentage of GNI, gross capital formation and central government expenditure and aid per capita provide a measure of the recipient country's dependency on aid. They are calculated using values in U.S. dollars converted at official exchange rates. Gross capital formation consists of outlays on additions to the fixed assets of the economy, net changes in the level of inventories, and net acquisitions of valuables. Central government expenditure includes both current and capital (development) expenditures and excludes lending minus repayments. For definitions of population and GNI, please see table 1.

Donor fragmentation index A Herfindahl index of donor concentration is calculated by summing the squared shares of aid over all donor agencies with positive gross disbursements of official development assistance (ODA/OA) in the recipient country during the year. This index, which ranges from 0 to 1, is then subtracted from 1, to form an index of donor fragmentation, with high values indicating greater fragmentation. Data, and list of donor agencies, are from the OECD DAC's *Geographical Distribution of Financial Flows to Aid Recipients.*

Table 6. Aid flows from Development Assistance Committee members

Net official development assistance and **net official aid** record the actual international transfer by the donor of financial resources or of goods or services valued at the cost to the donor, less any repayments of loan principal during the same period.

DAC maintains a list of countries and territories that are aid recipients. Part I of the list comprises developing countries and territories considered by DAC members to be eligible for ODA. Part II comprises economies in transition: more advanced countries of Central and Eastern Europe, the countries of the former Soviet Union, and certain advanced

developing countries and territories. Flows to these recipients that meet the criteria for ODA are termed official aid.

Measures of aid flows from the perspective of donors differ from recipients' perceived aid receipts for two main reasons. First, aid flows include expenditure items about which recipients may have no precise information, such as development-oriented research, stipends and tuition costs for aid-financed students in donor countries, or payment of experts hired by donor countries. Second, donors record their concessional funding (usually grants) to multilateral agencies when they make payments, while the agencies make funds available to recipients with a time lag and in many caes in the form of soft loans where donors' grants have been used to reduce the interest burden over the life of the loan. All data in this table—including GNI, population, general government disbursement—come from and are calculated by the OECD.

Data are shown at current prices and dollar exchange rates.

Aid as a percentage of GNI shows the donor's contributions of ODA or official aid as a share of its gross national income.

Average annual percentage change in volume and **aid per capita of donor country** are calculated using 2000 exchange rates and prices.

Aid as a percentage of general government disbursement shows the donor's contributions of ODA as a share of public spending.

Untied aid is the share of ODA that is not subject to restrictions by donors on procurement sources.

Table 7. Key indicators for other economies

Population is based on the de facto definition of population, which counts all residents regardless of legal status or citizenship—except for refugees not permanently settled in the country of asylum, who are generally considered part of the population of their country of origin. The values shown are midyear estimates for 2002.

Surface area is a country's total area, including areas under inland bodies of water and some coastal waterways.

Gross national income (GNI) is the sum of value added by all resident producers plus any product taxes (less subsidies) not included in the valuation of output plus net receipts of primary income (compensation of employees and property income) from abroad. Data are in current U.S. dollars converted using the World Bank Atlas method (see the technical notes for Table 1 and the section on statistical methods).

GNI per capita is gross national income divided by midyear population. GNI per capita in U.S. dollars is converted using the World Bank Atlas method.

PPP gross national income (GNI) is gross national income converted to international dollars using purchasin power parity rates. An international dollar has the same purchasing power over GNI as a U.S. dollar has in the United States. (See the technical notes for Table 1).

Gross domestic product (GDP) per capita growth is based on GDP measured in constant prices. GDP is the sum of value added by all resident producers plus any product taxes (less subsidies) not included in the valuation of output. Growth is calculated from constant price GDP data in local currency. (See the technical notes for Table 1).

Life expectancy at birth is the number of years a newborn infant would live if prevailing patterns of mortality at the time of its birth were to stay the same throughout its life.

Reduce child mortality—under-five mortality rate is the probability that a newborn baby will die before reaching age five, if subject to current age-specific mortality rates. The probability is expressed as a rate per 1,000.

Primary completion rate is the number of students successfully completing the last year of (or graduating from) primary school in a given year, divided by the number of children of official graduation age in the population.

Adult illiteracy rate is the percentage of adults ages 15 and above who cannot, with understanding, read and write a short, simple statement about their everyday life.

Statistical methods

This section describes the calculation of the least-squares growth rate, the exponential (endpoint) growth rate, and the World Bank's Atlas methodology for calculating the conversion factor used to estimate GNI and GNI per capita in U.S. dollars.

Least-squares growth rate. Least-squares growth rates are used wherever there is a sufficiently long time series to permit a reliable calculation. No growth rate is calculated if more than half the observations in a period are missing.

The least-squares growth rate, r, is estimated by fitting a linear regression trendline to the logarithmic annual values of the variable in the relevant period. The regression equation takes the form

$$\ln X_t = a + bt,$$

which is equivalent to the logarithmic transformation of the compound growth equation,

$$X_t = X_o (1 + r)^t.$$

In this equation, X is the variable, t is time, and $a = \log X_o$ and $b = ln (1 + r)$ are the parameters to be estimated. If b^* is the least-squares estimate of b, the average annual growth rate, r, is obtained as $[\exp(b^*)-1]$ and is multiplied by 100 to express it as a percentage.

The calculated growth rate is an average rate that is representative of the available observations over the entire period.

It does not necessarily match the actual growth rate between any two periods.

Exponential growth rate. The growth rate between two points in time for certain demographic data, notably labor force and population, is calculated from the equation

$$r = \ln (p_n /p_1)/n,$$

where p_n and p_1 are the last and first observations in the period, n is the number of years in the period, and ln is the natural logarithm operator. This growth rate is based on a model of continuous, exponential growth between two points in time. It does not take into account the intermediate values of the series. Note also that the exponential growth rate does not correspond to the annual rate of change measured at a one-year interval which is given by

$$(p_n - p_{n-1})/p_n - 1.$$

World Bank Atlas method. In calculating GNI and GNI per capita in U.S. dollars for certain operational purposes, the World Bank uses the Atlas conversion factor. The purpose of the Atlas conversion factor is to reduce the impact of exchange rate fluctuations in the cross-country comparison of national incomes.

The Atlas conversion factor for any year is the average of a country's exchange rate (or alternative conversion factor) for that year and its exchange rates for the two preceding years, adjusted for the difference between the rate of inflation in the country, and through 2000, that in the G-5 countries (France, Germany, Japan, the United Kingdom, and the United States). For 2001 onwards, these countries include the Euro Zone, Japan, the United Kingdom, and the United States. A country's inflation rate is measured by the change in its GDP deflator.

The inflation rate for G-5 countries (through 2000), or the Euro Zone, Japan, the United Kingdom, and the United States (for 2001 onwards), representing international inflation, is measured by the change in the SDR deflator. (Special drawing rights, or SDRs, are the IMF's unit of account.) The SDR deflator is calculated as a weighted average of the G-5 countries' (through 2000, and the Euro Zone, Japan, the United Kingdom, and the United States for 2001 onwards) GDP deflators in SDR terms, the weights being the amount of each country's currency in one SDR unit. Weights vary over time because both the composition of the SDR and the relative exchange rates for each currency change. The SDR deflator is calculated in SDR terms first and then converted to U.S. dollars using the SDR to dollar Atlas conversion factor. The Atlas conversion factor is then applied to a country's GNI. The resulting GNI in U.S. dollars is divided by the midyear population to derive GNI per capita.

When official exchange rates are deemed to be unreliable or unrepresentative of the effective exchange rate during a period, an alternative estimate of the exchange rate is used in the Atlas formula (see below).

The following formulas describe the calculation of the Atlas conversion factor for year t:

$$e_t^* = \frac{1}{3}\left[e_{t-2}\left(\frac{p_t}{p_{t-2}} \middle/ \frac{p_t^{S\$}}{p_{t-2}^{S\$}} \right) + e_{t-1}\left(\frac{p_t}{p_{t-1}} \middle/ \frac{p_t^{S\$}}{p_{t-1}^{S\$}} \right) + e_t \right]$$

and the calculation of GNI per capita in U.S. dollars for year t:

$$Y_t^\$ = (Y_t/N_t)/e_t^*$$

where e_t^* is the Atlas conversion factor (national currency to the U.S. dollar) for year t, e_t is the average annual exchange rate (national currency to the U.S. dollar) for year t, p_t is the GDP deflator for year t, p_t S\$ is the SDR deflator in U.S. dollar terms for year t, Y_t \$ is the Atlas GNI per capita in U.S. dollars in year t, Y_t is current GNI (local currency) for year t, and N_t is the midyear population for year t.

Alternative conversion factors

The World Bank systematically assesses the appropriateness of official exchange rates as conversion factors. An alternative conversion factor is used when the official exchange rate is judged to diverge by an exceptionally large margin from the rate effectively applied to domestic transactions of foreign currencies and traded products. This applies to only a small number of countries, as shown in *Primary Data Documentation* table in *World Development Indicators 2003*. Alternative conversion factors are used in the Atlas methodology and elsewhere in the *Selected World Development Indicators* as single-year conversion factors.